# QUANTITATIVE METHODS FOR MANAGEMENT DECISIONS

# QUANTITATIVE METHODS FOR MANAGEMENT DECISIONS

William P. Cooke

*University of Wyoming*

McGraw-Hill Book Company

*New York   St. Louis   San Francisco   Auckland
Bogotá   Hamburg   Johannesburg   London   Madrid
Mexico   Montreal   New Delhi   Panama   Paris
São Paulo   Singapore   Sydney   Tokyo   Toronto*

QUANTITATIVE METHODS FOR MANAGEMENT DECISIONS

1 2 3 4 5 6 7 8 9 0 DOCDOC 8 9 8 7 6 5

ISBN 0-07-012518-X

This book was set in Palatino by Monotype Composition Company, Inc.
The editors were Cheryl L. Mehalik and Laura D. Warner;
the designer was Robin Hessel;
the production supervisor was Diane Renda.
The drawings were done by Wellington Studios Ltd.
R. R. Donnelley & Sons Company was printer and binder.

**Library of Congress Cataloging in Publication Data**

Cooke, William P., date
    Quantitative methods for management decisions.

    Includes bibliographies and index.
    1. Management science.   I. Title.
T57.6.C658   1985      658.4'03      84-20082
ISBN 0-07-012518-X

To Alice

# CONTENTS

**CHAPTER 10  STATISTICAL ESTIMATION
AND FORECASTING                                 367**

**CHAPTER 11  INVENTORY MODELS                       439**

# PREFACE

This book provides an elementary introduction to the principal concepts and applications of quantitative management techniques. Key words that characterize it are readability and teachability. Equal emphasis is given to illustration of applications and promotion of conceptual understanding. Students completing a course based on this text should leave it knowing *when* to use a particular technique, *why* it works, and *how* to use it.

The text is addressed primarily to the *student* of business and economics. The writing is clear and direct, and the examples are intended to be both motivating and entertaining.

Thoughtful consideration has been given to the use of the text as a classroom tool. Quality and variety in examples and exercises are what make a quantitative methods text pedagogically sound. Instructors using this book should appreciate the more than 170 worked-out examples and the more than 370 end-of-chapter exercises—all together, over 540 illustrations of applications and concepts in management science. Brief answers to about half the exercises (marked with the symbol ◆) are included in an appendix, and an instructor's manual with complete solutions to all problems is available.

The only mathematical prerequisite for this material is a course at the level of college algebra. Certainly, exposure to some calculus and some probability and statistics would be helpful because of the mathematical maturity gained thereby, but it is not necessary. Chapters 8 and 10 include thorough discussions of probability and statistical estimation at the level of a beginning statistics course, and Chapters 8 through 10 constitute a very complete unit on basic applications of probability and statistics in management decision making. Students with prior background in statistics could skip Chapter 8 and the first part of Chapter 10, or else could use them for review. The latter portions of Chapter 10 contain more material on regression, time series, and forecasting than is in most elementary quantitative methods texts.

Chapters 2 through 7 comprise a particularly complete unit on linear programming. Throughout those chapters the emphasis is on formulation of problems, although LP solution techniques themselves are extensively discussed. The material ranges from simple graphical solutions through simplex tableaus; goal programming; duality and sensitivity analysis; computer solutions of larger applied problems; and integer, transportation, and assignment problems.

Chapter 6 presents examples illustrating very realistic applications of linear programming and makes much use of figures exhibiting computer input and output. The emphasis of the chapter is on interpretations of the output.

Within Chapter 5 is a very complete yet elementary discussion of the concept of duality and its implications for management decisions. The meaning of implicit value of a resource, how it is related to the objective and to all other resources, is exceptionally well developed.

Chapters 11 through 16 contain other selected topics frequently included in management science courses. They are arranged, however, so that nice two-chapter units are readily available in three major areas: inventory, networks, and queueing and simulation. Included in those chapters are the basic EOQ models; probabilistic inventory models; dynamic programming applied to network, inventory, and capital budgeting problems; minimal spanning tree, shortest route, and maximal flow problems; PERT networks, including probability, cost, and resource leveling; intuitive queueing situations as well as the basic results for single- and multiple-server Poisson queues; and simulation as essentially a model-sampling operation, with applications in queueing and inventory settings. Other ideas included in the text are a brief history of operations research, cutting planes, branch-and-bound, the transportation and assignment methods, binomial and normal distributions, decision trees, and utility.

Much flexibility is available for course design. A one-quarter course, for example, presuming students who have taken basic probability, could include Chapters 1 to 4, Chapter 6, Chapter 9, Chapter 11, and selected topics from Chapters 13 and 14. A one-semester course, assuming no previous statistics, might include Chapters 1 to 6, Chapters 8 to 10, Chapter 11, Chapter 14, and Chapter 15.

Beyond algebra, the book is self-contained both mathematically and statistically. While it is intended primarily for business and economics students, it could also be used profitably by students in industrial management, industrial engineering, agricultural economics, mathematics, and statistics. By way of its topical coverage in both breadth and depth, its readability, and its wide variety of exercises and examples, the book is meant to provide an excellent basis for any introductory course in management science.

I would like to express my thanks for the many useful comments and suggestions provided by colleagues who reviewed this text during the course of its development, especially to David Burkitt, Emory University; Joseph Glynn, Canisius College; Kirk Karwan, Duke University; John

Nicholas, Loyola University of Chicago; and Bill Verdini, University of Washington.

I would also like to acknowledge the influence of people who, although they had nothing directly to do with this book, did have a profound effect upon the way I think.  To Fletcher Moseley of West Texas State, for the example of teaching excellence; to Gordon Fuller of Texas Tech and H. O. Hartley of Texas A&M, for examples of distinguished scholarship; and to Timon Walther of Wyoming, for encouragement and for friendship; wherever you each may be now, I hope you can hear me say: Thank you.

**William P. Cooke**

# QUANTITATIVE METHODS FOR MANAGEMENT DECISIONS

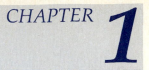

# INTRODUCTION

*T*he quantitative methods discussed in this book are primarily mathematical and statistical techniques used in managerial decision making. One of two names, often used interchangeably, is commonly used to designate this area of study: *operations research* or *management science*. A person who practices those techniques may be called a management scientist or an operations researcher. To indicate the division of an organization wherein quantitative studies of management decision problems take place, or to denote the general field of study itself, this text will use operations research (OR).

Basically, OR is problem solving pertaining to the operations of organizations. The organization may be a small business firm, a large industrial company, a nonprofit foundation, an agency of government, or a branch of the military. The questions range from a simple updating of solutions for small routine problems to make them compatible with current information to the planning of the next ten or fifteen years' effort in the organization. Only when the problem contains some new, unfamiliar feature does "research" in the usual sense of the word occur. Quite often the problem requires only the direct application of a well-known operations research technique of the type found in this book.

One of the key words in OR is *optimization;* as OR practitioners, or as managers who must have a basic understanding of the power and the limitations of OR, we ask for the *best* ways to conduct the operations of our firm. But since our solutions are usually for mathematical models of real-world situations, models which often fail to reflect the complexity of the problem, what we report as optimal in a mathematical sense may only be a "good" or a "preferred" solution. In fact, one of the principal uses of OR is the making of "sensitivity analyses," which compare alternative scenarios or strategies with a view to selection of a satisfactory (not necessarily optimal) solution. These remarks suggest the following definition:

*Operations research.* A quantitative science devoted to helping the management of organizations make good decisions.

In this introductory chapter you will find some simple, representative examples, a brief early history of OR, and a discussion of some of the distinguishing characteristics of the field. The remainder of the text is a working survey of the most important elementary OR techniques.

## 1.1 REAL PROBLEMS IN ABSTRACT SETTINGS: MATHEMATICAL MODELS

Business and industrial decisions often involve the selection from many alternatives that one choice which will achieve a specified objective, such as maximum profit or minimum cost. If a very large number of alternatives is involved, the best choice may not be immediately evident. However, it may be possible to simplify the decision problem by writing it out symbolically, so that all alternatives may be represented by one concise arrangement of mathematical symbols.

This symbolic formulation of the problem is called a *mathematical model.* It may or may not accurately represent the real problem. A solution for the model is expected to be only an approximate solution for the original problem. How good that solution is will depend upon how faithfully the model represents the real-life situation.

Clearly then, a very important aspect of problem solving is the mathematical modeling, or formulation, of the problem. At the formulation stage the manager (the person who has the problem), with an intimate familiarity with such situations, makes a large contribution toward the solution. This person is qualified by experience to supply much of the relevant input to the model (costs, demand, supply, and so on), and to offer a judgment about the relevance of the model to reality.

Rarely will the OR practitioner merely take the manager's statement of the real problem and go away to formulate the model in solitude. Usually the formulation stage involves a team effort, with the manager either intimately involved or else kept abreast of developments in the formulation and solution of the model. Part of the solution may be a sensitivity analysis which gives the changes that may be expected if some of the input parameters, like cost of materials, change. The manager will have to decide among a number of possibly equally attractive solutions, and ultimately any decision coming from an analysis of the model will be the manager's responsibility.

The preceding discussion has two immediate implications. First, one must strive for a model that depicts reality as accurately as possible, yet is simple enough to permit a mathematical solution. Second, modern managers must become acquainted with the basic principles and techniques of OR. Model building and mathematical solutions are not commonly a day-to-day responsibility of managers, but the making of decisions is. An OR solution of a modeled problem is used to assist the manager in the decision-making function, and he or she must be sufficiently conversant with OR to be able to evaluate that solution.

### Example 1.1
### Design of a Minimum-Cost Device

Rocky's Sand and Gravel wants a rectangular-based box which will hold exactly 81 cubic feet when filled level. The width must be half the length, and the box is to be open at the top. Material for the base of the box costs $4 per square foot, while the material for the sides and ends costs $3 per square foot. What are the dimensions (length, width, and height) of the minimum-cost box?

While this little problem may appear to be just a puzzle of the type often encountered in mathematics textbooks, it is in fact representative of a class of problems regularly faced in industrial operations. We might call them design problems—design at minimum cost a device that will meet certain specifications. Research on such design problems by Clarence Zener and others at Westinghouse in the 1960s led to the development of geometric programming, a powerful solution technique (for special types

**FIGURE 1.1**   Box specifications: Rocky's Sand and Gravel Company

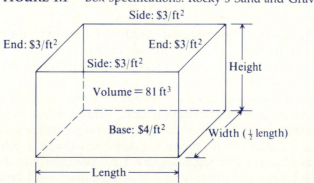

of models) that possesses a rather unique property: it will find the minimum cost for the box *before* it finds its optimal dimensions. However, we will not use geometric programming, considered a fairly advanced OR technique, to solve the problem. At this stage in your study of OR we are more interested in model formulation than in solution procedures.

In our mathematical model of Rocky's problem we will encounter three basic terms used in many OR problems: an *objective function*, *decision variables*, and *constraints* on those variables. Here the decision variables are $L$, $W$, and $H$, the length, width, and height of the box; the objective function will represent cost (our objective is to minimize cost); and the constraints come from the specifications that width must be half the length and the box must hold 81 cubic feet.

Reference to Figure 1.1 and the names of our decision variables tells us that the area of the base will be $LW$ square feet, the two ends each have area $HW$ square feet, and the two longer sides each have area $HL$ square feet. Since the base costs \$4 per square foot and the sides and ends cost \$3 per square foot, our objective function is

$$\text{Cost in dollars} = C = 4LW + 3(2HW + 2HL)$$

The specifications for the box give us the following two constraints:

$$LWH = 81 \quad \text{and} \quad W = 0.5L$$

Thus a mathematical model of the problem consists of the equations above and the statement: Find $L$, $W$, and $H$ which minimize $C$ subject to the two given constraints.

Because the two constraints are equations, the cost can be written as a function of only a single decision variable, say $L$. Since $W = 0.5L$ and $LWH = 81$, substitution of the width constraint into the volume constraint yields $L(0.5L)H = 81$, or $H = 81/0.5L^2$. Then substitution into the objective function of $W$ in terms of $L$ and $H$ in terms of $L$ gives

$$C = 2L^2 + \frac{1,458}{L}$$

Not only has the substitution produced a simpler form of the objective function, but the constraints are also incorporated into that function. Now our problem is only to minimize an unconstrained function of a single variable.

An exact solution can be achieved by either elementary calculus or the method of geometric programming. However, a very carefully drawn graph of $C$ versus $L$ will yield an approximate solution, and trial and error with a calculator could refine it. Approximating the minimum value of $C$ graphically is illustrated in Figure 1.2. We conclude that minimum cost is about \$310, occurring for a box approximately 7.1 feet long.

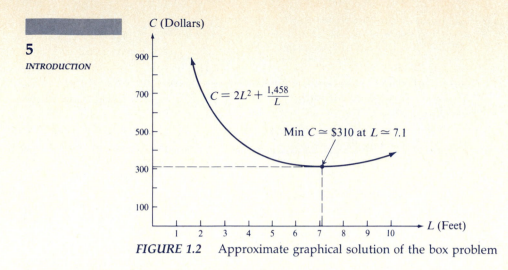

**FIGURE 1.2**    Approximate graphical solution of the box problem

The exact, optimal value for $L$ in the model turns out to be the cube root of 364.5.   To five-decimal accuracy the dimensions in feet of the minimum-cost box are

$$L = 7.14330 \qquad W = 3.57165 \qquad H = 3.17481$$

and the minimum cost is

$$\text{Min } C = \$306.16$$

This solution gives the absolute minimum cost achievable for the problem as described by our model and for the schematic of a box that we drew in Figure 1.1.   However, if Rocky's Sand and Gravel actually wants to build such a box so it will be sturdy enough to hold 3 yards (81 cubic feet) of sand, a couple of practical problems exist.

First, it would be next to impossible for Rocky to saw a board to the length of 7.1433 feet.   He would be lucky to cut it to within two-tenths of an inch of 7 feet.   The curve in Figure 1.2 tells us that would not be much of a problem; the curve is very "flat" for $L$ between 6 and 8, so the solution is not very sensitive to departures from optimality.   For instance, if the length of the box were exactly 7 feet, with $W$ and $H$ adjusted accordingly, the cost of the box would be $306.29, only $0.13 more than the theoretical minimum cost.   This is an example of a *sensitivity analysis*.

A second practical problem has more drastic consequences.   No overlap was included in the model; it would be impossible to nail together a box holding 81 cubic feet using our "optimal" dimensions.   This is an example of an *inadequate model*; given information about how the pieces are to overlap (does the base fit inside the end-pieces, or do they rest atop the base?) and about how much overlap is needed, a model that better depicts reality could easily be constructed.   The presence of a carpenter on the OR team might have precluded this impractical solution.

**TABLE 1.1**   YIELDS FOR FEELINGIZ MUTUAL INVESTMENTS

| Company | Yield, % |
| --- | --- |
| Old Conservative Life Insurance | 4 |
| Old Zinc Tobacco, Inc. | 5 |
| Old Great Aunt Distilleries, Consol. | 8 |
| Old Timer Discotheques, Ltd. | 12 |

**Example 1.2**
**Portfolio Selection**

The Feelingiz Mutual Fund has $500,000 available for investment. The board of directors has decided to restrict investment to the four companies indicated in Table 1.1, which also shows the current annual yields.

The chairperson of the board owns some personal shares of Old Conservative and insists that at least $100,000 be invested there. The other members agree, with the stipulation that regardless of the amount placed in Old Conservative, at least an equal amount be invested in the combination of Old Zinc and Old Great Aunt. Finally, it is decided that no more than $200,000 should be invested in Old Timer. If it is assumed that future yield will not differ from current yield, what investment decision will produce maximum overall yield?

This problem has a mathematical formulation that is known as a *linear programming model*. Such a model has a linear objective function and linear constraints (often inequalities instead of equations) on the decision variables, and usually involves the restriction that negative values of the decision variables are not permitted.

Let $X_1$, $X_2$, $X_3$, and $X_4$ be the amount in dollars to be invested in Old Conservative, Old Zinc, Old Great Aunt, and Old Timer, respectively. No more than $500,000 can be invested, $X_1$ must be at least $100,000, $X_2$ plus $X_3$ must be at least as large as $X_1$, and $X_4$ cannot exceed $200,000. Further, negative values for those variables make no sense practically. We write our mathematical model as

$$\text{Find } X_1, X_2, X_3, X_4 \text{ that maximize } Y$$

where

$$Y = 0.04X_1 + 0.05X_2 + 0.08X_3 + 0.12X_4$$

subject to the restrictions

$$X_1 + X_2 + X_3 + X_4 \leq 500{,}000$$

$$X_1 \geq 100{,}000$$

$$-X_1 + X_2 + X_3 \geq 0$$

$$X_4 \leq 200{,}000$$

$$X_1 \geq 0 \qquad X_2 \geq 0 \qquad X_3 \geq 0 \qquad X_4 \geq 0$$

The set of values for the four decision variables that satisfies all of the restrictions is called the *feasible region* for the problem. Even if the values of those variables were to be restricted to only integer, or whole-number, values, the number of feasible combinations is very, very large. Yet we must in some efficient way be able to search through all of those feasible combinations to find that one combination that produces maximum yield. A general procedure for that search, called the *simplex method*, is presented in Chapters 3 and 4 of this text.

The solution of the problem is

$$X_1 = 100,000 \qquad X_2 = 0 \qquad X_3 = 200,000 \qquad X_4 = 200,000$$

with the maximum yield in dollars being

$$\text{Max } Y = \$44,000$$

This represents an effective yield of 8.8 percent on the $500,000 investment.

While this solution is guaranteed by the simplex method to be optimal, in this instance it is easy to arrive at the same decision using common sense. We want to put as much as possible into the 12 percent yield but are allowed a maximum of only $200,000 for Old Timer. This leaves $300,000 available, but $100,000 must be put into Old Conservative. Obviously it is ridiculous to put more than that amount in the 4 percent investment when we could receive 8 percent on the remaining $200,000 by placing it in Old Great Aunt.

But what if the problem had involved 50 companies and 40 inequality constraints on the decision variables? What if many of those companies had the *same* highest-percentage yields and the constraints are so complicated that a rational choice between apparently equal investments becomes extremely difficult? In that case the standard simplex method will dutifully crank out an optimal solution, one that might violate your intuitive guess at an answer. And only a masochist would want to try to work out the answer using hand calculations. Instead, you would want to use a computer, which could give in a matter of seconds a solution that might take days to achieve with pencil and paper.

A model for a many-variable, many-constraint linear programming problem appears in Example 2.6 of Chapter 2. A glance ahead to that example might convince you that commonsense solutions of large, complex problems are not always easy to obtain. Examples of computer solutions of such problems are presented in Chapter 6.

Before leaving the Feelingiz Mutual example we should note that the simple solution for our model was highly dependent upon our assumption that the stated yields would be the actual yields. We have no guarantee that future dividends will be the same as current dividends. We might discover in retrospect that the investment decision based on the model we formulated was not the best decision, simply because the yields changed. Here again, a sensitivity analysis that considers the effect on the optimal decision of changes in yield rates could be a valuable contribution from the OR analyst.

### Example 1.3
### An Inventory Decision

Inventory decisions occur regularly in almost every kind of business organization. Apart from back orders, if items are not on hand then nothing can be sold. If too many items are on hand, however, storage costs, insurance, and maintenance costs become excessive, and space and capital that might otherwise be put to productive use are tied up in inventory.

Inventory decisions are often *ordering* decisions, with the decision variables usually being *quantity* and *time*. How many items should be ordered, and when should the order be placed? The objective is usually to minimize cost among all possible inventory decisions, although sometimes maximum profit is the target.

The following example treats an inventory problem where demand for items during a single time period is probabilistic; demand cannot be predicted exactly, but a probability distribution of demand is known or else can be assumed to hold approximately. It does not involve everything that might have to be considered when one is faced with a real ordering decision, but it will serve to illustrate that the solution of even a simple inventory problem is not always obvious.

Simpson's Discount Store stocks a popular parlor game. Demand for the game in the month of March has historically ranged from zero to six games, according to the probability distribution in Table 1.2. In that table, $d$ represents demand and $p(d)$ is the probability that demand will be $d$. For instance, the probability that four such games can be sold in March is 0.30. That probability is interpreted to mean that in 30 percent of the months of March for which records have been kept, four games have been requested by customers.

Ordering cost per game, including wholesale price, administrative cost, and shipping cost, is $10. It costs $5 per month to keep a game in stock—this includes space, insurance, and profit that might otherwise be made from capital. The store manager has concluded that the cost of a shortage (not having the game on hand when a customer wants it) is $20—this involves lost profit and the cost of offending a customer. What is Simpson's minimum-cost decision for the month of March?

For simplicity we assume that an order will be received on the day it is

**TABLE 1.2** *DISTRIBUTION OF MARCH DEMAND FOR GAME*

| $d$ | 0 | 1 | 2 | 3 | 4 | 5 | 6 |
|------|------|------|------|------|------|------|------|
| $p(d)$ | 0.05 | 0.10 | 0.15 | 0.20 | 0.30 | 0.10 | 0.10 |

placed and that the order will be placed on the first of March. In many inventory problems the time between placing an order and receiving it, called the *lead time,* is itself probabilistic. Here we ignore that extra complication. Thus time is not a decision variable in Simpson's problem. The optimal order quantity will depend only on the costs, the demand distribution, and the number of games on hand when the order is placed.

Our objective is really to minimize *expected* (average) cost, since actual demand is probabilistic. For example, there is a particular cost involved if we have six games on hand in March but demand is zero. However, if we have two games on hand when demand is four games, there is a different cost. Because of the uncertainty in the problem, measured by the probability distribution, we can never be sure what the actual cost of our decision will be. So we seek an ordering strategy that *on the average* will produce minimum cost over *many* such months of March.

Let $I$ be the number of games on hand when the order is placed and $X$ be the number on hand after the order is received, so that $X - I$ is the order quantity. We make those identifications because of the particular solution process to be used with our mathematical model (it is found in Chapter 11). The order quantity depends on $I$, the initial inventory, but $X$ itself does not. Thus $X$, the amount on hand after the order is received, is used as the decision variable to preclude the necessity of a separate solution for every possible value of $I$.

Let $E[C(X)]$ denote the expected cost as a function of $X$. Then our model may be written as

Find $X$ which minimizes $E[C(X)]$

where $\quad E[C(X)] = 10(X - I) + 5\sum_{d=0}^{X}(X - d)p(d) + 20\sum_{d=X+1}^{6}(d - X)p(d)$

The first term in $E[C(X)]$ is the cost of ordering $X - I$ games, the second term is the expected inventory cost (when $X$ exceeds $d$, some items are held in inventory), and the third term is the expected shortage cost (when $d$ exceeds $X$, there is a shortage).

We shall not at this point develop a solution procedure for this problem, nor shall we consider the fascinating manner in which the number $I$ disappears from the problem during the process of solution. This problem is worked out, based on the same numbers, but with a different scenario, as Example 11.9 in Chapter 11, with a more complete explanation of the model also being presented in that chapter. From the work in Example 11.9, we find the solution is

Optimal $X = 3$

Remember, $X$ is not the order quantity. It is the amount on hand after an order is received. Thus if initial inventory $I$ is fewer than three games, order $3 - I$, enough items to bring the inventory up to three. But if $I$ is three or more, order nothing (we do not want the amount on hand to get even farther away from the optimal value, three). In terms of the optimal order quantity for Simpson's Discount Store, the preceding two sentences report the solution.

The objective of this more difficult example and its possibly mystifying solution at such an early stage in your study of OR is quite frankly to motivate you to continue. Don't you want to know *how* the solution was obtained? How does one *prove* that this solution minimizes average cost over many such months of March? Why is *three* such a magic number when the most probable value of demand is *four* games?

## 1.2   SOME EARLY HISTORY OF OPERATIONS RESEARCH

Modern operations research is generally regarded as beginning with the onset of World War II in Europe. In England in 1939 a group of civilian scientists was assigned to the headquarters of the RAF Fighter Command, its task being the study of efficient ways to use the newly developed device called radar in a system providing early warning against air attack. This British group, and others subsequently during World War II, did *research* on military *operations*.

Nowadays *operations research* and *management science* are terms used interchangeably. But prior to World War II the designation *scientific management* was more synonymous with "industrial engineering," being devoted more narrowly to industrial production and the productivity of workers. In the late 1800s an American engineer named Frederick W. Taylor began work on the scientific analysis of manufacturing problems. This work was so important and sufficiently unique that Taylor is often called the "Father of Scientific Management." A student and colleague of Taylor, Henry L. Gantt, continued the work and made valuable contributions in the area of production scheduling. In the early 1900s the husband and wife team of Frank B. and Lillian Gilbreth became well known as "efficiency experts," consulting with management to improve worker productivity using the method of time and motion study originally proposed by Taylor. They and their philosophy were immortalized in 1949 with the appearance of *Cheaper by the Dozen*, a book written by Frank B. Gilbreth, Jr., and Ernestine Gilbreth Carey, two of their twelve children. That hilarious book, later made into a popular film, chronicled life in a family raised by the methods of scientific management.

Taylor, Gantt, the Gilbreths, and the Danish engineer A. K. Erlang (who established models underlying modern queuing theory) are regarded as the earliest practitioners of scientific management. Those pioneers most certainly used scientific methods in their work, but those methods did not take the broader, overall organizational viewpoint characteristic of modern OR. What they did, because of the limited extent of the problems they considered, is now only a small part of the field known as operations research.

In World War I two noteworthy studies that can be called forerunners of the OR work done in World War II were carried out by civilian scientists. F. W. Lanchester in England made a thorough study of the relationships between superiority of numbers and firepower to "victory" in war. In the United States, Thomas A. Edison used statistical techniques and a tactical game board to study the operational problems in antisubmarine warfare. However, neither of those studies produced any effect on actual military operations.

In World War II a different viewpoint was maintained by the military. Because of the early successes with radar-utilization studies by British OR teams, military commanders began to make significant operational decisions using recommendations of their civilian scientific advisors. One example is the research into the optimal size of merchant ship convoys and aircraft formations—optimal in the sense of minimizing losses due to enemy attack. OR groups, after intensive study of much wartime data, recommended very large convoys and formations as being better than the smaller groupings used early in the war. After those recommendations were transformed into actual military decisions the percentage of losses decreased substantially. The amount of decrease had been predicted rather accurately by the civilian scientists.

An "interdisciplinary team" Operations Research Group is often advocated as the best organization for conducting a large OR study. This brings many different points of view to the same problem. That approach is antedated by a British OR team organized in 1941. Put together by the Nobel laureate physicist P. M. S. Blackett, the group consisted of two mathematicians, three physiologists, three physicists, an army officer, an astrophysicist, and a surveyor. That heterogeneous team was known as "Blackett's Circus." Members were recruited on the basis of their talent and training in the basic sciences and their familiarity with the scientific method.

As the early successes of the British groups were reported to Allied commanders, interest in OR rapidly developed in the United States's military services. The Army Air Force and the Navy soon (1941) both organized their own OR teams. The thrust of American military operations research, however, seemed to be more offensive than defensive in nature. The island nation of England was necessarily more concerned with defense. It was dependent for critical supplies on merchant shipping, and being only 20 miles from continental Europe it was bombed almost nightly throughout World War II. The United States's OR groups were involved more with large logistical problems associated with offensive operations. Other examples of American OR efforts are analysis of sea and air attacks on German U-boats, study of the best way to mine the ocean from aircraft, and investigations of ship maneuvers to best avoid damage from Japanese kamikaze attacks.

We cannot assess the impact of the U.S. and British OR teams on shortening World War II, but we do know that the results of their scientific inquiries were translated into action. Research on operations in the military sector was more than just an intellectual exercise. The main contribution of OR to the war effort was the scientific management, analysis, and control of the complex operations of a large organization. Immediately after the war some members of those military OR groups were sought out by major industry to act as consultants.

In England, major industry was rapidly nationalized in an effort to rebuild from the rubble of war and to put the economy in order. Managers of the critical industries needed help in allocating limited resources. The organization-oriented graduate of military OR groups, accustomed to extremely large, complicated operational problems, was welcomed into the industrial fold.

The 1950s in both England and the United States is an important decade in the history of operations research. During this period the very practical techniques of linear and dynamic programming were being developed and extended. Great strides were made in pure research on production-inventory and queuing problems. More importantly, the decade of the 1950s introduced the computer into industry. The combination of new, sophisticated mathematical and statistical tools along with the data-management and arithmetic power of the computer suggested that OR would become a very profitable arm of industry.

Until the 1960s one became an operations researcher by way of training in one of the classical disciplines—mathematics, statistics, physics, engineering, chemistry, and so on, or else one drifted into the field from the ranks of middle management, being in need of solutions to OR-type problems but having no one in the company who was trained in the area. But the growing acceptance of OR in business, industry, and the military prompted a demand for people trained in the specific techniques of OR. Universities responded with courses and degrees in operations research. Now more and more talented people are drawn to OR as an initial choice of career, recognizing it as an area of work and study offering practical and intellectually stimulating problems.

## 1.3  SOME CHARACTERISTICS OF OPERATIONS RESEARCH

Production-inventory problems have received much attention from operations researchers. Within that framework we can discuss some of the tasks that characterize an OR approach to a management problem.

A manufacturing company will produce many products to meet anticipated demands. Someone must assess the extent of demand throughout a specified time period. Often demand over a number of months cannot be predicted exactly; a probability distribution of demand might be involved. Typically, someone assigned to the problem will be experienced at making statistical predictions. Further input comes from sales personnel in the field, economists in the home office, opinions of experienced managers, and others throughout the company. Often an operations research group is expected to coordinate and analyze those separate inputs so an accurate forecast of demand can be made.

Assume that a dependable prediction of demand is available. Now management must decide how best to respond to that demand. Here "best" is interpreted to mean that strategy which best advances the objectives of the organization. At this point the manager feels the pressure from varying viewpoints within the company.

Sales wants large inventories of each product. Then customers may expect immediate delivery and the selling job is made easier. On the other hand, Finance is concerned about too much capital being tied up in inventory. Finance might advocate "production on demand" as optimal from their viewpoint. Personnel, however, worries about training and morale problems among employees if heavy production occurs in some time periods and no production occurs in others. Optimal from the vantage of Personnel is continuous, regular production.

The executive who is responsible for the production decision must take into consideration all of those differing views. But each by itself could lead to a different production-inventory decision. The final decision should be good for the organization as a whole, not just for one or two of its divisions. When presenting the problem to an OR group, the executive knows that it will take the overall organizational view—optimizing system, not subsystem, performance.

Operations Research will look to Sales for assessments of minimum and maximum sales potential, to Finance for a judgment about available capital, to Accounting for analyses of cash-flow requirements, and to Personnel for information about worker availability and job-security expectations. All inputs will be viewed either as restrictions on the problem or as objectives or goals which are to be met as closely as is feasible. The restrictions become constraints in the model and the objectives are incorporated into it.

Note particularly that the model might be required to make provision for *multiple objectives*, such as cost minimization subject to maintenance of specified inventory levels *and* maximization of worker satisfaction subject to specified profit requirements. Often, multiple objectives will be in conflict with each other, so that the final solution might involve a production-inventory decision that is optimal for *no* particular single objective, but that represents a best compromise decision.

The model will include all of the restrictions mentioned above, as well as others such as limitations on time and on the availability of raw materials. Then OR will seek a solution for the problem that has been modeled. Thus an organizational orientation, a model, and a solution for the model characterize the OR approach.

Many different types of problems can be called operations research problems, and there may be many different approaches to solution for a particular problem. Yet certain tasks are common to all OR inquiries. Six critical stages of any OR investigation are:

1 Identifying the problem: its objectives, its constraints, and its decision variables
2 Formulating the model of the problem
3 Assessing model parameters
4 Determining a solution for the model
5 Testing and modifying (validating) the model
6 Exploiting the solution

In this text we will deal principally with the first five stages, with major emphasis on stages 2 and 4. The final stage, exploiting the solution, or putting the results of the study to good use, is mainly the province of the manager. The job of the OR group at this last stage is to make sure that the manager understands its recommendations.

Stage 3, the assessment of model parameters (unit cost, unit profit, demand, amount of resource available during production, time, and so on), may be the most difficult. Often the parameters simply reflect the best judgment of people who are supposed to be experts. The form of the model may be correct, but a bad decision can still result from inaccurate values being assigned to the parameters.

The fifth stage, testing and modifying the model, is very important. The conditions which prevailed when the model was formulated might have changed by the end of the fourth stage, when the solution for the model is obtained. We must continually assess the ability of the information available to adequately reflect the real problem. And even if conditions have not changed since the model-formulation stage, we should still test the performance of the model as applied to a practical situation. This might be done by using past data to see how well the model solution would have worked if it had been available then. Or the solution given by the model might be compared with the decision that would have been made in the absence of the model. This stage might also involve establishing controls whereby variations in critical model parameters could be incorporated into the model.

Most of the material in this text addresses only the formulation and solution of models for small but often quite realistic problems of the type one might encounter in business or industry. Those two stages, stages 2 and 4, require less actual business experience and so are more suitable for intensive study by a beginner in the field. Moreover, the practice acquired in model formulation and model solution will enhance your ability to reduce a real problem to a realistic model and will help you to know what information to seek for input of parameters.

In business and industry some kind of economic criterion is usually used to measure optimality. Superficially, the notion of an economic criterion is quite simple; we merely maximize profit or minimize the cost of a job that must be done. But minimizing cost in the short run might reduce the quality of the product so that the decision is not in the company's best long-run interests. We must be careful that relevant constraints precluding that type of decision, or multiple objectives where necessary, are incorporated into the model.

In problems encountered by educational or governmental organizations no profit may be measurable in a strict economic sense. The quantification of objectives of nonprofit institutions is extremely difficult and is one of the areas currently calling for more pure and applied research. For example, consider the following situations: locating and constructing parks within a city to achieve maximum benefit for its residents; allocating the water resources of a region so that everyone receives a fair share, socially as well as economically; the management of a national forest as a multiple-use resource, allowing for timbering, livestock grazing, hunting, fishing, mineral exploration and extraction, general recreational use, and the maintenance of wilderness areas. What is the optimal strategy for managing a national forest?

A new generation of problem solvers will be expected to suggest strategies for the management of public resources in the presence of pressures for exploitation, recreation, and conservation. If two of these viewpoints are overlooked to the advantage of a third, that forest could become a patch of barren ground adjacent to a gallery displaying photographs of trees, a teeming ghetto of contiguous campgrounds, or a beautiful wooded area which one is permitted to view but not enter. If something besides one of those extremes is to be achieved, certainly multiple objectives must be put into the model, and "benefit" will not be measured exclusively in terms of dollars.

## KEY WORDS AND PHRASES

**Operations research or management science**  A quantitative science which helps managers make good decisions.

**Mathematical model**  A symbolic statement of a decision problem, usually only a simplified approximation of the real situation.

**Model formulation**  Determining an objective function and incorporating constraints into the mathematical model, each stated in terms of the decision variables in the problem.

**Objective function**  A mathematical function which is to be optimized (maximized or minimized) according to the objective desired by the manager.

**Multiple objectives**  More than one objective in the same decision problem, often conflicting with each other.

**Decision variables**  The variables in the problem over which the manager has some control; their values may be specified by the manager, subject to constraints that may have been imposed upon those variables.

**Constraints**  Equations or inequalities that express mathematically the restrictions that have been imposed on the decision variables.

**Feasible region**   The set of values of the decision variables that permits all constraints to be satisfied.

**Sensitivity analysis**   Analysis of the effect upon the optimal decision of changes in the values of parameters used in the model.

**OR team**   A group of people trained in various scientific disciplines, brought together to attack a decision problem in such a way that their differing viewpoints may converge to the same rational solution.

## SELECTED REFERENCES

Ackoff, R. L., and M. W. Sasieni: *Fundamentals of Operations Research*, John Wiley & Sons, Inc., New York, 1968.

Churchman, C. W., R. L. Ackoff, and E. L. Arnoff: *Introduction to Operations Research*, John Wiley & Sons, Inc., New York, 1957.

Duffin, R. J., E. L. Peterson, and C. Zener: *Geometric Programming*, John Wiley & Sons, Inc., New York, 1967.

Gaver, D. P., and G. L. Thompson: *Programming and Probability Models in Operations Research*, Brooks/Cole Publishing Company, Monterey, Calif., 1973.

Hillier, F. S., and G. J. Lieberman: *Introduction to Operations Research*, 3d ed., Holden-Day, Inc., San Francisco, 1980.

Levin, R. I., C. A. Kirkpatrick, and D. S. Rubin: *Quantitative Approaches to Management*, 5th ed., McGraw-Hill Book Company, New York, 1982.

Richmond, S. B.: *Operations Research for Management Decisions*, The Ronald Press, New York, 1968.

Siemans, N., C. H. Marting, and F. Greenwood: *Operations Research*, The Free Press, New York, 1973.

Taha, H. A.: *Operations Research*, 3d ed., Macmillan Publishing Company, Inc., New York, 1982.

Thierauf, R. J., and R. C. Klekamp: *Decision Making Through Operations Research*, 2d ed., John Wiley & Sons, Inc., New York, 1975.

Thompson, W. W., Jr.: *Operations Research Techniques*, Charles E. Merrill Books, Inc., Columbus, Ohio, 1967.

Trefethen, F. N.: "A History of Operations Research," in McCloskey, J. F., and Trefethen, F. N. (eds.), *Operations Research for Management*, The Johns Hopkins Press, Baltimore, 1954.

Wagner, H. M.: *Principles of Operations Research*, Prentice-Hall, Inc., Englewood Cliffs, N.J., 1969.

# LINEAR PROGRAMMING MODELS

$O$ne of the most powerful OR techniques available to a business decision maker is *linear programming*. Although problems of this type have existed for centuries, it was not until the 1940s that George Dantzig developed a general solution technique for them, a procedure called the *simplex method*. Subsequent research, still going on today, has extended that original work to encompass both linear and nonlinear problems into a broad body of theory and methods known simply as *mathematical programming*. Here we consider only the *linear* models.

Linear programming models consist of a linear objective function and linear constraints, either equations or inequalities, on the decision variables. In the simple case of only two decision variables, linearity just means that the objective function (at a specified value) and the boundaries of all constraints may be graphed in two dimensions as *straight lines*.

Many different types of real business problems can be formulated as linear programming models. Examples are found in almost any division of a business organization: finance, production, accounting, personnel, distribution, and in many different types of businesses: manufacturing, service, banking, agriculture, mineral production, and so on. For this reason, an extended lesson in linear programming is a good starting point for your education in the procedures of quantitative management.

In this chapter only the *formulation* of linear programming models is introduced. Then Chapters 3 through 7 constitute a leisurely, elementary development of the concepts and mechanics in the simplex method. In addition to the basic solution procedures, in those chapters you will also see some very practical economic interpretations of numerical results, sensitivity analyses, and computer-based solutions with interpretations.

While this chapter is devoted exclusively to the mathematical formulation of realistic problems, you should not assume that it contains the last word on that subject. Correct formulation of linear programming models is extremely important, and opportunities to practice those formulations exist in all of the linear programming chapters.

## 2.1 FORMULATING SIMPLE LINEAR PROGRAMMING MODELS

In this section we will consider linear programming formulation by way of two examples, a specific small-business problem and a rather generic production problem. Then Section 2.2 will be a general, explanatory interlude before we return in Section 2.3 to other examples of model formulation.

### Example 2.1
### A Small-Business Application

Early Auto Sales stocks and sells two types of automobiles, model *A* and model *T*. During the next six-month period Mr. Early expects to have $600,000 available for purchasing cars, and this year dealer cost for a model *A* is $4,000 while a model *T* costs $3,000. Past experience indicates that it takes on the average 4 hours of sales time to sell a model *A* to a customer and 6 hours to sell a model *T*. Mr. Early and his son, the only other employee of the company, estimate that between them they will have available 960 hours during the next six months to devote exclusively to selling.

In the previous six-month period the average gross profit (selling price minus dealer cost) has been 15 percent of cost on model *A* and 10 percent of cost on model *T*. No reason exists to suppose those percentages will change in the near future, so the Earlys assume that profit per model *A* sold will be $600 and profit per model *T* sold will be $300. Only 100 model *A*'s and 300 model *T*'s will be available from the factory during the period of interest, and projected demand studies indicate that Mr. Early must buy at least 100 model *T*'s to maintain customer goodwill. Demand for model *A*'s is not predictable, so no lower bound other than zero is presumed.

Our objective is to discover how many cars of each model the company should purchase and sell during the next six months in order to maximize gross profit for the period. For ready reference, Table 2.1 shows the parameters mentioned in the problem description.

Now we begin formulating the linear programming model. Let the letter $A$ denote the number of model $A$ cars to purchase and let $T$ be the corresponding number of model $T$'s. We know the profit per car for each model, so the objective function is

$$\text{Profit} = P = 600A + 300T$$

That is, the profit on $A$ model $A$'s is \$600A, the profit on $T$ model $T$'s is \$300T, and the total profit is \$600A + \$300T.

We observe that \$4,000A is the cost per model $A$ times the number of model $A$'s purchased, \$3,000T is the cost per model $T$ times the number of model $T$'s purchased, and the sum of those two costs cannot exceed total available capital, \$600,000. Similar observations yield the time constraint in the model. Finally, the demand and availability constraints are easily written down, and it is obvious that the decision variables must be nonnegative. Thus the required linear programming model is

Find $A$ and $T$ which maximize $P$

where $\qquad P = 600A + 300T \qquad$ gross profit in dollars

subject to

$$4,000A + 3,000T \le 600,000 \qquad \text{capital constraint}$$
$$4A + \qquad 6T \le 960 \qquad \text{time constraint}$$
$$100 \le T \le 300 \qquad \text{demand and availability for model } T$$
$$A \le 100 \qquad \text{availability for model } A$$
$$A \ge 0 \qquad T \ge 0 \qquad \text{a negative number of cars is not permitted}$$

The solution is to stock 100 model $T$'s and 75 model $A$'s, producing a maximum gross profit for the six-month period of \$75,000. This answer is worked out in Example 3.6 of Chapter 3 as an illustration of the graphical

**TABLE 2.1**  *PARAMETERS FOR EARLY AUTO SALES PROBLEM*

| Type of car | Cost per car | Selling time per car | Profit per car | No. cars available | Minimum no. cars required |
|---|---|---|---|---|---|
| Model A | \$  4,000 | 4 hours | \$600 | 100 | 0 |
| Model T | \$  3,000 | 6 hours | \$300 | 300 | 100 |
| **Available** | \$600,000 | 960 hours | | | |

procedure for solving two-variable linear programming problems. An implicit assumption in the solution is that Early Auto Sales will be able to sell all automobiles stocked, including the 75 model $A$'s for which no demand could be predicted.

### Example 2.2
### A Generic Production Application

The word "generic" is used here to imply that many manufacturing problems have the same general form as this example. Instead of stating what specific items are being produced or what the actual raw materials are, we simply call them "product $B$" or "material III." For a particular case, of course, you would know what products you are making and what materials you are making them from.

A manufacturing company produces four products from three different types of materials. The amount in pounds of each raw material used in the manufacture of a unit of each product appears in Table 2.2.

Additionally, it takes 5 person-hours to produce a unit of product $A$, and the person-hours required for a unit of products $B$, $C$, and $D$, respectively, are 4, 3, and 6. The company has available 200 pounds of material I, 300 pounds of II, and 400 pounds of III, and will have 300 person-hours available during the current production period. If the profits per unit for products $A$, $B$, $C$, and $D$ are \$7, \$10, \$5, and \$6, respectively, formulate as a linear programming model the problem of discovering how many units of each product to manufacture in order to maximize profit for the current period.

The first thing to do is identify the decision variables.

Let $x_A$ = number of units of product $A$ to manufacture

$x_B$ = number of units of product $B$ to manufacture

$x_C$ = number of units of product $C$ to manufacture

$x_D$ = number of units of product $D$ to manufacture

**TABLE 2.2** POUNDS OF MATERIAL REQUIRED PER UNIT OF PRODUCT

| Product | Material | | |
|---------|-----|-----|-----|
|  | I | II | III |
| A | 2.0 | 3.5 | 4.0 |
| B | 4.0 | 2.0 | 1.0 |
| C | 2.5 | 2.0 | 3.0 |
| D | 1.0 | 3.5 | 2.5 |

Then the objective function is obvious, and the constraints are easy to write.

Consider, for instance, the constraint due to the limited amount of material II. One unit of product $A$ consumes 3.5 pounds of material II, so if $x_A$ units are produced, $3.5x_A$ pounds of material II are required. Likewise, $x_B$ units of product $B$ require $2.0x_B$ pounds of material II, and so on. Only 300 pounds of material II are available, so the constraint that arises because of that limitation is

$$3.5x_A + 2.0x_B + 2.0x_C + 3.5x_D \le 300$$

Constraints for the other two materials and for person-hours are similarly formulated.

With $P$ representing profit in dollars, the linear programming model (the source of each constraint being identified beside it) is

Maximize $P$

where $\qquad\qquad\qquad P = 7x_A + 10x_B + 5x_C + 6x_D$

subject to $\quad 2.0x_A + 4.0x_B + 2.5x_C + 1.0x_D \le 200 \qquad$ material I

$\qquad\qquad 3.5x_A + 2.0x_B + 2.0x_C + 3.5x_D \le 300 \qquad$ material II

$\qquad\qquad 4.0x_A + 1.0x_B + 3.0x_C + 2.5x_D \le 400 \qquad$ material III

$\qquad\qquad 5.0x_A + 4.0x_B + 3.0x_C + 6.0x_D \le 300 \qquad$ person-hours

$\qquad\qquad\qquad\quad x_A, x_B, x_C, x_D \ge 0 \qquad\qquad\qquad$ nonnegativity

The solution for this model is

$$x_A = 0 \qquad x_B = 45 \qquad x_C = 0 \qquad x_D = 20$$

giving a maximum profit of

$$\text{Max } P = \$570$$

That is, the company should make no units of products $A$ and $C$, but it should manufacture 45 units of product $B$ and 20 units of product $D$ for a maximum profit of $570 during the current period.

Does this answer violate your intuition about the problem? Why shouldn't the company make some units of product $A$ instead of product $D$, since the per-unit profit is a dollar higher for product $A$? Why shouldn't the company make as many units as possible (50) of product $B$, since that product is by far the most profitable per unit? The answer to these questions, of course, resides in the *constraints*.

Note, for example, that if $x_B = 50$, then all of material I is used up by the manufacture of product $B$ so that nothing else can be produced. But this only gives a profit of $500. With the *optimal* solution, however, *both* material I *and* available person-hours are totally consumed, and *more* of materials II and III are used. Naturally, if one may use more of the available profit-making potential of the time and materials, one should expect to be able to make more profit. This was basically a problem in the *optimal allocation of resources*, a subject which we will consider in more depth in the *duality* portion of Chapter 5.

## 2.2  CHARACTERISTICS REQUIRED FOR STRICT LINEARITY

A real-world problem should possess four specific characteristics if it is to be reduced to the simple mathematical formulation that permits solution by a linear programming technique. These characteristics are (1) exact knowledge of parameters, (2) additivity, (3) direct proportionality, and (4) fractionality. These terms are discussed in some detail in the next few paragraphs.

In our formulation of the Early Auto Sales problem (Example 2.1), for instance, we made some implicit assumptions. First, we assumed that all of the coefficients of decision variables in the model, and all of the boundary numbers in the constraints, were *known exactly*; they would not change during the period for which the problem was posed. We also assumed that profits and costs were purely *additive* in nature; total profit and total costs were just the sums of individual profits and costs that would have accrued if we had been marketing the two different models of cars separately. Further, we supposed that per-unit profit and cost remained fixed regardless of the number of units sold or purchased, or that there were no quantity discounts or premiums involved. This is the concept of *direct proportionality*. And finally, by not including in our model the obvious requirement that the decision variables must be integers (we buy and sell whole cars, not fractions of cars) we have implied that *fractionality* of decision variables was allowed. Nothing in our model required $A$ and $T$ to be whole numbers; we were only lucky that their optimal values involved no fractions.

### Exact Knowledge of Parameters

Rarely in a real decision problem will we know exactly the values of the input constants for the model, the parameters. We are usually making a decision about some future course of action, and the correct parameters will be those that exist then, not those that have existed in the past. For example, profit per car on model $A$ three months from now might not be the $600 figure used in our model for Example 2.1. Or costs could change, or available capital could. We only hope that our choices for these parameters will be close to their actual values so the solution for the model will be close to the correct solution for the problem.

Sometimes the parameters may be random variables, with known, or worse yet, unknown, probability distributions. In some instances we would simply use their expected values (average value over the entire distribution), treating expected values like known parameters. But other times the element of randomness may be so important that it must be incorporated into the model in a more complete fashion. Procedures for solving some versions of this *stochastic* (random) *programming* problem do exist, but we will not consider them in this text.

Even in the case that the parameters are known to be deterministic (nonrandom) but we are unsure of their exact values, something more can be done beyond merely finding a solution for the model as originally formulated. A feature of the simplex method called *sensitivity analysis* allows us to investigate the effect on the optimal solution of variations in values of the parameters. Examples of such analyses appear in Chapter 5.

### Additivity

In Example 2.1 the amount of money used to purchase model $A$'s was added to the amount used to purchase model $T$'s, producing an expression representing the total capital required to acquire the cars that will become available for sale. You might assume that the adding together of individual prices to produce total price is such an obvious thing to do that it need not be mentioned. But what about the terms in the objective function, the profit terms? Here, by adding the two individual profit terms, $600A$ and $300T$, we are assuming that the marketing of two competitive models simultaneously produces the same per-unit profit as if each model had been offered for sale separately. That is, if only model $A$'s are sold, profit per car is $600, while if both model $A$'s and model $T$'s are to be sold, there will be no "interactive" adjustment necessary in profit considerations. If such an adjustment had been required, it might have entered the objective function in the form of a cross-product term, like $-10AT$. Such a term in a mathematical function is a second-degree term, not linear, and must not appear in either the objective function or any of the constraints. The methods of linear programming cannot handle functions containing nonlinear terms.

### Direct Proportionality

The characteristic of direct proportionality refers to the coefficients of the decision variables in the model. For example, profit per model $A$ was assumed to be $600 and cost was assumed to be $4,000 regardless of the number of model $A$'s purchased and then sold. That is, profit and cost increase in direct proportion to the number of units involved. But if a quantity discount is offered, where the cost per unit is decreased if more than a specified number of units is purchased, then total cost is *not* directly proportional to number of units. This would be the case, for instance, if the first 50 model $A$'s purchased cost $4,000 apiece, but only $3,800 apiece for all model $A$'s purchased beyond that initial 50. Here $4,000A$ would not be the correct capital-consumption term if more than 50 model $A$'s are purchased, nor would $3,800A$ be correct either, since each of the first 50 cars costs $4,000. Such lack of direct proportionality can be handled in a model formulation, but the resulting model would not be strictly linear.

### Fractionality

By the term "fractionality" we simply mean that the decision variables are not required to be whole numbers (integers). For the model to be strictly a linear programming model, the decision variables must be permitted to range through all feasible values (all combinations of values of the decision variables which satisfy all constraints in the model). If some or all of the variables are restricted to integer values, we really have what is called an *integer programming* problem.

In our formulation of the problem in Example 2.1 we blithely ignored that obvious integer-valued feature of the decision variables, hoping that the optimal solution for the model would turn out to involve only integer values. In that case it did, with $A = 75$ and $T = 100$.

Very often in practice an integer restriction is ignored, with the answer simply rounded to integers and called an approximate solution. It is possible to get into big trouble by adopting that viewpoint, but usually a rounded solution will be a good approximation, especially if all of the values of the decision variables are large. In Chapter 7 the question of integer linear programming is considered, so you will have an opportunity to see what can be done if it is important to include the integer restriction in the model. And finally, it should be noted that there do exist special cases of integer linear programming models for which the ordinary simplex method automatically produces integer solutions. You will also see some of those problems in Chapter 7.

### 2.3 MORE FORMULATION EXAMPLES

Despite the fact that the mathematical modeling of real problems is the most critical skill in operations research, the emphasis in the next few chapters will be on the solution procedures for linear programming problems. The process of mathematical modeling becomes easier as you learn more about methods for solving the models and about why those methods work. But your ability to recognize important features which should be incorporated into models is also enhanced by formulation practice, so now we will consider some more examples of linear programming models.

### Example 2.3
### A Generic Diet Problem

Among the earliest kinds of problems to be worked using linear programming techniques are those which are generally called "diet" or "blending" problems. A nice thing about that type of problem is the fact that the variables may reasonably assume fractional values. That characteristic is evident in the following generic example.

A diet is to contain at least 8 ounces of nutrient $A$, 10 ounces of nutrient $B$, and 22 ounces of nutrient $C$. Some mixture of foods $F_1$, $F_2$, and $F_3$ will constitute the diet and is to supply the required nutrients. Each pound of $F_1$ costs $0.50 and contains 5 ounces of $A$, 2 ounces of $B$, and 1 ounce of $C$. Each pound of $F_2$ costs $0.80 and has 1 ounce of $A$, 2 ounces of $B$, and 5 ounces of $C$. A pound of $F_3$ costs $0.60 and has no $A$, but contains 1 ounce of $B$ and 4 ounces of $C$. In what quantity should each of the three foods be purchased in order to meet the specified dietary requirements at minimum cost?

Before formulating the model of this problem we note that all of the requirements for strict linearity seem to be satisfied. It is reasonable to suppose that $1\frac{1}{4}$ pounds of food could be as easily purchased as a pound, so fractionality makes sense. For additivity, observe that the amount of nutrient $A$ in the mixture is simply the sum of the amounts supplied by foods $F_1$, $F_2$, and $F_3$, and that costs are also additive. The amount of nutrient $B$ obviously increases in direct proportion to the amount of increase in any food in the mixture, and finally, the chemistry of the situation seems to assure exact knowledge of the parameters.

Let $x_1$, $x_2$, and $x_3$ be, respectively, the number of pounds of foods $F_1$, $F_2$, and $F_3$ to purchase. These are the decision variables. Table 2.3 gives a convenient organization of all the information in the problem.

Since we know the cost per pound of each food, have named the decision variables as number of pounds of food, and know that the objective is to minimize total cost of the diet, the objective function writes itself. Letting $C$ represent the cost of the diet in cents, we have

$$C = 50x_1 + 80x_2 + 60x_3$$

Since a pound of $F_1$ contributes 5 ounces of $A$ to the diet, the number of ounces of nutrient $A$ in the mix which come from $F_1$ is $5x_1$. Likewise, $F_2$ contributes $1x_2$ ounces of $A$, while $F_3$ contributes no nutrient $A$. The total number of ounces of nutrient $A$ in the diet must be at least 8, yielding the constraint

$$5x_1 + x_2 \geq 8$$

**TABLE 2.3**  VARIABLES AND PARAMETERS FOR THE DIET PROBLEM

| Food | Number of pounds | Cost per pound | Ounces of nutrient per pound of food | | |
|------|------------------|----------------|------|------|------|
| | | | A | B | C |
| $F_1$ | $x_1$ | $0.50 | 5 | 2 | 1 |
| $F_2$ | $x_2$ | $0.80 | 1 | 2 | 5 |
| $F_2$ | $x_3$ | $0.60 | 0 | 1 | 4 |
| **Minimum requirements, oz** | | | 8 | 10 | 22 |

The other two nutrient constraints are similarly determined. Realizing that negative amounts of food are impossible, we can now write the complete model.

$$\text{Minimize } C$$

where
$$C = 50x_1 + 80x_2 + 60x_3 \qquad \text{cost of diet}$$

subject to

$$
\begin{aligned}
5x_1 + x_2 &\geq 8 && \text{nutrient } A \\
2x_1 + 2x_2 + x_3 &\geq 10 && \text{nutrient } B \\
x_1 + 5x_2 + 4x_3 &\geq 22 && \text{nutrient } C \\
x_1 \geq 0 \qquad x_2 \geq 0 \qquad x_3 &\geq 0 && \text{nonnegativity}
\end{aligned}
$$

The set of values for $x_1$, $x_2$, and $x_3$ that gives the smallest value for $C$ subject to the condition that those values also satisfy all constraints (fall in the *feasible region*) is the optimal solution for the model. In this case, where the model is assumed to be an exact representation of reality, we assume that optimal solution is the solution of the real problem. That solution is $(x_1, x_2, x_3) = (0.75, 4.25, 0)$, where Min $C = 377.5$ cents ($3.775). You will be asked to verify that answer in an exercise in Chapter 4. In words, the minimum-cost diet consists of $\frac{3}{4}$ pound of food $F_1$ and $4\frac{1}{4}$ pounds of food $F_2$.

## Example 2.4
### A Distribution Application: Transportation Problem

This example is a special case of a linear programming problem called a *transportation problem*. The unique structure of its model permits us to use a special procedure, the *transportation method*, to obtain its solution. At the moment, however, we are only interested in formulating the model.

Monthly, Suregood Hardware ships units of the same product from two warehouses to three retail stores. Because of such things as different distances or different shipping methods, the cost of shipping a unit of product depends upon both the warehouse from which the shipment originates and the store which is to receive the unit. Further, each warehouse has a limited capacity for storing the product, and each store will require only a fixed number of units monthly.

Table 2.4 gives relevant cost, capacity, and requirements parameters. The body of the table shows costs per unit (in dollars) for shipping from each warehouse to each store, and the margins of the table give monthly warehouse capacities and store requirements. Total capacity has been made equal to total requirements; that is, supply equals demand. The more realistic case, where supply exceeds demand or vice versa, is reserved for Chapter 7, where transportation problems are considered in greater detail.

The objective is to determine how many units to ship from each

**TABLE 2.4**

**COSTS, CAPACITIES, AND REQUIREMENTS: SUREGOOD HARDWARE PROBLEM**

| | **Per-Unit Shipping Cost** | | | | |
|---|---|---|---|---|---|
| | **Store** | | | | (number |
| **Warehouse** | **1** | **2** | **3** | **Capacity** | of units) |
| 1 | 9 | 8 | 6 | 100 | |
| 2 | 7 | 4 | 3 | 200 | |
| **Requirement** (number of units) | 140 | 50 | 110 | 300 | (total) |

warehouse to each store in order to minimize overall transportation cost. This suggests six decision variables. Let $x_{ij}$ denote the number of units of product to ship from warehouse $i$ to store $j$, where $i = 1, 2$ and $j = 1, 2, 3$. Then, for example, $8x_{12}$ would be the total cost of shipping $x_{12}$ units from warehouse 1 to store 2. The objective function, total cost in dollars, is then easily seen to be

$$C = 9x_{11} + 8x_{12} + 6x_{13} + 7x_{21} + 4x_{22} + 3x_{23}$$

There are five constraints besides the usual nonnegativity restrictions: two come from limitations on capacity of warehouses, three from the store requirements. Each warehouse must exhaust its capacity, and each store must receive the number of units it requires.

The complete model is

$$\text{Minimize } C$$

where $\qquad C = 9x_{11} + 8x_{12} + 6x_{13} + 7x_{21} + 4x_{22} + 3x_{23} \qquad$ cost: dollars

$$\begin{aligned}
\text{subject to} \quad x_{11} + x_{12} + x_{13} \qquad\qquad\qquad &= 100 \qquad \text{warehouse 1} \\
x_{21} + x_{22} + x_{23} &= 200 \qquad \text{warehouse 2} \\
x_{11} \qquad\qquad + x_{21} \qquad\qquad &= 140 \qquad \text{store 1} \\
x_{12} \qquad\qquad + x_{22} \qquad &= 50 \qquad \text{store 2} \\
x_{13} \qquad\qquad + x_{23} &= 110 \qquad \text{store 3} \\
x_{ij} \geq 0 \quad i = 1, 2 \quad j = 1, 2, 3 \qquad\qquad & \qquad\qquad \text{nonnegativity}
\end{aligned}$$

Note that each constraint (except the nonnegativity constraints) in this problem is an equation. Generally, even in transportation problems similar to this one, the constraints will be inequalities because total capacity will not equal total requirements.

The optimal solution, discovered using the *transportation method* that will be presented in Chapter 7, is

$$x_{11} = 100 \qquad x_{12} = 0 \qquad x_{13} = 0$$

$$x_{21} = 40 \qquad x_{22} = 50 \qquad x_{23} = 110$$

$$\text{with Min } C = \$1,710$$

Observe the *integer* characteristic of the $x_{ij}$'s at optimality. The transportation method *always* gives an integer solution even though nothing in our model indicates that the $x_{ij}$'s should be integer-valued. This is due to the important "corner-point" characteristic of an optimal solution that you will learn about in Chapter 3. All of the "feasible corners" in a transportation problem happen to have integer-valued coordinates.

As an operations researcher reporting this solution to the distribution manager of Suregood Hardware, you would phrase the solution as follows:

Ship: 100 units from warehouse 1 to store 1
40 units from warehouse 2 to store 1
50 units from warehouse 2 to store 2
110 units from warehouse 2 to store 3

Note that all capacity and requirement constraints are satisfied. Further, you might be surprised to learn that 100 units are shipped at the highest rate ($9 per unit). Do you doubt the solution? An unbeliever is challenged to achieve a cheaper solution satisfying all the constraints.

**Example 2.5**
**An Accounting Application: Assignment Problem**

Chekov and Adams is a large accounting firm with a number of wealthy clients. One of its services is the preparation of tax returns. On April 14 four of its most valued clients finally bring in the necessary information for completion of their returns. To keep these clients happy, the firm will prepare their returns on a crash basis.

Four of Chekov and Adams's tax specialists—Brown, Green, White, and Black—are selected for assignment to the four returns. Intense, intimate consultation with each client is anticipated, so each specialist will work on only one return. Mr. Chekov has estimated the time required for each specialist to complete the return of each client, and of course he knows the hourly wage of each specialist. This information permits him to construct Table 2.5, which gives the estimated cost in dollars for each specialist's preparation of each client's return. Mr. Chekov wants to determine how to assign specialists to clients so the total estimated cost of preparing all four returns is minimized.

**TABLE 2.5**    COSTS: CHEKOV AND ADAMS PROBLEM

| | Client | | | |
|---|---|---|---|---|
| **Specialist** | **1** | **2** | **3** | **4** |
| 1 Brown | 231 | 378 | 252 | 168 |
| 2 Green | 240 | 384 | 216 | 160 |
| 3 White | 192 | 228 | 168 | 120 |
| 4 Black | 234 | 306 | 216 | 162 |

Note that once a specialist is assigned to a client, he or she cannot be assigned to another, and no client is assigned more than one specialist. This characteristic of an *assignment problem* suggests decision variables that will only assume one of two values: 0 or 1.  Let $x_{11}$ denote a Brown–client 1 association, $x_{23}$ a Green–client 3 association, and so on.  Then if $x_{11}$ = 1, this means Brown is assigned to client 1 (and that Brown cannot be assigned to another client), while if $x_{11}$ = 0, then Brown is *not* assigned to client 1.  Consequently, there will be 16 decision variables (and 8 constraints) in the model for this problem, but at any feasible solution only 4 of the $x_{ij}$'s can be 1 and the other 12 will be 0.

To formulate the objective function, we need only notice that $231x_{11}$ is equal to 231 if $x_{11}$ = 1 and is equal to zero if $x_{11}$ = 0, and so on for any of the other cost terms.  Therefore, the cost function is simply a 16-term function with each term being the product of cost and the associated $x_{ij}$.

To form a constraint, remember that Brown, for instance, can only be assigned to one client.  Thus

$$x_{11} + x_{12} + x_{13} + x_{14} = 1$$

would be the constraint associated with Brown.  If $x_{12}$ = 1, then Brown is assigned to client 2, so $x_{11} = x_{13} = x_{14} = 0$, since Brown can be assigned to no one else.  Likewise, consider the "client 3" constraint.  It is

$$x_{13} + x_{23} + x_{33} + x_{43} = 1$$

since if $x_{43}$ = 1, this means Black is assigned to client 3, and that $x_{13}$, $x_{23}$, and $x_{33}$ must each be 0 (a specialist is already assigned to client 3).  This reasoning produces the following model:

Minimize C

where    $C = 231x_{11} + 378x_{12} + 252x_{13} + 168x_{14} + 240x_{21} + 384x_{22} +$
$216x_{23} + 160x_{24} + 192x_{31} + 228x_{32} + 168x_{33} + 120x_{34} +$
$234x_{41} + 306x_{42} + 216x_{43} + 162x_{44}$

subject to

$$x_{11} + x_{12} + x_{13} + x_{14} = 1 \qquad \text{Brown}$$

$$x_{21} + x_{22} + x_{23} + x_{24} = 1 \qquad \text{Green}$$

$$x_{31} + x_{32} + x_{33} + x_{34} = 1 \qquad \text{White}$$

$$x_{41} + x_{42} + x_{43} + x_{44} = 1 \qquad \text{Black}$$

$$x_{11} + x_{21} + x_{31} + x_{41} = 1 \qquad \text{client 1}$$

$$x_{12} + x_{22} + x_{32} + x_{42} = 1 \qquad \text{client 2}$$

$$x_{13} + x_{23} + x_{33} + x_{43} = 1 \qquad \text{client 3}$$

$$x_{14} + x_{24} + x_{34} + x_{44} = 1 \qquad \text{client 4}$$

$$x_{ij} = 0 \text{ or } 1 \quad i = 1, 2, 3, 4 \quad j = 1, 2, 3, 4$$

This model is *not* strictly linear, since it violates the *fractionality* requirement. However, this is one type of problem where the ordinary simplex method, although designed for strictly linear problems, will automatically give an integer solution, with our specified "0-1" characteristic for all variables.

The solution is exhibited in Exercise 6.12 of Chapter 6 and is

$$x_{11} = 1 \qquad x_{24} = 1 \qquad x_{32} = 1 \qquad x_{43} = 1$$

with the 12 other $x_{ij}$'s being zero. The (minimum) estimated total cost of the assignment is $835. In words, the optimal solution is: Assign Brown to client 1, Green to client 4, White to client 2, and Black to client 3.

This problem may also be solved by a technique called the *assignment method*, which takes advantage of the very special structure of an assignment problem. You will be asked to solve it in one of the exercises in Chapter 7 using that simplified procedure.

### Example 2.6
### A Petroleum Industry Application: Blending Problem

This larger example is similar to the diet problem discussed in Example 2.3 except that the objective is to maximize profit. It is presented here to give you a feeling for the size and complexity of an actual industrial problem. It was first given to a professor in the Department of Petroleum Engineering at the University of Wyoming who was acting as consultant for an oil company. He in turn came to the author (analyst) for help with its formulation as a linear programming problem and for advice on obtaining its solution. The size of the problem dictated the use of a "canned" linear programming computer program, and the solution itself chewed up about $1\frac{1}{2}$ minutes of computer time on an old Xerox Sigma 7 computer.

The problem was first presented to the analyst in the form shown in Table 2.6. That original presentation is displayed here to point out a typical situation in business: the person with the problem is often unable to communicate it on a first try so that the analyst completely understands it. The expert in any field rarely appreciates the extent of the nonexpert's ignorance about the expert's chosen profession. Usually the analyst and the problem proposer must work jointly to obtain an adequate mathematical model of the problem.

The problem comes from an oil refinery which uses various "blending stocks" to produce products for eventual marketing. The three products involved here are aviation gasoline, premium gasoline, and regular gasoline. The problem is a bit dated now, having been posed in the early 1970s, prior to the general use of unleaded gasoline.

Table 2.6 represents the problem as received by the analyst in the mail. To clarify the problem, here are the questions the analyst had to ask over the telephone, along with their answers.

1 Can any one of the five kinds of blending stock be used to make, individually, any one product? *Answer:* Yes.

2 Don't you mean "lead" instead of "lean"? *Answer:* No. (The analyst still does not fully understand the meaning of "lean" in this context, but such understanding is not necessary for an adequate formulation of the problem.)

3 Does "Lean costs $0.14/bbl" mean $0.14/bbl *per unit of octane? Answer:* Yes.

---

**TABLE 2.6**   *ORIGINAL PRESENTATION OF REFINERY PROBLEM*

| Blending stock | Rate, bbl*/day | Cost/bbl, $ | Octane | |
|---|---|---|---|---|
| | | | No lean | Lean |
| 1 Motor polymer | 1,400 | 4.00 | 96 | 99 |
| 2 Alkylate | 1,800 | 3.60 | 98 | 108 |
| 3 Reformate | 6,900† | 4.50 | 93 | 100 |
| 4 Standard run gasoline | | 4.00 | 60 | 74 |
| 5 Grackate | 3,600 | 4.30 | 90 | 96 |

| Products | Min. rate | Max. rate | Octane | Value/bbl $ |
|---|---|---|---|---|
| 1 Aviation gasoline | 500 | 1,000 | 85 (no lean) | 6.30 |
| 2 Premium gasoline | 2,000 | 5,000 | 100 | 6.10 |
| 3 Regular gasoline | 5,000 | 10,000 | 92 | 5.70 |

Lean costs $0.14/bbl. Assume octanes blend linearly. All stock must be made into product. Question: What is the optimal blending policy?

* bbl = barrels.
† Combined total of standard run gasoline and reformate is 6,900; that is, standard run gasoline is used to make reformate.

**4** Does "(no lean)" opposite "Aviation gasoline" mean that aviation gas is to be made exclusively from "no lean" blending stock? *Answer:* Yes.

**5** Do "Min. rate" and "Max. rate" for products mean respectively the minimum and maximum daily production rate in barrels? *Answer:* Yes.

As one can see from the description of this problem, the modeling and solution of a reasonably large industrial problem is a team effort, where the team at the minimum consists of an expert in the field of application and an expert in mathematical modeling. In this case quite likely a third expert, such as an accountant, participated at some stage to supply the "value/bbl" and "cost/bbl" figures.

Conceptually the model was not difficult to formulate; it was only longer and more tedious to write out than the models for the preceding examples. Careful inspection of the problem statement reveals 25 decision variables required for a linear formulation. Premium gasoline, for example, can be made from any of the 5 stocks in any of 2 modes (lean or no lean), giving rise to 10 variables. Regular gas also involves 10 variables. Aviation gas, to be made only in the "no lean" mode, produces only 5 variables (from the 5 blending stocks). Thus a suitable concise notation for naming the variables is no trivial problem.

The decision was to use $A$, $P$, and $R$ to denote, respectively, aviation gas, premium gas, and regular gas. First subscripts 1, 2, 3, 4, and 5 denoted the correspondingly numbered blending stocks in Table 2.6, while second subscripts 1 and 2 denoted "lean" and "no lean," respectively. Thus $A_{12}$ denotes the number of barrels of aviation gas made from motor polymer in the "no lean" mode, while $R_{21}$ means the number of barrels of regular gas made with alkylate in the "lean" mode.

The objective function is simply the total value of products minus the total cost of products, or a gross profit figure since blending cost is being ignored. The profit contribution per barrel for aviation gas made in the 12 fashion is then $6.30 − $4.00, or $2.30, while the profit contribution per barrel for regular gas of the 21 type is $5.70 − $3.60 − 10($0.14) = $0.70, the last term on the left being the cost of 10 units of octane in the "lean" mode (108 − 98 = 10). By proceeding in this fashion you can obtain the 25 profit per barrel constants used in the objective function of the model to follow.

Apart from the 25 nonnegativity restrictions, an example of which is the inequality $A_{12} \geq 0$, there are three basic types of constraints in this problem. Some arise from the statement that all stock must be made into product, others from the "min rate–max rate" requirements, and still others from the octane requirements that were specified. Of these, the only ones that might be difficult for you to formulate are the octane restrictions.

A complete discussion of how every term in the model was determined is not in order here. An example of the formulation of an octane restriction should suffice to enable you to verify the complete model.

The easiest octane constraint to write out is that for aviation gasoline, since only five variables are involved. Consider the equation

$$\frac{96A_{12} + 98A_{22} + 93A_{32} + 60A_{42} + 90A_{52}}{A_{12} + A_{22} + A_{32} + A_{42} + A_{52}} = 85$$

This is the octane restriction for aviation gasoline, although it does not yet resemble a linear constraint of the type we have seen in the previous examples. It is simply a weighted sum of octanes for the various ways of making aviation gasoline (the weights being number of barrels) divided by the total number of barrels of aviation gas produced, set equal to the required 85 octane.

Multiplying both sides of the equation by the denominator of the fraction on the left puts this constraint into a more obviously linear form:

$$96A_{12} + 98A_{22} + 93A_{32} + 60A_{42} + 90A_{52} = 85(A_{12} + A_{22} + A_{32} + A_{42} + A_{52})$$

Then we subtract the right-hand side from both sides to obtain the more familiar form

$$11A_{12} + 13A_{22} + 8A_{32} - 25A_{42} + 5A_{52} = 0$$

Now we state the complete model for the refinery problem. It has an objective function, 25 decision variables, and 10 constraints. It is

Maximize P

where
$$\begin{aligned}
P = {} & 2.30A_{12} + 2.70A_{22} + 1.80A_{32} + 2.30A_{42} + 2.00A_{52} + \\
& 2.10P_{12} + 2.50P_{22} + 1.60P_{32} + 2.10P_{42} + 1.80P_{52} + \\
& 1.69P_{11} + 1.10P_{21} + 0.62P_{31} + 0.14P_{41} + 0.96P_{51} + \\
& 1.70R_{12} + 2.10R_{22} + 1.20R_{32} + 1.70R_{42} + 1.40R_{52} + \\
& 1.28R_{11} + 0.70R_{21} + 0.22R_{31} - 0.26R_{41} + 0.56R_{51}
\end{aligned}$$

subject to

$$A_{12} + P_{12} + P_{11} + R_{12} + R_{11} = 1{,}400$$

$$A_{22} + P_{22} + P_{21} + R_{22} + R_{21} = 1{,}800$$

$$A_{32} + A_{42} + P_{32} + P_{42} + P_{31} + P_{41} + R_{32} + R_{42} + R_{31} + R_{41} = 6{,}900$$

$$A_{52} + P_{52} + P_{51} + R_{52} + R_{51} = 3{,}600$$

$$11A_{12} + 13A_{22} + 8A_{32} - 25A_{42} + 5A_{52} = 0$$

$$-4P_{12} - 2P_{22} - 7P_{32} - 40P_{42} - 10P_{52} - P_{11} + 8P_{21} - 26P_{41} - 4P_{51} = 0$$

$$4R_{12} + 6R_{22} + R_{32} - 32R_{42} - 2R_{52} + 7R_{11} + 16R_{21} + 8R_{31} - 18R_{41} + 4R_{51} = 0$$

$$500 \leq A_{12} + A_{22} + A_{32} + A_{42} + A_{52} \leq 1{,}000$$

$$2{,}000 \leq P_{12} + P_{22} + P_{32} + P_{42} + P_{52} + P_{11} + P_{21} + P_{31} + P_{41} + P_{51} \leq 5{,}000$$

$$5{,}000 \leq R_{12} + R_{22} + R_{32} + R_{42} + R_{52} + R_{11} + R_{21} + R_{31} + R_{41} + R_{51} \leq 10{,}000$$

and each of the 25 variables is nonnegative

A solution for this model can be found by the simplex method of linear programming, a procedure which will be discussed during the next few chapters. Of course, a well-written computer program requiring not too much storage can handle a problem of this size quite easily. But even to use such a program, which may have been written by someone else and put onto your computer for the use of everyone, you would have to know *something* about the simplex method.

An optimal solution (with variable values to the nearest hundredth of a barrel) is

$$A_{42} = 166.67 \qquad A_{52} = 833.33$$

$$P_{11} = 900 \qquad P_{22} = 1,350 \qquad P_{21} = 450$$

$$R_{12} = 500 \qquad R_{32} = 6,636.36 \qquad R_{42} = 96.97 \qquad R_{52} = 2,766.67$$

with all of the other variables taking the value zero. The maximum profit produced by that solution is

$$\text{Max } P = \$20,292.82$$

This solution is reported in Exercise 6.7 of Chapter 6, which also indicates the existence of *alternate optimal solutions* for this problem, that is, alternative sets of values for the decision variables that produce the *same* maximum profit. But no other feasible solution gives a larger value for $P$. You are encouraged to convince yourself that the quoted optimal solution is feasible (does it satisfy all constraints?). It is advisable, however, to defer any attempt to verify that it is optimal or to discover one of the alternate solutions until after you have studied the next four chapters.

## 2.4  SUMMARY AND CONCLUSIONS

This chapter introduces linear programming models and their formulation. The subject of linear programming is discussed throughout the next five chapters, and it is important to have a good start by learning how to *construct* models for linear programming problems before learning how to *solve* them.

Linear functions in both the objective function and all the constraints are characteristic of linear programming models. Exact knowledge of parameters, additivity, direct proportionality, and fractionality are all required to have a strictly linear programming model. However, in some of the examples we observed that ignoring fractionality of decision variables could nevertheless lead to a practical solution. Still, ignoring any one of those four important characteristics without knowing a lot about the *simplex method* (to be discussed in the next few chapters) is not advisable.

Introductory examples were chosen to illustrate a variety of business applications as well as a variety of types of linear programming models. Business areas represented include a small business operation (automobile dealership), manufacturing, distribution, accounting, and the petroleum industry. Types of models exhibited include these generic types: production problem, diet problem, transportation problem, assignment problem, and blending problem.

In addition to the examples, the end-of-chapter exercises involve similar problem types and a few more application areas, including job shops, investment portfolios, banking, production-distribution scheduling, and shipping. The exercises to follow are perhaps the most important part of the chapter. Practicing a lot of them, using the examples as models when necessary, enhances understanding in immediately subsequent chapters.

## KEY WORDS AND PHRASES

**Linear function**   A function in which each variable appears in only one term, and only to the first power. A linear function in only two variables, set equal to a constant, gives an equation whose graph in two dimensions is a straight line.

**Linear constraint**   An equation or inequality which involves only a constant and a linear function of decision variables.

**Exact knowledge of parameters**   The situation in which we know the precise values of constants in the problem, such as costs, unit profit, or per-unit consumption of resources. Required for strict linearity.

**Additivity**   The situation in which all functions are simply sums of terms, with no cross-products or quotients of variables involved. For example, profit from sales of two items individually is added to obtain the profit when both items are sold simultaneously. Required for strict linearity.

**Direct proportionality**   The situation in which amount of profit, cost, or resource consumption increases by a constant increment per unit increase in the decision variable. Required for strict linearity.

**Fractionality**   The situation in which decision variables are not constrained to only whole-number (integer) values but may assume either integral or fractional values. Required for strict linearity.

**Nonnegativity**   The requirement that a decision variable be either positive-valued or zero-valued.

**Feasible solution**   A set of values for the decision variables that satisfies all the constraints in the problem.

**Optimal solution**   The best feasible choice of values for the decision variables; that choice which produces the highest (in the case of maximization) or lowest (in the case of minimization) value of the objective function.

## EXERCISES

**2.1** In order to produce three different products, $A$, $B$, and $C$, a company must use two processes, process I and process II. To manufacture one unit of product $A$, 0.2 hours of process I time and 0.4 hours of process II time are necessary.

Similarly, a unit of product $B$ demands 0.1 hours from process I and 0.3 hours from process II, while a unit of product $C$ requires only 0.5 hours from process I (product $C$ does not require process II during its manufacture).

During the next two months 300 hours of process I time and 240 hours of process II time will be available for manufacturing the three products. Profit contributions per unit of products $A$, $B$, and $C$ are, respectively, $2, $5, and $8. All units made can be sold. The company wants to know how many units of each product it should make in order to maximize profit from their production during the next two months.

    **a** Identify the resources which are to be allocated as well as the decision variables in the problem.

    **b** Formulate a linear programming model whose solution will answer the company's question.

    **c** Write that model so that no decimal numbers appear as coefficients of any of the variables. Is it still the same model; that is, will it have the same solution as the model in part $b$?

◆ **2.2** Universal Furniture Outlets (UFO) has just learned that the market for squidgets is about to boom. They have decided to manufacture as many squidgets as possible using labor power and material currently available.

As is well known, squidgets come in three sizes: yellow, thin, and smooth. The profit per yellow squidget is $3; profit on the more durable, everyday thin squidget is $6; and the profit per smooth squidget, suitable for framing, is $10.

On hand in inventory are 30,000 gallons of corn syrup and 50,000 board feet of fir. UFO has also decided that it can use up to 24,000 worker-hours of labor before the optimal marketing date arrives. Units of resource required to manufacture a squidget are given in the following table:

| | Required per squidget | | |
| Size | Worker-hours | Gallons of corn syrup | Board feet of fir |
| --- | --- | --- | --- |
| Yellow | 8 | 10 | 4 |
| Thin | 6 | 7 | 8 |
| Smooth | 4 | 3 | 12 |

UFO can sell all of the squidgets they can make and wishes to maximize profit. Develop a linear programming model which, when solved, will tell UFO how many of each size squidget to manufacture.

◆ **2.3** The Acme Trap Company has received a letter from a hungry coyote in Arizona. He states that he plans to order a substantial number of roadrunner traps in the near future. Reasoning that if this one coyote has that much of a problem, there must be others with similar difficulties, Acme decides to make a large number of roadrunner traps during its next production run. They expect to sell all of the traps they can make.

Acme manufactures two types of roadrunner traps, the Little Giant Trap and the Giant Little Trap. Producing a trap of either type requires three operations: stamping, assembly, and packaging. Time requirements for each type of trap, profit per trap, and available time for each operation during the production period are shown in the following table:

| Trap | Profit per trap | Hours per trap | | |
| --- | --- | --- | --- | --- |
| | | Stamping | Assembly | Packaging |
| Little Giant | $2 | 0.2 | 1.0 | 0.1 |
| Giant Little | $5 | 0.4 | 1.2 | 0.2 |
| **Hours available** | | 400 | 1,200 | 150 |

Acme employs an animal psychologist who is attached to their operations research division. She assures Acme they must produce at least 300 Giant Little Traps to meet anticipated demand.

**a** Formulate as a linear programming model Acme's problem of how many traps of each type to produce in order to maximize profit from that production run.

**b** Can you detect any redundant constraints in the problem as you have formulated it in part *a*? (A redundant constraint is one that need not be mentioned since it is superseded by another constraint.)

**2.4** Meanwhile our Arizona coyote from Exercise 2.3 is trying to determine an optimal strategy for ordering traps. He knows that the cost of a Little Giant is $3 and the cost of a Giant Little is $10. From bitter experience he has learned that on the average a Little Giant will produce 19 misses per 20 times set to catch a roadrunner, while a Giant Little averages only 4 misses per 5 settings.

The coyote has converted these averages into ratios: 19/20 misses per Little Giant and 4/5 misses per Giant Little. He figures his costs in the units "dollar-misses." For example, 20 Little Giants and 5 Giant Littles set cost (20)(19/20)(3) + (5)(4/5)(10), or 97 dollar-misses on the average.

It takes him 1 hour to set a Little Giant and 2 hours to set a Giant Little trap. He has determined that he will use at least 100 hours for trap setting before starvation begins to render him incapable of that task. He has $450 available for purchasing traps. Establish a linear programming model whose solution will tell the coyote how many of each type trap to order so that total expected dollar-misses will be minimized.

**2.5** The Clear Cut Corporation produces two types of laminated wood. The lamination involves layers of pine and maple, some glue, and two production processes. The table below gives the amount of resources required to produce a square foot of each type of laminate and the amounts of each resource available during the current production period.

| Type | Board feet of pine | Board feet of maple | Ounces of glue | Hours in process I | Hours in process II |
| --- | --- | --- | --- | --- | --- |
| LAM1 | 2 | 2 | 1 | 0.2 | 0.1 |
| LAM2 | 1 | 3 | 2 | 0.1 | 0.3 |
| **Available** | 10,000 | 9,000 | 6,000 | 600 | 800 |

Profit per square foot is $3 for LAM1 and $4 for LAM2. Clear Cut wants to know how many square feet of each laminate to manufacture in the current period. Formulate their problem as a linear programming model.

**2.6** Claude Grind has enrolled in two courses: beginning statistics, a 4-semester-hour course, and freshman English, a 2-hour course. His college uses a "4-point" system, where each semester hour of A grade earns 4 grade points, each hour of B earns 3 points, a C earns 2 points, a D earns 1 point, and an F earns 0 grade points per semester hour. He has determined that there are only 130 clock-hours during the semester that he can devote to the study of those two courses. Further, Claude has decided that he can study English no more than 40 hours and statistics no more than 100 hours.

He has estimated, using the experience of other students who have taken those courses, that if $X$ denotes the number of hours spent studying statistics and $Y$ is the number of hours spent studying English, then

$$\text{Grade in statistics} = \frac{X}{30} \qquad \text{Grade in English} = \frac{Y}{10}$$

Formulate a linear programming model whose solution will tell Claude how many hours he should study each subject in order to maximize his grade point average (GPA) for the two courses.

◆ **2.7** Centennial Machine Shop produces three types of parts for automatic washing machines. It purchases castings of the parts from a local foundry and then finishes the parts on drilling, shaping, and polishing machines.

The selling prices of parts $A$, $B$, and $C$, respectively, are $8, $10, and $14. All parts made can be sold. Castings for parts $A$, $B$, and $C$, respectively, cost $5, $6, and $10.

The shop possesses only one of each type of machine. Costs per hour to run each of the three machines are $20 for drilling, $30 for shaping, and $30 for polishing. The capacities (parts per hour) for each part on each machine are shown in the following table:

| Machine | Capacity per hour | | |
| --- | --- | --- | --- |
|  | Part $A$ | Part $B$ | Part $C$ |
| Drilling | 25 | 40 | 25 |
| Shaping | 25 | 20 | 20 |
| Polishing | 40 | 30 | 40 |

Centennial's shop manager wants to know how many parts of each type to produce per hour in order to maximize profit for the hour's run. Write the problem in a linear programming format.

◆ **2.8** A candy dealer wishes to market a 2-pound box of assorted chocolates. She may purchase at wholesale prices any of five types of chocolates. Types $A$ and $B$ have nougat centers, type $C$ is pure milk chocolate, and types $D$ and $E$ are fruit-centered.

The dealer may purchase in any quantity provided that her combined order exceeds 200 pounds. She wants to market at least 300 boxes of the candy assortment.

Wholesale price per pound for each of types $A$ through $E$, consecutively, are $0.80, $1.00, $1.50, $1.20, and $1.80. The dealer imposes the following requirements on the mix: (1) at least 40 percent of the assortment must consist of nougat-centered chocolates; (2) fruit-centered chocolates must comprise no more than 30 percent of the mix, but there must be at least $\frac{1}{4}$ pound of type $E$ chocolates in each box; (3) types $B$, $C$, and $D$ must total at least half the weight of the box.

   a Write the linear programming model which, when solved, will tell the candy dealer how many pounds of each type of chocolate to buy in order that a minimum-cost assortment may be marketed.

   b Suppose that as the quantity purchased exceeds 100 pounds for each type of chocolate, the wholesaler will discount the price 10 percent on all chocolates of that type purchased beyond the first 100-pound quantity. Will the problem now permit a linear programming formulation? If so, what is that new model? If not, why not?

✦ **2.9** Justin Case, the notorious jet set playboy, has been threatened with disinheritance if he does not change his frivolous lifestyle. During the past year he has been unobtrusively drinking a cheaper brand of champagne and occasionally flying coach, and has managed to save up $1 million out of his monthly allowances from his father. He plans to invest this money in some combination of the five areas listed in the table below, which also shows the percentage annual yield anticipated on each type of investment.

| Area | Yield, % |
|---|---|
| 1 Long-term certificates of deposit | 10 |
| 2 Florida real estate | 20 |
| 3 Frozen pork bellies | 30 |
| 4 A Libyan oil refinery | 40 |
| 5 The Wyoming numbers racket | 50 |

Justin decides that at least a quarter of his capital must be put into areas 1, 2, and 3 and that at least half that combined amount should go to area 1. No more money should be put in area 4 than in area 3, and the amount invested in area 5 cannot exceed the combined amounts placed in areas 1 and 4. Finally, so his father will know he is behaving with the conservatism befitting a Case, he plans to invest at least $200,000 in area 1.

   a Formulate a linear programming model of Justin's problem of how much to invest in each area in order to maximize his anticipated annual yield.

   b Merely by observation, can you decide upon an investment strategy for Justin which you think should be optimal? If so, what amount of money annually would that strategy produce?

✦ **2.10** Laramie-Tie Siding Express is a large trucking firm with four major terminals located at Bosler, Federal, Woods Landing, and Buford. They have managed to standardize the tire size on all of their tractors and trailers and are preparing to place a large order for tires with each of two rubber companies, Goodstone and Fireyear.

Laramie-Tie Siding requires in total 20,000 tires. They will be received at each of the four terminals in the quantities shown in the following table. Also shown is the price per tire bid by each company, delivered to each terminal (transportation costs are included).

| | No. tires | Price per tire in dollars | |
|---|---|---|---|
| Terminal | required | Goodstone | Fireyear |
| Bosler | 4,000 | 70 | 64 |
| Federal | 8,000 | 74 | 62 |
| Woods Landing | 3,000 | 62 | 68 |
| Buford | 5,000 | 62 | 72 |

Goodstone reports they can supply up to 16,000 tires while Fireyear has available only 8,000. The trucking firm wants to minimize the total cost of receiving the 20,000 tire order. Establish a linear programming model whose solution will tell Laramie-Tie Siding the number of tires to order for delivery by each company to each terminal.

**2.11** A restauranteur provides catered luncheons for departmental meetings in three colleges of the university in his town. He owns three restaurants: $X$, $Y$, and $Z$. Restaurant $X$ can cater 14 luncheons per week, $Y$ can cater 10 per week, and $Z$ is able to cater 8 luncheons per week. The College of Arts and Sciences (A&S) has 15 departmental luncheons weekly, Engineering (E) has 8, and Business Administration (B.Ad.) has 5.

Because of differences in types of lunches requested, as well as different locations and personnel for the three restaurants, profit per luncheon varies over restaurants and colleges. The following table shows the profit per luncheon for each restaurant catering to each college:

| | College | | |
|---|---|---|---|
| Restaurant | A&S | E | B.Ad. |
| X | $20 | $15 | $12 |
| Y | $14 | $20 | $16 |
| Z | $10 | $12 | $14 |

Formulate a linear programming model whose solution will tell the restauranteur how many luncheons each restaurant should provide each college so that maximum weekly profit is realized. (*Hint*: This looks like a transportation problem, except the objective function is to be maximized and the constraints will be inequalities, not equations.)

**2.12** A company has three plants, in each of which is manufactured the same product. Production costs at each plant differ. The company maintains two warehouses at different locations, with different prices being paid for the product at the two locations.

The company wants to establish a production-distribution schedule which will maximize profit for a particular planning period, assuming that sales will equal projected sales. The following tables give production costs, production capacities, selling prices, projected sales, and transportation costs during the planning period.

| | Plant | | | | Warehouse | |
|---|---|---|---|---|---|---|
| | A | B | C | | 1 | 2 |
| Production cost per unit of product | $10 | $14 | $12 | Selling price per unit of product | $25 | $28 |
| Production capacity, number of units | 200 | 400 | 300 | Projected sales, number of units | 400 | 300 |

*TRANSPORTATION COST PER UNIT FOR SHIPPING FROM PLANT TO WAREHOUSE*

| | Warehouse | |
|---|---|---|
| Plant | 1 | 2 |
| A | $8 | $4 |
| B | $6 | $9 |
| C | $2 | $7 |

Formulate the linear programming model which will lead to the optimum production-distribution schedule, that is, the number of units to produce at each plant for shipment to each warehouse in order to maximize profit.

**2.13** Mule Creek Junction Feed and Grain (MCJF&G), serving ranches between Red Bird, Wyoming, and Igloo, South Dakota, blends three types of feed for livestock. Profit per ton and percentages of ingredients in each type are shown below, along with the number of tons of each ingredient available:

| Feed | Profit per ton | Percentage in feed | | | |
|---|---|---|---|---|---|
| | | Molasses | Oats | Barley | Corn |
| Junction Standard | $10 | 2 | 8 | 10 | 80 |
| Creek's Best | $14 | 5 | 15 | 20 | 60 |
| Mule's Preferred | $20 | 10 | 30 | 20 | 40 |
| **Tons available** | | 2,000 | 5,000 | 5,000 | 10,000 |

Because of demand, MCJF&G must mix at least as much Junction Standard as Creek's Best and Mule's Preferred combined. Ignore blending costs. Formulate a linear programming model whose solution will yield the amount of each feed to mix in order to maximize profit if everything made is sold.

◆ **2.14** Patrician Patio Pieces manufactures a medium-priced line of outdoor furniture, using a combination of redwood and cedar along with ornamental cast iron fittings for extra strength. Patterns for the furniture have been standardized so that only 12-inch and 8-inch fittings are required, these fittings and the long bolts necessary to hold the furniture together being purchased in large lots from Custom Casting and Forging (see Exercise 2.18).

Patrician manufactures two sizes of tables and benches (long and short in both cases), armchairs, and smaller folding chairs suitable for indoor and outdoor use. Material and labor requirements during the coming month, resource availabilities, and profit per piece are given in the following table:

| | Long table | Short table | Long bench | Short bench | Arm-chair | Folding chair | Available |
|---|---|---|---|---|---|---|---|
| Redwood, board feet | 10 | 6 | 6 | 4 | 7 | 3 | 3,000 |
| Cedar, board feet | 8 | 5 | 3 | 2 | 4 | 1 | 2,000 |
| 12-inch fittings, number | 6 | 4 | 2 | 4 | 4 | 0 | 1,800 |
| 8-inch fittings, number | 4 | 6 | 6 | 0 | 0 | 4 | 1,400 |
| Bolts, number | 20 | 14 | 12 | 10 | 12 | 8 | 4,000 |
| Labor, labor hours | 8 | 4 | 5 | 3 | 8 | 6 | 2,400 |
| Unit profit | $50 | $35 | $25 | $20 | $45 | $15 | |

Because of a prior order at least 10 short tables and 20 short benches must be produced, and sales projections indicate that no more than 50 armchairs should be produced. Formulate a linear programming model whose solution will yield maximum profit from the month's production.

**2.15** Mr. Adams of Chekov and Adams (see Example 2.5) would prefer a minimum time assignment to a minimum-cost assignment. (The tax specialists earn different hourly wages, so the two solutions could differ.) He uses Mr. Chekov's time estimates to come up with the following table of the times in hours required for each specialist to complete each client's tax return:

| | Client | | | |
|---|---|---|---|---|
| Specialist | 1 | 2 | 3 | 4 |
| 1 Brown | 15 | 22 | 16 | 12 |
| 2 Green | 14 | 20 | 13 | 10 |
| 3 White | 20 | 23 | 18 | 14 |
| 4 Black | 17 | 21 | 16 | 13 |

Formulate a linear programming model for determining the minimum total estimated time for completing all four returns. (If you want to see the solution for comparison with Example 2.5, peek ahead to Exercise 6.13 of Chapter 6.)

◆ **2.16** First State Bank will make six types of loans to its customers. These loans and their associated interest rates are listed below:

| Type of loan | Interest rate, % |
|---|---|
| Home mortgage | 14 |
| Industrial | 15 |
| Commercial | 17 |
| Automobile | 18 |
| Otherwise secured | 20 |
| Unsecured | 22 |

Banking laws and the internal policies of First State Bank impose the following restrictions: (1) no more than 15 percent of the total dollar amount of loans may be unsecured; (2) at least 50 percent of the total dollar amount of loans must be home mortgage, industrial, or commercial loans; (3) the total of commercial, automobile, and otherwise secured loans cannot exceed 60 percent of the total dollar amount of loans.

First State Bank anticipates $20 million to be available for all loans this year and wishes to know how many dollars to allocate to each type of loan in order to maximize the annual earned interest. Formulate a linear programming model for this problem.

**2.17** Solidstate Manufacturing produces three types of transistors in two different plants. Each transistor can be made by one of three different methods. The selling price to the wholesaler and maximum quantities that could be purchased by the wholesaler follow:

| | Transistor type | | |
|---|---|---|---|
| | 1 | 2 | 3 |
| Selling price to wholesaler | $20 | $30 | $50 |
| Maximum quantity | 10,000 | 5,000 | 4,000 |

Production costs in dollars in each plant for each method and each type of transistor are given in the following two tables:

PLANT A

| Method | Transistor | | |
|---|---|---|---|
| | 1 | 2 | 3 |
| P | 8 | 15 | 28 |
| Q | 10 | 12 | 36 |
| R | 12 | 20 | 38 |

PLANT B

| Method | Transistor | | |
|---|---|---|---|
| | 1 | 2 | 3 |
| P | 7 | 20 | 35 |
| Q | 9 | 10 | 30 |
| R | 10 | 22 | 40 |

Available production time (hours) and time consumed by the manufacture of each transistor by each method are given in the next two tables:

PLANT A

| Method | Transistor | | | Available |
|--------|---|---|---|-----------|
| | 1 | 2 | 3 | |
| P | 1 | 2 | 4 | 60,000 |
| Q | 2 | 2 | 5 | 50,000 |
| R | 3 | 4 | 3 | 30,000 |

PLANT B

| Method | Transistor | | | Available |
|--------|---|---|---|-----------|
| | 1 | 2 | 3 | |
| P | 3 | 3 | 5 | 40,000 |
| Q | 4 | 2 | 3 | 30,000 |
| R | 2 | 3 | 4 | 20,000 |

The objective is to determine how many of each type of transistor to manufacture in each plant by each process in order to maximize total gross profit (selling price minus cost). Formulate the linear programming model for this problem.

◆ **2.18** Custom Casting and Forging is the innocuous name of a company which, although it does do some legitimate jobs (see Exercise 2.14), makes the bulk of its profit from the manufacture of "antique" bronzes, castings of bowls, bells, axes, swords, and so on, purported to date as far back as 2000 B.C. Because of a recent archeological discovery in China the current "hot" items in the antique bronze market are bells, gongs, and ceremonial vessels from the Chou dynasty (circa 1000 B.C.). The ancient Chinese formula for that bronze was 5 parts copper to 1 part tin, although in that period the metals were not available as pure copper and tin; lead and zinc were often present in significant amounts.

It has been decided that a bronze consisting of 70 percent copper, 16 percent tin, 10 percent lead, and 4 percent zinc will be suitable for duplicating Chou dynasty bronze artifacts. However, because of a current shortage of copper in the commodities market Custom Casting and Forging has decided to utilize existing bronze ingots (in stock) of types used previously for faking statues and weaponry of Phoenician, Greek, Etruscan, Assyrian, and Egyptian styles. Those five bronzes bear the constituent metals in the following percentages:

| Bronze | Percent copper | Percent tin | Percent lead | Percent zinc | Value per pound |
|--------|---------------|-------------|--------------|--------------|-----------------|
| Phoenician | 95 | 4 | 1 | 0 | $20 |
| Greek | 60 | 30 | 5 | 5 | $14 |
| Etruscan | 50 | 30 | 15 | 5 | $10 |
| Assyrian | 70 | 10 | 15 | 5 | $16 |
| Egyptian | 80 | 5 | 5 | 10 | $18 |

Formulate a linear programming model whose solution will determine the relative amounts (proportions) of each of the five existing bronzes that should be blended to yield the specified Chou dynasty bronze while achieving minimum value.

**2.19** USS Albatross is a freighter with four main cargo holds: upper forward, lower forward, upper stern, and lower stern. The floors of the two upper holds are removable for those occasions when larger holds are required, resulting in structural weaknesses requiring weight limitations on the upper holds in addition to the obvious volume restrictions. The lower holds's cargo capacities are restricted only by volume.

Hold capacities (weight in tons and volume in cubic feet) are given below:

| Hold | Weight | Volume |
|------|--------|--------|
| Lower forward | — | 48,000 |
| Upper forward | 960 | 64,000 |
| Lower stern | — | 32,000 |
| Upper stern | 600 | 40,000 |

The *Albatross* will embark from Boston with sequential ports of call at Glasgow, London, Casablanca, Rio de Janeiro, and Caracas. Potential cargo available for loading in Boston, weight (tons) and volume (cubic feet per ton), profit per cubic foot, and destination are indicated in the following table:

| Cargo | Weight | Volume | Profit | Destination |
|-------|--------|--------|--------|-------------|
| Bagpipes | 600 | 100 | $ 3 | Glasgow |
| Tweed suits | 800 | 90 | $ 2 | London |
| Blank passports | 500 | 40 | $10 | Casablanca |
| Bananas | 800 | 30 | $ 2 | Rio de Janeiro |
| Coal | 1,000 | 50 | $ 1 | Caracas |

In order to maintain initial trim of the freighter, four-sevenths of the total weight must be loaded into the forward holds. Any portion of any potential cargo may be loaded. The *Albatross*'s owners want to know how many tons of each type of cargo must be loaded into each hold in order to maximize total profit for the voyage.

  **a** If it may be assumed that cargo may be shifted so that any portion of any hold may be unloaded at any port of call, formulate a linear programming model for the problem.

  **b** Suppose that a lower hold cannot be unloaded until the entire upper hold above it is unloaded and the floor is removed. Keeping in mind the sequence of ports of call, can you now formulate a linear programming model for this modified problem? If so, do so; if you cannot, discuss the difficulties you encountered in the attempt.

**2.20** Reconsider Exercise 2.16. Suppose that First State Bank does not know how much money it will have available for loans (delete the $20 million). Formulate a linear programming model whose solution will tell First State Bank the *proportions* of total available money to allocate to the different loan types.

## SELECTED REFERENCES

Ackoff, R. L., and M. W. Sasieni: *Fundamentals of Operations Research*, John Wiley & Sons, Inc., New York, 1968.

Anderson, D. R., D. J. Sweeney, and T. A. Williams: *An Introduction to Management Science*, 3d ed., West Publishing Company, St. Paul, Minn., 1982.

Bierman, H., C. P. Bonini, and W. H. Hausman: *Quantitative Analysis for Business Decisions*, 6th ed., Richard D. Irwin, Inc., Homewood, Ill., 1981.

Dantzig, G. B.: *Linear Programming and Extensions*, Princeton University Press, Princeton, N.J., 1963.

Hillier, F. S., and G. J. Lieberman: *Introduction to Operations Research*, 3d ed., Holden-Day, Inc., San Francisco, 1980.

Kim, C.: *Introduction to Linear Programming*, Holt, Rinehart, and Winston, New York, 1971.

Naylor, T. H., E. T. Byrne, and J. M. Vernon: *Introduction to Linear Programming: Methods and Cases*, Wadsworth Publishing Company, Inc., Belmont, Calif., 1971.

Nicholson, T. A.: *Optimization in Industry*, vol. II, Longman Group Ltd., London, 1971.

di Roccaferrera, G. M. F.: *Introduction to Linear Programming Processes*, South-Western Publishing Company, Inc., Cincinnati, Ohio, 1967.

Thierauf, R. J., and R. C. Klekamp: *Decision Making Through Operations Research*, John Wiley & Sons, Inc., New York, 1975.

# GRAPHICAL AND ALGEBRAIC SOLUTIONS

*T*his chapter and Chapter 4 present some of the concepts and mechanics of the *simplex method*, the usual procedure by which solutions are obtained for linear programming models. In these two chapters you will see some problems being solved graphically, some being solved algebraically, and some being solved using tables (tableaus) that shorten the labor in the algebraic procedure. Although the manipulations will look different in each of those three cases, they are all based on the *same concepts*, and each can be called a version of the simplex method.

A graphical approach is easiest for solving problems with only two decision variables. When more than two decision variables are involved, most people prefer the tabular version discussed in Chapter 4, or a computer-based solution, of course, like you will see in Chapter 6. But to fully *understand* the simplex method—*why* it works as well as *how* it works—you should have a good appreciation of the graphical and algebraic principles discussed in this chapter. These arguments will show you how the simplex method takes full advantage of the *linearity* in linear programming (LP) problems.

No better setting exists than the arena of business and industry for observing the importance of *inequalities*. Look back in Chapter 2 at the models formulated in Example 2.1 (Early Auto Sales), Example 2.2 (production application), Example 2.3 (diet problem), and Example 2.6 (petroleum industry application). You see far more inequalities than equations in those models. Consider two other common situations: time *consumed* by a necessary task is usually less than time *available* to do the task (it certainly cannot be *more* than time available, or the task would not get done), or the amount of money on hand for capital construction should not be exhausted just because it is there; we would want to spend only what is required to complete the construction.

Since a manager of resources always operates in the realm of inequalities, it is important for him or her to be able to *visualize* their implications by way of graphs. But the first step in graphing a linear inequality is the more familiar act of graphing a straight line. In Example 3.1 an inventory problem motivates our review of that simple activity.

### Example 3.1
### Graphing Lines

Peerless Appliance Hospital stocks replacement parts for Swisher automatic washing machines. The most commonly required major parts for Swishers are motors and transmissions. Inventories of these parts must be maintained so that repairs can be made, but restrictions exist on capital and storage space and a few other constraints are involved. Peerless is preparing to place an order to replenish inventory of motors and transmissions.

The wholesale price of a Swisher motor is $50, and of a Swisher transmission is $80, and $800 is available for purchasing these two types of parts. Only 20 cubic feet of storage space may be allocated to them, and a motor (in its box) requires 2 cubic feet of space, while a boxed transmission requires 1 cubic foot of space. Further, when a motor breaks down, the transmission is often unaffected, but when a transmission goes out, often the motor does too. This phenomenon, along with recent repair experience, has suggested that at least twice as many motors as transmissions are needed. Finally, because of a backlog of repair work, at least three motors must be ordered.

The restrictions observed here produce inequalities whose boundaries are of the types most frequently encountered in linear programming problems. To look at these lines, first we need a statement of the inequalities. Let $x_1$ = number of motors to order and $x_2$ = number of transmissions to order. Then the five inequalities restricting the Peerless Appliance Hospital inventory order are

$$A: \qquad 50x_1 + 80x_2 \leq 800 \qquad \text{capital}$$

$$B: \qquad 2x_1 + \phantom{0} x_2 \leq \phantom{0}20 \qquad \text{storage space}$$

$$C: \qquad\qquad x_1 \geq 2x_2 \qquad \text{motors vs. transmission}$$

$$D: \qquad\qquad x_1 \geq \phantom{0}3 \qquad \text{lower bound for motors}$$

$$E: \qquad\qquad x_2 \geq \phantom{0}0 \qquad \text{nonnegativity}$$

Here the last inequality reminds us that we cannot order a negative number of transmissions, but the inequality $x_1 \geq 3$ already assures a nonnegative number of motors.

We will defer graphs of the inequalities to Example 3.2. Rather, at this stage we consider only the following associated *equations:*

$$A: \qquad\qquad\qquad 50x_1 + 80x_2 = 800$$

$$B: \qquad\qquad\qquad 2x_1 + \phantom{0} x_2 = \phantom{0}20$$

$$C: \qquad\qquad\qquad\qquad x_1 = 2x_2$$

$$D: \qquad\qquad\qquad\qquad x_1 = \phantom{0}3$$

$$E: \qquad\qquad\qquad\qquad x_2 = \phantom{0}0$$

Equations $A$ and $B$, associated, respectively, with the capital and space constraints, are examples of the most common type of equation one sees in linear programming. While any *two points* suffice to determine a line, the easiest way to graph one like equation $A$ is called the *intercept method*. The intercept method discovers the two points at which the line intersects the two coordinate axes and has the feature that the two points thus determined are usually sufficiently far apart to give an accurate resolution of the line.

Whenever one of the two variables $x_1$ or $x_2$ is zero, the associated point falls on a coordinate axis. For example, $(x_1, x_2) = (0, 5)$ is a point five units away from the origin on the $x_2$ axis, and $(x_1, x_2) = (3, 0)$ is a point three units from the origin on the $x_1$ axis. To apply the intercept method to graphing equation $A$ we use that idea.

In equation $A$ let $x_1 = 0$. Then the equation becomes

$$80x_2 = 800$$

or

$$x_2 = 10$$

This means that the pair $(x_1, x_2) = (0, 10)$ satisfies the equation, and is a point on the line that is the graph of that equation (it is the $x_2$ *intercept* of the line).

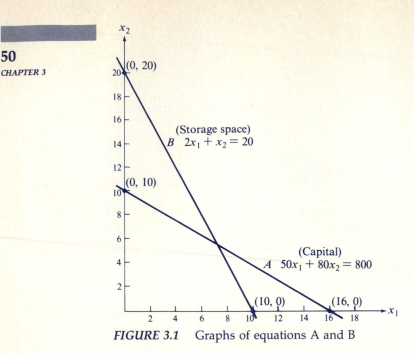

**FIGURE 3.1**   Graphs of equations A and B

Similarly, let $x_2 = 0$ in equation $A$.   Then the equation becomes

$$50x_1 = 800$$
or
$$x_1 = 16$$

and the point $(x_1, x_2) = (16, 0)$ is the $x_1$ intercept of the line.   These intercepts are plotted and the line is drawn in Figure 3.1.   Equation $B$, with the intercepts (0, 20) and (10, 0), is also shown in the same figure.

   Next consider equation $C$, associated with the statement that the number of motors must be at least twice as large as the number of transmissions. It is

$C$:                                   $x_1 = 2x_2$

Here, when we set $x_1 = 0$ we get $x_2 = 0$, and when we set $x_2 = 0$ we just get back $x_1 = 0$, or only *one point*, (0, 0), the *origin* of the coordinate system.   Any line passing through the origin intersects both axes at the same point, so the intercept method will not work (will not give two distinct points) for graphing a line that passes through the origin.   On the other hand, any other point can be determined very easily.   For instance, if we set $x_2 = 8$ then we know that $x_1$ has to be 2(8), or $x_1 = 16$. Thus the point (16, 8) is another point on the line in addition to (0, 0). Knowing *two* points on the line, we can now graph it, as shown in Figure 3.2.

   Finally, consider equations $D$ and $E$.   Such equations, where one of the

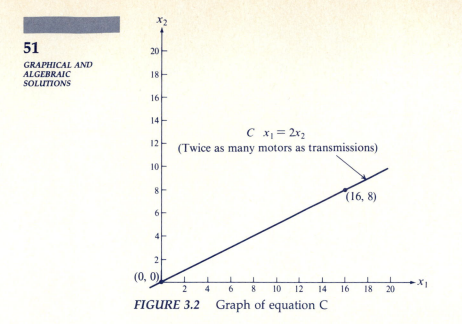

**FIGURE 3.2**    Graph of equation C

variables is not specifically included, are always lines that are *parallel to a coordinate axis*.   As a special case, when the constant on the right is 0 as in the case of equation $E$, the line could *be* one of the axes.   The equation

$$x_1 = 3$$

equation $D$, just tells us that regardless of the $x_2$ coordinate, the $x_1$ coordinate of any point on the line is the number 3.   Then *all* points with an $x_1$ coordinate of 3 are on the line, which then must be a *vertical line* parallel to the $x_2$ axis and three units to the right of it.   Similarly, equation $E$,

$$x_2 = 0$$

is a *horizontal* line representing all points whose $x_2$ coordinates are 0, in this case, just the $x_1$ axis.   These two lines are pointed out in Figure 3.3.

Just as the graph of a two-variable linear equation is always a line, the graph of a *linear inequality* is always a *half space*.   In two dimensions a half space is all of the plane (indicated by the two-dimensional coordinate system) that is on the *same side of the line* (usually, in LP, including the line itself).   Thus to graph a linear inequality, we need only graph the line that divides the plane into two half spaces, then determine which of the two half spaces contains the points satisfying the inequality.   To do that, we use the following rule:

*Rule for finding the correct half space.*   Choose any point *not* on the line bounding the two half spaces.   If the point satisfies the inequality, then

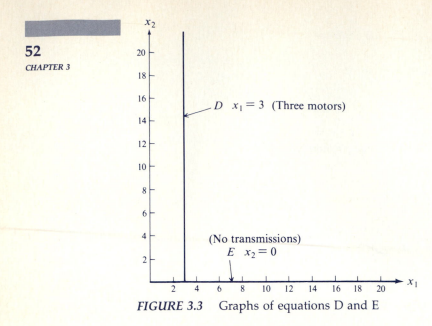

**FIGURE 3.3**    Graphs of equations D and E

*all* points in the *same* half space satisfy the inequality.  If the chosen point *does not* satisfy the inequality, then all points in the *other* half space will.  [*Note:* If the boundary line does not pass through the origin, then (0, 0) is the most convenient such "test point."]

**Example 3.2**
**Graphing Linear Inequalities**

The storage-space constraint for the Peerless Appliance Hospital scenario in Example 3.1 was

$$2x_1 + x_2 \leq 20$$

Refer to Figure 3.1 to see the graph of the line that divides the $x_1$, $x_2$ plane into two half spaces.  Use (0, 0) as a test point.  Since

$$2(0) + (0) = 0$$

which is less than 20, the test point *satisfies* the inequality.  Then *all* points on the *same side* of the line $2x_1 + x_2 = 20$ satisfy the inequality, and since (0, 0) is "below" the line, the appropriate half space is as indicated in Figure 3.4.

Now consider the constraint that required the number of motors ordered to be at least twice as large as the number of transmissions.  It was

$$x_1 \geq 2x_2$$

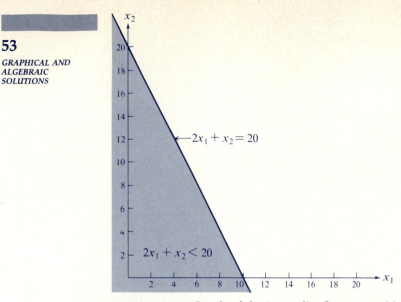

**FIGURE 3.4**   Graph of the inequality $2x_1 + x_2 \leq 20$

The graph of the boundary line (see Figure 3.2) goes through the origin, so (0, 0) is not an appropriate test point. Arbitrarily, we decide to use (8, 10). Is $x_1 = 8$ greater than $2x_2 = 2(10) = 20$? No. The point (8, 10) is "above" the line, which means that all points on the *other* side of the line *do* satisfy $x_1 \geq 2x_2$. The correct half space is shown in Figure 3.5.

**FIGURE 3.5**   Graph of the inequality $x_1 \geq 2x_2$

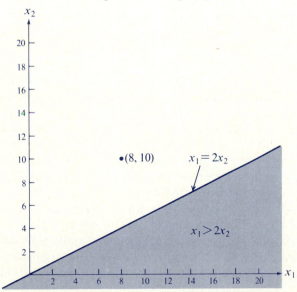

## 3.2 THE FEASIBLE REGION: SET OF ALL POTENTIAL SOLUTIONS

Constraints in linear programming problems often are described mathematically by linear inequalities. The entire set of constraints defines a *feasible region* for the problem. The first step in a graphical solution for a two-variable LP model is to sketch its feasible region.

**Example 3.3**
**Graphing a Feasible Region**

Since no objective function was specified, the Peerless Appliance Hospital situation (Example 3.1) did not describe a linear programming problem. Nevertheless, its five linear inequalities do constitute a feasible region for Peerless's inventory order. Remember, a feasible region is just the set of all points that satisfy all constraints.

The inequalities from Example 3.1 are repeated here for ease of reference. In that example, $x_1$ denotes the number of motors and $x_2$ the number of transmissions to order for replenishment of the inventory of Swisher washing-machine parts.

$$50x_1 + 80x_2 \leq 800 \qquad \text{capital}$$

$$2x_1 + \phantom{8}x_2 \leq 20 \qquad \text{storage space}$$

$$x_1 \geq 2x_2 \qquad \text{motors vs. transmissions}$$

$$x_1 \geq \phantom{2}3 \qquad \text{lower bound for motors}$$

$$x_2 \geq \phantom{2}0 \qquad \text{nonnegativity}$$

This set of inequalities is the feasible region for the inventory order. All pairs $(x_1, x_2)$ that satisfy all five inequalities are pairs that constitute *feasible* order quantities (ignoring any integer restriction, of course). Using the "rule for finding the correct half space," and following the procedures used in Example 3.2, we may graph this feasible region, as shown in Figure 3.6.

Notice the little arrows on both ends of each line segment in Figure 3.6. These point the way into the appropriate half space for each inequality, and thus to the feasible region itself. The shaded region in the figure delineates the largest set of points that will satisfy all five inequalities. Note further that the capital constraint, $50x_1 + 80x_2 \leq 800$, is *not a binding* constraint; that is, all points in the feasible region automatically satisfy the capital constraint in a strictly *unequal* sense. This means that the other constraints make it impossible to spend all the available capital. Such a nonbinding constraint is often referred to as *redundant*. If it had not been included in the constraint set, the feasible region would not have changed.

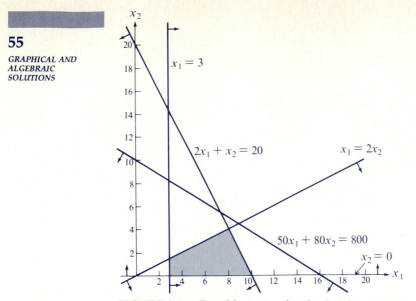

**FIGURE 3.6**    Feasible region for the Peerless inventory decision

### Example 3.4
### An Unbounded Feasible Region

A feasible region will not always be a closed polygon like the region exhibited in Figure 3.6. Particularly in LP problems involving cost minimization, feasible regions are sometimes not bounded. Following are inequalities that are two-variable analogs to the kinds of restrictions we observed in Example 2.3 of Chapter 2 (the diet problem):

$$2x + 3y \geq 6$$
$$3x + \phantom{3}y \geq 3$$
$$x \geq 0 \qquad y \geq 0$$

The set of pairs $(x, y)$ satisfying all four of those inequalities, the feasible region, is graphed in Figure 3.7.

The shaded region in Figure 3.7 is bounded below and on the left by straight lines but is not bounded from above or to the right. Both $x$ and $y$ may be very large, positive numbers, and the pair $(x, y)$ will still be in the feasible region. Such a region is said to be *unbounded.*

This *does not* imply, however, that the associated linear programming problem will have no solution. Because this type of region is usually associated with a *minimization* problem, the fact that the region is bounded from *below* usually assures the existence of a solution. In Example 3.7 we add an objective function to the problem and demonstrate that characteristic.

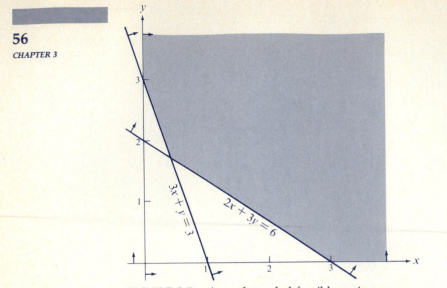

*FIGURE 3.7*    An unbounded feasible region

## 3.3   CORNER POINTS AND LINEAR CONTOURS: THE GRAPHICAL SOLUTION

As has been mentioned in Section 3.2, there is more to linear programming models than feasible regions.   Those models also involve objective functions.   Here, after appreciating the fact that the objective function may be depicted on a two-dimensional graph by *linear contours*, you will see examples of the complete graphical solution of LP models.

**Example 3.5**
**Contours of the Early Auto Sales Objective Function**
In Example 2.1, where $A$ was the number of model $A$'s to purchase and $T$ was the number of model $T$'s, the objective function was

$$P = 600A + 300T$$

Here $P$ represents gross profit in dollars, and the objective in the problem was to maximize $P$.

   A function of this type is not graphable in two dimensions, since *three* variables, $P$, $A$, and $T$, are involved.   Its graph is a *plane* in three dimensions.

   However, if we set $P$ equal to some specific number, say 36,000, we would see the equation

$$600A + 300T = 36,000$$

We recognize this as an ordinary two-variable equation whose graph is just a *line*.  Obviously that line is *related* to the objective function.  It is what the function would be if profits were $36,000, and its graph is called a *contour* of the objective function at $P = 36,000$.  Any pair $(A, T)$ that satisfies the equation, or that is a point on the contour, gives a profit of $36,000.

We could set $P$ equal to another number, say 60,000, and see the equation for the contour associated with a profit of $60,000.  That equation is

$$600A + 300T = 60,000$$

Similarly, the equation for the contour associated with a profit of $90,000 is

$$600A + 300T = 90,000$$

The three equations are graphed as *linear contours* in Figure 3.8.

*FIGURE 3.8*    Contours indicating the direction of increasing profit

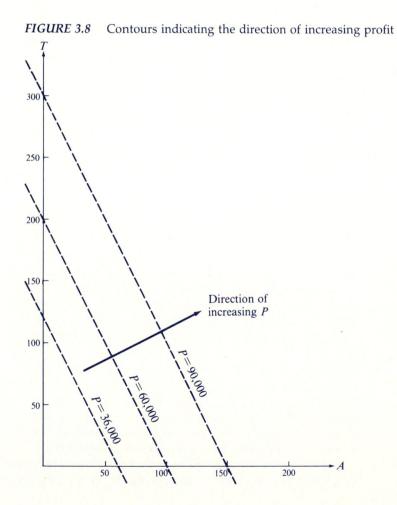

Two important characteristics of such linear contours are exhibited by Figure 3.8. First, the contours are *parallel lines*. Second, an arrow drawn perpendicular to the contours will indicate the *direction of increasing profit*. That is, if we use a ruler to draw another line parallel to the $P = 90,000$ contour, and to the right of it, we know that the associated profit will be more than $90,000.

These recent comments about objective functions and contours, along with what you learned earlier about graphing feasible regions, give us the key to graphical solutions for LP models. How those ideas all fit together will now be illustrated.

## Example 3.6
## Graphical Solution of the Early Auto Sales Model

The entire LP model for the Early Auto Sales problem of Example 2.1 follows:

$$\text{Maximize } P$$

where

$$P = 600A + 300T \qquad \text{profit}$$

subject to

$$4,000A + 3,000T \le 600,000 \qquad \text{capital}$$

$$4A + 6T \le 960 \qquad \text{time}$$

$$T \le 300 \qquad \text{availability of model } T\text{'s}$$

$$T \ge 100 \qquad \text{demand for model } T\text{'s}$$

$$A \le 100 \qquad \text{availability of model } A\text{'s}$$

$$A \ge 0 \quad T \ge 0 \qquad \text{nonnegativity}$$

Here the constraint originally written as $100 \le T \le 300$ is written instead as the two separate constraints $T \le 300$ and $T \ge 100$ to remind us that two separate boundary lines will be needed on the graph.

To solve this problem we will sketch its feasible region and draw some representative objective-function contours. The resulting picture, with the broken lines being contours of $P$, is shown in Figure 3.9.

The feasible region is shaded in Figure 3.9. Our approach was to draw it first, then to draw the contours for $P = 60,000$ and $P = 90,000$. We notice that $60,000 is a *feasible* profit since the contour line for $P = 60,000$ passes through the feasible region. That is, some points $(A, T)$ in the region are also on the contour. But that is not the case for the $P = 90,000$ contour. It misses the feasible region entirely, so there is *no* feasible way to make the profit $90,000. Thus we immediately observe that *maximum* $P$ must be somewhere between 60,000 and 90,000.

But we know much more than that just from observation of the graph. We know the direction of increasing $P$. If we just (in our imagination)

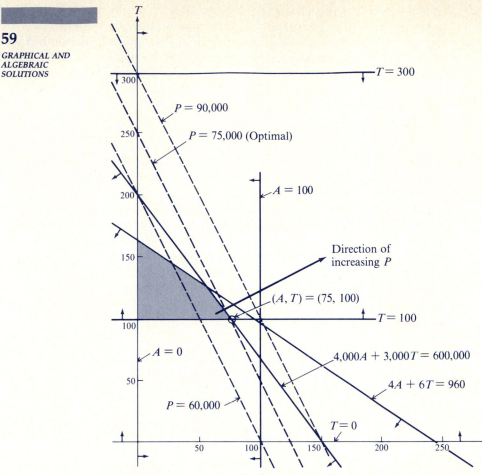

**FIGURE 3.9**  Graphical solution of the Early Auto Sales problem

move the $P = 60{,}000$ contour parallel to itself and toward the $P = 90{,}000$ contour (or in the direction of increasing $P$), we observe that the last point in the feasible region encountered (just before the line misses the region altogether) is the point $(A, T) = (75, 100)$. At that point, $P = 600(75) + 300(100) = 75{,}000$, so the point is on the $P = 75{,}000$ contour. Also, $75{,}000$ is the *maximum feasible profit.*

But that is what we wanted to know all along—the *solution* for the model. In words consistent with the original phrasing of the Early Auto Sales *problem* (not the model), the solution is:

To achieve maximum gross profit of $75{,}000$, purchase 75 model $A$'s and 100 model $T$'s.

Here it was not too difficult to read the coordinates of the optimal solution directly from the graph. However, we do want the exact coordinates, and sometimes it is not possible to get an accurate reading from just looking at the graph. That is, moving our contours through the region will identify *which* feasible point gives the optimal solution but will not tell us its precise coordinates. But the point happens to occur at the intersection of the lines whose associated equations are

$$4{,}000A + 3{,}000T = 600{,}000$$

$$T = 100$$

Solution of that system of equations [finding the pair $(A, T)$ that satisfies them both simultaneously] gives the exact solution for the model, $(A, T)$ = (75, 100).

Before we state a general graphical solution procedure, observe a critical feature of the optimal solution for the Early Auto Sales model. The values of the optimal decision variables were coordinates of a *corner point* of the feasible region. Think about that. If we move a straight line through a feasible region which is itself bounded by straight lines, the last point touched (or *one* of the last points, in the case of a boundary parallel to the contour) *must* be a *corner* of the feasible region. This line of reasoning yields the following general procedure.

**GENERAL GRAPHICAL SOLUTION PROCEDURE**

**1 Graph the feasible region.**

**2 Draw two different contours of the objective function in order to determine the direction of increase.**

**3 a If the problem is a *maximization* problem, move a ruler through the region in the direction of *increase*.**
**b If the problem is a *minimization* problem, move a ruler through the region in the *opposite* direction (the direction of *decrease*).**

**4 The last corner in the feasible region touched by the edge of the ruler will be the *optimal* solution. (If the ruler leaves the region parallel to a boundary line, then the model has *alternate optimal solutions*—see Example 3.7.)**

**5 The equations of the lines that intersect to form the optimal corner give a system whose solution yields the exact coordinates of that corner.**

This "edge of the ruler" technique is just a mechanical way of considering parallel contours. The procedure always works because in a linear programming model all boundaries of the feasible region and all objective-function contours are straight lines.

### Example 3.7
### A Minimization Problem with Alternate Optimal Solutions

A diet is to contain at least 6 ounces of nutrient $A$ and at least 3 ounces of nutrient $B$. Some mixture of food $X$ and food $Y$ will constitute the diet. A pound of food $X$ costs \$1 and contains 2 ounces of nutrient $A$ and 3 ounces of nutrient $B$. A pound of food $Y$ costs \$1.50 and contains 3 ounces of nutrient $A$ and 1 ounce of nutrient $B$. How many pounds of each food must be bought in order to meet the specified dietary requirements at minimum cost, and what is that minimum cost?

This problem has been constructed so that the feasible region for its model is just the unbounded region we saw in Figure 3.7. Let $x$ = number of pounds of food $X$ to buy and let $y$ = number of pounds of food $Y$ to buy. Then the LP model for this simple diet problem is

$$\text{Minimize } C$$

where $\qquad\qquad C = x + 1.5y \qquad$ cost in dollars

subject to $\qquad\qquad 2x + 3y \geq 6 \qquad$ nutrient $A$

$$3x + y \geq 3 \qquad \text{nutrient } B$$

$$x \geq 0 \qquad y \geq 0 \qquad \text{nonnegativity}$$

The feasible region and contours for a graphical solution are shown in Figure 3.10.

Here the contours for $C = 1.5$ and $C = 4$ were drawn to determine the

**FIGURE 3.10**   Alternate optimal solutions for the diet problem

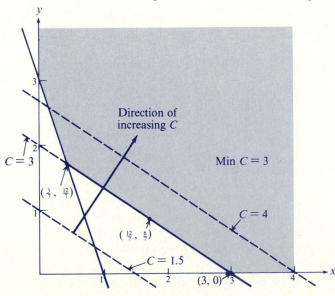

direction of increasing $C$. Then the edge of a ruler was moved from the $C = 4$ contour through the region, in the *opposite* direction since this is a minimization problem. The last points encountered before leaving the region were *all* points on the lower boundary that is indicated in Figure 3.10 by the bold line segment.

One point on that segment is the corner $(x, y) = (3, 0)$, and another is the corner determined by the intersection of the constraints for nutrient $A$ and nutrient $B$. The associated system of equations is

$$2x + 3y = 6$$
$$3x + y = 3$$

The solution of that system is the point $(x, y) = (\frac{3}{7}, \frac{12}{7})$.

When $x = 3$ and $y = 0$,

$$C = (3) + 1.5(0) = 3$$

and when $x = \frac{3}{7}$ and $y = \frac{12}{7}$,

$$C = \frac{3}{7} + 1.5(\frac{12}{7})$$
$$= \frac{3}{7} + (\frac{3}{2})(\frac{12}{7}) = \frac{3}{7} + \frac{18}{7} = \frac{21}{7} = 3$$

This is an algebraic verification that both corner points lie on the same contour, the contour for $C = 3$.

Thus a minimum-cost diet meeting specifications will cost $3. One minimum-cost diet is achieved by just using 3 pounds of food $X$, corresponding to the point $(3, 0)$. Another way is to buy $\frac{3}{7}$ pound of food $X$ and $\frac{12}{7}$ pounds of food $Y$. But there are also many other diets that will suffice. For example, the point on the $C = 3$ contour halfway between $(\frac{3}{7}, \frac{12}{7})$ and $(3, 0)$ is the point $(\frac{12}{7}, \frac{6}{7})$. At that point,

$$C = \frac{12}{7} + 1.5(\frac{6}{7}) = \frac{12}{7} + \frac{9}{7} = \frac{21}{7} = 3$$

All of the *feasible* points on the $C = 3$ contour would yield acceptable, *alternate optimal solutions*.

Finally, note that the feasible region was *unbounded* but that a solution (in fact, many of them) did exist for the problem. So an unbounded feasible region does not necessarily imply an unbounded, or "infinite," value of the objective function. Of course, if the problem has been stated illogically, so that we wanted to *maximize* cost subject to the same constraints, then we would have had an unbounded "solution." We would have moved the edge of the ruler in the other direction, and it would never have left the feasible region.

Now that you are acquainted with feasible regions, corner points, and contours of objective functions, you are ready to make a transition to algebraic reasoning in linear programming. Although most LP problems involve inequality constraints, not equations, we will be converting our inequalities to *related* equations. The basis for understanding the concepts in the algebraic simplex method is *Gauss-Jordan reduction* of a system of equations.

**Example 3.8**
**Two Equations in Two Unknowns**

Consider the following system of two equations in the two unknowns $x$ and $y$:

$A$: $$x + 3y = 17$$

$B$: $$4x - y = 3$$

We will find the pair $(x, y)$ that simultaneously satisfies both equations (that is, *solves* the system) by reducing the system to an *equivalent* system where (1) each equation involves only one unknown and (2) the coefficient of each unknown in each equation is 1. The method of Gauss-Jordan reduction is a mechanical way of doing that.

The coefficient of $x$ in equation $A$ is already 1 (if it had been 5, say, we would first divide the whole equation by 5 to make 1 the coefficient of $x$). Now we want to completely eliminate $x$ from equation $B$ (so $x$ is only seen in equation $A$). To do that, just multiply equation $A$ by 4 and subtract from equation $B$:

$B$: $$4x - y = 3$$
$4A$: $$4x + 12y = 68$$
$B - 4A$: $$-13y = -65$$

Divide the resulting equation by $-13$. This produces a 1 coefficient for $y$, and the new but equivalent system

$A_1$: $$x + 3y = 17$$

$B_1$: $$y = 5$$

Now we have a 1 coefficient of $x$ in equation $A_1$ and a 1 coefficient of $y$ in equation $B_1$. To make each equation involve only *one* unknown, we only need to eliminate $y$ from equation $A_1$. To do that, just multiply equation $B_1$ by 3 and subtract from equation $A_1$:

$$
\begin{array}{llr}
A_1\text{:} & x + 3y & = 17 \\
3B_1\text{:} & 3y & = 15 \\
\hline
A_1 - 3B_1\text{:} & x & = 2
\end{array}
$$

This gives the desired reduced system, equations $A_2$ and $B_2$:

$$
\begin{array}{ll}
A_2\text{:} & x = 2 \\
B_2\text{:} & y = 5
\end{array}
$$

It is easy to show that the reduced system is equivalent to the original system, since the pair $(x, y) = (2, 5)$ is a solution for the original system, equations $A$ and $B$.

### Example 3.9
### More Unknowns than Equations

In linear programming models, to make related equations out of inequalities we will be including an extra unknown for each inequality (see Section 3.5, following). Thus we will always be dealing with more unknowns than equations.

Consider the following system of two equations in three unknowns:

$$
\begin{array}{ll}
A\text{:} & 2x + 3y + 4z = 12 \\
B\text{:} & 3x + 5y - z = 20
\end{array}
$$

It will not be possible in this case to reduce the system so that every equation involves only one unknown, but let's go ahead and do a Gauss-Jordan reduction as far as possible.

First we want 1 as the coefficient of $x$ in the first equation. Just divide equation $A$ by 2. Then we see the new system

$$
\begin{array}{ll}
A_1\text{:} & x + \frac{3}{2}y + 2z = 6 \\
B_1\text{:} & 3x + 5y - z = 20
\end{array}
$$

Next, multiply equation $A_1$ by 3 and subtract from equation $B_1$. This eliminates $x$ from the second equation:

$$
\begin{array}{llr}
B_1\text{:} & 3x + 5y - z & = 20 \\
3A_1\text{:} & 3x + \frac{9}{2}y + 6z & = 18 \\
\hline
B_1 - 3A_1\text{:} & \frac{1}{2}y - 7z & = 2
\end{array}
$$

Now multiply the resulting equation by 2 to make 1 the coefficient of $y$. This gives the system

$A_2$: $\qquad\qquad\qquad\qquad x + \frac{3}{2}y + 2z = 6$

$B_2$: $\qquad\qquad\qquad\qquad\qquad\quad y - 14z = 4$

Continuing, we want to eliminate $y$ from equation $A_2$. Just multiply equation $B_2$ by $\frac{3}{2}$ and subtract from equation $A_2$:

$A_2$: $\qquad\qquad\qquad\qquad x + \frac{3}{2}y + 2z = 6$

$\frac{3}{2}B_2$: $\qquad\qquad\qquad\qquad\quad \underline{\frac{3}{2}y - 21z = 6}$

$A_2 - \frac{3}{2}B_2$: $\qquad\qquad\quad x \qquad\quad + 23z = 0$

Our final reduced system, as far as we can go using Gauss-Jordan reduction, is

$A_3$: $\qquad\qquad\qquad\qquad x \qquad + 23z = 0$

$B_3$: $\qquad\qquad\qquad\qquad\qquad y - 14z = 4$

This system has an infinity of solutions (as did the original system, since the reduced system is equivalent to it). We can arbitrarily assign $z$ *any* value and then solve for $x$ and $y$. For instance, if we let $z = 1$, then $x = -23$ and $y = 18$. Is the point $(x, y, z) = (-23, 18, 1)$ a solution of the original system? Yes.

$A$: $\qquad\qquad 2(-23) + 3(18) + 4(1) = -46 + 54 + 4 = 12$

$B$: $\qquad\qquad 3(-23) + 5(18) - (1) = -69 + 90 - 1 = 20$

What is the *easiest* point to find that satisfies both equations? Look at the system $[A_3, B_3]$ and let $z = 0$. Then immediately we see $x = 0$ and $y = 4$. So the point $(x, y, z) = (0, 4, 0)$ is also a solution.

This last solution, where we arbitrarily let $z = 0$, is the solution process used in the *simplex method* of linear programming. After a Gauss-Jordan reduction we call variables like $x$ and $y$ (the ones that appear only once in the system and whose coefficients are 1) *basic* variables, and variables like $z$ (which essentially has not been "reduced") *nonbasic* variables. Then we always give nonbasic variables the value 0 to find a solution.

## 3.5 CONVERTING INEQUALITIES TO EQUATIONS: SLACK AND SURPLUS VARIABLES

We are now ready for the first phase of the algebraic simplex method, the description of a feasible region using a system of equations. Our example involves three of the inequalities from Examples 2.1 and 3.6, where the Early Auto Sales problem was considered.

**Example 3.10**

Three of the constraints in the Early Auto Sales model were

I: $\qquad 4{,}000A + 3{,}000T \le 600{,}000 \qquad$ capital

II: $\qquad 4A + \quad 6T \le 960 \qquad$ time

III: $\qquad T \ge 100 \qquad$ demand for model $T$'s

Let's consider some implications of each constraint, and how to write a *related equation* for each one.

Look at constraint I, the capital constraint. Suppose $A$ and $T$ assume values such that $4000A + 3000T$ is *strictly less than* 600,000. That would mean we did not use all of our available capital, or we say there is some *slack* in the constraint. This means we would have to add some *positive* amount to the left side of constraint I to make the sum *equal* 600,000. Generally, we call this number the value of the *slack variable* for the constraint. Suppose we name this slack variable "$S_1$." Then we may write the related equation

I: $\qquad 4{,}000A + 3{,}000T + S_1 = 600{,}000$

Thus a slack variable "takes up the slack" in a "$\le$" type inequality. If $4{,}000A + 3{,}000T$ is *less than* 600,000, then we know $S_1$ would have to be a *positive* number. Suppose $A$ and $T$ are such that the constraint is satisfied with *equality*; that is, $4{,}000A + 3{,}000T = 600{,}000$. This just means that there is *no slack*, so $S_1$ would have to be *zero*. Then a slack variable is also a *nonnegative* variable, just like the variables $A$ and $T$. The equation can be related to the inequality only if

$$S_1 \ge 0$$

Remember the optimal solution for the Early Auto Sales model? Figure 3.9 reminds us that the maximum gross profit occurred when $A = 75$ and $T = 100$. That figure also showed us that the capital constraint was satisfied with *equality* (we were able to use all the available capital). Then the corresponding value of the slack variable $S_1$ at optimality is 0. That is, $(A, T, S_1) = (75, 100, 0)$ is the solution of the equation corresponding to the capital constraint when $A$ and $T$ assume their optimal values.

Similarly we can associate an equation and another slack variable, $S_2$, with the time constraint. The equation is

II: $\qquad 4A + 6T + S_2 = 960$

where we also require $S_2 \ge 0$. Again, $S_2$ is a nonnegative amount that would have to be added to $4A + 6T$ to make the total equal 960. It is also the amount of time we *did not use*, or it is the slack in the time constraint.

At optimality, where $A = 75$ and $T = 100$, $4A + 6T = 4(75) + 6(100) = 900$. Then at optimality $S_2 = 60$, or we were unable to use 60 hours of the available selling time. Figure 3.9 shows that lack of equality in the original constraint, since the point (75, 100) is not on the line whose equation is $4A + 6T = 960$.

Constraint III, related to the demand for model $T$'s since it requires the number purchased to be at least 100, takes a different modification to become an equation. The constraint is

III: $$T \geq 100$$

If $T$ is *strictly greater* than 100, we would have to *subtract* a positive amount from it to reach 100. If $T = 100$, we subtract zero from it. So the related equation is

III: $$T - S_3 = 100$$

where $S_3 \geq 0$. Here $S_3$ is called a *surplus* variable instead of a slack variable, since it represents the surplus, or excess, on the left-hand side that must be subtracted to achieve equality.

In the Early Auto Sales problem, $S_3$ would represent the number of model $T$'s purchased in excess of the minimum required, which is 100. Since at optimality $T = 100$, then the optimal value for the surplus variable is $S_3 = 0$.

Notice the convention that the subscript on a slack or surplus variable indicates the number of the constraint in which it appears. That convention is convenient for keeping track of variables while executing the mechanics of the simplex method. Another convention is the arrangement of variables in a system of equations so that they "line up" in columns for ease of reference (and to facilitate a Gauss-Jordan reduction of the system).

Then associated with a system of inequalities describing a feasible region is a related system of equations. With the inequality system

I: $$4{,}000A + 3{,}000T \leq 600{,}000$$

II: $$4A + 6T \leq 960$$

III: $$T \geq 100$$

we associate the equation system

I: $$4{,}000A + 3{,}000T + S_1 = 600{,}000$$

II: $$4A + 6T + S_2 = 960$$

III: $$T - S_3 = 100$$

where $S_1 \geq 0$, $S_2 \geq 0$, $S_3 \geq 0$.

Note the lining-up of variables into columns. Also note that the system looks like the end result of a Gauss-Jordan reduction of a three-equation, five-variable system, where the reduction was only applied to the variables $S_1$, $S_2$, and $S_3$. The coefficient of $S_3$ is $-1$ instead of 1, but otherwise the system could have come from a Gauss-Jordan reduction.

## 3.6   THE SIMPLEX METHOD

From your work with graphical solutions of LP models you will have learned that the key to linear programming is *corner points*. In fact, an alternative to the "edge of the ruler" technique would be to simply identify all corner points of the feasible region, put their coordinates into the objective function and evaluate the function at each corner, then choose as the optimal solution that corner which gives the largest (or smallest) value of the objective function. The preceding sentence *almost* describes the simplex method.

The simplex method of linear programming is an algebraic procedure designed to move from corner to *adjacent* corner of the feasible region, evaluating the objective function as it goes, and in such a way that the objective function must never decrease (for a maximization problem) if a move is to be made. When no adjacent corner gives a better value of the objective function, the simplex method declares the current corner the optimal solution. Thus rarely are *all* feasible corners considered by the simplex method. It is more efficient than the "brute force" method described in the previous paragraph.

When more than two decision variables are involved, then simply *identifying* corners (or their algebraic analogs in more than three dimensions) could be a formidable task. The identification of "corners" in higher-dimensional problems is a built-in feature of the simplex method. The principles of corner-identification and efficient moves to adjacent corners stem from the notion of Gauss-Jordan reduction of a system of equations.

### Example 3.11
### A Job-Shop Application: Small-Scale Production Problem

Warren Pease and his brother Leo make furniture in their spare time to supplement their income. Recently, Warren and Leo have contracted to supply unfinished pine furniture, tables and chairs, to a large local furniture store. The store can handle no more than the equivalent of 50 board feet of furniture per week, in any mix of tables and chairs. The Pease brothers have 52 worker-hours per week available to devote to the job.

It takes 5 board feet of pine and 2 worker-hours to make a table, and 2 board feet of pine and 4 worker-hours to make a chair (ignore any waste of pine). Profit per table is $8 and per chair is $4.

Warren thinks they should only make tables because of the higher per-unit profit; Leo thinks they should only make chairs because chairs consume much less lumber. You are called in as a consultant to settle the dispute.

With the objective being the maximization of weekly profit, what do you advise?

After formulating an LP model of their problem and solving it graphically, you are able to say that while Warren's approach does give more profit than Leo's, there is some merit in Leo's idea. The optimal solution involves both tables and chairs, but more chairs than tables.

Let Z denote weekly profit in dollars, and let $x_1$ = number of tables to make and $x_2$ = number of chairs to make per week. Then the LP model is

$$\text{Maximize } Z$$

where
$$Z = 8x_1 + 4x_2 \qquad \text{profit}$$

subject to
$$5x_1 + 2x_2 \leq 50 \qquad \text{board feet of pine}$$
$$2x_1 + 4x_2 \leq 52 \qquad \text{worker-hours}$$
$$x_1 \geq 0 \qquad x_2 \geq 0 \qquad \text{nonnegativity}$$

Its graphical solution is indicated by Figure 3.11.

The optimal solution, occurring at point C in Figure 3.11, is:

Make 6 tables and 10 chairs for maximum weekly profit of $88.

This solution satisfies both resource constraints with equality, so there is no slack at all at optimality.

You can show Warren that his solution is point B on Figure 3.11, where 10 tables and no chairs are made. It would yield a profit of $80 and would consume all 50 board feet of pine permitted, but if it is put into the left-hand side of the worker-hour constraint, we would see

$$2(10) + 4(0) = 20$$

So Warren's solution would leave $52 - 20 = 32$ worker-hours unused.

You can show Leo that his solution is point D on Figure 3.11, where no tables and 13 chairs are made. It would yield a profit of only $52, but it would permit the use of all 52 available worker-hours. However, if it is put into the left-hand side of the pine constraint, we would see

$$5(0) + 2(13) = 26$$

so Leo's solution would leave $50 - 26 = 24$ board feet of pine unused.

You congratulate both Leo and Warren for at least realizing that the optimal solution should occur at a corner point of the feasible region. You advise them, however, to make 6 tables and 10 chairs if they want to maximize weekly profit.

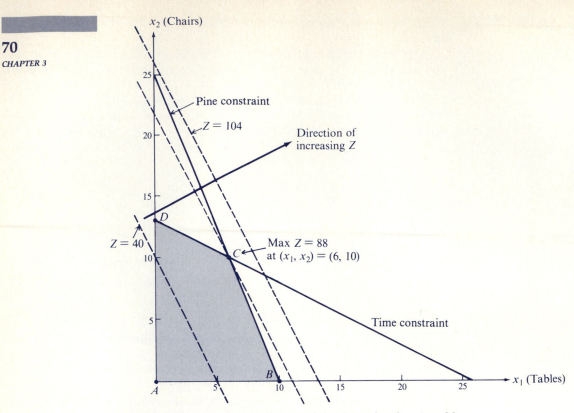

*FIGURE 3.11*  Graphical solution of the Pease brothers' problem

## Example 3.12
### Simplex-Method Solution of the Pease Brothers' Problem

Now we will rephrase the LP model in Example 3.11 using equations, and we will discuss its solution by the algebraic simplex method. During that process we will encounter some of the same corner points considered in Example 3.11, the graphical solution, and will observe how the two procedures are related to each other.

First of all, observe that while slack variables are needed to make equations out of the pine and worker-hour constraints, they will have no effect on the objective function. Yet they *will* be variables in the complete model formulation. Thus to incorporate slack variables into the original objective function, we should attach zero coefficients to them. With $S_1$ the slack variable for board feet of pine and $S_2$ the slack variable for worker-hours, the model in equation form becomes

$$\text{Maximize } Z$$

where
$$Z = 8x_1 + 4x_2 + 0S_1 + 0S_2$$

subject to
$$5x_1 + 2x_2 + S_1 \qquad = 50$$
$$2x_1 + 4x_2 \qquad + S_2 = 52$$
$$x_1, x_2, S_1, S_2 \geq 0$$

Suppose now we just look at all the *equations* in the model, just *remembering* that nonnegativity of all variables is required. Further we write all equations, including the objective-function equation, with the variables lined up in columns like we did in our Gauss-Jordan-reduction examples. This means we have to move the right-hand side of the objective-function equation to the left, leaving 0 on the right. Doing that, we see the system

$$\{Z\} - 8x_1 - 4x_2 \qquad\qquad = 0$$
$$5x_1 + 2x_2 + \{S_1\} \qquad = 50$$
$$2x_1 + 4x_2 \qquad + \{S_2\} = 52$$

Look at the variables that have been set off in braces ($\{S_1\}$, for example). They look as if a Gauss-Jordan reduction applied just to them produced the system we have in view. What is an obvious *solution* for this system? If we let $x_1$ and $x_2$ be *zero*, then $Z = 0$, $S_1 = 50$, and $S_2 = 52$. Thus the most obvious solution for this system of three equations in five variables is

$$(Z, x_1, x_2, S_1, S_2) = (0, 0, 0, 50, 52)$$

Relating this solution to the original problem, it means that if we make no tables and no chairs, we would make no profit ($Z = 0$) and would still have 50 board feet of pine and 52 worker-hours available ($S_1 = 50$, $S_2 = 52$). Thus this particular solution of the system of equations is equivalent to the *corner A* solution on Figure 3.11.

Can we rewrite the system so there is a correspondence of its most obvious solution to *another* corner of the feasible region? Yes. Before doing that, however, we want to introduce the ideas of *basic* and *nonbasic* variables and *basic feasible solutions*.

We decide to subscribe to the following convention: Call the variables in braces *basic variables* and the other variables *nonbasic variables* (mathematically, the notion is that of a basis of a vector space, an important topic in matrix theory). Further, decide that *all nonbasic variables will assume the value zero*. Applied to the current system of equations, this again gives us our solution $(Z, x_1, x_2, S_1, S_2) = (0, 0, 0, 50, 52)$, which we call a *basic feasible solution*. As we have already noticed, that basic feasible solution is associated with corner A in Figure 3.11. In fact, a basic feasible solution is the *algebraic analog of a corner point* on a graph of a feasible region.

A basic feasible solution permits only the basic variables to assume nonzero values (although a basic variable *can* be zero; here $Z = 0$, for instance). Now we want to use these ideas to construct *another* basic feasible solution with a higher value for Z (we are trying to maximize Z, remember).

Consider moving to a new basic feasible solution by bringing *one* new variable into the set of basic variables (there are always three basic variables in this problem—generally, one for each equation in the system) and making *one* formerly basic variable a nonbasic variable. Specifically, bring into that set of basic variables (called the *basis*) that currently nonbasic variable which will *increase Z the most per unit* of new variable brought in.

Look at the objective-function equation

$$\{Z\} - 8x_1 - 4x_2 = 0$$

The variables $x_1$ and $x_2$ are currently nonbasic variables, so one of them is a candidate for inclusion into the new basis. If we let $x_1 = 1$ and $x_2 = 0$ (make $x_1$ basic, with a nonzero value, but leave $x_2$ a nonbasic variable), then Z would have to become 8 to satisfy the equation. So Z would increase by 8 per *unit* increase in $x_1$ (if $x_2$ remains 0). What if we leave $x_1 = 0$ and make $x_2 = 1$? Then Z would have to be 4 or would increase by only 4 per unit increase in $x_2$. Thus $x_1$ is the currently nonbasic variable that could be brought into the basis so that Z experiences the *most* per-unit increase.

So that we do not lose contact with the original problem, what does this mean practically? Simply that if we wanted to make one item of furniture to increase profit the most, we would make *one table* instead of one chair. This presumes, of course, that at this point in time nothing has been made, or that we are currently at corner A in Figure 3.11.

Now we reason that if making one table does a little good, making a lot of tables will do a lot of good. If we are only going to make tables (no chairs yet, since we have to leave $x_2$ at the zero level to keep it nonbasic), how many can we make?

Look at the two resource constraints. They are

$$(5)x_1 + 2x_2 + \{S_1\} \qquad = 50 \qquad \text{pine}$$
$$(2)x_1 + 4x_2 \qquad + \{S_2\} = 52 \qquad \text{worker-hours}$$

Here the coefficients of $x_1$ are put in parentheses to call our attention to them, and the braces around $S_1$ and $S_2$ remind us that these are variables in the current basis.

Currently $x_1$ and $x_2$ are 0, $S_1$ is 50, and $S_2$ is 52. But we want to leave $x_2 = 0$ and increase $x_1$ as much as possible. The pine constraint says we could let $x_1 = 10$, leave $x_2 = 0$, change $S_1$ so that $S_1 = 0$, and still satisfy the constraint. What if we made $x_1$ *more than 10*? Then $5x_1$ would be more than 50, and since $x_2$ and $S_1$ are required to be nonnegative, that wouldn't work. Now if we only look at the *worker-hour* constraint using the same analysis, we could let $x_1$ be as much as 26 (we could leave $x_2 = 0$ and make $S_2 = 0$). But we have already learned from the *pine* constraint that $x_1$ cannot exceed 10. So to be able to satisfy *both* constraints, we bring $x_1$ into the basis with the value 10.

Before proceeding, let's look at a very *mechanical* way (as opposed to reasoning) to do the same thing. We want to bring $x_1$ into the basis. Consider the ratio of the right-hand side of a constraint to the coefficient of $x_1$. Look at those ratios for both constraints.

$$\text{Pine:} \qquad\qquad 50/5 = 10 \leftarrow \text{minimum}$$

$$\text{Worker-hours:} \qquad 52/2 = 26$$

The minimum (nonnegative) value of these two ratios is the *maximum* value permitted for the new basic variable $x_1$. Since sometimes a coefficient of an incoming basic variable (in another problem) might be negative, but we do not permit negative values of decision variables, this mechanical procedure for discovering the value of the new basic variable is called "determining the *minimum nonnegative ratio.*" Had the ratio been negative, it could not have been a suitable value for $x_1$. So we seek the minimum of *only* the *nonnegative* ratios.

What is the new basic feasible solution? We have to keep $x_2 = 0$ and we let $x_1 = 10$ (this is the new basic variable). If we do that, then from the objective-function equation, $Z - 8x_1 - 4x_2 = 0$, we see that $Z = 80$. From the worker-hour constraint, $2x_1 + 4x_2 + S_2 = 52$, if $x_1 = 10$ and $x_2 = 0$, then we must have $S_2 = 32$. Finally, the pine constraint tells us that $S_1 = 0$, or $S_1$ has become a *nonbasic* variable. The new basis consists of $Z$, $x_1$, and $S_2$ (with nonzero values), and the new set of nonbasic variables contains $x_2$ and $S_1$ (zero-valued). The *new basic feasible solution* is

$$(Z, x_1, x_2, S_1, S_2) = (80, 10, 0, 0, 32)$$

This is Warren's solution, or corner $B$ in Figure 3.11. It says to make 10 tables and no chairs for a profit of $80, and that if we do that, we will have 32 worker-hours left over but will have used up all the pine.

All of the reasoning behind the achievement of this new basic feasible solution may be replaced by a mechanical procedure that incorporates Gauss-Jordan reduction. Consider our original system of equations:

$$
\begin{array}{lll}
\{Z\} - 8x_1 - 4x_2 & = 0 & \\
(5)x_1 + 2x_2 + \{S_1\} & = 50 & 50/5 = 10 \leftarrow \min \\
(2)x_1 + 4x_2 + \{S_2\} & = 52 & 52/2 = 26
\end{array}
$$

Ratios

First we look at the objective-function equation to see which currently nonbasic variable should come into the basis. The fact that $Z$ will increase by 8 per unit increase in $x_1$ (and that this is the *most* per-unit increase among the variables $x_1$ and $x_2$) is equivalent to simply noticing that $-8$ is the *most negative coefficient* in the objective-function equation. This condition is indicated by the arrow that points to the coefficient $-8$ in the preceding system.

Now we know that $x_1$ is the *incoming* basic variable. But the basis must only have three basic variables, and currently they are $Z$, $S_1$, and $S_2$ (the variables in braces). If $x_1$ comes into the basis, something must go out. What is the *outgoing* variable (the currently basic variable that must become nonbasic, with zero value)? It is simply the currently basic variable in the equation associated with the *minimum nonnegative ratio,* or the variable $S_1$. This condition is indicated by the left-pointing arrow in the preceding system.

How do we immediately see the *new* basic feasible solution? *Write a new system of equations that has the same characteristics as the old system* with respect to basic and nonbasic variables. Those characteristics are

**1** The first equation (objective-function equation) contains only $Z$ and *nonbasic* variables.

**2** The coefficients of all *basic* variables in the other equations must be 1, and each basic variable must appear *only once* in the system.

This new system may be achieved by performing a Gauss-Jordan reduction on only the *new basic variable.*

The steps from here on are familiar. Divide the second equation by 5 to make the coefficient of $x_1$ be 1. Then multiply that new second equation by 8 and add to the first equation (removing the new basic variable $x_1$ from the first equation), and multiply the new second equation by 2 and subtract from the third equation (removing $x_1$ from the third equation). The resulting new system is

$$
\begin{array}{llll}
\{Z\} & \quad -\tfrac{4}{5}x_2 + \tfrac{8}{5}S_1 & = 80 & \text{Ratios} \\
& \{x_1\} + \tfrac{2}{5}x_2 + \tfrac{1}{5}S_1 & = 10 & 10/\tfrac{2}{5} = 25 \\
\leftarrow & \tfrac{16}{5}x_2 - \tfrac{2}{5}S_1 + \{S_2\} = 32 & & 32/\tfrac{16}{5} = 10 \leftarrow \text{min}
\end{array}
$$

Now let the nonbasic variables $x_2$ and $S_1$ be zero. Immediately we see that $Z = 80$, $x_1 = 10$, and $S_2 = 32$. We have that same basic feasible solution we observed by reasoning, corner $B$ of Figure 3.11.

The arrows and ratios appended to this new system tell us how to proceed from here. Just repeat the same steps.

The coefficient $-\tfrac{4}{5}$ in the first equation says that $Z$ must increase by $\tfrac{4}{5}$ per unit increase in the *incoming* basic variable, $x_2$. The minimum nonnegative ratio is 10, occurring with the third equation, so the *outgoing* variable is $S_2$. A Gauss-Jordan reduction applied only to the variable $x_2$, with the 1 coefficient of $x_2$ occurring in the third equation ($x_2$ replaces $S_2$ in the basis), gives the following new system:

$$\{Z\} \qquad\qquad + 3S_1 + \tfrac{1}{4}S_2 = 88$$

$$\{x_1\} \qquad + \tfrac{1}{4}S_1 - \tfrac{1}{8}S_2 = 6$$

$$\{x_2\} - \tfrac{1}{8}S_1 + \tfrac{5}{16}S_2 = 10$$

Let the nonbasic variables $S_1$ and $S_2$ be zero. Then $Z = 88$, $x_1 = 6$, and $x_2 = 10$. The new basic feasible solution is

$$(Z, x_1, x_2, S_1, S_2) = (88, 6, 10, 0, 0)$$

This corresponds to *corner C* of Figure 3.11, the *optimal solution.*

How can we tell in our algebraic approach that we have achieved optimality? Simple. Just try to proceed further and discover that we cannot. There is *no negative coefficient* in the first equation. If we let $S_1 = 1$, then $3S_1 = 3$, and Z would have to be 85 (Z would *decrease*). Likewise, Z would decrease if we let $S_2$ become basic. We don't want Z to decrease since we are trying to *maximize Z,* so we *stop here,* concluding that *there is no better basic feasible solution* than the one implied by our last system of equations.

But is there a better *solution* (*not* basic feasible)? No. Remember, basic feasible solutions are algebraic representations of corner points, and we already know that optimal solutions occur at the best corner-point solutions. Thus the best basic feasible solution, being also the best corner-point solution, is optimal.

Before we leave the Pease brothers' problem, one other point should be made. Observe the *sequence* of basic feasible solutions obtained by the algebraic simplex method. It moved from corner A to corner B to corner C (see Figure 3.11), always to an *adjacent* corner. The last step in the procedure, observing that Z could only decrease if we moved to the next adjacent corner, corner D (Leo's solution), precluded consideration of that corner. Thus the simplex method moves systematically from corner to *adjacent* corner but does not necessarily consider *all* corners.

The steps in the algebraic simplex method are easy to follow, but there are quite a few of them. Also, those steps must be executed in a very specific sequence. The following listing will help you keep everything straight.

## STEPS IN THE SIMPLEX METHOD

### Getting Started
1 Shift the right-hand side of the objective function to the left, and set the resulting function equal to zero.

2 Convert the inequalities to equations using slack variables, and regard $Z$ and all the slacks as initial basic variables.

3 Regarding the other variables as nonbasic, with zero values, determines an initial basic feasible solution.

### Finding the Next Basic Feasible Solution

4 The most negative coefficient in the first equation determines the incoming basic variable.

5 For all equations except the first, determine the ratios (right-hand side)/(coefficient of incoming variable).

6 For all those ratios that are nonnegative, determine the minimum. The currently basic variable in the equation associated with that minimum nonnegative ratio becomes a nonbasic variable in the new basic feasible solution.

7 Perform a Gauss-Jordan reduction on the new basic variable in the system.

8 Since now the new basic and new nonbasic variables are known, the next basic feasible solution may be determined.

### Determining the Optimal Solution

9 If after step 8 there remains a negative coefficient in the first equation, go back to step 4 and proceed to the next basic feasible solution.

10 If after step 8 there are no negative coefficients in the first equation, that current basic feasible solution is an optimal solution. STOP.

Ties could occur in steps 4 and 6. That is, there may be two or more negative coefficients in the first equation that are equal and also "most negative." Minimum nonnegative ratios could also occur in more than one of the other equations. In case of such ties, be arbitrary; just choose any one of the contenders for incoming or outgoing variable, and proceed.

Notice that these steps are designed only for LP models in which all constraints are of the "≤" type, requiring only slack variables. They must be modified, but only slightly, in the case where some of the constraints are equations or are inequalities of the "≥" type. A further slight modification is required if the problem calls for *minimization* of the objective function. The necessary modifications are introduced in Chapter 4.

### Example 3.13
### Practicing the Steps in the Simplex Method

The following LP model is not based on any particular business scenario. It is merely a symbolic model included here so you can practice following the steps in the algebraic simplex method. Its graphical solution is also indicated, in Figure 3.12, to reinforce the idea of corner points being basic feasible solutions.

$$\text{Maximize } Z$$

where
$$Z = 3x_1 + 2x_2$$

subject to
$$x_1 + x_2 \leq 15$$
$$2x_1 + x_2 \leq 28$$
$$x_1 + 2x_2 \leq 20$$
$$x_1 \geq 0 \qquad x_2 \geq 0$$

The first few steps involve setting up the related system of equations and finding an initial basic feasible solution. The system is

$$\{Z\} - 3x_1 - 2x_2 \qquad\qquad\qquad = 0$$
$$x_1 + x_2 + \{S_1\} \qquad\qquad = 15 \qquad 15/1 = 15$$
$$\leftarrow \quad 2x_1 + x_2 \qquad + \{S_2\} \qquad = 28 \qquad 28/2 = 14 \leftarrow \text{min}$$
$$x_1 + 2x_2 \qquad\qquad + \{S_3\} = 20 \qquad 20/1 = 20$$

Ratios (column heading, to the right of equations)

Since we let $x_1$ and $x_2$ be nonbasic initially, the first basic feasible solution is $(Z, x_1, x_2, S_1, S_2, S_3) = (0, 0, 0, 15, 28, 20)$. This is corner $A$ in Figure 3.12 following.

The coefficient $-3$ in the first equation says that $x_1$ should be the incoming basic variable. Since the minimum nonnegative ratio of right-hand sides to coefficients of $x_1$ is 14, occurring in the third equation, $S_2$ is the variable that first leaves the basis, the outgoing variable.

Next we must perform a Gauss-Jordan reduction on only the variable $x_1$. We want its coefficient in the third equation to be 1, and $x_1$ must disappear from all the other equations. The resulting new system is

$$\{Z\} \qquad - \tfrac{1}{2}x_2 \qquad + \tfrac{3}{2}S_2 \qquad\qquad = 42$$
$$\tfrac{1}{2}x_2 + \{S_1\} - \tfrac{1}{2}S_2 \qquad = 1 \qquad 1/\tfrac{1}{2} = 2 \leftarrow \text{min}$$
$$\{x_1\} + \tfrac{1}{2}x_2 \qquad + \tfrac{1}{2}S_2 \qquad = 14 \qquad 14/\tfrac{1}{2} = 28$$
$$\tfrac{3}{2}x_2 \qquad - \tfrac{1}{2}S_2 + \{S_3\} = 6 \qquad 6/\tfrac{3}{2} = 4$$

Ratios (column heading, to the right of equations)

The new basic feasible solution is $(Z, x_1, x_2, S_1, S_2, S_3) = (42, 14, 0, 1, 0, 6)$. Here $Z$ has become 42 with $x_1$ coming in at the level 14, or $Z$ has indeed been increased by 3 per unit of $x_1$. Further, we know that this is not yet the optimal solution, since there remains a negative coefficient in the first equation. This current basic feasible solution is corner $B$ on Figure 3.12, and we would expect the next one to be corner $C$.

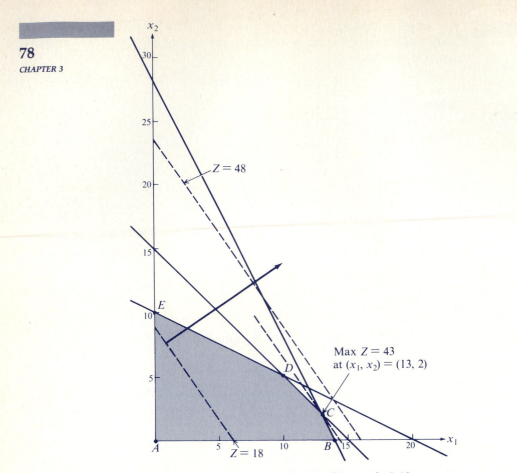

**FIGURE 3.12**   Graphical solution of Example 3.13

Sure enough, Gauss-Jordan reduction applied to the variable $x_2$ produces the following system, which we recognize as giving us the optimal basic feasible solution.   No negative coefficients remain in the first equation.

$$\{Z\} \qquad\qquad\quad + \; S_1 + S_2 \qquad\quad = 43$$

$$\{x_2\} + 2S_1 - S_2 \qquad\quad = 2$$

$$\{x_1\} \qquad\quad - \; S_1 + S_2 \qquad\quad = 13$$

$$- 3S_1 + S_2 + \{S_3\} = 3$$

The optimal basic feasible solution for this system is $(Z, x_1, x_2, S_1, S_2, S_3) = (43, 13, 2, 0, 0, 3)$.   It says that the first two constraints are satisfied with equality (having zero slack) but that there are three units of slack in the third constraint at optimality.   This solution, in terms of the original variables, is

$$\text{Max } Z = 43 \text{ at } (x_1, x_2) = (13, 2) \qquad \text{corner } C$$

## 3.7 SUMMARY AND CONCLUSIONS

The principal topic of this chapter is the simplex method of linear programming. Two ways of seeking the optimal solution of an LP model are discussed: graphical solution and the algebraic simplex method. Both approaches identify basic feasible solutions, or corner points, since an optimal solution will always be found at some corner of the feasible region.

The basic idea in the graphical solution is moving a contour of an objective function through a feasible region, locating the last corner touched as the contour moves in the direction of improving value. Necessary to this process is the graphing of lines and linear inequalities, so the early examples show how to do that. Later examples, mostly in realistic business settings, illustrate the complete technique.

For the algebraic simplex method, Gauss-Jordan reduction is the most important notion. This technique is used for moving from one basic feasible solution to the next (an adjacent corner) until further moves would only worsen the value of the objective function. The steps in the algebraic simplex method are formally listed to make that procedure easy to follow.

Emphasis in this chapter was placed on the logic of the processes involved. Further mechanical refinements will be included in Chapter 4. Only two-variable examples were considered in the body of the chapter so the relationships between the two techniques could be observed. The algebraic simplex method, however, is not restricted to two variables, so some of the exercises to follow include more than two variables.

In most real business problems a lot of decision variables are involved. Most often then, LP problems will be done algebraically, and usually on a computer. Chapter 2 discussed model formulation, and this chapter took you through the basic logic of their solutions. Subsequent chapters will include simpler algebraic manipulations, important economic interpretations of optimal solutions, computer applications, and special cases of LP models.

In Chapter 4 the tabular organization of simplex-method calculations is presented. This is a more convenient form for keeping track of computations, and it also facilitates consideration of minimization problems and problems involving surplus variables. Other LP topics such as artificial variables, infeasibility and unbounded solutions, and goal programming (for multiple objectives) are also considered in Chapter 4. Then, after the important interpretive topics of duality and sensitivity analysis are discussed in Chapter 5, you will see in Chapter 6 many examples of different linear programming applications and interpretations of computer output. In all of those chapters, exercises in model formulation, the most important aspect of all, are provided for your practice.

### KEY WORDS AND PHRASES

**Intercept method**  A method for graphing a linear equation by finding the two points where the line will intersect the two coordinate axes.

**Graph of an inequality**   The set of all points that satisfy the inequality. For a linear inequality the set is a half space.

**Feasible region**   The set of all points that satisfy every constraint in the problem.

**Objective function**   That function (a linear function in LP) which is to be optimized (maximized or minimized).

**Corner point** (of a feasible region)   The intersection of two or more boundaries of a feasible region.   Equivalent to basic feasible solution.

**Contour** (of objective function)   The straight line resulting from setting a linear objective function equal to a constant.

**Optimal solution**   That point (or points) in the feasible region which yields the optimal value of the objective function.

**Alternate optimal solution**   A point in the feasible region that gives the same optimal value of the objective function that occurred at another feasible point.

**Gauss-Jordan reduction**   A method for reducing a system of equations to an equivalent system in which as many variables as there are equations appear only once and each with coefficient 1.

**Slack variable**   A nonnegative variable which when added to the left-hand side of a "less-than-or-equal" constraint, makes that constraint an equation.

**Surplus variable**   A nonnegative variable which when subtracted from the left-hand side of a "greater-than-or-equal" constraint, makes that constraint an equation.

**Basic variable**   A variable with coefficient 1 that appears exactly once, in one row and one column, in the system of equations representing a linear programming problem.

**Nonbasic variable**   Any variable in the system of equations that is not a basic variable.   A nonbasic variable always takes the value zero.

**Basic feasible solution**   A solution of the system of equations in which only basic variables are allowed to have nonzero values.   Equivalent to corner point.

**The simplex method**   An algebraic procedure for moving from one corner point to an adjacent corner point in such a way that the value of the objective function is never worsened.

**Most negative coefficient** (in first equation of system)   Determines the incoming basic variable for the next system.

**Minimum nonnegative ratio**   The criterion whereby the current basic variable that will become nonbasic in the next system is determined.


**EXERCISES**

◆ **3.1** Solve graphically.

$$\text{Maximize } Z$$

where

$$Z = x_1 + x_2$$

subject to

$$3x_1 + 2x_2 \leq 6$$
$$x_1 \geq 0 \qquad x_2 \geq 0$$

**3.2** Solve graphically.

Maximize $Z$

where

$$Z = x_1 + x_2$$

subject to

$$3x_1 + 2x_2 \leq 6$$
$$2x_1 + 3x_2 \leq 6$$
$$x_1 \geq 0 \qquad x_2 \geq 0$$

◆ **3.3** Solve graphically.

Maximize $P$

where

$$P = x + 3y$$

subject to

$$x + 2y \leq 12$$
$$x - y \geq 0$$
$$2x - 5y \leq 10$$
$$x \geq 0 \qquad y \geq 0$$

◆ **3.4** Solve graphically.

Minimize $C$

where

$$C = 10A + 20B$$

subject to

$$4A + 15B \geq 60$$
$$A \qquad \geq 5$$
$$B \geq 2$$

**3.5** Solve graphically.

Maximize $P$

where

$$P = 2x_1 + 8x_2$$

subject to

$$4x_1 + 5x_2 \leq 40$$
$$x_1 + 4x_2 \leq 12$$
$$x_1 \qquad \geq 2$$
$$x_2 \geq 0$$

**3.6** Use the same feasible region as the one indicated by the constraints in Exercise 3.5, but change the objective function to $P = 2x_1 - 8x_2$. **(a)** Maximize $P$, graphically, and **(b)** minimize $P$, graphically.

✦ **3.7** A small company makes two types of leather belts: type $A$ and type $B$. It is preparing to produce a day's run of belts, with all belts made being the same size.

A belt of type $A$ contributes $1 toward profit, takes 2 minutes of production time, and requires 100 square inches of leather. A belt of type $B$ contributes $0.75 to profit, takes 3 minutes of production time, and requires 60 square inches of leather. There are available 7 hours of production time and 12,000 square inches of leather for the day. Find the number of each type of belt to produce in order to maximize profit contribution for the day's production run **(a)** graphically and **(b)** using the algebraic simplex method.

**3.8** A merchant has 2,400 square feet of floor space for storing units of products I and II. To gain the advantage of a good price he must purchase his stock now. A unit of product I costs $8 and requires 8 square feet of space, while a unit of product II costs $12 and requires 4 square feet of space. The merchant must stock at least 50 units of product II.

He expects to make a profit of $3 on each unit of product I he stocks and $4 on each unit of product II. If he has $3,000 available for purchasing stock, how many units of each product should he buy so as to maximize profit? Solve graphically. (A fractional number of units is permitted.)

**3.9** A bird's nest is located 500 feet from a worm bed (bed 1) containing nightcrawlers of type 1 and 1,000 feet from a bed (bed 2) containing type 2 nightcrawlers. It takes one minute for the bird to travel to bed 1 and return with one worm (the bird cannot carry more than one type 1 crawler). It takes two minutes for the bird to travel to bed 2 and return with two type 2 worms. The bird will work no more than four hours per day at supplying worms to her family.

Type 1 nightcrawlers weigh 0.5 ounces and type 2 nightcrawlers weigh 0.3 ounces, so a trip to bed 1 yields 0.5 ounces of worms, while a trip to bed 2 yields 0.6 ounces. On any day there are only 120 type 1 worms in bed 1 and 160 type 2 worms in bed 2.

The bird would like to maximize total worm weight gathered per day. She is in the habit of cleaning out all of bed 2 before making any trips to bed 1. Whether she knows it or not, is the bird behaving rationally?

✦ **3.10** The production manager for Kitchen Brite Cookware wants to schedule a day's production run for two types of electric toaster, the Plain and the Gaudy. The production of a Plain toaster requires 1.0 person-hours, 2.0 square feet of sheet metal, and 0.5 pounds of wiring. Making a Gaudy toaster uses up 2.0 person-hours, 2.5 square feet of sheet metal, and 0.4 pounds of wiring.

Available for the day's run are 300 person-hours, 500 square feet of sheet metal, and 120 pounds of wiring. The profit per Plain toaster is $5, while the profit per Gaudy toaster is $8. The run is to be scheduled in order to maximize profit.

The manager wants to know how many Plain and how many Gaudy toasters to produce. A fraction of a toaster produced at the end of the run is all right, since the rest of the toaster could just be part of tomorrow's run. Solve the problem **(a)** graphically and **(b)** using the algebraic simplex method.

**3.11** Consider the following objective function and set of constraints:

$$Z = 3x + y$$

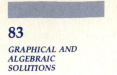
$$A: \qquad\qquad 6x + 11y \leq 66$$
$$B: \qquad\qquad 2x + \phantom{1}y \leq 8$$
$$C: \qquad\qquad -x + \phantom{1}y \leq 2$$
$$x \geq 0 \qquad y \geq 0$$

**a** Sketch the feasible region. Find the point $(x, y)$ that maximizes Z. Find the point $(x, y)$ that minimizes Z.

**b** Suppose the sense of inequality B is reversed. Now which point maximizes Z? Which point minimizes Z?

**c** Reverse the sense of both inequalities B and C. Sketch the new feasible region and find max Z and min Z.

◆ **3.12** This problem anticipates the *sensitivity analyses* of Chapter 5, or what is often called *ranging* in commercially available computer packages for LP. How sensitive is the optimal solution to changes of an objective-function coefficient?

Reconsider Exercise 3.3 of this section.

**a** Suppose the objective function is changed to $P = x + 4y$. Is the solution, the optimal $(x, y)$, changed?

**b** With $P = x + 2y$, what is the solution?

**c** With $P = x + y$, what is the solution?

**d** In general, if the coefficient of $x$ in the objective function is left unchanged, describe the effect of changes in the coefficient of $y$. Particularly, note *ranges* of the coefficient producing identical solutions $(x, y)$.

**3.13** Solve the Acme Trap Company problem: Exercise 2.3 of Chapter 2.

◆ **3.14** Solve the Clear Cut Corporation problem: Exercise 2.5 of Chapter 2.

**3.15** Solve Claude Grind's problem of maximizing his GPA: Exercise 2.6 of Chapter 2.

**3.16** Refer to the Kitchen Brite Cookware problem, Exercise 3.10 in this section. Change the profit per Gaudy toaster to $6, leaving everything else the same. Solve the problem. If the answer does not involve integer values for the decision variables, what do you think will be the best feasible, integer-valued solution? What is maximum daily profit in that case?

◆ **3.17** Refer to the Kitchen Brite Cookware problem, Exercise 3.10 in this section. Change the profit per Plain toaster to $4 and the profit per Gaudy toaster to $5, leaving everything else the same. You should encounter alternate optimal solutions. Can you discover an integer-valued optimal solution?

**3.18** Archaic Bakery (Logo: "You can have Archaic and eat it too.") makes edible centerpieces for decorating holiday tables. It makes two types of centerpieces: Delicious and Scrumptious. Profit per Delicious centerpiece is $2, while a Scrumptious centerpiece yields a $5 profit.

A Delicious centerpiece requires 4 pounds of flour, 1 pound of sugar, 6 teaspoons of salt, 1 hour to mix and bake, and 10 minutes to decorate. A Scrumptious centerpiece requires 6 pounds of flour, 2 pounds of sugar, 3 teaspoons of salt, 1 hour to mix and bake, and 30 minutes to decorate. For the current planning period, Archaic has available 4,800 pounds of flour, 2,000 pounds of sugar, 3,600 teaspoons of salt, 800 hours for mixing and baking, and 300 hours for decorating.

**a** How many of each type centerpiece must be produced in order to maximize profit for the period?

**b** Is the salt constraint a binding constraint? (If less salt were available, would less profit be earned?) How about the decorating-time constraint?

**c** How many pounds of flour and sugar could be diverted to other uses within the bakery without changing the maximum profit possible from the production of centerpieces?

**d** Suppose the profit per Scrumptious centerpiece had been $6 while profit for a Delicious centerpiece remained at $2. How does this affect your reporting of an optimal solution? What can you say about the problem if it is known that profit per Delicious centerpiece is fixed at $2, but profit per Scrumptious centerpiece may vary from $5 to $6?

**e** Suppose you are told that profit on each type is usually the same, but that sometimes profit on a Delicious centerpiece will slightly exceed that for a Scrumptious one. What would be your instructions to bakery personnel regarding how many of each type to make?

◆ **3.19** A retail candy store sells two types of mixed nuts: Family Mix and Party Mix. Family Mix consists of 50 percent cashews and 50 percent peanuts. Party Mix has 20 percent pecans, 60 percent cashews, and 20 percent peanuts.

Costs per pound to the retailer are $1.20, $1.00, and $0.50 for pecans, cashews, and peanuts, respectively. The retailer makes up her stock of mixed nuts weekly, and the maximum amounts of nuts available to her weekly are 500 pounds of pecans, 3,000 pounds of cashews, and 2,500 pounds of peanuts.

Family Mix is sold at retail for $1.50 per pound and Party Mix sells for $2.00 a pound. Assuming that the retailer can sell all of the nuts she offers during a week, find the number of pounds of each type mix required to maximize weekly profit. Would it be to her advantage to have more pecans available? To have more peanuts?

**3.20** Pull, Inc., a wire and cable manufacturer, has received an order for at least 10,000 feet of cable consisting of twisted steel and copper wire. Specifications call for there to be at least three times as much steel in the cable as copper (three strands to one). Steel costs $2 per pound while copper costs $3 per pound. The twisting operation shortens the steel wire by 4 inches per foot and the copper wire by 3 inches per foot (1 foot of steel wire becomes 8 inches in the cable, while 1 foot of copper wire becomes 9 inches).

Pull, Inc., must manufacture the wire as well as the cable. In the extrusion process a pound of steel becomes 6 feet of wire, and a pound of copper becomes 8 feet of wire. There are 10,000 pounds of steel and 3,000 pounds of copper available for the project. The extrusion equipment will be available for 600 hours, and it takes 1 minute to make a foot of steel wire and 0.5 minutes to make a foot of copper wire.

The purchaser is willing to receive more than the required 10,000 feet of cable if it will make Pull, Inc.'s, production run more efficient. How many feet of steel and copper wire will be produced if Pull, Inc., makes the ordered cable at minimum cost?

✦ **3.21** Solve the following problem by the algebraic simplex method. Verify that the optimal values reported for the original variables and the slack variables are consistent with the original inequalities describing the feasible region.

$$\text{Maximize } Z$$

where

$$Z = x_1 + 2x_2 + 3x_3$$

subject to

$$2x_1 + 3x_2 + x_3 \leq 6$$

$$x_1 + 2x_2 + 2x_3 \leq 10$$

$$x_1 \geq 0 \qquad x_2 \geq 0 \qquad x_3 \geq 0$$

**3.22** Solve the following problem by the algebraic simplex method. Do not be alarmed if the incoming basic variable from one stage immediately becomes a leaving variable in the next stage. The simplex method permits this.

$$\text{Maximize } Z$$

where

$$Z = 2x_1 + 5x_2 + 3x_3$$

subject to

$$x_1 + x_2 + x_3 \leq 10$$

$$3x_1 + 6x_2 + 2x_3 \leq 60$$

$$x_1, x_2, x_3 \geq 0$$

✦ **3.23** Solve the Universal Furniture Outlet's problem: Exercise 2.2 at the end of Chapter 2.

**3.24** In order to produce three different products, A, B, and C, a company must use two processes, process I and process II. Also involved in the operation are person-hours and storage space.

To manufacture one unit of product A, 0.1 hours of process I time, 0.3 hours of process II time, 1 person-hour, and 3 cubic feet of storage space are required. A unit of product B demands 0.2 hours from process I, 0.1 hours from process II, 2 person-hours, and 4 cubic feet of storage. One unit of product C requires 0.1 hours from process I, 0.1 hours from process II, 2 person-hours, and 2 cubic feet of storage.

During the next production period there will be available 200 hours of process I time, 300 hours of process II time, 1,000 person-hours, and 1,200 cubic feet of storage space. Profit contributions per unit of products A, B, and C, respectively, are $10, $8, and $6.

  **a** How many units of each product should be made in order to maximize profit for the production period?
  **b** Which is the binding constraint in the problem, in the sense that it is the most restrictive on the amount of profit that can accrue?

✦ **3.25** Solve the Generic Production Application problem that was posed as Example 2.2 in the early pages of Chapter 2.

## SELECTED REFERENCES

Bowen, E. K.: *Mathematics with Applications in Management and Economics*, Richard D. Irwin, Inc., Homewood, Ill., 1972.

Cooke, W. P.: "Two-Dimensional Graphical Solution of Higher-Dimensional Linear Programming Problems," *Mathematics Magazine*, vol. 46, 1973, pp. 70–76.

Frazer, J. R.: *Applied Linear Programming*, Prentice-Hall, Inc., Englewood Cliffs, N.J., 1968.

Kim, C.: *Introduction to Linear Programming*, Holt, Rinehart, and Winston, New York, 1971.

Lapin, L. L.: *Management Science for Business Decisions*, Harcourt Brace Jovanovich, Inc., New York, 1980.

Loomba, N. P.: *Linear Programming: An Introductory Analysis*, McGraw-Hill Book Company, New York, 1964.

Naylor, T. H., E. T. Byrne, and J. M. Vernon: *Introduction to Linear Programming: Methods and Cases*, Wadsworth Publishing Company, Inc., Belmont, Calif., 1971.

di Roccaferrera, G. M. F.: *Introduction to Linear Programming Processes*, South-Western Publishing Company, Inc., Cincinnati, Ohio, 1967.

Thierauf, R. J., and R. C. Klekamp: *Decision Making Through Operations Research*, John Wiley & Sons, Inc., New York, 1975.

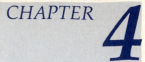

# SIMPLEX TABLEAUS AND GOAL PROGRAMMING

*I*n this chapter the manipulative chores of the simplex method will be made easier by standard tabular organizations of the work. Minimization problems, surplus variables, and what are called artificial variables will also be considered, as well as other features of the algebraic simplex method, such as detecting alternate optimal solutions and recognizing when a model as formulated has no solution. These and other extensions of ideas presented in Chapter 3 are easier to follow if the arithmetic tedium is reduced by use of simplex tableaus.

The last section of the chapter presents a method of handling multiple objectives, a procedure called *goal programming*. The principal difference between a goal programming problem and an ordinary (single-objective) LP problem is in the model formulation stage, not in the solution process. Tableaus like those exhibited in the earlier parts of the chapter will also apply to goal programming.

You will recall that in Chapter 3 every time a system of equations appeared the variables were "lined up" in columns. This standard way of displaying a system clearly brings out its important characteristics. Also, it suggests that one need not write down all the variables in every equation in order to see those characteristics.

Reconsider Example 3.13 of Chapter 3. The model was

$$\text{Maximize } Z$$

where

$$Z = 3x_1 + 2x_2$$

subject to

$$x_1 + x_2 \leq 15$$

$$2x_1 + x_2 \leq 28$$

$$x_1 + 2x_2 \leq 20$$

$$x_1 \geq 0 \qquad x_2 \geq 0$$

The related system of equations which initiated the simplex method (with all variables now assumed to be nonnegative) was

$$\{Z\} - 3x_1 - 2x_2 \qquad\qquad\qquad = 0$$

$$x_1 + x_2 + \{S_1\} \qquad\qquad = 15$$

$$2x_1 + x_2 \qquad + \{S_2\} \qquad = 28$$

$$x_1 + 2x_2 \qquad\qquad + \{S_3\} = 20$$

Table 4.1 gives the same information in a different format. Here the braces are left off the basic variables because the organization of the table itself clearly identifies them.

The left-most column in Table 4.1 gives the current basic variables, and the right-most column shows their values in the initial basic feasible solution. Since $x_1$ and $x_2$ are not specified as basic variables, they are understood to be nonbasic. Observe that the columns associated with

**TABLE 4.1** *INITIAL SIMPLEX TABLEAU*

| Basic | Z | $x_1$ | $x_2$ | $S_1$ | $S_2$ | $S_3$ | Solution |
|-------|---|-------|-------|-------|-------|-------|----------|
| Z | 1 | −3 | −2 | 0 | 0 | 0 | 0 |
| $S_1$ | 0 | 1 | 1 | 1 | 0 | 0 | 15 |
| $S_2$ | 0 | 2 | 1 | 0 | 1 | 0 | 28 |
| $S_3$ | 0 | 1 | 2 | 0 | 0 | 1 | 20 |

basic variables contain only zeros and ones. Also, in each such column the 1 occurs at the intersection of the row and column associated with the basic variable. Particularly notice that the $Z$-row (first row) coefficients of the *basic* variables (except for $Z$ itself) are zero. Clearly Table 4.1 just shows the same initial system of equations without the variables being specifically written for every equation.

With this new tabular organization being available, the statement of the steps in the simplex method can be condensed. The six steps that follow constitute the "programming" part of linear programming.

---

### STEPS IN THE SIMPLEX METHOD

1 **Form the initial tableau, depicting the first system encountered after the addition of extra variables.**

2 **The most negative coefficient in the $Z$ row of the table indicates the new incoming basic variable.**

3 **Divide the elements in the "Solution" column by the corresponding elements in the incoming variable's column (except for the $Z$ row). The smallest nonnegative ratio indicates what variable leaves the basis. The row in which that minimum nonnegative ratio occurs is called the *pivot row*. The intersection of that row and the column for the incoming variable falls on the *pivot element*.**

4 **In the next tableau, replace the outgoing variable by the incoming variable in the "Basic" column and in the pivot-row position. Divide all elements in that row by the pivot element, and put the resulting row of elements in the same position in the new tableau that they occupied in the previous tableau.**

5 **Complete the Gauss-Jordan reduction on the incoming variable. This means to use the new row from step 4 to create zeros in the column associated with the incoming basic variable. This step makes the new tableau appear similar to the old tableau and indicates the new basic feasible solution.**

6 **Continue steps 2 through 5 until no negative coefficients are observed in the $Z$ row. This final basic feasible solution will be an optimal solution.**

---

### Example 4.1

The complete solution for our introductory model is given in Table 4.2. The steps listed preceding were used to generate each successive tableau.

The final tableau, tableau III, tells us that the optimal solution has been achieved since there remain no negative coefficients in the $Z$ row. Again we have obtained the solution of Example 3.13: Max $Z = 43$ at $(x_1, x_2) = (13, 2)$.

**TABLE 4.2**   TABULAR SIMPLEX SOLUTION

| | Basic | Z | $x_1$ | $x_2$ | $S_1$ | $S_2$ | $S_3$ | Solution | Ratios |
|---|---|---|---|---|---|---|---|---|---|
| | Z | 1 | ↓ $-3$ | $-2$ | 0 | 0 | 0 | 0 | |
| | $S_1$ | 0 | 1 | 1 | 1 | 0 | 0 | 15 | $15/1 = 15$ |
| I. ← | $S_2$ | 0 | (2) | 1 | 0 | 1 | 0 | 28 | $28/2 = 14$ ← min |
| | $S_3$ | 0 | 1 | 2 | 0 | 0 | 1 | 20 | $20/1 = 20$ |
| | Z | 1 | 0 | ↓ $-\frac{1}{2}$ | 0 | $\frac{3}{2}$ | 0 | 42 | |
| | ← $S_1$ | 0 | 0 | $(\frac{1}{2})$ | 1 | $-\frac{1}{2}$ | 0 | 1 | $1/\frac{1}{2} = 2$ ← min |
| II. | $x_1$ | 0 | 1 | $\frac{1}{2}$ | 0 | $\frac{1}{2}$ | 0 | 14 | $14/\frac{1}{2} = 28$ |
| | $S_3$ | 0 | 0 | $\frac{3}{2}$ | 0 | $-\frac{1}{2}$ | 1 | 6 | $6/\frac{3}{2} = 4$ |
| | Z | 1 | 0 | 0 | 1 | 1 | 0 | 43 ← optimal | |
| | $x_2$ | 0 | 0 | 1 | 2 | $-1$ | 0 | 2 | |
| III. | $x_1$ | 0 | 1 | 0 | $-1$ | 1 | 0 | 13 | |
| | $S_3$ | 0 | 0 | 0 | $-3$ | 1 | 1 | 3 | |

Tableaus I, II, and III in Table 4.2 are called, respectively, the initial tableau, first revised tableau, and second revised tableau. The pivot elements in tableaus I and II are indicated by parentheses, while the arrows show the incoming and outgoing variables for proceeding to the next tableau.

The tableaus were generated by Gauss-Jordan reduction. Let's review what that means. There are two basic rules for creating a revised tableau. After the pivot row and pivot element are discovered,

**A** Obtain the *new* row for the incoming variable by dividing every element in the *old* pivot row by the pivot element.

**B** Obtain the *new* row for the remaining basic variables (including Z) by (1) multiplying the *new* row from rule A by the coefficient of the new basic variable in the *old* tableau and (2) subtracting, element by element, from the *old* row.

Rules A and B may be converted to formulas quite easily.

Let $a_{ij}$ = element in $i$th row and $j$th column of current tableau

$a_{ij}'$ = element in $i$th row and $j$th column of next tableau

$I$ = column number associated with incoming variable

$R$ = row number associated with outgoing variable

Then rule A becomes

$$a'_{Rj} = \frac{a_{Rj}}{a_{RI}}$$

and rule B becomes

$$a'_{ij} = a_{ij} - \frac{a_{iI}a_{Rj}}{a_{RI}} \qquad i \neq R$$

For emphasis, remember that the "primed" elements $a'_{ij}$ are elements of the new revised tableau you want to construct, and the "unprimed" elements $a_{ij}$ are elements of the previous tableau, which you will already have. A move from one tableau to the next revised tableau is called an *iteration* of the process, and the formulas work for any iteration.

If you are comfortable with Gauss-Jordan reduction as we have been doing it, you may not want to use those formulas. However, they do have an advantage for checking entries in a tableau; you don't have to recall how you reasoned through an entire row; with the formulas, you can easily check individual elements.

Let's check a few of the elements in Table 4.2. Number the rows 0 through 3, with the Z row being row 0. Number the columns 0 through 6, with the Z column being column 0, the $x_1$ column being column 1, and so on up to the "Solution" column, which is column 6. (Designating the Z row and Z column by the number 0 makes our notation consistent with that to be used in Section 4.2, where we consider another tabular scheme that does not explicitly display the Z column and that handles the Z row differently.) Suppose the initial tableau (tableau I) is our current tableau and the first revised tableau (tableau II) is the one we want to construct. We see that $x_1$ is the incoming variable and $S_2$ is the outgoing variable, so $I = 1$ and $R = 2$.

From the formula $a'_{Rj} = a_{Rj}/a_{RI}$ (rule A), some of the elements in the new $x_1$ row of tableau II are

$$a'_{21} = \frac{a_{21}}{a_{21}} = \tfrac{2}{2} = 1 \qquad \text{under } x_1$$

$$a'_{22} = \frac{a_{22}}{a_{21}} = \tfrac{1}{2} = \tfrac{1}{2} \qquad \text{under } x_2$$

$$a'_{23} = \frac{a_{23}}{a_{21}} = \tfrac{0}{2} = 0 \qquad \text{under } S_1$$

$$a'_{26} = \frac{a_{26}}{a_{21}} = \tfrac{28}{2} = 14 \qquad \text{under "Solution"}$$

From the formula $a'_{ij} = a_{ij} - (a_{il}a_{Rj})/a_{RI}$ (rule B), some of the elements in the new $S_3$ row of tableau II are

$$a'_{30} = a_{30} - \frac{a_{31}a_{20}}{a_{21}} = 0 - \frac{(1)(0)}{2} = 0 \qquad \text{under } Z$$

$$a'_{32} = a_{32} - \frac{a_{31}a_{22}}{a_{21}} = 2 - \frac{(1)(1)}{2} = \tfrac{3}{2} \qquad \text{under } x_2$$

$$a'_{34} = a_{34} - \frac{a_{31}a_{24}}{a_{21}} = 0 - \frac{(1)(1)}{2} = -\tfrac{1}{2} \qquad \text{under } S_2$$

$$a'_{36} = a_{36} - \frac{a_{31}a_{26}}{a_{21}} = 20 - \frac{(1)(28)}{2} = 6 \qquad \text{under "Solution"}$$

If you are moving from tableau II to tableau III in Table 4.2, the incoming variable is $x_2$ and the outgoing variable is $S_1$, so $I = 2$ and $R = 1$ (thus $a_{RI} = a_{21} = \tfrac{1}{2}$). The element in the new $x_2$ row and under $S_1$ in tableau III would be

$$a'_{13} = \frac{a_{13}}{a_{12}} = \frac{1}{\tfrac{1}{2}} = 2 \qquad \text{rule A}$$

and the element in the $S_3$ row and under $S_2$ in tableau III would be

$$a'_{34} = a_{34} - \frac{a_{32}a_{14}}{a_{12}} = -\tfrac{1}{2} - \frac{\tfrac{3}{2}\left(-\tfrac{1}{2}\right)}{\tfrac{1}{2}} = \tfrac{2}{2} = 1 \qquad \text{rule B}$$

Don't forget that the $a_{ij}$'s, on the right-hand sides of the formulas, now come from tableau II since we are constructing elements for tableau III.

If you have worked through and understood these examples, you should have no trouble applying these pivoting formulas. Regardless of the particular format of a simplex tableau (you will see another one in Section 4.2), the methods you have just studied will be involved.

## 4.2   AN ALTERNATE TABULAR FORMAT: $c_j - z_j$ APPROACH

The tabular simplex organization displayed in Tables 4.1 and 4.2 was a direct consequence of the type of mathematical analyses we did in Chapter 3. Because basic feasible solutions were identified as corner points, and optimal solutions occur at corner points, we wanted an efficient way to move from one corner to an adjacent corner, improving $Z$ as we go. Writing a complete system of equations, including an objective-function equation (the $Z$ row in a tableau), gave us one such efficient technique.

Another popular organization of simplex-method computations derives from the "$c_j - z_j$ approach" to determining an incoming basic variable.

Here $c_j$ will be an original objective-function coefficient, and $z_j$ will represent (in a profit-maximization problem) the profit *given up* by changing from one basic variable to another. As we shall see, since $c_j$ will represent profit *gained* by making the same change, the difference, $c_j - z_j$, is a *net gain*.

The following problem, Example 4.2, provides a convenient vehicle for demonstrating this line of reasoning. Also, since it involves three decision variables, not two, it reminds us that a tabular simplex method is designed for efficient handling of larger problems that cannot be solved graphically.

## Example 4.2

Yummy Cereal Company makes three kinds of breakfast cereals: Crunchies, Chewies, and Gummies. A pound of Crunchies consists of 6 ounces of wheat, 6 ounces of corn, and 4 ounces of bran. A pound of Chewies contains 4 ounces of wheat, 7 ounces of corn, and 5 ounces of bran. A pound of Gummies contains 1 ounce of wheat, 3 ounces of corn, and 12 ounces of bran.

In a given production period, Yummy Cereal Company has available 2,000 pounds of wheat, 1,000 pounds of corn, and 1,500 pounds of bran. Profit contributions are $0.40 per pound of Crunchies, $0.30 per pound of Chewies, and $0.50 per pound of Gummies. The problem is this: How many pounds of each kind of cereal must the company make to maximize profit for that period?

Let $x_1$, $x_2$, and $x_3$ denote, respectively, the number of pounds of Crunchies, Chewies, and Gummies to be made. Then the LP model is easily written as

$$\text{Maximize } Z$$

where
$$Z = 40x_1 + 30x_2 + 50x_3 \qquad \text{profit in cents}$$

subject to
$$6x_1 + 4x_2 + x_3 \leq 2{,}000(16) \qquad \text{wheat}$$
$$6x_1 + 7x_2 + 3x_3 \leq 1{,}000(16) \qquad \text{corn}$$
$$4x_1 + 5x_2 + 12x_3 \leq 1{,}500(16) \qquad \text{bran}$$
$$x_1, x_2, x_3 \geq 0 \qquad \text{nonnegativity}$$

Before introducing the $c_j - z_j$ approach, it is worthwhile to go ahead and solve this problem using the tabular organization and mechanics presented in Section 4.1. Not only will this be an opportunity for you to practice the technique, but also it will enable you to compare the two methods. There are only minor differences in the two kinds of tabular organization, and it enhances understanding to see them both being used on the same problem.

The system of equations which initiates the simplex method is

$$\{Z\} - 40x_1 - 30x_2 - 50x_3 = 0$$

$$6x_1 + 4x_2 + x_3 + \{S_1\} = 32{,}000$$

$$6x_1 + 7x_2 + 3x_3 + \{S_2\} = 16{,}000$$

$$4x_1 + 5x_2 + 12x_3 + \{S_3\} = 24{,}000$$

A complete tabular solution is shown in Table 4.3.

Following through the information provided by Table 4.3, we see that $x_3$ is the first entering variable and that $S_3$ first leaves the basis. Since $x_3$ came in with the value 2,000 (see the first revised tableau), and profit per pound of Gummies was $0.50, this solution is to make only 2,000 pounds of Gummies, and if we do that, profit is $1,000 (100,000 cents, in the solution column). But the negative coefficients in the $Z$ row of the second tableau (first revised tableau) tell us that this is not the optimal solution.

Continuing our interpretation of Table 4.3, we note that since $-\frac{70}{3}$ is the most negative coefficient in the $Z$ row of the first revised tableau, and it is under the variable $x_1$, then $x_1$ is the next incoming basic variable. The minimum nonnegative ratio in that tableau occurs in the $S_2$ row, so $S_2$ is the outgoing variable. The second revised tableau (last tableau in Table 4.3) indicates that $x_1$ came in with value 2,000, but that the value of $x_3$ then had to be changed to $\frac{4{,}000}{3}$ (1,333.3). No negative coefficients were observed in the $Z$ row of this tableau, so the optimal solution has been achieved. It is:

**TABLE 4.3**  SOLUTION OF YUMMY CEREAL COMPANY PROBLEM

| Basic | z | $x_1$ | $x_2$ | $x_3$ | $S_1$ | $S_2$ | $S_3$ | Solution | Ratio | |
|---|---|---|---|---|---|---|---|---|---|---|
| Z | 1 | $-40$ | $-30$ | $\downarrow$ $-50$ | 0 | 0 | 0 | 0 | | |
| $S_1$ | 0 | 6 | 4 | 1 | 1 | 0 | 0 | 32,000 | 32,000 | |
| $S_2$ | 0 | 6 | 7 | 3 | 0 | 1 | 0 | 16,000 | 5,333+ | |
| ←$S_3$ | 0 | 4 | 5 | (12) | 0 | 0 | 1 | 24,000 | 2,000 | ← min |
| Z | 1 | $\downarrow$ $-\frac{70}{3}$ | $-\frac{55}{6}$ | 0 | 0 | 0 | $\frac{25}{6}$ | 100,000 | | |
| $S_1$ | 0 | $\frac{17}{3}$ | $\frac{43}{12}$ | 0 | 1 | 0 | $-\frac{1}{12}$ | 30,000 | 5,294+ | |
| ←$S_2$ | 0 | (5) | $\frac{23}{4}$ | 0 | 0 | 1 | $-\frac{1}{4}$ | 10,000 | 2,000 | ← min |
| $x_3$ | 0 | $\frac{1}{3}$ | $\frac{5}{12}$ | 1 | 0 | 0 | $\frac{1}{12}$ | 2,000 | 6,000 | |
| Z | 1 | 0 | $\frac{53}{3}$ | 0 | 0 | $\frac{14}{3}$ | 3 | $\frac{440{,}000}{3}$ ← max | | |
| $S_1$ | 0 | 0 | $-\frac{44}{15}$ | 0 | 1 | $-\frac{17}{15}$ | $\frac{1}{5}$ | $\frac{56{,}000}{3}$ | | |
| $x_1$ | 0 | 1 | $\frac{23}{20}$ | 0 | 0 | $\frac{1}{5}$ | $-\frac{1}{20}$ | 2,000 | | |
| $x_3$ | 0 | 0 | $\frac{1}{30}$ | 1 | 0 | $-\frac{1}{15}$ | $\frac{1}{10}$ | $\frac{4{,}000}{3}$ | | |

Make 2,000 pounds of Crunchies, no Chewies, and 1,333.3 pounds of Gummies for a maximum profit of $1,466.67 (440,000/3 cents).

In so doing, Yummy Cereal Company will have used all of the corn and bran available ($S_2 = 0$ and $S_3 = 0$ at optimality), but it would still have 1,166.7 pounds of wheat left over (56,000/3 ounces, divided by 16). Notice that while the variables $x_1$, $x_2$, and $x_3$ are *pounds* of cereal, the slack variables $S_1$, $S_2$, and $S_3$ represent *ounces* of resource (wheat, corn, bran).

You should take the time to start from the initial tableau in Table 4.3 and work through the computation of all the numbers in the two subsequent revised tableaus, using the procedure outlined in Section 4.1. That practice will serve to verify your understanding of the method.

Now we want to look at the same problem with the $c_j - z_j$ approach. That approach amounts to handling constraint rows as we have been, but changing the way we incorporate the objective function into the tableaus. Its method of determining the incoming basic variable is a more intuitive process that is intimately related to the particular problem under consideration. Its key feature is the reference to *original* objective-function coefficients regardless of the tableau that is currently being revised.

To use that procedure we must think of the subscript "*j*" as representing the column associated with a *potentially* incoming basic variable. Then

$c_j$ = original objective-function coefficient of the potentially incoming variable, or the increase in $Z$ per unit of value of the "incoming" variable

Further,

$z_j$ = the decrease in $Z$ per unit of value of the "incoming" variable

The quotation marks around "incoming" serve to remind us that each variable under consideration will only be a potentially incoming variable; only one of them can actually come into the basis on any iteration.

With these definitions available (we will consider how to *determine* $z_j$ forthwith), then

$c_j - z_j$ = *net increase* in $Z$ per unit of value of "incoming" variable

Then the actual incoming variable should be the variable associated with the *maximum* net increase, provided, of course, the maximum $c_j - z_j$ is positive.

Now we want to find out how to determine values of $z_j$. To do that, it will be most instructive to consider that process at some iteration *after* the initial tableau. So we will look at the middle (first revised) tableau of Table 4.3, except we will not include the $Z$ row or the $Z$ column. Further, it is helpful here to recall the original objective function, since our $c_j$'s will come from it. It was

$$Z = 40x_1 + 30x_2 + 50x_3 + 0S_1 + 0S_2 + 0S_3$$

The zero coefficients of slack variables remind us that only pounds of cereal *made* (out of the available grains, of course) contribute toward profit, not ounces of *unused* grain.

Think of the $j$ subscript as ranging from 1 through 6, associated sequentially with the variables $x_1$, $x_2$, $x_3$, $S_1$, $S_2$, and $S_3$. Then Table 4.4 organizes information from the first revised tableau in Table 4.3 and indicates the implied correspondence of the $c_j$'s.

Remember, in the alternate tabular approach we want to develop, we said we would handle constraint rows the way we always have, but we will be determining the incoming basic variable differently. So we need the constraint rows but not the Z row (or the Z column). Instead, we put all the $c_j$'s where the Z row used to be, just to remind us of original objective-function coefficients, and we further put *some* of the $c_j$'s in a column alongside the corresponding basic variables.

Now let's ask the question: If $x_1$ were to come into the basis with value 1, what decrease in Z would ensue? That is, what is $z_1$?

To consider this question, we remember that the constraint rows in Table 4.4 actually represent equations. These equations are

$$\tfrac{17}{3}x_1 + \tfrac{43}{12}x_2 + 0x_3 + 1S_1 + 0S_2 - \tfrac{1}{12}S_3 = 30{,}000$$

$$5x_1 + \tfrac{23}{4}x_2 + 0x_3 + 0S_1 + 1S_2 - \tfrac{1}{4}S_3 = 10{,}000$$

$$\tfrac{1}{3}x_1 + \tfrac{5}{12}x_2 + 1x_3 + 0S_1 + 0S_2 + \tfrac{1}{12}S_3 = 2{,}000$$

What happens if we let $x_1 = 1$ but change no other previously nonbasic variable? In the first equation, since $x_2$ and $S_3$ are nonbasic, with the value 0, and the coefficients of the basic variables $x_3$ and $S_2$ are 0, letting $x_1 = 1$ means we reduce $S_1$ by the amount $\tfrac{17}{3}$ in order to preserve the equality. That is, we would use $\tfrac{17}{3}$ ounces *less wheat* than before, since $S_1$ was the slack variable for wheat. From the second equation, a similar analysis says $S_2$ must be reduced by 5, or that we use 5 ounces *less corn* than before. In the third equation the coefficients of $S_1$ and $S_2$ are 0, while the values of $x_2$ and $S_3$ are 0 since they are nonbasic. Then an equivalent equation would be

$$\tfrac{1}{3}x_1 + 1x_3 = 2{,}000$$

**TABLE 4.4**   *A PARTIAL FIRST REVISED TABLEAU*

| Basic | $c_j$ | $x_1$ 40 | $x_2$ 30 | $x_3$ 50 | $S_1$ 0 | $S_2$ 0 | $S_3$ 0 | Solution |
|-------|-------|----------|----------|----------|---------|---------|---------|----------|
| $S_1$ | 0 | $\tfrac{17}{3}$ | $\tfrac{43}{12}$ | 0 | 1 | 0 | $-\tfrac{1}{12}$ | 30,000 |
| $S_2$ | 0 | 5 | $\tfrac{23}{4}$ | 0 | 0 | 1 | $-\tfrac{1}{4}$ | 10,000 |
| $x_3$ | 50 | $\tfrac{1}{3}$ | $\tfrac{5}{12}$ | 1 | 0 | 0 | $\tfrac{1}{12}$ | 2,000 |

If we let $x_1 = 1$, we reduce $x_3$ by $\frac{1}{3}$. But that means we would produce $\frac{1}{3}$ pound *less Gummies* than before.

So we have given up $\frac{17}{3}$ ounces of wheat, 5 ounces of corn, and $\frac{1}{3}$ pound of Gummies in order to make 1 pound of Crunchies (that is, to let $x_1 = 1$). What is the corresponding *reduction in Z?*

Profit coefficients associated with wheat, corn, and Gummies are 0, 0, and 50, respectively (see the $c_j$ column in Table 4.4). Thus the decrease in Z per unit increase in $x_1$, the number $z_1$, is

$$z_1 = (0)(\tfrac{17}{3}) + (0)(5) + (50)(\tfrac{1}{3}) = \tfrac{50}{3}$$

That is, making an extra pound of Crunchies at this stage reduces our *previous* profit by $\frac{50}{3}$ cents.

But we did not consider the *gain,* the *extra* profit that would accrue from having a pound of Crunchies. That is just $c_1$, the profit per pound of Crunchies, or

$$c_1 = 40 \qquad \text{from top row of Table 4.4}$$

Then the *net increase* in Z per unit increase in $x_1$ is

$$\begin{aligned}
c_1 - z_1 &= 40 - \tfrac{50}{3}\\
&= \tfrac{120}{3} - \tfrac{50}{3}\\
&= \tfrac{70}{3} \qquad \text{cents}
\end{aligned}$$

Does that number look familiar? It should, since $-\frac{70}{3}$ was the coefficient in the Z row, under the variable $x_1$, in the first revised tableau of Table 4.3. And how was that *negative* coefficient interpreted? It was interpreted as the increase in Z per unit increase in $x_1$. That is, in our previous tabular format a negative coefficient was associated with the potential for increasing Z. With our $c_1 - z_1$ calculation we have just *verified* that interpretation by determining the increase using another procedure. Note the simple algebraic correspondence between the two numbers:

$$c_1 - z_1 = -(z_1 - c_1)$$

This implies that the numbers in the Z rows of tableaus like those in Table 4.3 are just $z_j - c_j$'s instead of $c_j - z_j$'s.

We have accomplished much more than just a verification of what we already knew, however. In order to determine $c_1 - z_1$ we have had to analyze the entire problem at an intermediate stage. That is, if we had first decided to make only Gummies, 2,000 pounds of them, what is the effect of the decision to throw in a pound of Crunchies? To answer that question we had to look at the objective function and every constraint, and our appreciation of the problem from a *managerial viewpoint* has been enhanced. We were determining that net increase by *reasoning* our way through the entire problem. Don't forget, of course, that the same kind of reasoning was done in Chapter 3 as a prelude to the more manipulative approach of Section 4.1.

Can the $c_j - z_j$ approach be made similarly manipulative? Of course. Now that you understand the reasoning, if all you want is a *solution*, you can achieve it by a mechanical process that has been *suggested* by the reasoning you have already done. Consider, for example, the remaining $c_j - z_j$'s for the first revised tableau of Table 4.3.

Look at Table 4.4. A computational scheme for $z_1$ would be to just *multiply the elements in the $c_j$ column by the elements in the $x_1$ column, and add*. Do the same thing for the other $z_j$'s, and you see

$$z_1 = (0)(\tfrac{17}{3}) + (0)(5) + (50)(\tfrac{1}{3}) = \tfrac{50}{3}$$

$$z_2 = (0)(\tfrac{43}{12}) + (0)(\tfrac{23}{4}) + (50)(\tfrac{5}{12}) = \tfrac{125}{6}$$

$$z_3 = (0)(0) + (0)(0) + (50)(1) = 50$$

$$z_4 = (0)(1) + (0)(0) + (50)(0) = 0$$

$$z_5 = (0)(0) + (0)(1) + (50)(0) = 0$$

$$z_6 = (0)(-\tfrac{1}{12}) + (0)(-\tfrac{1}{4}) + (50)(\tfrac{1}{12}) = \tfrac{25}{6}$$

Obtaining $c_j$'s from the $c_j$ row of Table 4.4, you see the corresponding net increases in Z:

$$c_1 - z_1 = 40 - \tfrac{50}{3} = \tfrac{120}{3} - \tfrac{50}{3} = \tfrac{70}{3}$$

$$c_2 - z_2 = 30 - \tfrac{125}{6} = \tfrac{180}{6} - \tfrac{125}{6} = \tfrac{55}{6}$$

$$c_3 - z_3 = 50 - 50 = 0$$

$$c_4 - z_4 = 0 - 0 = 0$$

$$c_5 - z_5 = 0 - 0 = 0$$

$$c_6 - z_6 = 0 - \tfrac{25}{6} = -\tfrac{25}{6}$$

Compare these numbers with the entries in the Z row of the first revised tableau in Table 4.3.

Thus the *largest* net increase is $\tfrac{70}{3}$, suggesting that $x_1$ should be the new incoming basic variable. The new outgoing variable would be determined the usual way, by finding the *minimum nonnegative ratio* of "Solution" column numbers to coefficients of the incoming variable.

By the way, this $c_j - z_j$ approach affords an excellent *check* of the elements in tableaus like those of Table 4.3 that were obtained using Gauss-Jordan reduction. If the $c_j - z_j$ is *not* the negative of the corresponding element in the Z row, something is wrong somewhere in the *column* associated with that element. It doesn't find the mistake for you, but it does tell you where to look.

The process we have most recently described suggests an alternate format for the simplex method. That alternative tabular procedure is illustrated by Table 4.5. In that display the $c_j - z_j$ row is at the *bottom* of a tableau and is called the *net evaluation row*.

To use the format in Table 4.5, first you evaluate the *bottom two rows* of a tableau, the $z_j$ row and the $c_j - z_j$ row. Note that the number in the $z_j$ row under the "Solution" column is now the *current value of Z*. It is obtained by multiplying the elements in the $c_j$ column by the elements in the "Solution" column, since those $c_j$'s are profit contributions for the basic variables whose values are given in the "Solution" column.

The *most positive* $c_j - z_j$ indicates the incoming basic variable. Then you find the outgoing variable by determining the "minimum nonnegative ratio," just as we did in Section 4.1 and Table 4.3. Finally, when no positive $c_j - z_j$ is found for a tableau, that tableau is the optimal tableau.

These rules, as well as those given in Section 4.1, are for *maximization* problems. If the LP problem is a *minimization* problem, the "minimum nonnegative ratio" rule still applies, but now you would look for the *most negative* $c_j - z_j$ (a negative net increase is a net decrease) to determine the incoming basic variable, and you would stop when no negative $c_j - z_j$ is found in a tableau. With the format of Table 4.3, of course, you would

**TABLE 4.5**　　*ALTERNATE TABULAR FORMAT: YUMMY CEREAL COMPANY PROBLEM*

| Basic | $c_j$ | $x_1$ 40 | $x_2$ 30 | $x_3$ 50 | $S_1$ 0 | $S_2$ 0 | $S_3$ 0 | Solution | Ratio | |
|---|---|---|---|---|---|---|---|---|---|---|
| $S_1$ | 0 | 6 | 4 | 1 | 1 | 0 | 0 | 30,000 | 32,000 | |
| $S_2$ | 0 | 6 | 7 | 3 | 0 | 1 | 0 | 16,000 | 5,333$^+$ | |
| $\leftarrow S_3$ | 0 | 4 | 5 | (12) | 0 | 0 | 1 | 24,000 | 2,000 | $\leftarrow$ min |
| $z_j$ | | 0 | 0 | 0 $\downarrow$ | 0 | 0 | 0 | 0 | | |
| $c_j - z_j$ | | 40 | 30 | 50 | 0 | 0 | 0 | | | |
| $S_1$ | 0 | $\frac{17}{3}$ | $\frac{43}{12}$ | 0 | 1 | 0 | $-\frac{1}{12}$ | 30,000 | 5,294$^+$ | |
| $\leftarrow S_2$ | 0 | (5) | $\frac{23}{4}$ | 0 | 0 | 1 | $-\frac{1}{4}$ | 10,000 | 2,000 | $\leftarrow$ min |
| $x_3$ | 50 | $\frac{1}{3}$ | $\frac{5}{12}$ | 1 | 0 | 0 | $\frac{1}{12}$ | 2,000 | 6,000 | |
| $z_j$ | | $\frac{50}{3}$ $\downarrow$ | $\frac{125}{6}$ | 50 | 0 | 0 | $\frac{25}{6}$ | 100,000 | | |
| $c_j - z_j$ | | $\frac{70}{3}$ | $\frac{55}{6}$ | 0 | 0 | 0 | $-\frac{25}{6}$ | | | |
| $S_1$ | 0 | 0 | $-\frac{44}{15}$ | 0 | 1 | $-\frac{17}{15}$ | $\frac{1}{5}$ | $\frac{56,000}{3}$ | | |
| $x_1$ | 40 | 1 | $\frac{23}{20}$ | 0 | 0 | $\frac{1}{5}$ | $-\frac{1}{20}$ | 2,000 | | |
| $x_3$ | 50 | 0 | $\frac{1}{30}$ | 1 | 0 | $-\frac{1}{15}$ | $\frac{1}{10}$ | $\frac{4,000}{3}$ | | |
| $z_j$ | | 40 | $\frac{143}{3}$ | 50 | 0 | $\frac{14}{3}$ | 3 | $\frac{440,000}{3}$ $\leftarrow$ optimal | | |
| $c_j - z_j$ | | 0 | $-\frac{53}{3}$ | 0 | 0 | $-\frac{14}{3}$ | $-3$ | (no positive $c_j - z_j$) | | |

look for the *most positive* element in the Z row and stop when no positive element is found.

Which tabular format should you use? Take your choice; being just different organizations of the same reasoning process, the simplex method, either can be used to solve any linear programming problem. However, in an LP model involving *artificial variables* (to be discussed in Section 4.3), most people prefer the $c_j - z_j$ procedure (Table 4.5). This is because of a bit of preliminary algebra that must be done to set up such a problem in the format of Table 4.3. No such preliminaries are required for the format of Table 4.5. But if the LP model only involves slack variables, many people would prefer the first format (Table 4.3) since one less row is involved in each tableau.

## 4.3  SURPLUS AND ARTIFICIAL VARIABLES:
## THE BIG-*M* METHOD

A constraint such as $2x_1 + 3x_2 + 4x_3 \geq 12$ requires a *surplus variable* to make it an equation. The equation is

$$2x_1 + 3x_2 + 4x_3 - S_1 = 12 \qquad S_1 \geq 0$$

When only *slack* variables are involved, they always form a convenient set of initial basic variables. But suppose we try to use $S_1$ (the surplus variable) as a basic variable in the equation. This means that $x_1$, $x_2$, and $x_3$ are nonbasic (only one basic variable per equation is allowed) and have zero values. Then $-S_1 = 12$, or $S_1 = -12$. This violates the nonnegativity restriction on $S_1$. Thus, because they always enter the system with negative coefficients, surplus variables are not convenient initial basic variables.

A similar situation occurs when one of the original constraints is an *equation* (no slack *or* surplus variable required). For example, suppose one of the constraints is

$$4x_1 - 5x_2 + 2x_3 = 28$$

None of the coefficients on the left-hand side of the equation is 1, and the other constraints will probably involve at least one of the variables $x_1$, $x_2$, $x_3$, so again there is no convenient initial basic variable.

In such cases, the standard technique for obtaining a convenient initial basic feasible solution involves the use of *artificial variables*. While slack and surplus variables are used to create equations in the system, artificial variables are employed to provide a *convenient initial basis*.

For instance, in the equation containing the surplus variable, we merely introduce the artificial variable $A_1$, with $A_1 \geq 0$, to obtain

$$2x_1 + 3x_2 + 4x_3 - S_1 + A_1 = 12$$

Then $A_1$ is a convenient initial basic variable. The variables $x_1$, $x_2$, $x_3$, and $S_1$ would be nonbasic, with zero values, and $A_1 = 12$ does not violate the nonnegativity restriction on $A_1$. We made $A_1$ nonnegative because it will become involved in a simplex-method solution, and all variables must be nonnegative for the simplex method to work.

Likewise, for the constraint that was *already* an equation, we include another nonnegative artificial variable, $A_2$. Looking at the two modified equations with the variables lined up in columns like we usually write them, and with braces indicating basic variables, we would see the system

$$2x_1 + 3x_2 + 4x_3 - S_1 + \{A_1\} \qquad = 12$$

$$4x_1 - 5x_2 + 2x_3 \qquad + \{A_2\} = 28$$

"Now wait just a minute," you say. "We already had equations *before* incorporating the artificial variables. How can you add some *more* nonnegative numbers and retain the equalities? Wouldn't both $A_1$ and $A_2$ have to be *zero*?"

Very true. In order to have an *equivalent* system (equivalent to the original two constraints), $A_1$ would have to be zero since $S_1$ has already accounted for all the surplus on the left-hand side of the first constraint, and $A_2$ would have to be zero because the second constraint was originally an equation. What we are really doing is creating an "artificial problem" that is *related* to the original one, and we will be solving it because it is more convenient to do so. We act, therefore, in an "artificial" manner, thinking of $A_1$ and $A_2$ as being nonnegative when we know they must both be zero at optimality. In fact, that knowledge is the key to the "Big-M method" (discussed in Example 4.3), which *forces* the artificial variables to become zero before we are able to declare optimality.

### Example 4.3

Happy Heifer Feed Company has received an order from Cheyenne Dairy for 1,000 tons of cattle feed. The order may be a mixture of Happy Heifer's three regular brands of feed: Standard, Special, and Super.

Cheyenne Dairy has specified that at least 200 tons of Super must be included in the order and that they will accept no more than 400 tons of Standard feed. Manufacturing costs per ton for Standard, Special, and Super are, respectively, $120, $160, and $240.

The feed company wants to minimize manufacturing cost of the 1,000-ton order (ignoring any blending cost). How many tons of each brand should be included?

Let $x_1$ = number of tons of Standard to include

$\quad x_2$ = number of tons of Special to include

$\quad x_3$ = number of tons of Super to include

Note that the 1,000-ton order implies an *equality* constraint, $x_1 + x_2 + x_3 = 1,000$. The LP model for this problem is

$$\text{Minimize } Z$$

where

$$Z = 120x_1 + 160x_2 + 240x_3$$

subject to

$$x_1 + x_2 + x_3 = 1,000$$
$$x_3 \geq 200$$
$$x_1 \leq 400$$
$$x_1, x_2, x_3 \geq 0$$

We will ignore the objective function for the moment, only writing the corresponding equations for the constraints. Note the two artificial variables $A_1$ and $A_2$, the surplus variable $S_2$, and the slack variable $S_3$, with the subscripts indicating the number of the constraint in which the extra variable appears.

$$x_1 + x_2 + x_3 \qquad\qquad + \{A_1\} \qquad\qquad = 1,000$$
$$x_3 \qquad - S_2 \qquad + \{A_2\} = 200$$
$$x_1 \qquad\qquad + \{S_3\} \qquad\qquad = 400$$

All variables, including the artificial variables, are nonnegative. The braces indicate the basic variables that will be used in the initial simplex tableau.

As has been noted earlier, the artificial variables will have to be zero-valued at optimality. Yet, being initial basic variables, they will not start out with zero values (initially, $A_1 = 1,000$, $A_2 = 200$, and $S_3 = 400$). In fact, that initial solution will not even be *feasible* for the original problem; it does not become feasible until the artificial variables become zero. So somehow we must tell the simplex method to *force* the artificial variables to have zero values. The *Big-M method* is one way to do that.

Write the objective function, but include the artificial variables, each with coefficient $M$, as follows:

$$Z = 120x_1 + 160x_2 + 240x_3 + 0S_3 + 0S_2 + MA_1 + MA_2$$

Think of $M$ as being an *extremely large, positive* number (hence, "Big-M"). Since we are trying to *minimize* $Z$, and $M$ is very, very large (although unspecified), the simplex method will try to get rid of the terms involving $M$. If either artificial variable is just a little bit positive, say $A_1$, then $MA_1$ is still going to be very large. One way to get rid of such a large, positive term is to make $A_1 = 0$.

We are ready to begin solution of the problem. We will use the $c_j - z_j$ format and will look at each tableau separately for clarity. The initial tableau appears as Table 4.6.

TABLE 4.6    INITIAL TABLEAU: FEED COMPANY PROBLEM

## TABLE 4.6    INITIAL TABLEAU: FEED COMPANY PROBLEM

| Basic | $c_j$ | $x_1$ 120 | $x_2$ 160 | $x_3$ 240 | $S_3$ 0 | $S_2$ 0 | $A_1$ M | $A_2$ M | Solution | Ratio |
|-------|-------|-----------|-----------|-----------|---------|---------|---------|---------|----------|-------|
| $A_1$ | M | 1 | 1 | 1 | 0 | 0 | 1 | 0 | 1,000 | 1,000 |
| ← $A_2$ | M | 0 | 0 | (1) | 0 | −1 | 0 | 1 | 200 | 200 ← min |
| $S_3$ | 0 | 1 | 0 | 0 | 1 | 0 | 0 | 0 | 400 | 400/0 |
| $z_j$ | | M | M | 2M ↓ | 0 | −M | M | M | 1,200M | |
| $c_j - z_j$ | | 120 − M | 160 − M | 240 − 2M | 0 | M | 0 | 0 | | |

The values of the initial basic variables are $A_1 = 1,000$, $A_2 = 200$, and $S_3 = 400$.   The current value of $Z$ for this solution is $1,200M$, a very large positive value.   We are trying to minimize $Z$, so we look for the *most* negative $c_j - z_j$.   Since $-2M$ is extremely negative, that number is $240 - 2M$, occurring in the $x_3$ column, so $x_3$ is the incoming basic variable.   The minimum nonnegative ratio is 200, occurring in the second row of the tableau, so $A_2$ is the outgoing variable.   Proceed to the next tableau, Table 4.7.    Observe that because of all the 0s and 1s in the initial tableau, determining the new rows for Table 4.7 is very easy.

The value of $Z$ has been reduced from $1,200M$ to $800M + 48,000$ (remember, $M$ is very large, so $1,200M$ is *much* larger than $800M + 48,000$).   Although there is little difference between $120 - M$ and $160 - M$, $120 - M$ is a bit more negative and is in fact the most negative $c_j - z_j$, indicating that $x_1$ is the incoming basic variable.   The minimum nonnegative ratio 400 occurs in the third row, so $S_3$ is the outgoing variable (Surprise!   You thought it would be $A_1$, didn't you?).   On to the next tableau in Table 4.8.

Now $Z$ is reduced to $400M + 96,000$.   The unspecified number $M$ is still part of its value because the artificial variable $A_1$ is still in the basis.

## TABLE 4.7    FIRST REVISED TABLEAU: FEED COMPANY PROBLEM

| Basic | $c_j$ | $x_1$ 120 | $x_2$ 160 | $x_3$ 240 | $S_3$ 0 | $S_2$ 0 | $A_1$ M | $A_2$ M | Solution | Ratio |
|-------|-------|-----------|-----------|-----------|---------|---------|---------|---------|----------|-------|
| $A_1$ | M | 1 | 1 | 0 | 0 | 1 | 1 | −1 | 800 | 800 |
| $x_3$ | 240 | 0 | 0 | 1 | 0 | −1 | 0 | 1 | 200 | 200/0 |
| ← $S_3$ | 0 | (1) | 0 | 0 | 1 | 0 | 0 | 0 | 400 | 400 ← min |
| $z_j$ | | M ↓ | M | 240 | 0 | M − 240 | M | −M + 240 | 800M + 48,000 | |
| $c_j - z_j$ | | 120 − M | 160 − M | 0 | 0 | 240 − M | 0 | 2M − 240 | | |

**TABLE 4.8    SECOND REVISED TABLEAU: FEED COMPANY PROBLEM**

| | | $x_1$ | $x_2$ | $x_3$ | $S_3$ | $S_2$ | $A_1$ | $A_2$ | | |
|---|---|---|---|---|---|---|---|---|---|---|
| Basic | $c_j$ | 120 | 160 | 240 | 0 | 0 | $M$ | $M$ | Solution | Ratio |
| ←$A_1$ | $M$ | 0 | (1) | 0 | $-1$ | 1 | 1 | $-1$ | 400 | 400 ← min |
| $x_3$ | 240 | 0 | 0 | 1 | 0 | $-1$ | 0 | 1 | 200 | 200/0 |
| $x_1$ | 120 | 1 | 0 | 0 | 1 | 0 | 0 | 0 | 400 | 400/0 |
| | $z_j$ | 120 | $M$ ↓ | 240 | $120 - M$ | $M - 240$ | $M$ | $240 - M$ | $400M + 96,000$ | |
| | $c_j - z_j$ | 0 | $160 - M$ ↓ | 0 | $M - 120$ | $240 - M$ | 0 | $2M - 240$ | | |

As soon as $A_1$ becomes zero, however (on the next iteration), $M$ will have to disappear from the value of $Z$.

The next (optimal) tableau is determined by the usual rules. It is shown as Table 4.9. In it no negative $c_j - z_j$ is found. This solution, the first one that has been *feasible* for the original problem (both artificial variables are now 0), is also the *optimal* solution. This often happens in problems like this, but not always; sometimes more iterations are required, even after the artificial variables have left the basis. Also, in any such problem, once an artificial variable has left the basis, it can never return to it.

In the phrasing of the original problem, the optimal solution given by Table 4.9 is:

Happy Heifer Feed Company should prepare for Cheyenne Dairy:

400 tons of Standard feed

400 tons of Special feed

200 tons of Super feed

This will fill the 1,000-ton order at a minimum cost of $160,000.

**TABLE 4.9    THIRD REVISED (OPTIMAL) TABLEAU: FEED COMPANY PROBLEM**

| | | $x_1$ | $x_2$ | $x_3$ | $S_3$ | $S_2$ | $A_1$ | $A_2$ | | |
|---|---|---|---|---|---|---|---|---|---|---|
| Basic | $c_j$ | 120 | 160 | 240 | 0 | 0 | $M$ | $M$ | Solution | Ratio |
| $x_2$ | 160 | 0 | 1 | 0 | $-1$ | 1 | 1 | $-1$ | 400 | |
| $x_3$ | 240 | 0 | 0 | 1 | 0 | $-1$ | 0 | 1 | 200 | |
| $x_1$ | 120 | 1 | 0 | 0 | 1 | 0 | 0 | 0 | 400 | |
| | $z_j$ | 120 | 160 | 240 | $-40$ | $-80$ | 160 | 80 | 160,000 ← min | |
| | $c_j - z_j$ | 0 | 0 | 0 | 40 | 80 | $M - 160$ | $M - 80$ | | |

Reference to the original problem statement in Example 4.3 should convince you of the correctness of this solution. It simply uses as little as possible of the most costly feed and as much as possible of the least costly feed, but must total 1,000 tons, the amount ordered.

A specific value for $M$ need never be stated for any such LP problem. $M$ is always very large and positive, so that a number like $M - 240$ is always very positive, and a number like $160 - M$ is always very negative. Further, $M$ will always disappear from all the relevant (interior) positions in the tableaus after all artificial variables have been forced to zero. It is never part of the optimal value of $Z$, nor is it ever involved in the value of any variable at optimality.

## 4.4   ALTERNATE OPTIMAL SOLUTIONS

In Example 3.7 of Chapter 3 we encountered a two-variable problem with alternate optimal solutions. This situation can occur whenever the contours of the objective function are parallel to one of the lines bounding the feasible region (see Figure 3.10 of Chapter 3). Since the algebraic simplex method employs no graphs, how does it detect alternate optimal solutions?

Fortunately, detection is very easy. One simply looks for a *zero* value of $c_j - z_j$ under a *nonbasic* variable in the *optimal* tableau (or, in the other tabular format, a zero coefficient in the $Z$ row under a nonbasic variable). These numbers, $c_j - z_j$'s or $Z$-row coefficients, give the per-unit change in $Z$. Then such a zero associated with a nonbasic variable at optimality says that the currently nonbasic variable can come into the basis with *no effect* on $Z$. Thus another basic feasible solution giving the *same* optimal value for $Z$ is possible. It will be an *alternate optimal solution*.

### Example 4.4

In Exercise 3.5 of Chapter 3 we saw the following LP model:

$$\text{Maximize } Z$$

where
$$Z = 2x_1 + 8x_2$$

subject to
$$4x_1 + 5x_2 \le 40$$
$$x_1 + 4x_2 \le 12$$
$$x_1 \qquad\ \ge 2$$
$$x_1, x_2 \ge 0$$

The third constraint requires both a surplus and an artificial variable if we are to use the algebraic simplex method. Thus notice that the use of artificial variables is not restricted to minimization problems.

Equations we will need to set up an initial tableau follow:

$$Z = 2x_1 + 8x_2 + 0S_1 + 0S_2 + 0S_3 - MA_3$$

$$4x_1 + 5x_2 + S_1 \qquad\qquad\qquad = 40$$

$$x_1 + 4x_2 \qquad + S_2 \qquad\qquad = 12$$

$$x_1 \qquad\qquad\qquad - S_3 + A_3 = 2$$

Here, since our objective is to *maximize Z*, the coefficient of $A_3$ in the objective-function equation is $-M$. Then if $A_3$ is anything positive, $Z$ will be *very negative*. The simplex method notices this and works diligently to drive $A_3$ to zero, since maximum $Z$ will not be a large negative number. A solution for this LP model is given in Table 4.10.

At the second revised tableau we have reached an optimal solution, since there remain no positive $c_j - z_j$'s. Thus *an* optimal solution is

$$\text{Max } Z = 24 \qquad \text{at } (x_1, x_2) = (2, \tfrac{5}{2})$$

However, the arrow in the second revised tableau that points to the 0 $c_j - z_j$ underneath the *nonbasic* variable $S_3$ indicates the existence of an

**TABLE 4.10  ONE OPTIMAL SOLUTION FOR EXAMPLE 4.4**

| Basic | $c_j$ | $x_1$ 2 | $x_2$ 8 | $S_1$ 0 | $S_2$ 0 | $S_3$ 0 | $A_3$ $-M$ | Solution | Ratio | |
|---|---|---|---|---|---|---|---|---|---|---|
| $S_1$ | 0 | 4 | 5 | 1 | 0 | 0 | 0 | 40 | 10 | |
| $S_2$ | 0 | 1 | 4 | 0 | 1 | 0 | 0 | 12 | 12 | |
| $\leftarrow A_3$ | $-M$ | (1) | 0 | 0 | 0 | $-1$ | 1 | 2 | 2 | $\leftarrow$ min |
| $z_j$ | | $-M$ $\downarrow$ | 0 | 0 | 0 | $M$ | $-M$ | $-2M$ | | |
| $c_j - z_j$ | | $2 + M$ | 8 | 0 | 0 | $-M$ | 0 | | | |
| $S_1$ | 0 | 0 | 5 | 1 | 1 | 4 | $-4$ | 32 | 32/5 | |
| $\leftarrow S_2$ | 0 | 0 | (4) | 0 | 1 | 1 | $-1$ | 10 | 5/2 | $\leftarrow$ min |
| $x_1$ | 2 | 1 | 0 | 0 | 0 | $-1$ | 1 | 2 | 2/0 | |
| $z_j$ | | 2 | 0 $\downarrow$ | 0 | 0 | $-2$ | 2 | 4 | | |
| $c_j - z_j$ | | 0 | 8 | 0 | 0 | 2 | $-2 - M$ | | | |
| $\leftarrow S_1$ | 0 | 0 | 0 | 1 | $-\tfrac{1}{4}$ | $(\tfrac{11}{4})$ | $-\tfrac{11}{4}$ | $\tfrac{39}{2}$ | 78/11 | $\leftarrow$ min |
| $x_2$ | 8 | 0 | 1 | 0 | $\tfrac{1}{4}$ | $\tfrac{1}{4}$ | $-\tfrac{1}{4}$ | $\tfrac{5}{2}$ | 10 | |
| $x_1$ | 2 | 1 | 0 | 0 | 0 | $-1$ | 1 | 2 | $-2$ | |
| $z_j$ | | 2 | 8 | 0 | 2 | 0 $\downarrow$ | 0 | 24 $\leftarrow$ optimal | | |
| $c_j - z_j$ | | 0 | 0 | 0 | $-2$ | 0 | $-M$ | | | |

**TABLE 4.11    AN ALTERNATE OPTIMAL SOLUTION FOR EXAMPLE 4.4**

| Basic | $c_j$ | $x_1$ 2 | $x_2$ 8 | $S_1$ 0 | $S_2$ 0 | $S_3$ 0 | $A_3$ $-M$ | Solution | Ratio |
|---|---|---|---|---|---|---|---|---|---|
| $\leftarrow S_3$ | 0 | 0 | 0 | $(\frac{4}{11})$ | $-\frac{1}{11}$ | 1 | $-1$ | $\frac{78}{11}$ | 39/2 $\leftarrow$ min |
| $x_2$ | 8 | 0 | 1 | $-\frac{1}{11}$ | $\frac{3}{11}$ | 0 | 0 | $\frac{8}{11}$ | $-8$ |
| $x_1$ | 2 | 1 | 0 | $\frac{4}{11}$ | $-\frac{1}{11}$ | 0 | 0 | $\frac{100}{11}$ | 25 |
| $z_j$ | | 2 | 8 | 0 $\downarrow$ | 2 | 0 | 0 | 24 $\leftarrow$ optimal | |
| $c_j - z_j$ | | 0 | 0 | 0 | $-2$ | 0 | $-M$ | | |

alternate optimal solution. This zero-valued $c_j - z_j$ tells us that $S_3$ can come into the basis without changing the value of Z.

To *find* the new basic feasible solution that is an alternate optimal solution, simply bring $S_3$ into the basis in the usual way; that is, do one more simplex iteration. The minimum nonnegative ratio in the second revised tableau of Table 4.10 occurs in the first row, so when $S_3$ comes into the basis, $S_1$ will leave. The new revised tableau is shown as Table 4.11.

Again we see no positive $c_j - z_j$, so we know that this alternate solution is indeed optimal. The presence of the 0 in the $c_j - z_j$ row under $S_1$ tells us that $S_1$ could come back into the basis without changing the value of Z. But if we performed the next iteration to find *that* alternate optimal solution, we see that $S_3$ would be the outgoing variable and we would be right back to the previous optimal solution found in Table 4.10. The new (alternate optimal) solution from Table 4.11 is

$$\text{Max } Z = 24 \qquad \text{at } (x_1, x_2) = (\tfrac{100}{11}, \tfrac{8}{11})$$

We have found, of course, the two *corner points* describing the line segment along which Z is maximum. To find *other* alternate optima requires a linear interpolation between those two corners. The simplex method only locates corner-point solutions.

Figure 4.1 indicates the four iterations of the simplex method: points A, B, and C on the figure are the solutions from, respectively, the initial tableau, the first revised tableau, and the second revised tableau in Table 4.10. Point D in Figure 4.1 is the alternate optimal solution from Table 4.11.

Notice first that the graph of $2x_1 + 8x_2 = 24$ is the line through points C and D. It is the last contour of the objective function to touch feasible points as contours of Z move through the feasible region in the direction of increasing Z.

Further, point A is *not feasible*. This characteristic reflects the manner in which the simplex method handles nonnegative artificial variables until

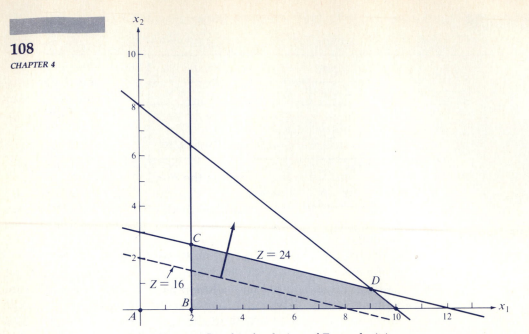

**FIGURE 4.1**  Graphical solution of Example 4.4

they become zero. The artificial variable must be zero at a feasible solution. We allow it to be positive only to start with a convenient basis. After $A_3$ became zero, the remaining simplex iterations did produce feasible solutions.

## 4.5  OTHER IMPORTANT FEATURES OF SIMPLEX TABLEAUS

The work up to this point in the chapter gives you most of the basics of the algebraic simplex method in its tabular format. Certain features that are sometimes encountered, however, have not turned up in the examples, which were designed to illustrate other points. In this section appear brief discussions of four of those features: *degeneracy, negative zeros, unbounded solutions,* and *no feasible solution.*

### Degeneracy and Negative Zeros

Very often in an LP model or one of its revised tableaus, a zero will occur as the right-hand side of a constraint. Initially this condition could occur as a natural consequence of the type of constraint in a model. For example, the constraint

$$x_1 \leq 2x_2$$

when put in equation form using a slack variable, will become

$$x_1 - 2x_2 + S_1 = 0$$

Since this equation will appear in the initial tableau of a simplex procedure, one of the initial *basic* variables ($S_1$ in this case) will have the value *zero* (which will appear in the "Solution" column of the tableau). This condition, a *zero-valued basic variable*, is called *degeneracy*.

In an intermediate tableau, a tableau that is not the initial one, degeneracy can also occur when there is a *tie* between two or more variables as choices for outgoing variables. Consider, for instance, the tableaus of the Z-row type shown in Table 4.12.

In the first of the two tableaus of Table 4.12, $x_2$ is the incoming basic variable (maximization problem). Two of the ratios, for the $S_1$ row and the $x_1$ row, are *both* equal to 6, which is the minimum nonnegative ratio. In such a case we *arbitrarily* choose the outgoing variable. Suppose we choose $S_1$, making the (2) in that row the pivot element. Then when we move to the next tableau, the row-revision rules produce a *zero* value for the *basic* variable $x_1$. This is a degenerate solution.

Degeneracy *does not* mean "bad." Ordinarily a degenerate solution causes no problems at all. We just proceed merrily along to the next tableau, or we accept a degenerate solution as optimal if it occurs in an optimal tableau. There is some danger that the zero in the "Solution" column could cause "cycling" in the tableaus, a flip-flopping back and forth between the same two tableaus. Such cycling is very rare, however, especially when we use the "negative-zero" convention discussed in the following paragraph. Further, most good computer codes for LP make provision for the possibility of cycling.

Now consider the second of the two tableaus in Table 4.12 for a different reason. Notice that to determine numbers in the "Ratio" column, in the $x_1$ row a division of 0 by $-\frac{15}{2}$ was involved. That number was called "$-0$" in the "Ratio" column and is regarded as a *negative ratio*. This is a *convention* adopted for the simplex method. Any time a zero right-hand side is divided by a negative coefficient of an incoming basic variable, the resulting ratio is considered to be negative and the corresponding current

---

**TABLE 4.12**    INTERMEDIATE TABLEAUS: DEGENERACY AND A NEGATIVE ZERO

| Basic | Z | $x_1$ | $x_2$ | $x_3$ | $S_1$ | $S_2$ | $S_3$ | Solution | Ratio | |
|---|---|---|---|---|---|---|---|---|---|---|
| Z | 1 | 0 | $-10$ ↓ | 0 | 0 | 3 | $-8$ | 28 | | |
| ← $S_1$ | 0 | 0 | (2) | 0 | 1 | 6 | 1 | 12 | 6 | ← min |
| $x_1$ | 0 | 1 | 3 | 0 | 0 | 5 | $-6$ | 18 | 6 | ← min |
| $x_3$ | 0 | 0 | 4 | 1 | 0 | $-3$ | 2 | 36 | 9 | |
| Z | 1 | 0 | 0 | 0 | 5 | 33 | $-3$ ↓ | 88 | | |
| ← $x_2$ | 0 | 0 | 1 | 0 | $\frac{1}{2}$ | 3 | $(\frac{1}{2})$ | 6 | 12 | ← min |
| $x_1$ | 0 | 1 | 0 | 0 | $-\frac{3}{2}$ | $-4$ | $-\frac{15}{2}$ | 0 | $-0$ | |
| $x_3$ | 0 | 0 | 0 | 1 | $-2$ | $-15$ | 0 | 12 | 12/0 | |

basic variable cannot become the outgoing variable. We call this situation a *negative zero*. It can only occur in conjunction with degeneracy.

## Unbounded Solution

Sometimes one or more of the variables in an LP model may be increased without bound, accompanied by a corresponding increase in the objective function. In a maximization problem, this situation usually occurs when the problem has been modeled incorrectly (perhaps a constraint was overlooked) or when a computational error has been made.

### Example 4.5

Consider the following maximization model:

$$\text{Maximize } Z$$

where

$$Z = 2x_1 + 5x_2 + x_3$$

subject to

$$3x_1 - 4x_2 - x_3 \leq 12$$

$$x_1 + x_2 - x_3 \leq 6$$

$$x_1, x_2, x_3 \geq 0$$

A careful first look at this problem suggests letting $x_1$ and $x_2$ be zero while making $x_3$ large. Clearly, because of the negative coefficients of $x_3$ in both constraints, feasibility is maintained no matter how large $x_3$ becomes. But $Z$ is increased as $x_3$ is increased, so there is an *unbounded*, yet feasible, solution.

Suppose, however, that we fail to notice that characteristic and just proceed automatically to the simplex tableaus. Is there something inherent in those tableaus that will warn us about the unbounded solution? Fortunately, yes. Consider the tableaus in Table 4.13. Tilt! The standard

**TABLE 4.13**   *DETECTING AN UNBOUNDED SOLUTION FOR EXAMPLE 4.5*

| | Basic | $z$ | $x_1$ | $x_2$ | $x_3$ | $S_1$ | $S_2$ | Solution | Ratio | |
|---|---|---|---|---|---|---|---|---|---|---|
| | $Z$ | 1 | $-2$ | $-5$ ↓ | $-1$ | 0 | 0 | 0 | | |
| | $S_1$ | 0 | 3 | $-4$ | $-1$ | 1 | 0 | 12 | $-3$ | ← negative |
| ← | $S_2$ | 0 | 1 | (1) | $-1$ | 0 | 1 | 6 | 6 | ← min |
| | $Z$ | 1 | 8 | 0 | $-6$ ↓ | 0 | 5 | 30 | | |
| | $S_1$ | 0 | 7 | 0 | $-5$ | 1 | 4 | 36 | $-36/5$ | ← negative |
| ? | $x_2$ | 0 | 1 | 1 | $-1$ | 0 | 1 | 6 | $-6$ | ← negative ? |

simplex manipulations have stalled at the second iteration. The negative coefficient under $x_3$ in the $Z$ row of the second tableau indicates that $Z$ can be increased by bringing $x_3$ into the basis. But *both* ratios used to determine the outgoing variable are *negative*. There is no way to proceed by the ordinary simplex rules.

This situation will always occur in the presence of an unbounded solution. The simplex method will stall because it cannot decide upon an outgoing variable. Either all ratios will be negative, or else divisions by zero will occur along with other ratios that are all negative.

### No Feasible Solution

Sometimes a problem has so many restrictions on the variables that no feasible solution exists at all. In other words, some of the constraints are incompatible and the feasible region is an empty set. This cannot happen if all constraints are the "≤" type and all right-hand sides and all decision variables are nonnegative, since then the *origin* (all decision variables zero-valued) must be a feasible solution. But when artificial variables are required, infeasibility is possible.

Recall that in those problems requiring artificial variables for an initial basis, we were dealing with "artificial feasibility." For instance, in Example 4.4 we observed that the first basic "feasible" solution was in reality not feasible for the original problem.

In this case the simplex method has a built-in way to point out the infeasibility. It will simply report an *optimal* solution with a *nonzero artificial variable still in the basis*. Since artificial variables must go to zero before feasibility is achieved, a "no feasible solution" answer is suggested by that situation.

### 4.6 GOAL PROGRAMMING

The linear programming problems we have considered up to this point have all had only a *single* objective, such as maximization of profit or minimization of cost. Often, however, management will have *more than one* objective in the same problem. For example, a firm may want to achieve at least a specified profit *and* keep capital outlay below a certain level because of cash-flow requirements. Or perhaps management wants to minimize cost while maintaining a reasonably constant work force, possibly *competing* objectives.

A number of approaches to such *multiple-objective* problems may be tried. One procedure would be to combine all objectives into a single function using some reasonable weighting scheme for each objective. Another might be to identify the most important objective, use it as the objective function, and incorporate the less-important objectives into the constraints. A third approach is to use a method called *goal programming*.

In goal programming we refer to the objectives as *goals*, some or all of which might be impossible to achieve because of other constraints in the problem. We either attempt to *minimize a weighted sum of deviations* from the goals or else we rank the goals in order of *priority* and attempt to satisfy as many goals as possible sequentially, from high-priority goals on down through the ranked list.

In this section we consider only the "weighted sum of deviations" version of goal programming, and only in the setting of *linear* models (goal programming also applies to some nonlinear situations). Example 4.6 provides an elementary framework for learning that basic goal programming procedure.

### Example 4.6

The basic input for this example comes from Exercise 3.10 at the end of Chapter 3. Here we restate that exercise for ease of reference but include a second objective to make it a goal programming problem.

The production manager for Kitchen Brite Cookware wants to schedule a day's production run for two types of electric toaster, the Plain and the Gaudy. Production of a Plain toaster requires 1.0 person-hours, 2.0 square feet of sheet metal, and 0.5 pounds of wiring. Making a Gaudy toaster uses up 2.0 person-hours, 2.5 square feet of sheet metal, and 0.4 pounds of wiring. Available for a day's run are 300 person-hours, 500 square feet of sheet metal, and 120 pounds of wiring.

The manager would like to maximize profit but is also concerned about maintaining the related work force at a nearly constant level in the interest of employee morale. The Plain and the Gaudy toasters are new designs, replacing earlier models of toasters whose production has been discontinued. Before the changeover to the new designs, the production of toasters was associated with a work force of 72 people (not all involved in production, of course; sales staff, secretaries, truck drivers, and other support personnel are included).

Studies within the OR Division of Kitchen Brite indicate that production of one Plain toaster per day would maintain 0.2 persons in the work force, and one Gaudy toaster per day is associated with 0.5 persons. Profit per Plain toaster is expected to be $5, and per Gaudy toaster, $8.

Kitchen Brite's manager knows that if the objective had only been to maximize profit, the solution would be to produce 166.67 Plain toasters and 66.67 Gaudy toasters (fractions allowed, since the rest of a toaster could be produced in the next day's run). This solution, based on the daily availability of the three resources, would yield $1,366.67 profit per day. However, it would only maintain $(0.2)(166.67) + (0.5)(66.67) = 66.67$ people in the work force. Perhaps if a slightly lower profit were to be accepted, a work-force objective of 72 people could be achieved.

Accordingly, the following two goals are established:

*Goal 1:* Profit of $1,350 per day
*Goal 2:* Work force of 72 people

We will now proceed to a goal-programming formulation of this problem.

Let $x_1$ = number of Plain toasters to produce per day

$x_2$ = number of Gaudy toasters to produce per day

Writing the goals and the resource constraints, we see

$$5x_1 + 8x_2 = 1{,}350 \qquad \text{goal 1: profit}$$
$$0.2x_1 + 0.5x_2 = 72 \qquad \text{goal 2: work force}$$
$$x_1 + 2x_2 \le 300 \qquad \text{person-hours}$$
$$2x_1 + 2.5x_2 \le 500 \qquad \text{sheet metal}$$
$$0.5x_1 + 0.4x_2 \le 120 \qquad \text{wiring}$$

However, we know it might be impossible to find a feasible solution that meets both goals exactly, and besides, we need an objective function to be able to solve this problem using the simplex method. The way to handle both of those difficulties is to quantify the notions of *underachievement* and *overachievement* of the two goals.

Let $U_1$ = number of dollars *under* the profit goal of $1,350

$O_1$ = number of dollars *over* the profit goal of $1,350

$U_2$ = number of people *under* the work-force goal of 72 people

$O_2$ = number of people *over* the work-force goal of 72 people

Then, presuming no penalty for overachievement of either goal, we decide that our objective will be to *minimize total underachievement*. This produces the following LP model, written in equation form as a prelude to use of simplex tableaus:

$$\text{Minimize } Z = U_1 + U_2$$

subject to
$$5x_1 + 8x_2 + U_1 - O_1 = 1{,}350$$
$$0.2x_1 + 0.5x_2 + U_2 - O_2 = 72$$
$$x_1 + 2x_2 + S_3 = 300$$
$$2x_1 + 2.5x_2 + S_4 = 500$$
$$0.5x_1 + 0.4x_2 + S_5 = 120$$

Note that the two goals are written as constraints, and the fact that the simplex method will be employed assures nonnegativity of all variables, including $U_1$, $U_2$, $O_1$, and $O_2$. Expressing the deviation from a goal as the difference between two nonnegative variables gives the model sufficient flexibility to permit *either* overachievement or underachievement of the goal. The objective function implies that we are putting *equal weight* on a $1 underachievement of the profit goal and a one-person underachievement of the work-force goal. This may look unreasonable but would not necessarily be bad, especially if it turns out to be possible to achieve both goals. In Example 4.7 we will look at essentially the same problem, but with *different* weights.

Ordinarily when equality constraints are involved, we would use artificial variables to achieve an initial basis. In this case, however, $U_1$ in the first constraint and $U_2$ in the second will serve just as well. Table 4.14 shows an initial simplex tableau for this problem. Columnal arrangement is such that the last five columns go with initial basic variables. Here, since the model is a minimization problem, we look for the most negative $c_j - z_j$. That number, $-8.5$, occurs under $x_2$, so $x_2$ is the first incoming variable. The minimum nonnegative ratio occurs in the $U_2$ row, so $U_2$ is the outgoing variable.

The variable $U_2$ represents underachievement of the work-force goal, and since it immediately becomes nonbasic, with zero value, the solution given by the first revised tableau will meet that goal. However, that solution will not be optimal, and in fact $U_2$ returns to the basis with positive value during a later iteration.

Four revised tableaus are required to achieve optimality (in Exercise 4.30 you will be asked to verify the solution). The basic variables and their values at optimality (minimum total underachievement) are

$$U_2 = \quad 4.5 \qquad \text{underachievement of work-force goal}$$

$$x_2 = \quad 75 \qquad \text{produce 75 Gaudy toasters}$$

$$x_1 = \quad 150 \qquad \text{produce 150 Plain toasters}$$

$$S_4 = \quad 12.5 \qquad \text{12.5 square feet of sheet metal unused}$$

$$S_5 = \quad 15 \qquad \text{15 pounds of wiring unused}$$

The other variables are nonbasic, so all of the available person-hours were used ($S_3 = 0$), neither goal was overachieved ($O_1 = 0$, $O_2 = 0$), and since the profit goal was not underachieved either ($U_1 = 0$), it was met exactly.

Let's check out these conclusions about the two goals. Profit is

$$5(150) + 8(75) = 1{,}350$$

and the associated work force is

$$0.2(150) + 0.5(75) = 67.5$$

or 4.5 persons fewer than the goal of 72. On the other hand, we note

TABLE 4.14 INITIAL TABLEAU: KITCHEN BRITE GOAL-PROGRAMMING PROBLEM

| Basic | $c_j$ | $x_1$ 0 | $x_2$ 0 | $O_1$ 0 | $O_2$ 1 | $U_1$ 1 | $U_2$ 1 | $S_3$ 0 | $S_4$ 0 | $S_5$ 0 | Solution | Ratio |
|---|---|---|---|---|---|---|---|---|---|---|---|---|
| $U_1$ | 1 | 5 | 8 | −1 | 0 | 1 | 0 | 0 | 0 | 0 | 1,350 | 168.75 |
| ← $U_2$ | 1 | 0.2 | (0.5) | 0 | −1 | 0 | 1 | 0 | 0 | 0 | 72 | 144 ← min |
| $S_3$ | 0 | 1 | 2 | 0 | 0 | 0 | 0 | 1 | 0 | 0 | 300 | 150 |
| $S_4$ | 0 | 2 | 2.5 | 0 | 0 | 0 | 0 | 0 | 1 | 0 | 500 | 200 |
| $S_5$ | 0 | 0.5 | 0.4 | 0 | 0 | 0 | 0 | 0 | 0 | 1 | 120 | 300 |
| $z_j$ | | 5.2 | 8.5 ↓ | −1 | −1 | 1 | 1 | 0 | 0 | 0 | 1,422 | |
| $c_j - z_j$ | | −5.2 | −8.5 | 1 | 1 | 0 | 0 | 0 | 0 | 0 | | |

that by reducing profit from $1,366.67 to $1,350 ($16.67 less profit), we are able to increase the work force by 0.83 persons (from 66.67 to 67.5).

It is instructive to consider this problem graphically. The solution reported by the simplex tableaus is indicated in Figure 4.2. The dashed lines in Figure 4.2 represent the two goals, and the shaded area is the feasible region determined only by the three resource constraints. Note particularly that the solution obtained by goal programming is *not a corner point* of that two-dimensional region. However, it would be a corner point in the six-dimensional space of $x_1$, $x_2$, $U_1$, $O_1$, $U_2$, and $O_2$.

The picture in Figure 4.2 also shows that the profit goal was achieved exactly, but the work-force goal was not achieved. If you will consider the direction of increase for a work-force contour (say, use a goal of 80 persons instead of 72), you will be convinced by the picture that the work-force goal is *under*achieved.

Finally, the little square on the picture contains the point of simultaneous achievement of both goals. Since that point is not in the feasible region described by the resource constraints, it is *not possible* to achieve both goals simultaneously. There do exist feasible points permitting *over*achievement of *one* goal, but again, overachievement of both is precluded. The picture also points out the bottleneck in the problem: Given a few more person-hours for production, we *could* achieve both goals. How many? Well, the two goal lines intersect at the point $(x_1, x_2) = (110, 100)$, and $(1)(110) + 2(100) = 310$. So we need only 10 more person-hours to be able to meet both goals.

### Example 4.7

For another example of goal-programming analysis, this time with different weights attached to the two goals, consider a modified version of Example 4.6. Suppose the profit goal is changed to $1,400, while the work-force goal is left at 72 people. Suppose further that a one-person underachieve-

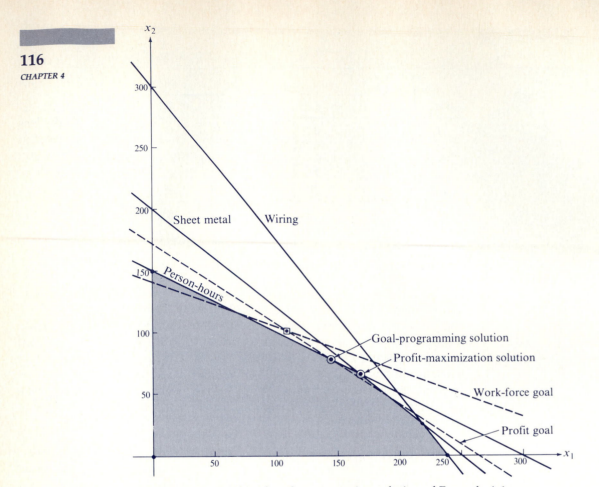

**FIGURE 4.2**   Exhibit of goal-programming solution of Example 4.6

ment is deemed roughly equal to $30 in profit.  This is a managerial assessment of the "tradeoff" between the two goals.  It means that we would be willing to give up about $30 to get one more person into the work force or that we would be willing to give up a person in exchange for an extra $30 (daily) profit.

Then the only changes from Example 4.6 are in the objective function and the first goal constraint.  The new objective function is

$$Z = U_1 + 30U_2$$

and the new goal constraint for profit is

$$5x_1 + 8x_2 + U_1 - O_1 = 1{,}400$$

Everything else would remain the same in the model formulation.

The solution of this problem is

$$(x_1, x_2) = (60, 120)$$

where the work-force goal is satisfied exactly but the profit goal is underachieved by $140. That is, now we would make 60 Plain toasters and 120 Gaudy toasters, and the work force associated with that decision is $(0.2)(60) + (0.5)(120) = 72$ but the profit is only $(5)(60) + (8)(120) = $1,260$, or $140 less than the goal of $1,400.

The main thing to notice here is that we could have chosen $1,366.67 profit (the maximum possible profit), but instead we elected to take less profit in order to meet the work-force goal. The reason for that decision resides in our estimate of a $30 tradeoff; that is, in our objective function we indicated that a one-person underachievement of the work-force goal was 30 times as important as a $1 underachievement of the profit goal.

In Exercise 4.31 you will be asked to verify this solution to Example 4.7. Further examples of goal-programming applications appear in Chapter 6.

## 4.7  SUMMARY AND CONCLUSIONS

The primary purpose of this chapter has been to illustrate convenient tabular formats for the simplex method, along with simplified rules and formulas for moving from one tableau to the next revised tableau. Two formats, identified as the Z-row format and the $c_j - z_j$ format, were used, with example problems being worked to illustrate each procedure.

Particular attention was given to the use of artificial variables and the Big-$M$ method, and to the detection and determination of alternate optimal solutions. Both of these situations occur quite frequently in practice, and separate, completely solved examples were included to exhibit the solution techniques.

The special cases of degeneracy, negative zeros, unbounded solutions, and the detection of infeasibility were briefly discussed. These situations occur less frequently, but whenever one of them does occur, you need to be equipped to recognize it.

A further word about the two tabular formats is in order here. The ability to use both approaches will enhance your understanding of all the nuances of the simplex method. That ability is assumed in the interpretive material of Chapter 5. However, if you only want to learn *one* way of organizing the work in the simplex method, then the $c_j - z_j$ format is recommended as being the more versatile of the two.

Multiple objectives and goal programming were introduced at the end of the chapter. The examples were small problems with only two objectives and two original decision variables, just to familiarize you with the notions in goal programming and to provide a bit more practice in the use of simplex tableaus. Larger-sized applications of goal programming, along with their computer solutions, are discussed in Chapter 6.

With all of the necessary tools at hand for efficient solution of LP models, you are now ready for some more interpretive features of linear programming and for larger problems in a greater variety of applied settings. Discussions of duality, economic interpretations of optimal solutions, and sensitivity of optimal solutions to changes in parameters are presented in Chapter 5. There the algebraic manipulations will be fairly simple so you can devote your attention to interpretations. Then Chapter 6 exhibits a wide variety of linear programming applications, where again, because of the computer solutions that are provided, you can concentrate on understanding solutions, not merely obtaining them.

## KEY WORDS AND PHRASES

**Simplex tableau**  A table displaying in an efficient manner all of the coefficients representing one iteration of the simplex method and concisely organizing some of the calculations for tableau revision.

**Pivot row**  The row of a simplex tableau in which the minimum nonnegative ratio occurs. This row is associated with the variable that will leave the basis in the next simplex iteration.

**Pivot element**  The element of a simplex tableau occurring at the intersection of the column associated with an incoming basic variable and the pivot row.

**Artificial variable**  An extra variable that is added to a constraint to help supply a convenient initial basis. Its value at optimality must be zero.

**Big-$M$ method**  A method for assuring that the simplex method will force all artificial variables to zero.

**Z-row format**  Tabular format for the simplex method that includes at the top of a tableau the negatives of the coefficients in the objective function. It is the most convenient format for a model involving no artificial variables.

$c_j - z_j$  Net increase in Z per unit of value of "incoming" variable.

$c_j - z_j$ **format**  Tabular format for the simplex method that determines the incoming basic variable using a net evaluation row at the bottom of a tableau. It is the most convenient format for a model involving artificial variables.

**Alternate optimal solution**  Another feasible solution of an LP model that yields the same value for the objective function as the solution reported by an optimal simplex tableau. It is detected by observing a zero coefficient in the Z row or a zero $c_j - z_j$ under a nonbasic variable in an optimal tableau.

**Degeneracy**  The condition of a solution of an LP model characterized by a zero-valued basic variable.

**Unbounded solution**  The condition in which increasing the value of a variable will maintain feasibility while increasing the value of the objective function indefinitely.

**No feasible solution**  The condition in which the LP problem as stated permits no feasible combination of variable values.

**Goal**  One of the objectives in a multiple-objective problem.

**Goal programming**  A procedure for solving a multiple-objective problem. In this text, the specific method of goal programming involves minimizing a weighted sum of underachievements of the goals.

## EXERCISES

✦ **4.1**                                   Maximize $Z$

where                          $Z = x_1 + 2x_2 + 3x_3$

subject to                   $2x_1 + x_2 + 4x_3 \leq 32$

$3x_1 + 2x_2 + 5x_3 \leq 30$

$x_1, x_2, x_3 \geq 0$


**4.2**                                      Maximize $Z$

where                          $Z = 10x_1 + 8x_2 + 5x_3$

subject to                   $2x_1 + 4x_2 + 3x_3 \leq 60$

$2x_1 \qquad\quad + 8x_3 \leq 40$

$x_2 + x_3 \leq 10$

$x_1, x_2, x_3 \geq 0$


✦ **4.3** Solve the production problem described in Exercise 2.1 at the end of Chapter 2.

✦ **4.4** Solve Universal Furniture Outlet's problem: Exercise 2.2 at the end of Chapter 2.

✦ **4.5** A manufacturer has two machines, $A$ and $B$, which are used to make three products, I, II, and III.   A unit of product I requires 2 minutes on machine $A$ and 4 minutes on machine $B$.   A unit of product II requires 1 minute on machine $A$ and 4 minutes on machine $B$, and a unit of product III requires 3 minutes on machine $A$ and 2 minutes on machine $B$.

Profit contributions per unit of products I, II, and III, respectively, are $1, $2, and $3.   During a given production period there are available to devote to the three products 80 hours on machine $A$ and 60 hours on machine $B$.   How many units of each product should be made in order to maximize profit contribution for the period, and what is that maximum profit?

✦ **4.6** Using simplex tableaus, solve the Clear Cut Corporation problem, stated in Exercise 2.5 at the end of Chapter 2.   Verify the solution graphically.

**4.7** Solve the Mule Creek Junction Feed and Grain problem, stated in Exercise 2.13 at the end of Chapter 2.

✦ **4.8** Using simplex tableaus, solve the original Kitchen Brite Cookware problem, as stated in Exercise 3.10 at the end of Chapter 3.

**4.9** Solve the problem described in Exercise 3.24 at the end of Chapter 3.

**4.10** Using simplex tableaus, solve the Archaic Bakery problem described in Exercise 3.18 at the end of Chapter 3.   Verify the solution graphically.

**4.11** Solve the Feelingiz Mutual Fund portfolio selection problem that was given as Example 1.2 near the beginning of Chapter 1.

◆ **4.12** Solve Justin Case's investment problem: Exercise 2.9 at the end of Chapter 2.

◆ **4.13** Using simplex tableaus, solve the minimization problem that was given as Exercise 3.4 at the end of Chapter 3. Verify the solution graphically.

◆ **4.14** Solve the diet problem that was stated as Example 2.3 in the body of Chapter 2.

**4.15** Alternate optimal solutions exist for the following problem:

$$\text{Maximize } Z$$

where

$$Z = 5x_1 + 2x_2$$

subject to

$$4x_1 + x_2 \leq 12$$
$$10x_1 + 4x_2 \leq 20$$
$$x_1, x_2 \geq 0$$

Use simplex tableaus to find all alternate optimal basic feasible solutions. Then find one *other* optimal solution. Locate all of these solutions on a graph.

◆ **4.16** Find all alternate optimal basic feasible solutions for the following problem:

$$\text{Maximize } Z$$

where

$$Z = 2x_1 + 6x_2 + 4x_3$$

subject to

$$x_1 + 3x_2 + 2x_3 \leq 12$$
$$x_1 + x_2 + x_3 \leq 20$$
$$x_1, x_2, x_3 \geq 0$$

◆ **4.17** Use simplex tableaus to solve the following problem. Discuss any unusual characteristics.

$$\text{Maximize } Z$$

where

$$Z = 8x_1 + 6x_2 + 10x_3$$

subject to

$$x_1 + 2x_2 + 3x_3 \leq 24$$
$$4x_1 + 3x_2 + 5x_3 \leq 60$$
$$x_1, x_2, x_3 \geq 0$$

**4.18** Use simplex tableaus to solve the following problem. Discuss any unusual characteristics.

Maximize $Z$

where

$$Z = x_1 + 3x_2 + 2x_3$$

subject to

$$4x_1 + 5x_2 + 6x_3 \leq 12$$
$$x_1 + x_2 \qquad \geq 20$$
$$x_1, x_2, x_3 \geq 0$$

✦ **4.19** Use simplex tableaus to solve the following problem. Discuss any unusual characteristics.

Maximize $Z$

where

$$Z = 3x_1 + x_2 + 2x_3$$

subject to

$$x_1 - 2x_2 + 6x_3 \leq 12$$
$$x_1 - x_2 \qquad \leq 0$$
$$x_1 \qquad + x_3 \leq 5$$
$$x_1, x_2, x_3 \geq 0$$

✦ **4.20** Use simplex tableaus to solve the following problem. Discuss any unusual characteristics.

Minimize $Z$

where

$$Z = 5x_1 + 4x_2 + 7x_3 + 6x_4$$

subject to

$$3x_1 + 2x_2 + 6x_3 + x_4 \leq 48$$
$$x_1 + 2x_2 + x_3 + x_4 \geq 60$$
$$2x_1 + 3x_2 + 5x_3 + 5x_4 \leq 30$$
$$x_1, x_2, x_3, x_4 \geq 0$$

**4.21** Use simplex tableaus to solve the following problem. Discuss any unusual characteristics.

Maximize $Z$

where

$$Z = 3x_1 - 4x_2 + 5x_3 - x_4$$

subject to

$$2x_1 + x_2 - 3x_3 + 4x_4 \leq 48$$
$$x_1 - 2x_2 + 2x_3 + x_4 \geq 10$$
$$x_1, x_2, x_3, x_4 \geq 0$$

**4.22** Sometimes not all of the variables in an LP model are required to be nonnegative. Particularly, in Chapter 5 you will encounter dual variables which are unrestricted in sign. When this situation occurs, one must change the statement of the model so the standard simplex rules will work.

Suppose, for instance, that $x_1$ is unrestricted in sign. Then we can let $x_1 = v_1 - w_1$, where $v_1 \geq 0$ and $w_1 \geq 0$ (note the similarity to $U_1 - O_1$ in a goal-programming problem). That is, whether $x_1$ is a positive number or a negative number, it is always possible to express $x_1$ as a difference between two *nonnegative* numbers. Then we just substitute $v_1 - w_1$ in place of $x_1$ throughout the original model. When the optimal solution is achieved, it will be reported by the simplex tableau in terms of the optimal $v_1$ and $w_1$. Then opt $x_1 = $ opt $v_1 - $ opt $w_1$.

Apply that substitution to solve the following problem using simplex tableaus. Ignore the apparent alternate optimal solution. The substituted variables $v_1$ and $w_1$ will always *both* have zero coefficients in the Z row (or zero $c_j - z_j$'s) whenever *either* is in the basis. You may check the final $x_1$, $x_2$ solution graphically, of course.

$$\text{Maximize } Z$$

where

$$Z = 2x_1 + 5x_2$$

subject to

$$2x_1 + 3x_2 \leq 18$$

$$-x_1 + 2x_2 \leq 10$$

$$x_2 \geq 0 \qquad x_1 \text{ unrestricted in sign}$$

◆ **4.23** Solve Exercise 4.22 using the same feasible region but the objective function $Z = -2x_1 + x_2$.

**4.24** Work Exercise 4.22, except change the objective to that of minimizing Z.

◆ **4.25** Work Exercise 4.23, except change the objective to that of minimizing Z.

◆ **4.26** Reconsider the Happy Heifer Feed Company problem, Example 4.3 of this chapter. To the problem as stated there, add the further restriction that the combined total of Standard and Super brands of feed cannot exceed 500 tons. Solve this augmented problem.

**4.27** Reconsider the Happy Heifer Feed Company problem, Example 4.3 of this chapter. Suppose you try to work that problem using the Z-row format suggested by the tableaus in Table 4.3. That approach starts off by shifting the right-hand side of the objective function to the left, leaving zero on the right. For the feed company problem with its two artificial variables, that new form of the objective-function equation would be

$$Z - 120x_1 - 160x_2 - 240x_3 + 0S_3 + 0S_2 - MA_1 - MA_2 = 0$$

Is something awry here? This is a *minimization* problem, and back at the end of Section 4.2 we observed that to determine the incoming basic variable we would look for the *most positive* coefficient in the Z-row of a tableau. But here we see *no* positive coefficients in the Z equation. Does this say that our *initial* solution is also *optimal*? That can't be right, since initially $x_1 = 0$, $x_2 = 0$, and $x_3 = 0$, but 1,000 tons of feed *must* be manufactured.

This apparent contradiction can be resolved quite easily. Remember, the artificial variables $A_1$ and $A_2$ are initial *basic* variables, and the coefficient of a basic variable in the Z row of a tableau must be zero. Thus some adjusting of the system of equations must be done before we start on the problem using Z-row-type simplex tableaus. The correct equation from which coefficients are abstracted for the Z row of the initial tableau is

$$Z + (M - 120)x_1 + (M - 160)x_2 + (2M - 240)x_3 + 0S_3 - MS_2 + 0A_1 + 0A_2 = 1,200M$$

**a** Discuss the line of reasoning used to obtain this version of the objective-function equation prior to establishing the initial simplex tableau.
**b** Solve the feed company problem using tableaus in the Z-row format.

**4.28** Solve the augmented feed company problem of Exercise 4.26 using tableaus in the Z-row format.

✦ **4.29** The local dealer for Suhonaha motorcycles is planning to place the order for the next six-months' inventory. Suhonaha makes three types of street-trail bikes: S125, S175, and S250. The dealer must consider capital, storage space (including space for spare parts), sales time, and mechanics' time (for servicing the bikes sold). He has estimated the amounts of each of these four resources that he will have available during the next six months. Also he has estimated the amount of each resource that will be consumed by the stocking and selling of each type of bike. These estimates, as well as the selling price and dealer cost of each unit, appear below.

| | Type of bike | | | Resource availability |
|---|---|---|---|---|
| | S125 | S175 | S250 | |
| Dealer cost | $400 | $500 | $ 800 | $72,200 |
| Selling price | $700 | $900 | $1,400 | — |
| Storage, cubic feet | 3 | 4 | 5 | 600 |
| Sales time, hours | 2 | 4 | 10 | 1,000 |
| Mechanic time, hours | 15 | 9 | 5 | 750 |

Suhonaha is such a popular motorcycle that the dealer can sell every one that he receives. How many of each type of bike should he order so as to maximize gross profit (selling price minus dealer cost) for the six-month period, and what is that maximum gross profit?

**4.30** Verify the solution of Example 4.6, the initial goal-programming formulation of the Kitchen Brite Cookware problem.

**4.31** Verify the solution of Example 4.7, the modified goal-programming formulation of the Kitchen Brite Cookware problem.

✦ **4.32** Reconsider the goal-programming problem in example 4.7, one of the Kitchen Brite Cookware examples. Leave the profit goal at $1,400 and the work-force goal at 72 people, but now assume the following tradeoff: a one-person underachievement of the work-force goal is equivalent to a $10 underachievement of the profit goal.
Solve this goal-programming problem. Is either goal achieved? Exhibit your solution graphically.

Ackoff, R. L., and M. W. Sasieni: *Fundamentals of Operations Research*, John Wiley & Sons, Inc., New York, 1968.

Anderson, D. R., D. J. Sweeney, and T. A. Williams: *An Introduction to Management Science*, 3d ed., West Publishing Company, St. Paul, Minn., 1982.

Bierman, H., C. P. Bonini, and W. H. Hausman: *Quantitative Analysis for Business Decisions*, 6th ed., Richard D. Irwin, Inc., Homewood, Ill., 1981.

Hillier, F. S., and G. J. Lieberman: *Introduction to Operations Research*, 3d ed., Holden-Day, Inc., San Francisco, 1980.

Lee, S. M.: *Goal Programming for Decision Analysis*, Van Nostrand Reinhold Company, New York, 1973.

Levin, R. I., C. A. Kirkpatrick, and D. S. Rubin: *Quantitative Approaches to Management*, 5th ed., McGraw-Hill Book Company, New York, 1982.

Loomba, N. P.: *Linear Programming: An Introductory Analysis*, McGraw-Hill Book Company, New York, 1964.

Thierauf, R. J., and R. C. Klekamp: *Decision Making Through Operations Research*, 2d ed., John Wiley & Sons, Inc., New York, 1975.

# DUALITY AND SENSITIVITY ANALYSIS

*T*his chapter deals with implications of the simplex method to managerial decisions. Up until this point we have just been solving "static" problems; all of the coefficients have been fixed; our only problem has been to *discover* the optimum levels for the decision variables given those particular coefficients. But in a sense, no decision has been required of us. We have only been *finding* the optimal levels of the variables, and those levels have been *fixed* from the moment the model was formulated. There must be more to management science than merely the discovery of solutions for mathematical models.

In a practical setting it is extremely unusual for all of the constants in an LP model to be known exactly. Profit contributions per unit of product, for instance, are seldom precisely known; often the manager can quote them only within certain ranges. Furthermore, a manager exerts much control over the quantities of resources made available, but even the amounts of resources consumed per unit of product may only be estimates.

In the first parts of this chapter we consider economic interpretations of optimal simplex tableaus, interpretations that permit some managerial input that might improve upon the solutions; that is, managerial decisions that make available more of a scarce resource so that more profit can be earned, or that divert to other uses some resources that exist in abundance. Managerial insights into the structure of LP models gained from understanding the important concept known as *duality* can produce better decisions.

The latter sections of the chapter consider the process of *sensitivity analysis*. That analysis considers the effect upon optimal solutions of changes in some of the coefficients in the model; that is, it considers the sensitivity of the optimal solution to the numbers that were input to the model. This is also known as *postoptimality* analysis. The manager who fully understands the implications of duality and postoptimality analyses will be in a position to gain maximum information from the simplex method of linear programming.

## 5.1 IMPLICIT VALUES OF RESOURCES: SHADOW PRICES

Linear programming is generally concerned with the optimal allocation of resources to competing activities. In determining the number of units of each product to manufacture in order to maximize profit, we are specifying the way in which our resources are to be used. We know how much of each resource will be consumed by a unit of each product, so we can determine the exact amount of each resource to be allocated to each product in order to yield maximum profit. The implication is this: There is *value* in our resources, and we want to use that value to its fullest.

Each resource has a certain *worth* to the company if all resources are used optimally. That implied worth, on a per-unit basis, is called the *implicit value* of the resource. (Synonyms are shadow price, imputed value, incremental value, and intrinsic value.) Further, if the company acts optimally, then the total profit should equal the total worth of the scarce resources made available to generate that profit. So we see that the implicit value of a resource reflects its ability to contribute to profit.

Another way of looking at the implicit value of a resource might help you understand the concept. Think of implicit value as the maximum price a company should be willing to pay for an extra unit of that resource in order to acquire its profit-making capacity (or else the price the company pays by giving up a unit of the resource). The company would certainly wish to minimize the total price of all resources used to generate maximum profit. Then the operation of maximizing profit is the same thing as that of minimizing the price paid by making those resources available to generate the profit. The set of prices for all resources that minimizes the total price is a set of *shadow prices* for the individual resources.

Note particularly that if at optimality the resource has not been exhausted, then the company would *not* want to have *additional* units of the resource. Such a resource would have *zero* implicit value, since in that instance extra units are of no value. That is, if a resource is in excess supply, then the lack of demand forces its price (implicit value) to zero. Thus implicit value is definitely *not* the same thing as *cost* of a unit of resource. Cost is merely the amount that one pays to acquire a unit of resource, while implicit value is the worth of a unit of resource for contributing to profit.

## 5.2 THE CONCEPT OF DUALITY

The concept of *duality* in linear programming is best introduced by way of an example problem. We will formulate the usual LP model directly from the statement of the problem and will call that formulation the *primal* problem. Then we will formulate the same problem another way, using as variables the implicit values of the resources. That alternative formulation will be called the *dual* problem.

### Example 5.1

Dooley Corporation wants to produce two products, I and II, which will be kept in a storage area whose capacity is 30,000 square feet. Product I requires 3 square feet of space per unit; product II requires 4 square feet. It takes 4 machine-hours to manufacture a unit of product I, while 8 machine-hours are needed for a unit of product II. There are available 48,000 machine-hours during the production period. Also available are 36,000 person-hours for finishing the products, and a unit of product I takes 4 person-hours for finishing, with a unit of product II needing 3 person-hours.

Profit contributions are $2 per unit of product I and $6 per unit of product II. In order to maximize profit for the period, how many units of each product should Dooley manufacture?

This example is no different from many of the others you have seen so far in this text. The resources are storage space, machine-hours, and person-hours. The primal decision variables are the number of units of each product to manufacture. Each resource is available in only a limited quantity.

Let $x_1$ = number of units of product I to manufacture

$x_2$ = number of units of product II to manufacture

Then the problem is easily modeled as follows.

$$\text{Maximize } Z$$

where $\qquad\qquad Z = 2x_1 + 6x_2 \qquad$ profit in dollars

subject to
$$3x_1 + 4x_2 \leq 30{,}000 \qquad \text{storage space}$$
$$4x_1 + 8x_2 \leq 48{,}000 \qquad \text{machine-hours}$$
$$4x_1 + 3x_2 \leq 36{,}000 \qquad \text{person-hours}$$
$$x_1, x_2 \geq 0 \qquad\qquad \text{nonnegativity}$$

The graphical solution of this primal problem (shown in Figure 5.1) is

$$\text{Max } Z = \$36{,}000 \qquad \text{at } (x_1, x_2) = (0, 6{,}000)$$

Notice that at optimality the machine-hour constraint is the only resource constraint satisfied with equality. This implies there will be value in extra machine-hours, but *additional* space or person-hours are worthless since these resources are already in excess.

What would happen if we had one *extra* machine-hour (48,001 instead of 48,000)? Then in Figure 5.1 the $x_2$ intercept of the machine-hour line would be $48{,}001/8 = 6{,}000.125$, and it is clear that the optimal solution would occur at the corner $(x_1, x_2) = (0, 6{,}000.125)$. Then maximum $Z$ would be $\$6(6{,}000.125) = \$36{,}000.75$. Thus an *additional* machine-hour

**FIGURE 5.1** Graphical solution: Dooley Corporation problem

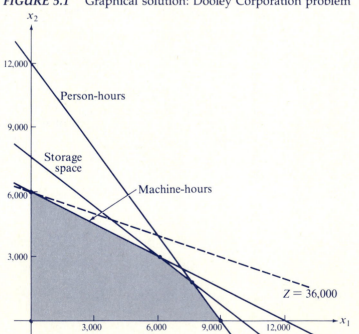

can contribute $0.75 *more* toward profit, or the *implicit value* of a machine-hour is $0.75. We can further say that since they are already *abundant* resources, the implicit values of an additional square foot of space or an additional person-hour are both *zero*.

However, very few real problems involve only two decision variables, so usually this type of graphical argument will be unavailable to us. Another approach is to formulate the problem differently, with the *decision variables* being the *implicit values* of the resources, and to solve that (dual) problem with simplex tableaus. As we will soon see, it turns out that such a formulation and solution is totally unnecessary if we already have the tabular solution of the *primal* problem. Nevertheless, it is instructive to work through the formulation and solution of the dual.

Let $y_1$ = implicit value of 1 square foot of storage space

$y_2$ = implicit value of 1 machine-hour

$y_3$ = implicit value of 1 person-hour

Now we want to *minimize* the total *price* paid by making those resources available to generate profit.

We know the number of units of each resource that the Dooley Company has made available, so our objective is to minimize $Y$, where

$$Y = 30{,}000y_1 + 48{,}000y_2 + 36{,}000y_3$$

That is, we are giving up resources with implicit values (shadow prices) $y_1$, $y_2$, and $y_3$ in order to realize our profit, but we maximize the profit by minimizing the *price* paid by allocating those resources to the manufacture of products I and II.

The three variables $y_1$, $y_2$, and $y_3$ are values of resources, and those values cannot be unlimited. They too are constrained. To understand the constraints in this dual problem, one must realize that *the profit contribution of a unit of product cannot exceed the value of the resources used to make it.* We are consuming resources, each of which has a certain *value* in the sense of its contribution toward profit. If those resources are used rationally, then we want to receive *full value* from them during the manufacture of a unit of product. But we cannot receive more value than is intrinsically there, so it is impossible for the profit per unit to exceed that value.

What is the value of all resources used to make one unit of product I? Each unit of product I consumes 3 square feet of space, 4 machine-hours, and 4 person-hours. Then the total value of the resources used to make a unit of product I is $3y_1 + 4y_2 + 4y_3$. Since the profit contribution ($2) of one unit of product I cannot exceed the value of the resources used to make it, we have the constraint

$$3y_1 + 4y_2 + 4y_3 \geq 2$$

That is, the value of those resources must be *at least* $2, for otherwise it would be impossible to earn a $2 profit on a unit of product I.

If the implicit values are such that this constraint is satisfied with *equality*, then it will be all right to manufacture some units of product I. In that case we receive full value from the resources used. If, however, the left-hand side of the constraint *exceeds* 2, then the value of the necessary resources is *larger* than the profit realizable from their use. The resources should be diverted to other, more profitable, products. Evidently, from the solution to the primal problem, they should be used to make product II, since $x_1 = 0$ at optimality. A similar analysis of the resources used to make product II will yield a second constraint on the dual variables $y_1$, $y_2$, and $y_3$.

Finally, we suppose that excess resources will not penalize us. That is, even if a resource is in excess supply, its implicit value is no less than zero. The *excess* resource has no value, but on the other hand, it has no detrimental effect either. Thus in this setting the $y$'s are nonnegative. The model of the dual problem follows.

### The Dual Problem

$$\text{Minimize } Y$$

where

$$Y = 30{,}000y_1 + 48{,}000y_2 + 36{,}000y_3$$

subject to

$$3y_1 + 4y_2 + 4y_3 \geq 2 \qquad \text{product I}$$

$$4y_1 + 8y_2 + 3y_3 \geq 6 \qquad \text{product II}$$

$$y_1, y_2, y_3 \geq 0$$

The solution of this problem for $y_1$, $y_2$, and $y_3$ will yield the actual implicit values of the resources. In fact,

$$\text{Min } Y = \text{Max } Z$$

that is, the minimum total value of the resources will equal the maximum possible profit in this manufacturing setting. The solution of the dual problem is given in Table 5.1.

In Table 5.1, since our objective was to *minimize Y*, to determine the incoming basic variable in each tableau we look for the *most negative* $c_j - z_j$. At the bottom of the second revised tableau we observe *no* negative $c_j - z_j$, so we know we have reached optimality. Since $y_2$ is the only original variable in the basis, we know that $y_1 = 0$ and $y_3 = 0$ because they are nonbasic variables. Thus

$$\text{Min } Y = 36{,}000 \qquad \text{at } (y_1, y_2, y_3) = (0, \tfrac{3}{4}, 0)$$

This solution is completely consistent with the primal solution obtained in Figure 5.1, where Max $Z = 36{,}000$. Since $y_2$ was defined to be the

**TABLE 5.1**  SIMPLEX SOLUTION OF THE DUAL PROBLEM

| Basic | $c_j$ | $y_1$ | $y_2$ | $y_3$ | $S_1$ | $S_2$ | $A_1$ | $A_2$ | Solution | Ratio |
|---|---|---|---|---|---|---|---|---|---|---|
| | | 30,000 | 48,000 | 36,000 | 0 | 0 | M | M | | |
| ← $A_1$ | M | 3 | (4) | 4 | −1 | 0 | 1 | 0 | 2 | 1/2 ← min |
| $A_2$ | M | 4 | 8 | 3 | 0 | −1 | 0 | 1 | 6 | 3/4 |
| $z_j$ | | 7M | 12M ↓ | 7M | −M | −M | M | M | 8M | |
| $c_j - z_j$ | | 30,000 − 7M | 48,000 − 12M | 36,000 − 7M | M | M | 0 | 0 | | |
| $y_2$ | 48,000 | $\frac{3}{4}$ | 1 | 1 | −$\frac{1}{4}$ | 0 | $\frac{1}{4}$ | 0 | $\frac{1}{2}$ | −2 |
| ← $A_2$ | M | −2 | 0 | −5 | (2) | −1 | −2 | 1 | 2 | 1 ← min |
| $z_j$ | | 36,000 − 2M | 48,000 | 48,000 − 5M | −12,000 + 2M ↓ | −M | 12,000 − 2M | M | 24,000 + 2M | |
| $c_j - z_j$ | | 2M − 6,000 | 0 | 5M − 12,000 | 12,000 − 2M | M | 3M − 12,000 | 0 | | |
| $y_2$ | 48,000 | $\frac{1}{2}$ | 1 | $\frac{3}{8}$ | 0 | −$\frac{1}{8}$ | 0 | $\frac{1}{8}$ | $\frac{3}{4}$ | |
| $S_1$ | 0 | −1 | 0 | −$\frac{5}{2}$ | 1 | −$\frac{1}{2}$ | −1 | $\frac{1}{2}$ | 1 | |
| $z_j$ | | 24,000 | 48,000 | 18,000 | 0 | −6,000 | 0 | 6,000 | 36,000 ← optimal | |
| $c_j - z_j$ | | 6,000 | 0 | 18,000 | 0 | 6,000 | M | M − 6,000 | | |

implicit value of one machine-hour, the value $y_2 = \frac{3}{4} = 0.75$ agrees with our graphical analysis of the effect of an extra machine-hour, and $y_1 = 0$, $y_3 = 0$ agree with our graphical observation that storage space and person-hours have not been exhausted at optimality.

Must we solve *both* the primal *and* the dual to realize maximum economic information? Fortunately, no. An algebraic simplex solution of *either* the primal or the dual formulation automatically gives the solution for the *other* formulation, provided one knows where to look in the tableaus. Section 5.3 gives the key to such interpretations.

## 5.3 DUAL SOLUTION FROM PRIMAL TABLEAU

Table 5.2 shows the simplex solution of the *primal* problem. The Z-row format is used because of its simplicity for this type of maximization problem. The primal problem formulation is repeated here for reference.

$$\text{Maximize Z}$$

where
$$Z = 2x_1 + 6x_2 \qquad \text{profit in dollars}$$

subject to
$$3x_1 + 4x_2 \leq 30{,}000 \qquad \text{storage space}$$
$$4x_1 + 8x_2 \leq 48{,}000 \qquad \text{machine-hours}$$
$$4x_1 + 3x_2 \leq 36{,}000 \qquad \text{person-hours}$$
$$x_1, x_2 \geq 0$$

Only one revised tableau was necessary to reach the optimal solution. It is

$$\text{Max Z} = 36{,}000 \qquad \text{at } (x_1, x_2) = (0, 6{,}000)$$

**TABLE 5.2**  *SIMPLEX SOLUTION OF THE PRIMAL PROBLEM*

| Basic | Z | $x_1$ | $x_2$ | $S_1$ | $S_2$ | $S_3$ | Solution | Ratio |
|-------|---|-------|-------|-------|-------|-------|----------|-------|
| Z | 1 | $-2$ | $-6$ | 0 | 0 | 0 | 0 | |
| $S_1$ | 0 | 3 | 4 | 1 | 0 | 0 | 30,000 | 7,500 |
| $\leftarrow S_2$ | 0 | 4 | (8) | 0 | 1 | 0 | 48,000 | 6,000 ← min |
| $S_3$ | 0 | 4 | 3 | 0 | 0 | 1 | 36,000 | 12,000 |
| Z | 1 | 1 | 0 | 0 | $\frac{3}{4}$ | 0 | 36,000 | ← optimal |
| $S_1$ | 0 | 1 | 0 | 1 | $-\frac{1}{2}$ | 0 | 6,000 | |
| $x_2$ | 0 | $\frac{1}{2}$ | 1 | 0 | $\frac{1}{8}$ | 0 | 6,000 | |
| $S_3$ | 0 | $\frac{5}{2}$ | 0 | 0 | $-\frac{3}{8}$ | 1 | 18,000 | |

We have already obtained this solution graphically, of course, in Figure 5.1. However, since ordinarily we will have to interpret simplex tableaus because graphical solutions are not possible when many decision variables are involved, the basis of our subsequent analysis will be the numbers in Table 5.2.

Clearly, some of the resources were not fully utilized. In the optimal basis of Table 5.2 we see $S_1 = 6,000$ and $S_3 = 18,000$. Now $S_1$ was the slack in the original storage-space constraint, so 6,000 of the available square feet were not utilized in our manufacture of 6,000 units of product II. Further, since $S_3$ was the slack in the person-hour constraint, we see that 18,000 of the available person-hours were not used. *Why* were these amounts not utilized? Because of a *scarcity of machine-hours*. We came up against the machine-hour restriction before we could reach the boundaries of either of the other two constraints.

The implication to the manager is clear. The limiting factor on profit is the paucity of machine-hours. If the number of machine-hours could be increased, then more units of product II could be made and stored, with a corresponding increase in profit.

Of course, a unit of product II requires more than machine-hours. Some person-hours and some storage space are also needed. Here we gain a little more insight into the meaning of *implicit value* of a scarce resource. The value of an extra machine-hour is not just its individual monetary cost; an extra machine-hour would allow us to use a little more space and a little more of the available person-hours. In other words, when we have more of a *scarce* resource, we are able to utilize more of the profit potential inherent in those resources which are in *abundance*. Thus the implicit value of a machine-hour resides in its ability to allow the use of more of *all* the resources.

Now let's see how to find the numerical implicit value of a resource by merely inspecting the optimal tableau for the *primal* problem. First we concentrate on discovering the optimal value for $y_2$, the implicit value of one machine-hour in the formulation of the dual problem. Here our reasoning is the same as that used when we wanted to discover what currently nonbasic variable could enter the basis and increase $Z$. Only this time, since we will consider only the *optimal* tableau, we ask what currently nonbasic variables could enter the basis and *decrease* $Z$. The optimal tableau from Table 5.2 is repeated here as Table 5.3 for convenient reference.

Remember that the tableau in Table 5.3 is in the $Z$-row format and that this format just reports coefficients in a system of equations. So the $Z$ row of the optimal tableau merely represents the following equation:

$$Z + 1x_1 + 0x_2 + 0S_1 + \tfrac{3}{4}S_2 + 0S_3 = 36,000$$

The only nonzero coefficients in this equation (except for the 1 coefficient of $Z$) are coefficients of the *nonbasic* variables $x_1$ and $S_2$. Thus the coefficient of $x_1$ in the optimal $Z$ row, the number 1, tells us that if we decide to

TABLE 5.3   OPTIMAL TABLEAU FOR PRIMAL PROBLEM

| Basic | Z | $x_1$ | $x_2$ | $S_1$ | $S_2$ | $S_3$ | Solution |
|-------|---|-------|-------|-------|-------|-------|----------|
| Z | 1 | 1 | 0 | 0 | $\frac{3}{4}$ | 0 | 36,000 |
| $S_1$ | 0 | 1 | 0 | 1 | $-\frac{1}{2}$ | 0 | 6,000 |
| $x_2$ | 0 | $\frac{1}{2}$ | 1 | 0 | $\frac{1}{8}$ | 0 | 6,000 |
| $S_3$ | 0 | $\frac{5}{2}$ | 0 | 0 | $-\frac{3}{8}$ | 1 | 18,000 |

make one unit of product I, we would decrease profit by $1, since then we would have $x_1 = 1$ and the equation would become

$$Z + (1)(1) = 36,000$$

or Z would have to be 35,999 if we are to add 1 to it and get 36,000 (either the coefficients or the variables in all the other terms are 0).

Apply that same line of reasoning to the current nonbasic variable $S_2$. It is the slack variable for the machine-hour constraint. If we include a unit of slack in the machine-hour constraint, that is, if we let $S_2 = 1$ (it is currently 0), then the Z-row equation would become

$$Z + (\tfrac{3}{4})(1) = 36,000$$

Then Z would have to be 35,999.25, or it would be *decreased* by 0.75. But at optimality we used *all* of the machine-hours that were available, since at optimality $S_2 = 0$. So what we are really saying is that if we elect to use *one less* machine-hour, our profit would be reduced by $0.75. That is, for each machine-hour *not* available, we decrease profit by $\frac{3}{4}$ dollars. Thus $\frac{3}{4}$ is the *implicit value of a machine-hour*, since *use* of that extra unit would regain the $0.75 profit.

So the Z-row coefficient of $S_2$ in the optimal tableau, where $S_2$ is the slack in the machine-hour constraint, is the implicit value of a machine-hour. Similarly, the Z-row coefficients of $S_1$ and $S_3$ are, respectively, the implicit values of a square foot of storage space and of one person-hour. The values of those two slack variables are 6,000 and 18,000, or neither resource was exhausted at optimality. This means the implicit values associated with extra units of those two resources are both zero.

The full economic implication of the first row of the optimal primal tableau is now evident. The *coefficients of the slack variables* in the Z row of the *optimal* tableau are the *implicit values* of the corresponding resources. That is, $S_1$ is associated with space, and $y_1 = 0$. Similarly, since $S_2$ is associated with machine hours, $y_2 = \frac{3}{4}$, while $y_3 = 0$ because $S_3$ is associated with person-hours.

This is the same solution obtained for the dual problem in Table 5.1. Let's look again at the formulation of that dual problem. It was

$$\text{Minimize } Y$$

where
$$Y = 30{,}000y_1 + 48{,}000y_2 + 36{,}000y_3$$

subject to
$$3y_1 + 4y_2 + 4y_3 \geq 2 \qquad \text{product I}$$
$$4y_1 + 8y_2 + 3y_3 \geq 6 \qquad \text{product II}$$
$$y_1, y_2, y_3 \geq 0$$

According to Table 5.1 or, equivalently, to the analysis of the optimal primal tableau we have just completed, the solution is

$$\text{Min } Y = 36{,}000 \qquad \text{at } (y_1, y_2, y_3) = (0, \tfrac{3}{4}, 0)$$

We see that indeed the value of the objective function is

$$Y = 30{,}000(0) + 48{,}000(\tfrac{3}{4}) + 36{,}000(0) = 36{,}000$$

Now consider the two constraints. The product I constraint, in which the left-hand side represents the value of all resources used to make one unit of product I, becomes

$$3(0) + 4(\tfrac{3}{4}) + 4(0) = 3 > 2$$

so the constraint is satisfied in the *inequality* sense. This means that the value of the resources used to make a unit of product I *exceeds* the $2 profit per unit of product I, so it would be uneconomical to manufacture product I. Sure enough, at optimality $x_1 = 0$, or we decide not to make any units of product I. We would not wish to make a product which would not return to us full value of the resources it consumes.

Now look at the product II constraint in the dual. It is

$$4(0) + 8(\tfrac{3}{4}) + 3(0) = 6$$

or it is satisfied with *equality*. This means that the value of the resources used to make a unit of product II is precisely equal to the profit per unit of product II or that the manufacture of product II *does* return full value of the resources consumed. So we would want to make as many units of product II as the resources permit, in this case, $x_2 = 6{,}000$ units.

Let's review what we have observed so far about the primal and dual problems. We have seen that we can formulate the dual directly, with the decision variables being implicit values of the resources, and that we can solve the dual using simplex tableaus (Table 5.1). But we have also

**TABLE 5.4**   *THE* $c_j - z_j$ *ROW OF THE OPTIMAL DUAL TABLEAU*

| | $y_1$ | $y_2$ | $y_3$ | $S_1$ | $S_2$ | $A_1$ | $A_2$ |
|---|---|---|---|---|---|---|---|
| $c_j - z_j$ | 6,000 | 0 | 18,000 | 0 | 6,000 | $M$ | $M - 6,000$ |

noticed that the dual solution can simply be read out of the appropriate positions in the optimal *primal* tableau.

Then can we read the primal solution directly off the optimal *dual* tableau? Yes. As you might have guessed, the dual of the dual problem will be the primal problem. So we ought to be able to obtain the primal solution from the $c_j - z_j$ row of the optimal dual tableau (or from its Z row, if that alternate tabular format had been used). Table 5.4 shows that final $c_j - z_j$ row from Table 5.1, along with the associated variables.

Look under $S_1$ and $S_2$ in Table 5.4. $S_1$ is the surplus variable associated with the product I constraint in the dual, and the 0 $c_j - z_j$ under $S_1$ implies that $x_1 = 0$. The number 6,000 under $S_2$, associated with product II, tells us that $x_2 = 6,000$. Sure enough, the optimal solution for the primal problem may be obtained by looking at the optimal dual tableau.

## 5.4   A DEMONSTRATION OF IMPLICIT VALUE

By saying that the implicit value of a machine-hour is $\frac{3}{4}$, we imply that we can increase profit by \$0.75 per extra machine-hour we can make available. But it takes 8 machine-hours to make an entire unit of product II, so our conclusion is that if those 8 hours were made available, profit should increase by (\$0.75)(8) = \$6. Let us see *how* that profit increase is brought about.

Act as if in the original problem we had started with 48,008 machine-hours instead of 48,000. Then the second primal constraint would be

$$4x_1 + 8x_2 \leq 48,008$$

Table 5.5 shows the simplex solution of the primal problem with this modified constraint. The only change from Table 5.2 has been to increase the right-hand side of the second constraint by 8 in the initial tableau. The same incoming and outgoing variables are involved in obtaining the first revised (optimal) tableau, and the same implicit values of resources are observed. The only changes are in the values of the basic variables and the optimal value for Z.

Clearly we have improved profit by exactly the predicted \$6. But how? Remember, to make and store a unit of product II requires not only 8 machine-hours but also 4 square feet of space and 3 person-hours. The additional 8 machine-hours have the effect of freeing exactly the necessary space and person-hours. In the final tableau we now have $S_1 = 5,996$ instead of 6,000; the slack in the space constraint has been reduced by 4 units, meaning that 4 more square feet were used. $S_3$ has been reduced from 18,000 to 17,997, implying that 3 more person-hours were used. Finally, $x_2 = 6,001$ instead of 6,000; exactly 1 more unit of product II was made.

That is the meaning of "implicit value of a resource." Only a *scarce* resource has a nonzero implicit value and that value resides in its ability to free up *all* resources so their profit potential can be utilized. Thus while $Y$, the objective function in the dual, is evaluated at optimality by simply computing the total value of the *scarce* resources, the preceding analysis has shown how the worth of the *other* resources is also included.

## 5.5 SUBSTITUTION COEFFICIENTS

The demonstration of implicit value presented in Table 5.5 was designed to show *how* the implicit value of a *scarce* resource was intimately related to the value of *all* resources. However, suppose all we want to know is how the optimal solution would *change* if we made available more units of the scarce resource. The analysis we have already done suggests an easy way to do that *without* having to go back and rework the entire problem. All we have to do is look at the appropriate column in the original optimal tableau.

Remember how the coefficient $\frac{3}{4}$ in the $Z$ row and the $S_2$ column of Table 5.3 was interpreted? It was the implicit value of an extra machine-hour. But it also may be interpreted as the change in the *basic variable* $Z$ per extra machine-hour. Then *all* coefficients in the $S_2$ column of the optimal tableau have the same interpretation. Each is the *change in the basic variable per unit increase in the scarce resource.* Those coefficients, often called *substitution*

**TABLE 5.5**    DEMONSTRATING IMPLICIT VALUE

| Basic | Z | $x_1$ | $x_2$ | $S_1$ | $S_2$ | $S_3$ | Solution | Ratio |
|-------|---|-------|-------|-------|-------|-------|----------|-------|
| Z | 1 | −2 | ↓ −6 | 0 | 0 | 0 | 0 | |
| $S_1$ | 0 | 3 | 4 | 1 | 0 | 0 | 30,000 | 7,500 |
| ← $S_2$ | 0 | 4 | (8) | 0 | 1 | 0 | 48,008 | 6,001 ← min |
| $S_3$ | 0 | 4 | 3 | 0 | 0 | 1 | 36,000 | 12,000 |
| Z | 1 | 1 | 0 | 0 | $\frac{3}{4}$ | 0 | 36,006 | ← optimal |
| $S_1$ | 0 | 1 | 0 | 1 | $-\frac{1}{2}$ | 0 | 5,996 | |
| $x_2$ | 0 | $\frac{1}{2}$ | 1 | 0 | $\frac{1}{8}$ | 0 | 6,001 | |
| $S_3$ | 0 | $\frac{5}{2}$ | 0 | 0 | $-\frac{3}{8}$ | 1 | 17,997 | |

**TABLE 5.6** SUBSTITUTION COEFFICIENTS FOR $S_2$

| Basic | $S_2$ | Solution |
|-------|-------|----------|
| $Z$ | $\frac{3}{4}$ | 36,000 |
| $S_1$ | $-\frac{1}{2}$ | 6,000 |
| $x_2$ | $\frac{1}{8}$ | 6,000 |
| $S_3$ | $-\frac{3}{8}$ | 18,000 |

*coefficients,* are shown in the reduced display of Table 5.6, along with associated values of the basic variables at optimality. Note that the substitution coefficients come from the *optimal* tableau in Table 5.3.

We already know that $S_2$ is associated with machine-hours and that if we include an *extra* machine-hour, the optimal value of the basic variable $Z$ (profit) will change from 36,000 to 36,000.75. Then correspondingly, the optimal $S_1$ (slack in the storage-space constraint) would change from 6,000 to 5,999.5 (reduced by $\frac{1}{2}$), $x_2$ (number of units of product II) would move from 6,000 to 6,000.125 (increased by $\frac{1}{8}$), and $S_3$ (slack in the person-hour constraint) would change from 18,000 to 17,999.625 (reduced by $\frac{3}{8}$).

Is that analysis consistent with the results in Table 5.5, where we looked at the effect of 8 extra machine-hours? Yes. All we have to do is multiply each substitution coefficient by 8 and add to the numbers in the "Solution" column. This will give the new optimal solution that would have been obtained had we started with 48,008 machine-hours instead of 48,000. The calculation is shown in Table 5.7.

The importance of this procedure is twofold. First, it is unnecessary to reformulate and resolve the entire problem to investigate the change due to additional units of resource; we only need to look at the optimal tableau for the original problem. Second, this approach is the basis for one type of *sensitivity* (postoptimality) *analysis* that will be presented subsequently.

To finish up our consideration of the original Dooley Corporation problem posed as Example 5.1, let's do one more thing with it. The substitution coefficient $-\frac{1}{2}$, associated with $S_1$, the slack for the storage-space constraint,

**TABLE 5.7** EFFECT OF 8 EXTRA MACHINE-HOURS

| Basic | Substitution coefficient | Previous solution | New solution |
|-------|--------------------------|-------------------|--------------|
| $Z$ | $\frac{3}{4}$ | 36,000 | $36,000 + (\frac{3}{4})(8) = 36,006$ |
| $S_1$ | $-\frac{1}{2}$ | 6,000 | $6,000 + (-\frac{1}{2})(8) = 5,996$ |
| $x_2$ | $\frac{1}{8}$ | 6,000 | $6,000 + (\frac{1}{8})(8) = 6,001$ |
| $S_3$ | $-\frac{3}{8}$ | 18,000 | $18,000 + (-\frac{3}{8})(8) = 17,997$ |

says that slack will be reduced by $\frac{1}{2}$ square foot per additional machine-hour. How many additional machine-hours are required to reduce $S_1$ to 0, that is, to permit the use of *all* the available storage space *as well as* all the machine-hours? Well, $S_1$, which was originally 6,000, is reduced by $\frac{1}{2}$ unit for each additional machine-hour, so the addition of *12,000* machine-hours would reduce $S_1$ to 0. Corresponding changes in the other basic variables, including $Z$, the value of the objective function, are shown in Table 5.8.

This says that making 12,000 *more* machine-hours available, so that we start with 60,000 machine-hours instead of 48,000, will increase profit from $36,000 to $45,000. In the process we would consume all 60,000 machine-hours ($S_2 = 0$ since it is nonbasic) *and* all of the original 30,000 square feet of storage space ($S_1 = 0$), but we would still have in excess supply 13,500 person-hours ($S_3 = 13,500$). The extra 12,000 machine-hours permits the use of more of the other resources as well; in fact, we can produce an extra 1,500 units of product II, since $x_2$ has changed from 6,000 to 7,500. However, the addition of *more than* 12,000 machine-hours would not produce a similar increase in profit, since now we will have consumed all of the *storage space* as well. That is, more machine-hours than an extra 12,000 would not help unless we could *also* obtain more storage space.

To illustrate that last observation, let's look at this new Dooley Corporation problem graphically. The new primal problem is

$$\text{Maximize } Z$$

where
$$Z = 2x_1 + 6x_2 \qquad \text{profit}$$

subject to
$$3x_1 + 4x_2 \leq 30,000 \qquad \text{storage space}$$
$$4x_1 + 8x_2 \leq 60,000 \qquad \text{machine-hours}$$
$$4x_1 + 3x_2 \leq 36,000 \qquad \text{person-hours}$$
$$x_1, x_2 \geq 0$$

The graphical solution of that model is shown in Figure 5.2.
Now the optimal solution is

$$\text{Max } Z = 45,000 \qquad \text{at } (x_1, x_2) = (0, 7,500)$$

**TABLE 5.8** EFFECT OF 12,000 EXTRA MACHINE-HOURS

| Basic | Substitution coefficient | Previous solution | New solution |
|---|---|---|---|
| $Z$ | $\frac{3}{4}$ | 36,000 | $36,000 + (\frac{3}{4})(12,000) = 45,000$ |
| $S_1$ | $-\frac{1}{2}$ | 6,000 | $6,000 + (-\frac{1}{2})(12,000) = 0$ |
| $x_2$ | $\frac{1}{8}$ | 6,000 | $6,000 + (\frac{1}{8})(12,000) = 7,500$ |
| $S_3$ | $-\frac{3}{8}$ | 18,000 | $18,000 + (-\frac{3}{8})(12,000) = 13,500$ |

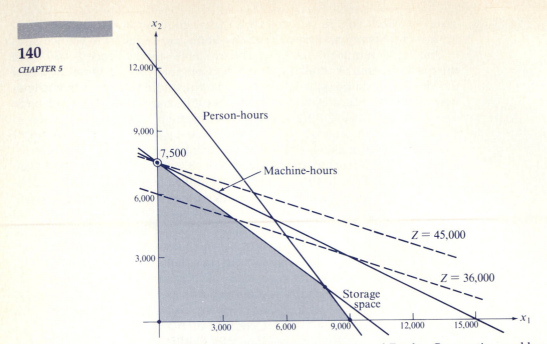

**FIGURE 5.2**  Graphical solution: Augmented Dooley Corporation problem

This solution occurs at the intersection of the machine-hour constraint and the storage-space constraint in Figure 5.2. Unless we increase *both* machine-hours and storage space, we cannot improve upon the solution.

As a manager, what would you be willing to pay for each additional machine-hour above 48,000 (until you reach 60,000)? Anything up to $0.75 per machine-hour. That is, if you could acquire extra machine-hours at a price less than the *implicit value* of a machine-hour, it would be profitable to do so. Of course, you would not wish to acquire more than 12,000 additional machine-hours unless you could also (profitably) acquire more storage space.

## 5.6  SENSITIVITY ANALYSIS

In the previous section the concept of substitution coefficients was used to investigate the effect of a change in the amount of a scarce resource. This general area, investigating the effect of changes in any of the parameters in the model, is known as *sensitivity* or *postoptimality analysis*.

The process is called sensitivity analysis because it considers how "sensitive" the optimal solution is to such changes. If a minor change in an input parameter causes a drastic change in the solution, we say the solution is very *sensitive* to the value of that parameter. This would imply that careful assessment of model parameters, like profit per unit or amount of resource available, is extremely important. On the other hand, if some of the parameters may change considerably without major effect on the nature of the optimal solution, we say the solution is relatively *insensitive* to the values of those parameters.

The process is also called postoptimality analysis because it can occur *after* an optimal solution, assuming a given set of parameters, has been obtained for the model. Instead of reworking the entire problem as a new model with new parameters, we may take the original optimal tableau as a *starting point* for the analysis.

Five types of changes in the original problem may be investigated during a sensitivity analysis. They are

1 Availability of resources (right-hand sides of constraints)

2 Profit contributions or cost per unit of decision variable (coefficients in the objective function)

3 Consumption of resources per unit of decision variable (coefficients in left-hand sides of constraints)

4 The inclusion of a new constraint

5 The inclusion of a new variable

Changes of types 1 and 2 are most frequently investigated in a sensitivity analysis. While the amount of resources on hand will usually be known, a manager may be most interested in the effect of a type 1 change. It is the manager who makes those resources available, and the more that is known about their profit-making potential, the better the decision that will result from the analysis. A change in an objective-function coefficient (profit or cost per unit, usually; type 2) will always be of interest because some portions of a profit or cost parameter will depend upon the marketplace; these parameters cannot be precisely assessed or controlled by management; they change with fluctuations in demand and with the general state of the economy.

In a production problem, coefficients of type 3, those on the left-hand sides of the constraints, are often called *technological coefficients*, being indicators of resource consumption per unit of product. These coefficients are much more likely to be known exactly or to be subject to only minor changes. Usually the inclusion of a new constraint or a new variable (types 4 and 5) is considered because of errors in the original model formulation or because more information has become available. Thus sensitivity analyses for changes of types 3, 4, and 5 occur much less frequently than for changes of types 1 and 2.

Only changes of types 1 and 2 will be discussed here. Most computer codes for LP that include "ranging" (sensitivity analysis) only consider objective-function coefficients and right-hand sides of constraints.

A change in the right-hand side of a constraint (type 1) cannot affect the coefficients in the Z row of the original optimal tableau (or the optimal $c_j - z_j$'s). Thus a change of type 1 affects only the *feasibility* of what was previously the optimal solution. A change of type 2, in an objective-function coefficient, has no effect on the feasible region. The solution originally quoted as optimal will still be feasible (although not necessarily optimal).   Thus a change of type 2 only affects *optimality* of the previous solution.   Example 5.2, with its accompanying Figures 5.3, 5.4, and 5.5, exhibits those features graphically.

**Example 5.2**

Consider the following two-variable LP model:

$$\text{Maximize } Z$$

where
$$Z = 3x_1 + 4x_2$$

subject to
$$4x_1 + 3x_2 \leq 24$$
$$2x_1 + 3x_2 \leq 18$$
$$x_1 \quad\quad \leq 4$$
$$x_1, x_2 \geq 0$$

Its graphical solution,

$$\text{Max } Z = 25 \quad\quad \text{at } (x_1, x_2) = (3, 4)$$

is shown in Figure 5.3.

   Now suppose we change the right-hand side of the first constraint (a type 1 change) from 24 to 18.   Then the first constraint would be

$$4x_1 + 3x_2 \leq 18$$

**FIGURE 5.3**   Graphical solution of Example 5.2

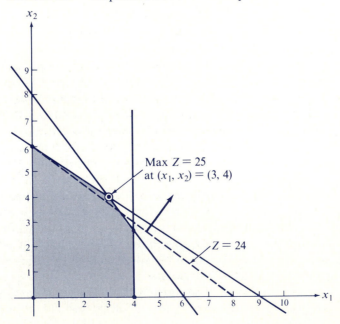

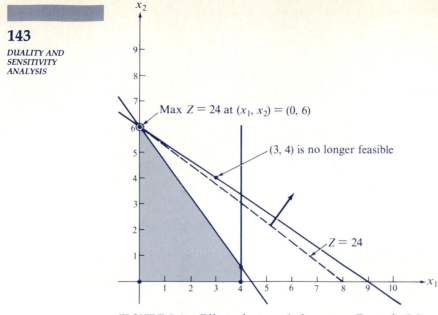

**FIGURE 5.4**    Effect of a type 1 change on Example 5.2

The new feasible region and new solution are indicated in Figure 5.4. The slope of the boundary line for the first constraint was unchanged, but the change in its right-hand side gave different intercepts for that boundary line.   The feasible region was changed so that the previous optimal solution is now no longer feasible.

Now let's change one of the objective-function coefficients (a type 2 change), leaving everything else in Example 5.2 just like it was originally. Changing the objective-function coefficient of $x_2$ from 4 to 5 gives the new function

$$Z = 3x_1 + 5x_2$$

but does not change the original feasible region shown in Figure 5.3. Since the slope of objective-function contours has changed, however, although the previous optimal solution is still feasible, it is no longer optimal.   This condition is shown in Figure 5.5.

## 5.7   CHANGES IN RIGHT-HAND SIDES OF CONSTRAINTS

In Section 5.5, where substitution coefficients were discussed, we considered the effect of extra machine-hours upon the optimal solution of the Dooley Corporation problem, originally stated as Example 5.1.   That analysis only required reference to the final (optimal) tableau.   Here we look at another problem using a similar analysis, but with a slightly different phrasing of our objective.

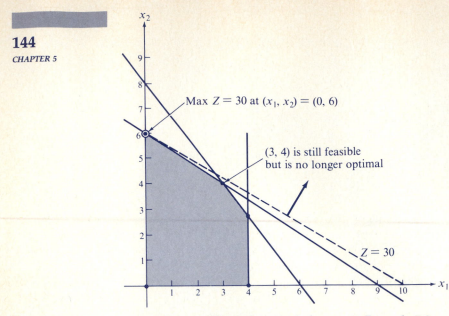

**FIGURE 5.5**    Effect of a type 2 change on Example 5.2

### Example 5.3

In Exercise 2.16 at the end of Chapter 2 an investment problem was stated. Its basic scenario is retained here, but the statements of its constraints are modified to provide a simple first example of the standard approach to sensitivity analysis.

First State Bank will make six types of loans to its customers.   These loans and their associated interest rates are listed in Table 5.9.

First State Bank expects to have $20 million available for loans during the year.   Banking laws and the internal policies of First State Bank impose the following restrictions:

**1** No more than $3 million may be allocated to unsecured loans.

**2** At least $10 million must be allocated to some combination of home mortgage, industrial, and commercial loans.

**3** The total amount allocated to commercial, automobile, and otherwise-secured loans cannot exceed $12 million.

The basic question is: How much money should be allocated to each type of loan in order to maximize annual earned interest?

We will formulate the model and solve the problem, reporting in Tables 5.10 and 5.11 only the initial and optimal tableaus.   Then we will consider sensitivity analyses related to right-hand sides of the constraints—in this problem, monetary amounts.

TABLE 5.9 TYPE OF LOAN AND INTEREST RATE

| Type of loan | Interest rate, % |
|---|---|
| 1 Home mortgage | 14 |
| 2 Industrial | 15 |
| 3 Commercial | 17 |
| 4 Automobile | 18 |
| 5 Otherwise-secured | 20 |
| 6 Unsecured | 22 |

Let $x_1$ = number of millions of dollars allocated to home mortgage loans, and so on according to the numbering scheme in Table 5.9, up to $x_6$ = number of millions of dollars allocated to unsecured loans. To avoid one artificial variable, we observe that restriction 2, which says that at least $10 million must be allocated to home mortgage, industrial, and commercial loans, can also be stated as: "No more than $10 million may be allocated to some combination of automobile, otherwise-secured, and unsecured loans," since the total available capital is $20 million. This converts what would have been a "≥" constraint to a "≤" constraint. Note, however, that one *equality* constraint is implied by the availability of $20 million and the fact that we want to maximize annual earned interest; the more we loan, the more interest we earn, so we would want to loan the entire $20 million. Thus one artificial variable, associated with this equality constraint, will appear in the simplex tableaus.

The model for this investment problem is

$$\text{Maximize } Z$$

where

$$Z = 0.14x_1 + 0.15x_2 + 0.17x_3 + 0.18x_4 + 0.20x_5 + 0.22x_6$$

subject to

$$x_1 + x_2 + x_3 + x_4 + x_5 + x_6 = 20$$

$$x_6 \leq 3$$

$$x_4 + x_5 + x_6 \leq 10$$

$$x_3 + x_4 + x_5 \leq 12$$

$$x_1, x_2, x_3, x_4, x_5, x_6 \geq 0$$

Remember, the $x$'s are numbers of *millions* of dollars, not numbers of dollars. The initial tableau, in the $c_j - z_j$ format, is shown as Table 5.10.

Four revised tableaus are required to achieve the optimal solution (you may easily work through them; the 0s and 1s in the body of the table make that work very simple). The fourth revised (optimal) tableau is shown here as Table 5.11.

## TABLE 5.10  INITIAL TABLEAU FOR FIRST STATE BANK PROBLEM

| Basic | $c_j$ | $x_1$ 0.14 | $x_2$ 0.15 | $x_3$ 0.17 | $x_4$ 0.18 | $x_5$ 0.20 | $x_6$ 0.22 | $A_1$ $-M$ | $S_2$ 0 | $S_3$ 0 | $S_4$ 0 | Solution |
|---|---|---|---|---|---|---|---|---|---|---|---|---|
| $A_1$ | $-M$ | 1 | 1 | 1 | 1 | 1 | 1 | 1 | 0 | 0 | 0 | 20 |
| $\leftarrow S_2$ | 0 | 0 | 0 | 0 | 0 | 0 | (1) | 0 | 1 | 0 | 0 | 3 $\leftarrow$ |
| $S_3$ | 0 | 0 | 0 | 0 | 1 | 1 | 1 | 0 | 0 | 1 | 0 | 10 |
| $S_4$ | 0 | 0 | 0 | 1 | 1 | 1 | 0 | 0 | 0 | 0 | 1 | 12 |
| $z_j$ | | $-M$ | $-M$ | $-M$ | $-M$ | $-M$ | $-M$ $\downarrow$ | $-M$ | 0 | 0 | 0 | $-20M$ |
| $c_j - z_j$ | | $0.14+M$ | $0.15+M$ | $0.17+M$ | $0.18+M$ | $0.20+M$ | $0.22+M$ | 0 | 0 | 0 | 0 | |

The optimal strategy is to allocate:

$5 million to industrial loans
$5 million to commercial loans
$7 million to otherwise-secured loans
$3 million to unsecured loans

That allocation will yield maximum annual interest of $3.66 million, an effective overall yield of 18.3 percent. Note that no home mortgage or automobile loans are permitted, a situation not conducive to maintenance of customer goodwill. Nevertheless, if the *only* objective is maximum interest, that decision is optimal. If other objectives, such as making at least $1 million available for automobile loans, are desirable, then you might want to use a goal-programming formulation (see Example 6.5 of Chapter 6).

Now let's investigate the sensitivity of the optimal solution to changes in right-hand sides of constraints. We will be particularly interested in

## TABLE 5.11  OPTIMAL TABLEAU FOR FIRST STATE BANK PROBLEM

| Basic | $c_j$ | $x_1$ 0.14 | $x_2$ 0.15 | $x_3$ 0.17 | $x_4$ 0.18 | $x_5$ 0.20 | $x_6$ 0.22 | $A_1$ $-M$ | $S_2$ 0 | $S_3$ 0 | $S_4$ 0 | Solution |
|---|---|---|---|---|---|---|---|---|---|---|---|---|
| $x_2$ | 0.15 | 1 | 1 | 0 | 0 | 0 | 0 | 1 | $-1$ | 0 | $-1$ | 5 |
| $x_6$ | 0.22 | 0 | 0 | 0 | 0 | 0 | 1 | 0 | 1 | 0 | 0 | 3 |
| $x_5$ | 0.20 | 0 | 0 | 0 | 1 | 1 | 0 | 0 | $-1$ | 1 | 0 | 7 |
| $x_3$ | 0.17 | 0 | 0 | 1 | 0 | 0 | 0 | 0 | 1 | $-1$ | 1 | 5 |
| $z_j$ | | 0.15 | 0.15 | 0.17 | 0.20 | 0.20 | 0.22 | 0.15 | 0.04 | 0.03 | 0.02 | 3.66 |
| $c_j - z_j$ | | $-0.01$ | 0 | 0 | $-0.02$ | 0 | 0 | $-M-0.15$ | $-0.04$ | $-0.03$ | $-0.02$ | optimal |

where the *form* of the optimal solution will change, which in turn is associated with the set of *basic variables*. A change in a right-hand side which produces only a change in *value* of the *current* basic variables, like the changes produced in Table 5.7 of Section 5.5, does not represent a significant change in the form of the solution. But a change in the entire *set* of basic variables is a definite change of form, representing a major change in the overall decision. That is, if after the change in right-hand-side coefficient our optimal decision is still to allocate money for industrial, commercial, otherwise-secured, and unsecured loans, there has been no significant change in the decision. But if after the change the optimal decision is to allocate money to home mortgage, industrial, commercial, and unsecured loans (replacing otherwise-secured loans by home mortgage loans), a significant change in the *type* of decision has occurred.

Mathematically then, the notions discussed in the previous paragraph boil down to consideration of the *set of basic variables*. We wonder by how much a right-hand-side coefficient can change before the current basic solution (original optimal basic variables) would no longer be feasible. In Example 5.4 we see how easily such a question can be answered.

### Example 5.4
### Change in Only One Right-Hand Side

Unsecured loans (Example 5.3) provide the highest interest rate, 22 percent, but we are only allowed $3 million for unsecured loans (the associated constraint is $x_6 \leq 3$). We should be able to earn more interest if more money is permitted for unsecured loans, and we would expect to earn less interest if less money is permitted for unsecured loans. We are also interested in knowing the effect on the overall decision of any change in that amount. Thus we ask:

By how much can the right-hand side of the constraint $x_6 \leq 3$ change before the current optimal basis becomes infeasible?

Let $\delta$ represent the change in that right-hand side. Here $\delta$ might be either positive or negative, representing an increase or a decrease in the amount of money permitted for unsecured loans. We wish to determine limits for $\delta$ so that the current optimal basic variables all remain in the basis, or, equivalently, so that any change, $\delta$, outside of those limits causes the set of optimal basic variables to change.

Consider the initial tableau of Table 5.10, with the 3 in the solution column, the right-hand side of the second constraint, replaced by $3 + \delta$ (see Table 5.12). What would happen to $\delta$ as we move through successive revised tableaus toward optimality?

That question appears to be impossible to answer, since $\delta$ is unspecified. Ratios of right-hand sides to coefficients of incoming variables determine outgoing variables, and with $\delta$ unspecified, how would we determine the minimum nonnegative ratio? We don't. In this version of a sensitivity

**TABLE 5.12**

ANALOGY OF δ COLUMN TO
$S_2$ COLUMN: INITIAL TABLEAU

| Basic | $S_2$ | Solution |
|-------|-------|----------|
| $A_1$ | 0 | $20 + 0\delta$ |
| $S_2$ | 1 | $3 + 1\delta$ |
| $S_3$ | 0 | $10 + 0\delta$ |
| $S_4$ | 0 | $12 + 0\delta$ |

analysis we merely ask: What would the optimal tableau look like if we had simply carried out the *same sequence of algebraic operations* as before, except with 3 replaced by $3 + \delta$? To answer *that* question, consider Table 5.12, a truncation of Table 5.10, as well as Table 5.10 itself.

The replacement of 3 by $3 + \delta$ in the solution column of Table 5.12 is represented by $3 + 1\delta$. In all the *other* right-hand sides, initially we have $0\delta$ added in, or no change. However, that new δ column involves the *same coefficients* as the initial $S_2$ column. Then what happens to the coefficients in the δ column by the time we reach the optimal tableau of Table 5.11? *The same thing that happens to the $S_2$ column.*

Gauss-Jordan reduction only manipulates *rows* of the tableaus, so everything that happens to a 0 in the $S_2$ column would also happen to the corresponding 0 in the δ column. Similarly, whatever happens to the 1 in the $S_2$ column must happen to the 1 in the δ column. Further, we know that the original system of equations would still be satisfied by the numbers in the solution column, since Gauss-Jordan reduction always produces a system *equivalent* to the original system.

Table 5.13 shows the corresponding look of part of Table 5.11, the optimal tableau, after carrying out of the same operations as before. Note that the *only* change in the optimal tableau occurs in the *solution* column. The $c_j - z_j$'s are unaffected, so our solution is still optimal, *provided* it is still feasible.

We know all of the equations in the final system of Table 5.11 are satisfied by this solution since Gauss-Jordan reduction gives equivalent systems. Consider, for example, the first equation in Table 5.11 (the $x_2$ row). It is now

$$x_1 + x_2 + A_1 - S_2 - S_4 = 5 - \delta$$

**TABLE 5.13**

ANALOGY OF δ COLUMN TO
$S_2$ COLUMN: OPTIMAL TABLEAU

| Basic | $S_2$ | Solution |
|-------|-------|----------|
| $x_2$ | $-1$ | $5 - 1\delta$ |
| $x_6$ | $1$ | $3 + 1\delta$ |
| $x_5$ | $-1$ | $7 - 1\delta$ |
| $x_3$ | $1$ | $5 + 1\delta$ |

But the only basic variable in the equation is $x_2$, which happens to equal $5 - \delta$, so the equation is certainly satisfied by this new solution. Likewise are all other equations satisfied.

But to have a *feasible* solution, the values of all variables must be *nonnegative* in addition to being values that satisfy all equations. For what values of $\delta$ are all *basic* variables nonnegative? (The nonbasic variables are still 0, which is all right.) That is, for what values of $\delta$ are $x_2 \geq 0$, $x_6 \geq 0$, $x_5 \geq 0$, and $x_3 \geq 0$? Clearly, for values such that *all* of the following inequalities are satisfied (see Table 5.13):

| | | |
|---|---|---|
| 1: | $5 - \delta \geq 0$ | $(\delta \leq 5)$ |
| 2: | $3 + \delta \geq 0$ | $(-\delta \leq 3 \text{ or } \delta \geq -3)$ |
| 3: | $7 - \delta \geq 0$ | $(\delta \leq 7)$ |
| 4: | $5 + \delta \geq 0$ | $(-\delta \leq 5 \text{ or } \delta \geq -5)$ |

The graphical solution of this system of inequalities is indicated by Figure 5.6. That solution is

$$-3 \leq \delta \leq 5$$

That is, if we do not reduce the permitted allocation to unsecured loans by more than $3 million or do not increase that allocation by more than $5 million, the current optimal basis will remain feasible. Another way to say the same thing is that the current optimal basis will remain feasible if the permitted allocation for unsecured loans ranges from 0 to $8 million (the original $3 million plus or minus $5 or $3 million). In many LP computer programs this process is called *ranging* the right-hand sides.

Thus the form of the optimal solution is *not very sensitive* to changes in the right-hand side of the second constraint. The decision, in this case the choice of industrial, commercial, otherwise-secured, and unsecured

**FIGURE 5.6**  Range for change in amount allocated to unsecured loans

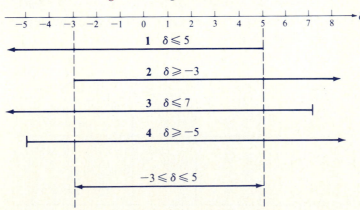

loans, remains the same throughout an $8 million range of allocation permitted for unsecured loans.

Refer once more to Table 5.13 to observe that for $-3 \leq \delta \leq 5$, an optimal basic feasible solution is given by $x_2 = 5 - \delta$, $x_3 = 5 + \delta$, $x_5 = 7 - \delta$, and $x_6 = 3 + \delta$. This means that if $\delta = 4$, or an extra $4 million ($7 million altogether) had originally been permitted for unsecured loans, then our solution would have been to allocate:

$1 million to industrial loans

$9 million to commercial loans

$3 million to otherwise-secured loans

$7 million to unsecured loans

The associated maximum annual interest would have been $(0.15)(\$1$ million) $+ (0.17)(\$9$ million) $+ (0.20)(\$3$ million) $+ (0.22)(\$7$ million) $=$ $3.82 million. This is consistent with our interpretation of $c_j - z_j = -0.04$ in the optimal tableau of Table 5.11. The implicit value of an extra $1 million permitted in unsecured loans is $0.04 million, so the extra interest associated with $4 million more in unsecured loans is $(4)(\$0.04$ million) $=$ $0.16 million. Adding this $0.16 million to the original Max $Z = \$3.66$ million gives $3.82 million.

## Example 5.5
## Changes in Two Right-Hand Sides

Suppose we want to consider effects of changes in right-hand sides of *both* the first and the second constraints. That is, let $\delta_1 =$ change in total amount made available for *all* loans, and let $\delta_2 =$ change in amount permitted for *unsecured* loans. The analysis is just a logical extension of the approach used in Example 5.4.

First, look at analogies of $\delta$ columns to columns in the initial tableau of Table 5.10. These are shown in Table 5.14.

Next we look at the resulting analogies for Table 5.11, the optimal tableau, if the same sequence of algebraic operations had been carried out. These are shown in Table 5.15.

From Table 5.15 we see that for the current basic optimal solution to remain feasible, the following system of inequalities must be satisfied by the pair $(\delta_1, \delta_2)$:

**TABLE 5.14**   $\delta$ COLUMN ANALOGIES: INITIAL TABLEAU

| Basic | $A_1$ | $S_2$ | Solution |
|-------|-------|-------|----------|
| $A_1$ | 1 | 0 | $20 + 1\delta_1 + 0\delta_2$ |
| $S_2$ | 0 | 1 | $3 + 0\delta_1 + 1\delta_2$ |
| $S_3$ | 0 | 0 | $10 + 0\delta_1 + 0\delta_2$ |
| $S_4$ | 0 | 0 | $12 + 0\delta_1 + 0\delta_2$ |

**TABLE 5.15**   δ COLUMN ANALOGIES: OPTIMAL TABLEAU

| Basic | $A_1$ | $S_2$ | Solution |
|-------|-------|-------|----------|
| $x_2$ | 1 | $-1$ | $5 + 1\delta_1 - 1\delta_2$ |
| $x_6$ | 0 | 1 | $3 + 0\delta_1 + 1\delta_2$ |
| $x_5$ | 0 | $-1$ | $7 + 0\delta_1 - 1\delta_2$ |
| $x_3$ | 0 | 1 | $5 + 0\delta_1 + 1\delta_2$ |

1:    $5 + \delta_1 - \delta_2 \geq 0$     $(-\delta_1 + \delta_2 \leq 5)$

2:    $3\phantom{ + \delta_1} + \delta_2 \geq 0$     $(\delta_2 \geq -3)$

3:    $7\phantom{ + \delta_1} - \delta_2 \geq 0$     $(\delta_2 \leq 7)$

4:    $5\phantom{ + \delta_1} + \delta_2 \geq 0$     $(\delta_2 \geq -5)$

The graphical solution of that system is shown in Figure 5.7.

For any pair $(\delta_1, \delta_2)$ falling in the shaded region of Figure 5.7, the current optimal basis is still feasible. For example, suppose $(\delta_1, \delta_2) = (-4, -2)$. That is a point within the shaded region of Figure 5.7. It means that we have \$4 million less total capital than before, or \$20 $-$ \$4 = \$16 million made available for all loans, and \$2 million less is allowed for unsecured

**FIGURE 5.7**   Solution for simultaneous changes in total capital and amount allocated to unsecured loans

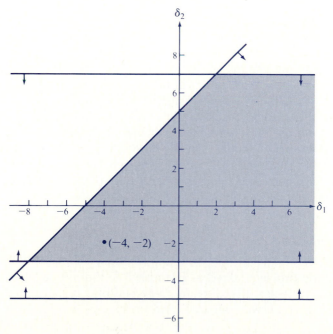

loans (we start with a maximum of $3 - $2 = $1 million). The form of the decision is unchanged; we still make only industrial, commercial, otherwise-secured, and unsecured loans (the optimal basis is unchanged). But the amounts of those loans are, respectively, $x_2 = 5 + \delta_1 - \delta_2 = 5 - 4 - (-2) = 3$, $x_3 = 5 + \delta_2 = 5 - 2 = 3$, $x_5 = 7 - \delta_2 = 7 - (-2) = 9$, $x_6 = 3 + \delta_2 = 3 - 2 = 1$. So the new solution is to allocate:

> $3 million to industrial loans
>
> $3 million to commercial loans
>
> $9 million to otherwise-secured loans
>
> $1 million to unsecured loans

The associated maximum total interest is $(0.15)(\$3$ million$) + (0.17)(\$3$ million$) + (0.20)(\$9$ million$) + (0.22)(\$1$ million$) = \$2.98$ million. This is lower than the original $3.66 million interest, but remember that we are loaning only $16 million now, not $20 million. The effective interest rate, $(2.98/16)(100$ percent$) = 18.625$ percent, is actually *higher* than the 18.3 percent achieved in the original phrasing of the problem.

Because this new solution is the result of *simultaneous* changes in *two* constraints, no analogy with implicit values can be made. Our optimal $c_j - z_j$'s are the negatives of the implicit values of extra units on only *one* right-hand side, when nothing else is changed.

## 5.8 CHANGES IN OBJECTIVE-FUNCTION COEFFICIENTS

Another important type of sensitivity analysis considers the effect of changes in one or more of the coefficients in the objective function. Often a manager will have less control over the "profit per unit" constants than over the availability of resources. In fact, part of the manager's job may be to estimate those profit contributions. A sensitivity analysis will indicate how good those estimates need to be.

If the current basic solution will remain optimal throughout a rather wide range on a particular profit contribution, then a seat-of-the-pants estimate may suffice. On the other hand, if the optimality of the current feasible solution is extremely sensitive to a deviation from the estimated contribution, then a major effort (perhaps statistical in nature) may need to be devoted to obtaining a precise estimate.

### Example 5.6
### Change in One Objective-Function Coefficient: *Nonbasic* Variable

For the problem stated as Example 5.3, the optimal solution involved the basic variables $x_2$, $x_3$, $x_5$, $x_6$, representing, respectively, industrial, commercial, otherwise-secured, and unsecured loans. Note particularly that automobile loans, with a fairly high interest rate of 18 percent, were not included in the optimal solution.

Let's ask the question:

By how much would the interest rate for automobile loans have to change before the current feasible solution is no longer optimal?

We presume, of course, that change would mean an improved solution, involving making auto loans, would result. Notice that the variable $x_4$, the number of millions of dollars allocated to automobile loans, is currently a *nonbasic* variable, with zero value. The following very simple sensitivity analysis only applies to nonbasic variables.

As you might suspect, in view of the analyses of right-hand sides in the previous section, we need only consider the initial and optimal tableaus. But now we observe that a change in an objective-function coefficient can only affect *optimality*, not feasibility, of the current solution (see Figure 5.5). This is true because the constraint equations are not affected by a change in the objective function.

Let $\delta$ be the amount added to 0.18, the original objective-function coefficient of $x_4$. Then the $c_j$ row of the initial tableau would be as shown in Table 5.16 (obtained from Table 5.10).

Now, as before, consider carrying out through all intermediate tableaus the *same algebraic operations* that yielded the optimal solution given by Table 5.11. From Table 5.11 we see that starting from an initial $c_j$ of 0.18 under $x_4$ we wound up with a final $c_j - z_j$ of $-0.02$. Since none of the algebra involved manipulations of the number $\delta$, if we had started with $0.18 + \delta$ we would have finished with $-0.02 + \delta$. That is, the $c_j - z_j$ row of the optimal tableau, Table 5.11, would have been the row shown in Table 5.17.

What is the range of values for $\delta$ such that the current basic feasible solution remains optimal? Simply that range which leaves all the $c_j - z_j$'s nonpositive (the optimality criterion in the $c_j - z_j$ format). So we just write

$$-0.02 + \delta \leq 0$$

or, equivalently,

$$\delta \leq 0.02$$

**TABLE 5.16**   $c_j$ *ROW OF INITIAL TABLEAU*

|       | $x_1$ | $x_2$ | $x_3$ | $x_4$ | $x_5$ | $x_6$ | $A_1$ | $S_2$ | $S_3$ | $S_4$ |
|-------|-------|-------|-------|-------|-------|-------|-------|-------|-------|-------|
| $c_j$ | 0.14  | 0.15  | 0.17  | $0.18 + \delta$ | 0.20 | 0.22 | $-M$ | 0 | 0 | 0 |

**TABLE 5.17**     $c_j - z_j$ ROW OF OPTIMAL TABLEAU

| | $x_1$ | $x_2$ | $x_3$ | $x_4$ | $x_5$ | $x_6$ | $A_1$ | $S_2$ | $S_3$ | $S_4$ |
|---|---|---|---|---|---|---|---|---|---|---|
| $c_j - z_j$ | $-0.01$ | $0$ | $0$ | $-0.02 + \delta$ | $0$ | $0$ | $-M - 0.15$ | $-0.04$ | $-0.03$ | $-0.02$ |

That is, as long as the rate on automobile loans is not increased by more than 0.02, or as long as that interest rate is no more than 20 percent, the current feasible solution remains optimal.

What happens if $\delta$ exceeds 0.02, or if the interest rate for auto loans *exceeds* 20 percent? The associated $c_j - z_j$ in Table 5.17 becomes *positive*, implying that the current solution is not optimal. Moreover, because that positive $c_j - z_j$ is in the $x_4$ column, that number says that $x_4$ can come into the basis and *increase* the value of Z. Suspicion confirmed: Bringing $x_4$ into the basis (at a nonzero level) means that we would then want to allocate money to automobile loans.

How *sensitive* is the current solution to changes in interest rate for auto loans? It is not at all sensitive to decreases in that rate, but it would change with an increase of more than 2 percent. Simply stated, we know that as long as the auto-loan rate is 20 percent or less, we would not change the original decision.

### Example 5.7
### A Convenient Application of Duality

Here we will answer the same question posed in Example 5.6, but applying the notion of *duality*. It will not be necessary to formulate the entire dual of the original investment problem stated as Example 5.3; we only need to form the dual constraint that is associated with the variable $x_4$.

Remember that right-hand sides of dual constraints are just objective-function coefficients in the primal problem. Furthermore, coefficients of dual variables for that constraint are just the original coefficients of $x_4$ in the primal constraints. Thus the dual constraint associated with automobile loans is

$$1y_1 + 0y_2 + 1y_3 + 1y_4 \geq 0.18$$

There are four dual variables, of course, since there were four constraints in the primal problem.

If we change the number 0.18 to the number $0.18 + \delta$, the only change in the whole dual problem is in the right-hand side of the auto-loan constraint. It becomes

$$y_1 + y_3 + y_4 \geq 0.18 + \delta$$

Then the question about optimality in the primal converts to a question about *feasibility* in the dual. From Table 5.11 we find that the optimal dual-variable values are

$$y_1 = 0.15 \qquad y_2 = 0.04 \qquad y_3 = 0.03 \qquad y_4 = 0.02$$

(ignore the $-M$ under $A_1$ in the optimal $c_j - z_j$ row). Then we ask:

For what values of $\delta$ do these optimal dual-variable values remain feasible?

Substitution gives

$$0.15 + 0.03 + 0.02 \geq 0.18 + \delta$$

or
$$\delta \leq 0.02$$

This is the same answer obtained in Example 5.6. When one is investigating a change in a coefficient of a *nonbasic* variable, this duality approach will always give the same result as the slightly more complicated analysis involving primal tableaus.

**Example 5.8**
**Change in One Objective-Function Coefficient: *Basic* Variable**

Let's change scenarios and return to the Dooley Corporation problem. It was stated as Example 5.1. Its tabular simplex solution is given in Table 5.2. There the variables $x_1$ and $x_2$ were the numbers of units of product I and product II to manufacture, respectively, and the resource constraints involved storage space, machine-hours, and person-hours. For ease of reference, Table 5.2 is repeated here as Table 5.18.

**TABLE 5.18**    *SIMPLEX SOLUTION OF THE DOOLEY CORPORATION PROBLEM*

| Basic | Z | $x_1$ | $x_2$ | $S_1$ | $S_2$ | $S_3$ | Solution | Ratio |
|---|---|---|---|---|---|---|---|---|
| Z | 1 | $-2$ | $-6$ ↓ | 0 | 0 | 0 | 0 | |
| $S_1$ | 0 | 3 | 4 | 1 | 0 | 0 | 30,000 | 7,500 |
| $\leftarrow S_2$ | 0 | 4 | (8) | 0 | 1 | 0 | 48,000 | 6,000 ← min |
| $S_3$ | 0 | 4 | 3 | 0 | 0 | 1 | 36,000 | 12,000 |
| Z | 1 | 1 | 0 | 0 | $\frac{3}{4}$ | 0 | 36,000 | ← optimal |
| $S_1$ | 0 | 1 | 0 | 1 | $-\frac{1}{2}$ | 0 | 6,000 | |
| $x_2$ | 0 | $\frac{1}{2}$ | 1 | 0 | $\frac{1}{8}$ | 0 | 6,000 | |
| $S_3$ | 0 | $\frac{5}{2}$ | 0 | 0 | $-\frac{3}{8}$ | 1 | 18,000 | |

From Table 5.18 (in the Z-row format) we observe that the original objective-function coefficient of $x_1$ was 2 and of $x_2$ was 6. At optimality, $x_2$ was a basic variable while $x_1$ was nonbasic. We want to investigate the effect of a change in the objective-function coefficient of a *basic* variable, so we look at the coefficient of $x_2$. Suppose it had been $6 + \delta$ instead of 6. Then in the Z row of the initial tableau we would have seen $-6 - \delta$, and the Z row of the optimal tableau would be as shown in Table 5.19. That row would have been the result of application of the same algebraic operations used before. However, this time those operations do not give the correct Z row for the simplex method, which always requires a *zero coefficient of a basic variable*. Thus before doing our sensitivity analysis we have to multiply the $x_2$ row of the optimal tableau in Table 5.18 by $\delta$ and add to the new Z row. This gives the row shown in Table 5.20.

The Z row in Table 5.20 takes into account the effect of a change of the amount $\delta$ in the original objective-function coefficient of $x_2$. Note that the optimal Z, under the solution column, would also be changed. This is only sensible to expect, since a different objective-function coefficient of a *basic* variable would have to produce a different value for Z (not so for a *nonbasic* variable, which is zero-valued).

For what values of $\delta$ is the current basic feasible solution still optimal? For values of $\delta$ such that all coefficients in the Z row of Table 5.20 are nonnegative (optimality criterion for Z-row format). Thus the desired range on $\delta$ is the solution of the system:

1: $\qquad\qquad 1 + \tfrac{1}{2}\delta \geq 0$

2: $\qquad\qquad \tfrac{3}{4} + \tfrac{1}{8}\delta \geq 0$

The system can be rewritten as

1: $\qquad\qquad 2 + \delta \geq 0$

2: $\qquad\qquad 6 + \delta \geq 0$

or, equivalently,

1: $\qquad\qquad -2 \leq \delta$

2: $\qquad\qquad -6 \leq \delta$

**TABLE 5.19** *NEW Z ROW: PRELIMINARY*

| Basic | Z | $x_1$ | $x_2$ | $S_1$ | $S_2$ | $S_3$ | Solution |
|---|---|---|---|---|---|---|---|
| Z | 1 | 1 | $0 - \delta$ | 0 | $\tfrac{3}{4}$ | 0 | 36,000 |

**TABLE 5.20** *NEW Z ROW: FINAL*

| Basic | Z | $x_1$ | $x_2$ | $S_1$ | $S_2$ | $S_3$ | Solution |
|-------|---|-------|-------|-------|-------|-------|----------|
| Z | 1 | $1 + (\tfrac{1}{2})\delta$ | 0 | 0 | $\tfrac{3}{4} + (\tfrac{1}{8})\delta$ | 0 | $36{,}000 + 6{,}000\delta$ |

That equivalent system has the obvious solution

$$-2 \le \delta$$

Therefore, as long as the original $6 profit contribution of a unit of product II is not reduced by more than $2, the current basic feasible solution remains optimal. If that $6 contribution were to be reduced by more than $2, however, the final tableau would still have a negative coefficient in the $Z$ row, and another iteration would be required. For instance, if $\delta = -3$, then the coefficient under $x_1$ in Table 5.20 would be

$$1 + (\tfrac{1}{2})(-3) = -\tfrac{1}{2}$$

which says $Z$ could be improved by bringing the variable $x_1$ into the basis. Thus reducing profitability of a unit of product II by $3 (to $6 − $3 = $3) means that it would now be worthwhile to manufacture some units of product I. Before that change, only units of product II were manufactured, basically because $6 was quite a lot more per-unit profit than the $2 per unit of product I. That condition (high per-unit profit for product II) is also the reason there was no upper bound on $\delta$. *Increasing* the profitability of product II does not change the *current* decision to manufacture *only* product II.

Finally, how *sensitive* is the current solution to changes in the objective-function coefficient of $x_2$? The inequality $-2 \le \delta$ tells us that if we have estimated the profit per unit of product II as $6 and are pretty sure that it is correct to within at least $2, then our decision would not change; we would still manufacture as many units of product II as possible. But if our estimate of $6 per unit only reflects a belief that might be phrased as "$6 ± $3," that is, we think the profit per unit is somewhere in the range $3 to $9, then we realize we could have made the wrong decision. In that case we should devote more time and effort to obtaining a better estimate of the profitability of product II.

### Example 5.9
### Simultaneous Changes in Objective-Function Coefficients

For a final example of a sensitivity analysis, let's investigate the effect of simultaneous changes in profitability for units of product I *and* product II in the Dooley Corporation problem (Example 5.1). The procedure is just a natural extension of the ideas presented in Examples 5.7 and 5.8.

TABLE 5.21   PRELIMINARY Z ROW

| Basic | Z | $x_1$ | $x_2$ | $S_1$ | $S_2$ | $S_3$ | Solution |
|-------|---|-------|-------|-------|-------|-------|----------|
| Z | 1 | $1 - \delta_1$ | $-\delta_2$ | 0 | $\frac{3}{4}$ | 0 | 36,000 |

Let $\delta_1$ be the change in the objective-function coefficient of $x_1$ and $\delta_2$ be the change in the objective-function coefficient of $x_2$. Then the Z row of the original optimal tableau (Table 5.18) would become as shown in Table 5.21.

Because $x_2$ is a *basic* variable, we must obtain a zero coefficient under $x_2$. So we multiply the optimal $x_2$ row in Table 5.18 by $\delta_2$ and add to the Z row in Table 5.21. This gives the correct Z row for the simplex method, as shown in Table 5.22.

The nonnegativity requirement for all coefficients in an optimal Z row produces the system:

1: $$1 - \delta_1 + \tfrac{1}{2}\delta_2 \geq 0$$

2: $$\tfrac{3}{4} + \tfrac{1}{8}\delta_2 \geq 0$$

or, equivalently,

1: $$2\delta_1 - \delta_2 \leq 2$$

2: $$\delta_2 \geq -6$$

The graphical solution of that system is shown in Figure 5.8.

Any pair $(\delta_1, \delta_2)$ that falls in the shaded region of Figure 5.8 is associated with the current feasible solution still remaining optimal. Consider, for instance, the point

$$(\delta_1, \delta_2) = (-1, -3)$$

This means that the profit per unit of product I is reduced by $1 (from $2 to $1), while the profit per unit of product II is reduced by $3 (from $6 to $3). According to Table 5.22, the new value of Z will be reduced to

TABLE 5.22   FINAL Z ROW

| Basic | Z | $x_1$ | $x_2$ | $S_1$ | $S_2$ | $S_3$ | Solution |
|-------|---|-------|-------|-------|-------|-------|----------|
| Z | 1 | $1 - \delta_1 + \tfrac{1}{2}\delta_2$ | 0 | 0 | $\frac{3}{4} + \tfrac{1}{8}\delta_2$ | 0 | $36,000 + 6,000\delta_2$ |

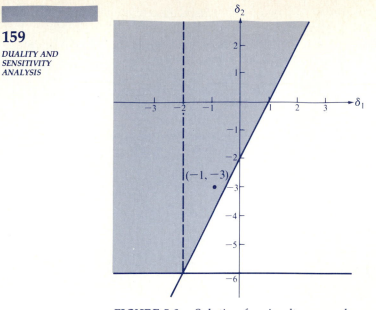

**FIGURE 5.8**   Solution for simultaneous changes in profitability of
units of product I and product II

$$Z = 36{,}000 + 6{,}000(-3)$$

$$= 36{,}000 - 18{,}000$$

$$= 18{,}000$$

But the *decision* will still be to manufacture $x_2 = 6{,}000$ units of product II
and no product I (see Table 5.18).

Finally, notice the dashed vertical line in Figure 5.8, the line $\delta_1 = -2$.
This just reminds us that if $\delta_1$ is *less* than $-2$ (some of the shaded points
have smaller $\delta_1$ coordinates), we would be talking about negative profit,
or *loss* associated with the manufacture of product I.  Note that *all* points
in Figure 5.8 to the left of that line are in the shaded region (provided $\delta_2$
$\geq -6$), which just says that we *never* change the decision (manufacture
only product II) whenever the manufacture of product I results in a loss.

## 5.9   FORMULATING AND EXPLOITING DUAL PROBLEMS

To conclude this chapter we return to the concept of duality in linear
programming.  You have already seen dual variables interpreted as implicit
values of resources, and you have seen one other use of the dual in a
sensitivity analysis (Example 5.7).  These notions were economic ones,
and although the primary advantage in duality resides in the enhancement
of one's comprehension of the economics of a problem, there exists a
secondary advantage.  Often the dual will be a much easier problem to

solve than the primal. Thus a *computational* advantage may sometimes be realized by formulating and solving the dual.

It is not necessary to be able to reason through the economics of the problem to be able to formulate a dual. One may simply learn some standard rules which allow an easy formulation of the dual of *any* LP problem. The rules, of course, are based upon general economic interpretations.

---

**RULES FOR DUAL FORMULATION**

**1 If the primal is a maximization problem, the dual is a minimization problem.**

**2 Objective-function coefficients in the primal become right-hand sides of dual constraints.**

**3 Columns of constraint coefficients in the primal become rows of constraint coefficients in the dual.**

**4 If a primal variable is nonnegative, the associated dual constraint is a "greater-than-or-equal-to" type.**

**5 If a primal variable is unrestricted in sign, the associated dual constraint is an equation.**

**6 If a primal constraint is an equation, the associated dual variable is unrestricted in sign.**

**7 If a primal constraint is a "less-than-or-equal-to" type, the associated dual variable is nonnegative.**

**8 The dual of the dual is the primal.**

---

Note particularly that no rule was stated for the case that the primal constraint is a "greater-than-or-equal-to" type. This is because such a constraint may always be multiplied by $-1$ to change the sense of the inequality. For instance, the constraint

$$2x_1 + 4x_2 + 5x_3 \geq 8$$

in Example 5.10 following is equivalent to the constraint

$$-2x_1 - 4x_2 - 5x_3 \leq -8$$

**Example 5.10**

*Primal*                                                    *Dual*

        Maximize Z                                  Minimize Y

where                                                       where

$$Z = 3x_1 - 2x_2 + x_3 \qquad\qquad Y = 6y_1 + 7y_2 - 8y_3$$

subject to

$$2x_1 + 3x_2 - x_3 = 6$$

$$x_1 - 2x_2 + 3x_3 \leq 7$$

$$2x_1 + 4x_2 + 5x_3 \geq 8$$

$$x_1 \geq 0 \qquad x_2 \geq 0$$

$$x_3 \text{ unrestricted in sign}$$

subject to

$$2y_1 + y_2 - 2y_3 \geq 3$$

$$3y_1 - 2y_2 - 4y_3 \geq -2$$

$$-y_1 + 3y_2 - 5y_3 = 1$$

$$y_1 \text{ unrestricted in sign}$$

$$y_2 \geq 0 \qquad y_3 \geq 0$$

Since there are three "resource" constraints in the primal, there are three variables in the dual. Note in particular the third column of coefficients in the dual constraints and the $-8$ coefficient of $y_3$ in the dual objective function. These come from having multiplied the third primal constraint by $-1$ (see the inequality immediately preceding Example 5.10), that modification also making $y_3$ nonnegative in the dual formulation. Also, observe that the first (equality) constraint in the primal means that $y_1$ is unrestricted in sign, and the third (equality) constraint in the dual comes from $x_3$ being unrestricted in sign.

The $-2$ right-hand side of the second dual constraint comes from the $-2$ coefficient in the primal objective function. That negative right-hand side is perfectly allowable at this stage, since all we are doing is *formulating* the dual, not attempting to solve it. If we were to set up the dual problem for simplex solution, then we would multiply that constraint by $-1$, or we would use the following equivalent version:

$$-3y_1 + 2y_2 + 4y_3 \leq 2$$

**Example 5.11**

*Primal*

Minimize $Z$

where

$$Z = 2x_1 + 5x_2$$

subject to

$$x_1 + 3x_2 \geq 4$$

$$3x_1 + 5x_2 \geq 7$$

$$x_1 + x_2 \geq 3$$

$$x_1, x_2 \geq 0$$

*Dual*

Maximize $Y$

where

$$Y = 4y_1 + 7y_2 + 3y_3$$

subject to

$$y_1 + 3y_2 + y_3 \leq 2$$

$$3y_1 + 5y_2 + y_3 \leq 5$$

$$y_1, y_2, y_3 \geq 0$$

This primal problem, involving only two variables, could of course be solved graphically. But suppose one intended using simplex tableaus. The dual offers a distinct computational advantage in that case. Its constraints each require only a single slack variable, while each constraint in the primal requires both a surplus and an artificial variable to set the problem up for solution by the simplex method. Since this primal is a type usually associated with "blending" or "diet" problems, which involve cost minimization, this computational advantage would often be encountered in practice.

The solution for the primal, of course, can be found in the optimal $Y$ row of the final tableau of the dual solution, underneath the slack variables. For instance, three revised tableaus give the final tableau shown as Table 5.23, from which the optimal dual-variable values are found to be

$$y_1 = \tfrac{3}{2} \qquad y_2 = 0 \qquad y_3 = \tfrac{1}{2}$$

The solution for the primal, obtained from the $Y$ row of Table 5.23, is

$$\text{Min } Z = \tfrac{15}{2} \qquad \text{at } (x_1, x_2) = (\tfrac{5}{2}, \tfrac{1}{2})$$

## 5.10  SUMMARY AND CONCLUSIONS

Central to the economic interpretation of an optimal LP solution is the notion of implicit value of a resource and the concept of duality. The implicit value (shadow price) of a resource is its value to the company for generating profit if all available resources are used optimally. Another way of looking at the same concept is to regard the shadow price (implicit value) as the price the company pays by giving up a unit of resource to acquire its profit-making capacity.

The dual is an alternate formulation of an LP problem, with decision variables being implicit values. The solution of the dual, which is itself an LP problem, yields the implicit values directly, but those values can also be obtained by inspecting the optimal tableau for the original (primal) problem. Although the most important benefit of the concept of duality is its enhancement of economic understanding, sometimes a dual formulation of the problem offers a computational advantage as well.

Simplex tableaus can also be used efficiently for investigating the effect of changes in input coefficients of the problem. The coefficients may not be known precisely, but only within certain ranges. It is important to

**TABLE 5.23**  *OPTIMAL TABLEAU FOR THE DUAL*

| Basic | $Y$ | $y_1$ | $y_2$ | $y_3$ | $S_1$ | $S_2$ | Solution | |
|---|---|---|---|---|---|---|---|---|
| $Y$ | 1 | 0 | 3 | 0 | $\tfrac{5}{2}$ | $\tfrac{1}{2}$ | $\tfrac{15}{2}$ | ← optimal |
| $y_3$ | 0 | 0 | 2 | 1 | $\tfrac{3}{2}$ | $-\tfrac{1}{2}$ | $\tfrac{1}{2}$ | |
| $y_1$ | 0 | 1 | 1 | 0 | $-\tfrac{1}{2}$ | $\tfrac{1}{2}$ | $\tfrac{3}{2}$ | |

determine the sensitivity of the optimal solution to small changes in the assumed values of those coefficients. Only the initial and optimal tableaus are required to carry out that process, known as sensitivity or postoptimality analysis.

Both duality and sensitivity analyses have important managerial implications. Their most important contribution is a thorough appreciation of the economics of the problem. Implicit values tell the manager what price would be reasonable for acquisition of scarce resources, or which resources are in abundance and could be diverted to other uses within the firm. Sensitivity analysis lets the manager know if more effort should be given to estimating certain parameters of the problem, and when changes in those estimated parameters might produce a change in the basic nature of the decision.

Most computer codes for LP recognize the importance of duality and postoptimality analyses. In Chapter 6, where a variety of applications of linear programming are considered using computer-generated solutions, implicit values are called *opportunity costs,* and the two types of sensitivity analyses done here are called *ranging* analyses. As you will see, in almost every LP example presented in Chapter 6, it is deemed important to request at least one type of ranging analysis, and opportunity costs are quoted for every example.

## KEY WORDS AND PHRASES

**Implicit value**  The implied worth of an extra unit of resource if all resources are used optimally. The same thing as shadow price.

**Shadow price**  The price paid by giving up a unit of resource to realize its optimal profit-making potential. The same thing as implicit value.

**Primal problem**  The mathematical formulation of an LP problem that uses as decision variables the variables associated with the primary objective of the problem, such as units of product or amount of investment.

**Dual problem**  The mathematical formulation of an LP problem that uses implicit values as decision variables.

**Scarce resource**  A resource that is completely exhausted if the optimal solution of an LP problem is implemented. Only a scarce resource can have a nonzero implicit value.

**Primal-dual analysis**  The simultaneous consideration of both the primal and dual optimal solutions with a view to enhancing the quality of managerial decisions.

**Sensitivity analysis**  An investigation of the effect on a current optimal solution of changes in some of the coefficients of the LP problem.

**Resource availability**  A phrase used to indicate consideration of right-hand sides of constraints. A change here only affects the feasibility of the current optimal solution.

**Profit contribution**   A phrase used to indicate consideration of objective-function coefficients.   A change here only affects the optimality of the current feasible solution.

**Initial and final tableaus**   The only two simplex tableaus required for the sensitivity analyses discussed here.

**Simultaneous changes**   A phrase implying a sensitivity analysis involving changes in two or more coefficients in the original LP problem.


## EXERCISES

◆ **5.1** The Small-Time Can Company makes three types of frozen food containers, types $A$, $B$, and $C$, with respective profit contributions of $0.005, $0.007, and $0.008 per container.   A container of type $A$ requires 0.5 ounces of aluminum, 10 square inches of cardboard, and 0.1 minutes during its production. A type $B$ container requires 0.8 ounces of aluminum, 12 square inches of cardboard, and 0.2 minutes, while a type $C$ container requires 1 ounce of aluminum, 16 square inches of cardboard, and 0.2 minutes.

Available are 1,200 ounces of aluminum, 32,000 square inches of cardboard, and 7,200 minutes during a given production period.   The objective is to maximize profit contribution for the period.

Formulate the problem directly as a minimization problem, using as variables the implicit values of 1 ounce of aluminum, 1 square inch of cardboard, and 1 minute.

◆ **5.2** Formulate and solve the Small-Time Can Company problem of Exercise 5.1 as a primal problem with variables being the number of units of type $A$, $B$, and $C$ containers to produce.   State the implicit values for the three resources, and verify that they give the solution for the problem you formulated in Exercise 5.1.

**5.3** Formulate the problem posed as Exercise 4.5 at the end of Chapter 4 directly as a minimization problem.   Use as variables the implicit values of a minute of machine $A$ time and a minute of machine $B$ time.   Solve for these implicit values by solving the primal problem; that is, use the tableaus from your solution of Exercise 4.5 (or solve it now if you have not done so previously) to determine the optimal dual-variable values.

**5.4** Formulate the Suhonaha motorcycle dealer's problem, Exercise 4.29 at the end of Chapter 4, directly as a minimization problem.   Use as variables the implicit values of $1 of capital, 1 cubic foot of storage space, 1 hour of sales time, and 1 hour of mechanic time.   Set up the initial simplex tableau for both the primal and dual versions of the problem, and comment on which you would prefer to use (and why) if you had to solve the problem.

◆ **5.5** Solve the diet problem, Example 2.3 in the body of Chapter 2, by formulating and solving its dual.   Compare this solution with your work on Exercise 4.14 at the end of Chapter 4.

**5.6** The city manager of Repellent, Wyoming, is making preparations for the annual pretourist mosquito-spraying operation.   The spray consists of two chemicals, $A$ and $B$. A consulting biologist has recommended that at least 15,000 pounds of chemical $A$ and 5,000 pounds of chemical $B$ must be dispensed if the spraying operation is to be effective.

A premixed spray may be purchased in any quantity from any of three chemical companies: $D$, $M$, and $P$. Costs and fractions of chemicals $A$ and $B$ per pound of each company's spray are given in the accompanying table.

|  | Company | | |
|---|---|---|---|
|  | D | M | P |
| Cost per pound | $1.00 | $1.50 | $2.00 |
| Pounds of A | 0.25 | 0.50 | 0.80 |
| Pounds of B | 0.75 | 0.50 | 0.20 |

The city manager wants to know how many pounds of spray to purchase from each company so that the biologist's recommendation is satisfied at minimum cost. Formulate both the primal and the dual of this problem, and solve it by whatever means seems easiest. State the optimal number of pounds to purchase from each company, as well as the minimum cost.

✦ **5.7** Refer to the Archaic Bakery problem, Exercise 3.18 at the end of Chapter 3. During the current planning period, Archaic has the opportunity to purchase extra flour, sugar, and salt from a competitor who is going out of business. The competitor will sell a pound of flour for $0.20, a pound of sugar for $0.50, and a teaspoon of salt for $0.01. Is it to Archaic's advantage to buy any ingredients from the defunct competitor?

Also, Archaic can hire out-of-work mixers and bakers or out-of-work cake decorators on a part-time basis. They can get mixers and bakers for $0.75 per hour and cake decorators for $1.00 per hour. Should Archaic Bakery hire any such extra help?

**5.8** Refer to Exercise 5.7. Suppose that the competitor only has available 600 pounds of flour, 200 pounds of sugar, and 400 teaspoons of salt. The out-of-work people, however, are available for an unlimited number of hours. Completely analyze the Archaic Bakery problem under all conditions that have now been stated, recommending a strategy which will produce the maximum possible profit for the current planning period.

✦ **5.9** Formulate the dual of the following primal problem:

$$\text{Maximize } Z$$

where

$$Z = 100x_1 + 70x_2 + 30x_3$$

subject to

$$20x_1 + 10x_2 + 5x_3 \le 1{,}000$$

$$x_1 + x_2 + x_3 \le 50$$

$$x_1, x_2, x_3 \ge 0$$

**5.10** Formulate the dual of the following primal problem:

Minimize C

where
$$C = 10x_1 + 4x_2 + 25x_3 + 15x_4$$

subject to
$$5x_1 + 10x_2 + x_3 - 2x_4 \geq 5,000$$
$$x_1 - 2x_2 + x_4 \geq 1,000$$
$$6x_1 + 2x_3 + 3x_4 \geq 2,000$$
$$x_1, x_2, x_3, x_4 \geq 0$$

✦ **5.11** Formulate the dual of the following primal problem:

Maximize Y

where
$$Y = 6y_1 + y_2 + 5y_3$$

subject to
$$y_1 + y_2 + y_3 \leq 400$$
$$2y_1 + 3y_2 - 4y_3 \geq 800$$
$$y_1 - 10y_2 + 20y_3 = 200$$
$$y_1 \geq 0 \qquad y_2 \text{ unrestricted in sign} \qquad y_3 \geq 0$$

**5.12** Formulate the dual of the following primal problem:

Minimize Z

where
$$Z = 2x_1 + 6x_2 - 4x_3$$

subject to
$$x_1 + x_2 + x_3 \leq 300$$
$$2x_1 - 2x_2 + 7x_3 \geq 10$$
$$x_1 - x_2 + 3x_3 = 50$$
$$x_1 + x_2 \geq 20$$
$$x_1 \geq 0 \qquad x_2 \geq 0 \qquad x_3 \text{ unrestricted in sign}$$

Exercises 5.13 through 5.18 are based on the tableaus that are presented in Table 5.24. They come from the problem described as Exercise 4.5 at the end of Chapter 4.

Let $x_1$ = the number of units of product I to manufacture

$x_2$ = the number of units of product II to manufacture

$x_3$ = the number of units of product III to manufacture

Then the model for that problem is

$$\text{Maximize } Z$$

where

$$Z = x_1 + 2x_2 + 3x_3 \qquad \text{profit in dollars}$$

subject to

$$2x_1 + x_2 + 3x_3 \leq 4,800 \qquad \text{minutes: machine } A$$

$$4x_1 + 4x_2 + 2x_3 \leq 3,600 \qquad \text{minutes: machine } B$$

$$x_1, x_2, x_3 \geq 0$$

✦ **5.13 a** By how much can the 4,800 minutes available on machine $A$ change so that the current optimal basic solution will remain feasible?

**b** If 5 hours (300 minutes) are added to those currently available for the use of machine $A$, what would be the new optimal solution? (Use the results of your analysis in part $a$ above; do not re-solve the problem with new simplex tableaus.)

**5.14 a** By how much can the 3,600 minutes available on machine $B$ change so that the current optimal basic solution will remain feasible?

**b** If 2 hours (120 minutes) are deducted from those currently available for the use of machine $B$, what will be the new optimal solution?

✦ **5.15 a** By how much can the right-hand sides of the original two constraints change simultaneously with the effect that the current optimal solution remains feasible?

**b** If 5 hours are deducted from the machine $A$ availability and 20 hours are added to the machine $B$ availability, is the current basic optimal solution still feasible? If so, what is the new optimal solution?

**5.16 a** By how much can the original objective-function coefficient of $x_1$ change so that the current basic feasible solution remains optimal?

**b** By how much can the original objective-function coefficient of $x_2$ change so that the current basic feasible solution remains optimal?

**TABLE 5.24** INITIAL AND OPTIMAL TABLEAUS

| Basic | Z | $x_1$ | $x_2$ | $x_3$ | $S_1$ | $S_2$ | Solution | |
|-------|---|-------|-------|-------|-------|-------|----------|---|
| Z | 1 | $-1$ | $-2$ | $-3$ | 0 | 0 | 0 | ← initial |
| $S_1$ | 0 | 2 | 1 | 3 | 1 | 0 | 4,800 | |
| $S_2$ | 0 | 4 | 4 | 2 | 0 | 1 | 3,600 | |
| . | . | . | . | . | . | . | . | |
| . | . | . | . | . | . | . | . | |
| . | . | . | . | . | . | . | . | |
| Z | 1 | $\frac{9}{5}$ | 0 | 0 | $\frac{4}{5}$ | $\frac{3}{10}$ | 4,920 | ← optimal |
| $x_3$ | 0 | $\frac{2}{5}$ | 0 | 1 | $\frac{2}{5}$ | $-\frac{1}{10}$ | 1,560 | |
| $x_2$ | 0 | $\frac{4}{5}$ | 1 | 0 | $-\frac{1}{5}$ | $\frac{3}{10}$ | 120 | |

◆ **5.17** By how much can the objective-function coefficients of $x_1$ and $x_2$ change simultaneously with the effect that the current basic feasible solution remains optimal?

**5.18** By how much can the objective-function coefficients of $x_2$ and $x_3$ change simultaneously so that the current basic feasible solution remains optimal?

Exercises 5.19 through 5.24 are based on the following problem.

Kuttum Corporation produces four types of chain saw: Economy, Standard, Deluxe, and Super. Although the housings, finishes, and general quality of the saws differ, they have many parts in common. Parts A, B, and C are interchangeable among the four saws, although they occur in different quantities. Assume that profit contributions of each saw depend only on parts A, B, and C.

For the current month, these parts are in limited supply. Table 5.25 gives the number of parts used per type of saw, the profit contributions per saw, and the availability of the parts.

Kuttum's objective is to maximize profit from the month's production of chain saws. How many of each type of saw should be produced?

The mathematical model of the Kuttum Corporation problem follows.

Let $x_1$ = the number of Economy saws to produce

$x_2$ = the number of Standard saws to produce

$x_3$ = the number of Deluxe saws to produce

$x_4$ = the number of Super saws to produce

Then the problem is

$$\text{Maximize } Z$$

where

$$Z = 30x_1 + 50x_2 + 60x_3 + 72x_4$$

subject to

$$2x_1 + 3x_2 + 4x_3 + 6x_4 \leq 300$$

$$4x_1 + 2x_2 + 3x_3 + 3x_4 \leq 450$$

$$6x_1 + 4x_2 + 4x_3 + 2x_4 \leq 250$$

$$x_1, x_2, x_3, x_4 \geq 0$$

**TABLE 5.25**

| | Number of parts per saw | | | | Number of |
| | Economy | Standard | Deluxe | Super | parts available |
|---|---|---|---|---|---|
| Part A | 2 | 3 | 4 | 6 | 300 |
| Part B | 4 | 2 | 3 | 3 | 450 |
| Part C | 6 | 4 | 4 | 2 | 250 |
| Profit per saw | $30 | $50 | $60 | $72 | |

## TABLE 5.26  INITIAL AND OPTIMAL TABLEAUS

| Basic | Z | $x_1$ | $x_2$ | $x_3$ | $x_4$ | $S_1$ | $S_2$ | $S_3$ | Solution |
|---|---|---|---|---|---|---|---|---|---|
| Z | 1 | $-30$ | $-50$ | $-60$ | $-72$ | 0 | 0 | 0 | 0 |
| $S_1$ | 0 | 2 | 3 | 4 | 6 | 1 | 0 | 0 | 300 |
| $S_2$ | 0 | 4 | 2 | 3 | 3 | 0 | 1 | 0 | 450 |
| $S_3$ | 0 | 6 | 4 | 4 | 2 | 0 | 0 | 1 | 250 |
| . | . | . | . | . | . | . | . | . | . |
| . | . | . | . | . | . | . | . | . | . |
| . | . | . | . | . | . | . | . | . | . |
| Z | 1 | $\frac{170}{9}$ | 0 | $\frac{4}{9}$ | 0 | $\frac{94}{9}$ | 0 | $\frac{14}{3}$ | 4,300 |
| $x_4$ | 0 | $-\frac{5}{9}$ | 0 | $\frac{2}{9}$ | 1 | $\frac{2}{9}$ | 0 | $-\frac{1}{6}$ | 25 |
| $S_2$ | 0 | $\frac{19}{9}$ | 0 | $\frac{5}{9}$ | 0 | $-\frac{4}{9}$ | 1 | $-\frac{1}{6}$ | 275 |
| $x_2$ | 0 | $\frac{16}{9}$ | 1 | $\frac{8}{9}$ | 0 | $-\frac{1}{9}$ | 0 | $\frac{1}{3}$ | 50 |

The initial and optimal tableaus are shown in Table 5.26.

◆ **5.19** By how much can the number of parts $A$ change so that the current optimal basic solution will remain feasible?  The number of parts $C$?

**5.20** By how much can the number of parts $A$ and parts $C$ change simultaneously so that the current optimal basic solution remains feasible?

◆ **5.21 a** By how much can the original \$60 profit per Deluxe saw change so that the current basic feasible solution remains optimal?
  **b** Suppose that the profit per Deluxe saw increased to \$62.  Now what is the optimal solution?

◆ **5.22** By how much can the original profit per Standard saw change so that the current basic feasible solution remains optimal?

**5.23** Suppose that the profit per Economy saw is increased to \$40 while the profit per Super saw is decreased to \$65.  Is the current basic feasible solution still optimal?  If not, what is the optimal solution?

**5.24** Suppose that the profit per Economy saw is increased to \$35, the profit per Standard saw is increased to \$60, and the profit per Deluxe saw is decreased to \$60.  Is the current basic feasible solution still optimal?  If not, what is the optimal solution?

## SELECTED REFERENCES

Anderson, D. R., D. J. Sweeney, and T. A. Williams: *An Introduction to Management Science*, 3d ed., West Publishing Company, St. Paul, Minn., 1982.

Bierman, H., C. P. Bonini, and W. H. Hausman: *Quantitative Analysis for Business Decisions*, 6th ed., Richard D. Irwin, Inc., Homewood, Ill., 1981.

Eck, R. D.: *Operations Research for Business*, Wadsworth Publishing Company, Belmont, Calif., 1976.

Hillier, F. S., and G. J. Lieberman: *Introduction to Operations Research*, 3d ed., Holden-Day, Inc., San Francisco, 1980.

Kim, C.: *Introduction to Linear Programming*, Holt, Rinehart, and Winston, New York, 1971.

Levin, R. I., C. A. Kirkpatrick, and D. S. Rubin: *Quantitative Approaches to Management*, 5th ed., McGraw-Hill Book Company, New York, 1982.

Loomba, N. P.: *Linear Programming: An Introductory Analysis*, McGraw-Hill Book Company, New York, 1964.

Strum, J. E.: "Note on Two-Sided Shadow Prices," *Journal of Accounting Research*, vol. 7, 1969.

Taha, H. A.: *Operations Research*, 3d ed., Macmillan Publishing Company, Inc., New York, 1982.

Wagner, H. M.: *Principles of Operations Research*, Prentice-Hall, Inc., Englewood Cliffs, N.J., 1969.

# APPLIED LINEAR PROGRAMMING MODELS WITH COMPUTER SOLUTIONS

Now we are ready to consider linear programming analyses done as they would actually be done in the modern world of computer-assisted business management. From previous chapters you have learned how to formulate models and interpret optimal tableaus, tasks that require creative thinking and consequently cannot be done for you by computers. But computers excel at doing arithmetic rapidly, and the steps in the tabular simplex method are sufficiently mechanical that they may be conveniently programmed. By appealing to computers we can speed up the solution process, reduce the chance of arithmetic error, and relegate the tedium to a machine. Most importantly, we are thus freed to devote our energy only to formulation and interpretation.

Be assured, however, that all the hard work you have done up to this point has not been in vain. Without your ability to formulate an LP problem in mathematical terms a program for its solution is useless, since you have to be able to tell the computer what specific problem you wish to solve. Without your ability to interpret numbers in optimal tableaus and to further analyze those tableaus postoptimally, the printed output of a computer is just an impressive but meaningless array of numbers. And without your appreciation of the justification for and the mechanics of the simplex method, you would never know what methods the computer used to obtain its answers. That is, and this point cannot be emphasized too strongly, your ability to gain maximum benefit from a computer-generated solution depends upon your complete understanding of the processes involved. Intimate familiarity with all aspects of the simplex method—its theory, its limitations, and its mechanics—means that you are unlikely to commit a formulation error or to misinterpret the computer output.

Further, because of the computer solutions to be utilized in this chapter we are free to consider larger, more complex problems. Partly because of that new freedom, you will also see a wider variety of LP applications in the sections to follow, applications that could not be presented earlier, at least along with their solutions, since their intrinsic nature demands more variables and more constraints than could be managed conveniently with just pencil and paper. Some of these applications also anticipate the specialized models and solution algorithms to be presented in Chapter 7.

The emphasis in this chapter is on interpretation of solutions instead of the mechanics of obtaining them. The examples to follow and most of the exercises at the end of the chapter come complete with computer output from a standard software system. The end-of-chapter exercises are of equal importance to the examples selected for inclusion in the body of the chapter, with the entire problem selection indicating the broad applicability of linear programming.

## 6.1 COMPUTER PACKAGES FOR LINEAR PROGRAMMING

Commercially and academically originated computer programs for linear programming are nowadays widely distributed and readily available. Computer manufacturers like International Business Machines (IBM) and Control Data Corporation (CDC) not only produce computer hardware, but also are heavily involved in designing and marketing software compatible with their machines. Many other companies specialize only in producing such software, packages of efficient programs adaptable to various brands of computers. A number of university computer centers have developed their own packages of programs for whatever type of computer they may own, and some of these packages have been distributed to other computer centers and businesses possessing the same basic hardware.

Examples of well-known mathematical programming systems, which do linear programming but which also have some nonlinear capabilities, include IBM's MPSX and CDC's APEX systems, the LP codes in IMSL (International Mathematical & Statistical Libraries), and Northwestern University's MPOS (Multi Purpose Optimization System). Each of these

**173**

*APPLIED LINEAR
PROGRAMMING
MODELS WITH
COMPUTER
SOLUTIONS*

systems, and the numerous other systems that are available commercially, comes with its own documentation: instructions on how to use the system.

Regardless of the particular system, minimum documentation must inform the user about two things: input and output. That is, the user must be told how to input her or his problem so the system can correctly interpret the data and execute the solution process, and the user must be told how to read the final output from the system. Note the occurrence of the two main problems in LP: formulation and interpretation. The formulated LP problem is input into the system, and system output is read, then interpreted.

In order to demonstrate features common to such packaged systems the author has chosen to use the MPOS* code. Specifically, the computer input and output to be observed in the following applications is for MPOS, Version 4.0, originating in 1978 from Vogelback Computing Center at Northwestern University (see Cohen and Stein, 1978). That system was designed to solve optimization problems on CDC 6000/CYBER computers such as the CDC CYBER computer currently in operation at the University of Wyoming. This choice of MPOS was made for three reasons. First, it is the system most familiar to the author, so the potential for erroneous decription is minimized. Second, input to MPOS is in a format almost identical to the mathematical formulations with which you are already well acquainted. Third, the output from MPOS can be requested in tabular form very similar to the tableaus for hand calculations used in earlier chapters of this text. MPOS, like all other good LP codes, also has the capability for sensitivity analyses.

Even though a specific software package, MPOS, is being used here, you may anticipate little difficulty converting your thinking to some other system, such as IBM's MPSX. All good software systems for linear programming have well-documented input-output features that are easy to understand if one first understands completely the general linear programming problem.


## 6.2 FAMILIARIZATION VIA A FAMILIAR PROBLEM

Before we move on to consideration of LP applications, you must become familiar with the basic instructions for MPOS. The best way to learn any new solution technique is to apply it to a problem you have already solved some other way. Then you will be able to recognize the answer and to determine the location in the output of other helpful numbers. Familiarization with input-output for MPOS will be accomplished herein by way

---

* MPOS (Multi Purpose Optimization System) is a proprietary computer software product of Northwestern University and is currently available for use by license only on CDC 6000 and Cyber series computers.

of a small three-variable problem that you have considered more than once in earlier chapters.

### Example 6.1
### Yummy Cereal Company

In Chapters 4 and 5 you saw the Yummy Cereal Company problem, the complete description of which occurs in Example 4.2 of Chapter 4. Recall that $x_1$, $x_2$, and $x_3$ are, respectively, the number of pounds of Crunchies, Chewies, and Gummies to be produced in order to maximize profit, where constraints reflect the consumption and availability, in ounces, of wheat, corn, and bran. The complete LP model follows:

$$\text{Maximize } Z$$

where            $Z = 40x_1 + 30x_2 + 50x_3$            profit in cents

subject to            $6x_1 + 4x_2 + \phantom{0}x_3 \leq 32{,}000$            wheat

$6x_1 + 7x_2 + \phantom{0}3x_3 \leq 16{,}000$            corn

$4x_1 + 5x_2 + 12x_3 \leq 24{,}000$            bran

$x_1, x_2, x_3 \geq 0$            nonnegativity

Table 6.1 gives the MPOS input. On the CDC CYBER computer this is simply a little control program that is written and stored in file, then MPOS is called up to execute the instructions on file. This job was done

**TABLE 6.1**  *MPOS CONTROL PROGRAM FOR YUMMY CEREAL COMPANY PROBLEM*

```
TITLE
YUMMY CEREAL COMPANY
REGULAR
VARIABLES
X1 TO X3
MAXIMIZE
40X1 + 30X2 + 50X3
CONSTRAINTS
6X1 + 4X2 + X3 .LE. 32000
6X1 + 7X2 + 3X3 .LE. 16000
4X1 + 5X2 + 12X3 .LE. 24000
RNGOBJ
RNGRHS
PRINT
OPTIMIZE
STOP
```

**175**

*APPLIED LINEAR*
*PROGRAMMING*
*MODELS WITH*
*COMPUTER*
*SOLUTIONS*

from a remote cathode-ray terminal (CRT), but it could have been submitted on punched cards. In either mode the first letter in each line of the program occurs in column 1, a convenient feature of MPOS.

The commands in Table 6.1 represent all of the input necessary to work our little problem with MPOS. The MPOS system has been told what variables are involved, that the problem involves maximization, what the objective function and the constraints are, and to do sensitivity analyses on coefficients in the objective function and the right-hand sides of the constraints.

Note particularly the middle instructions in the program. The objective function and the constraints are simply written out as they appear in the mathematical formulation, except that "≤" has clearly been replaced by ".LE." Thus only a few lines of Table 6.1 remain to be described for you.

The first two lines are like a "comment" in FORTRAN or a "remark" in BASIC: they give a title to the problem, a title that MPOS will print at the top of each page of output. The command REGULAR tells MPOS that you want the LP problem solved under the REGULAR option, which produces tableaus like the simplex tableaus of Chapter 4, using the two-phase method whenever artificial variables are necessary. In addition to seven nonlinear programming options, MPOS offers the choice of six LP procedures, including the revised simplex method (a matrix-algebra version) and a procedure for using generalized upper bounds when the constraints take on a particular form. For our purposes the REGULAR option will usually be adequate.

Following the last constraint in Table 6.1 you see the command RNGOBJ, which mnemonically stands for "range the objective-function coefficients" and produces the one-at-a-time sensitivity analyses for those coefficients. Likewise, RNGRHS ranges the right-hand sides of the constraints, or produces individual sensitivity analyses on the resources.

The PRINT command tells MPOS to print only the initial and final tableaus. If this had been replaced by PRINT 1, MPOS would have printed every intermediate tableau. If PRINT is deleted from the program, no tableaus are printed but a compact output of the solution is provided. This last option will be the one we will use in most of the applications to follow, since the compact output will contain everything we need to know. Here PRINT was included so you could compare the computer output to tableaus from Chapters 4 and 5, thus enhancing your understanding of the output.

The word OPTIMIZE is a "run" command. It tells MPOS you are ready to execute the previous instructions. Finally, STOP says you are finished, so MPOS returns control of the computer to you. If you want to run a *sequence* of LP problems, you would simply put TITLE after OPTIMIZE, state the new problem, and continue doing this until the end of the last problem is reached, where you would then put STOP.

Simple, isn't it? Of course, MPOS comes to a computer installation with a 154-page user's guide (see Cohen and Stein, 1978), so obviously the system has many capabilities we have not utilized here. But for reasonably large LP problems, the instructions you have seen are all you will need.

Now to the MPOS output. The little control program we have written produces the following information, a separate page of output being devoted to each to facilitate reference: the control program that was input (with the constraint lines numbered), the initial simplex tableau, the final (optimal) tableau, a "summary of results" table, the objective-function sensitivity analysis, and finally the sensitivity analysis for resources. In a packed format (computer-page spacings reduced), what you see is depicted in Figure 6.1.

For comparative purposes, you can find the tableaus for our hand-generated solution to the Yummy Cereal Company problem in Table 4.3 of Chapter 4. For convenient reference the optimal tableau is repeated as Table 6.2, with the common fractions having been converted to decimal fractions.

Recall that in the mathematical formulation $x_1$, $x_2$, and $x_3$ were measured in pounds of cereal, while the resources were measured in ounces. Thus the maximum profit of $1,466.67 (146,666.67 cents) is achieved by making 2,000 pounds of Crunchies, no Chewies, and 1,333.3 pounds of Gummies. All of the corn and bran was used, but 18,666.7 ounces of wheat (1,166.7 pounds) was left over.

First compare Table 6.2 to the FINAL TABLEAU in the computer output of Figure 6.1. All of the numbers are there, with the exception of those in the Z column of Table 6.2, omitted as unnecessary information. The "Solution" column of Table 6.2 appears as the VALUES column in the output, occurring just after the BASIC column, which tells us which variables were basic variables at optimality. Obviously $S_1$, $S_2$, and $S_3$ were called variables 4, 5, and 6 by MPOS, and the optimal Z row appears at the bottom of the FINAL TABLEAU instead of at the top as in Table 6.2.

All of the pertinent information from the FINAL TABLEAU is repeated in the table called SUMMARY OF RESULTS. The optimal values of the decision and slack variables appear under ACTIVITY LEVEL, the coefficients in the optimal Z row appear in the column headed OPPORTUNITY COST (another name for optimal dual-variable values or implicit values), and maximum Z is reported directly below the table. The two right-most columns just give the original bounds on decision variables, in this case the nonnegativity restrictions (INF means "infinite," the "upper bound" in the constraint $x_1 \geq 0$, for example).

So if no sensitivity analysis is desired, the SUMMARY OF RESULTS table gives us all the information we need, including optimal dual-variable values:

$y_1$ = value in cents of an extra ounce of wheat = 0

$y_2$ = value in cents of an extra ounce of corn = 4.667

$y_3$ = value in cents of an extra ounce of bran = 3.000

```
TITLE
YUMMY CEREAL COMPANY
REGULAR
VARIABLES
X1 TO X3
MAXIMIZE
40X1+30X2+50X3
CONSTRAINTS
1.   6X1+4X2+X3.LE.32000
2.   6X1+7X2+3X3.LE.16000
3.   4X1+5X2+12X3.LE.24000
RNGOBJ
RNGRHS
PRINT 1
OPTIMIZE
```

```
       INITIAL TABLEAU

ROW      BASIC   VALUES    (   1)      (   2)      (   3)
  1   VAR-  0   32000.    6.0000     4.0000     1.0000
  2   VAR-  0   16000.    6.0000     7.0000     3.0000
  3   VAR-  0   24000.    4.0000     5.0000     12.000
  4      -Z   0.         40.000     30.000     50.000
```

```
     FINAL TABLEAU

ROW    BASIC   VALUES     (  1)      (   2)      (  3)      (  4)      (   5)      (   6)
  1  VAR-  4  18667.    0.        -2.9333    0.        1.0000    -1.1333    .20000
  2  VAR-  1  2000.0    1.0000    1.1500     0.        0.        .20000     -.50000E-01
  3  VAR-  3  1333.3    0.        .33333E-01 1.0000    0.        -.66667E-01 .10000E+00
  4     -Z   .14667E+06 0.        17.667     0.        0.        4.6667     3.0000
```

```
                    SUMMARY OF RESULTS

VAR  VAR        ROW STATUS   ACTIVITY        OPPORTUNITY      LOWER      UPPER
NO   NAME       NO            LEVEL             COST          BOUND      BOUND
 1   X1         --    B     2000.0000000      0.0000000      0.0000      INF
 2   X2         --    LB       0.0000000     17.6666667      0.0000      INF
 3   X3         --    B     1333.3333333      0.0000000      0.0000      INF
 4   SLACK-- D- 1     B    18666.6666667      0.0000000      0.0000      INF
 5   SLACK-- D- 2     LB       0.0000000      4.6666667      0.0000      INF
 6   SLACK-- D- 3     LB       0.0000000      3.0000000      0.0000      INF
```

```
MAXIMUM VALUE OF THE OBJECTIVE FUNCTION =    146666.666667
```

```
                      RNGOBJ
                      ******
          (OPTIMALITY RANGE FOR COST COEFFICIENTS)
                 BASIC VARIABLES ONLY

CJ   XIN    MIN CJ       ORIGINAL CJ      MAX CJ       XIN
            -------      -----------      -------
            Z-LOWER          Z            Z-UPPER


 1    2    24.638        40.000          100.00         6
           .11594E+06    .14667E+06      .26667E+06

 3    6    20.000        50.000          120.00         5
           .10667E+06    .14667E+06      .24000E+06
```

```
                      RNGRHS
                      ******
       (OPTIMALITY RANGE FOR RIGHT-HAND-SIDE CONSTANTS)
                 NON-SLACK RESOURCES ONLY

BI   XOUT   MIN BI       ORIGINAL BI      MAX BI       XOUT
            -------      -----------      -------
            Z-LOWER          Z            Z-UPPER


 2    1    6000.0        16000.          32471.         4
           .10000E+06    .14667E+06      .22353E+06

 3    3    10667.        24000.          64000.         1
           .10667E+06    .14667E+06      .26667E+06
```

**FIGURE 6.1**    MPOS solution of Yummy Cereal Company problem

TABLE 6.2 OPTIMAL TABLEAU FROM CHAPTER 4: YUMMY CEREAL COMPANY

| Basic | Z | $x_1$ | $x_2$ | $x_3$ | $S_1$ | $S_2$ | $S_3$ | Solution |
|-------|---|-------|-------|-------|-------|-------|-------|----------|
| Z | 1 | 0 | 17.667 | 0 | 0 | 4.667 | 3 | 146,666.67 |
| $S_1$ | 0 | 0 | -2.933 | 0 | 1 | -1.133 | 0.200 | 18,667.7 |
| $x_1$ | 0 | 1 | 1.150 | 0 | 0 | 0.200 | -0.050 | 2,000 |
| $x_3$ | 0 | 0 | 0.033 | 1 | 0 | -0.067 | 0.100 | 1,333.3 |

Note that the number 17.667 is the *reduction* in profit (in cents) that would occur if we decided to make a pound of Chewies; optimal dual-variable values are found only under slack and artificial variables in an optimal tableau.

The last two tables in the computer output of Figure 6.1 report sensitivity analyses on objective-function coefficients and resource availabilities. The following discussion shows how these tables should be interpreted.

Refer to the last table in Figure 6.1, headed RNGRHS. Here BI is the name given to amount of resource. Look at the last two rows of the table: since the original amount of bran was 24,000 ounces and bran was represented by the third constraint in the problem (observe the "3" at the left of the page), we know that this is the sensitivity analysis for bran. The numbers tell us that as long as the amount of bran remains between 10,667 ounces and 64,000 ounces, the current optimal basic solution will remain feasible. This is precisely the type of information gained from the sensitivity analyses performed in Chapter 5. However, RNGRHS also gives us the range of optimal Z under these conditions: as bran availability ranges from 10,667 to 64,000 ounces, optimal Z ranges from 106,670 cents to 266,670 cents. Obviously, the other numbers in the RNGRHS table give similar information about the amount of corn, the only other "nonslack resource" in the problem.

Now the table headed RNGOBJ should be easy enough for you to interpret. There CJ is the name given to an objective-function coefficient. Since the original coefficient of $x_1$ was 40 (and this is variable number 1), we see that as long as the profit per pound of Crunchies stays between 24.638 cents and 100 cents, the current basic feasible solution remains optimal, with corresponding optimal Z values ranging between 115,940 cents and 266,670 cents. Similarly, the profit contribution per pound of Gummies may range from 20 cents to 120 cents without changing the optimality of the current basic feasible solution.

Note that RNGOBJ only considers the sensitivity of the solution to changes in *basic* variable coefficients. But remember that the corresponding sensitivity analysis for a nonbasic variable is extremely simple, given the optimal tableau. See Section 5.8 of Chapter 5 for a review of the process, which is merely a process of observation, with no calculations required.

**179**

*APPLIED LINEAR
PROGRAMMING
MODELS WITH
COMPUTER
SOLUTIONS*

By now, if you have diligently studied Example 6.1 and have dutifully made your comparisons of tableaus, you should understand the input-output features of MPOS. We are ready to use this knowledge to analyze the applied problems in the next section.

## 6.3 APPLIED LINEAR PROGRAMMING MODELS

### Example 6.2
### Patrician Patio Pieces: A Production Application

Patrician Patio Pieces manufactures a medium-priced line of outdoor furniture, using a combination of redwood and cedar along with ornamental cast iron fittings for extra strength. Patterns for the furniture have been standardized so that only 12-inch and 8-inch fittings are required. Bolts of uniform size are used to hold the furniture together.

Patrician manufactures two sizes of tables and benches, armchairs, and smaller folding chairs suitable for indoor and outdoor use. Material and labor requirements during the coming month, resource availabilities, and profit per piece are given in Table 6.3.

Because of a prior order at least 10 short tables and at least 20 short benches must be produced. Sales projections indicate that no more than 50 armchairs should be produced. We desire a linear programming analysis of this problem, with the primary objective being the maximization of profit from the month's production.

The mathematical model for this problem has a straightforward formulation. Since the MPOS output reports this formulation by printing out the control file, we can just look at the output shown in Figure 6.2 to appreciate the formulation as well as the solution. Here the variable LTAB is the number of long tables, STAB is the number of short tables, and so on.

In the SUMMARY OF RESULTS table we find the optimal solution.

**TABLE 6.3** *PARAMETERS FOR PATRICIAN PATIO PIECES PROBLEM*

| | Long table | Short table | Long bench | Short bench | Arm-chair | Folding chair | Available |
|---|---|---|---|---|---|---|---|
| Redwood, board feet | 10 | 6 | 6 | 4 | 7 | 3 | 3,000 |
| Cedar, board feet | 8 | 5 | 3 | 2 | 4 | 1 | 2,000 |
| 12-inch fittings, number | 6 | 4 | 2 | 4 | 4 | 0 | 1,800 |
| 8-inch fittings, number | 4 | 6 | 6 | 0 | 0 | 4 | 1,400 |
| Bolts, number | 20 | 14 | 12 | 10 | 12 | 8 | 4,000 |
| Labor, work-hours | 8 | 4 | 5 | 3 | 8 | 6 | 2,400 |
| Unit profit | $50 | $35 | $25 | $20 | $45 | $15 | |

```
TITLE
PATRICIAN PATIO PIECES
REGULAR
VARIABLES
LTAB STAB LBEN SBEN ARMC FCHA
MAXIMIZE
50LTAB + 35STAB + 25LBEN + 20SBEN + 45ARMC + 15FCHA
CONSTRAINTS
1.  10LTAB + 6STAB + 6LBEN + 4SBEN + 7ARMC + 3FCHA .LE. 3000
2.  8LTAB + 5STAB + 3LBEN + 2SBEN + 4ARMC + FCHA .LE. 2000
3.  6LTAB + 4STAB + 2LBEN + 4SBEN + 4ARMC .LE. 1800
4.  4LTAB + 6STAB + 6LBEN + 4FCHA .LE. 1400
5.  20LTAB + 14STAB + 12LBEN + 10SBEN + 12ARMC + 8FCHA .LE. 4000
6.  8LTAB + 4STAB + 5LBEN + 3SBEN + 8ARMC + 6FCHA .LE. 2400
7.  STAB .GE. 10
8.  SBEN .GE. 20
9.  ARMC .LE. 50
RNGOBJ
RNGRHS
PRINT
OPTIMIZE
```

SUMMARY OF RESULTS

| VAR NO | VAR NAME | ROW NO | STATUS | ACTIVITY LEVEL | OPPORTUNITY COST | LOWER BOUND | UPPER BOUND |
|---|---|---|---|---|---|---|---|
| 1 | LTAB | -- | B | 153.0000000 | 0.0000000 | 0.0000 | INF |
| 2 | STAB | -- | B | 10.0000000 | 0.0000000 | 0.0000 | INF |
| 3 | LBEN | -- | LB | 0.0000000 | 5.0000000 | 0.0000 | INF |
| 4 | SBEN | -- | B | 20.0000000 | 0.0000000 | 0.0000 | INF |
| 5 | ARMC | -- | B | 50.0000000 | 0.0000000 | 0.0000 | INF |
| 6 | FCHA | -- | LB | 0.0000000 | 5.0000000 | 0.0000 | INF |
| 7 | SLACK-- D- | 1 | B | 980.0000000 | 0.0000000 | 0.0000 | INF |
| 8 | SLACK-- D- | 2 | B | 486.0000000 | 0.0000000 | 0.0000 | INF |
| 9 | SLACK-- D- | 3 | B | 562.0000000 | 0.0000000 | 0.0000 | INF |
| 10 | SLACK-- D- | 4 | B | 728.0000000 | 0.0000000 | 0.0000 | INF |
| 11 | SLACK-- D- | 5 | LB | 0.0000000 | 2.5000000 | 0.0000 | INF |
| 12 | SLACK-- D- | 6 | B | 676.0000000 | 0.0000000 | 0.0000 | INF |
| 13 | SLACK-- | 7 | LB | 0.0000000 | 0.0000000 | 0.0000 | INF |
| 22 | ARTIF-- D- | 7 | LB | 0.0000000 | 0.0000000 | 0.0000 | INF |
| 14 | SLACK-- | 8 | LB | 0.0000000 | 5.0000000 | 0.0000 | INF |
| 23 | ARTIF-- D- | 8 | LB | 0.0000000 | -5.0000000 | 0.0000 | INF |
| 15 | SLACK-- D- | 9 | LB | 0.0000000 | 15.0000000 | 0.0000 | INF |

MAXIMUM VALUE OF THE OBJECTIVE FUNCTION =     10650.000000

RNGOBJ
******

(OPTIMALITY RANGE FOR COST COEFFICIENTS)
BASIC VARIABLES ONLY

| CJ | XIN | MIN CJ — Z-LOWER | ORIGINAL CJ — Z | MAX CJ — Z-UPPER | XIN |
|---|---|---|---|---|---|
| 1 | 13 | 50.000 10650. | 50.000 10650. | 75.000 14475. | 15 |
| 2 | | *INF* | 35.000 10650. | 35.000 10650. | 13 |
| 4 | | *INF* | 20.000 10650. | 25.000 10750. | 14 |
| 5 | 15 | 30.000 9900.0 | 45.000 10650. | *INF* | |

RNGRHS
******

(OPTIMALITY RANGE FOR RIGHT-HAND-SIDE CONSTANTS)
NON-SLACK RESOURCES ONLY

| BI | XOUT | MIN BI — Z-LOWER | ORIGINAL BI — Z | MAX BI — Z-UPPER | XOUT |
|---|---|---|---|---|---|
| 5 | 1 | 940.00 3000.0 | 4000.0 10650. | 5215.0 13688. | 8 |
| 7 | 2 | 0. 10650. | 10.000 10650. | 228.57 10650. | 1 |
| 8 | 4 | 0. 10750. | 20.000 10650. | 326.00 9120.0 | 1 |
| 9 | 5 | 0. 9900.0 | 50.000 10650. | 261.25 13819. | 12 |

*FIGURE 6.2*   Solution of Patrician Patio Pieces problem

**181**

*APPLIED LINEAR
PROGRAMMING
MODELS WITH
COMPUTER
SOLUTIONS*

Our decision is to produce 153 long tables, 10 short tables, no long benches, 20 short tables, 50 armchairs, and no folding chairs. The corresponding maximum profit is $10,650.

Note that we should produce only the minimum required numbers of short tables and short benches, and the maximum permitted number of armchairs, 50. This suggests that even though armchairs are $5 per unit less profitable than long tables, their production is still worthwhile. A glance at Table 6.3 confirms a suspicion: the $45 per armchair is obtained with much less consumption of resources than the $50 per long table. But once the quota of armchairs is reached, and the required numbers of short tables and short benches have been made, the remainder of the resources should be devoted to the production of long tables, the most profitable item.

Now look at the OPPORTUNITY COST column in the SUMMARY OF RESULTS table. Variable number 11 is the slack variable for the fifth constraint, so the opportunity cost (or implicit value) associated with an extra unit of the fifth resource is $2.50. The fifth constraint is the *bolt* constraint, so an extra bolt would permit the utilization of $2.50 more of the value of all resources toward generation of maximum profit. All other implicit values for *resource* constraints are zero, meaning that the "bottle-neck" in the process is the limited number of bolts. If more bolts could be made available, more profit, at the rate of $2.50 per bolt, would accrue.

Up to a point, that is. The RNGRHS table says that the optimal solution would no longer be feasible if more than 5,215 bolts were available. The new profit if we had an extra 1,215 bolts (over the original 4,000) should be

$$\$10,650 + (\$2.50)(1,215) = \$10,650 + \$3,037.50 = \$13,687.50$$

Rounded to the nearest even dollar, this is the $13,688 shown as Z-UPPER for constraint 5 in the RNGRHS table.

Other implicit values and sensitivity analyses for constraints are not keyed to the basic resources in the problem, but rather to the minimum-order and maximum-sales-potential restrictions, that is, constraints 7, 8, and 9 in the model. For constraint 7, a ".GE." constraint, the associated opportunity cost (implicit value) is found opposite the *artificial* variable (variable number 22 in the SUMMARY OF RESULTS table) and is zero. This suggests that we could produce one more short table and not change the optimal solution, or that an *alternate optimal solution* does exist for this problem.

Constraint 8 is also a ".GE." constraint, with associated opportunity cost of −$5.00. This means that if we had to make 21 short benches instead of 20, our maximum profit would be *reduced* by $5.00.

The last constraint, constraint 9, is a ".LE." constraint, so the opportunity cost of $15 looks very attractive. But since this was associated with sales projections of number of armchairs, we see that the only way to take advantage of the opportunity implied by an extra unit of that "resource" is to guarantee the sale of more than 50 armchairs.

The RNGOBJ table also contains some interesting information. Note first of all that a reduction of the profit per long table to any number below $50 will mean that the current feasible solution would no longer be optimal. Thus we must be very careful to assure that the $50-per-unit profit for long tables has not been overestimated; otherwise, we would have a different solution (not necessarily a less-profitable one, only a *different* one than indicated by this MPOS output). Likewise, the $35-per-unit profit for short tables cannot have been underestimated or the solution would change. That is, the optimality of this feasible solution is *very sensitive* to the profit contributions from long tables and short tables. Any changes in those numbers could mean major changes in the production decision, so they should be monitored very carefully.

Another implication of this analysis is that effort aimed at producing long tables more efficiently, at less cost so at more profit, could be very worthwhile. Not only is our optimal solution extremely sensitive to profits per unit near $50, but an increase in profitability for long tables presents great opportunity for increasing profit; note the $14,475 associated with a $75-per–long table profit.

Do not become overly excited by the "*INF*" in the MIN CJ column of the RNGOBJ table. This should be interpreted as "*minus* infinity." An *INF* under MAX CJ is "plus infinity," but clearly if profitability per unit is increased indefinitely, so is overall profit.

The managerial implications of the preceding analysis include the following observations. If you can acquire a bolt for substantially less than $2.50, buy at least 1,215 of them, thus permitting $3,037.50 more profit (less the cost of bolt acquisition) through the use of more of *all* the resources. If you can promote more efficient production procedures for long tables, do so (although you might first want to look at an alternate optimal solution to check for suggestions of similar actions). Finally, you might consider spending some money advertising armchairs.

### Example 6.3
### Amalgamated Metals: A Blending Application

Amalgamated Metals has been marketing manganese bronze, an alloy of copper and zinc with some manganese included to increase strength. The formula has been 56 percent copper, 41 percent zinc, and 3 percent manganese.

Recently the price of copper has increased drastically, while the market for tin and lead has been depressed, leading to lower prices for those two commodities. Company metallurgists recall that the ancient Chinese formula for bronze was five parts copper to one part tin (Chou dynasty, circa 1000 B.C.), but that in that period, the metals were not available in pure form; significant amounts of lead and zinc were often present. Acting upon this information the metallurgists have determined a new formula for manganese bronze that uses less copper, zinc, and manganese because of the introduction of tin and lead, yet which has properties similar to the

**183**

*APPLIED LINEAR
PROGRAMMING
MODELS WITH
COMPUTER
SOLUTIONS*

manganese bronze made by the previous formula. The new formula calls for an alloy that is 46 percent copper, 23 percent zinc, 18 percent tin, 11 percent lead, and 2 percent manganese.

Large inventories of six other alloys containing these metals are on hand, and these alloys have not been in great demand. Amalgamated's management has decided to make their stock of these alloys available for the blending of the new manganese bronze. Table 6.4 gives the percentage of metal and the current market value per pound for the six alloys.

A blend from the six alloys is desired so the resulting manganese bronze has minimum value, since for a fixed market price of the bronze, profit is maximized if the bronze consumes a minimum value of resources. Amalgamated Metals wants to know what fraction of the blend should come from each alloy.

Let $P_i$ denote the proportion of the manganese bronze that comes from alloy $i$, $i = 1, \ldots, 6$. Note that the sum of these six proportions will have to be unity, since 100 percent of the manganese bronze is made from the six alloys. Note also that $P_i$ can be regarded as the number of pounds (a fraction less than 1) of alloy $i$ in 1 pound of manganese bronze, a viewpoint that will make model formulation easier.

For the objective function, observe that if $P_1$ is the number of pounds of alloy 1 in the bronze, then $32P_1$ is the portion of the value of a pound of bronze from alloy 1. Other value terms are similarly determined, yielding for the objective function

$$Z = 32P_1 + 26P_2 + 38P_3 + 20P_4 + 14P_5 + 44P_6$$

and we want to minimize $Z$.

Now look at the formulation of one of the resource constraints, the one for copper. Alloy 1 is 56 percent copper and $P_1$ is the number of pounds of alloy 1 in a pound of the bronze, so $0.56P_1$ is the number of pounds of copper that comes from alloy 1. Likewise, $0.40P_2$ is the number of pounds of copper contributed by alloy 2, and so on. Further, the amount of

**TABLE 6.4**   *CHARACTERISTICS AND VALUES OF ALLOYS*

| Alloy | Percent copper | Percent zinc | Percent tin | Percent lead | Percent manganese | Value per pound |
|-------|---------|------|-----|------|-----------|-----------|
| 1 | 56 | 40 | 0 | 0 | 3 | $32 |
| 2 | 40 | 20 | 20 | 15 | 5 | $26 |
| 3 | 65 | 5 | 25 | 5 | 0 | $38 |
| 4 | 20 | 0 | 40 | 39 | 1 | $20 |
| 5 | 0 | 40 | 30 | 30 | 0 | $14 |
| 6 | 70 | 20 | 0 | 0 | 10 | $44 |

copper in a pound of this manganese bronze is required to be 0.46 pounds. Thus the copper constraint is

$$0.56P_1 + 0.40P_2 + 0.65P_3 + 0.20P_4 \qquad\qquad + 0.70P_6 = 0.46$$

The other four resource constraints are similarly formed. Notice that the number 0.46 on the right-hand side of the copper constraint represents 46 percent of the blend being copper, so it is actually $0.46(P_1 + P_2 + P_3 + P_4 + P_5 + P_6)$, but the sum of the $P_i$'s is unity.

The complete mathematical model is

$$\text{Minimize } Z$$

where

$$Z = 32P_1 + 26P_2 + 38P_3 + 20P_4 + 14P_5 + 44P_6$$

subject to

$$
\begin{array}{lll}
56P_1 + 40P_2 + 65P_3 + 20P_4 \qquad\quad + 70P_6 = 46 & \text{copper} \\
41P_1 + 20P_2 + \phantom{0}5P_3 \qquad\quad + 40P_5 + 20P_6 = 23 & \text{zinc} \\
\phantom{41P_1 +} 20P_2 + 25P_3 + 40P_4 + 30P_5 \qquad\quad = 18 & \text{tin} \\
\phantom{41P_1 +} 15P_2 + \phantom{0}5P_3 + 39P_4 + 30P_5 \qquad\quad = 11 & \text{lead} \\
\phantom{0}3P_1 + \phantom{0}5P_2 \qquad\quad + \phantom{0}P_4 \qquad\quad + 10P_6 = \phantom{0}2 & \text{manganese}
\end{array}
$$

with all of the $P_i$'s being nonnegative. Here each constraint was multiplied by 100 to remove decimals. The sum of all five constraints in this model is $100 \, \Sigma \, P_i = 100$, or simply $\Sigma \, P_i = 1$. Thus a constraint that specifically mentions the sum of the proportions being unity is redundant, being already implied by the model. Figure 6.3 gives the MPOS solution of this equality-constrained problem.

Since the formula for the new manganese bronze involves very specific percentages, no sensitivity analysis was done on the right-hand sides of constraints. The values per pound of the available alloys might change with changing market conditions, however, so RNGOBJ was included in the control program.

The optimal solution, with proportions rounded to the third decimal place, is

$$P_1 = 0.308 \qquad P_2 = 0.200 \qquad P_3 = 0.296$$

$$P_4 = 0.073 \qquad P_5 = 0.122 \qquad P_6 = 0$$

and the minimum value per pound of resources consumed to make the manganese bronze is $29.50. Note that the most valuable alloy, alloy 6, is not used at all, but that approximately 60 percent of the blend comes from alloys 1 and 3, the next two most valuable alloys. Clearly at least one of those alloys must be used if alloy 6 is not, since the manganese

*APPLIED LINEAR
PROGRAMMING
MODELS WITH
COMPUTER
SOLUTIONS*

SUMMARY OF RESULTS

| VAR NO | VAR NAME | ROW NO | STATUS | ACTIVITY LEVEL | OPPORTUNITY COST | LOWER BOUND | UPPER BOUND |
|--------|----------|--------|--------|---------------|------------------|-------------|-------------|
| 1 | P1 | -- | B | .3082707 | 0.0000000 | 0.0000 | INF |
| 2 | P2 | -- | B | .2003759 | 0.0000000 | 0.0000 | INF |
| 3 | P3 | -- | B | .2962406 | 0.0000000 | 0.0000 | INF |
| 4 | P4 | -- | B | .0733063 | 0.0000000 | 0.0000 | INF |
| 5 | P5 | -- | B | .1218045 | C.0000000 | 0.0000 | INF |
| 6 | P6 | -- | LB | 0.0000000 | -10.2631579 | 0.0000 | INF |
| 7 | ARTIF-- D- | 1 | LB | 0.0000000 | .4766541 | 0.0000 | INF |
| 8 | ARTIF-- D- | 2 | LB | 0.0000000 | .1484586 | 0.0000 | INF |
| 9 | ARTIF-- D- | 3 | LB | 0.0000000 | .2465789 | 0.0000 | INF |
| 10 | ARTIF-- D- | 4 | LB | 0.0000000 | .0221429 | 0.0000 | INF |
| 11 | ARTIF-- D- | 5 | LB | 0.0000000 | -.2598120 | 0.0000 | INF |

MINIMUM VALUE OF THE OBJECTIVE FUNCTION = 29.503008

RNGOBJ
******
(OPTIMALITY RANGE FOR COST COEFFICIENTS)
BASIC VARIABLES ONLY

| CJ | XIN | MIN CJ ------- Z-LOWER | ORIGINAL CJ ----------- Z | MAX CJ ------- Z-UPPER | XIN |
|----|-----|--------|-------------|--------|-----|
| 4 | | *INF* | 20.000 29.503 | 254.00 46.657 | 6 |
| 1 | | *INF* | 32.000 29.503 | 51.500 35.514 | 6 |
| 3 | 6 | 13.625 22.282 | 38.000 29.503 | *INF* | |
| 5 | 6 | 1.5532 27.987 | 14.000 29.503 | *INF* | |
| 2 | | *INF* | 26.000 29.503 | 32.126 30.730 | 6 |

**FIGURE 6.3** Solution of Amalgamated Metals problem

bronze must contain 46 percent copper and these are the only other alloys with at least that percentage of copper.

RNGOBJ gives optimality ranges for the cost coefficients in the objective function. The entire RNGOBJ table conveys a rough impression of the effect on value of the manganese bronze due to changes in values of the alloys. Note particularly that a drastic drop in the value of alloy 5 does not produce a proportional decrease in the value of the bronze, and that a $6 increase in the value per pound of alloy 2 only increases the value of the manganese bronze by $1.23 per pound.

## Example 6.4
### First Intrastate Banks: A Financial Application

Until recently, Bank of Bosler has been a local, home-owned bank that makes seven different types of loans available to its customers. These loans and their associated interest rates are listed in Table 6.5.

A statewide banking group, First Intrastate Banks, has acquired Bank of Bosler. First Intrastate's board of directors is concerned that the casual, folksy attitude that has prevailed at Bank of Bosler is not consistent with their group's corporate philosophy. Consequently, the following guide-

TABLE 6.5    LOAN TYPE AND INTEREST RATE

| Type of loan | Interest rate, % |
|---|---|
| 1 Agricultural | 12 |
| 2 Home mortgage | 14 |
| 3 Industrial | 15 |
| 4 Commercial | 17 |
| 5 Automobile | 18 |
| 6 Otherwise secured | 20 |
| 7 Unsecured | 23 |

lines have been established for the allocation of money loaned by this new local branch:

1 No more than 10 percent of the total dollar amount of loans may be unsecured.

2 At least 50 percent of the total dollar amount of loans must be agricultural, home mortgage, or commercial loans.

3 The total of agricultural, automobile, and unsecured loans cannot exceed 30 percent of the total dollar amount of loans.

4 The total of industrial and otherwise-secured loans must be less than the total of agricultural and commercial loans.

Further, the bottom line in a statement of First Intrastate Banks's corporate philosophy would read: "Maximize interest."

The president of the new Bosler branch of First Intrastate anticipates $20 million being available for all loans this year. She wants to know how many dollars to allocate to each type of loan in order to remain consistent with the guidelines and to maximize annual interest. Her initial formulation of the model is

$$\text{Maximize } Z$$

where

$$Z = 0.12x_1 + 0.14x_2 + 0.15x_3 + 0.17x_4 + 0.18x_5 + 0.20x_6 + 0.23x_7$$

subject to

$$x_1 + x_2 + x_3 + x_4 + x_5 + x_6 + x_7 \leq 20{,}000{,}000$$

$$x_7 \leq 0.10(x_1 + x_2 + x_3 + x_4 + x_5 + x_6 + x_7)$$

$$x_1 + x_2 + x_4 \geq 0.50(x_1 + x_2 + x_3 + x_4 + x_5 + x_6 + x_7)$$

$$x_1 + x_5 + x_6 \leq 0.30(x_1 + x_2 + x_3 + x_4 + x_5 + x_6 + x_7)$$

$$x_3 + x_6 \leq x_1 + x_4$$

$$x_1, x_2, x_3, x_4, x_5, x_6, x_7 \geq 0$$

**187**

*APPLIED LINEAR*
*PROGRAMMING*
*MODELS WITH*
*COMPUTER*
*SOLUTIONS*

Here of course the subscripts on the $x$'s are consistent with the numbering of loan type in Table 6.5; $x_1$ is the number of dollars made available for agricultural loans, and so on.

Assuming that demand is sufficient to exhaust the entire $20 million available, it would be reasonable to presume that the sum of the seven variables will in fact *equal* $20 million if annual interest is to be maximized. This presumption, and a bit of algebra, permits the use of the following simpler constraints:

$$x_1 + x_2 + x_3 + x_4 + x_5 + x_6 + x_7 = 20{,}000{,}000$$

$$x_7 \leq 2{,}000{,}000$$

$$x_1 + x_2 \quad\quad + x_4 \quad\quad\quad\quad \geq 10{,}000{,}000$$

$$x_1 \quad\quad\quad\quad\quad\quad + x_5 + x_6 \quad \leq 6{,}000{,}000$$

$$-x_1 \quad\quad + x_3 - x_4 \quad\quad + x_6 \quad \leq 0$$

Figure 6.4 gives the MPOS solution.

The optimal mix of loans produces a maximum annual interest of $3,700,000, with $x_4 = \$12{,}000{,}000$, $x_6 = \$6{,}000{,}000$, and $x_7 = \$2{,}000{,}000$. All the other $x_i$'s are zero. Thus only commercial, otherwise-secured, and unsecured loans are made if the single objective is the maximization of

**FIGURE 6.4**  Solution: First Intrastate Banks problem

USING REGULAR
FIRST INTRASTATE BANK

SUMMARY OF RESULTS

| VAR NO | VAR NAME | ROW STATUS | NO | | ACTIVITY LEVEL | OPPORTUNITY COST | LOWER BOUND | UPPER BOUND |
|---|---|---|---|---|---|---|---|---|
| 1 | X1 | -- | | LB | 0.0000000 | .0800000 | 0.0000 | INF |
| 2 | X2 | -- | | LB | 0.0000000 | .0300000 | 0.0000 | INF |
| 3 | X3 | -- | | LB | 0.0000000 | .0200000 | 0.0000 | INF |
| 4 | X4 | -- | | B | 12000000.0000000 | 0.0000000 | 0.0000 | INF |
| 5 | X5 | -- | | LB | 0.0000000 | .0200000 | 0.0000 | INF |
| 6 | X6 | -- | | B | 6000000.0000000 | 0.0000000 | 0.0000 | INF |
| 7 | X7 | -- | | B | 2000000.0000000 | 0.0000000 | 0.0000 | INF |
| 8 | ARTIF-- D- | 1 | LB | | 0.0000000 | .1700000 | 0.0000 | INF |
| 9 | SLACK-- D- | 2 | LB | | 0.0000000 | .0600000 | 0.0000 | INF |
| 10 | SLACK-- | 3 | B | | 2000000.0000000 | 0.0000000 | 0.0000 | INF |
| 15 | ARTIF-- D- | 3 | LB | | 0.0000000 | 0.0000000 | 0.0000 | INF |
| 11 | SLACK-- D- | 4 | LB | | 0.0000000 | .0300000 | 0.0000 | INF |
| 12 | SLACK-- D- | 5 | B | | 6000000.0000000 | 0.0000000 | 0.0000 | INF |

MAXIMUM VALUE OF THE OBJECTIVE FUNCTION =    3700000.000000

RNGOBJ
******
(OPTIMALITY RANGE FOR COST COEFFICIENTS)
BASIC VARIABLES ONLY

| CJ | XIN | MIN CJ | ORIGINAL CJ | MAX CJ | XIN |
|---|---|---|---|---|---|
| | | ------- | ----------- | ------ | |
| | | Z-LOWER | Z | Z-UPPER | |
| 4 | 3 | .15000 | .17000 | .20000 | 11 |
| | | .34600E+07 | .37000E+07 | .40600E+07 | |
| 7 | 9 | .17000 | .23000 | *INF* | |
| | | .35800E+07 | .37000E+07 | | |
| 6 | 5 | .18000 | .20000 | *INF* | |
| | | .35800E+07 | .37000E+07 | | |

interest earnings. No agricultural, home mortgage, industrial, or automobile loans are permitted by this combination of guidelines and interest rates.

For the time being, we ignore the opportunity costs and optimality ranges for objective-function coefficients given in the RNGOBJ table. You will be asked to consider them in an exercise.

The more serious problem, from the viewpoint of the bank president, is the elimination by the optimal solution of some of the loan types that have traditionally been made by Bank of Bosler. Many of its customers are ranchers, needing agricultural loans, and the complete elimination of all home mortgage and automobile loans will cause extreme hardship for many of its valued clients. This solution, while optimal in terms of maximum interest and feasible in terms of the guidelines, is simply unacceptable.

The bank president notices that the maximum interest of $3.7 million means that the effective interest rate on the available $20 million is 18.5 percent. Bank of Bosler, before its acquisition by First Intrastate, had been averaging 14.8 percent on all loans. She reasons that the board of directors of First Intrastate Banks might accept from her a recommendation of at least 16.5 percent effective interest if thereby the goodwill of their clients, and, in fact, the clients themselves, are to be retained. Consequently, she prepares a proposal that will lead to a goal-programming analysis.

## Example 6.5
## First Intrastate Banks: A Goal-Programming Application

Bank of Bosler's president (see Example 6.4) submits the following proposal to First Intrastate's board of directors. Her bank will meet all of the restrictions they have imposed but would like to reserve $5 million for agricultural loans, $2 million for home mortgages, and $2 million for automobile loans. Since the economy of Bosler is principally agriculturally and commercially based, she expects no adverse effects from canceling industrial loans. If this proposal is acceptable to the board, she will endeavor to assure an effective overall interest rate of at least 16.5 percent.

First Intrastate's board responds favorably, except they would like to know if her effective interest rate is feasible under the conditions of her proposal. To reassure the board, the president formulates and solves the problem using a goal-programming model.

Four goals are proposed. They are:

*Goal 1:* Total interest of at least $3.3 million (16.5 percent of $20 million)

*Goal 2:* At least $5 million for agricultural loans

*Goal 3:* At least $2 million for home mortgages

*Goal 4:* At least $2 million for automobile loans

**189**

APPLIED LINEAR
PROGRAMMING
MODELS WITH
COMPUTER
SOLUTIONS

At the outset of the analysis, all goals are regarded as having the same priorities, since it may be possible to achieve every goal. Letting $U$'s denote underachievements and $O$'s denote overachievements for the goals, the following four constraints are added to the original five constraints in Example 6.4:

$$0.12x_1 + 0.14x_2 + 0.15x_3 + 0.17x_4 + 0.18x_5 + 0.20x_6 + 0.23x_7$$
$$+ U_1 - O_1 = 3{,}300{,}000$$

$$x_1 + U_2 - O_2 = 5{,}000{,}000$$

$$x_2 + U_3 + O_3 = 2{,}000{,}000$$

$$x_5 + U_4 - O_4 = 2{,}000{,}000$$

The objective is to minimize the sum of the $U_i$'s, the total underachievement in dollars for all goals. Then the objective function that must be minimized is

$$U = U_1 + U_2 + U_3 + U_4$$

The SUMMARY OF RESULTS table in Figure 6.5 gives the optimal goal-programming solution. The values of the original decision variables are

| | | |
|---|---|---|
| $x_1 =$ | \$4,000,000 | agricultural loans |
| $x_2 =$ | \$2,000,000 | home mortgages |
| $x_3 =$ | 0 | industrial loans |
| $x_4 =$ | \$10,000,000 | commercial loans |
| $x_5 =$ | \$2,000,000 | automobile loans |
| $x_6 =$ | 0 | otherwise-secured loans |
| $x_7 =$ | \$2,000,000 | unsecured loans |

Note that the mix of loan amounts is now substantially different from that advocated by the maximum-interest solution of Example 6.4. The entire \$6 million in otherwise-secured loans and \$2 million of the amount originally allocated to commercial loans have now been reallocated in an attempt to achieve all goals.

Not all goals were attained, however. The ACTIVITY LEVEL for $U_1$ is \$20,000, meaning that the interest goal of \$3.3 million lacked \$20,000 of being achieved. Likewise, $U_2$ is \$1 million, meaning that where \$5 million was desired for agricultural loans, only \$4 million was allocated.

The bank president might be able to manage the \$1 million shortfall in the money she wanted available for agricultural loans, especially since goals 3 and 4 are met exactly by this solution. Further, since total interest is \$3,280,000 instead of \$3,300,000, or the effective overall interest rate is

SUMMARY OF RESULTS

| VAR NO | VAR NAME | ROW NO | STATUS | ACTIVITY LEVEL | OPPORTUNITY COST | LOWER BOUND | UPPER BOUND |
|---|---|---|---|---|---|---|---|
| 1 | X1 | -- | B | 4000000.0000000 | 0.0000000 | 0.0000 | INF |
| 2 | X2 | -- | B | 2000000.0000000 | 0.0000000 | 0.0000 | INF |
| 3 | X3 | -- | LB | 0.0000000 | -.0200000 | 0.0000 | INF |
| 4 | X4 | -- | B | 9999999.9999999 | 0.0000000 | 0.0000 | INF |
| 5 | X5 | -- | B | 2000000.0000000 | 0.0000000 | 0.0000 | INF |
| 6 | X6 | -- | LB | 0.0000000 | -.9200000 | 0.0000 | INF |
| 7 | X7 | -- | B | 2000000.0000000 | 0.0000000 | 0.0000 | INF |
| 8 | U1 | -- | B | 20000.0000000 | 0.0000000 | 0.0000 | INF |
| 9 | U2 | -- | B | 1000000.0000000 | 0.0000000 | 0.0000 | INF |
| 10 | U3 | -- | LB | 0.0000000 | -.9700000 | 0.0000 | INF |
| 11 | U4 | -- | LB | 0.0000000 | -.0600000 | 0.0000 | INF |
| 12 | O1 | -- | LB | 0.0000000 | -1.0000000 | 0.0000 | INF |
| 13 | O2 | -- | LB | 0.0000000 | -1.0000000 | 0.0000 | INF |
| 14 | O3 | -- | LB | 0.0000000 | -.0300000 | 0.0000 | INF |
| 15 | O4 | -- | LB | 0.0000000 | -.9400000 | 0.0000 | INF |
| 16 | ARTIF-- D- | 1 | LB | 0.0000000 | 1.0000000 | 0.0000 | INF |
| 17 | ARTIF-- D- | 2 | LB | 0.0000000 | 1.0000000 | 0.0000 | INF |
| 18 | ARTIF-- D- | 3 | LB | 0.0000000 | .0300000 | 0.0000 | INF |
| 19 | ARTIF-- D- | 4 | LB | 0.0000000 | .9400000 | 0.0000 | INF |
| 20 | ARTIF-- D- | 5 | LB | 0.0000000 | -.1700000 | 0.0000 | INF |
| 21 | SLACK-- D- | 6 | LB | 0.0000000 | -.0600000 | 0.0000 | INF |
| 22 | SLACK-- | 7 | B | 6000000.0000000 | 0.0000000 | 0.0000 | INF |
| 31 | ARTIF-- D- | 7 | LB | 0.0000000 | 0.0000000 | 0.0000 | INF |
| 23 | SLACK-- D- | 8 | LB | 0.0000000 | -.9500000 | 0.0000 | INF |
| 24 | SLACK-- D- | 9 | B | 13999999.9999999 | 0.0000000 | 0.0000 | INF |

MINIMUM VALUE OF THE OBJECTIVE FUNCTION = 1020000.000000

FIGURE 6.5   Goal-programming solution: First Intrastate Banks

16.4 percent, the board of directors of First Intrastate Banks might be satisfied as well.

In the end-of-chapter exercises you will see this problem again. Some of the goals might be changed, or different priorities might be assigned to them.

## Example 6.6
### Span-America Pipelines: An Advertising Application

Span-America Pipelines has been experiencing difficulty convincing members of the Wyoming legislature to support enabling legislation releasing state water for use in a proposed coal-slurry pipeline. Public resistance in the arid western states to any diversion of water for out-of-state uses runs high. A Wyoming citizen's lobby has been running ads on radio and television and in newspapers, announcements that keep the public aware of developments pertaining to the proposed pipeline and that are slanted toward an opposition viewpoint.

The management of Span-America decides that it must reach the public with its own story; mere lobbying efforts in the legislature do not seem to be enough. Consequently, it allocates a budget of $200,000 to an intensive advertising campaign, slated to run during the month prior to convening of the regular legislative session. These ads will not emphasize the company's interest in the coal-slurry pipeline; rather, they will be informative ads designed to enhance Span-America's corporate image.

Contact is made with the advertising departments of two television stations, two radio stations, and three newspapers to determine their respective numbers of viewers, listeners, and readers. The number of

**191**

APPLIED LINEAR
PROGRAMMING
MODELS WITH
COMPUTER
SOLUTIONS

times during the month that prime-time spots on television and radio are available is also determined, as is the availability of space for half-page ads in Sunday supplements to the newspapers. Costs for the spots and the space are also considered, as are measures of the relative effectiveness per person of the different types of advertisements.

TV1 is a Wyoming television station based in Casper, the state's largest city, while TV2 is a Denver station that is viewed in Wyoming by means of a cable connection. R1 is a Casper radio station; R2 is a radio station based in Cheyenne, the state capital. N1 is a Casper newspaper, N2 a Cheyenne paper, and N3 a Colorado paper with wide Sunday circulation in Wyoming.

To facilitate tabular presentation of cost and other parameters, radio and television spots and newspaper space are called simply "spots" in Table 6.6. A television spot runs 30 seconds, a radio spot runs 45 seconds, and a newspaper "spot" is a half-page color ad in a Sunday supplement. Table 6.6 shows costs, spot availabilities, public contact, and relative effectiveness factors for the month. The two Wyoming newspapers are the basis for the relative-effectiveness factors, which will just be multiplied by numbers of people to measure total effectiveness of a spot.

Span-America's management believes that some of the money should be spent in Wyoming even if this decision would tend to reduce total effectiveness. The goodwill of the Wyoming media is certainly going to be important in the long run. Management decides that the amount of money spent in Wyoming must be at least 35 percent of the amount spent in Colorado.

The objective is to maximize total effectiveness subject to the previous constraint, while spending no more than $200,000. Span-America's management wants to know how many spots of each type to purchase.

Let $x_1$ be the number of spots purchased on station TV1, $x_2$ be the number of spots purchased on station TV2, and so on according to the media numbering in the left-most column of Table 6.6, up to $x_7 = $ the

**TABLE 6.6** PARAMETERS FOR SPAN-AMERICA'S ADVERTISING DECISION

| Advertising medium | | People contacted per spot | Relative effectiveness | Number of spots available | Cost: Dollars per spot |
|---|---|---|---|---|---|
| 1 TV1 | (WY) | 25,000 | 2.0 | 35 | 3,000 |
| 2 TV2 | (CO) | 75,000 | 2.5 | 45 | 10,000 |
| 3 R1 | (WY) | 4,000 | 0.7 | 55 | 200 |
| 4 R2 | (WY) | 8,000 | 0.8 | 45 | 400 |
| 5 N1 | (WY) | 10,000 | 1.0 | 3 | 550 |
| 6 N2 | (WY) | 15,000 | 1.0 | 4 | 850 |
| 7 N3 | (CO) | 30,000 | 1.2 | 3 | 2,200 |

number of spots purchased in newspaper N3. Also note that (WY) means a Wyoming location while (CO) means a Colorado location.

The total effectiveness of the campaign (with multiple contacts of the same person ignored) is

$$Z = (25,000)(2.0)x_1 + (75,000)(2.5)x_2 + (4,000)(0.7)x_3 + (8,000)(0.8)x_4$$
$$+ (10,000)(1.0)x_5 + (15,000)(1.0)x_6 + (30,000)(1.2)x_7$$

The cost constraint is simply stated and can be easily identified in the MPOS printout in Figure 6.6. The restriction that some of the money be spent in Wyoming may be stated initially as

$$3,000x_1 + 200x_3 + 400x_4 + 550x_5 + 850x_6 \geq (0.35)(10,000x_2 + 2,200x_7)$$

This can be rewritten as

$$3,000x_1 - 3,500x_2 + 200x_3 + 400x_4 + 550x_5 + 850x_6 - 770x_7 \geq 0$$

In this problem are seven additional "upper bound" constraints that come from the number of spots that are available from each of the seven advertising outlets. These constraints are listed as BOUNDS in the MPOS input. Figure 6.6 gives the complete formulation and solution of the model.

Constraint 1 represents the restriction on money distribution between Wyoming and Colorado. Constraint 2 just says that no more than $200,000

**FIGURE 6.6**  Solution: Span-America Pipelines problem

```
TITLE
SPAN-AMERICA PIPELINE
REGULAR
VARIABLES
X1 TO X7
MAXIMIZE
50000X1+18750JX2+2800X3+6400X4+10000X5+15000X6+36000X7
CONSTRAINTS
1.  3000X1-3500X2+200X3+400X4+550X5+850X6-770X7.GE.0
2.  3000X1+10000X2+200X3+400X4+550X5+850X6+2200X7.LE.200000
BOUNDS
X1.LE.35
X2.LE.45
X3.LE.55
X4.LE.45
X5.LE.3
X6.LE.4
X7.LE.3
OPTIMIZE
```

SUMMARY OF RESULTS

| VAR NO | VAR NAME | ROW NO | STATUS | ACTIVITY LEVEL | OPPORTUNITY COST | LOWER BOUND | UPPER BOUND |
|---|---|---|---|---|---|---|---|
| 1 | X1 | -- | B | 15.6006173 | 0.0000000 | 0.0000 | 35.0000 |
| 2 | X2 | -- | B | 14.8148148 | 0.0000000 | 0.0000 | 45.0000 |
| 3 | X3 | -- | LB | 0.0000000 | 533.3333333 | 0.0000 | 55.0000 |
| 4 | X4 | -- | LB | 0.0000000 | 266.6666667 | 0.0000 | 45.0000 |
| 5 | X5 | -- | UB | 3.0000000 | 833.3333333 | 0.0000 | 3.0000 |
| 6 | X6 | -- | UB | 4.0000000 | 833.3333333 | 0.0000 | 4.0000 |
| 7 | X7 | -- | LB | 0.0000000 | 5250.0000000 | 0.0000 | 3.0000 |
| 8 | SLACK-- | 1 | LB | 0.0000000 | 0.0000000 | 0.0000 | INF |
| 10 | ARTIF-- D- | 1 | LB | 0.0000000 | 1.5432099 | 0.0000 | INF |
| 9 | SLACK-- D- | 2 | LB | 0.0000000 | -1.5432099 | 0.0000 | INF |
| | | | | | 18.2098765 | | |

MAXIMUM VALUE OF THE OBJECTIVE FUNCTION =   3647808.641975

**193**

*APPLIED LINEAR
PROGRAMMING
MODELS WITH
COMPUTER
SOLUTIONS*

may be spent. The seven other constraints are listed as BOUNDS so MPOS can use a "bounded variables" version of the simplex method to gain some computational efficiency. This BOUNDS designation also produces a shorter SUMMARY OF RESULTS table than would have occurred if the seven bounds had been designated CONSTRAINTS (note the absence from the summary of any slack variables for those bounding constraints).

From the slack-variable ACTIVITY LEVELS in the SUMMARY OF RESULTS table of Figure 6.6 we see that both monetary constraints are satisfied with strict equality. Exactly $200,000 would be spent, and the money going to Wyoming is exactly 35 percent of the money going to Colorado.

The "optimal" solution is

$$x_1 = 15.6006173 = \text{number of TV1 spots (WY)} \qquad \text{Cost: \$ 46,801.85}$$

$$x_2 = 14.8148148 = \text{number of TV2 spots (CO)} \qquad \text{Cost: \$148,148.15}$$

$$x_5 = 3.0 \qquad = \text{number of ads in N1 (WY)} \qquad \text{Cost: \$ 1,650.00}$$

$$x_6 = 4.0 \qquad = \text{number of ads in N2 (WY)} \qquad \text{Cost: \$ 3,400.00}$$

$$(x_3 = x_4 = x_7 = 0) \qquad\qquad\qquad\qquad \text{Total cost: \$200,000.00}$$

Colorado expenditure: $148,148.15

Wyoming expenditure: $ 51,851.85

($51,851.85 is precisely 35 percent of $148,148.15)

Maximum total effectiveness = 3,347,808.641975

Mathematically, then, everything is just fine. Practically, however, Span-America cannot use this solution. Television spots and newspaper ads are sold only as complete units, not fractions of units.

Suppose we simply round off the solution for the $x$'s to the nearest integers. Then $x_1 = 16$ and $x_2 = 15$, while $x_5$ and $x_6$ remain at 3 and 4, respectively. Total cost would be $203,050, or $3,050 over budget. This is not acceptable.

Then let's round $x_1$ to 15 and $x_2$ to 15. Total cost is now $200,050. Still over budget, but only by $50. However, the expenditure in Colorado would be $150,000 while that in Wyoming would only be $50,050, just a little more than 33 percent of Colorado expenditure, whereas at least 35 percent was required.

We can take care of that by rounding both $x_1$ and $x_2$ *down*. If $x_1 = 15$, $x_2 = 14$, $x_5 = 3$, $x_6 = 4$, then total cost is $190,050 while Colorado money is $140,000 and Wyoming money is $50,050, 35.75 percent of the expenditure in Colorado. This is a *feasible* solution involving *integers*.

But it is certainly not an *optimal* integer solution. Span-America would have $9,950 still available, some or all of which could simply be spent in

Wyoming, thus increasing effectiveness while still satisfying all constraints. But even though we might through trial and error come up with a "pretty good" solution relative to the optimal noninteger solution, we would not be able to say that it was optimal unless we tried all possibilities. If you want to guarantee optimality of your integer solution, you will have to use an *integer-programming* technique (see Chapter 7).

To satisfy your curiosity before we move to another application, be advised that the optimal integer solution is $x_1 = 18$, $x_2 = 14$, $x_3 = 1$, $x_4 = 4$, $x_5 = 3$, $x_6 = 3$, $x_7 = 0$. Quite a bit different from any rounding-type solution you might have tried, isn't it? This produces maximum effectiveness (over the set of all integer solutions) of 3,638,400, 99.5 percent of the original noninteger maximum. The cost is exactly $200,000, and the money spent in Wyoming is about 43 percent of the money spent in Colorado. This is Span-America Pipelines's optimal *practical* decision for allocating its advertising budget.

### Example 6.7
### Family Theaters: A Small Business Application

In Example 6.6 you observed an LP application in which an integer solution was desired but for which a specialized new algorithm would be required to assure optimality. Here we present another application requiring integer-valued variables, but only the integers 0 and 1 are permitted. You will see that the simplex method will in this case give the correct integer values. However, in Chapter 7 you will learn a better algorithm for achieving the same solution, called the *assignment method*.

Family Theaters is a locally owned business that operates the only five motion-picture theaters in Middletown. They are Bijou, Paramount, Esquire, Capitol, and Rex. To welcome schoolchildren to summer vacation, Family Theaters' owner plans to provide a program of five horror movies. The movies will be shown simultaneously over a two-week period. The selection of movies is "I Was a Teenage Vegetarian" (ITV), "Attack of the Killer Harpsichords" (AKH), "The Incredible Shrinking Asset" (ISA), "The Oklahoma Roto-Rooter Massacre" (ORM), and "It Came from Peoria" (ICP).

The owner of Family Theaters was born and raised in Middletown and has been in the theater business there for 40 years. Because of his intimate knowledge of the movie-going habits of his customers, he is able to make quite accurate predictions of attendance, and thereby of gross revenue. He simply measures the type of movie against the characteristics of the neighborhood surrounding the theater in which the movie will be shown. After due consideration of these factors he has established gross revenue predictions for each movie shown in each theater. These revenue predictions are given in Table 6.7.

A movie will be run at the same theater for the entire two-week period. The owner's problem is the assignment of movies to theaters in a manner that will maximize total gross revenue. Only 5 assignments are to be

TABLE 6.7

**GROSS REVENUE PER THEATER-MOVIE ASSIGNMENT, IN HUNDREDS OF DOLLARS**

| Theater | Movie | | | | |
|---------|-------|-------|-------|-------|-------|
| | **1**<br>**ITV** | **2**<br>**AKH** | **3**<br>**ISA** | **4**<br>**ORM** | **5**<br>**ICP** |
| **1** Bijou | 47 | 46 | 45 | 40 | 41 |
| **2** Paramount | 56 | 52 | 55 | 54 | 50 |
| **3** Esquire | 61 | 60 | 58 | 56 | 57 |
| **4** Capitol | 54 | 52 | 49 | 48 | 50 |
| **5** Rex | 48 | 51 | 47 | 46 | 49 |

made, but 25 potential assignments exist. Notice that if ITV is assigned to the Paramount, then ITV cannot be assigned to any other theater, nor can any other movie be assigned to the Paramount.

The theater owner decides to formulate his problem in an LP model, letting $x_{ij}$ be the variable for the $i$th theater and the $j$th movie. This variable can only assume the values 0 or 1; if $x_{13} = 0$, for example, then ISA is *not* assigned to the Bijou, while if $x_{24} = 1$, then ORM *is* assigned to the Esquire. Thus only 5 of the 25 variables will take on the value 1, with the other 20 being 0.

This will become a 25-variable, 10-constraint linear programming problem. As an example of one constraint, consider

$$x_{21} + x_{22} + x_{23} + x_{24} + x_{25} = 1$$

This simply says that one movie will be assigned to the Paramount, with the associated $x_{2j}$ being 1 and the other four $x_{2j}$'s being 0. Figure 6.7 shows the complete formulation and solution of this assignment problem.

In the SUMMARY OF RESULTS table in Figure 6.7 we see the "0-1" characteristic of the optimal solution. While nothing we said to the computer told it to make the variables either 0s or 1s, the structure of an assignment problem of this type forces that kind of solution. That is, the simplex method takes care of itself since in an assignment problem there is no better solution than the best 0-1 solution.

The five variables with the value 1 are $x_{13}$, $x_{24}$, $x_{32}$, $x_{41}$, and $x_{55}$. Reference to Table 6.7 tells the theater owner that the optimal assignment is

Bijou ↔ ISA

Paramount ↔ ORM

Esquire ↔ AKH

Capitol ↔ ITV

Rex ↔ ICP

```
TITLE
FAMILY THEATERS
REGULAR
VARIABLES
X11 TO X15 X21 TO X25 X31 TO X35 X41 TO X45 X51 TO X55
MAXIMIZE
47X11 + 46X12 + 45X13 + 40X14 + 41X15
+ 56X21 + 52X22 + 55X23 + 54X24 + 50X25
+ 61X31 + 60X32 + 58X33 + 56X34 + 57X35
+ 54X41 + 52X42 + 49X43 + 48X44 + 50X45
+ 48X51 + 51X52 + 47X53 + 46X54 + 49X55
CONSTRAINTS
 1.   X11 + X12 + X13 + X14 + X15 = 1
 2.   X21 + X22 + X23 + X24 + X25 = 1
 3.   X31 + X32 + X33 + X34 + X35 = 1
 4.   X41 + X42 + X43 + X44 + X45 = 1
 5.   X51 + X52 + X53 + X54 + X55 = 1
 6.   X11 + X21 + X31 + X41 + X51 = 1
 7.   X12 + X22 + X32 + X42 + X52 = 1
 8.   X13 + X23 + X33 + X43 + X53 = 1
 9.   X14 + X24 + X34 + X44 + X54 = 1
10.   X15 + X25 + X35 + X45 + X55 = 1
OPTIMIZE
```

SUMMARY OF RESULTS

| VAR NO | VAR NAME | ROW NO | STATUS | ACTIVITY LEVEL | OPPORTUNITY COST | LOWER BOUND | UPPER BOUND |
|---|---|---|---|---|---|---|---|
| 1 | X11 | -- | LB | 0.0000000 | 2.0000000 | 0.0000 | INF |
| 2 | X12 | -- | LB | 0.0000000 | 1.0000000 | 0.0000 | INF |
| 3 | X13 | -- | B | 1.0000000 | 0.0000000 | 0.0000 | INF |
| 4 | X14 | -- | LB | 0.0000000 | 3.0000000 | 0.0000 | INF |
| 5 | X15 | -- | LB | 0.0000000 | 4.0000000 | 0.0000 | INF |
| 6 | X21 | -- | LB | 0.0000000 | 4.0000000 | 0.0000 | INF |
| 7 | X22 | -- | LB | 0.0000000 | 6.0000000 | 0.0000 | INF |
| 8 | X23 | -- | LB | 0.0000000 | 1.0000000 | 0.0000 | INF |
| 9 | X24 | -- | B | 1.0000000 | 0.0000000 | 0.0000 | INF |
| 10 | X25 | -- | LB | 0.0000000 | 6.0000000 | 0.0000 | INF |
| 11 | X31 | -- | LB | 0.0000000 | 1.0000000 | 0.0000 | INF |
| 12 | X32 | -- | B | 1.0000000 | 0.0000000 | 0.0000 | INF |
| 13 | X33 | -- | B | 0.0000000 | 0.0000000 | 0.0000 | INF |
| 14 | X34 | -- | B | 0.0000000 | 0.0000000 | 0.0000 | INF |
| 15 | X35 | -- | LB | 0.0000000 | 1.0000000 | 0.0000 | INF |
| 16 | X41 | -- | B | 1.0000000 | 0.0000000 | 0.0000 | INF |
| 17 | X42 | -- | B | 0.0000000 | 0.0000000 | 0.0000 | INF |
| 18 | X43 | -- | LB | 0.0000000 | 1.0000000 | 0.0000 | INF |
| 19 | X44 | -- | LB | 0.0000000 | 0.0000000 | 0.0000 | INF |
| 20 | X45 | -- | LB | 0.0000000 | 0.0000000 | 0.0000 | INF |
| 21 | X51 | -- | LB | 0.0000000 | 5.0000000 | 0.0000 | INF |
| 22 | X52 | -- | B | 0.0000000 | 0.0000000 | 0.0000 | INF |
| 23 | X53 | -- | LB | 0.0000000 | 2.0000000 | 0.0000 | INF |
| 24 | X54 | -- | LB | 0.0000000 | 1.0000000 | 0.0000 | INF |
| 25 | X55 | -- | B | 1.0000000 | 0.0000000 | 0.0000 | INF |
| 26 | ARTIF-- | D- 1 | LB | 0.0000000 | 45.0000000 | 0.0000 | INF |
| 27 | ARTIF-- | D- 2 | LB | 0.0000000 | 56.0000000 | 0.0000 | INF |
| 28 | ARTIF-- | D- 3 | LB | 0.0000000 | 58.0000000 | 0.0000 | INF |
| 29 | ARTIF-- | D- 4 | LB | 0.0000000 | 50.0000000 | 0.0000 | INF |
| 30 | ARTIF-- | D- 5 | LB | 0.0000000 | 49.0000000 | 0.0000 | INF |
| 31 | ARTIF-- | D- 6 | LB | 0.0000000 | 4.0000000 | 0.0000 | INF |
| 32 | ARTIF-- | D- 7 | LB | 0.0000000 | 2.0000000 | 0.0000 | INF |
| 33 | ARTIF-- | D- 8 | LB | 0.0000000 | 0.0000000 | 0.0000 | INF |
| 34 | ARTIF-- | D- 9 | LB | 0.0000000 | -2.0000000 | 0.0000 | INF |
| 45 | ARTIF-- | D- 10 | B | 0.0000000 | 0.0000000 | 0.0000 | INF |

MAXIMUM VALUE OF THE OBJECTIVE FUNCTION = 262.000000

**FIGURE 6.7** Solution: Family Theaters problem

This assignment of movies to theaters generates a maximum gross revenue of $26,200 for the two-week period during which these movies are to be shown.

For another special type of problem, called the transportation problem, ordinary simplex-method iterations also give optimal integer solutions. However, in Chapter 7 you will see more efficient algorithms for obtaining solutions for assignment and transportation problems.

### Example 6.8
**Auditrol Associates: An Accounting Application of Goal Programming**

Auditrol Associates has been invited to bid for the contract to do an inventory audit for a large, centralized Air Force supply depot. Involved

**197**

*APPLIED LINEAR
PROGRAMMING
MODELS WITH
COMPUTER
SOLUTIONS*

in the audit will be the checking of computer entries against actual inventories on hand in the depot. The Air Force advises Auditrol that the combination of cost and anticipated error rate within the audit will form the basis for its awarding of the contract.

No information about competitors for the contract is available. Auditrol decides to determine its bid purely on the basis of the capabilities of the firm itself, with no consideration given to underbidding a competitor. That is, they will simply bid at a cost figure that will generate acceptable profit for the job while attempting to assure the Air Force of a low rate of error within the audit.

Three types of personnel are available for assignment to the auditing job: senior partners in the firm, CPAs with experience on similar audits, and accounting associates, who are either recently hired employees or else older employees with less training in modern auditing procedures than the CPAs.

Parameters central to determination of a reasonable bid are the number of person-hours available from each of the three categories, the anticipated error rate per hour for the three types of personnel, and cost per hour for each type in amounts consistent with attainment of a respectable profit on the job. Because of the type of linear programming analysis that is planned, knowledge of one other kind of parameter is of prime importance. It is the fraction of the total job that can be done in one hour. That is, if the fraction per hour for a senior partner is 0.00030, then $10,000/3 = 3,333.3$ hours of senior partner time would suffice to complete the entire job.

Table 6.8 gives these fractions, error rates, costs, and availabilities for each of the three categories of personnel, where SP denotes senior partners, CPA denotes the experienced CPAs, and AA denotes the accounting associates. Table 6.8 also shows the decision variables $x_1$, $x_2$, $x_3$, which are the number of hours on the job assigned to each of the three categories.

Two competing objectives are desired for the project: minimum cost and minimum error rate. The figures for cost and error rate in Table 6.8 make it clear that increasing the time of senior partners reduces the error rate but increases the cost. Consequently, Auditrol decides to phrase its problem in a goal-programming format.

**TABLE 6.8** *PARAMETERS AND VARIABLES FOR AUDITROL'S DECISION PROBLEM*

| | Personnel category | | |
|---|---|---|---|
| Parameter-variable | SP | CPA | AA |
| Fraction of audit/hour | 0.00030 | 0.00025 | 0.00015 |
| Hours available | 500 | 3000 | 1200 |
| Cost/hour | $70 | $40 | $15 |
| Errors/hour | 0.1 | 0.2 | 0.4 |
| Number hours on audit | $x_1$ | $x_2$ | $x_3$ |

Auditrol's senior partners agree that a cost quotation of $130,000 at an error rate of 0.5 percent would most likely be a contract-winning bid. Since the Air Force has furnished them a job description indicating 180,000 entries in the supply depot's computer files, and 0.5 percent of 180,000 is 900, Auditrol establishes the following goals:

*Goal 1:* 900 errors in the audit

*Goal 2:* Audit cost of $130,000

These specifications generate the following two constraints:

$$0.1x_1 + 0.2x_2 + 0.4x_3 + U_1 - O_1 = 900 \qquad \text{errors}$$

$$70x_1 + 40x_2 + 15x_3 + U_2 - O_2 = 130,000 \qquad \text{cost}$$

Here $U_1$ and $U_2$ represent underachievements of the goals, while $O_1$ and $O_2$ are the corresponding overachievements.

The senior partners further conclude that low error rate is certainly twice as important as low cost, so they decide that the objective function should be

$$Z = 2O_1 + O_2$$

which should be minimized. A preliminary calculation has indicated that resources are insufficient to meet either goal, so zero values are anticipated for both $U_1$ and $U_2$.

Upper bounds for $x_1$, $x_2$, and $x_3$ come from the available amounts of time and are obvious. The only other constraint in the problem arises from the fact that the audit must be completed; that is, the fraction of the audit done by all personnel assigned must total 1.0. This constraint is

$$0.00030x_1 + 0.00025x_2 + 0.00015x_3 = 1.0$$

Figure 6.8 gives the complete formulation and MPOS solution of this goal-programming problem.

The SUMMARY OF RESULTS table in Figure 6.8 displays a solution that comes as a mild surprise to Auditrol's senior partners. Even though the error rate was deemed twice as important as cost, the linear programming decision is to assign all 1,200 available hours to the accounting associates, who have high error rates, and only 233 hours, 20 minutes to the senior partners, whose error rate is a quarter of the associates' rate. All of the available CPA time, 3,000 hours, is assigned to the audit.

On a second look at this solution, however, Auditrol decides it is not too bad for bidding purposes. The error goal was overachieved by 203.3 (ACTIVITY LEVEL for $O_1$), meaning that $900 + 203.3 = 1,103.3$ is the predicted number of errors, a rate of 0.613 percent, whereas 0.5 percent was desired. Further, $O_2 = 24,333.3$, so the implied cost of the audit is

**199**

APPLIED LINEAR
PROGRAMMING
MODELS WITH
COMPUTER
SOLUTIONS

```
TITLE
AUDITROL ASSOCIATES
REGULAR
VARIABLES
X1 X2 X3 U1 U2 O1 O2
MINIMIZE
2O1 + O2
CONSTRAINTS
1.   .1X1 + .2X2 + .4X3 + U1 - O1 = 900
2.   70X1 + 40X2 + 15X3 + U2 - O2 = 130000
3.   .0003X1 + .00025X2 + .00015X3 = 1.0
BOUNDS
X1.LE.500
X2.LE.3000
X3.LE.1200
OPTIMIZE
```

SUMMARY OF RESULTS

| VAR NO | VAR NAME | ROW STATUS | ROW NO | ACTIVITY LEVEL | OPPORTUNITY COST | LOWER BOUND | UPPER BOUND |
|---|---|---|---|---|---|---|---|
| 1 | X1 | -- | B | 233.3333333 | 0.0000000 | 0.0000 | 500.0000 |
| 2 | X2 | -- | UB | 3000.0000000 | -18.1000000 | 0.0000 | 3000.0000 |
| 3 | X3 | -- | UB | 1200.0000000 | -19.3000000 | 0.0000 | 1200.0000 |
| 4 | U1 | -- | LB | 0.0000000 | -2.0000000 | 0.0000 | INF |
| 5 | U2 | -- | LB | 0.0000000 | -1.0000000 | 0.0000 | INF |
| 6 | O1 | -- | B | 203.3333333 | 0.0000000 | 0.0000 | INF |
| 7 | O2 | -- | B | 24333.3333333 | 0.0000000 | 0.0000 | INF |
| 8 | ARTIF-- D- | 1 | LB | 0.0000000 | -2.0000000 | 0.0000 | INF |
| 9 | ARTIF-- D- | 2 | LB | 0.0000000 | -1.0000000 | 0.0000 | INF |
| 10 | ARTIF-- D- | 3 | LB | 0.0000000 | 234000.0000000 | 0.0000 | INF |

```
MINIMUM VALUE OF THE OBJECTIVE FUNCTION =    24740.000000
```

**FIGURE 6.8** Goal-programming solution: Auditrol Associates

$130,000 + $24,333 = $154,333. The senior partners deem the decision acceptable and inform their colleagues that they plan to bid at $154,333 with an anticipated error rate of 0.613 percent.

One of the accounting associates, a bright young graduate of the University of Wyoming who included operations research courses in her accounting program, offers a different proposal. Her campus experience with goal programming has taught her that the solutions are often insensitive to coefficients in the objective function. She decides to presume that error rate is 75 times as important as cost. Begging access to the Auditrol computer, she re-runs the problem with the only change from the input of Figure 6.8 being to make the objective function $75O_1 + O_2$ rather than $2O_1 + O_2$. Her solution is shown in Figure 6.9.

Now $O_1 = 16.67$ and $O_2 = 35,000$. This means that Auditrol could bid

**FIGURE 6.9** Second solution: Auditrol Associates

```
USING REGULAR
AUDITROL ASSOCIATES
```

SUMMARY OF RESULTS

| VAR NO | VAR NAME | ROW STATUS | ROW NO | ACTIVITY LEVEL | OPPORTUNITY COST | LOWER BOUND | UPPER BOUND |
|---|---|---|---|---|---|---|---|
| 1 | X1 | -- | UB | 500.0000000 | -12.5000000 | 0.0000 | 500.0000 |
| 2 | X2 | -- | UB | 3000.0000000 | -20.0000000 | 0.0000 | 3000.0000 |
| 3 | X3 | -- | B | 666.6666667 | 0.0000000 | 0.0000 | 1200.0000 |
| 4 | U1 | -- | LB | 0.0000000 | -75.0000000 | 0.0000 | INF |
| 5 | U2 | -- | LB | 0.0000000 | -1.0000000 | 0.0000 | INF |
| 6 | O1 | -- | B | 16.6666667 | 0.0000000 | 0.0000 | INF |
| 7 | O2 | -- | B | 35000.0000000 | 0.0000000 | 0.0000 | INF |
| 8 | ARTIF-- D- | 1 | LB | 0.0000000 | -75.0000000 | 0.0000 | INF |
| 9 | ARTIF-- D- | 2 | LB | 0.0000000 | -1.0000000 | 0.0000 | INF |
| 10 | ARTIF-- D- | 3 | LB | 0.0000000 | 300000.0000000 | 0.0000 | INF |

```
MINIMUM VALUE OF THE OBJECTIVE FUNCTION =    36250.000000
```

$165,000 but assure an error rate of only 0.510 percent. All of the senior partner time is utilized by this solution, but only 666 hours, 40 minutes of accounting associate time is required. That is, the greater importance attached to the error rate has meant the assignment of more time from the most competent personnel, increasing the cost, but not by a significant amount relative to monies available in military budgets.

The senior partners of Auditrol congratulate her perspicacity and decide to go with her solution, reasoning that the Air Force will also be much more concerned about error rate than about cost. An empty chair in the Senior Partner Meeting Room is dusted off in anticipation of her passing the CPA exam next month.

## 6.4  SUMMARY AND CONCLUSIONS

The main purpose of this chapter is the illustration of the utility of LP computer programs for assisting management decisions. A variety of applications are suggested, including production, blending, financial, advertising, small business, and accounting decisions. The value of goal-programming formulations is demonstrated by two of the examples.

Computer-generated solutions of the examples are exhibited, as well as computer printouts of problem formulations and tables showing the results of sensitivity analyses. Only formulation and interpretation effort is expended, not computational effort. Thus, the power and the limitations of a company computer are made apparent.

By no means do the examples chosen exhaust all of the possibilities for application of linear programming. Other realistic applications, along with their computer solutions, will appear in the exercises below. Whether or not all of these exercises are assigned to you by your instructor as homework or test problems, you should at least scan them all to appreciate the broad applicability of linear programming to management decision problems.

Many of the earlier exercises of this chapter are based on problems you may have already formulated, since they were exercises in Chapter 2. Now you will be able to appreciate their solutions without having to do hand computations.

## KEY WORDS AND PHRASES

**Application**  An example of a realistic business decision problem wherein a linear programming computer analysis is very helpful.

**MPOS**  Multi Purpose Optimization System. A proprietary computer software product of Northwestern University that is currently available for use by license only on CDC 6000 and Cyber series computers.

**SUMMARY OF RESULTS**  The table in the MPOS output where one finds the optimal values for decision variables, the optimum objective-function value, and implicit values of resources.

**201**

APPLIED LINEAR
PROGRAMMING
MODELS WITH
COMPUTER
SOLUTIONS

**ACTIVITY LEVEL**   The name given in the MPOS output to the optimum value of a decision variable.

**OPPORTUNITY COST**   The name given in the MPOS output to the implicit value of an extra unit of resource.

**RNGOBJ**   The table in the MPOS output that gives the one-at-a-time sensitivity analyses for objective-function coefficients of basic variables.

**RNGRHS**   The table in the MPOS output that gives individual sensitivity analyses for the availability of scarce resources.

**Familiarization**   Key word in the heading of Section 6.2, wherein interpretation of MPOS input and output is discussed relative to a problem you have already solved.

**Goal programming**   A way of handling multiple objectives, used in Examples 6.5 and 6.8.


## EXERCISES

◆ **6.1** (*Product mix application*)   In Exercise 2.5 of Chapter 2 is the statement of the Clear Cut Corporation problem.   Refer to that statement to verify the model formulation implied by the MPOS output on page 202.   The variables LAM1 and LAM2 are the number of square feet of the two laminated woods to produce in order to maximize profit.

   **a** How many square feet of each laminate should be produced, and what is the maximum profit for the production period?

   **b** Identify the scarce resources and their associated implicit values.   Discuss the implications of the implicit values and the RNGRHS table.

   **c** Discuss the RNGOBJ table.

**6.2** (*Product mix application*)   Determination of an optimal product mix was discussed in Example 2.2 of Chapter 2.   The problem was also formulated in that example, so only solution portions of the MPOS output are given on page 203.   Write a brief report to company management, explaining the implications of this solution.

◆ **6.3** (*Production-distribution application*)   The MPOS output on page 204 exhibits the formulation and SUMMARY OF RESULTS table for the problem that was stated in Exercise 2.12 of Chapter 2.   Here XA1 is the number of units produced in plant *A* for shipment to warehouse 1, XC2 is the number of units produced in plant *C* for shipment to warehouse 2, and so on.

   **a** Verify the model formulation, being particularly certain that you agree with the coefficients in the objective function.

   **b** What is the maximum profit?

   **c** How many units of product are to be produced in plant *B*?

   **d** How many units of product are to be shipped to warehouse 2?

◆ **6.4** (*Production scheduling application*)   Refer to the Solidstate Manufacturing problem, Exercise 2.17 of Chapter 2.   The MPOS output (page 204) reports the formulation and solution, where *AP*1 denotes the number of type 1 transistors produced by method *P* in plant *A*, *BQ*3 denotes the number of type 3 transistors produced by method *Q* in plant *B*, and so on for all 18 variables in the problem.

   **a** Verify the model formulation, being particularly certain that you agree to all the constraints.

*EXERCISE 6.1*

```
TITLE
CLEAR CUT CORPORATION
REGULAR
VARIABLES
LAM1 LAM2
MAXIMIZE
3LAM1 + 4LAM2
CONSTRAINTS
1.  2LAM1 + LAM2 .LE. 10000.
2.  2LAM1 + 3LAM2 .LE. 9000.
3.  LAM1 + 2LAM2 .LE. 6000.
4.  2LAM1 + LAM2 .LE. 6000
5.  LAM1 + 3LAM2 .LE. 8000
RNGOBJ
RNGRHS
OPTIMIZE
```

### SUMMARY OF RESULTS

| VAR NO | VAR NAME | ROW NO | STATUS | ACTIVITY LEVEL | OPPORTUNITY COST | LOWER BOUND | UPPER BOUND |
|---|---|---|---|---|---|---|---|
| 1 | LAM1 | -- | B | 2250.0000000 | 0.0000000 | 0.0000 | INF |
| 2 | LAM2 | -- | B | 1500.0000000 | 0.0000000 | 0.0000 | INF |
| 3 | SLACK-- D- | 1 | B | 4000.0000000 | 0.0000000 | 0.0000 | INF |
| 4 | SLACK-- D- | 2 | LB | 0.0000000 | 1.2500000 | 0.0000 | INF |
| 5 | SLACK-- D- | 3 | B | 750.0000000 | 0.0000000 | 0.0000 | INF |
| 6 | SLACK-- D- | 4 | LB | 0.0000000 | .2500000 | 0.0000 | INF |
| 7 | SLACK-- D- | 5 | B | 1250.0000000 | 0.0000000 | 0.0000 | INF |

```
MAXIMUM VALUE OF THE OBJECTIVE FUNCTION =    12750.000000
```

### RNGOBJ
******
(OPTIMALITY RANGE FOR COST COEFFICIENTS)
BASIC VARIABLES ONLY

| CJ | XIN | MIN CJ Z-LOWER | ORIGINAL CJ Z | MAX CJ Z-UPPER | XIN |
|---|---|---|---|---|---|
| 1 | 6 | 2.6667 12000. | 3.0000 12750. | 8.0000 24000. | 4 |
| 2 | 4 | 1.5000 9000.0 | 4.0000 12750. | 4.5000 13500. | 6 |

### RNGRHS
******
(OPTIMALITY RANGE FOR RIGHT-HAND-SIDE CONSTANTS)
NON-SLACK RESOURCES ONLY

| BI | XOUT | MIN BI Z-LOWER | ORIGINAL BI Z | MAX BI Z-UPPER | XOUT |
|---|---|---|---|---|---|
| 2 | 2 | 6000.0 9000.0 | 9000.0 12750. | 10000. 14000. | 7 |
| 4 | 7 | 4333.3 12333. | 6000.0 12750. | 9000.0 13500. | 2 |

**b** In words rather than symbols, what is the optimal solution?

**c** If the optimal solution is implemented, will all of the plants be involved in production and will all processes be used?

**6.5** (*Job shop application*)  You will recognize the setting of this problem from Exercise 2.7 of Chapter 2.  To make the problem more interesting, however, some of its requirements have been changed.  It is restated here, with modifications, for easy reference during the model-formulation stage.

Centennial Machine Shop makes three types of parts for automatic washing machines.  It purchases castings of the parts from a local foundry and then finishes the parts on drilling, shaping, and polishing machines.

The selling prices of parts *A*, *B*, and *C*, respectively, are $8, $10, and $14.

**EXERCISE 6.2**

**203**

**APPLIED LINEAR
PROGRAMMING
MODELS WITH
COMPUTER
SOLUTIONS**

```
                              SUMMARY OF RESULTS
VAR  VAR        ROW STATUS      ACTIVITY     OPPORTUNITY      LOWER        UPPER
NO NAME          NO             LEVEL          COST          BOUND        BOUND
 1 XA        --   LB          0.0000000      .1000000       0.0000        INF
 2 XB        --   B          45.0000000      0.0000000      0.0000        INF
 3 XC        --   LB          0.0000000     1.6000000       0.0000        INF
 4 XD        --   B          20.0000000      0.0000000      0.0000        INF
 5 SLACK-- D-  1  LB          0.0000000     1.8000000       0.0000        INF
 6 SLACK-- D-  2  B         140.0000000      0.0000000      0.0000        INF
 7 SLACK-- D-  3  B         305.0000000      0.0000000      0.0000        INF
 8 SLACK-- D-  4  LB          0.0000000      .7000000       0.0000        INF


        MAXIMUM VALUE OF THE OBJECTIVE FUNCTION =        570.000000


                              RNGOBJ
                              ******
              (OPTIMALITY RANGE FOR COST COEFFICIENTS)
                        BASIC VARIABLES ONLY


  CJ   XIN        MIN  CJ      ORIGINAL CJ      MAX  CJ       XIN
                  -------      -----------      -------
                  Z-LOWER          Z           Z-UPPER


   2    1         9.7143        10.000          24.000         8
                  557.14        570.00          1200.0

   4    1         5.8333        6.0000          15.000         5
                  566.67        570.00          750.00



                              RNGRHS
                              ******
            (OPTIMALITY RANGE FOR RIGHT-HAND-SIDE CONSTANTS)
                        NON-SLACK RESOURCES ONLY


  BI   XOUT       MIN  BI      ORIGINAL BI      MAX  BI       XOUT
                  -------      -----------      -------
                  Z-LOWER          Z           Z-UPPER


   1    2         50.000        200.00          300.00         4
                  300.00        570.00          750.00

   4    4         200.00        300.00          533.33         6
                  500.00        570.00          733.33
```

Castings for parts $A$, $B$, and $C$, respectively, cost $4.35, $6, and $10, delivered from the foundry.

The shop possesses only one of each type of machine. Including labor costs, costs per hour to run each of the three machines are $20 for drilling, $30 for shaping, and $30 for polishing. The capacities (parts per hour) for each part on each machine are shown in the following table:

|                | Capacity per hour | | |
|----------------|--------|--------|--------|
| **Machine**    | Part $A$ | Part $B$ | Part $C$ |
| Drilling       | 25     | 40     | 25     |
| Shaping        | 25     | 20     | 20     |
| Polishing      | 40     | 30     | 40     |

At least three of each type of part must be made per hour. No more than eight parts $A$ should be made per hour. If these restrictions are met, every part that is made can be sold. Centennial Machine Shop's manager wants to know how many parts of each type to make per hour in order to maximize hourly profit.

Formulation of an LP model for this problem is not trivial. The key idea is the consideration of the time per part required on each machine. For example, since the shaping machine has the capacity to handle 20 parts $B$ per hour, then one-twentieth of an hour (3 minutes) is required for shaping one part $B$.

## EXERCISE 6.3

```
       TITLE
       PLANT-WAREHOUSE DISTRIBUTION
       REGULAR
       MAXIMIZE
       7XA1 + 14XA2 + 5XB1 + 5XB2 + 11XC1 + 9XC2
       CONSTRAINTS
   1.  XA1 + XB1 + XC1 = 400
   2.  XA2 + XB2 + XC2 = 300
   3.  XA1 + XA2 .LE. 200
   4.  XB1 + XB2 .LE. 400
   5.  XC1 + XC2 .LE. 300
       OPTIMIZE
```

### SUMMARY OF RESULTS

| VAR NO | VAR NAME | ROW NO | STATUS | ACTIVITY LEVEL | OPPORTUNITY COST | LOWER BOUND | UPPER BOUND |
|---|---|---|---|---|---|---|---|
| 1 | XA1 | -- | LB | 0.0000000 | 7.0000000 | 0.0000 | INF |
| 2 | XA2 | -- | B | 200.0000000 | 0.0000000 | 0.0000 | INF |
| 3 | XB1 | -- | B | 100.0000000 | 0.0000000 | 0.0000 | INF |
| 4 | XB2 | -- | B | 100.0000000 | 0.0000000 | 0.0000 | INF |
| 5 | XC1 | -- | B | 300.0000000 | 0.0000000 | 0.0000 | INF |
| 6 | XC2 | -- | LB | 0.0000000 | 2.0000000 | 0.0000 | INF |
| 7 | ARTIF-- D- | 1 | LB | 0.0000000 | 5.0000000 | 0.0000 | INF |
| 8 | ARTIF-- D- | 2 | LB | 0.0000000 | 5.0000000 | 0.0000 | INF |
| 9 | SLACK-- D- | 3 | LB | 0.0000000 | 9.0000000 | 0.0000 | INF |
| 10 | SLACK-- D- | 4 | B | 200.0000000 | 0.0000000 | 0.0000 | INF |
| 11 | SLACK-- D- | 5 | LB | 0.0000000 | 6.0000000 | 0.0000 | INF |

MAXIMUM VALUE OF THE OBJECTIVE FUNCTION = 7100.000000

## EXERCISE 6.4

```
       TITLE
       SOLIDSTATE MANUFACTURING
       REVISED
       MAXIMIZE
       12AP1 + 10AQ1 + 8AR1 + 15AP2 + 18AQ2 + 10AR2
       + 22AP3 + 14AQ3 + 12AR3 + 13BP1 + 11BQ1 + 10BR1
       + 10BP2 + 20BQ2 + 8BR2 + 15BP3 + 20BQ3 + 10BR3
       CONSTRAINTS
   1.  AP1 + 2AP2 + 4AP3 .LE. 60000
   2.  2AQ1 + 2AQ2 + 5AQ3 .LE. 50000
   3.  3AR1 + 4AR2 + 3AR3 .LE. 30000
   4.  3BP1 + 3BP2 + 5BP3 .LE. 40000
   5.  4BQ1 + 2BQ2 + 3BQ3 .LE. 30000
   6.  2BR1 + 3BR2 + 4BR3 .LE. 20000
   7.  AP1 + AQ1 + AR1 + BP1 + BQ1 + BR1 .LE. 10000
   8.  AP2 + AQ2 + AR2 + BP2 + BQ2 + BR2 .LE. 5000
   9.  AP3 + AQ3 + AR3 + BP3 + BQ3 + BR3 .LE. 4000
       OPTIMIZE
```

### SUMMARY OF RESULTS

| VAR NO | VAR NAME | ROW NO | STATUS | ACTIVITY LEVEL | OPPORTUNITY COST | LOWER BOUND | UPPER BOUND |
|---|---|---|---|---|---|---|---|
| 1 | AP1 | -- | LB | 0.0000000 | 1.0000000 | 0.0000 | INF |
| 2 | AQ1 | -- | LB | 0.0000000 | 3.0000000 | 0.0000 | INF |
| 3 | AR1 | -- | LB | 0.0000000 | 5.0000000 | 0.0000 | INF |
| 4 | AP2 | -- | LB | 0.0000000 | 5.0000000 | 0.0000 | INF |
| 5 | AQ2 | -- | LB | 0.0000000 | 2.0000000 | 0.0000 | INF |
| 6 | AR2 | -- | LB | 0.0000000 | 10.0000000 | 0.0000 | INF |
| 7 | AP3 | -- | B | 4000.0000000 | 0.0000000 | 0.0000 | INF |
| 8 | AQ3 | -- | LB | 0.0000000 | 8.0000000 | 0.0000 | INF |
| 9 | AR3 | -- | LB | 0.0000000 | 10.0000000 | 0.0000 | INF |
| 10 | BP1 | -- | B | 10000.0000000 | 0.0000000 | 0.0000 | INF |
| 11 | BQ1 | -- | LB | 0.0000000 | 2.0000000 | 0.0000 | INF |
| 12 | BR1 | -- | LB | 0.0000000 | 3.0000000 | 0.0000 | INF |
| 13 | BP2 | -- | LB | 0.0000000 | 10.0000000 | 0.0000 | INF |
| 14 | BQ2 | -- | B | 5000.0000000 | 0.0000000 | 0.0000 | INF |
| 15 | BR2 | -- | LB | 0.0000000 | 12.0000000 | 0.0000 | INF |
| 16 | BP3 | -- | LB | 0.0000000 | 7.0000000 | 0.0000 | INF |
| 17 | BQ3 | -- | LB | 0.0000000 | 2.0000000 | 0.0000 | INF |
| 18 | BR3 | -- | LB | 0.0000000 | 12.0000000 | 0.0000 | INF |
| 19 | --SLACK D- | 1 | B | 44000.0000000 | 0.0000000 | 0.0000 | INF |
| 20 | --SLACK D- | 2 | B | 50000.0000000 | 0.0000000 | 0.0000 | INF |
| 21 | --SLACK D- | 3 | B | 30000.0000000 | 0.0000000 | 0.0000 | INF |
| 22 | --SLACK D- | 4 | B | 10000.0000000 | 0.0000000 | 0.0000 | INF |
| 23 | --SLACK D- | 5 | B | 20000.0000000 | 0.0000000 | 0.0000 | INF |
| 24 | --SLACK D- | 6 | B | 20000.0000000 | 0.0000000 | 0.0000 | INF |
| 25 | --SLACK D- | 7 | LB | 0.0000000 | 13.0000000 | 0.0000 | INF |
| 26 | --SLACK D- | 8 | LB | 0.0000000 | 20.0000000 | 0.0000 | INF |
| 27 | --SLACK D- | 9 | LB | 0.0000000 | 22.0000000 | 0.0000 | INF |

MAXIMUM VALUE OF THE OBJECTIVE FUNCTION = 318000.000000

205

APPLIED LINEAR
PROGRAMMING
MODELS WITH
COMPUTER
SOLUTIONS

Thus the cost of shaping per part $B$ is $(\frac{1}{20})(\$30)$ = $1.50. Likewise, drilling cost is $(\frac{1}{40})(\$20)$ = $0.50 and polishing cost is $(\frac{1}{30})(\$30)$ = $1.00 for one part $B$, so that total machining cost per part $B$ is $3. Since selling price is $10 and purchase price from the foundry is $6, profit per part $B$ is $10 − $6 − $3 = $1.00. Other profits per part are similarly determined.

Now consider the constraint for the drilling machine. If $XA$ is the number of parts $A$ made per hour, then $\frac{1}{25}XA$ is the time in hours consumed by parts $A$ on the drilling machine. Likewise, $\frac{1}{40}XB$ is the time consumed by parts $B$ and $\frac{1}{25}XC$ is the time consumed by parts $C$ during the hour. These times cannot exceed one hour, so the drilling-machine constraint is

$$\tfrac{1}{25}XA + \tfrac{1}{40}XB + \tfrac{1}{25}XC \leq 1$$

In the MPOS output on page 206, the first constraint is just this drilling-machine constraint, multiplied by 200 to clear fractions.

a Verify the correctness of the objective-function coefficients and each of the constraints in the model formulation.
b How many of each type of part should be made per hour, and what is the associated hourly profit?
c Would the optimal production decision (number of each type of part per hour) change if the profit per part $A$ could be increased?
d Is all of the available capacity on all of the machines utilized by the optimal solution? If not, for which machine(s) would an increase in capacity be advantageous? How would you propose to increase that capacity, and do you suppose the increase would cost something?
e Interpret the .20 OPPORTUNITY COST associated with variable 5 in the SUMMARY OF RESULTS table. Be careful; this constraint was originally multiplied by 100 before it was input to MPOS.

✦ 6.6 (Blending application) In Exercise 2.8 of Chapter 2 a candy dealer was attempting to determine a minimum-cost assortment of chocolates. Refer to that original problem, but note the following modifications.

Let the objective be the number of pounds of each type of chocolate the dealer should purchase from the wholesaler. $XA$ denotes the number of pounds of type $A$ chocolates to purchase, $XB$ the number of pounds of type $B$, and so on. Include all of the original constraints, but also include the following restrictions in the model formulation: at least 10 percent of the assortment must be type $C$ chocolates, and at least 10 percent must be type $D$.

The model is shown in the MPOS output on page 207. Only the SUMMARY OF RESULTS table is exhibited; no sensitivity analysis was done.

a Verify the correctness of the model.
b State in words the optimal solution.
c What percentage of the total order consists of each type of chocolate?
d Suppose the candy dealer purchases 600 pounds of chocolates for $657. Will she be able to market exactly 300 two-pound boxes of an assortment containing the percentages in part c?
e The candy dealer decided she would like to satisfy all the original conditions except that at least 20 percent, not 10 percent, of the mix must consist of type $D$ chocolates. This means that constraint 7 would be

$$-0.2XA - 0.2XB - 0.2XC + 0.8XD - 0.2XE \text{ .GE. } 0$$

## EXERCISE 6.5

```
TITLE
CENTENNIAL MACHINE SHOP
REGULAR
VARIABLES
XA XB XC
MAXIMIZE
0.90XA+ 1.00XB + .95XC
CONSTRAINTS
1.   8XA + 5XB + 8XC .LE. 200
2.   4XA + 5XB + 5XC .LE. 100
3.   3XA + 4XB + 3XC .LE. 120
4.   XA .GE. 3
5.   XB .GE.3.
6.   XC .GE. 3
7.   XA .LE. 8
RNGOBJ
RNGRHS
OPTIMIZE
```

### SUMMARY OF RESULTS

| VAR NO | VAR NAME | ROW NO | STATUS | ACTIVITY LEVEL | OPPORTUNITY COST | LOWER BOUND | UPPER BOUND |
|---|---|---|---|---|---|---|---|
| 1 | XA | -- | B | 8.0000000 | 0.0000000 | 0.0000 | INF |
| 2 | XB | -- | B | 10.6000000 | 0.0000000 | 0.0000 | INF |
| 3 | XC | -- | B | 3.0000000 | 0.0000000 | 0.0000 | INF |
| 4 | SLACK-- D- | 1 | B | 59.0000000 | 0.0000000 | 0.0000 | INF |
| 5 | SLACK-- D- | 2 | LB | 0.0000000 | .2000000 | 0.0000 | INF |
| 6 | SLACK-- D- | 3 | B | 44.6000000 | 0.0000000 | 0.0000 | INF |
| 7 | SLACK-- | 4 | B | 5.0000000 | 0.0000000 | 0.0000 | INF |
| 14 | ARTIF-- D- | 4 | LB | 0.0000000 | 0.0000000 | 0.0000 | INF |
| 8 | SLACK-- | 5 | B | 7.6000000 | 0.0000000 | 0.0000 | INF |
| 15 | ARTIF-- D- | 5 | LB | 0.0000000 | 0.0000000 | 0.0000 | INF |
| 9 | SLACK-- | 6 | LB | 0.0000000 | .0500000 | 0.0000 | INF |
| 16 | ARTIF-- D- | 6 | LB | 0.0000000 | -.0500000 | 0.0000 | INF |
| 10 | SLACK-- D- | 7 | LB | 0.0000000 | .1000000 | 0.0000 | INF |

MAXIMUM VALUE OF THE OBJECTIVE FUNCTION = 20.650000

### RNGOBJ
******
#### (OPTIMALITY RANGE FOR COST COEFFICIENTS)
#### BASIC VARIABLES ONLY

| CJ | XIN | MIN CJ / Z-LOWER | ORIGINAL CJ / Z | MAX CJ / Z-UPPER | XIN |
|---|---|---|---|---|---|
| 1 | 10 | .80000 / 19.850 | .90000 / 20.650 | *INF* | |
| 2 | 9 | .95000 / 20.120 | 1.0000 / 20.650 | 1.1250 / 21.975 | 10 |
| 3 | | *INF* / | .95000 / 20.650 | 1.0000 / 20.800 | 9 |

### RNGRHS
******
#### (OPTIMALITY RANGE FOR RIGHT-HAND-SIDE CONSTANTS)
#### NON-SLACK RESOURCES ONLY

| BI | XOUT | MIN BI / Z-LOWER | ORIGINAL BI / Z | MAX BI / Z-UPPER | XOUT |
|---|---|---|---|---|---|
| 2 | 8 | 62.000 / 13.050 | 100.00 / 20.650 | 155.75 / 31.800 | 6 |
| 6 | 3 | 0. / 20.800 | 3.0000 / 20.650 | 10.600 / 20.270 | 8 |
| 7 | 7 | 3.0000 / 20.150 | 8.0000 / 20.650 | 17.500 / 21.600 | 8 |

## 207

APPLIED LINEAR
PROGRAMMING
MODELS WITH
COMPUTER
SOLUTIONS

## EXERCISE 6.6

```
TITLE
CANDY MIXTURE
REGULAR
VARIABLES
XA XB XC XD XE
MINIMIZE
.8XA + 1.0XB + 1.5XC + 1.2XD + 1.8XE
CONSTRAINTS
1.   XA + XB + XC + XD + XE .GE. 600
2.   .6XA + .6XB - .4XC - .4XD - .4XE .GE. 0
3.   -.3XA - .3XB - .3XC + .7XD + .7XE .LE. 0
4.   -.125XA-.125XB-.125XC-.125XD+.875XE .GE. 0
5.   -.5XA+.5XB+.5XC+.5XD-.5XF .GE. 0
6.   -.1XA -.1XB + .9XC - .1XD - .1XE .GE. 0
7.   -.1XA - .1XB - .1XC + .9XD - .1XE .GE. 0
RNGOBJ
RNGRHS
OPTIMIZE
```

### SUMMARY OF RESULTS

| VAR NO | VAR NAME | ROW NO | STATUS | ACTIVITY LEVEL | OPPORTUNITY COST | LOWER BOUND | UPPER BOUND |
|---|---|---|---|---|---|---|---|
| 1 | XA | -- | B | 225.0000000 | 0.0000000 | 0.0000 | INF |
| 2 | XB | -- | B | 180.0000000 | 0.0000000 | 0.0000 | INF |
| 3 | XC | -- | B | 60.0000000 | 0.0000000 | 0.0000 | INF |
| 4 | XD | -- | B | 50.0000000 | 0.0000000 | 0.0000 | INF |
| 5 | XE | -- | B | 75.0000000 | 0.0000000 | 0.0000 | INF |
| 6 | SLACK-- | 1 | LB | 0.0000000 | -1.0950000 | 0.0000 | INF |
| 13 | ARTIF-- D- | 1 | LB | 0.0000000 | 1.0950000 | 0.0000 | INF |
| 7 | SLACK-- | 2 | B | 165.0000000 | 0.0000000 | 0.0000 | INF |
| 14 | ARTIF-- D- | 2 | LB | 0.0000000 | 0.0000000 | 0.0000 | INF |
| 8 | SLACK-- D- | 3 | B | 45.0000000 | 0.0000000 | 0.0000 | INF |
| 9 | SLACK-- | 4 | LB | 0.0000000 | -1.0000000 | 0.0000 | INF |
| 16 | ARTIF-- D- | 4 | LB | 0.0000000 | 1.0000000 | 0.0000 | INF |
| 10 | SLACK-- | 5 | LB | 0.0000000 | -.2000000 | 0.0000 | INF |
| 17 | ARTIF-- D- | 5 | LB | 0.0000000 | .2000000 | 0.0000 | INF |
| 11 | SLACK-- | 6 | LB | 0.0000000 | -.2000000 | 0.0000 | INF |
| 18 | ARTIF-- D- | 6 | LB | 0.0000000 | .5000000 | 0.0000 | INF |
| 12 | SLACK-- | 7 | LB | 0.0000000 | -.2000000 | 0.0000 | INF |
| 19 | ARTIF-- D- | 7 | LB | 0.0000000 | .2000000 | 0.0000 | INF |

MINIMUM VALUE OF THE OBJECTIVE FUNCTION = 657.000000

The resulting MPOS run concludes with the statement "***ARTIFICIAL VARIABLES COULD NOT BE SUPPRESSED   NO FEASIBLE SOLUTION EXISTS"  What is the meaning of the word "SUPPRESSED" in this context?

**6.7** (*Blending application*)  Example 2.6 of Chapter 2 exhibited a large gasoline-blending problem faced by a refinery.  The complete model formulation and the solution were stated therein, along with the comment that an alternate optimal solution exists.  Use the SUMMARY OF RESULTS table on page 208 to verify the solution, and tell how the existence of an alternate optimal solution could be detected.  Also, since the MPOS input is not reported here, verify that the solution does satisfy all the original constraints.

◆ **6.8** (*Transportation application*)  See page 209 for the MPOS input and output for the problem described in Exercise 2.10 of Chapter 2.  This was the Laramie-Tie Siding Express problem, involving purchases of truck tires from two companies for shipment to each of four terminals.  Note the integer-valued characteristic of the optimal solution, a characteristic always found in such transportation problems (see Chapter 7).

  **a** Identify in words the meaning of each of the eight variables in the model formulation.

  **b** How many tires are purchased from each of the two tire companies?

  **c** Does an alternate optimal solution exist for this problem?  If so, can you determine one by inspection?  If so, what is it, and how do you know it is also an optimal solution?

  **d** Interpret the negative OPPORTUNITY COST associated with constraint 6.

### EXERCISE 6.7

USING REVISED
REFINERY: GASOLINE BLENDING PROBLEM

SUMMARY OF RESULTS

| VAR NO | VAR NAME | ROW NO | STATUS | ACTIVITY LEVEL | OPPORTUNITY COST | LOWER BOUND | UPPER BOUND |
|---|---|---|---|---|---|---|---|
| 1 | A12 | -- | LB | 0.0000000 | 0.0000000 | 0.0000 | INF |
| 2 | A22 | -- | LB | 0.0000000 | .2396970 | 0.0000 | INF |
| 3 | A32 | -- | LB | 0.0000000 | 0.0000000 | 0.0000 | INF |
| 4 | A42 | -- | B | 166.6666667 | 0.0000000 | 0.0000 | INF |
| 5 | A52 | -- | B | 833.3333333 | 0.0000000 | 0.0000 | INF |
| 6 | P12 | -- | LB | 0.0000000 | .0100000 | 0.0000 | INF |
| 7 | P22 | -- | B | 1350.0000000 | 0.0000000 | 0.0000 | INF |
| 8 | P32 | -- | LB | 0.0000000 | .3845455 | 0.0000 | INF |
| 9 | P42 | -- | LB | 0.0000000 | 4.5045455 | 0.0000 | INF |
| 10 | P52 | -- | LB | 0.0000000 | .7590909 | 0.0000 | INF |
| 11 | P11 | -- | B | 900.0000000 | 0.0000000 | 0.0000 | INF |
| 12 | P21 | -- | B | 450.0000000 | 0.0000000 | 0.0000 | INF |
| 13 | P31 | -- | LB | 0.0000000 | .3845455 | 0.0000 | INF |
| 14 | P41 | -- | LB | 0.0000000 | 4.5045455 | 0.0000 | INF |
| 15 | P51 | -- | LB | 0.0000000 | .7590909 | 0.0000 | INF |
| 16 | R12 | -- | B | 500.0000000 | 0.0000000 | 0.0000 | INF |
| 17 | R22 | -- | LB | 0.0000000 | .2396970 | 0.0000 | INF |
| 18 | R32 | -- | B | 6636.3636364 | 0.0000000 | 0.0000 | INF |
| 19 | R42 | -- | B | 96.9696970 | 0.0000000 | 0.0000 | INF |
| 20 | R52 | -- | B | 2766.6666667 | 0.0000000 | 0.0000 | INF |
| 21 | R11 | -- | LB | 0.0000000 | .3745455 | 0.0000 | INF |
| 22 | R21 | -- | LB | 0.0000000 | 1.4881818 | 0.0000 | INF |
| 23 | R31 | -- | LB | 0.0000000 | .8739394 | .0000 | INF |
| 24 | R41 | -- | LB | 0.0000000 | 1.7478788 | 0.0000 | INF |
| 25 | R51 | -- | LB | 0.0000000 | .7490909 | 0.0000 | INF |
| 26 | --SLACK D- | 8 | LB | 0.0000000 | .9166667 | 0.0000 | INF |
| 27 | --SLACK | 9 | B | 500.0000000 | 0.0000000 | 0.0000 | INF |
| 28 | --SLACK D- | 10 | B | 2300.0000000 | 0.0000000 | 0.0000 | INF |
| 29 | --SLACK | 11 | B | 700.0000000 | 0.0000000 | 0.0000 | INF |
| 30 | --SLACK D- | 12 | LB | 0.0000000 | .2106061 | 0.0000 | INF |
| 31 | --SLACK | 13 | B | 5000.0000000 | 0.0000000 | 0.0000 | INF |
| 32 | --ARTIF D- | 1 | LB | 0.0000000 | 1.5500000 | 0.0000 | INF |
| 33 | --ARTIF D- | 2 | LB | 0.0000000 | 2.2200000 | 0.0000 | INF |
| 34 | --ARTIF D- | 3 | LB | 0.0000000 | 1.0045455 | 0.0000 | INF |
| 35 | --ARTIF D- | 4 | LB | 0.0000000 | 1.1590909 | 0.0000 | INF |
| 36 | --ARTIF D- | 5 | LB | 0.0000000 | -.0151515 | 0.0000 | INF |
| 37 | --ARTIF D- | 6 | LB | 0.0000000 | -.1400000 | 0.0000 | INF |
| 38 | --ARTIF D- | 7 | LB | 0.0000000 | -.0151515 | 0.0000 | INF |
| 39 | --ARTIF D- | 9 | LB | 0.0000000 | 0.0000000 | 0.0000 | INF |
| 40 | --ARTIF D- | 11 | LB | 0.0000000 | 0.0000000 | 0.0000 | INF |
| 41 | --ARTIF D- | 13 | LB | 0.0000000 | 0.0000000 | 0.0000 | INF |

MAXIMUM VALUE OF THE OBJECTIVE FUNCTION = 20292.818182

**6.9** (*Personnel application: Management trainees*)  Four major industrial firms have agreed to cooperate with the United States government (in return for certain subsidies) in a trial management-training program for high school dropouts (HSD), high school graduates (HSG), and college dropouts (CD).  An exception is that firm $C$ will not be able to train high school dropouts.  The government subsidies for training each type of applicant in each firm are given in the following table in thousands of dollars:

| Type of applicant | Firm | | | |
|---|---|---|---|---|
| | A | B | C | D |
| HSD | 12 | 14 | — | 15 |
| HSG | 10 | 10 | 11 | 12 |
| CD | 11 | 9 | 12 | 9 |

Firm $A$ will be allotted 8 trainees, 10 will go to firm $B$, 8 to firm $C$, and 12 to firm $D$.  The government's personnel officers have screened the applicants to the program and have accepted as potential participants 20 high school dropouts, 15 high school graduates, and 15 college dropouts.  The 38 trainees will be selected from this pool of 50 people.

The government wishes to allocate trainees to firms so that total subsidy is

**209**

*APPLIED LINEAR
PROGRAMMING
MODELS WITH
COMPUTER
SOLUTIONS*

*EXERCISE 6.8*

```
TITLE
  TRUCK TIRES PROBLEM
  REGULAR
  MINIMIZE
  70X11+64X12+74X21+62X22+62X31+68X32+62X41+72X42
  CONSTRAINTS
1.  X11+X12=4000
2.  X21+X22=8000
3.  X31+X32=3000
4.  X41+X42=5000
5.  X11+X21+X31+X41.LE.16000
6.  X12+X22+X32+X42.LE.8000
  OPTIMIZE
```

```
                      SUMMARY OF RESULTS

VAR  VAR      ROW STATUS     ACTIVITY      OPPORTUNITY      LOWER      UPPER
NO NAME       NO              LEVEL           COST          BOUND      BOUND
 1 X11        --   B      4000.0000000     0.0000000      0.0000       INF
 2 X12        --   LB        0.0000000    -6.0000000      0.0000       INF
 3 X21        --   B         0.0000000     0.0000000      0.0000       INF
 4 X22        --   B      8000.0000000     0.0000000      0.0000       INF
 5 X31        --   B      3000.0000000     0.0000000      0.0000       INF
 6 X32        --   LB        0.0000000   -18.0000000      0.0000       INF
 7 X41        --   B      5000.0000000     0.0000000      0.0000       INF
 8 X42        --   LB        0.0000000   -22.0000000      0.0000       INF
 9 ARTIF-- D-  1   LB        0.0000000    70.0000000      0.0000       INF
10 ARTIF-- D-  2   LB        0.0000000    74.0000000      0.0000       INF
11 ARTIF-- D-  3   LB        0.0000000    62.0000000      0.0000       INF
12 ARTIF-- D-  4   LB        0.0000000    62.0000000      0.0000       INF
13 SLACK-- D-  5   B      4000.0000000     0.0000000      0.0000       INF
14 SLACK-- D-  6   LB        0.0000000   -12.0000000      0.0000       INF
```

MINIMUM VALUE OF THE OBJECTIVE FUNCTION = 1272000.000000

minimized. Note that this is a transportation-type problem (see Exercise 6.8), so integer values of decision variables are assured.

Let *DA* denote the number of high school dropouts allocated to firm *A*, *GB* denote the number of high school graduates allocated to firm *B*, *CC* denote the number of college dropouts allocated to firm *C*, and so on. The MPOS input and output appear on page 210.

**a** State in words the optimal solution.

**b** Is there an alternate optimal solution? If so, state one.

**c** Remembering that this is a minimization problem, interpret one of the negative OPPORTUNITY COSTS.

**6.10** (*Shipping application*) In Exercise 2.19 of Chapter 2 a cargo-loading problem was stated for the freighter *USS Albatross*. Refer to that exercise for an initial statement of the problem.

Additionally, suppose that some of every type of cargo must be loaded. Specifically, at least 100 tons of bagpipes (1), 50 tons of tweed suits (2), 50 tons of blank passports (3), 200 tons of bananas (4), and 100 tons of coal (5) must be aboard the *Albatross* when it leaves Boston.

Presume cargo types to be numbered according to the designations in the preceding paragraph. Let X1LF be the number of tons of bagpipes to be loaded into the lower forward hold, X4US be the number of tons of bananas to be loaded into the upper stern hold, and so on. The model formulation and MPOS solution are given on pages 211 and 212.

**a** Verify the correctness of the model.

**b** Write up a set of loading instructions for the supervisor of the stevedores who will load the freighter.

**c** How many tons of bagpipes will be aboard? Tons of bananas? Cubic feet of tweed suits?

**d** What do you conclude from all of those "0's" in the OPPORTUNITY COST column? (*Hint:* Take a close look at the RNGOBJ table.)

*EXERCISE 6.9*

```
TITLE
MANAGEMENT TRAINEES
REGULAR
MINIMIZE
12DA + 14DB + 15DD + 10GA + 10GB + 11GC
+ 12GD + 11CA + 9CB + 12CC + 9CD
CONSTRAINTS
1.  DA + GA + CA = 8
2.  DB + GB + CB = 10
3.  GC + CC = 8
4.  DD + GD + CD = 12
5.  DA + DB + DD .LE. 20
6.  GA + GB + GC + GD .LE. 15
7.  CA + CB + CC + CD .LE. 15
OPTIMIZE
```

```
                    SUMMARY OF RESULTS


VAR  VAR     ROW STATUS       ACTIVITY      OPPORTUNITY      LOWER        UPPER
NO   NAME    NO                LEVEL           COST          BOUND        BOUND
 1   DA      --    B        8.0000000       0.0000000       0.0000         INF
 2   DB      --    B        0.0000000       0.0000000       0.0000         INF
 3   DD      --    LB       0.0000000      -1.0000000       0.0000         INF
 4   GA      --    LB       0.0000000      -2.0000000       0.0000         INF
 5   GB      --    B        7.0000000       0.0000000       0.0000         INF
 6   GC      --    B        8.0000000       0.0000000       0.0000         INF
 7   GD      --    LB       0.0000000      -2.0000000       0.0000         INF
 8   CA      --    LB       0.0000000      -4.0000000       0.0000         INF
 9   CB      --    B        3.0000000       0.0000000       0.0000         INF
10   CC      --    LB       0.0000000      -2.0000000       0.0000         INF
11   CD      --    B       12.0000000       0.0000000       0.0000         INF
12   ARTIF-- D-  1 LB       0.0000000      12.0000000       0.0000         INF
13   ARTIF-- D-  2 LB       0.0000000      14.0000000       0.0000         INF
14   ARTIF-- D-  3 LB       0.0000000      15.0000000       0.0000         INF
15   ARTIF-- D-  4 LB       0.0000000      14.0000000       0.0000         INF
16   SLACK-- D-  5 B       12.0000000       0.0000000       0.0000         INF
17   SLACK-- D-  6 LB       0.0000000      -4.0000000       0.0000         INF
18   SLACK-- D-  7 LB       0.0000000      -5.0000000       0.0000         INF


MINIMUM VALUE OF THE OBJECTIVE FUNCTION =        389.000000
```

**e** Which of the original weight and volume constraints were satisfied with equality?

**f** Discuss the RNGRHS table.

**g** (*Information only*) The revised simplex method (a matrix version) was used to solve this problem. Nine iterations were required just to remove the 6 artificial variables from the basis, and 13 more iterations gave the optimal solution. The problem contained 20 variables and 17 constraints.

♦ **6.11** (*Small business application: Assignment problem*) AAA Signs has contracted to erect four different types of billboards to advertise the impending appearance in Mudville of a well-known rock group. Since the performance will be two days hence, the contract requires that all four billboards be erected tomorrow.

Four construction crews have been assembled to do the work. Each crew will erect only one billboard.

The construction supervisor has estimated the time required for each crew to put up each billboard. Those expected times are shown in the table below:

| | Expected time in hours | | | |
|---|---|---|---|---|
| Crew | Board 1 | Board 2 | Board 3 | Board 4 |
| 1 Red | 13 | 11 | 12 | 8 |
| 2 White | 13 | 11 | 10 | 7 |
| 3 Blue | 14 | 12 | 10 | 8 |
| 4 Mauve | 9 | 7 | 7 | 6 |

## 211

**APPLIED LINEAR
PROGRAMMING
MODELS WITH
COMPUTER
SOLUTIONS**

## EXERCISE 6.10

```
TITLE
FREIGHTER CARGO
REVISED
MAXIMIZE
300X1LF + 300X1UF + 300X1LS + 300X1US
+ 180X2LF + 180X2UF + 180X2LS + 180X2US
+ 400X3LF + 400X3UF + 400X3LS + 400X3US
+ 60X4LF + 60X4UF + 60X4LS + 60X4US
+ 50X5LF + 50X5UF + 50X5LS + 50X5US
CONSTRAINTS
1.  X1UF + X2UF + X3UF + X4UF + X5UF .LE. 900
2.  X1US + X2US + X3US + X4US + X5US .LE. 600
3.  100X1LF + 90X2LF + 40X3LF + 30X4LF + 50X5LF .LE. 48000
4.  100X1UF + 90X2UF + 40X3UF + 30X4UF + 50X5UF .LE. 84000
5.  100X1LS + 90X2LS + 40X3LS + 30X4LS + 50X5LS .LE. 32000
6.  100X1US + 90X2US + 40X3US + 30X4US + 50X5US .LE. 40000
7.  3X1LF + 3X1UF + 3X2LF + 3X2UF + 3X3LF + 3X3UF
    + 3X4LF + 3X4UF + 3X5LF + 3X5UF - 4X1LS - 4X1US
    - 4X2LS - 4X2US - 4X3LS - 4X3US - 4X4LS - 4X4US
    - 4X5LS - 4X5US = 0
8.  X1LF + X1UF + X1LS + X1US .GE. 100
9.  X2LF + X2UF + X2LS + X2US .GE. 50
10. X3LF + X3UF + X3LS + X3US .GE. 50
11. X4LF + X4UF + X4LS + X4US .GE. 200
12. X5LF + X5UF + X5LS + X5US .GE. 100
13. X1LF + X1UF + X1LS + X1US .LE. 600
14. X2LF + X2UF + X2LS + X2US .LE. 600
15. X3LF + X3UF + X3LS + X3US .LE. 500
16. X4LF + X4UF + X4LS + X4US .LE. 300
17. X5LF + X5UF + X5LS + X5US .LE. 1000
RNGOBJ
RNGRHS
OPTIMIZE
```

### SUMMARY OF RESULTS

| VAR NU | VAR NAME | ROW NO | STATUS | ACTIVITY LEVEL | OPPORTUNITY COST | LOWER BOUND | UPPER BOUND |
|---|---|---|---|---|---|---|---|
| 1 | X1LF | -- | LB | 0.0000000 | 0.0000000 | 0.0000 | INF |
| 2 | X1UF | -- | B | 232.4489795 | 0.0000000 | 0.0000 | INF |
| 3 | X1LS | -- | LB | 0.0000000 | 0.0000000 | 0.0000 | INF |
| 4 | X1US | -- | B | 317.5510204 | 0.0000000 | 0.0000 | INF |
| 5 | X2LF | -- | B | 259.3877551 | 0.0000000 | 0.0000 | INF |
| 6 | X2UF | -- | B | 397.2789116 | 0.0000000 | 0.0000 | INF |
| 7 | X2LS | -- | B | 133.3333333 | 0.0000000 | 0.0000 | INF |
| 8 | X2US | -- | LB | 0.0000000 | 0.0000000 | 0.0000 | INF |
| 9 | X3LF | -- | LB | 0.0000000 | 0.0000000 | 0.0000 | INF |
| 10 | X3UF | -- | LB | 0.0000000 | 0.0000000 | 0.0000 | INF |
| 11 | X3LS | -- | B | 500.0000000 | 0.0000000 | 0.0000 | INF |
| 12 | X3US | -- | LB | 0.0000000 | 0.0000000 | 0.0000 | INF |
| 13 | X4LF | -- | B | 525.1700680 | 0.0000000 | 0.0000 | INF |
| 14 | X4UF | -- | LB | 0.0000000 | 0.0000000 | 0.0000 | INF |
| 15 | X4LS | -- | LB | 0.0000000 | 0.0000000 | 0.0000 | INF |
| 16 | X4US | -- | B | 274.8299320 | 0.0000000 | 0.0000 | INF |
| 17 | X5LF | -- | B | 160.0000000 | 0.0000000 | 0.0000 | INF |
| 18 | X5UF | -- | LB | 0.0000000 | 0.0000000 | 0.0000 | INF |
| 19 | X5LS | -- | LB | 0.0000000 | 0.0000000 | 0.0000 | INF |
| 20 | X5US | -- | LB | 0.0000000 | 0.0000000 | 0.0000 | INF |
| 21 | --SLACK D- | 1 | B | 290.2721088 | 0.0000000 | 0.0000 | INF |
| 22 | --SLACK D- | 2 | B | 7.6190476 | 0.0000000 | 0.0000 | INF |
| 23 | --SLACK D- | 3 | LB | 0.0000000 | 1.0000000 | 0.0000 | INF |
| 24 | --SLACK D- | 4 | LB | 0.0000000 | 1.0000000 | 0.0000 | INF |
| 25 | --SLACK D- | 5 | LB | 0.0000000 | 1.0000000 | 0.0000 | INF |
| 26 | --SLACK D- | 6 | LB | 0.0000000 | 1.0000000 | 0.0000 | INF |
| 27 | --SLACK | 8 | B | 500.0000000 | 0.0000000 | 0.0000 | INF |
| 28 | --SLACK | 9 | B | 750.0000000 | 0.0000000 | 0.0000 | INF |
| 29 | --SLACK | 10 | B | 450.0000000 | 0.0000000 | 0.0000 | INF |
| 30 | --SLACK | 11 | B | 600.0000000 | 0.0000000 | 0.0000 | INF |
| 31 | --SLACK | 12 | B | 60.0000000 | 0.0000000 | 0.0000 | INF |
| 32 | --SLACK D- | 13 | LB | 0.0000000 | 200.0000000 | 0.0000 | INF |
| 33 | --SLACK D- | 14 | LB | 0.0000000 | 90.0000000 | 0.0000 | INF |
| 34 | --SLACK D- | 15 | LB | 0.0000000 | 360.0000000 | 0.0000 | INF |
| 35 | --SLACK D- | 16 | LB | 0.0000000 | 30.0000000 | 0.0000 | INF |
| 36 | --SLACK D- | 17 | B | 840.0000000 | 0.0000000 | 0.0000 | INF |
| 37 | --ARTIF D- | 7 | LB | 0.0000000 | 0.0000000 | 0.0000 | INF |
| 38 | --ARTIF D- | 8 | LB | 0.0000000 | 0.0000000 | 0.0000 | INF |
| 39 | --ARTIF D- | 9 | LB | 0.0000000 | 0.0000000 | 0.0000 | INF |
| 40 | --ARTIF D- | 10 | LB | 0.0000000 | 0.0000000 | 0.0000 | INF |
| 41 | --ARTIF D- | 11 | LB | 0.0000000 | 0.0000000 | 0.0000 | INF |
| 42 | --ARTIF D- | 12 | LB | 0.0000000 | 0.0000000 | 0.0000 | INF |

MAXIMUM VALUE OF THE OBJECTIVE FUNCTION = 280000.000000

### EXERCISE 6.10 (Continued)

```
                         RNGOBJ
                         ******
              (OPTIMALITY RANGE FOR COST COEFFICIENTS)
                      BASIC VARIABLES ONLY
```

| CJ | XIN | MIN CJ / Z-LOWER | ORIGINAL CJ / Z | MAX CJ / Z-UPPER | XIN |
|---|---|---|---|---|---|
| 13 | 3 | 60.000 / .58000E+06 | 60.000 / .58000E+06 | 60.000 / .58000E+06 | 8 |
| 5 | 1 | 180.00 / .58000E+06 | 180.00 / .58000E+06 | 180.00 / .58000E+06 | 3 |
| 7 | 3 | 180.00 / .58000E+06 | 180.00 / .58000E+06 | 180.00 / .58000E+06 | 9 |
| 17 | 18 | 50.000 / .58000E+06 | 50.000 / .58000E+06 | 100.00 / .58800E+06 | 33 |
| 11 | 9 | 400.00 / .58000E+06 | 400.00 / .58000E+06 | *INF* | |
| 4 | 3 | 300.00 / .58000E+06 | 300.00 / .58000E+06 | 300.00 / .58000E+06 | 15 |
| 6 | 8 | 180.00 / .58000E+06 | 180.00 / .58000E+06 | 180.00 / .58000E+06 | 1 |
| 2 | 1 | 300.00 / .58000E+06 | 300.00 / .58000E+06 | 300.00 / .58000E+06 | 8 |
| 16 | 8 | 60.000 / .58000E+06 | 60.000 / .58000E+06 | 60.000 / .58000E+06 | 3 |

```
                         RNGRHS
                         ******
         (OPTIMALITY RANGE FOR RIGHT-HAND-SIDE CONSTANTS)
                   NON-SLACK RESOURCES ONLY
```

| BI | XOUT | MIN BI / Z-LOWER | ORIGINAL BI / Z | MAX BI / Z-UPPER | XOUT |
|---|---|---|---|---|---|
| 3 | 31 | 45000. / .57700E+06 | 48000. / .58000E+06 | 48889. / .58089E+06 | 22 |
| 4 | 31 | 61000. / .57700E+06 | 64000. / .58000E+06 | 64889. / .58089E+06 | 22 |
| 5 | 22 | 29000. / .57700E+06 | 32000. / .58000E+06 | 53865. / .60187E+06 | 5 |
| 6 | 31 | 37000. / .577C0E+06 | 40000. / .58000E+06 | 40889. / .58089E+06 | 22 |
| 7 | 22 | -53.333 / .58000E+06 | 0. / .58000E+06 | 1346.7 / .58000E+06 | 16 |
| 13 | 22 | 592.22 / .57644E+06 | 600.00 / .58000E+06 | 630.00 / .58600E+06 | 31 |
| 14 | 22 | 777.78 / .57800E+06 | 800.00 / .58000E+06 | 833.33 / .58300E+06 | 31 |
| 15 | 22 | 483.73 / .57416E+06 | 500.00 / .58000E+06 | 575.00 / .60700E+06 | 31 |
| 16 | 30 | 200.00 / .55200E+06 | 800.00 / .58000E+06 | 844.44 / .58133E+06 | 22 |

The supervisor wants to know which crew to assign to which billboard in order to minimize total expected crew hours. MPOS input and solution are shown at the top of page 213.

Let the objective-function coefficients be your key to the meaning of each of the 16 original variables. What is the optimal assignment, and what is the minimum total expected crew hours?

◆ **6.12** (*Accounting application: Assignment problem*) Chekov and Adams is an accounting firm with a number of wealthy clients. One of its services is the preparation

**213**

*APPLIED LINEAR
PROGRAMMING
MODELS WITH
COMPUTER
SOLUTIONS*

## EXERCISE 6.11

```
TITLE
CREW ASSIGNMENT
REGULAR
MINIMIZE
13X11 + 11X12 + 12X13 + 8X14 + 13X21 + 11X22
+ 10X23 + 7X24 + 14X31 + 12X32 + 10X33
+ 8X34 + 9X41 + 7X42 + 7X43 + 6X44
CONSTRAINTS
1.    X11 + X12 + X13 + X14 = 1
2.    X21 + X22 + X23 + X24 = 1
3.    X31 + X32 + X33 + X34 = 1
4.    X41 + X42 + X43 + X44 = 1
5.    X11 + X21 + X31 + X41 = 1
6.    X12 + X22 + X32 + X42 = 1
7.    X13 + X23 + X33 + X43 = 1
8.    X14 + X24 + X34 + X44 = 1
OPTIMIZE
```

### SUMMARY OF RESULTS

| VAR NO | VAR NAME | ROW NO | STATUS | ACTIVITY LEVEL | OPPORTUNITY COST | LOWER BOUND | UPPER BOUND |
|---|---|---|---|---|---|---|---|
| 1 | X11 | -- | B | 0.0000000 | 0.0000000 | 0.0000 | INF |
| 2 | X12 | -- | B | 1.0000000 | 0.0000000 | 0.0000 | INF |
| 3 | X13 | -- | LB | 0.0000000 | -3.0000000 | 0.0000 | INF |
| 4 | X14 | -- | LB | 0.0000000 | -1.0000000 | 0.0000 | INF |
| 5 | X21 | -- | B | 0.0000000 | 0.0000000 | 0.0000 | INF |
| 6 | X22 | -- | LB | 0.0000000 | 0.0000000 | 0.0000 | INF |
| 7 | X23 | -- | LB | 0.0000000 | -1.0000000 | 0.0000 | INF |
| 8 | X24 | -- | B | 1.0000000 | 0.0000000 | 0.0000 | INF |
| 9 | X31 | -- | LB | 0.0000000 | 0.0000000 | 0.0000 | INF |
| 10 | X32 | -- | B | 0.0000000 | 0.0000000 | 0.0000 | INF |
| 11 | X33 | -- | B | 1.0000000 | 0.0000000 | 0.0000 | INF |
| 12 | X34 | -- | LB | 0.0000000 | 0.0000000 | 0.0000 | INF |
| 13 | X41 | -- | B | 1.0000000 | 0.0000000 | 0.0000 | INF |
| 14 | X42 | -- | LB | 0.0000000 | 0.0000000 | 0.0000 | INF |
| 15 | X43 | -- | LB | 0.0000000 | -2.0000000 | 0.0000 | INF |
| 16 | X44 | -- | LB | 0.0000000 | -3.0000000 | 0.0000 | INF |
| 17 | ARTIF-- 0- | 1 | LB | 0.0000000 | 7.0000000 | 0.0000 | INF |
| 18 | ARTIF-- 0- | 2 | LB | 0.0000000 | 7.0000000 | 0.0000 | INF |
| 19 | ARTIF-- 0- | 3 | LB | 0.0000000 | 8.0000000 | 0.0000 | INF |
| 20 | ARTIF-- 0- | 4 | LB | 0.0000000 | 3.0000000 | 0.0000 | INF |
| 21 | ARTIF-- 0- | 5 | LB | 0.0000000 | 6.0000000 | 0.0000 | INF |
| 22 | ARTIF-- 0- | 6 | LB | 0.0000000 | 4.0000000 | 0.0000 | INF |
| 23 | ARTIF-- 0- | 7 | LB | 0.0000000 | 2.0000000 | 0.0000 | INF |
| 32 | ARTIF-- 0- | 8 | B | 0.0000000 | 0.0000000 | 0.0000 | INF |

MINIMUM VALUE OF THE OBJECTIVE FUNCTION =     37.000000

of income tax returns. On April 14, at the busiest time of the year, four of its most valued clients finally bring in the necessary papers for completion of their tax returns. To keep these clients happy, the firm agrees to prepare their returns on a crash basis.

Four of Chekov and Adams's tax specialists, Brown, Greene, White, and Black, are selected for assignment to the four returns. Intense, intimate consultation with each client is anticipated, so each specialist will work on only one return. Mr. Adams and Mr. Chekov have estimated the time required for each specialist to complete the return of each client. These times, in hours, are given in the table below:

| | Time table | | | |
|---|---|---|---|---|
| | Client | | | |
| Specialist | 1 | 2 | 3 | 4 |
| 1 Brown | 15 | 22 | 16 | 12 |
| 2 Greene | 14 | 20 | 13 | 10 |
| 3 White | 20 | 23 | 18 | 14 |
| 4 Black | 17 | 21 | 16 | 13 |

The jobs will begin at noon on April 14, and the returns must be in the mail by midnight, April 15. Thus any of the four tax specialists will be working overtime after 12 hours on the job. Hourly wages for Brown, Greene, White, and Black, respectively, are $14, $16, $8, and $12. Each receives time-and-a-half for overtime.

Mr. Chekov wants to know which specialist to assign to which client in order to minimize the estimated total cost of preparing all returns. With this objective the problem becomes just a simple assignment problem, using cost instead of time as coefficients in the objective function. The cost for Brown's preparation of client 1's return, for example, is 12($14) + 3($21) = $231. Similar calculations produce all the entries in the following cost table, with the entries being in dollars.

### Cost table

| Specialist | Client 1 | 2 | 3 | 4 |
|---|---|---|---|---|
| 1 Brown | 231 | 378 | 252 | 168 |
| 2 Greene | 240 | 384 | 216 | 160 |
| 3 White | 192 | 228 | 168 | 120 |
| 4 Black | 234 | 306 | 216 | 162 |

Let X11 denote a Brown–client 1 association, X23 a Greene–client 3 association, and so on. These variables will each take on only the values 0 and 1, and only 4 of the 16 X's will be 1s.

The MPOS input and output follow on page 215. What is the assignment schedule, and what is the minimum estimated total cost?

**6.13** (*Accounting application: Assignment problem with goal programming*) Mr. Adams would prefer a minimum-time assignment to a minimum-cost assignment (see Exercise 6.12). That way he might be able to utilize the specialists on other jobs, thus increasing revenue to the firm. Accordingly, he works the problem using the same variables and constraints that were used by Mr. Chekov, but with the following different objective function:

$$T = 15X11 + 22X12 + 16X13 + 12X14 + 14X21 + 20X22 + 13X23 + 10X24 + 20X31 + 23X32 + 18X33 + 14X34 + 17X41 + 21X42 + 16X43 + 13X44$$

The new computer run gives the results $X11 = 1$, $X23 = 1$, $X34 = 1$, $X42 = 1$, with all the other X's being 0.

a What is Adams's assignment schedule and the associated minimum estimated time?
b What is the cost of Adams's minimum-time assignment?
c Compare time and cost for Chekov's assignment (Exercise 6.12) and Adams's assignment. Could goal programming be used to resolve the differences in a problem like this? How would you formulate the goal-programming version?
d Consider the two competing assignments and your goal-programming model. Do you believe the effort required to solve this last version is worthwhile in this particular case? Cite two possible solutions to your goal-programming model (by inspection; do not try to solve it except on a computer). Do you think a different problem of this type would be as easy? Why or why not?

**215**

*APPLIED LINEAR
PROGRAMMING
MODELS WITH
COMPUTER
SOLUTIONS*

## EXERCISE 6.12

```
TITLE
MR. CHEKOV'S PROBLEM
REGULAR
MINIMIZE
   231X11 + 378X12 + 252X13 + 168X14 + 240X21 + 384X22
   + 216X23 + 160X24 + 192X31 + 228X32 + 168X33 + 120X34
   + 234X41 + 306X42 + 216X43 + 162X44
CONSTRAINTS
1.   X11 + X12 + X13 + X14 = 1
2.   X21 + X22 + X23 + X24 = 1
3.   X31 + X32 + X33 + X34 = 1
4.   X41 + X42 + X43 + X44 = 1
5.   X11 + X21 + X31 + X41 = 1
6.   X12 + X22 + X32 + X42 = 1
7.   X13 + X23 + X33 + X43 = 1
8.   X14 + X24 + X34 + X44 = 1
OPTIMIZE
```

### SUMMARY OF RESULTS

| VAR NO | VAR NAME | ROW NO | STATUS | ACTIVITY LEVEL | OPPORTUNITY COST | LOWER BOUND | UPPER BOUND |
|---|---|---|---|---|---|---|---|
| 1 | X11 | -- | B | 1.0000000 | 0.0000000 | 0.0000 | INF |
| 2 | X12 | -- | LB | 0.0000000 | -105.0000000 | 0.0000 | INF |
| 3 | X13 | -- | LB | 0.0000000 | -39.0000000 | 0.0000 | INF |
| 4 | X14 | -- | LB | 0.0000000 | -11.0000000 | 0.0000 | INF |
| 5 | X21 | -- | LB | 0.0000000 | -6.0000000 | 0.0000 | INF |
| 6 | X22 | -- | LB | 0.0000000 | -108.0000000 | 0.0000 | INF |
| 7 | X23 | -- | B | 0.0000000 | 0.0000000 | 0.0000 | INF |
| 8 | X24 | -- | B | 1.0000000 | 0.0000000 | 0.0000 | INF |
| 9 | X31 | -- | LB | 0.0000000 | -6.0000000 | 0.0000 | INF |
| 10 | X32 | -- | B | 1.0000000 | 0.0000000 | 0.0000 | INF |
| 11 | X33 | -- | B | 0.0000000 | 0.0000000 | 0.0000 | INF |
| 12 | X34 | -- | LB | 0.0000000 | -8.0000000 | 0.0000 | INF |
| 13 | X41 | -- | B | 0.0000000 | 0.0000000 | 0.0000 | INF |
| 14 | X42 | -- | LB | 0.0000000 | -30.0000000 | 0.0000 | INF |
| 15 | X43 | -- | B | 1.0000000 | 0.0000000 | 0.0000 | INF |
| 16 | X44 | -- | LB | 0.0000000 | -2.0000000 | 0.0000 | INF |
| 17 | ARTIF-- | D- 1 | LB | 0.0000000 | 157.0000000 | 0.0000 | INF |
| 18 | ARTIF-- | D- 2 | LB | 0.0000000 | 160.0000000 | 0.0000 | INF |
| 19 | ARTIF-- | D- 3 | LB | 0.0000000 | 112.0000000 | 0.0000 | INF |
| 20 | ARTIF-- | D- 4 | LB | 0.0000000 | 160.0000000 | 0.0000 | INF |
| 21 | ARTIF-- | D- 5 | LB | 0.0000000 | 74.0000000 | 0.0000 | INF |
| 22 | ARTIF-- | D- 6 | LB | 0.0000000 | 116.0000000 | 0.0000 | INF |
| 23 | ARTIF-- | D- 7 | LB | 0.0000000 | 56.0000000 | 0.0000 | INF |
| 32 | ARTIF-- | D- 8 | B | 0.0000000 | 0.0000000 | 0.0000 | INF |

MINIMUM VALUE OF THE OBJECTIVE FUNCTION = 835.000000

◆ **6.14** (*Small business application*)  Refer to Exercise 4.29 at the end of Chapter 4. This is the Suhonaha motorcycle dealer problem, which has a straightforward formulation.  If we let $X1$ be the number of S125 motorcycles to order, and $X2$ and $X3$ be the numbers of S175 and S250 motorcycles, respectively, then the MPOS output on page 216 shows the formulation and solution.

Although the SUMMARY OF RESULTS table shows noninteger values for $X2$ and $X3$, be assured that the optimal integer solution is $X1 = 0$, $X2 = 51$, and $X3 = 58$, a result obtained using the Gomory cutting-plane algorithm to be discussed in the first part of Chapter 7.  The maximum profit with the integer solution is $55,200, very near the $55,276.60 given as the noninteger maximum.  Thus we may presume that the analyses in RNGOBJ and RNGRHS are fairly dependable guidelines even for an integer solution.

**a** Refer to the RNGOBJ table.  What does it say to the Suhonaha dealer about reductions in selling price (due to "haggling" or special sales, for instance) on S175 and S250 motorcycles?

**b** Consider the 0.72 OPPORTUNITY COST associated with an extra dollar of capital.  Since a dollar is worth a dollar, does this mean the dealer would expect *less* net profit if he could acquire more capital?  If not, what *does* it mean?

**c** What is the rate of return on the dealer's investment?

*EXERCISE 6.14*

```
TITLE
SUHONAHA MOTORCYCLE DEALER
REGULAR
MAXIMIZE
300X1 + 400X2 + 600X3
CONSTRAINTS
1.  400X1 + 500X2 + 800X3 .LE. 72000
2.  3X1 + 4X2 + 5X3 .LE. 600
3.  2X1 + 4X2 + 10X3 .LE. 1000
4.  15X1 + 9X2 + 5X3 .LE. 750
RNGRHS
RNGOBJ
OPTIMIZE
```

### SUMMARY OF RESULTS

| VAR NO | VAR NAME | ROW NO | STATUS | ACTIVITY LEVEL | OPPORTUNITY COST | LOWER BOUND | UPPER BOUND |
|--------|----------|--------|--------|----------------|------------------|-------------|-------------|
| 1 | X1 | -- | LB | 0.0000000 | 53.1914894 | 0.0000 | INF |
| 2 | X2 | -- | B | 51.0638298 | 0.0000000 | 0.0000 | INF |
| 3 | X3 | -- | B | 58.0851064 | 0.0000000 | 0.0000 | INF |
| 4 | SLACK-- D- | 1 | LB | 0.0000000 | .7234043 | 0.0000 | INF |
| 5 | SLACK-- D- | 2 | B | 105.3191489 | 0.0000000 | 0.0000 | INF |
| 6 | SLACK-- D- | 3 | B | 214.8936170 | 0.0000000 | 0.0000 | INF |
| 7 | SLACK-- D- | 4 | LB | 0.0000000 | 4.2553191 | 0.0000 | INF |

MAXIMUM VALUE OF THE OBJECTIVE FUNCTION = 55276.595745

### RNGOBJ
******
(OPTIMALITY RANGE FOR COST COEFFICIENTS)
BASIC VARIABLES ONLY

| CJ | XIN | MIN CJ / Z-LOWER | ORIGINAL CJ / Z | MAX CJ / Z-UPPER | XIN |
|----|-----|--------|-------------|--------|-----|
| 3 | 4 | 222.22 / 33333. | 600.00 / 55277. | 640.00 / 57600. | 7 |
| 2 | 1 | 375.00 / 54000. | 400.00 / 55277. | 1080.0 / 90000. | 4 |

### RNGRHS
******
(OPTIMALITY RANGE FOR RIGHT-HAND-SIDE CONSTANTS)
NON-SLACK RESOURCES ONLY

| BI | XOUT | MIN BI / Z-LOWER | ORIGINAL BI / Z | MAX BI / Z-UPPER | XOUT |
|----|------|--------|-------------|--------|------|
| 1 | 3 | 41667. / 33333. | 72000. / 55277. | 86429. / 65714. | 6 |
| 4 | 2 | 450.00 / 54000. | 750.00 / 55277. | 1296.0 / 57600. | 3 |

**d** Among the three resource constraints—storage space, sales time, and mechanic time—which is a binding constraint? Up to what amount should the dealer be willing to spend to acquire an extra unit of that scarce resource? Convert that information to practical advice to the dealer.

**e** What are the implications to the dealer of the positive-valued slack variables for constraints 2 and 3?

♦ **6.15** (*Financial application: Investment portfolio*) Refer to Justin Case's investment problem, Exercise 2.9 in Chapter 2. MPOS input and output are on page 217.

  **a** How much is invested in each of the five areas, and what is the rate of return on investment?

  **b** Since Justin was to put at least a quarter of his capital ($250,000) into areas 1, 2, and 3, and at least half that amount ($125,000) into area 1, why was the constraint X1 .GE. 125000 not part of the input to MPOS?

  **c** Interpret the 150,000 value of the SLACK variable 7.

**217**

APPLIED LINEAR
PROGRAMMING
MODELS WITH
COMPUTER
SOLUTIONS

**6.16** (*Financial application*) Discuss the RNGOBJ table for Example 6.4, the First Intrastate Banks problem. What would be the effective interest rate at optimality if the rate for otherwise-secured loans were 18 percent instead of 20 percent? If the rate for commercial loans were to fall to just below 15 percent, what other type of loan would be made as part of the optimal solution?

**6.17** (*Financial application: Goal-programming formulation*) Refer to the First Intrastate Banks problems, Examples 6.4 and 6.5. Suppose that the requirements imposed by the board of directors remain the same as those stated in Example 6.4, but that the president of Bank of Bosler establishes the following different set of goals:

> *Goal 1:* Effective interest rate of at least 17 percent.
>
> *Goal 2:* At least $2 million for home mortgages.
>
> *Goal 3:* At least $1 million for agricultural loans.
>
> *Goal 4:* The combined total of agricultural and industrial loans is at least $5 million.

The president further decides that goal 1 is twice as important as goal 4 and that goal 2 is twice as important as goal 1, while goal 3 and goal 4 are equally important.
  **a** Formulate the goal-programming LP model for this problem.
  **b** The optimal x values, obtained from an MPOS run, are these: $x_1 = $1 million, $x_2 = $2 million, $x_3 = $4 million, $x_4 = $7 million, $x_5 = 0$, $x_6 = $4 million, $x_7 = $2 million. Consider the four goals. Which ones are not achieved? Which, if any, are overachieved?

✦ **6.18** (*Inventory-production application*) American Engines has the contract to manufacture 4,000 engines for snowblowers over the four months preceding the winter

*EXERCISE 6.15*

```
TITLE
     JUSTIN CASE'S INVESTMENT PORTFOLIO
     REGULAR
     VARIABLES
     X1 TO X5
     MAXIMIZE
     .1X1 + .2X2 + .3X3 + .4X4 + .5X5
     CONSTRAINTS
 1.   X1 + X2 + X3 + X4 + X5 .LE. 1000000
 2.   X1 + X2 + X3 .GE. 250000
 3.   X1 .GE. 200000
 4.   -X3 + X4 .LE. 0
 5.   -X1 - X4 + X5 .LE. 0
     OPTIMIZE
```

SUMMARY OF RESULTS

| VAR NO | VAR NAME | ROW STATUS | NO | | ACTIVITY LEVEL | OPPORTUNITY COST | LOWER BOUND | UPPER BOUND |
|---|---|---|---|---|---|---|---|---|
| 1 | X1 | -- | | B | 200000.0000000 | 0.0000000 | 0.0000 | INF |
| 2 | X2 | -- | | LB | 0.0000000 | .2000000 | 0.0000 | INF |
| 3 | X3 | -- | | B | 200000.0000000 | 0.0000000 | 0.0000 | INF |
| 4 | X4 | -- | | B | 200000.0000000 | 0.0000000 | 0.0000 | INF |
| 5 | X5 | -- | | B | 400000.0000000 | 0.0000000 | 0.0000 | INF |
| 6 | SLACK-- D- | 1 | | LB | 0.0000000 | .4000000 | 0.0000 | INF |
| 7 | SLACK-- | 2 | | B | 150000.0000000 | 0.0000000 | 0.0000 | INF |
| 12 | ARTIF-- D- | 2 | | LB | 0.0000000 | 0.0000000 | 0.0000 | INF |
| 8 | SLACK-- | 3 | | LB | 0.0000000 | .2000000 | 0.0000 | INF |
| 13 | ARTIF-- D- | 3 | | LB | 0.0000000 | -.2000000 | 0.0000 | INF |
| 9 | SLACK-- D- | 4 | | LB | 0.0000000 | .1000000 | 0.0000 | INF |
| 10 | SLACK-- D- | 5 | | LB | 0.0000000 | .1000000 | 0.0000 | INF |

MAXIMUM VALUE OF THE OBJECTIVE FUNCTION =    360000.000000

season. American must deliver the engines to the snowblower manufacturer according to the following schedule. Deliveries are to be made at the end of each month.

| Month | Number of engines |
|---|---|
| July | 500 |
| August | 1,200 |
| September | 1,500 |
| October | 800 |

Any number of engines may be produced in any month. Production costs per engine per month differ because of escalating prices of commodities and a new contract with the union. The production cost per engine is $50 in July, $55 in August, $63 in September, and $74 in October.

Including cost of capital, storage space, maintenance, and insurance, inventory cost is $10 per engine on hand at the end of any month (after delivery to fill demand). Because of warehouse capacity not more than 600 engines may be stored in any one month.

Suppose that American Engines has 100 of the engines in inventory at the first of July. Its management wants to know the production schedule that will minimize total cost of inventory and production over the four-month period. Zero inventory is desired at the end of October.

Let $XJ$, $XA$, $XS$, and $XO$ be the number of engines to produce in July, August, September, and October, respectively. Then production cost in dollars is

$$50XJ + 55XA + 63XS + 74XO$$

To determine inventory cost, proceed in the following manner. At the end of July there will be $100 + XJ$ engines on hand, but demand is 500, so inventory cost at the end of July, in dollars, is

$$10(100 + XJ - 500) = 10XJ - 4,000$$

By the end of August, $100 + XJ + XA$ engines will have been available to fill demand of 1,700 engines, and so on. You should verify that total inventory cost in dollars is

$$30XJ + 20XA + 10XS - 51,000$$

keeping in mind that inventory at the end of October will be zero.

Demand requirements and warehouse capacity supply the constraints. In the MPOS output (page 219) is the model formulation and the solution. Note that $51,000 should be subtracted from the minimum value reported in the SUMMARY OF RESULTS table.

  a Verify the formulation of the model that was input to MPOS.
  b What is the optimum production schedule?
  c What inventory is on hand at the end of each month?
  d What is the cost associated with this optimal production-inventory strategy?

**6.19** (*Assembly-line balancing application*) A company manufactures a device that consists of four components. The components are produced and then the device

**219**

APPLIED LINEAR
PROGRAMMING
MODELS WITH
COMPUTER
SOLUTIONS

*EXERCISE 6.18*

```
TITLE
AMERICAN ENGINES: INVENTORY-PRODUCTION PROBLEM
REGULAR
MINIMIZE
80XJ + 75XA + 73XS + 74XO
CONSTRAINTS
1.   XJ .GE. 400
2.   XJ .LE. 1000
3.   XJ + XA .GE. 1600
4.   XJ + XA .LE. 2200
5.   XJ + XA + XS .GE. 3100
6.   XJ + XA + XS .LE. 3700
7.   XJ + XA + XS + XO = 3900
     OPTIMIZE
```

```
                      SUMMARY OF RESULTS

VAR  VAR     ROW STATUS      ACTIVITY     OPPORTUNITY    LOWER      UPPER
NO   NAME    NO               LEVEL         COST         BOUND      BOUND
 1  XJ        --     B       400.0000000    0.0000000    0.0000      INF
 2  XA        --     B      1200.0000000    0.0000000    0.0000      INF
 3  XS        --     B      2100.0000000    0.0000000    0.0000      INF
 4  XO        --     B       200.0000000    0.0000000    0.0000      INF
 5  SLACK--    1  LB         0.0000000     -5.0000000    0.0000      INF
12  ARTIF--  D- 1  LB         0.0000000      5.0000000    0.0000      INF
 6  SLACK-- D- 2  B        600.0000000      0.0000000    0.0000      INF
 7  SLACK--    3  LB         0.0000000     -2.0000000    0.0000      INF
14  ARTIF--  D- 3  LB         0.0000000      2.0000000    0.0000      INF
 8  SLACK-- D- 4  B        600.0000000      0.0000000    0.0000      INF
 9  SLACK--    5  B        600.0000000      0.0000000    0.0000      INF
16  ARTIF--  D- 5  LB         0.0000000      0.0000000    0.0000      INF
10  SLACK-- D- 6  LB         0.0000000     -1.0000000    0.0000      INF
11  ARTIF--  D- 7  LB         0.0000000     74.0000000    0.0000      INF
```

MINIMUM VALUE OF THE OBJECTIVE FUNCTION =    290100.000000

is assembled. The components are produced in three facilities. Production rates for each component in each facility are given in the following table:

| Facility | Production rate, components per hour | | | |
| --- | --- | --- | --- | --- |
| | Component 1 | Component 2 | Component 3 | Component 4 |
| 1 | 10 | 12 | 5 | 3 |
| 2 | 8 | 10 | 14 | 4 |
| 3 | 7 | 11 | 6 | 9 |

During an impending two-week production period, facility 1 will be available for 160 hours, facility 2 for 200 hours, and facility 3 for 150 hours. Decision variables will be $x_{ij}$'s, the number of hours that facility $i$ is assigned to production of component $j$.

The company would like to have equal numbers of all components at the end of the two-week period. Each device uses one of each of the four components, and if the numbers produced are not equal, some unusable components are left over. But since production rates differ, it may not be possible to achieve that objective. An alternate approach is to minimize the number of excess components or, equivalently, to maximize the final number of devices.

Following are expressions representing the numbers of each type component that will be produced:

*Number of components 1:* $10x_{11} + 8x_{21} + 7x_{31}$
*Number of components 2:* $12x_{12} + 10x_{22} + 11x_{32}$
*Number of components 3:* $5x_{13} + 14x_{23} + 6x_{33}$
*Number of components 4:* $3x_{14} + 4x_{24} + 9x_{34}$

Since the final device consists of one each of the four components, the total number of devices that may be assembled equals the minimum of the previously listed four expressions. Thus to maximize the number of devices we must *maximize the minimum* among these four numbers of components. Then at the outset of the formulation process the problem looks like this:

$$\text{Maximize } Z$$

where

$$Z = \text{minimum } [(10x_{11} + 8x_{21} + 7x_{31}), (12x_{12} + 10x_{22} + 11x_{32}),$$
$$(5x_{13} + 14x_{23} + 6x_{33}), (3x_{14} + 4x_{24} + 9x_{34})]$$

subject to

$$x_{11} + x_{12} + x_{13} + x_{14} \leq 160$$

$$x_{21} + x_{22} + x_{23} + x_{24} \leq 200$$

$$x_{31} + x_{32} + x_{33} + x_{34} \leq 150$$

Bother! The objective function is not an ordinary linear function. The standard approach to handling that difficulty is to let

$$F = \text{Final number of assembled devices}$$

Then we maximize $F$ subject to the condition that each of the four numbers of components is at least $F$. MPOS input and output are shown on page 221.
   **a** Discuss the final model formulation.
   **b** To the nearest integer, how many final devices may be assembled?
   **c** How many of each type of component are produced? (Use integers.)
   **d** If the maximum integer value for $F$ is desired, discuss any special difficulties that might be encountered, even if you had available a computer program for integer programming.

**6.20** (*Trim loss application*) Conglomerated Paper Products markets rolls of Christmas gift wrap. The rolls are made in three widths: 48 inches, 36 inches, and 30 inches. In the mill is a machine that makes standard-width rolls 100 inches wide, a machine that is used for newsprint ordinarily, but which is utilized for gift wrap during the holiday season.
   These standard 100-inch rolls are cut into rolls of gift wrap with the desired smaller widths. The standard rolls can be cut in a number of ways; for example, a standard roll could be cut into three 30-inch rolls, with 10 inches of waste left over. This and other cutting schemes are shown in the table below. While not all feasible cutting schemes are illustrated, these are the only ones that Conglomerated deems reasonable.

| Width | Cutting scheme, number of rolls | | | | | |
| | A | B | C | D | E | F |
| --- | --- | --- | --- | --- | --- | --- |
| 48 inches | 0 | 0 | 0 | 2 | 1 | 1 |
| 36 inches | 0 | 1 | 2 | 0 | 1 | 0 |
| 30 inches | 3 | 2 | 0 | 0 | 0 | 1 |
| Waste, inches | 10 | 4 | 28 | 4 | 16 | 22 |

**221**

*APPLIED LINEAR*
*PROGRAMMING*
*MODELS WITH*
*COMPUTER*
*SOLUTIONS*

## EXERCISE 6.19

```
TITLE
ASSEMBLY-LINE BALANCING
REGULAR
MAXIMIZE
F
CONSTRAINTS
1.   10X11 + 8X21 + 7X31 - F .GE. 0
2.   12X12 + 10X22 + 11X32 - F .GE. 0
3.   5X13 + 14X23 + 6X33 - F .GE. 0
4.   3X14 + 4X24 + 9X34 - F .GE. 0
5.   X11 + X12 + X13 + X14 .LE. 160
6.   X21 + X22 + X23 + X24 .LE. 200
7.   X31 + X32 + X33 + X34 .LE. 150
OPTIMIZE
```

```
                         SUMMARY OF RESULTS
```

| VAR NO | VAR NAME | ROW NO | STATUS | ACTIVITY LEVEL | OPPORTUNITY COST | LOWER BOUND | UPPER BOUND |
|---|---|---|---|---|---|---|---|
| 1 | F | -- | B | 1346.5464313 | 0.0000000 | 0.0000 | INF |
| 2 | X11 | -- | B | 134.6546431 | 0.0000000 | 0.0000 | INF |
| 3 | X21 | -- | LB | 0.0000000 | .0966999 | 0.0000 | INF |
| 4 | X31 | -- | LB | 0.0000000 | .6285495 | 0.0000 | INF |
| 5 | X12 | -- | B | 25.3453569 | 0.0000000 | 0.0000 | INF |
| 6 | X22 | -- | B | 103.8181120 | 0.0000000 | 0.0000 | INF |
| 7 | X32 | -- | B | .3837299 | 0.0000000 | 0.0000 | INF |
| 8 | X13 | -- | LB | 0.0000000 | 2.0376055 | 0.0000 | INF |
| 9 | X23 | -- | B | 96.1818880 | 0.0000000 | 0.0000 | INF |
| 10 | X33 | -- | LB | 0.0000000 | 1.6231773 | 0.0000 | INF |
| 11 | X14 | -- | LB | 0.0000000 | 2.0145817 | 0.0000 | INF |
| 12 | X24 | -- | LB | 0.0000000 | 1.2356101 | 0.0000 | INF |
| 13 | X34 | -- | B | 149.6162701 | 0.0000000 | 0.0000 | INF |
| 14 | SLACK-- | 1 | LB | 0.0000000 | .2900998 | 0.0000 | INF |
| 21 | ARTIF-- D- | 1 | LB | 0.0000000 | -.2900998 | 0.0000 | INF |
| 15 | SLACK-- | 2 | LB | 0.0000000 | .2417498 | 0.0000 | INF |
| 22 | ARTIF-- D- | 2 | LB | 0.0000000 | -.2417498 | 0.0000 | INF |
| 16 | SLACK-- | 3 | LB | 0.0000000 | .1726784 | 0.0000 | INF |
| 23 | ARTIF-- D- | 3 | LB | 0.0000000 | -.1726784 | 0.0000 | INF |
| 17 | SLACK-- | 4 | LB | 0.0000000 | .2954720 | 0.0000 | INF |
| 24 | ARTIF-- D- | 4 | LB | 0.0000000 | -.2954720 | 0.0000 | INF |
| 18 | SLACK-- D- | 5 | LB | 0.0000000 | 2.9009977 | 0.0000 | INF |
| 19 | SLACK-- D- | 6 | LB | 0.0000000 | 2.4174981 | 0.0000 | INF |
| 20 | SLACK-- D- | 7 | LB | 0.0000000 | 2.6592479 | 0.0000 | INF |

```
MAXIMUM VALUE OF THE OBJECTIVE FUNCTION =     1346.546431
```

The order for the month of November has just come in from Conglomerated's wholesalers. It calls for 2,000 rolls 48 inches wide, 3,500 rolls 36 inches wide, and 1,400 rolls 30 inches wide. Conglomerated Paper Products wants to know how many times to use each cutting scheme so the November order is filled but total waste is minimized.

**a** Let $XA$ denote the number of 100-inch standard rolls cut by scheme $A$, $XB$ the number cut by scheme $B$, and so on. Formulate the LP model for the problem.

**b** A management trainee at Conglomerated Paper Products is given the task of formulating the LP model. He reasons that although he might use equality constraints, if he permits some overproduction, his solution might take advantage of any opportunity to use a small-waste cutting scheme. Accordingly, his LP model is

$$\text{Minimize } W$$

where
$$W = 10XA + 4XB + 28XC + 4XD + 16XE + 22XF$$

subject to
$$2XD + XE + XF \geq 2{,}000$$
$$XB + 2XC + XE \geq 3{,}500$$
$$3XA + 2XB + XF \geq 1{,}400$$

EXERCISE 6.20

```
TITLE
CONGLOMERATED PAPER PRODUCTS
REGULAR
MINIMIZE
10XA + 4XB + 28XC + 4XD + 16XE + 22XF + 48S1 + 36S2 +30S3
CONSTRAINTS
1.  2XD + XE + XF - S1 = 2000
2.  XB + 2XC + XE - S2 = 3500
3.  3XA + 2XB + XF - S3 = 1400
RNGOBJ
RNGRHS
OPTIMIZE
```

SUMMARY OF RESULTS

| VAR NO | VAR NAME | ROW NO | STATUS | ACTIVITY LEVEL | OPPORTUNITY COST | LOWER BOUND | UPPER BOUND |
|---|---|---|---|---|---|---|---|
| 1 | XA | -- | LB | 0.0000000 | -25.0000000 | 0.0000 | INF |
| 2 | XB | -- | B | 700.0000000 | 0.0000000 | 0.0000 | INF |
| 3 | XC | -- | B | 1400.0000000 | 0.0000000 | 0.0000 | INF |
| 4 | XD | -- | B | 1000.0000000 | 0.0000000 | 0.0000 | INF |
| 5 | XE | -- | LB | 0.0000000 | 0.0000000 | 0.0000 | INF |
| 6 | XF | -- | LB | 0.0000000 | -25.0000000 | 0.0000 | INF |
| 7 | S1 | -- | LB | 0.0000000 | -50.0000000 | 0.0000 | INF |
| 8 | S2 | -- | LB | 0.0000000 | -50.0000000 | 0.0000 | INF |
| 9 | S3 | -- | LB | 0.0000000 | -25.0000000 | 0.0000 | INF |
| 10 | ARTIF-- D- | 1 | LB | 0.0000000 | 2.0000000 | 0.0000 | INF |
| 11 | ARTIF-- D- | 2 | LB | 0.0000000 | 14.0000000 | 0.0000 | INF |
| 12 | ARTIF-- D- | 3 | LB | 0.0000000 | -5.0000000 | 0.0000 | INF |

MINIMUM VALUE OF THE OBJECTIVE FUNCTION =     46000.000000

with nonnegativity of all variables presumed. Does his model look like yours? Discuss the differences, if any.

c The solution for the model in part b is $XA = 0$, $XB = 3,500$, $XD = 1,000$, $XE = 0$, $XF = 0$, with minimum total waste being 18,000 inches. The management trainee begins to feel pretty good about this solution until he takes a closer look. It will yield 2,000 rolls 48 inches wide and 3,500 rolls 36 inches wide, the numbers desired, but 7,000 rolls 30 inches wide are to be cut when only 1,400 were ordered for November. Unless the 5,600 extra rolls can be sold later on, the combined total of waste and excess 30-inch rolls is 18,000 + 30(5,600) = 186,000 inches.

d Above are the input and output of an MPOS run with the model having been modified to take care of the overproduction problem. It would still permit some overproduction, but as you see, at optimality there is none.

Discuss this last model. How does it penalize overproduction yet make overproduction feasible? What is the minimum total waste? How many 100-inch rolls should be produced in order for this optimal solution to apply?

## SELECTED REFERENCES

Anderson, D. R., D. J. Sweeney, and T. A. Williams: *An Introduction to Management Science*, 3d ed., West Publishing Company, St. Paul, Minn., 1982.

Bierman, H., C. P. Bonini, and W. H. Hausman: *Quantitative Analysis for Business Decisions*, 6th ed., Richard D. Irwin, Inc., Homewood, Ill., 1981.

Bradley, S. P., A. C. Hax, and T. L. Magnanti: *Applied Mathematical Programming*, Addison-Wesley, Reading, Mass., 1977.

Cohen, C., and J. Stein: *Multi Purpose Optimization System: User's Guide*, Vogelback Computing Center, Northwestern University, Evanston, Ill., 1978.

Cooper, L., U. N. Bhat, and L. J. LeBlanc: *Introduction to Operations Research Models*, W. B. Saunders Company, Philadelphia, 1977.

**223**

*APPLIED LINEAR
PROGRAMMING
MODELS WITH
COMPUTER
SOLUTIONS*

Hillier, F. S., and G. J. Lieberman: *Introduction to Operations Research*, 3d ed., Holden-Day, Inc., San Francisco, 1980.

Lapin, L. L.: *Management Science for Business Decisions*, Harcourt Brace Jovanovich, Inc., New York, 1980.

Levin, R. I., C. A. Kirkpatrick, and D. S. Rubin: *Quantitative Approaches to Management*, 5th ed., McGraw-Hill Book Company, New York, 1982.

# INTEGER PROGRAMMING, TRANSPORTATION PROBLEMS, AND ASSIGNMENT PROBLEMS

*I*n Chapter 6 you encountered some applications in which integer-valued variables were involved, and you also saw examples of transportation and assignment problems. But the unique solution procedures for those examples were not described; only computer outputs were made available for interpretation.

In this chapter we consider the basic reasoning behind integer-programming solutions using two widely used approaches: *Gomory's cutting-plane algorithm* and a powerful technique known as *branch-and-bound*. We further look at specialized computational algorithms that have been designed for both transportation problems and assignment problems. Here all of those procedures will be illustrated by fairly small but realistic examples, with the understanding that for larger, more complex problems you would want to use your computer. The objective is to increase your understanding of those problems by showing you the logic underlying their solution and by giving you more opportunities to formulate their models.

**225**

INTEGER
PROGRAMMING,
TRANSPORTATION
PROBLEMS, AND
ASSIGNMENT
PROBLEMS

## 7.1   INTEGER PROGRAMMING

An *integer programming* problem is a problem with a linear objective function and linear inequality constraints, but with the restriction that some or all of the decision variables must be nonnegative integers. It looks just like an ordinary linear programming problem except for the integer restriction. Then it is no surprise to learn that a modified version of the simplex method can be used to solve it.

In practice an approximate solution of an integer programming problem is often attempted by the ordinary simplex method. If any fractional values are obtained for some decision variables they may be just rounded to the nearest integer. Sometimes they are truncated; that is, their fractional part is merely lopped off. However, a truncated answer might well be far from optimal, and rounding often gives an infeasible solution. Example 7.1 shows a simple case in which both rounding and truncation give nonoptimal solutions.

**Example 7.1**

$$\text{Maximize } Z$$

where

$$Z = 3x_1 + 4x_2$$

subject to

$$5x_1 + 3x_2 \leq 15$$

$$3x_1 + 5x_2 \leq 15$$

$$x_1, x_2 = 0 \text{ or } 1 \text{ or } 2 \text{ or } \ldots$$

Figure 7.1 shows the feasible region if the problem is approached using an ordinary graphical procedure. It also shows a "lattice" of points with integer-valued coordinates. Those points of the lattice that are in or on the border of the shaded region are the only feasible points for the problem.

In Figure 7.1 the last corner of the shaded region touched by a contour of $Z$ is the point $(x_1, x_2) = (1.875, 1.875)$. That is not an integer solution. If each coordinate is rounded to the nearest integer, we get $(2, 2)$; this is not feasible, so it cannot be the optimal solution. If the decimal part of each coordinate is truncated, we get $(1, 1)$. But at $(1, 1)$ the objective function $Z$ is only 7, while obviously the feasible points $(1, 2)$ and $(2, 1)$ give higher values for $Z$ (11 and 10, respectively). Thus neither rounding nor truncation gives the optimal integer solution.

In fact, the optimal solution is not very close at all to the point $(1.875, 1.875)$. It occurs at $(x_1, x_2) = (0, 3)$, the last feasible (integer coordinates) point touched by a contour of $Z$ as it moves in its direction of increase. There $Z = 12$, the maximum of $Z$ for integer-valued $x_1$ and $x_2$.

## 7.2   CUTTING PLANES

The graphical approach to the solution of Example 7.1 cannot be used in a problem involving more than two variables. However, a convenient

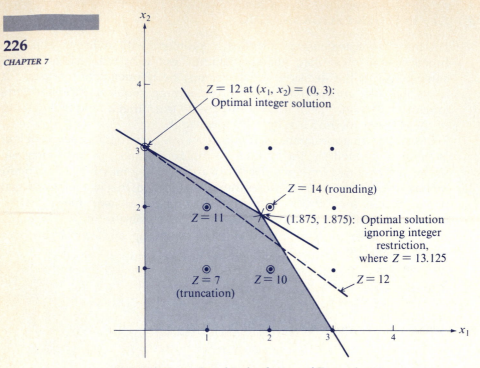

**FIGURE 7.1**    Graphical solution of Example 7.1

algorithm, called *Gomory's cutting-plane method*, has been created to handle integer programming problems using the simplex method. This method begins by solving the problem ignoring the integer restrictions. If the optimal basic variables happen to have integer values, then the problem is solved. If not, then a new "cutting-plane" constraint is created and included in the problem. The new problem is then solved by the simplex method, and the process is continued until an all-integer optimal solution is achieved. The method is best understood by way of example.

### Example 7.2

Molly's Maple Market is a small shop which produces and sells fine maple tables, chairs, and lamps. Each item is handmade by Molly herself. The respective profits per table, chair, and lamp are $100, $40, and $8.

During the coming month Molly will have on hand 200 board feet of maple and will be able to devote 80 hours to building her products. Each table made consumes 20 board feet of maple and requires 10 hours. Each chair takes 5 board feet of maple and 3 hours, while a lamp uses 2 board feet of maple and 1 hour.

A fraction of a product cannot be sold, so only an integral number of each will be produced. How many of each product should Molly make in order to maximize profit for the month's production?

**227**

*INTEGER
PROGRAMMING,
TRANSPORTATION
PROBLEMS, AND
ASSIGNMENT
PROBLEMS*

Let $x_1$ = number of tables to make

$x_2$ = number of chairs to make

$x_3$ = number of lamps to make

Then the model is

$$\text{Maximize } Z$$

where

$$Z = 100x_1 + 40x_2 + 8x_3$$

subject to

$$20x_1 + 5x_2 + 2x_3 \leq 200$$

$$10x_1 + 3x_2 + x_3 \leq 80$$

$$x_1, x_2, x_3 \text{ must be nonnegative integers}$$

First we solve the problem with simplex tableaus, ignoring the integer restrictions. After two simplex iterations we reach the optimal tableau of Table 7.1. It says that Molly should make $\frac{80}{3} = 26\frac{2}{3}$ chairs, no tables, and no lamps. If she could sell a fraction of a chair at a proportionate profit figure her profit would be \$3,200/3 = \$1,066.67. But a fraction of a product is not allowed by the original integer restrictions; we must use cutting-plane constraints to search for the best integer solution.

Since the decision variables $x_1$, $x_2$, and $x_3$ must be integers at optimality, the slack variables $S_1$ and $S_2$ must also be integers. The two inequality restrictions, with integral coefficients and integral right-hand sides, make that characteristic clear.

We seek the variable with the *largest fractional part*. Now $\frac{200}{3} = 66\frac{2}{3}$ while $\frac{80}{3} = 26\frac{2}{3}$. Both basic variables have the same fractional part, so we arbitrarily select $S_1$. The associated constraint equation, from Table 7.1, is

$$\tfrac{10}{3}x_1 + 0x_2 + \tfrac{1}{3}x_3 + 1S_1 - \tfrac{5}{3}S_2 = \tfrac{200}{3}$$

**TABLE 7.1**   *OPTIMAL NONINTEGER SOLUTION*

| Basic | Z | $x_1$ | $x_2$ | $x_3$ | $S_1$ | $S_2$ | Solution |
|-------|---|-------|-------|-------|-------|-------|----------|
| Z | 1 | $\frac{100}{3}$ | 0 | $\frac{16}{3}$ | 0 | $\frac{40}{3}$ | $\frac{3,200}{3}$ |
| $S_1$ | 0 | $\frac{10}{3}$ | 0 | $\frac{1}{3}$ | 1 | $-\frac{5}{3}$ | $\frac{200}{3}$ |
| $x_2$ | 0 | $\frac{10}{3}$ | 1 | $\frac{1}{3}$ | 0 | $\frac{1}{3}$ | $\frac{80}{3}$ |

Now rewrite the constraint so that *all coefficients are the sum of an integer and a nonnegative fraction*. Thus we have

$$(3 + \tfrac{1}{3})x_1 + (0 + 0)x_2 + (0 + \tfrac{1}{3})x_3 + (1 + 0)S_1 + (-2 + \tfrac{1}{3})S_2 = 66 + \tfrac{2}{3}$$

Rearrange the equation so that all of the integer coefficients appear on the right-hand side. This gives

$$\tfrac{1}{3}x_1 + 0x_2 + \tfrac{1}{3}x_3 + 0S_1 + \tfrac{1}{3}S_2 = \tfrac{2}{3} + (66 - 3x_1 - 0x_2 - 0x_3 - 1S_1 + 2S_2)$$

Consider the term in parentheses on the right-hand side. With the integer restriction on all variables (including slacks), it must be an integer. It *cannot* be a *negative* integer. If it is, then when it is added to $\tfrac{2}{3}$, the result would be a negative number. But the left-hand side is nonnegative since none of the variables can be negative.

This is the key to forming a cutting-plane restriction. The right-hand side is $\tfrac{2}{3}$ plus a *nonnegative* number. Thus we can write the following inequality:

$$\tfrac{1}{3}x_1 + 0x_2 + \tfrac{1}{3}x_3 + 0S_1 + \tfrac{1}{3}S_2 \geq \tfrac{2}{3}$$

Make an equation out of this constraint by including a surplus variable $S_3$. This produces the equation

$$\tfrac{1}{3}x_1 + 0x_2 + \tfrac{1}{3}x_3 + 0S_1 + \tfrac{1}{3}S_2 - S_3 = \tfrac{2}{3}$$

Now we want to include this new constraint. This means adding a row to the tableau of Table 7.1 and a column for the new variable $S_3$. However, just adding the row and column does not give a tableau showing a *basic* solution. We will have to choose another basic variable.

All of the coefficients in the $Z$ row of Table 7.1 are nonnegative. Thus bringing any currently nonbasic variable into the basis can only *decrease* $Z$. (This makes sense; the integer restrictions constrain the problem even more.) Then we will choose as the new basic variable that one which will *decrease Z the least*. This is obviously the variable $x_3$, since that variable has the smallest positive coefficient in the $Z$ row.

We want the new constraint to show a 1 coefficient of the basic variable $x_3$. Multiplying the new equation by 3 gives

$$x_1 + 0x_2 + x_3 + 0S_1 + S_2 - 3S_3 = 2$$

Include this equation as a new row in the tableau. This gives the tableau of Table 7.2.

But Table 7.2 is not yet a complete simplex tableau. Zero coefficients of $x_3$ are needed everywhere except in the last row. A Gauss-Jordan reduction gives the correct tableau, shown as Table 7.3.

TABLE 7.2 *INTERMEDIATE TABLEAU WITH CUTTING PLANE*

| Basic | Z | $x_1$ | $x_2$ | $x_3$ | $S_1$ | $S_2$ | $S_3$ | Solution |
|-------|---|-------|-------|-------|-------|-------|-------|----------|
| Z | 1 | $\frac{100}{3}$ | 0 | $\frac{16}{3}$ | 0 | $\frac{40}{3}$ | 0 | $\frac{3,200}{3}$ |
| $S_1$ | 0 | $\frac{10}{3}$ | 0 | $\frac{1}{3}$ | 1 | $-\frac{5}{3}$ | 0 | $\frac{200}{3}$ |
| $x_2$ | 0 | $\frac{10}{3}$ | 1 | $\frac{1}{3}$ | 0 | $\frac{1}{3}$ | 0 | $\frac{80}{3}$ |
| $x_3$ | 0 | 1 | 0 | 1 | 0 | 1 | $-3$ | 2 |

The tableau of Table 7.3 shows the optimal integer solution. It is

$$\text{Max } Z = 1{,}056 \qquad \text{at } (x_1, x_2, x_3) = (0, 26, 2)$$

Molly should make 26 chairs and 2 lamps (no tables) for a maximum profit of $1,056. She will use up all of her available time ($S_2 = 0$) but will have 66 board feet of maple left over. This solution is better than the truncated solution (26 chairs, yielding $1,040), and the rounded solution is infeasible (27 chairs, requiring 81 hours).

If one of the basic variables in Table 7.3 had remained fractional, we would have had to create another cutting-plane constraint and repeat the process. This would have added another row and column to the tableau. Thus Gomory's cutting-plane method requires the solution of successively larger and larger linear programming problems (but only one tableau is required for each). However, it permits the use of the familiar simplex method to solve an integer programming problem.

**Example 7.3**

Why is Gomory's method called a method of "cutting planes"? We demonstrate that designation by partially solving Example 7.1 with simplex tableaus, looking at the first cutting-plane restriction graphically. That problem was

TABLE 7.3 *COMPLETE NEW SIMPLEX TABLEAU (OPTIMAL)*

| Basic | Z | $x_1$ | $x_2$ | $x_3$ | $S_1$ | $S_2$ | $S_3$ | Solution |
|-------|---|-------|-------|-------|-------|-------|-------|----------|
| Z | 1 | 28 | 0 | 0 | 0 | 8 | 16 | 1,056 |
| $S_1$ | 0 | 3 | 0 | 0 | 1 | $-2$ | 1 | 66 |
| $x_2$ | 0 | 3 | 1 | 0 | 0 | 0 | 1 | 26 |
| $x_3$ | 0 | 1 | 0 | 1 | 0 | 1 | $-3$ | 2 |

Maximize Z

where

$$Z = 3x_1 + 4x_2$$

subject to

$$5x_1 + 3x_2 \leq 15$$
$$3x_1 + 5x_2 \leq 15$$

$x_1$, $x_2$ must be nonnegative integers

Table 7.4 shows the optimal tableau if the integer restrictions are ignored.

Again the fractional parts of each basic variable are equal. We arbitrarily choose variable $x_1$ for forming the cutting-plane restriction. The corresponding equation is

$$x_1 + 0x_2 + \tfrac{5}{16}S_1 - \tfrac{3}{16}S_2 = \tfrac{15}{8}$$

We rewrite it as follows:

$$(1 + 0)x_1 + (0 + 0)x_2 + (0 + \tfrac{5}{16})S_1 + (-1 + \tfrac{13}{16})S_2 = 1 + \tfrac{7}{8}$$

Using only the fractional parts of the coefficients, we obtain

$$0x_1 + 0x_2 + \tfrac{5}{16}S_1 + \tfrac{13}{16}S_2 \geq \tfrac{7}{8}$$

Instead of finishing the simplex solution by Gomory's method, let's look at this new restriction graphically. The original graph in Figure 7.1 is drawn on an $x_1$, $x_2$ plane. Then first we need to express the new constraint in terms of $x_1$ and $x_2$.

The original inequality constraints tell us that $S_1$ and $S_2$ must be as follows:

$$S_1 = 15 - 5x_1 - 3x_2$$
$$S_2 = 15 - 3x_1 - 5x_2$$

Then substitution yields the constraint

$$\tfrac{5}{16}(15 - 5x_1 - 3x_2) + \tfrac{13}{16}(15 - 3x_1 - 5x_2) \geq \tfrac{7}{8}$$

**TABLE 7.4**  *OPTIMAL NONINTEGER SOLUTION*

| Basic | Z | $x_1$ | $x_2$ | $S_1$ | $S_2$ | Solution |
|-------|---|-------|-------|-------|-------|----------|
| Z | 1 | 0 | 0 | $\frac{3}{16}$ | $\frac{11}{16}$ | $\frac{105}{8} = 13.125$ |
| $x_1$ | 0 | 1 | 0 | $\frac{5}{16}$ | $-\frac{3}{16}$ | $\frac{15}{8} = 1.875$ |
| $x_2$ | 0 | 0 | 1 | $-\frac{3}{16}$ | $\frac{7}{80}$ | $\frac{15}{8} = 1.875$ |

**231**

*INTEGER
PROGRAMMING,
TRANSPORTATION
PROBLEMS, AND
ASSIGNMENT
PROBLEMS*

Multiplying by 16 for convenience, collecting like terms, then multiplying by $-\frac{1}{8}$ puts the new constraint in the following form:

$$8x_1 + 10x_2 \leq 32$$

Now we graph the feasible region including the cutting-plane constraint. It is shown in Figure 7.2.

The new constraint cuts off a portion of the original shaded area in Figure 7.1. The part that is cut off is shown in Figure 7.2 as the smaller shaded region. This produces a new "feasible" region that still includes all of the original integer-coordinate feasible points. One of the two new corners that have been created, the circled corner in Figure 7.2, is the solution to the problem with the cutting plane included. Its $x_1$ coordinate is 1, an integer, but its $x_2$ coordinate is still fractional. At least one more cutting plane would have to be determined before the problem could be finished with the Gomory algorithm. Always, one of the corners through which a cutting plane passes will have at least one integral coordinate.

### 7.3  BRANCH-AND-BOUND

Gomory's cutting-plane method requires the solution of successively larger and larger LP problems, one problem per cutting-plane restriction that is

**FIGURE 7.2**    The effect of the cutting plane

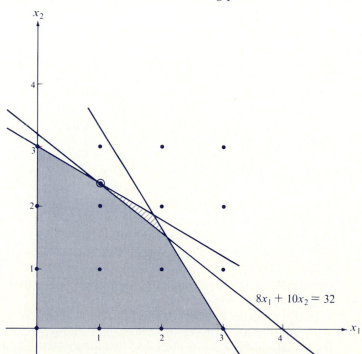

added. It was the first completely general algorithm to guarantee that an optimal integer solution could be found. Its development (around 1958) encouraged researchers to seek other, more efficient integer-programming procedures. One of the best approaches to come from those efforts is the concept of *branch-and-bound*. Branch-and-bound procedures, although they often also require solution of a succession of LP problems, are generally regarded as more efficient than the classic Gomory method.

The basic idea of branch-and-bound is twofold. The "branch" portion involves successively subdividing the original feasible region into smaller regions. The "bound" portion recognizes that the solution obtained by simply ignoring the integer restrictions must yield an upper bound for the objective function of the integer programming problem, while any feasible point with integer coordinates must provide a lower bound. These notions are best appreciated by consideration of a simple example.

## Example 7.4

Here we will solve the little problem used in Examples 7.1 and 7.3 by a branch-and-bound procedure. The model was

$$\text{Maximize } Z$$

where

$$Z = 3x_1 + 4x_2$$

subject to

$$5x_1 + 3x_2 \leq 15$$

$$3x_1 + 5x_2 \leq 15$$

$$x_1, x_2 \text{ must be nonnegative integers}$$

Of course, we already know how to find its integer solution graphically. The following discussion is provided only to illustrate the steps in branch-and-bound. It is not meant to imply that branch-and-bound is the easiest way to solve this particular problem.

Reference to Figure 7.1 reminds us that the optimal solution if we *ignore* the integer restrictions was

$$\text{Max } Z = 13.125 \quad \text{at } (x_1, x_2) = (1.875, 1.875)$$

Thus any *integer* solution cannot produce a larger value for $Z$, so 13.125 is an upper bound. In fact, since $Z = 3x_1 + 4x_2$ (coefficients of $x_1$ and $x_2$ are integers) and both $x_1$ and $x_2$ must be integers, Max $Z$ for an integer solution must itself be an integer. Since it cannot exceed 13.125, then the number 13 is an *upper bound* for integer solutions. This solution also forms the basis for the first *branching* operation, or a first subdivision of the original feasible region.

In the original solution we see $x_1 = 1.875$ and $x_2 = 1.875$. Eventually we want to make both of these variables integer-valued, but first let's just try to make *one* of them an integer. Suppose we think about $x_1$. Reasoning that its optimal integer value may be near the number 1.875, and noting

**233**

INTEGER
PROGRAMMING,
TRANSPORTATION
PROBLEMS, AND
ASSIGNMENT
PROBLEMS

that 1.875 is between the integers 1 and 2, we decide to subdivide the original feasible region into two smaller regions, one where $x_1 \leq 1$, and one where $x_1 \geq 2$. This division is implied by Figure 7.3. Notice that the two shaded regions in Figure 7.3, $R_1$ and $R_2$, do not contain all the points in the original feasible region (say $R_0$), but that they *do* contain all points in $R_0$ having *integer* coordinates.

This is the first *branching* operation. Now we look at *one* of the two subdivisions, say $R_1$, and find Max Z in that region. Reference to Figure 7.3 and consideration of contours of the objective function tells us that the maximum Z in $R_1$ occurs at the intersection of the lines $x_1 = 2$ and $5x_1 + 3x_2 = 15$. Then the $x_2$ coordinate of the point of intersection is obtained by substituting $x_1 = 2$ into the equation $5x_1 + 3x_2 = 15$. This gives $x_2 = \frac{5}{3} \simeq 1.667$. At that point $Z = 3(2) + 4(\frac{5}{3}) = 6 + \frac{20}{3} \simeq 12.667$.

Let's record what we know up to this point. Figure 7.4 shows the first branching operation and the results of graphical solutions in $R_0$ and $R_1$. It also contains the comment "Max $Z \leq 13$" beside the $R_0$ box to remind us of the upper bound on integer solutions.

We seek integer solutions, specifically at this stage an integer solution in $R_1$. The variable $x_1$ in the $R_1$ box of Figure 7.4 is integer-valued, but $x_2 = 1.667$ is not. Thus we decide to further subdivide $R_1$ into two regions, where $x_2 \leq 1$ and where $x_2 \geq 2$ ($1 < 1.667 < 2$). We are aware that sometime in the future we will have to look at region $R_2$, but here we are using a version of branch-and-bound called *last-generated, first-analyzed*.

**FIGURE 7.3**  Subdividing the feasible region

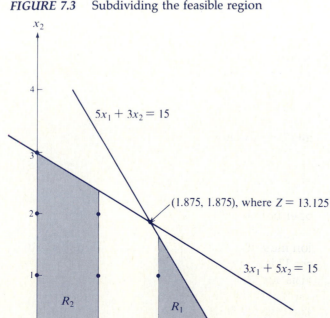

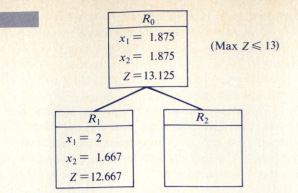

$$R_0$$
$$x_1 = 1.875$$
$$x_2 = 1.875$$
$$Z = 13.125$$

(Max $Z \leqslant 13$)

$$R_1$$
$$x_1 = 2$$
$$x_2 = 1.667$$
$$Z = 12.667$$

$$R_2$$

**FIGURE 7.4**    Results after first branching

That is, we continue to subdivide the most recently considered region. Figure 7.5 shows the result of this next subdivision as well as a subsequent one, which will also be discussed.

The region $R_3$ is that part of $R_1$ associated with $x_2 \leq 1$. A region $R_4$ is implied by $x_2 \geq 2$, but since this includes *no* points in $R_1$ (or in $R_0$, for that matter), that region is infeasible. The contour for Max $Z$ in $R_3$ touches the point $(x_1, x_2) = (2.4, 1)$, where $Z = 11.2$. So we have an integer value

**FIGURE 7.5**    Subdivisions of $R_1$ and $R_3$

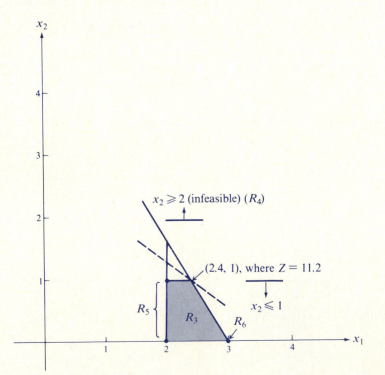

**235**

INTEGER
PROGRAMMING,
TRANSPORTATION
PROBLEMS, AND
ASSIGNMENT
PROBLEMS

for $x_2$ but not for $x_1$, and $R_3$ must be further subdivided. However, since $2 < 2.4 < 3$, that subdivision would be based on $x_1 \leq 2$ and $x_1 \geq 3$. The only points in $R_3$ where $x_1 \leq 2$ are on the vertical *line* indicated in Figure 7.5 as $R_5$, and only a single *point* in $R_3$ satisfies $x_1 \geq 3$ ("region" $R_6$ in Figure 7.5). Max $Z$ in $R_5$ occurs at $(x_1, x_2) = (2, 1)$ and is $3(2) + 4(1) = 10$. Max $Z$ in $R_6$ occurs at the only point in $R_6$, $(x_1, x_2) = (3, 0)$, and is $3(3) + 4(0) = 9$. Among those two *integer* solutions, $Z = 10$ is largest, so we have found a *lower bound* for integer solutions in $R_0$. That is, now we know that for integer solutions in the original feasible region, $10 \leq$ Max $Z \leq 13$. This illustrates the *bounding* aspect of branch-and-bound.

These observations are condensed in Figure 7.6. The asterisks below the boxes for $R_4$, $R_5$, and $R_6$ indicate that further branching is unnecessary.

We have learned that the best integer solution for the region $R_1$ occurs at $(x_1, x_2) = (2, 1)$, where $Z = 10$. But we have not yet considered the other region that resulted from the first branching operation, the region $R_2$. Since no more branching is required for $R_4$, $R_5$, and $R_6$, the "last-generated" region is now that region $R_2$.

We see from Figure 7.3 that Max $Z$ in $R_2$ occurs where the line $x_1 = 1$

**FIGURE 7.6**    Results after second and third branchings

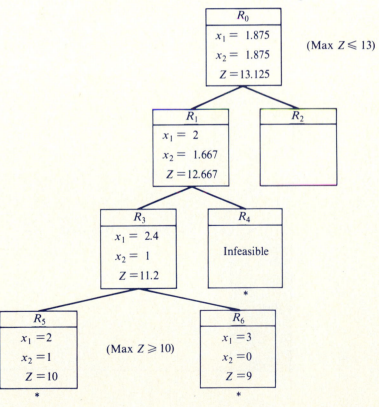

intersects the line $3x_1 + 5x_2 = 15$, or the optimal (noninteger) solution in $R_2$ occurs at $(x_1, x_2) = (1, 2.4)$, where $Z = 12.6$. Since this is not completely an integer solution and since $2 < 2.4 < 3$, we subdivide $R_2$ using $x_2 \leq 2$ and $x_2 \geq 3$. This gives regions $R_7$ and $R_8$ as shown in Figure 7.7, where the region $R_8$ contains only the single point $(x_1, x_2) = (0, 3)$.

From Figure 7.7 we see that Max $Z$ in $R_7$ is 11, occurring at $(x_1, x_2) = (1, 2)$, while Max $Z$ in $R_8$ is 12, occurring at $(x_1, x_2) = (0, 3)$, the only point in $R_8$. Since both of those solutions are *integer* solutions, we know that Max $Z$ for integer solutions in $R_2$ is 12, occurring at $(x_1, x_2) = (0, 3)$. This is a better solution than Max (integer) $Z$ in $R_1$, which was 10, and since the original feasible region was initially subdivided into only $R_1$ and $R_2$, we have completed the branch-and-bound solution. For integer-valued $x_1$ and $x_2$, the optimal solution is

$$\text{Max } Z = 12 \qquad \text{at } (x_1, x_2) = (0, 3)$$

Results of the entire branch-and-bound analysis are shown in Figure 7.8.

Recall that the *sequence* of subdivisions in our branch-and-bound analysis of Example 7.4 depended upon our *arbitrary* decision to consider $R_1$ first. Suppose we had first considered the region $R_2$. Then after subdividing $R_2$ we would have known that Max $Z \geq 12$ for integer solutions in $R_0$.

**FIGURE 7.7**  Subdivisions of $R_2$

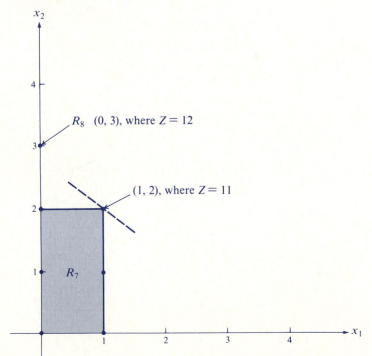

**237**

INTEGER
PROGRAMMING,
TRANSPORTATION
PROBLEMS, AND
ASSIGNMENT
PROBLEMS

We would have then returned to $R_1$, discovered a value for $Z$ greater than 12 (12.667), and subdivided $R_1$. However, in the subdivisions of $R_1$ we would have learned that Max $Z$ for integer solutions in $R_1$ *could not exceed* 12, so we would have stopped without further analysis, knowing that we had already found the optimal integer solution in the $R_2$ branch. That analysis, with the regions renumbered to indicate the sequence of subdivisions, is suggested by Figure 7.9.

The feature of branch-and-bound analysis indicated in Figure 7.9, the *bounding* feature illustrated by our knowledge that Max $Z \geq 12$, is the reason why branch-and-bound is usually, at least for large problems, more efficient than the cutting-plane method. It permits (although it does not assure) early elimination of branches that could not possibly contain the optimal integer solution.

As implied at the outset of work on Example 7.4, branch-and-bound was certainly not the easiest way to work that two-variable example. The graphical solution is much to be preferred. But a graphical analysis is not possible if the LP model involves lots of variables. Generally, branch-and-bound becomes more and more attractive, relative to graphical or

*FIGURE 7.8* Complete branch-and-bound analysis of Example 7.4

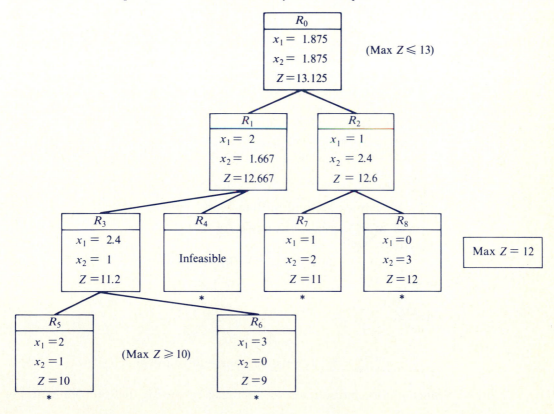

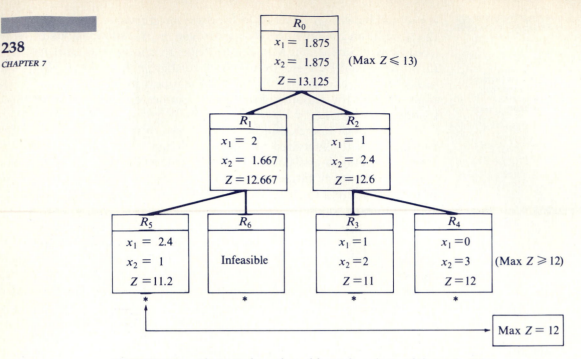

**FIGURE 7.9**   Alternate branch-and-bound analysis of Example 7.4

cutting-plane methods, as the numbers of variables in integer LP problems get larger.

A similarity does exist between branch-and-bound and the cutting-plane method. In each approach we have to solve a sequence of LP problems. For Example 7.4, graphical solutions of each of those little problems were possible. In problems involving more variables, however, we must resort to the algebraic (tabular) simplex method to solve each LP problem in the sequence. Example 7.5 suggests the type of work that would be involved.

### Example 7.5
### Algebraic Simplex Method in Branch-and-Bound

The problem addressed in Example 7.4 was

$$\text{Maximize } Z$$

where

$$Z = 3x_1 + 4x_2$$

subject to

$$5x_1 + 3x_2 \leq 15$$

$$3x_1 + 5x_2 \leq 15$$

$$x_1, x_2 \text{ must be nonnegative integers}$$

Branch-and-bound solution was initiated by solving that problem with the integer restrictions ignored. In a larger problem (more variables), simplex iterations would be used to do that.

Region $R_1$ in the first branching operation was defined by the original constraints and the extra constraint $x_1 \geq 2$ (see Figure 7.3). Then the feasible region for simplex solution in $R_1$ would be

$$5x_1 + 3x_2 \leq 15$$
$$3x_1 + 5x_2 \leq 15$$
$$x_1 \qquad \geq 2$$

Next we considered region $R_3$ (Figure 7.5). It was part of $R_0$ and of $R_1$, and was further defined by the extra constraint $x_2 \leq 1$. Thus the feasible region to use for simplex solution in $R_3$ is

$$5x_1 + 3x_2 \leq 15$$
$$3x_1 + 5x_2 \leq 15$$
$$x_1 \qquad \geq 2$$
$$x_2 \leq 1$$

Note the "nesting" of the constraints as we proceed through successive subdivisions. Each successive problem is an LP problem containing the original objective function, the original constraints, and *all* of the *extra* constraints used to reach a particular region. Thus, as long as we continue subdividing one earlier region, each successive LP problem gets larger and larger (more constraints). Of course, when we terminate the work and return to another basic branch (such as looking at $R_2$), then we start over. For instance, to analyze $R_2$ using simplex iterations we would use the constraints

$$5x_1 + 3x_2 \leq 15$$
$$3x_1 + 5x_2 \leq 15$$
$$x_1 \qquad \leq 1$$

Consequently, you might anticipate a lot of tedium when applying branch-and-bound (or the cutting-plane method) to large problems, especially if you limit your resources to only pencil, paper, and time. Enter the computer. You could incorporate branch-and-bound subroutines into a program for the simplex method, or you could hope that a branch-and-bound package is already available on your computer. MPOS (Multi Purpose Optimization System), the package used to obtain solutions for the problems in Chapter 6, does have branch-and-bound capabilities, including the capability to handle *mixed-integer* problems, where only *some* of the variables must be integers while others are allowed to range over some continuum of numbers. Again, all good LP packages will have similar capabilities.

## 7.4 TRANSPORTATION PROBLEMS

A *transportation problem* is a very special type of integer programming problem. As its name implies, it usually involves the physical transporting of commodities from various *sources* to multiple *destinations*. The objective is to carry out that shipping operation at minimum cost.

A transportation problem may be solved using the ordinary simplex method *without* resort to any particular integer programming scheme such as cutting planes or branch-and-bound. This simplicity occurs because all extreme points (corner points) in a transportation problem will have integer coordinates. But even small transportation problems will involve lots of variables and lots of constraints, so if you want to use the ordinary simplex method, you would also want to use the computer (see Exercise 6.8 at the end of Chapter 6).

However, a transportation problem has a special structure which permits it to be solved by a fairly efficient technique that can easily be executed by hand. That is called the *transportation method*. It will be discussed in Section 7.5.

### Example 7.6
### A Balanced Transportation Problem

Shippum Corporation operates three factories, in different locations, that monthly ship quantities of the *same product* to four warehouses in still different locations. Each factory has a maximum production capacity per month and each warehouse demands a specific number of units of that product per month. Capacities, demands, and shipping costs per unit from each factory to each warehouse are known. The problem is to determine how many units to ship from each factory to each warehouse so the total transportation cost for a month is minimized.

Let $c_{ij}$ denote the cost of shipping one unit from the $i$th factory to the $j$th warehouse, and let $x_{ij}$ be the corresponding number of units shipped. Thus there are 12 variables in the problem, for $i = 1, 2, 3$ and $j = 1, 2, 3, 4$. Table 7.5 shows a convenient organization of the known constants and the variables $x_{ij}$. The numbers in the upper-right-hand corners of the cells are the $c_{ij}$'s, while the margins of the table give factory capacities and warehouse demands. Such a table is called a *transportation table*.

Notice that the problem is *balanced*; that is, total demand equals total capacity (400 units). This balance is admittedly unusual in the real world. However, the more common unbalanced problem is not difficult to handle. In fact, we can just introduce some slack variables to convert it to a balanced version. Then if you can solve a balanced transportation problem, you can solve *any* transportation problem.

**TABLE 7.5**   *TRANSPORTATION TABLE: SHIPPUM CORPORATION*

| Factory | Warehouse 1 | Warehouse 2 | Warehouse 3 | Warehouse 4 | Capacity |
|---|---|---|---|---|---|
| 1 | 6 $x_{11}$ | 2 $x_{12}$ | 6 $x_{13}$ | 12 $x_{14}$ | 120 |
| 2 | 4 $x_{21}$ | 4 $x_{22}$ | 2 $x_{23}$ | 4 $x_{24}$ | 200 |
| 3 | 13 $x_{31}$ | 8 $x_{32}$ | 7 $x_{33}$ | 2 $x_{34}$ | 80 |
| Demand | 50 | 80 | 90 | 180 | 400 |

**Example 7.7**
**A General Model**

Let $C_i$ be the capacity of the $i$th source, $D_j$ be the demand at the $j$th destination, and suppose that there are $m$ sources and $n$ destinations. Then in general any balanced transportation problem can be formulated as

Minimize cost

where
$$\text{Cost} = \sum_{j=1}^{n} \sum_{i=1}^{m} c_{ij} x_{ij}$$

subject to
$$\sum_{j=1}^{n} x_{ij} = C_i \qquad i = 1, 2, \ldots, m$$

$$\sum_{i=1}^{m} x_{ij} = D_j \qquad j = 1, 2, \ldots, n$$

where every $x_{ij}$ is a nonnegative integer.

Here we see a total of $mn$ variables, $m + n$ constraints, and all linear functions. With the notable exception that all the $x_{ij}$'s must be integers (we will not transport a fraction of a unit), the problem looks like an ordinary linear programming problem.

**Example 7.8**
**A Specific Model**

To illustrate the appearance of such a model, let's formulate Shippum Corporation's transportation problem directly, using constants which are suggested by Table 7.5. This formulation also serves to define the summation notation used in the general model. The specific model is

Minimize cost

where

$$Cost = 6x_{11} + 2x_{12} + 6x_{13} + 12x_{14} + 4x_{21} + 4x_{22}$$
$$+ 2x_{23} + 4x_{24} + 13x_{31} + 8x_{32} + 7x_{33} + 2x_{34}$$

subject to

$$
\begin{array}{lllll}
x_{11} + x_{12} + x_{13} + x_{14} & & & & = 120 \\
& x_{21} + x_{22} + x_{23} + x_{24} & & & = 200 \\
& & x_{31} + x_{32} + x_{33} + x_{34} & = & 80 \\
x_{11} & + x_{21} & + x_{31} & & = & 50 \\
x_{12} & + x_{22} & + x_{32} & & = & 80 \\
x_{13} & + x_{23} & + x_{33} & & = & 90 \\
x_{14} & + x_{24} & + x_{34} & = & 180 \\
\end{array}
$$

and all $x_{ij}$'s are nonnegative integers.

Here we have what appears to be a linear problem in twelve variables, seven constraints, and the integer-valued restriction on the variables. The problem is linear and does have twelve variables, but there are only six *independent* constraints. The sum of the first three equations gives the same equation as the sum of the last four. Each sum just reminds us that the sum of all twelve $x_{ij}$'s is 400. Thus there is some dependence in the constraints. In general a transportation problem always has $m + n - 1$ independent constraints.

Because all linear programming problems have as many basic variables as they have *independent* constraints (a characteristic not specifically mentioned before but certainly implied by the simplex tableaus), a basic feasible solution for this problem will include at most *six* positive-valued $x_{ij}$'s. There are only six independent constraints, thus only six basic variables.

Notice the special structure of the model. All coefficients are 1, and all constraints are *equations*. In subsequent discussions and examples we study the transportation method, which takes advantage of that structure.

### Example 7.9
### Initial Solution by the Northwest-Corner Rule

Here we begin to solve the Shippum Corporation problem using transportation tables. Table 7.6 presents all of the original data along with an easily determined initial basic feasible solution. That initial solution is obtained using the *northwest-corner rule*, described following.

Start in the upper-left (northwest) corner of the table. Allocate as many units as possible to that cell. Since the capacity of factory 1 is 120 units but the demand of warehouse 1 is only 50 units, let $x_{11} = 50$. More than 50 units cannot be put there because that would exceed the demand at warehouse 1.

**243**

INTEGER
PROGRAMMING,
TRANSPORTATION
PROBLEMS, AND
ASSIGNMENT
PROBLEMS

Now the total demand in column 1 is met. Move to the right and consider column 2. Factory 1 has a remaining capacity of 70 units, but warehouse 2 demands 80. Let $x_{12} = 70$. This completes the allocation to row 1 since the capacity of factory 1 is now exhausted. Letting $x_{22} = 10$ will satisfy the remaining demand at warehouse 2. Continue in that fashion, along a generally left-to-right diagonal path. Make the requirement that *each allocation must complete either a row or a column*. Thus $x_{23} = 90$, $x_{24} = 100$, and $x_{34} = 80$ completes the northwest-corner initial allocation.

There were $3 + 4 = 7$ rows and columns, but the final allocation ($x_{34} = 80$) completed *both* a row and a column. Thus exactly six positive $x_{ij}$'s have been determined, and along with the zero-valued $x_{ij}$'s implied by the cells to which no allocation was made, the solution satisfies all constraints. So we have six zero-valued variables (nonbasic) and six positive-valued variables (basic), or a *basic feasible solution*.

You can verify that this initial allocation is indeed a feasible solution for the model which was formulated as Example 7.8. However, if we had considered that model using ordinary simplex procedures, six artificial variables would have been needed. Then the northwest-corner rule not only is a convenient way to obtain an initial basic feasible solution, but it also gives that solution in terms of the original variables.

## 7.5   THE TRANSPORTATION METHOD

The cost for the allocation suggested by Table 7.6 is

$$\text{Cost} = 6(50) + 2(70) + 4(10) + 2(90) + 4(100) + 2(80)$$

$$= 300 + 140 + 40 + 180 + 400 + 160$$

$$= 1{,}220$$

**TABLE 7.6**   *INITIAL BASIC FEASIBLE SOLUTION*

| Factory | Warehouse 1 | | Warehouse 2 | | Warehouse 3 | | Warehouse 4 | | Capacity |
|---------|---|---|---|---|---|---|---|---|----------|
| **1** | | 6 | | 2 | | 6 | | 12 | 120 |
| | 50 | | 70 | | | | | | |
| **2** | | 4 | | 4 | | 2 | | 4 | 200 |
| | | | 10 | | 90 | | 100 | | |
| **3** | | 13 | | 8 | | 7 | | 2 | 80 |
| | | | | | | | 80 | | |
| **Demand** | 50 | | 80 | | 90 | | 180 | | 400 |

This is not expected to be the optimal solution. It is the cost associated with a rather arbitrarily chosen initial solution. Now, *by changing only one basic variable at a time*, we want to find a new basic feasible solution with a lower cost. Note that this is the same general approach used by the ordinary simplex method.

The transportation method investigates the effect of allocating one unit to one of the currently empty cells (associated with a nonbasic variable). This is done for each empty cell in turn. If any such allocation has the effect that a reduction in cost ensues, then the $x_{ij}$ for that cell is a contender for an incoming basic variable. The new basic variable is the $x_{ij}$ associated with the maximum per-unit cost reduction.

Consider cell (1, 3), the first empty cell in row 1 of Table 7.6. The per-unit cost for that cell is 6. Suppose we simply say: Ship one unit from factory 1 to warehouse 3. If we do, then clearly "something's got to give" in the initial solution. The capacity of factory 1 has already been used up by shipping 50 units to warehouse 1 and 70 units to warehouse 2. So to supply one unit to warehouse 3 from factory 1 requires the shipment of one less unit to either warehouse 1 or warehouse 2.

Let's decide to leave 50 in cell (1, 1), put 1 in cell (1, 3), and change the allocation to cell (1, 2) from 70 to 69. Then $50 + 69 + 1 = 120$, and the capacity of factory 1 is satisfied. However, there is now a problem with warehouse 2. The demand at that warehouse is not satisfied, since $69 + 10 = 79$, not 80. Further, with 1 in cell (1, 3) we have $1 + 90 = 91$ in column 3. Both of these difficulties are easily resolved by replacing the 10 in cell (2, 2) by 11 and the 90 in cell (2, 3) by 89. In this fashion feasibility is maintained. The process of shifting a single unit around to maintain feasibility is suggested by Table 7.7.

What is the effect on *cost* of these changes? Consider the $+1$s and $-1$s

**TABLE 7.7**   *EVALUATING CELL (1, 3)*

| Factory | Warehouse | | | | Capacity |
|---|---|---|---|---|---|
| | 1 | 2 | 3 | 4 | |
| 1 | 6 \ 50 | $-1$ 2 \ 70 | $+1$ 6 | 12 | 120 |
| 2 | 4 | $+1$ 4 \ 10 | $-1$ 2 \ 90 | 4 \ 100 | 200 |
| 3 | 13 | 8 | 7 | 2 \ 80 | 80 |
| Demand | 50 | 80 | 90 | 180 | 400 |

**245**

INTEGER
PROGRAMMING,
TRANSPORTATION
PROBLEMS, AND
ASSIGNMENT
PROBLEMS

in Table 7.7. They indicate the changes we have suggested in the initial solution. The two +1s suggest that one unit will be added into the associated cells, at an increase of 10 (6 + 4) in cost. The two −1s indicate the subtraction of a unit from each of the associated cells, with a resulting decrease in cost of 4 (2 + 2). The net effect is to *increase* overall cost by 10 − 4 = 6 per unit of product so shifted about. Conclusion: Do not allocate anything to cell (1, 3) at this stage.

Here the number 10 − 4 = 6 is called the *value* of cell (1, 3). A positive value for a cell implies an increase in cost if a unit is allocated to it. We are interested in cells with *negative* values.

> *Rule for evaluating cells.* To evaluate any *empty* cell, put a +1 in that empty cell and then maintain feasibility by putting +1s and −1s only in other *filled* cells.

Notice that of the four cells used in Table 7.7, only cell (1, 3) was originally empty. This way the effect of allocating to only *one* empty cell is assessed. This is the same thing as considering only one nonbasic variable at a time for entry into the solution as a basic variable. Table 7.8 shows the application of the rule for the value of cell (1, 4).

First, place a +1 in the empty cell of interest, in this case cell (1, 4). Then maintain feasibility by placing +1s and −1s only in *filled* cells. We could try balancing column 4 by putting −1 in cell (3, 4), but then there is no other filled cell in row 3 where a +1 could be put to keep the row balanced. Thus we put −1 in cell (2, 4), balancing column 4. For row 2 balance, we must put +1 in cell (2, 2). Note that there is both a +1 and a −1 in each of rows 1 and 2 and columns 2 and 4. Feasibility is maintained, and cell (1, 4) may now be evaluated. Its value is 12 − 4 +

**TABLE 7.8** *EVALUATING CELL (1, 4)*

| Factory | Warehouse 1 | 2 | 3 | 4 | Capacity |
|---------|-------------|---|---|---|----------|
| 1 | 6<br>50 | −1 ← 2<br>70 ↓ | 6 | +1 → 12 ↑ | 120 |
| 2 | 4 | +1<br>4<br>10 | 2<br>90 | −1 →<br>4<br>100 | 200 |
| 3 | 13 | 8 | 7 | 2<br>80 | 80 |
| Demand | 50 | 80 | 90 | 180 | 400 |

$4 - 2 = 10$. This is a positive cell value, so $x_{14}$ is *not* a good choice for an incoming basic variable. It would only increase cost to change $x_{14}$ from its current zero value.

The cell evaluations in Tables 7.7 and 7.8 have suggested that the $+1$s and $-1$s occur in rectangular patterns. But that is not always the case. Sometimes we have to use a pattern like the one indicated in Table 7.9. There we are evaluating cell (3, 1). Patterns of $+1$s and $-1$s like those shown in Tables 7.7, 7.8, and 7.9 are called *closed loops*. If the current solution is *basic*, it is always possible to find a *unique* closed loop for evaluating any empty cell.

The value of cell (3, 1) is $13 - 2 + 4 - 4 + 2 - 6 = 7$, again positive. If $x_{31}$ is brought into the basis, the cost would only increase.

Similarly you can verify that the values of cells (3, 2) and (3, 3) are, respectively, 6 and 7. Only the empty cell (2, 1) remains to be evaluated. Its closed loop is indicated by the $+1$s and $-1$s in Table 7.10.

The value of cell (2, 1) is $4 - 4 + 2 - 6 = -4$. Thus the effect of allocating one unit to that cell is a *decrease* in overall cost. It is advantageous to allow $x_{21}$ to become positive. Then $x_{21}$ is the *incoming basic variable* for the next revised solution.

Now we know *which* variable should come into the basis. Next, just as in the ordinary simplex method, we want to know the *level* at which the variable should come in. If $x_{21} = 1$, cost is decreased by 4. Then if $x_{21} = 2$, cost is decreased by 8, and so on. Thus we want to make $x_{21}$ as large as possible.

How many units may be allocated to cell (2, 1)? The answer is obvious after consideration of the two cells in Table 7.10 that contain $-1$s. The $x_{ij}$'s must be nonnegative integers. For each unit that is added to cell (2, 1), a unit must be subtracted from each of those cells which contain $-1$s

**TABLE 7.9** *EVALUATING CELL (3, 1)*

| Factory | Warehouse 1 | | 2 | | 3 | | 4 | | Capacity |
|---|---|---|---|---|---|---|---|---|---|
| 1 | $-1$ ⟵ 6 | | $+1$ ↑ 2 | | 6 | | 12 | | 120 |
| | 50 | | 70 | | | | | | |
| 2 | | 4 | $-1$ ⟵ 4 | | 2 | | $+1$ ↑ 4 | | 200 |
| | | | 10 | | 90 | | 100 | | |
| 3 | $+1$ 13 | | 8 | | 7 | | ⟶ $-1$ 2 | | 80 |
| | | | | | | | 80 | | |
| Demand | 50 | | 80 | | 90 | | 180 | | 400 |

**TABLE 7.10   EVALUATING CELL (2, 1)**

| Factory | Warehouse 1 | Warehouse 2 | Warehouse 3 | Warehouse 4 | Capacity |
|---|---|---|---|---|---|
| 1 | $-1$ ← 6, 50 ↓ | $+1$ ↑ 2, 70 | 6 | 12 | 120 |
| 2 | $+1$ 4 | $-1$ 4, 10 | 2, 90 | 4, 100 | 200 |
| 3 | 13 | 8 | 7 | 2, 80 | 80 |
| Demand | 50 | 80 | 90 | 180 | 400 |

in the closed loop for evaluating cell (2, 1). Our attention is thus directed to the one of those two cells currently containing the *smaller* number of units, cell (2, 2). If $x_{21}$ is allowed to be more than 10 units, then $x_{22}$ would become negative. This violates feasibility. But if $x_{21}$ is set *equal* to 10, then $x_{22}$ becomes zero. This is all right. Table 7.11 shows the result of the preceding analysis.

Table 7.11 has the same characteristics as Table 7.6, the initial solution produced by the northwest-corner rule: six basic variables, six nonbasic (zero-valued) variables, and satisfaction of all seven equality constraints. The previously basic variable $x_{22}$ is now nonbasic with zero value, while the previously nonbasic variable $x_{21}$ is positive, thus basic. We have created a first revised table that displays a basic feasible solution.

**TABLE 7.11   FIRST REVISED TABLE (OPTIMAL)**

| Factory | Warehouse 1 | Warehouse 2 | Warehouse 3 | Warehouse 4 | Capacity |
|---|---|---|---|---|---|
| 1 | 6, 40 | 2, 80 | 6 | 12 | 120 |
| 2 | 4, 10 | 4 | 2, 90 | 4, 100 | 200 |
| 3 | 13 | 8 | 7 | 2, 80 | 80 |
| Demand | 50 | 80 | 90 | 180 | 400 |

The revised solution in Table 7.11 yields a smaller cost than did the northwest-corner-rule initial solution of Table 7.6. Specifically, the new transportation cost is

$$Cost = 1,180$$

Now we had already noted that cost should decrease by 4 per unit of $x_{21}$ brought into the solution. Sure enough, when we let $x_{21} = 10$, the cost decreased by 40, from 1,220 to 1,180.

Is this the optimal solution? Here we find ourselves in the same place we would have been upon completion of a first revised tableau using the ordinary simplex method; we ask the same question we would have asked then. Can we decrease cost further by introducing a new basic variable?

Once more investigate the effect of adding one unit to an empty cell. Do this for all empty cells, seeking the one which will permit the most decrease in cost. However, upon evaluating all empty cells in Table 7.11 you will find that all cell values are *positive*. Those values are shown in Table 7.12.

We see that the effect of changing any currently nonbasic variable from its zero value is only to *increase* cost. No further improvement is possible, so Table 7.11 shows the optimal solution for the Shippum Corporation's transportation problem. A clear statement of that solution appears as Table 7.13. The cost of that strategy is 1,180. No other strategy will yield as low a transportation cost.

Then what is the transportation method? A compact set of rules follows:

1 Obtain an initial basic feasible solution. (We have used the north-west-corner rule, but any initial basic feasible solution will suffice, including one obtained by the VAM procedure to be discussed in Section 7.8.)

2 Find cell values for every empty cell (either by the procedure discussed in this section or by the MODI method to be presented in Section 7.6 following).

3 If any cell values are negative, allocate as many units as possible to the cell with the most negative value.

4 Step 3 generates a revised basic feasible solution. Repeat step 2. If negative cell values are found, repeat step 3. If no negative cell values are found, the current solution is the optimal solution.

## 7.6 CELL EVALUATION BY THE MODI METHOD

We have already observed that, although it would involve lengthy computations, the simplex method could be used to solve the Shippum

**TABLE 7.12** CELL VALUES FOR TABLE 7.11

| Cell | Value | Cell | Value |
|------|-------|------|-------|
| (1, 3) | 2 | (3, 1) | 11 |
| (1, 4) | 6 | (3, 2) | 10 |
| (2, 2) | 4 | (3, 3) | 7 |

Corporation problem presented as Example 7.6. If so, then there would be a *dual* of the primal problem which was formulated in that example. A method for evaluating empty cells called the *modified distribution* (MODI) *method* can be developed from duality theory. That entire development will not be attempted here; only the MODI *method* will be presented, along with some discussion of its relationship to the dual problem. It should be noted here that the word "distribution" in "modified distribution method" only means that a transportation problem is a problem involving the distribution of items from various sources to other destinations; that is, the method is used in a "distribution of commodities" setting.

The dual problem will have as many variables as there are constraints in the primal. Let $u_i$ be the dual variable associated with the *i*th *source constraint* and $v_j$ be the dual variable associated with the *j*th *destination constraint*. The MODI method is based upon the fact that dual constraints corresponding to primal *basic* variables will be satisfied with *equality*. This line of reasoning produces the system of equations

$$u_i + v_j = c_{ij}$$

for every *basic* variable $x_{ij}$. The solution of that system (having as many equations as the current basic feasible solution has basic variables) gives values for all $u_i$'s and $v_j$'s. Then the cell values for *empty* cells are given by

$$V_{ij} = \text{value of empty cell } (i, j) = c_{ij} - u_i - v_j$$

**TABLE 7.13** SOLUTION OF SHIPPUM CORPORATION PROBLEM

| | | |
|------|------|------|
| From: Factory 1 ship | 40 units to warehouse 1 | |
| | 80 units to warehouse 2 | |
| Factory 2 ship | 10 units to warehouse 1 | |
| | 90 units to warehouse 3 | |
| | 100 units to warehouse 4 | |
| Factory 3 ship | 80 units to warehouse 4 | |

for all empty cells (associated with *nonbasic* variables). This last result you may recognize as the association of the difference in left- and right-hand sides of dual constraints with coefficients in the "Z row" of a simplex tableau.

### Example 7.10

Here we use the MODI method to evaluate the empty cells in the two primary tables used in the solution of the Shippum Corporation problem, Tables 7.6 and 7.11. First consider Table 7.6.

Basic variables for that table are $x_{11}$, $x_{12}$, $x_{22}$, $x_{23}$, $x_{24}$, and $x_{34}$. The corresponding system of equations in the $u_i$'s and $v_j$'s is

$$u_1 + v_1 = c_{11} = 6$$

$$u_1 + v_2 = c_{12} = 2$$

$$u_2 + v_2 = c_{22} = 4$$

$$u_2 + v_3 = c_{23} = 2$$

$$u_2 + v_4 = c_{24} = 4$$

$$u_3 + v_4 = c_{34} = 2$$

Now this is a system of six equations in the *seven* unknowns $u_1$, $u_2$, $u_3$ and $v_1$, $v_2$, $v_3$, $v_4$. This means we can arbitrarily assign *any* value to one of the unknowns. In the MODI method we usually let

$$u_1 = 0$$

With $u_1 = 0$, the first equation gives $v_1 = 6$ and the second equation gives $v_2 = 2$. Then knowing that $v_2 = 2$, we get $u_2 = 2$ from the third equation, and so on. The solution of the system is

$$u_1 = 0 \qquad v_1 = 6$$

$$u_2 = 2 \qquad v_2 = 2$$

$$u_3 = 0 \qquad v_3 = 0$$

$$v_4 = 2$$

Then the cell values for the *empty* cells are

$$V_{13} = c_{13} - u_1 - v_3 = 6 - 0 - 0 = 6$$

$$V_{14} = c_{14} - u_1 - v_4 = 12 - 0 - 2 = 10$$

$$V_{21} = c_{21} - u_2 - v_1 = 4 - 2 - 6 = -4 \leftarrow \text{negative}$$

$$V_{31} = c_{31} - u_3 - v_1 = 13 - 0 - 6 = 7$$

$$V_{32} = c_{32} - u_3 - v_2 = 8 - 0 - 2 = 6$$

$$V_{33} = c_{33} - u_3 - v_3 = 7 - 0 - 0 = 7$$

**251**

INTEGER
PROGRAMMING,
TRANSPORTATION
PROBLEMS, AND
ASSIGNMENT
PROBLEMS

If you will read back through Section 7.5, checking the cell values which were determined there, you will find that these values are the same.

Notice that with the MODI method it was not necessary to find a closed loop for the evaluation of any empty cell. This is a clear advantage of the MODI method over the "stepping stone," closed-loop procedure used in Section 7.5. On the other hand, the negative cell value $V_{21} = -4$ again tells us that $x_{21}$ can come into the basis to decrease cost by 4 per unit, but nothing in the MODI method tells us how much $x_{21}$ will be or how to reallocate to the other cells once the level of $x_{21}$ is determined. We must still use the closed loop for cell $(2, 1)$ as demonstrated in Table 7.10. Thus with the MODI method we do eventually have to consider *one* closed loop to continue toward the solution of the problem, whereas we needed six such loops using the method introduced in Section 7.5.

The point is this: The MODI method is simply an alternative way to evaluate empty cells, not an alternative to the entire transportation method. The MODI method is only step 2 of the four-step transportation method outlined at the end of Section 7.5.

Now consider the empty cells in Table 7.11. We will determine their values with the MODI method, but this time we will do all of the work using the transportation table itself. It isn't really necessary to write down the entire system of equations involving the $u_i$'s and $v_j$'s once the pattern evident in the MODI method has been observed. All of our work to determine values of $u_i$'s and $v_j$'s will be built around Table 7.14.

Notice that only the *locations* of the basic variables, not their values, are needed for the determination of the $u_i$'s and $v_j$'s. Thus in Table 7.14 we merely mark a cell associated with a basic variable with an "X" and do not need to include demand or capacities.

First we write, in the left margin of the table, the arbitrary choice $u_1 = 0$. Then, since cell $(1, 1)$ is marked with an X and $c_{11} = 6$, we know that $v_1 = 6$ (since $u_i + v_j = c_{ij}$). Put $v_1 = 6$ in the upper margin. Likewise, if $u_1 = 0$ and $c_{21} = 2$, we know that $v_2 = 2$. Put $v_2 = 2$ in the upper

**TABLE 7.14**    *A SHORTENED VERSION OF MODI*

| | Factory | $v_1 = 6$ <br> 1 | $v_2 = 2$ <br> 2 | $v_3 = 4$ <br> 3 | $v_4 = 6$ <br> 4 |
|---|---|---|---|---|---|
| | | | | **Warehouse** | |
| $u_1 = 0$ | 1 | 6 <br> X | 2 <br> X | 6 | 12 |
| $u_2 = -2$ | 2 | 4 <br> X | 4 | 2 <br> X | 4 <br> X |
| $u_3 = -4$ | 3 | 13 | 8 | 7 | 2 <br> X |

margin. Next look at cell (2, 1), the next cell which contains an X (meaning that a basic variable occupies that spot, so $u_2 + v_1 = c_{21}$). We know now that $v_1 = 6$ and $c_{21} = 4$, so this says, "put $u_2 = -2$ in the left margin." Continuing in this fashion we find, sequentially, $v_3 = 4$, $v_4 = 6$, and $u_3 = -4$. This analysis completes the development of all the information to be found in Table 7.14.

Now, to evaluate *empty* cells, simply refer to the costs and marginal $u_i$'s and $v_j$'s in Table 7.14. We obtain

$$V_{13} = 6 - 0 - 4 = 2$$

$$V_{14} = 12 - 0 - 6 = 6$$

$$V_{22} = 4 - (-2) - 2 = 4$$

$$V_{31} = 13 - (-4) - 6 = 11$$

$$V_{32} = 8 - (-4) - 2 = 10$$

$$V_{33} = 7 - (-4) - 4 = 7$$

These are the same values that were exhibited in Table 7.12 back in Section 7.5, the values which indicated that the optimal solution to the Shippum Corporation problem had been achieved.

## 7.7 ALTERNATE OPTIMAL SOLUTIONS AND DEGENERACY

In the standard simplex method an alternate optimal solution is indicated by a zero in the Z row and under a nonbasic variable in an optimal tableau. In the transportation method, if no empty cell has a negative value but at least one of them has a *zero* value, an alternate optimal solution exists.

### Example 7.11

Consider the transportation problem suggested by Table 7.15. Cell (2, 1) has value 2, while cell (1, 2) has a zero value. This is an optimal solution, with Cost = 880. However, because of the zero-valued cell, there exists an alternate optimal solution. Let's find it.

Treat cell (1, 2) as if it had a negative value. The locations of the $-1$s in Table 7.15 suggest that as many as 70 units can be allocated to cell (1, 2) without violating nonnegativity. Accordingly, we can construct the solution shown in Table 7.16.

Because in Table 7.16 there are no negative-valued empty cells, we have an optimal solution. The cost, of course, is 880 for this alternate solution. Note finally that cell (2, 2) is now zero-valued. This suggests another alternate optimal solution, but it will be the one shown already in Table 7.15.

There can be no more than $m + n - 1$ positive-valued variables in a basic feasible solution ($m$ = number of rows, $n$ = number of columns).

TABLE 7.15    TABLE INDICATING ALTERNATE OPTIMAL SOLUTION

| Factory | Warehouse 1 | Warehouse 2 | Warehouse 3 | Capacity |
|---|---|---|---|---|
| 1 | 2<br>20 | +1 ← 8 | −1 ↑ 4<br>80 | 100 |
| 2 | 3 | −1 → 7<br>70 | +1 3<br>10 | 80 |
| Demand | 20 | 70 | 90 | 180 |

However, one can obtain a basic feasible solution with *fewer* than $m + n - 1$ positive-valued variables. There will still be $m + n - 1$ *basic* variables in the solution, but one or more of them will have the value zero. In the ordinary simplex method that situation was called *degeneracy*. It bears the same name in the transportation problem.

Degeneracy may be encountered in an initial basic feasible solution, at an intermediate table, or at optimality. Just as in ordinary LP problems, degeneracy is not a "bad" feature; it simply means that one or more basic variables are zero-valued. However, in the transportation method this zero-valued basic variable is not distinguishable from the nonbasic variables; all we see is an empty cell. Example 7.12 shows one way of handling this difficulty in the transportation method.

**Example 7.12**
**Handling Degeneracy**

Consider the problem suggested by Table 7.17. It is a two-destination, four-source transportation problem with a degenerate initial solution.

TABLE 7.16    ALTERNATE OPTIMAL SOLUTION

| Factory | Warehouse 1 | Warehouse 2 | Warehouse 3 | Capacity |
|---|---|---|---|---|
| 1 | 2<br>20 | 8<br>70 | 4<br>10 | 100 |
| 2 | 3 | 7 | 3<br>80 | 80 |
| Demand | 20 | 70 | 90 | 180 |

Here the northwest-corner rule gives an initial solution with only *four* positive basic variables. But $m + n - 1$ is $4 + 2 - 1 = 5$. This initial solution is degenerate; there are five basic variables, but one of them has the value zero. The cost for this initial allocation is $C = 2,750$.

We want to know which currently nonbasic variable may come into the basis to promote a decrease in cost. But which *are* the nonbasic variables? While there are four zero-valued variables $x_{12}$, $x_{22}$, $x_{31}$, and $x_{41}$, one of them is *basic*.

Which one? From Table 7.17 there is no way to tell. So, let's just *arbitrarily* decide that $x_{12}$ will be the basic variable having zero value. We now want to evaluate cells (2, 2), (3, 1), and (4, 1). But the standard procedure of putting $+1$ in the empty cell and then balancing the allocation using only filled cells will not work. Feasibility cannot be maintained without using another empty cell. Neither can we find all of the $u_i$'s and $v_j$'s in the MODI method.

The way around this difficulty is obvious. Since we have arbitrarily decided that $x_{12}$ will be basic, treat cell (1, 2) as if it is a filled cell. To make that decision easy to remember while evaluating the other empty cells, place a small positive number $\epsilon$ (epsilon) in cell (1, 2). Epsilon is so small that when it is multiplied by 10, the cost per unit for $x_{12}$, the result is an insignificant contribution to cost. The initial table to use for cell evaluations is shown as Table 7.18.

The $\epsilon$ in cell (1, 2) is to remind us to regard that cell just like we would any other filled cell. Then the value of cell (2, 2) is 5, of cell (3, 1) is 5, and of cell (4, 1) is $-20$. Thus we can save 20 per unit of $x_{41}$. The "$+1$, $-1$" scheme in Table 7.18 indicates that we can let $x_{41} = 50$ without violating feasibility. Also, $x_{12}$ would now become $50 + \epsilon$, but since $\epsilon$ is

**TABLE 7.17  A DEGENERATE INITIAL SOLUTION**

| Source | Destination 1 | Destination 2 | Supply |
|---|---|---|---|
| 1 | 20   50 | 10 | 50 |
| 2 | 15   40 | 10 | 40 |
| 3 | 20 | 5   30 | 30 |
| 4 | 10 | 20   50 | 50 |
| Demand | 90 | 80 | 170 |

**TABLE 7.18** *OVERCOMING THE DENERACY PROBLEM*

| Source | Destination 1 | Destination 2 | Supply |
|---|---|---|---|
| 1 | −1 ← 20 / 50 | +1 ↑ 10 / ε | 50 |
| 2 | 15 / 40 | 10 | 40 |
| 3 | 20 / 30 | 5 | 30 |
| 4 | +1 → 10 / 50 | −1 20 | 50 |
| Demand | 90 | 80 | 170 |

infinitesimal anyway, we will just call it 50.  The first revised table is given as Table 7.19.

The solution shown in Table 7.19 is also degenerate.  The location of the epsilon in cell (3, 1) shows how one would continue the process of cell evaluation as one proceeds from Table 7.19 on toward the optimal transportation table.

Since not just any variable can be a basic variable, we need to be careful about our positioning of the epsilon.  It is sufficient that the epsilon be located so that *all the remaining empty cells may be evaluated*.

## 7.8  VAM: OBTAINING A BETTER INITIAL SOLUTION

The basic transportation method has been presented throughout the immediately previous sections of this chapter.  It depended only upon our having any initial basic feasible solution, regardless of the means used to achieve it.

The northwest-corner rule may or may not yield a near-optimal initial solution.  That rule does not consider cell costs; only if the low-cost cells tend to run along the main diagonal of the table would you expect the initial solution to be nearly optimal.

An initial solution which takes costs into consideration is desirable.  Such an initial allocation may be obtained using Vogel's approximation method (VAM).  VAM is also called the "penalty matrix" approach to an initial solution.

**TABLE 7.19**   FIRST REVISED TABLE

| Source | Destination 1 | Destination 2 | Supply |
|---|---|---|---|
| 1 | +1 [ 20 ] | −1 [ 10 ] 50 | 50 |
| 2 | [ 15 ] 40 | [ 10 ] | 40 |
| 3 | −1 [ 20 ] ε | +1 [ 5 ] 30 | 30 |
| 4 | [ 10 ] 50 | [ 20 ] | 50 |
| Demand | 90 | 80 | 170 |

The rationale of VAM is simple.   Consider any particular row or column of a transportation table.   If you initially allocate units to a cell other than the low-cost cell of that row or column, you "penalize" yourself by incurring more per-unit cost.   You want to avoid that penalty by allocating to the low-cost cell.

Of course, such a line of reasoning promotes the following strategy: Allocate as much as possible to the lowest-cost cell in the table, then to the next lowest, and so on.   This is not a bad procedure for obtaining an initial solution, but it has one drawback.   Sometimes you will find that you are forced to use one of the highest-cost cells near the end of your initial allocations.

VAM is a procedure which tries to avoid high penalties as well as high-cost cells in the "end game" of the initial allocations.   Often the initial solution obtained by VAM will be the optimal solution.

**Example 7.13**

Consider the $3 \times 3$ transportation problem suggested by Table 7.20.   The usual tabular format has been bordered by an extra row and column; these are "scratch pads" for recording penalties.

Calculate a penalty for each row and column by *subtracting the cost for the low-cost cell from that for the second-low-cost cell.*   Thus we have $9 - 8 = 1$ in row 1, $9 - 6 = 3$ in row 2, $6 - 5 = 1$ in row 3, $6 - 5 = 1$ in column 1, $9 - 7 = 2$ in column 2, and $8 - 6 = 2$ in column 3.

Each of these numbers is the penalty incurred by deciding to allocate to the second-low-cost cell instead of the low-cost cell in the corresponding

**257**

INTEGER
PROGRAMMING,
TRANSPORTATION
PROBLEMS, AND
ASSIGNMENT
PROBLEMS

row or column. Now reason that you would like to *avoid the maximum penalty*.

In this case the maximum penalty, 3, occurs if in the second row we allocate to cell (2, 2) instead of to cell (2, 1). How can that maximum penalty be avoided? By allocating to cell (2, 1). So initially we put as many units as possible into cell (2, 1); this means that we let $x_{21} = 30$.

With $x_{21} = 30$, all of the demand at destination 1 has been met. The remaining allocations will be made as if we had a 3 × 2 instead of a 3 × 3 transportation problem. Delete column 1 and change the supply for row 2 from 50 to 50 − 30 = 20. Table 7.21 includes those changes and incorporates the next round of penalty calculations.

Here there are three *ties* for maximum penalty. Instead of arbitrarily picking a cell, let's decide to allocate to the cell which allows us to avoid a penalty of 2 *and* to which the most units may be allocated. That cell is cell (1, 3), so let $x_{13} = 80$. Demand at destination 3 is met. The new reduced table is shown in Table 7.22.

To maintain feasibility, there is no choice but to let $x_{12} = 20$, $x_{22} = 20$, and $x_{32} = 70$. This completes the initial solution. It is shown in Table 7.23 in the usual transportation problem format.

Upon evaluating the empty cells in Table 7.23 you will find that this initial solution is in fact the (unique) *optimal* solution. At the expense of some preliminary calculations we have arrived at an initial solution which precludes subsequent revised tables. Now an initial VAM solution will not always be optimal. But surprisingly often it is, and other times it should be very nearly optimal.

To demonstrate the efficiency of VAM, two competing initial solutions for Example 7.13 are shown in Table 7.24. Neither is optimal. In fact, using the initial solution provided by the northwest-corner rule, at least

**TABLE 7.20**    THE FIRST STEP IN VAM

| Source | Destination 1 | | Destination 2 | | Destination 3 | | Supply | Penalty | |
|---|---|---|---|---|---|---|---|---|---|
| 1 | | 9 | | 10 | | 8 | 100 | 1 | |
| 2 | | 6 | | 9 | | 10 | 50 | {3} | ← max |
| 3 | | 5 | | 7 | | 6 | 70 | 1 | |
| Demand | 30 | | 110 | | 80 | | 220 | | |
| Penalty | 1 | | 2 | | 2 | | | | |

TABLE 7.21   *THE SECOND STEP IN VAM*

| Source | Destination 2 | Destination 3 | Supply | Penalty |
|--------|-----|-----|--------|---------|
| 1 | 10 | 8 | 100 | {2}  ← max |
| 2 | 9 | 10 | 20 | 1 |
| 3 | 7 | 6 | 70 | 1 |
| Demand | 110 | 80 | 190 | |
| Penalty | 2 max | 2 max | | |

three more revised tables are necessary to reach optimality.   With the low-cost allocation, at least two more revisions are required.

## 7.9   UNBALANCED TRANSPORTATION PROBLEMS

Almost always in the real world of business, supply will not equal demand. The problems will start out as *unbalanced*.   All that is necessary here is the incorporation of additional variables to take up the slack in the problem. We simply include the slack variables in such a way that the problem becomes balanced.

TABLE 7.22   *THE FINAL STEP IN VAM*

| Source | Destination 2 | Supply |
|--------|-----|--------|
| 1 | 10 | 20 |
| 2 | 9 | 20 |
| 3 | 7 | 70 |
| Demand | 110 | 110 |

**TABLE 7.23** INITIAL SOLUTION BY VAM

| Source | Destination 1 | Destination 2 | Destination 3 | Supply |
|---|---|---|---|---|
| 1 | 9 | 10   20 | 8   80 | 100 |
| 2 | 6   30 | 9   20 | 10 | 50 |
| 3 | 5 | 7   70 | 6 | 70 |
| Demand | 30 | 110 | 80 | 220 |

### Example 7.14

Table 7.25 shows the original information for an unbalanced transportation problem. The supply is 450 units while the destinations demand only 305 units.

Now we want an equivalent problem which is balanced. To achieve that, include a *dummy destination* with a "demand" of 145 units. The cost per unit of "shipping" from any source to that destination is zero. Thus units shipped to the dummy destination at optimality do not contribute to cost, since they are not really shipped at all. Table 7.26 shows the new setup. This is equivalent to including $x_{15}$, $x_{25}$, and $x_{35}$ as slack variables. They make equations out of the three inequality constraints on supply.

**TABLE 7.24** COMPETING INITIAL SOLUTIONS

Northwest-Corner Rule

| Source | Destination 1 | Destination 2 | Destination 3 | Supply |
|---|---|---|---|---|
| 1 | 9   30 | 10   70 | 8 | 100 |
| 2 | 6 | 9   40 | 10   10 | 50 |
| 3 | 5 | 7 | 6   70 | 70 |
| Demand | 30 | 110 | 80 | 220 |

Low-Cost Cell Allocation

| Source | Destination 1 | Destination 2 | Destination 3 | Supply |
|---|---|---|---|---|
| 1 | 9 | 10   60 | 8   40 | 100 |
| 2 | 6 | 9   50 | 10 | 50 |
| 3 | 5   30 | 7 | 6   40 | 70 |
| Demand | 30 | 110 | 80 | 220 |

**TABLE 7.25**    AN UNBALANCED TRANSPORTATION PROBLEM

| | Destination | | | | |
| Source | 1 | 2 | 3 | 4 | Supply |
|---|---|---|---|---|---|
| 1 | 5 | 20 | 7 | 10 | 100 |
| 2 | 14 | 15 | 9 | 4 | 200 |
| 3 | 16 | 5 | 12 | 8 | 150 |
| Demand | 50 | 75 | 100 | 80 | 305  450 |

Now we will solve this problem using an initial solution obtained by a condensed version of VAM. In Table 7.27 the largest penalty for a first allocation is in column 2. Let $x_{32} = 75$ and change the supply of source 3 to $150 - 75 = 75$, striking out column 2. Next the largest penalty is the 9 which is indicated in braces under column 1, so $x_{11} = 50$, column 1 is deleted, and the supply at source 1 becomes $100 - 50 = 50$. Now the largest penalty is 8 in row 3. Thus $x_{35} = 75$, row 3 is deleted, and the demand at destination 5 is now $145 - 75 = 70$. The next round of penalty calculations produces a maximum of 7 in row 1. Then $x_{15} = 50$, row 1 is deleted, and the demand at destination 5 becomes $70 - 50 = 20$. At this

**TABLE 7.26**    THE PROBLEM INCLUDING DUMMY DESTINATION

| | Destination | | | | | |
| Source | 1 | 2 | 3 | 4 | 5 | Supply |
|---|---|---|---|---|---|---|
| 1 | 5 | 20 | 7 | 10 | 0 | 100 |
| 2 | 14 | 15 | 9 | 4 | 0 | 200 |
| 3 | 16 | 5 | 12 | 8 | 0 | 150 |
| Demand | 50 | 75 | 100 | 80 | 145 | 450 |

TABLE 7.27 INITIAL SOLUTION BY VAM

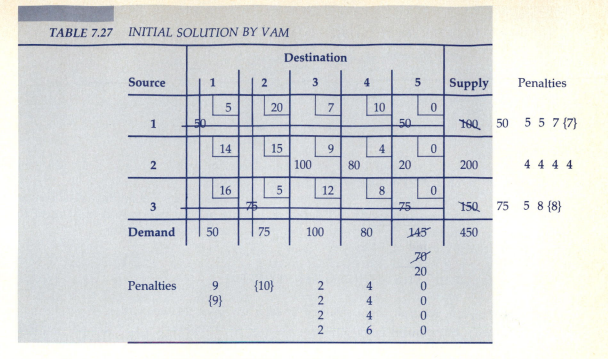

point only row 2 remains. We are forced to the remaining allocations $x_{23}$ = 100, $x_{24}$ = 80, and $x_{25}$ = 20.

Here VAM has produced an initial basic feasible solution which is not optimal. The value of cell (1, 3) is −2. Allocating 50 units to cell (1, 3) gives the optimal solution, shown in Table 7.28.

The cost of the optimal policy is 1,745. It is reported in Table 7.29.

**TABLE 7.28  THE OPTIMAL SOLUTION**

| Source | Destination 1 | 2 | 3 | 4 | 5 | Supply |
|---|---|---|---|---|---|---|
| 1 | 5<br>50 | 20 | 7<br>50 | 10 | 0 | 100 |
| 2 | 14 | 15 | 9<br>50 | 4<br>80 | 0<br>70 | 200 |
| 3 | 16 | 5<br>75 | 12 | 8 | 0<br>75 | 150 |
| Demand | 50 | 75 | 100 | 80 | 145 | 450 |

**TABLE 7.29**  *REPORTING THE OPTIMAL SOLUTION*

| Ship | 50 | from | Source 1 | to | Destination 1 |
|------|----|----|----|----|----|
| | 50 | | Source 1 | | Destination 3 |
| | 50 | | Source 2 | | Destination 3 |
| | 80 | | Source 2 | | Destination 4 |
| | 75 | | Source 3 | | Destination 2 |

Units shipped to dummy destinations, of course, are not really shipped at all. They are not included in the report.

In Example 7.14 supply exceeded demand and a dummy destination was incorporated. If demand exceeds supply, we would only need to include a dummy source and proceed in the same manner.

## 7.10   THE ASSIGNMENT PROBLEM

In general, the *assignment problem* involves the delegation of workers to jobs in order to minimize the cost of completing all of the jobs. Here "workers" could be machines, or even time, and "cost" could be replaced by time, distance, or some other measure of effectiveness. The important thing about an assignment problem is this: *Only one worker is assigned to each job, and every job has one worker assigned to it.* In Example 6.7 of Chapter 6 you considered a standard assignment problem, so you will have already noticed that again the ordinary simplex method will apply and will produce the appropriate integer-type solution (only this time the decision variables can only assume the values 0 or 1). But a much simpler procedure, called the *assignment method,* may be used to solve these problems.

The assignment problem is just a very special case of the transportation problem. Its salient features can be presented in a transportation table such as Table 7.30. In particular, note the capacity column and the demand row which border the table. Each job demands only one worker, and each worker will do only one job. This means that each $x_{ij}$ must be either 0 or 1. For instance, if worker 2 is assigned to job 3, then $x_{23} = 1$. Moreover, then $x_{21} = 0$, $x_{22} = 0$ and $x_{24} = 0$ since worker 2 cannot be assigned to more than one job. Also notice that the table is *square*. The number of workers equals the number of jobs to be done.

Of course, such a problem may be solved by the transportation method. But consider any allocation. Each assignment would complete *both* a row and a column in Table 7.30. A 1 in any cell would satisfy the capacity and demand for the corresponding row and column. Thus any trial solution would be *completely degenerate*. There can only be 4 positive-valued basic variables, but there must be $4 + 4 - 1 = 7$ basic variables. Then the transportation method would require *three* "epsilons" for evaluating empty cells. The larger the problem, the worse the difficulty because of degeneracy.

**263**

INTEGER
PROGRAMMING,
TRANSPORTATION
PROBLEMS, AND
ASSIGNMENT
PROBLEMS

The *assignment method,* on the other hand, allows us to take advantage of the unique characteristics of an assignment problem. For example, since we know that all $x_{ij}$'s must be either 0 or 1, there is no need to allow space in the table for them. Therefore, the assignment method only considers the *cost* associated with each cell.

The assignment method is built upon two principles. First, the optimal assignment remains the same if a constant is subtracted from every cost in any row or column. Second, if all of the $c_{ij}$'s are nonnegative, and if any feasible assignment can be made using only cells with *zero costs,* then that assignment is optimal. These principles have produced the following mechanical process for solving assignment problems:

1 Lay out a two-way table containing only the costs for every assignment.

2 In each row, subtract the smallest cost in the row from every cost in the row.

3 Consider the table resulting from step 2. In every column of that table, subtract the smallest cost in the column from every cost in the column.

4 Consider the table resulting from step 3. It will contain a number of zeros. Draw horizontal and vertical lines through all the zeros in such a way that you have used the minimum number of lines required to cover all of the zeros.

5 If the table is *n* by *n*, and if the minimum number of lines used in step 4 is exactly *n*, then an optimal assignment can be made. This optimal assignment uses only cells containing zeros. If the minimum number of lines used in step 4 is less than *n*, proceed to step 6.

6 Again, consider the table resulting from step 4. Find the smallest number in that table that is not covered by a line.
  a Subtract that number from every number that is not covered by a line.
  b Add that number to every number that is covered by two lines.
  c Leave the other numbers in the table as they were.

7 Step 6 gives a new table. Go back to step 4 and apply it to this new table. Eventually you will reach a table for which step 5 assures an optimal assignment.

## Example 7.15

Floatum Boat Company wants to fill the rush order of a regular customer for a small dinghy to carry on her yacht. To fill the order, four tasks remain: securing the hardware, painting, installing seats, and sewing the sail. Four workers, Amy, Bill, Cathy, and John, are available for the job. Each will be uniquely assigned to one of the tasks.

TABLE 7.30 TRANSPORTATION TABLE FOR AN ASSIGNMENT PROBLEM

| Worker | Job 1 | Job 2 | Job 3 | Job 4 | Capacity |
|--------|-------|-------|-------|-------|----------|
| 1 | $c_{11}$ | $c_{12}$ | $c_{13}$ | $c_{14}$ | 1 |
| 2 | $c_{21}$ | $c_{22}$ | $c_{23}$ | $c_{24}$ | 1 |
| 3 | $c_{31}$ | $c_{32}$ | $c_{33}$ | $c_{34}$ | 1 |
| 4 | $c_{41}$ | $c_{42}$ | $c_{43}$ | $c_{44}$ | 1 |
| Demand | 1 | 1 | 1 | 1 | 4 |

Floatum wishes to minimize the total estimated worker-hours required to complete the dinghy. The supervisor has estimated the times required for each worker to complete each task. These times are shown in Table 7.31. Assume that any of the tasks may be done concurrently with any others. How should Floatum assign workers to tasks?

Proceed to step 2 of the assignment method. Subtract from every number in each row of Table 7.31 the smallest number in that row. This gives Table 7.32.

Proceed to step 3. From every number in each column of Table 7.32, subtract the smallest number in that column. Then draw the lines required by step 4. This produces Table 7.33.

Now go to step 5. Table 7.33 is 4 × 4, but only three lines were required to cover all the zeros. Optimality is not yet implied, so go to step 6.

The smallest *uncovered* number in Table 7.33 is 2. Thus subtract 2 from

**TABLE 7.31** COMPLETION TIMES IN HOURS: STEP 1

| Worker | Task Hardware | Painting | Seats | Sail |
|--------|---------------|----------|-------|------|
| Amy | 5 | 3 | 1 | 5 |
| Bill | 6 | 6 | 2 | 7 |
| Cathy | 5 | 5 | 3 | 8 |
| John | 8 | 2 | 4 | 3 |

**TABLE 7.32**    THE RESULT OF STEP 2

| Worker | Hardware | Painting | Seats | Sail | Number subtracted |
|--------|----------|----------|-------|------|-------------------|
|        |          | **Task** |       |      |                   |
| Amy    | 4        | 2        | 0     | 4    | 1                 |
| Bill   | 4        | 4        | 0     | 5    | 2                 |
| Cathy  | 2        | 2        | 0     | 5    | 3                 |
| John   | 6        | 0        | 2     | 1    | 2                 |

all uncovered numbers, add 2 to all numbers covered by two lines, and leave the other numbers alone.  Next, go back to step 4 and draw your lines.  This gives Table 7.34.

It is not possible to cover all of the zeros in Table 7.34 with fewer than four lines.  Therefore, step 5 tells us that we can now make the optimal assignment of workers to tasks.

The assignment will be made using only the cells containing zeros in Table 7.34.  First, note that the only zero in the "Sail" column is opposite John.  So John is assigned to sew the sail.  Now since John will be sewing the sail, he cannot also do the painting.  The only feasible zero left in the "Painting" column is opposite Amy.  Amy is assigned to paint the dinghy. The only zero opposite Cathy is under "Hardware," so Cathy is assigned to secure the hardware.  This leaves Bill to install the seats.

The optimal assignment is shown in Table 7.35, along with the estimated completion times for each task.  The minimum number of worker-hours required to complete the dinghy is $5 + 3 + 2 + 3 = 13$ hours.

Finally, be advised that it is possible to have alternate optimal solutions for an assignment problem.  That is, there may be more than one way to use the zeros in a table like Table 7.34 to come up with assignments which are different but which give the same minimum cost.  In the Floatum Boat Company example, however, the optimal assignment quoted in Table 7.35 is unique.

**TABLE 7.33**    THE RESULT OF STEPS 3 AND 4

| Worker | Hardware | Painting | Seats | Sail |
|--------|----------|----------|-------|------|
|        |          | **Task** |       |      |
| Amy    | 2        | 2        | 0     | 3    |
| Bill   | 2        | 4        | 0     | 4    |
| Cathy  | 0        | 2        | 0     | 4    |
| John   | 4        | 0        | 2     | 0    |
| Number subtracted | 2 | 0 | 0 | 1 |

TABLE 7.34    THE RESULT OF STEPS 6, 7, AND 4

| Worker | Hardware | Task Painting | Seats | Sail |
|--------|----------|---------------|-------|------|
| Amy | 0 | 0 | 0 | 1 |
| Bill | 0 | 2 | 0 | 2 |
| Cathy | 0 | 2 | 2 | 4 |
| John | 4 | 0 | 4 | 0 |

## 7.11    SUMMARY AND CONCLUSIONS

Integer programming procedures apply to problems that would otherwise be ordinary LP problems except that some or all of the decision variables must be integer-valued. Historically, Gomory's cutting-plane method was the first approach that could guarantee an optimal integer solution. Research since the late 1950s has produced other procedures for integer programming, the most versatile and popular of which has been the branch-and-bound procedure that was discussed early on in this chapter.

Both the cutting-plane method and the branch-and-bound method require sequences of solutions of successively larger and larger LP problems. However, the bounding feature of branch-and-bound generally makes it a more efficient approach for most integer programming problems.

Two very special kinds of integer programming problems are the transportation problem and the assignment problem. Both problems can be solved by the ordinary simplex method since extreme points of their feasible regions must be points with only feasible integer coordinates. However, because of the simple structure of both of those special problems, efficient algorithms, called, respectively, the transportation method and the assignment method, have been invented for their solution. Each of those methods requires the working through of a succession of tables to achieve the optimal solution.

In the MPOS computer runs back in Chapter 6, examples of integer

TABLE 7.35    THE OPTIMAL ASSIGNMENT

| Worker | Hardware | Task Painting | Seats | Sail |
|--------|----------|---------------|-------|------|
| Amy | | 3 | | |
| Bill | | | 2 | |
| Cathy | 5 | | | |
| John | | | | 3 |

**267**

*INTEGER
PROGRAMMING,
TRANSPORTATION
PROBLEMS, AND
ASSIGNMENT
PROBLEMS*

programming solutions, transportation problem solutions, and assignment problem solutions were included. Unless you find yourself in a situation where an LP computer package is not available, computer solution of problems like those found in this chapter is advised.

While transportation problems have been introduced here as problems of minimizing shipping costs of items from sources to destinations, other problems may be modeled so that they fit the transportation-problem format. In the exercises to follow you will see examples involving production, food service, site selection, and personnel training.

The assignment problem is a simple example of what is generally called *0-1 programming*. All of its decision variables could only assume one of two values, 0 or 1. Other decision problems may be formulated as 0-1 problems. Questions such as "buy–don't buy" or "expand–don't expand" may be embedded in models with the number 0 associated with a "no" decision and the number 1 associated with a "yes" decision. The general approach to solution of such problems is a modified version of the branch-and-bound method. Often, however, a procedure called dynamic programming can be used. Examples of dynamic programming solutions of 0-1 decision problems will appear in Chapter 12.

## KEY WORDS AND PHRASES

**Integer programming problem**   A linear programming problem in which some or all of the decision variables must be integers.

**Gomory's cutting-plane method**   A modification of the ordinary simplex method that incorporates extra constraints that are associated with basic variables having the largest fractional part. It is used to solve integer programming problems.

**Cutting plane**   The constraint associated with the basic variable having the largest fractional part. It occurs as an extra constraint in one of the iterations of Gomory's cutting-plane method.

**Branch-and-bound method**   A procedure for solving integer programming problems. The branching operation subdivides the original feasible region, while the bounding feature simply recognizes that any feasible integer solution bounds the optimal value of the objective function.

**Upper bound**   In branch-and-bound, the optimal value of the objective function if the integer restrictions are ignored (maximization problem).

**Lower bound**   In branch-and-bound, any integer-valued feasible solution (maximization problem).

**Transportation problem**   The problem of determining routes to minimize the cost of shipping commodities from various sources to many destinations.

**Transportation table**   A convenient tabular organization of the given information in a transportation problem. It is also used when solving the problem using the transportation method.

**Balanced transportation problem**  A transportation problem in which total capacity equals total demand.

**Northwest-corner rule**  A method for obtaining a convenient initial basic feasible solution which does not take into account the costs associated with the cells in a transportation table.

**The transportation method**  The standard method for solving a transportation problem utilizing transportation tables.

**Cell value**  The per-unit amount by which transportation cost will be increased or decreased if an allocation is made to that cell.

**Closed loop**  A unique path for cell evaluation in any current solution that is basic.

**The MODI method**  A method for cell evaluation based on the dual variables in a transportation problem.  This method precludes the necessity for finding a different closed loop to evaluate each empty cell.

**Degeneracy**  The situation in which one or more of the basic variables in a trial solution will assume the value zero.

**VAM** (Vogel's approximation method)  A method for obtaining an initial basic feasible solution of a transportation problem, based on the avoidance of high penalties and high-cost cells.  The initial solution so obtained is often the optimal solution.

**Penalty** (for a row or column)  The difference between the cost for the low-cost cell and the second-low-cost cell in a row or column in which the allocations are as yet incomplete.

**Unbalanced transportation problem**  A transportation problem in which total capacity does not equal total demand.

**Dummy source or destination**  An extra row or column in a transportation table, with zero cost in each of its cells, used to balance an unbalanced problem.

**Assignment problem**  The problem of assigning $n$ workers to $n$ jobs in such a way that only one worker is assigned to each job, every job has a worker assigned to it, and the cost of completing all jobs is minimized.

**Assignment method**  The standard procedure for tabular solution of an assignment problem.

## EXERCISES

◆ **7.1** Consider the following integer programming problem:

Maximize $Z$

where

$$Z = 4x_1 + 5x_2$$

subject to

$$3x_1 + 4x_2 \leq 12$$

$$4x_1 + 3x_2 \leq 12$$

$x_1, x_2$ must be nonnegative integers

**269**

*INTEGER
PROGRAMMING,
TRANSPORTATION
PROBLEMS, AND
ASSIGNMENT
PROBLEMS*

Solve the problem **(a)** graphically, **(b)** using Gomory's cutting-plane method, and **(c)** using branch-and-bound.

◆ **7.2** Consider the following integer programming problem:

$$\text{Maximize } Z$$

where

$$Z = 5x_1 + 4x_2$$

subject to

$$x_1 + x_2 \geq 2$$
$$5x_1 + 3x_2 \leq 15$$
$$3x_1 + 5x_2 \leq 15$$

$$x_1, x_2 \text{ must be nonnegative integers}$$

Solve the problem **(a)** graphically, **(b)** using Gomory's cutting-plane method, and **(c)** using branch-and-bound.

**7.3** Good Sports, Inc., manufactures three types of tennis rackets: Basic, Custom, and Expert. To build a Basic racket requires 1 person-hour and 3 machine-hours. A Custom racket calls for $\frac{3}{2}$ person-hours and 4 machine-hours, and an Expert racket demands 3 person-hours and 7 machine-hours. The respective profits per Basic, Custom, and Expert rackets are $10, $14, and $20.

During the current planning period Good Sports will have available 2,000 person-hours and 2,300 machine-hours. A fraction of a racket produces no profit. How many of each type of racket should be made in order to maximize profit for the period? Solve it **(a)** using Gomory's cutting-plane method and **(b)** using branch-and-bound.

**7.4** Solve Example 7.2, the Molly's Maple Market problem, using branch-and-bound.

◆ **7.5** Following is a transportation table for a cost-minimization problem. Solve it **(a)** starting from an initial solution by the northwest-corner rule and **(b)** starting from an initial solution by VAM.

| Factory | Warehouse 1 | Warehouse 2 | Warehouse 3 | Capacity |
|---|---|---|---|---|
| 1 | 12 | 8 | 10 | 300 |
| 2 | 7 | 9 | 12 | 200 |
| Required | 250 | 150 | 100 | 500 |

**7.6** Following is a transportation table for a cost-minimization problem. Solve it, **(a)** starting from an initial solution by the northwest-corner rule and **(b)** starting from an initial solution by VAM.

| | Destination | | |
|---|---|---|---|
| Source | 1 | 2 | Supply |
| 1 | 40 | 35 | 50 |
| 2 | 45 | 30 | 70 |
| 3 | 20 | 25 | 40 |
| 4 | 10 | 20 | 60 |
| Demand | 160 | 60 | 220 |

✦ **7.7** Following is a transportation table for a cost-minimization problem. Solve it **(a)** starting from an initial solution by the northwest-corner rule and **(b)** starting from an initial solution by VAM.

| | Destination | | | | |
|---|---|---|---|---|---|
| Source | 1 | 2 | 3 | 4 | Supply |
| 1 | 23 | 31 | 27 | 40 | 500 |
| 2 | 30 | 44 | 28 | 36 | 300 |
| 3 | 36 | 21 | 45 | 25 | 420 |
| Demand | 250 | 360 | 320 | 170 | 1,100 / 1,220 |

**7.8** Solve the transportation problem described as Example 2.4 of Chapter 2.

✦ **7.9** Solve the Laramie-Tie Siding Express problem. It is described in Exercise 2.10 at the end of Chapter 2.

✦ **7.10** Solve the production-distribution problem described in Exercise 2.12 at the end of Chapter 2. *Note:* This is a maximization problem.

✦ **7.11** Solve the management-trainee problem described as Exercise 6.9 at the end of Chapter 6 using the transportation method.

**7.12** The Gas-Hog Car Rental Company wishes to move 50 cars: 25 from assembly plant *A*, 15 from plant *B*, and 10 from plant *C*, to two cities: Los Angeles and

**271**

INTEGER
PROGRAMMING,
TRANSPORTATION
PROBLEMS, AND
ASSIGNMENT
PROBLEMS

Dallas. Their agency in Los Angeles will get 30 cars and Dallas will receive 20 cars. College students in the three assembly plant areas will be hired to drive the cars to their destinations.

Gas-Hog's management reasons that transportation costs should be minimized if total distance driven is minimized. Distances between plants and agencies are shown below. Find how many cars to drive from each plant to each agency in order to minimize total distance driven.

|  |  |
|---|---|
| A to Los Angeles: 1,200 miles | A to Dallas: 600 miles |
| B to Los Angeles: 800 miles | B to Dallas: 1,000 miles |
| C to Los Angeles: 600 miles | C to Dallas: 900 miles |

**7.13** A manufacturing concern has three assembly lines, each capable of producing any of four different products. Setup costs from each assembly line making any product are negligible.

During a given production period, 50 units of product A, 100 of product B, 70 of product C, and 80 of product D are required. Assembly line 1 has a capacity of 100 units of any product or combination of products; the capacity of line 2 is 200 units, and of line 3 is 100 units.

Production costs per unit for products A, B, C, and D, respectively, are $10, $8, $9, and $5 on line 1; on line 2, $5, $7, $10, and $12; on line 3, $8, $11, $9, and $6. Using the transportation method, find out how many units of each product to make on each assembly line so that production cost for the period is minimized.

◆ **7.14** Suppose we modify Exercise 7.13 slightly, assuming that line 1 cannot handle product B and that line 2 cannot handle product C. Then in the associated transportation table you could put a "Big M" in the appropriate cost cells to assure that at optimality there are no allocations made to those two cells. Solve the problem as described using transportation tables.

**7.15** A local restauranteur provides catered luncheons for departmental meetings in three colleges of the university in town. He owns three restaurants: X, Y, and Z. Restaurant X can cater 14 luncheons per week, Y can cater 10 per week, and Z is able to cater 8 luncheons per week. The College of Arts and Sciences (A&S) has 15 departmental luncheons weekly, Engineering (E) has 8, and Commerce and Industry (C&I) has 5.

Because of differences in types of lunches requested, as well as different locations and personnel for the three restaurants, profit per luncheon varies over restaurants and colleges. The following table shows the profit per luncheon for each restaurant catering to each college. Use the transportation method to determine how many lunches each restaurant should provide for each college so that maximum weekly profit is realized.

PROFIT PER LUNCHEON

| Restaurant | College | | |
|---|---|---|---|
|  | A&S | E | C&I |
| X | $20 | $15 | $12 |
| Y | $14 | $20 | $16 |
| Z | $10 | $12 | $14 |

**7.16** A company currently manufactures three products: X, Y, and Z, at two plants, located in Detroit and Houston. A new plant is planned for either St. Louis or Atlanta. The company has decided to select the site for the new plant on the basis of maximizing aggregate monthly profit accruing from the three plants.

Profit per unit for the three products, because of differences in operating costs, depends upon the location of the production source. Monthly capacities of plants (included projected capacity for the new plant), monthly demand for products, and profit per unit of product are given in the following table.

### PROFIT, DEMAND, AND CAPACITY

| Plant | Profit per unit of product | | | Capacity |
|---|---|---|---|---|
| | X | Y | Z | |
| Detroit | 27 | 35 | 15 | 300 |
| Houston | 32 | 40 | 20 | 500 |
| St. Louis | 24 | 34 | 26 | 400 |
| Atlanta | 20 | 44 | 18 | 400 |
| Demand | 250 | 400 | 300 | |

Select the site for the new plant using the transportation method in the analysis. (*Hint:* You might want to consider two separate transportation problems.)

**7.17** Use the assignment method to solve the assignment problem suggested by the following cost table:

| Machine | Job | | |
|---|---|---|---|
| | 1 | 2 | 3 |
| A | 23 | 16 | 14 |
| B | 25 | 14 | 12 |
| C | 22 | 16 | 15 |

◆ **7.18** Use the assignment method to solve the problem described as Exercise 6.11 at the end of Chapter 6.

◆ **7.19** Use the assignment method to solve the Family Theaters problem, Example 6.7 of Chapter 6.

◆ **7.20** Use the assignment method to solve the minimum-time assignment problem of Chekov and Adams's accounting firm that is described in Exercise 6.12 at the end of Chapter 6.

◆ **7.21** Use the assignment method to solve the minimum-cost assignment problem of Chekov and Adams's accounting firm that is described in Exercise 6.12 at the end of Chapter 6.

**7.22** Laramie's Jubilee Days Committee has decided to hold a special event during this July's rodeo. Teams composed of two men and one woman will compete in three events: calf roping, steer wrestling, and barrel racing. Each event is timed, and the winning team will be the one which turns in the lowest combined time for the three events. Each member of a team must compete in only one event, and every event must be entered by some team member.

Bronk Ryder, Chuck Wagner, and Lariette Roper have decided to enter the special event as a team. They have been practicing each individual event and have determined an average time for each member in each event. Those average times, in seconds, are shown below.

| Person | Average time per person per event | | |
|--------|-------------|----------------|--------------|
| | Calf roping | Steer wrestling | Barrel racing |
| Bronk | 18 | 11 | 16 |
| Chuck | 20 | 15 | 20 |
| Lariette | 21 | 12 | 19 |

Bronk, Chuck, and Lariette will enter events using minimum combined average time as a criterion. Who should be assigned to each of the three events?

## SELECTED REFERENCES

Ackoff, R. L., and M. W. Sasieni: *Fundamentals of Operations Research,* John Wiley & Sons, Inc., New York, 1968.

Anderson, D. R., D. J. Sweeney, and T. A. Williams: *An Introduction to Management Science,* 3d ed., West Publishing Company, St. Paul, Minn., 1982.

Balinski, M. L.: "Integer Programming: Methods, Uses, Computation," *Management Science,* vol. 12, 1965, pp. 253–313.

Bierman, H., C. P. Bonini, and W. H. Hausman: *Quantitative Analysis for Business Decisions,* 6th ed., Richard D. Irwin, Inc., Homewood, Ill., 1981.

Gomory, R. E.: "An Algorithm for the Mixed Integer Problem," The Rand Corporation, RM-2597, 1960.

Hesse, R., and G. Woolsey: *Applied Management Science,* SRA, Chicago, 1980.

Levin, R. I., C. A. Kirkpatrick, and D. S. Rubin: *Quantitative Approaches to Management,* 5th ed., McGraw-Hill Book Company, New York, 1982.

Thierauf, R. J., and R. C. Klekamp: *Decision Making Through Operations Research,* 2d ed., John Wiley & Sons, Inc., New York, 1975.

Thompson, W. W., Jr.: *Operations Research Techniques,* Charles E. Merrill Books, Inc., Columbus, Ohio, 1967.

# BASIC PROBABILITY CONCEPTS

$A$ll of the models and solutions for problems from Chapters 2 through 7 have involved only *deterministic* notions; we have assumed *exact* knowledge of parameters such as cost per unit or amount of available resource. Particularly in the transportation problems of Chapter 7 demand at a specific destination was assumed to be known precisely. But demand is a type of variable that usually cannot be predicted exactly. We might know average demand per month, or an average demand rate per unit time for a certain season of the year, but not usually the *actual* level of demand that will occur during some time period in the future.

However, we might possess good information about the fraction of the time demand has assumed certain values during that period. Consider Example 8.1.

### Example 8.1
### Probability Distribution for Demand

A heating contractor in a town with a fairly stable population is attempting to assess December demand for new or replacement furnaces. His records for the past 40 years show 4 years in which no furnaces were sold in December, 9 years in which one furnace was sold, 21 years when two furnaces were sold, and 6 years in which three furnaces were sold in December. Then he has information about past *relative frequencies* of demand levels. Such relative frequencies may be interpreted as *probabilities*.

If the contractor believes that his past experience is a dependable guide to the future, he can say, for instance, that the probability that two furnaces will be required this December is $\frac{21}{40} = 0.525$, or that the probability that no furnaces will be required this December is $\frac{4}{40} = 0.100$. In fact, if he lets

$$X = \text{December demand for furnaces}$$

he can establish the *probability distribution* for December demand that is shown in Table 8.1.

Table 8.1 shows the contractor at a glance the way that December demand is distributed probabilistically, or in a relative frequency sense. For example, he immediately sees that the *most likely* demand is for 2 furnaces, since that value of demand is associated with the highest probability in the table. He would also know that if he has two furnaces in stock in December, the probability that he can meet demand from inventory is 0.850, the sum of the first three probabilities in Table 8.1. That is, in 85 percent of past Decembers an inventory of two furnaces would have been sufficient to meet demand. The probability distribution of Table 8.1 also shows *variability* in December demand, and it even permits a convenient calculation of *average* December demand, questions that will be considered more formally later on in this chapter.

Perhaps Example 8.1 has convinced you that a knowledge of basic probability concepts can be a valuable tool for assisting us in the making of business and industrial decisions. As you will see throughout the remainder of this book, the marriage of economic factors and probability considerations is often the only rational way to approach a particular decision-making problem.

In this chapter you will be introduced to some elementary notions about probability and random variables. Then these basic ideas will be imme-

**TABLE 8.1** PROBABILITY DISTRIBUTION OF DECEMBER DEMAND FOR FURNACES

| Demand $x$ | Probability $P(X = x)$ |
|------------|------------------------|
| 0 | $\frac{4}{40} = 0.100$ |
| 1 | $\frac{9}{40} = 0.225$ |
| 2 | $\frac{21}{40} = 0.525$ |
| 3 | $\frac{6}{40} = 0.150$ |

diately exploited in the problems of subsequent chapters. Usually most realistic business situations involve a blend of probabilistic and deterministic information.

## 8.1 INTERPRETATIONS OF PROBABILITY

The local television weatherperson announces, ''The probability of measurable precipitation tomorrow is 50 percent.'' Just what does that person mean by that statement?

Many people, perhaps even the majority, who hear that announcement won't really know how the weatherperson intends for it to be interpreted. Some will snort, ''Ha! What does 50 percent chance mean? It either rains tomorrow or it doesn't.'' Others may react as does the author's mother, who is wont to gaze out the window at the rain and remark, ''Well, there's that 50 percent chance of measurable precipitation!''

Actually, there are two meanings that could have been intended by the weatherperson, neither of which is entirely conveyed by the responses reported in the previous paragraph. One of those meanings has to do with the interpretation of a probability as a *relative frequency*. The other possibility is that the weatherperson may be giving us a *subjective estimate* of the probability based upon that person's qualifications as an expert in the field of weather forecasting. Let's consider the difference in those two interpretations.

If the weatherperson reached that conclusion using the concept of relative frequency, an *objective* statement of probability, based on accumulated data, is being reported. That data could occur in the following way. A particular pattern of atmospheric conditions has been observed. Consulting records accumulated over many years, the weatherperson observes that during this particular season, whenever that pattern of conditions has existed, about half the time it has rained the next day.

If on the other hand the weatherperson is giving us a *subjective* probability, we are being told the odds at which that person would bet that it rains tomorrow. Although accumulated data provide part of that person's background as an expert in the field, those records may not have actually been consulted. Having been in the business of weather forecasting for a long time, the weatherperson merely inspects the available maps and instruments, gazes outside, and remarks, ''If I had to bet on rain tomorrow, I would expect even-money odds.''

Either way, the result of the analysis was the quotation of a 50 percent chance, or a probability of 0.50 for rain. Not knowing how the forecast was made, of course, we must then interpret this number for ourselves, planning our own actions for tomorrow around that interpretation.

Most of us will probably be more comfortable with the relative-frequency interpretation. Betting and odds are foreign to many people, while anyone can appreciate the concept embodied in the statement: Half the time in the past it has rained on a day such as this. In fact, most probabilities permit this easy relative-frequency interpretation.

But sometimes relative frequency just doesn't make sense. Perhaps the situation of interest simply has not arisen before, so no data have been accumulated to cover it.

Consider a public utilities company awaiting a decision giving it permission to begin construction of a nuclear power plant. The company has had other nuclear plants approved in the past, but the last approval was granted more than seven years ago; conditions have changed since then. The Department of Energy is reflecting the more cautious attitude of a new administration, public awareness of potential dangers has increased, a pronuclear lobby is having trouble selling Congress on the benefits to be derived from less dependence on foreign oil, and that anticipated technological breakthrough which was supposed to solve the problem of waste disposal has not occurred.

There is no past experience available for assessing the probability that the proposed plant will be approved before 1988. Yet that probability is important to the decision that will have to be made in 1986: Shall we anticipate building the nuclear plant or shall we initiate plans for a more conventional coal-fired facility? Top management arrives at a consensus: The odds are 3 to 1 that the nuclear plant will not be approved by 1988. This converts to a probability of $\frac{1}{4}$, or 0.25, for 1988 approval. It is obviously a subjective probability that does not permit any long-run relative-frequency interpretation. The decision is one-of-a-kind.

So we have seen relative-frequency probabilities that are based on data or observation, and subjective probabilities of an "expert judgment" nature. Yet a third kind of probability, called *a priori* probability, exists. This is the type of probability usually associated with games of chance, like coin flipping or dice tossing, where the probability of an event may be determined without guesswork and without experimentation. The probability comes from physical laws governing the behavior of the coin or dice and may be obtained by *reasoning*. For instance, if we know that a coin is balanced, so that no bias toward either heads or tails is present, and excluding the possibility of the coin landing on edge, we reason that a 50/50 chance exists for tossing either a head or a tail. That is, we know in advance of any experimentation that $P(\text{Head}) = \frac{1}{2}$ and $P(\text{Tail}) = \frac{1}{2}$. Likewise, consider one fair (balanced), six-sided die, with faces (sides) numbered 1 through 6. Since the die is fair, we immediately know that the probability that any particular face will show is $\frac{1}{6}$.

These a priori probabilities are obtained through reasoning, but they are *interpreted* as relative frequencies. That is, a probability of $\frac{1}{2}$ for tossing a head is interpreted to mean that in the long run, after many, many tosses of the balanced coin, about one-half of the outcomes will have been heads.

Yet regardless of the process whereby probabilities are assessed or interpreted, their manipulation by the formulas to appear in Section 8.2 will be the same. That is, our formulas will not care whether they are dealing with relative frequencies, subjective probabilities, or a priori probabilities. The quality of the final results will only depend upon how accurately those probability assessments are made, or to borrow an acronym from the field of computer science, GIGO (garbage in, garbage out).

To formalize the discussions presented above, the following three working definitions of probability are provided:

*Relative-frequency probability.* If the event $A$ is given $n$ opportunities (trials) to occur, and if after those $n$ trials the number of times event $A$ has occurred is $a$, then the *estimated* probability for event $A$, in a *relative-frequency* sense, is

$$P(A) = \frac{a}{n}$$

*Subjective probability.* If the odds are $a$ to $b$ that event $A$ will occur, where these odds are anticipated without access to relative-frequency-type data or a priori reasoning, then the *subjective probability* for event $A$ is

$$P(A) = \frac{a}{a + b}$$

*A priori probability.* Given $n$ equally likely outcomes of some experiment, if $a$ of those outcomes are associated with the occurrence of event $A$, then the *a priori probability* for event $A$ is

$$P(A) = \frac{a}{n}$$

### Example 8.2
### Relative Frequency

Britetooth Company has kept records on the monthly demand per capita for Britetooth toothpaste in a particular marketing area. Suppose that over a period of 100 months the per-capita demand has been 0.5 tubes of Britetooth during 30 months, 0.4 tubes during 40 months, 0.3 tubes during 25 months, and 0.2 tubes during 5 months. If these past 100 months are a good indicator for demand in future months, then we could say for the next month

$$P(\text{demand is 0.3 tubes per capita}) = \tfrac{25}{100} = 0.25$$

or

$$P(\text{demand is 0.5 tubes per capita}) = \tfrac{30}{100} = 0.30$$

Here the probabilities are just relative frequencies that have been estimated from historical data.

### Example 8.3
### Subjective Probability

Harley Goldentouch, the famous wildcatter, is offering for sale an oil lease about which he is known to have remarked, "I'll bet there's oil down there if you'll give me 15 to 1 odds." Reasoning that Harley knows the oil business pretty well, we might peg the probability of that lease paying off with an oil well at one-sixteenth, or

$$P(\text{oil}) = \frac{1}{1 + 15} = \tfrac{1}{16}$$

Here we are using Harley's subjective assessment of the probability based on his stated betting odds.

### Example 8.4
### A Priori Probability

We are at the crap table in Las Vegas, contemplating betting that the next toss of the dice produces the number 7. We were attracted by the prominently displayed odds of 4 to 1 for a 7. We have available no historical data about dice tossing, but reason that the dice are probably fair. To see if betting on 7 is a good idea at 4 to 1 odds, we construct the diagram shown in Figure 8.1.

The dice are two separate objects, which we call die #1 and die #2. The diagram in Figure 8.1 shows that die #1 can show any of its six faces

*FIGURE 8.1* Possible outcomes on one toss of two dice

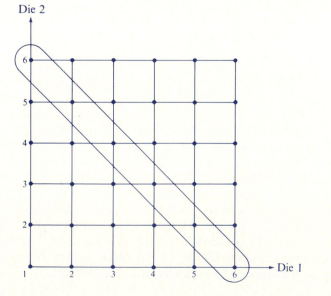

after the toss, as can die #2. Thus there are 36 possible outcomes of one toss of two dice, and the six enclosed points in Figure 8.1 represent those outcomes which produce a total of seven: 1 on die #1 and 6 on die #2, 2 on die #1 and 5 on die #2, and so on. Since the dice are fair, there is no reason to favor any one of the 36 points over any other, so we reason that out of 36 equally likely outcomes, 6 represent the event of interest, tossing a 7. Thus we say

$$P(\text{tossing a 7}) = \tfrac{6}{36} = \tfrac{1}{6}$$

Are the quoted odds of 4 to 1 "fair" odds? No. For a probability of $\tfrac{1}{6}$ we would need $1/(1 + 5)$, suggesting that 5 to 1 would be fair odds for that wager.

We may give the $\tfrac{1}{6}$ probability a relative-frequency interpretation, even though it was determined by a priori reasoning. It means that in the long run, over many, many tosses of a pair of fair dice, the number 7 should occur about one-sixth of the time. Note further, however, that our assessment of the fairness of the offered odds took advantage of ideas we used when interpreting subjective probabilities. Thus all of the previous discussions of different types of probabilities and their interpretations have been used in our analysis of the original question.

**Example 8.5**
**The Need for Probability Formulas**

Suppose that in a group of 200 people at a political gathering there are 100 Democrats, 80 Republicans, and 20 Independents. If we randomly select one person from that group, then

$$P(\text{selecting a Democrat}) = \tfrac{100}{200} = \tfrac{1}{2}$$

$$P(\text{selecting a Republican}) = \tfrac{80}{200} = \tfrac{2}{5}$$

$$P(\text{selecting an Independent}) = \tfrac{20}{200} = \tfrac{1}{10}$$

Here of course the probabilities come from a priori reasoning.

Probabilities associated with the random selection of a single person from that group were easy to determine. But what if we consider selecting *five* people, and ask: "What is the probability that we will obtain two Democrats, two Republicans, and one Independent?" We could try considering all possible outcomes of a first selection, then all possible outcomes of the second selection, and so on, but this analysis might lead to our having to envision the characteristics of a five-dimensional diagram of the type shown in Figure 8.1. A better approach is resort to probability formulas like those to appear in the next section.

Probabilities are numbers (fractions) between zero and unity, inclusive. That characteristic is clear when you consider a probability as a relative frequency, or a proportion of times out of many trials that a particular event, say event $A$, will occur. Thus if $A$ is any event, then always

$$0 \leq P(A) \leq 1$$

The probability zero may be assigned to an *impossible* event; that is, if an event cannot occur it has "zero chance" of occurring. Likewise, an event that is *certain* to occur is given a probability of unity (100 percent chance of occurring). All other probabilities are numbers that fall between those two extremes.

*Mutually exclusive events.* Events that cannot occur together (the occurrence of one of them precludes the occurrence of any of the others) are called *mutually exclusive* events.

Consider an event $A$ which is comprised entirely of the mutually exclusive events $A_1$, $A_2$, and $A_3$, a situation depicted schematically in Figure 8.2. Since the occurrence of event $A$ means that either $A_1$, $A_2$, or $A_3$ has occurred, and since $A_1$, $A_2$, and $A_3$ are mutually exclusive, then a natural way to compute $P(A)$ is suggested by the formula

$$P(A) = P(A_1) + P(A_2) + P(A_3)$$

This formula (or its natural extension for fewer or more constituent events in $A$) will always apply when the subevents comprising event $A$ are mutually exclusive and *exhaustive* (comprise *all* of $A$).

Now reconsider Figure 8.2 from a different perspective. The rectangle

**FIGURE 8.2**   Composition of event $A$

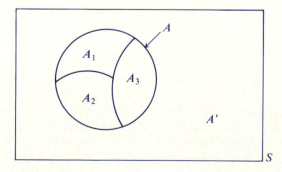

labeled $S$ is intended to suggest every possibility that could have occurred, and as such is a *certain* event.  So

$$P(S) = 1$$

But the event $A'$ of Figure 8.2 represents the *nonoccurrence* of event $A$ and is called the *complement* of event $A$.  Since $A$ and $A'$ (read "$A$-complement") are mutually exclusive, exhaustive events comprising all of event $S$, then

$$P(A) + P(A') = P(S) = 1$$

This reasoning gives us the first of our principal probability formulas.

> *Formula 1: The complementary event formula.*
> $$P(A) = 1 - P(A')$$

Sometimes one of the two probabilities $P(A)$ and $P(A')$ is easier to obtain directly than the other.  The complementary event formula enables us to obtain the harder probability by subtracting the easier one from unity.

### Example 8.6
### Using the Complementary Event Formula

Reconsider the dice-tossing problem of Example 8.4.  What is the probability of *not* tossing a 7 on one toss of a pair of fair dice?  Since $P$(tossing a 7) $= \frac{1}{6}$,

$$P(\text{not tossing a 7}) = 1 - \tfrac{1}{6} = \tfrac{5}{6}$$

This is much easier than computing the sum of all probabilities for outcomes other than 7, using the notion that they are mutually exclusive.  For that analysis, we would have

$P(\text{not tossing a 7})$
$$= P(2) + P(3) + \cdots + P(6) + P(8) + \cdots + P(11) + P(12)$$
$$= \tfrac{1}{36} + \tfrac{2}{36} + \cdots + \tfrac{5}{36} + \tfrac{5}{36} + \cdots + \tfrac{2}{36} + \tfrac{1}{36} = \tfrac{30}{36}$$
$$= \tfrac{5}{6}$$

Of course one could just refer again to Figure 8.1, counting all the points *not* associated with the total 7.  This would also give $\frac{30}{36} = \frac{5}{6}$ as the probability of not tossing a 7.  The advantage of the complementary event formula is not great in this example.  However, later on you will see other examples wherein you will be very glad to have that formula available.

   On many occasions we will find it necessary to calculate probabilities for *compound events*, events that are combinations of two or more other events that may not be mutually exclusive.  To keep things simple we

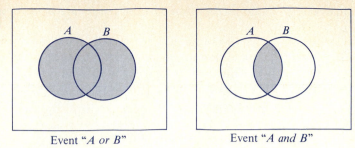

Event "*A or B*"      Event "*A and B*"

***FIGURE 8.3***    Two basic combined events

consider here only combinations of *two* events, say event *A* and event *B*. It is very easy to extend to combinations of three or more events the basic formulas for two combined events.

Only two types of combinations of events will be considered, these types being indicated by the key words "or" and "and." That is, we may know *P(A)* and *P(B)* individually, but we wish to know either *P(A or B)* or *P(A and B)*. Here the event "*A or B*" means either event *A* or event *B* or both events *A* and *B* occur. The "or" is an "inclusive or"; we say event *A* or event *B* has occurred if either or both of those events occur. However, the event "*A and B*" occurs only if *both* event *A* and event *B* occur. Figure 8.3 illustrates those meanings.

Usually we associate "or" with the algebraic operation of addition and "and" with the operation of multiplication. Computing probabilities for combined events involves those two operations, but in a unique way that will be illustrated as we consider the *addition formula* and the *multiplication formula* for probabilities.

### Example 8.7
### Prelude to the Addition Formula

Figure 8.4 exhibits a collection of 18 possible outcomes of some experiment (denoted by the 18 points in the figure), this collection being called the set *S* as it was in Figure 8.2. Suppose that all 18 points represent equally likely outcomes and notice that 8 points are in event *A* while 7 points are

***FIGURE 8.4***    The plausibility of the addition formula

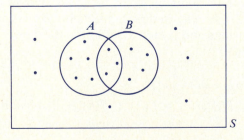

in event $B$. Note further that 3 of the points are in *both* event $A$ and event $B$.

Since all of the 18 points in $S$ are equally likely and since these are the only possible outcomes of the experiment, each must be assigned the probability $\frac{1}{18}$. Then the sum of the probabilities for the 18 simple constituent events in $S$ is unity (the sum of 18 fractions, each of which is $\frac{1}{18}$). Thus again we see that

$$P(S) = 1$$

Further, there are 8 mutually exclusive points (simple events) comprising event $A$, and they all have the probability $\frac{1}{18}$ associated with them, so the sum of those 8 probabilities is $P(A)$. Thus

$$P(A) = \tfrac{8}{18} = \tfrac{4}{9}$$

Likewise, $$P(B) = \tfrac{7}{18}$$

Probabilities for the events "$A$ *or* $B$" and "$A$ *and* $B$" are also easy to determine. By counting we see that there are 12 points in the event "$A$ *or* $B$" and 3 points making up event "$A$ *and* $B$." Thus

$$P(A \text{ or } B) = \tfrac{12}{18} = \tfrac{2}{3}$$

and $$P(A \text{ and } B) = \tfrac{3}{18} = \tfrac{1}{6}$$

Already it has been mentioned that "or" is associated with addition. But we observe that

$$P(A) + P(B) = \tfrac{8}{18} + \tfrac{7}{18} = \tfrac{15}{18} = \tfrac{5}{6}$$

which is certainly not the same number as the fraction $\frac{2}{3}$ ($= \frac{4}{6}$), the probability associated with event "$A$ *or* $B$." Now recall, however, that when you counted up points in Figure 8.4 to verify that 12 of them comprised event "$A$ *or* $B$," you only counted *once* the 3 points in event "$A$ *and* $B$." But when we determined $P(A)$, those 3 points were included, and when we determined $P(B)$, the same 3 points were *also* counted. Thus attempting to compute $P(A \text{ or } B)$ by simply adding $P(A)$ and $P(B)$ would mean that the 3 points in event "$A$ *and* $B$" would be counted *twice*, obviously not the right way to determine $P(A \text{ or } B)$. A simple ratification of that error is obvious and is embodied in the third term of our next basic probability formula.

*Formula 2: The addition formula.*
$$P(A \text{ or } B) = P(A) + P(B) - P(A \text{ and } B)$$

Applying this formula to the situation depicted by Figure 8.4 gives the correct value for $P(A \text{ or } B)$. That is,

$$P(A \text{ or } B) = P(A) + P(B) - P(A \text{ and } B)$$

$$= \tfrac{8}{18} + \tfrac{7}{18} - \tfrac{3}{18}$$

$$= \frac{8 + 7 - 3}{18}$$

$$= \tfrac{12}{18} = \tfrac{2}{3}$$

Notice that in the third line of equations appears the operation $(8 + 7 - 3)$. This reflects the fact that in the "$8 + 7$" portion three points have been counted twice. The "$-3$" portion corrects that error.

Formula 2, the addition formula, is quite general. Although we have only considered here points that were equally likely, the formula applies to *any* pair of events $A$ and $B$. A general proof is within the grasp of anyone familiar with the algebra of sets, but a proof will not be included here.

Notice that to use the addition formula it is necessary not only to know $P(A)$ and $P(B)$, but also to know $P(A \text{ and } B)$. Yet in many situations $P(A \text{ and } B)$ itself must be computed using algebraic combinations of probabilities for simpler events. In Example 8.8 you will see more illustrations of the addition formula, but also you will be acquiring some background necessary for appreciating the multiplication formula from which one obtains $P(A \text{ and } B)$. That background consists of your understanding the concept of *conditional probability*.

**Example 8.8**

Consider Table 8.2, which gives a cross-classification by sex and class of the enrollment in a typical large beginning statistics course at the University of Wyoming. Suppose we randomly select one name from the list of 298 names on the roll for that class. Then the probability of selecting a sophomore is

$$P(\text{sophomore}) = \tfrac{69}{298}$$

The probability of selecting a male is

$$P(\text{male}) = \tfrac{157}{298}$$

and the probability of selecting a male sophomore is

$$P(\text{male } and \text{ sophomore}) = \tfrac{33}{298}$$

**TABLE 8.2** CROSS-CLASSIFICATION OF ENROLLMENT

| Class | Sex | | Total |
|-------|--------|------|-------|
| | Female | Male | |
| Freshman | 12 | 9 | 21 |
| Sophomore | 36 | 33 | 69 |
| Junior | 57 | 68 | 125 |
| Senior | 36 | 47 | 83 |
| Total | 141 | 157 | 298 |

Note that both $P$(sophomore) and $P$(male) were obtained using numbers found in the margins of the table. But the events "select a sophomore" and "select a male," here abbreviated to simply "sophomore" and "male," are similar in concept to the events $A$ and $B$ of Figure 8.4 and the addition formula. In fact, probabilities like $P(A)$ and $P(B)$ are in general referred to as *marginal probabilities*. That generic name serves to distinguish them from conditional probabilities, to be discussed shortly. First of all, however, let's observe an application of the addition formula.

What is the probability that we select a name associated with either a male or a sophomore or both? According to the addition formula, it is

$P$(male *or* sophomore)

$$= P(\text{male}) + P(\text{sophomore}) - P(\text{male } and \text{ sophomore})$$

$$= \tfrac{157}{298} + \tfrac{69}{298} - \tfrac{33}{298}$$

$$= \frac{157 + 69 - 33}{298}$$

$$= \tfrac{193}{298}$$

That probability could have been obtained by counting all the males, adding to that all of the sophomores who are not males (the male sophomores already having been counted), then dividing by 298. That approach gives

$$P(\text{male } or \text{ sophomore}) = \frac{157 + 36}{298}$$

$$= \tfrac{193}{298}$$

the same fraction obtained by using the addition formula.

**Example 8.9**

Now let's look at a different kind of probability. Suppose we ask the question: Given that the person selected is male, what is the probability that he is a sophomore?

This type of probability is known as a *conditional probability*. In general, the conditional probability of the occurrence of event $A$ *given* that event $B$ has occurred (or will occur) is denoted by $P(A|B)$. Here the vertical line is read "given." Note we are asking for the probability of the event $A$ all right, but *conditioned* by the occurrence of event $B$. Thus $P(A|B)$, the conditional probability for event $A$ given $B$ has occurred, may be different from the marginal probability for $A$, denoted more simply by $P(A)$.

In this notation, then, the probability of obtaining a sophomore given that a male was selected is $P(\text{sophomore}|\text{male})$. Is this conditional probability really different from the marginal probability $P(\text{sophomore})$?

Since we are given that the person selected was male, we know that he is one of only 157 possibilities, not of the original 298. There are only 157 males in the class. Of those, we know that 33 are sophomores. Thus

$$P(\text{sophomore}|\text{male}) = \tfrac{33}{157} \simeq 0.2102$$

but
$$P(\text{sophomore}) = \tfrac{69}{298} \simeq 0.2315$$

certainly a different fraction. Further, by referring again to Table 8.2 we see that

$$P(\text{sophomore}|\text{female}) = \tfrac{36}{141} \simeq 0.2553$$

a number different still from the previous two.

So we see that the probability of selecting a sophomore depends upon the given condition. Even the marginal probability $P(\text{sophomore})$ is, in a way, conditioned upon the fact that we are selecting from the entire list of 298 names. But when no condition is implied by the probability statement, it will simply be understood that we are to consider the probability of the event over the entire set of all possible outcomes. Only when the condition *reduces* that set do we specifically mention the *conditional* nature of the probability. So the condition "male" reduced the number of possibilities to 157, while the condition "female" reduced that number to the 141 females in the class.

The previous discussion gives the meaning for conditional probability. When asked for a probability like $P(A|B)$, we know that the condition "event $B$ has occurred" reduces the original overall number of possible outcomes to just those contained in event $B$.

A couple of paragraphs earlier it was mentioned that the probability of selecting a sophomore *depends* upon the given condition. If it had *not* depended upon the condition, say, that we are selecting from the male list, then we would have said that the event "male" and the event "sophomore" were *independent* events. In that case we would have seen

$P(\text{sophomore}|\text{male}) = P(\text{sophomore})$, but since $P(\text{sophomore}|\text{male}) \simeq 0.2102$ while $P(\text{sophomore}) \simeq 0.2315$, the probabilities were *not equal* so the events were *not independent*. This suggests the following general definition.

> *Independent events.* Events $A$ and $B$ are *independent* if $P(A|B) = P(A)$ or if $P(B|A) = P(B)$. Furthermore, if one of these equations holds, then so must the other.

Thus two events are independent when the conditional probability of the first, given the second, is equal to the marginal probability of the first. Later on, after we have considered the multiplication formula, we will return to this important concept of independence.

### Example 8.10
### Prelude to the Multiplication Formula

Now reconsider the event "male *and* sophomore." We already know, from observation of Table 8.2, that the probability for that event is $\frac{33}{298}$. Notice that

$$P(\text{sophomore}|\text{male})P(\text{male}) = (\tfrac{33}{157})(\tfrac{157}{298})$$

$$= \tfrac{33}{298}$$

the numbers 157 in the denominator and numerator of the two fractions in the product having canceled out.

Is it merely happenstance that $P(\text{sophomore}|\text{male})P(\text{male}) = P(\text{male}$ *and* sophomore)? Let's look at a different product, again involving one conditional and one marginal probability. This time we observe, from Table 8.2, that

$$P(\text{male}|\text{sophomore}) = \tfrac{33}{69}$$

while

$$P(\text{sophomore}) = \tfrac{69}{298}$$

then

$$P(\text{male}|\text{sophomore})P(\text{sophomore}) = (\tfrac{33}{69})(\tfrac{69}{298})$$

$$= \tfrac{33}{298}$$

again the same fraction as $P(\text{male}$ *and* sophomore).

This suggests that the *joint* probability of two events is the conditional probability of one of them, given the other, times the marginal probability of the other. That is, we have observed that

$$P(\text{male }and\text{ sophomore}) = P(\text{sophomore}|\text{male})P(\text{male})$$

$$= P(\text{male}|\text{sophomore})P(\text{sophomore})$$

Another illustration of the same idea follows.

$$P(\text{junior } and \text{ female}) = P(\text{junior}|\text{female})P(\text{female})$$
$$= \left(\tfrac{57}{141}\right)\left(\tfrac{141}{298}\right)$$
$$= P(\text{female}|\text{junior})P(\text{junior})$$
$$= \left(\tfrac{57}{125}\right)\left(\tfrac{125}{298}\right)$$
$$= \tfrac{57}{298}$$

two results that may be verified by observing that in Table 8.2 there are 57 female juniors in the class of 298 students. The implication of all this is our third basic probability formula:

*Formula 3: The multiplication formula.*
$$P(A \text{ and } B) = P(A|B)P(B)$$
$$= P(B|A)P(A)$$

Thus the joint probability for the occurrence of two events, $P(A \text{ and } B)$, is the conditional probability of one event, given the other, times the marginal probability of the given event. The multiplication formula shows how the probability for the joint event "$A$ and $B$" may be computed if the right pair of conditional and marginal probabilities is known.

### Example 8.11

Back in Example 8.5 we considered the selection of one person from a group of 200 containing 100 Democrats, 80 Republicans, and 20 Independents. The discussion following Example 8.5 also suggested that if we were to make *more than one* selection, then probability formulas such as the ones we have recently observed would come in handy.

Suppose we select *two* names from the list of 200, without replacing the first name drawn, so that on the second draw we are selecting from a list of only 199 names. What is the probability that two Republicans will be selected?

Let $A$ = the event that a Republican is selected on the first draw

$B$ = the event that a Republican is selected on the second draw

Obviously, the only way to obtain two Republicans in two successive draws is for events $A$ and $B$ both to occur, or for $A$ and $B$ to occur jointly.

Thus we want $P(A \text{ and } B)$. We know, from the multiplication formula, that

$$P(A \text{ and } B) = P(A|B)P(B) = P(B|A)P(A)$$

It seems a little awkward to use $P(A|B)P(B)$ since the event $A|B$ is the event that a Republican is selected on the first draw given that a Republican was selected on the second. But event $B|A$, the event that a Republican is selected on the second draw given that a Republican was selected on the first, seems reasonable. We elect to use the second version of the multiplication formula, which is $P(A \text{ and } B) = P(B|A)P(A)$.

On the first draw, clearly

$$P(A) = P(\text{Republican first}) = \tfrac{80}{200} = \tfrac{2}{5}$$

For $P(B|A)$, however, we must remember that we are given the information that a Republican was selected on the first draw, so we know that only 79 Republicans remain on the list of 199 names available for the second draw. Thus

$$P(B|A) = P(\text{Republican second}|\text{Republican first}) = \tfrac{79}{199}$$

and
$$P(A \text{ and } B) = P(B|A)P(A)$$
$$= \left(\tfrac{79}{199}\right)\left(\tfrac{2}{5}\right)$$
$$= \tfrac{158}{995} \simeq 0.1588$$

This is the probability of selecting two Republicans on two successive draws if the first name is not replaced before the second draw.

### Example 8.12
### Using *Both* the Addition and Multiplication Formulas

Consider making two draws without replacement from the same list of names as in Example 8.11, but this time ask for the probability of selecting one Republican and one Democrat. At first glance this may look like the same kind of calculation as that of Example 8.11, but a second appraisal tells us there is a little more to be done. We could get a Republican on the first draw and a Democrat on the second *or* a Democrat on the first draw and a Republican on the second.

Let $R_1$ = the event of selecting a Republican first

$D_2$ = the event of selecting a Democrat second

$D_1$ = the event of selecting a Democrat first

$R_2$ = the event of selecting a Republican second

Then the probability we want is

$$P(\text{``}R_1 \text{ and } D_2\text{''} \text{ or } \text{``}D_1 \text{ and } R_2\text{''})$$

But this is just $P(A \text{ or } B)$, where $A = R_1 \text{ and } D_2$ and $B = D_1 \text{ and } R_2$. Thus the addition formula applies to $P(A \text{ or } B)$, while the multiplication formula will yield $P(A) = P(R_1 \text{ and } D_2)$ and $P(B) = P(D_1 \text{ and } R_2)$.

However, the way we have defined events $A$ and $B$ makes it clear that these events are mutually exclusive. $A$ and $B$ cannot *both* occur, since on only two draws from the list we cannot get a Republican first and a Democrat second *and* a Democrat first and a Republican second. That is, $P(A \text{ and } B) = 0$ in this case. So for *mutually exclusive* events the addition formula is just

$$P(A \text{ or } B) = P(A) + P(B)$$

Thus

$$
\begin{aligned}
P(\text{one Republican, one Democrat}) &= P(A) + P(B) \\
&= P(R_1 \text{ and } D_2) + P(D_1 \text{ and } R_2) \\
&= P(D_2|R_1)P(R_1) + P(R_2|D_1)P(D_1) \\
&= \left(\tfrac{100}{199}\right)\left(\tfrac{80}{200}\right) + \left(\tfrac{80}{199}\right)\left(\tfrac{100}{200}\right) \\
&= \tfrac{40}{199} + \tfrac{40}{199} = \tfrac{80}{199} \\
&\approx 0.40201
\end{aligned}
$$

### Example 8.13
### Demonstrating Independence

Back in Example 8.9 we observed events that were *not* independent, observations that led to the *definition of independence*: $A$ and $B$ are independent if $P(A|B) = P(A)$ or if $P(B|A) = P(B)$. Now let's consider a pair of events that *are* independent. The schematic in Figure 8.5 depicts two events $A$ and $B$ that are not mutually exclusive. Suppose further that we are given the following probabilities, which are in turn split into their constituent parts in Figure 8.5,

$$P(A) = 0.50$$
$$P(B) = 0.40$$
$$P(A \text{ and } B) = 0.20$$

One version of the multiplication formula is

$$P(A \text{ and } B) = P(A|B)P(B)$$

If we divide both sides by $P(B)$ and write $P(A|B)$ on the left of the equation, we obtain

$$P(A|B) = \frac{P(A \text{ and } B)}{P(B)}$$

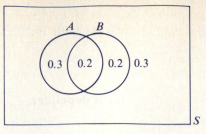

**FIGURE 8.5**   Two independent, non–mutually exclusive events

This version of the multiplication formula, by the way, is often quoted as the *definition of conditional probability.*

For the information depicted in Figure 8.5 we see that

$$P(A|B) = \frac{0.2}{0.4}$$

$$= 0.5$$

But we were given the information that $P(A) = 0.5$.  So

$$P(A|B) = P(A) = 0.5$$

and events $A$ and $B$ are indeed independent.  The probability for event $A$ was not changed by the fact that event $B$ was given to have occurred.
   You might also note that

$$P(B|A) = \frac{P(A \text{ and } B)}{P(A)}$$

$$= \frac{0.2}{0.5}$$

$$= 0.40$$

$$= P(B)$$

That is, we have observed that $P(A|B) = P(A)$ *and* $P(B|A) = P(B)$.  In the definition of independence it was stated that if $A$ and $B$ are independent, *both* of those equations must hold.
   One other result follows from the above analysis.  In the presence of independent events, the multiplication formula becomes simpler.  Since in general $P(A \text{ and } B) = P(A|B)P(B)$, but if $A$ and $B$ are independent, we know that $P(A|B) = P(A)$, then for *independent events* the multiplication formula is

$$P(A \text{ and } B) = P(A)P(B)$$

This is an extremely practical result.  Whenever we know that two events are independent (often the physical characteristics of the experiment being performed tell us that), then we may find the joint probability of the two independent events by just multiplying their individual marginal probabilities.

### Example 8.14
### Computing the Joint Probability for Independent Events

Suppose that we again consider drawing 2 names from the list of 200 people on which 100 are Democrats, 80 are Republicans and 20 are Independents. But this time we *replace* the first name drawn before making the second draw. Now if $R_1$ denotes a Republican on the first draw and $R_2$ denotes a Republican on the second, the manner in which the selection is made, "with-replacement selection," tells us that the events $R_1$ and $R_2$ are independent. Whatever occurs on the first draw can in no way influence the outcome on the second draw. So now the probability of selecting two Republicans (permitting the possibility of drawing the same name twice) is

$$P(R_1 \text{ and } R_2) = P(R_1)P(R_2)$$
$$= \left(\tfrac{80}{200}\right)\left(\tfrac{80}{200}\right)$$
$$= \left(\tfrac{2}{5}\right)\left(\tfrac{2}{5}\right) = \tfrac{4}{25}$$
$$= 0.16$$

This joint probability of 0.16 is different from the probability of approximately 0.1588 that was obtained in Example 8.11, where the drawing was done *without* replacement.

### Example 8.15
### A Wager You Should Definitely Avoid

The gambling game of Chuck-a-Luck is played with three ordinary six-sided dice. The dice are usually tumbled in an hourglass-shaped "squirrel cage" and then let come to rest at the base of the cage. Among the variety of bets that one may place is the wager: At least one 6 will show up among the three dice. For this wager you are offered even-money odds; if at least one 6 shows, you are returned the amount of money you wager plus an equal amount for winning the bet.

Let's investigate the fairness or unfairness of the wager. To do that we need to compute the probability of tossing at least one 6 on three fair dice. One rather lengthy way would be to compute the probabilities for three 6s, for two 6s and one non-6, for one 6 and two non-6s, and then add the probabilities for those three mutually exclusive events.

The concept of independence and the special version of the multiplication formula would be used in computing the separate probabilities mentioned above, but let's do this the easy way. The complementary event to "at least one 6" is the event "no 6." Further, since three dice are certainly three physically different objects, and what shows on one of them should in no way influence what shows on another, the outcomes on each of the three dice are certainly independent. Thus

$$P(\text{at least one 6}) = 1 - P(\text{no 6})$$

$$= 1 - (\tfrac{5}{6})(\tfrac{5}{6})(\tfrac{5}{6})$$

$$= 1 - \tfrac{125}{216}$$

$$= \tfrac{91}{216} \approx 0.4213$$

Here we have noticed that the probability of no 6 on one die is $\tfrac{5}{6}$, and independence tells us that the probability of no 6 on *three* dice is just the product of the individual marginal probabilities, or $(\tfrac{5}{6})(\tfrac{5}{6})(\tfrac{5}{6})$. Then the complementary event formula gives us the probability of at least one 6 by subtraction. Note that the outcome has a probability less than $\tfrac{1}{2}$, or has less than a 50/50 chance of occurring. Since the quoted odds of even money are only fair for a 50/50 chance, the wager is not a fair wager. Just how unfair is it?

Interpreting this probability as a relative frequency we can say that *on the average*, out of every \$216 wagered \$1 at a time, one would win 91 times. Since each time we win we get back the dollar invested plus another, for each \$216 invested we retain \$182 in the long run. That is, we lose on the average \$34 per \$216 invested. The fraction of our capital retained by the gambling house over the long haul is $\tfrac{34}{216} \approx 0.1574$, or the house retains about 16 percent of all money invested in that wager. Definitely not a fair game.

This little gambling example involved a marriage of probabilistic and economic considerations. Many business decision problems have similar characteristics. Business is a legal gambling activity where risk of loss and hope of gain occurs, and where frequently the outcome of the activity is uncertain but measurable, at least in part, by probabilities. In Chapter 9 you will see applications to business decisions of the same notions used in our Chuck-a-Luck analysis.

## 8.3   RANDOM VARIABLES AND PROBABILITY DISTRIBUTIONS

The annual dividend for a particular share of stock, the daily price per ton of cast aluminum ingots, the number of people in a market survey of 200 consumers who say they would try orange-flavored oatmeal, the proportion of the nine races per day at Santa Anita that are won by the betting favorite, the time required to complete the foundation of a new building: What do all of these things have in common? Answer: Each is an example of a random variable.

*Random variable.* A *random variable* is a function that takes on values according to the outcome of a random experiment.

Here "random experiment" is left undefined, being any of a myriad of processes whereby outcomes that cannot be predicted exactly are generated. The experiment could be one toss of two dice, with the random variable being the total showing after the toss; it could be the reading of a thermometer at a specified time of day, with temperature the random variable; it could be the selection of a random sample of 100 accounts from a large group of accounts receivable, with the random variable being the average account balance for accounts in the sample.

Random variables are of two types: discrete and continuous. A *discrete* random variable may assume any of only a finite or countably infinite number of values (a countably infinite set is one that may be placed in one to one correspondence with the set of positive integers). Examples are the total showing after the toss of a pair of dice (a finite set ranging through the integers from 2 to 12), the annual demand for Eldorados at the Cadillac dealership in Laramie, Wyoming (no one is expected to order half an Eldorado), and the number of particles striking the sensor of a particle counter during a 10-minute interval (a countably infinite situation). A *continuous* random variable, on the other hand, is a random variable that may assume any value in some interval or set of intervals. Examples of continuous random variables include the time required to complete a necessary task in a project, the weight of the contents of a box of breakfast cereal, the error made in the measurement of the diameter of a ball bearing, and the distance traveled by a salesperson in a day (although the number of stops made daily is a *discrete* random variable).

Later on in this chapter continuous random variables will be considered more formally. For the time being, however, our attention will center on discrete random variables because related probability concepts for the discrete case are easier to discuss at an elementary level.

Usually when talking about a random variable we will want to distinguish between the random variable itself and one of the values it may take on (a function is not a number, but the *value* of a function is). Convention dictates the use of a capital letter to denote the random variable (function) and a lowercase letter to denote a value that may be assumed by the random variable. Thus we often say that $X$ is a random variable that may assume a value $x$; for example, $x = 1, 2, 3, 4, 5$ could represent a list of possible values for the random variable $X$.

If along with each value that a random variable may assume, we also know the probability that it will assume that value, then we know the entire *probability distribution* for that random variable. The symbol $p(x)$ will be used to denote an individual one of those probabilities. That is,

$$P(X \text{ will assume the value } x) = p(x)$$

If we have a list of all the values $X$ may assume and a list of all the $p(x)$'s, then in a probabilistic sense we know how the values of $X$ are distributed over the entire range of its permissible values. If $p(1) = 0.20$ and $p(2) = 0.50$, we know there are $2\frac{1}{2}$ times as many ways $X$ could become 2 than there are for it to become 1, or 2 is $2\frac{1}{2}$ times more likely than 1 to be the value assumed by X. That is the meaning of the distribution of X in a probabilistic sense.

*Probability distribution.* The *probability distribution* for a *discrete* random variable is a list of values that the random variable may assume and an associated list of probabilities for each of those values.

### Example 8.16
### Characteristics of a Probability Distribution

The following list gives the number of television sets sold per day by a large discount store during each of the 26 shopping days in September: 3, 5, 1, 4, 3, 0, 0, 2, 7, 4, 3, 2, 5, 3, 1, 0, 6, 1, 3, 3, 5, 5, 4, 4, 5, 1. Let

$X$ = the number of sets sold on a day in September

Then the values that the random variable X could assume are 0, 1, 2, 3, 4, 5, 6, 7. Table 8.3 shows the probability distribution for the random variable X, where $p(x)$ is just the proportion of days in September when the sales were $x$, or $p(x)$ is an observed relative frequency that is interpreted as a probability.

Notice that each probability $p(x)$ is a number between zero and unity and that the sum of the $p(x)$'s over all possible values of X is unity. These two conditions must be satisfied by the probabilities involved in any probability distribution; that is,

1:
$$0 \le p(x) \le 1$$

2:
$$\sum_{\text{all } x} p(x) = 1$$

The probability distribution in Table 8.3 gives a better visual impression of the way X varies in value than does the simple list from which we constructed the distribution. But Figure 8.6, a graph of the probability distribution, makes an even more vivid visual impact. This bar graph has the special characteristic that the area of each bar (each of unit width) is equal to the associated probability $p(x)$, so the area of all the bars is the sum of the $p(x)$'s—unity. Now a bar graph for which the areas of the bars are merely *proportional* to the associated relative frequencies is called

**TABLE 8.3** PROBABILITY DISTRIBUTION FOR X

| $x$ | 0 | 1 | 2 | 3 | 4 | 5 | 6 | 7 | Total |
|-----|---|---|---|---|---|---|---|---|-------|
| $p(x)$ | $\frac{3}{26}$ | $\frac{4}{26}$ | $\frac{2}{26}$ | $\frac{6}{26}$ | $\frac{4}{26}$ | $\frac{5}{26}$ | $\frac{1}{26}$ | $\frac{1}{26}$ | $\frac{26}{26} = 1$ |

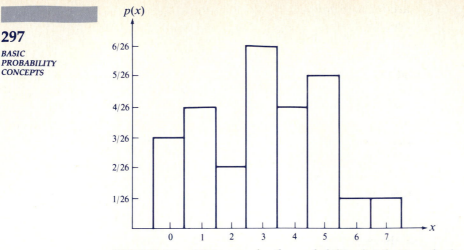

**FIGURE 8.6** Histogram for the probability distribution of sales

a *histogram*. Here we have a special histogram for which the proportionality constant is unity; that is, the areas are *exactly* equal (numerically) to the relative frequencies. When using a histogram to depict a probability distribution, you should use that specialized version.

Associated with any probability distribution is another function, called the *cumulative distribution function*, or more simply, the *distribution function*. Here we will retain the word "cumulative" when discussing the function because there will then be less potential for confusing it with the probability distribution.

The cumulative distribution function simply accumulates the probabilities for values of $x$ up to and including some number, say $r$. It gives the probability that the random variable $X$ will assume a value less than or equal to $r$. Thus

$$F(r) = P(X \text{ will take on a value less than or equal to } r)$$

$$= P(X \le r)$$

$$= \sum_{x \le r} p(x)$$

The probabilities $p(x)$ are summed from the smallest value that $X$ may assume up to and including $r$ to obtain $F(r)$. Table 8.4 shows the values of the cumulative distribution function related to the probability distribution of Table 8.3.

Now recall that $X$ was the number of television sets sold on a day in September. Thus $F(2) = \frac{9}{26}$ is the probability that on a randomly selected September shopping day, two or fewer sets will be sold.

To obtain $F(0)$, from Table 8.3 we note that

$$F(0) = \sum_{x \le 0} p(x) = p(0) = \tfrac{3}{26}$$

Likewise,
$$F(1) = \sum_{x \le 1} p(x) = p(0) + p(1)$$
$$= F(0) + p(1) = \tfrac{3}{26} + \tfrac{4}{26} = \tfrac{7}{26}$$

and
$$F(2) = \sum_{x \le 2} p(x)$$
$$= \sum_{x \le 1} p(x) + p(2)$$
$$= F(1) + p(2) = \tfrac{7}{26} + \tfrac{2}{26} = \tfrac{9}{26}$$

That is, instead of adding up probabilities already summed to obtain a previous value of $F$, we can simply note the relation

$$F(r) = F(r-1) + p(r)$$

Note that when $r = 0$, this becomes $F(0) = F(-1) + p(0)$. But since $X$ cannot assume a value less than zero, $F(-1) = 0$ and $F(0) = p(0)$.

The relation above also allows us to construct a probability distribution if we are given only the cumulative distribution, since

$$p(r) = F(r) - F(r-1)$$

This relationship is extremely useful when we deal with probability tables for standard (commonly encountered) distributions. Such tables often quote cumulative probabilities, not probabilities for individual values of $X$. But determining such a probability $p(x)$ only involves subtracting two adjacent cumulative probabilities in the table.

### Example 8.17

Table 8.5 gives the cumulative distribution for the number of sales representatives in a small firm who attend the weekly Friday afternoon sales meetings. The company only employs five sales reps.

We want to construct from the cumulative distribution the probability distribution for the random variable

$$Y = \text{number of sales reps who attend meetings}$$

**TABLE 8.4**   *CUMULATIVE DISTRIBUTION FOR X*

| $r$ | 0 | 1 | 2 | 3 | 4 | 5 | 6 | 7 |
|------|------|------|------|------|------|------|------|------|
| $F(r)$ | $\tfrac{3}{26}$ | $\tfrac{7}{26}$ | $\tfrac{9}{26}$ | $\tfrac{15}{26}$ | $\tfrac{19}{26}$ | $\tfrac{24}{26}$ | $\tfrac{25}{26}$ | $\tfrac{26}{26}$ |

TABLE 8.5   CUMULATIVE DISTRIBUTION FOR ATTENDANCE

| r | 0 | 1 | 2 | 3 | 4 | 5 |
|---|---|---|---|---|---|---|
| F(r) | 0.10 | 0.25 | 0.50 | 0.80 | 0.95 | 1.00 |

We start by observing that

$$p(0) = F(0) = 0.10$$

Then

$$p(1) = F(1) - F(0)$$
$$= 0.25 - 0.10 = 0.15$$
$$p(2) = F(2) - F(1)$$
$$= 0.50 - 0.25 = 0.25$$

and so on.   Table 8.6 exhibits the desired probability distribution.

Interpreting probabilities in Table 8.6 as relative frequencies we know that all five sales reps attend the meetings only 5 percent of the time, for example, or that exactly three sales reps show up at 30 percent of the meetings.   Further,

$$P(1 \le Y \le 3) = p(1) + p(2) + p(3)$$
$$= 0.15 + 0.25 + 0.30$$
$$= 0.70$$

or from one to three sales reps, inclusive, will be found in attendance at 70 percent of the meetings.

This last probability was obtained by adding up individual probabilities from Table 8.6, the probability distribution.   But it also may be computed from the cumulative distribution of Table 8.5.

$$P(1 \le Y \le 3) = F(3) - F(0)$$
$$= 0.80 - 0.10$$
$$= 0.70$$

TABLE 8.6   PROBABILITY DISTRIBUTION FOR ATTENDANCE

| y | 0 | 1 | 2 | 3 | 4 | 5 | Total |
|---|---|---|---|---|---|---|-------|
| p(y) | 0.10 | 0.15 | 0.25 | 0.30 | 0.15 | 0.05 | 1.00 |

Another use of a probability distribution, apart from its obvious information about individual or accumulated probabilities, is for the determination of measures of central tendency or variability of the associated random variable. Such measures are discussed in the next section.

## 8.4 EXPECTATION: MEAN, VARIANCE, AND STANDARD DEVIATION

### Example 8.18

With reference to Table 8.6 of Example 8.17 we might ask: What is the *average* number of sales reps attending the meetings? It should be obvious that the average is not simply the sum of the numbers 0, 1, 2, 3, 4, 5 divided by 6, since the probability distribution of Table 8.6 says that some of those numbers occur with greater frequency than others. The more frequently occurring numbers should be given more weight than those occurring less frequently. The correct weights for the calculation of the average turn out to be the associated probabilities, a fact that will be made plausible in the argument to follow.

Consider a representative set of 100 such meetings. If that set faithfully represents the probability distribution, then we would expect no sales reps to attend 10 of the meetings, one sales rep at 15 of the meetings, and so on. So to count the total number of sales reps who attended all 100 meetings, we would count 10 zeros, 15 ones, 25 twos, 30 threes, 15 fours, and 5 fives. The average number of sales reps per meeting would be that total divided by 100. Thus

$$\text{Average of } Y = \frac{0(10) + 1(15) + 2(25) + 3(30) + 4(15) + 5(5)}{100}$$

$$= 0(\tfrac{10}{100}) + 1(\tfrac{15}{100}) + 2(\tfrac{25}{100}) + 3(\tfrac{30}{100}) + 4(\tfrac{15}{100}) + 5(\tfrac{5}{100})$$

$$= 0(0.10) + 1(0.15) + 2(0.25) + 3(0.30) + 4(0.15) + 5(0.05)$$

$$= 0 + 0.15 + 0.50 + 0.90 + 0.60 + 0.25$$

$$= 2.40$$

So in the long run, over a representative 100 meetings, the number of sales reps in attendance averages 2.4.

Notice that during one stage of the calculation above we observed

$$\text{Average of } Y = 0(0.10) + 1(0.15) + 2(0.25) + 3(0.30) + 4(0.15) + 5(0.05)$$

or more concisely,

$$\text{Average } Y = \sum_{y=0}^{5} y p(y)$$

Thus the average of the random variable was just a weighted sum of its values, with the weights being the associated probabilities for those values.

In the language of probability and statistics the average of a random variable is called its *expected value*, or its *expectation*, denoted by $E(X)$ if $X$ is the name of the random variable, or its *mean*, denoted by $\mu$.

> *Expectation, mean, expected value.* The *expectation* (mean, expected value) of a random variable $X$ is obtained from its probability distribution by computing
>
> $$\mu = E(X) = \sum_{\text{all } x} xp(x)$$

The mean of a random variable is a *measure of central tendency* of values of the random variable, in the same sense that the average of an ordinary set of numbers is a centrally located number in the midst of that set. However, just as an average is not always a number in the set (the average of 1, 2, and 6 is 3), so the mean, or expected value, of a random variable does not have to be one of the values it may assume. For instance, in Example 8.18 we observed that

$$\text{Average } Y = \mu = E(Y) = 2.40$$

but the only possible values of $Y$ were the numbers 0, 1, 2, 3, 4, 5. Thus an expected value is not a value for the variable that we "expect" to see. Rather, it is a long-run average value.

Another interpretation of a mean is a *moment* interpretation. The mean is called the *first moment of the random variable,* the physical concept known as "center of gravity." To appreciate the mean as a center of gravity, consider the histogram for the probability distribution of Table 8.6, as shown in Figure 8.7.

The mean, here $\mu = 2.40$, is that location on the horizontal axis which would be a balance point for a cardboard cutout of the histogram. That is, the area represented by the histogram would balance on a knife edge located at $\mu$.

Since the histogram in Figure 8.7 represents a probability distribution, we have been careful to draw it so the area of each bar equals the associated probability. In fact, sometimes we choose to call that histogram the *graph of the probability distribution,* and we say that a probability of interest is simply the appropriate *area* from that graph. Particularly when we consider the distribution of a *continuous* random variable, such as a variable that has the *normal distribution* to be discussed in Section 8.6, this association of an area with a probability becomes a very useful notion. The mean, $\mu$, for a continuous random variable may also be interpreted as a center of gravity.

Another concept of great importance in probability and statistics is the second moment about the mean, called the *variance* of the random variable (or the variance of the probability distribution). The variance is a *measure*

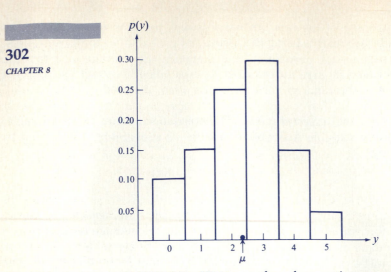

**FIGURE 8.7** Histogram for sales meeting attendance

*of variability* (or of spread, or dispersion) of the values of X about the centrally located mean, μ. Distributions with lots of spread (variability) have large variances; distributions with a heavy concentration of values about the mean (little variability) have small variances.

> *Variance.* The *variance* of a random variable X is the expected (average) squared deviation of values of X from their mean, μ. It is denoted by $\sigma^2$.

$$\sigma^2 = E[(X - \mu)^2] = \sum_{\text{all } x} (x - \mu)^2 p(x)$$

**Example 8.19**

For the probability distribution in Table 8.6 the mean is μ = 2.40. So the variance is

$$\sigma^2 = E[(Y - \mu)^2] = \sum_{y=0}^{5} (y - 2.4)^2 p(y)$$

$$= (0 - 2.4)^2(0.10) + (1 - 2.4)^2(0.15) + (2 - 2.4)^2(0.25)$$
$$+ (3 - 2.4)^2(0.30) + (4 - 2.4)^2(0.15) + (5 - 2.4)^2(0.05)$$

$$= (5.76)(0.10) + (1.96)(0.15) + (0.16)(0.25)$$
$$+ (0.36)(0.30) + (2.56)(0.15) + (6.76)(0.05)$$

$$= 1.74$$

This is the weighted average of the squared differences (deviations) of the values of Y from their mean, 2.4. Since y represents a number of sales representatives, as does the mean, then the difference $y - \mu$ is in units of "sales reps." So the squared difference $(y - \mu)^2$ is the units "squared sales reps," as is the variance, since it is the weighted sum of such units. It is difficult to interpret "squared sales reps" in a meaningful way. For that reason the variance, useful in many theoretical investigations but often difficult to interpret, is usually replaced by its square root, called the *standard deviation*. Since the variance is a measure of spread, so is its square root. But the square root of the variance will be in the *original units* of the data (the square root of "squared sales reps" is "sales reps").

> *Standard deviation.* The *standard deviation* of a random variable X is the square root of its variance and is denoted by σ:
>
> $$\sigma = \sqrt{\sigma^2}$$

For the random variable Y of Example 8.19 then, the standard deviation is

$$\sigma = \sqrt{1.74} \simeq 1.32$$

Thus Y, the number of sales reps attending weekly meetings, has a mean of 2.4 sales reps and a standard deviation of 1.32 sales reps. Both the measure of central tendency, μ, and σ, the measure of spread, have been expressed in the same units as the random variable.

In Example 8.19 the computation of the variance using its definitional formula was tedious. If the values of the random variable are integers while their mean is some decimal number, the variance computation is awkward. For this reason you will find it handy to have available the more convenient, but equivalent, formula given as

$$\sigma^2 = E(X^2) - \mu^2$$
$$= \sum_{\text{all } x} x^2 p(x) - \mu^2$$

That is, the variance may be computed by determining the average value of the squares of x and then subtracting from that number the square of the mean.

**Example 8.20**
**Alternate Computation of the Variance**
For the probability distribution shown in Table 8.6,

$$E(Y^2) = 0^2(0.10) + 1^2(0.15) + 2^2(0.25) + 3^2(0.30) + 4^2(0.15) + 5^2(0.05)$$

$$= 0(0.10) + 1(0.15) + 4(0.25) + 9(0.30) + 16(0.15) + 25(0.05)$$

$$= 7.50$$

From Example 8.18 we know that the mean is $\mu = 2.40$. Then the variance is

$$\sigma^2 = E(Y^2) - \mu^2$$
$$= 7.50 - (2.4)^2$$
$$= 7.50 - 5.76$$
$$= 1.74$$

the same result obtained in Example 8.19 when we used the definitional formula for a variance.

## 8.5   THE BINOMIAL DISTRIBUTION

With the possible exception of the normal distribution to be discussed in the next section of this chapter, the binomial distribution is the most useful of the so-called "standard" distributions, those that occur frequently in practice. Among the standard probability distributions for *discrete* random variables, it wins first place handily.

The binomial distribution pertains to repeated trials for which the outcome on any one trial can be classified in one of only two ways. For convenience we refer to those two categories as "success" and "failure." If the number of trials is fixed, say we will make $n$ trials, then the random variable for which the binomial distribution gives probabilities is

$X =$ the number of successes in $n$ trials

However, a specific set of conditions, or assumptions, must be satisfied before the binomial distribution will apply.

---

**ASSUMPTIONS FOR THE BINOMIAL DISTRIBUTION**

1 The outcome of each trial may be classified in one of two ways: success or failure.

2 The probability of success on a single trial, $p$, remains the same from trial to trial.

3 Successive trials are independent (the outcome on one trial does not influence the outcome on any other trial).

4 The number of trials, $n$, is fixed.

---

We are interested in the probability that $X$ will assume the value $x$. That probability will be denoted by $b(x; n, p)$. Thus

$$P(X = x) = b(x; n, p)$$

is the probability that the number of successes in $n$ trials is $x$ when the probability of success on a single trial is $p$. This is just like the symbol $p(x)$ we have been using, except here the $b$ reminds us we are dealing with the binomial probability distribution, and $n$ and $p$ give us the values of the number of trials and the success probability for a single trial.

By starting from the assumptions given for the binomial distribution and using the concept of independent events developed earlier in this chapter, it is a fairly straightforward matter to determine a general formula for binomial probabilities. To have exactly $x$ successes in $n$ trials, we must also have exactly $n - x$ failures, each occurring with probability $q = 1 - p$, since on any trial we can only have a success or a failure (failure is the complementary event to success). Because of independence, the probability of $x$ successes and $n - x$ failures in any particular order is $p^x q^{n-x}$, and the number of such orders turn out to be $C_x^n$, the number of combinations of $n$ things taken $x$ at a time. Thus a general formula from which binomial probabilities may be computed is

$$b(x; n, p) = C_x^n p^x q^{n-x} \qquad x = 0, 1, 2, \ldots, n$$

Since the binomial distribution is a probability distribution, it has associated with it a cumulative distribution. Values of this cumulative function are denoted by $B(r; n, p)$, where

$$B(r; n, p) = P(X \le r) = \sum_{x=0}^{r} b(x; n, p)$$

Values of this cumulative probability function are tabulated in Table A.1 of the Appendix. Since Table A.1 gives the cumulative probabilities for a binomial random variable (for selected values of $n$ and $p$), and since we can always get individual probabilities $b(x; n, p)$ by subtracting adjacent cumulative probabilities for values of $n$ and $p$ in Table A.1, it is never necessary to actually evaluate $b(x; n, p)$ using the formula $C_x^n p^x q^{n-x}$. Further, often we will only be interested in the cumulative probability itself, which is found in Table A.1.

### Example 8.21
### Using Table A.1 to Find Binomial Probabilities

Suppose that in a batch of 100 light bulbs 20 are defective. We randomly select, *with* replacement, 5 bulbs from that batch. Let's answer some probability questions about $X$, the number of defective bulbs observed among the 5 selected (some of which could be the same bulbs, since we are selecting with replacement).

Selection with replacement assures two things: the probability of drawing a defective bulb remains the same on each draw, and successive draws are independent. The number of draws (trials) is fixed at 5, and on each draw we will either get a defective bulb (a success) or a nondefective bulb. The assumptions for the binomial distribution are satisfied.

Here the number of trials is $n = 5$, and $p = 0.2$ since the proportion of defectives in the batch is $\frac{20}{100} = 0.2$, or this would be the probability of selecting a defective bulb on any one draw. Suppose we ask for the probability that the number of defective bulbs observed in the set of 5 selected is less than or equal to 2. That is, we want

$$P(X \leq 2) = B(2; 5, 0.2)$$

This is $B(r; n, p)$ in Table A.1, where $r = 2$, $n = 5$, and $p = 0.2$. On the first page of Table A.1 we find the probabilities associated with $n = 5$. We read under $p = 0.2$ and opposite $r = 2$ to obtain

$$B(2; 5, 0.2) = 0.94208$$

This is the probability of observing 2 or fewer defective bulbs in the set of 5 that are selected.

What is the probability that *exactly* 2 defective bulbs would be observed in the set of 5 selected? This is just $b(2; 5, 0.2)$, or the probability that $X = 2$ in a binomial distribution with $n = 5$ and $p = 0.2$. We obtain this probability by subtracting adjacent cumulative probabilities found in Table A.1:

$$P(X = 2) = b(2; 5, 0.2)$$
$$= B(2; 5, 0.2) - B(1; 5, 0.2)$$
$$= 0.94208 - 0.73728$$
$$= 0.20480$$

What is the probability that *more than 1* defective bulb is observed in the set of 5 selected? Here we use the idea of *complementary events*. The event "more than 1" is the complementary event to the event "less than or equal to 1." Then the desired probability is

$$P(X > 1) = 1 - P(X \leq 1)$$
$$= 1 - B(1; 5, 0.2)$$
$$= 1 - 0.73728$$
$$= 0.26272$$

**Example 8.22**
**Practical Application of the Binomial Distribution**

Earlier the claim was made that the binomial distribution is one of the most useful of standard probability distributions. The following problem is presented to illustrate one of its practical applications. Other such problems will be encountered in Chapter 10.

Kiddiecorp, a large manufacturer of backyard play equipment for children, must purchase a supply of machine bolts for inclusion in assembly kits for "jungle gyms." A particular supplier of these bolts claims that no more than 5 percent of his bolts are oversized. To test that claim Kiddiecorp is permitted to select a random sample of 20 bolts from a large bin at the supplier's warehouse. Four oversized bolts are observed in the sample. Would Kiddiecorp tend to agree or disagree with the supplier's claim that 5 percent or fewer are oversized?

We observe that 4 oversized bolts out of 20 means that 20 percent of the bolts in the sample are oversized. But is that really unusual? After all, there were lots of bolts in that bin and we only selected 20 of them. Perhaps the supplier's claim of 5 percent defective is true and we just happened to get an unusual sample.

What would be the probability of such an unusual sample, or an even worse one, with more oversized bolts, if in fact exactly 5 percent of the bolts in the bin had been oversized? We reason as follows: The binomial assumptions are not strictly satisfied since we did not sample with replacement, but there were so many thousands of bolts in that bin that our small sample of 20 would not significantly change the mix of good and bad bolts; the probability of obtaining an oversized bolt on one draw remains nearly 0.05 on each draw, and independence of draws seems a reasonable assumption. So the binomial distribution should supply a very good approximation of the desired probability.

Let $X$ be the number of oversized bolts in a sample of size $n = 20$ when $p = 0.05$ is the probability of selecting an oversized bolt on one draw. Then

$$P(X \geq 4) = 1 - P(X \leq 3)$$
$$= 1 - B(3; 20, 0.05)$$
$$= 1 - 0.9841$$
$$= 0.0159$$

So if the proportion oversized in the bin really had been $p = 0.05$, the probability Kiddiecorp would have seen 4 or more of them in a sample of size 20 is only 0.0159. And clearly if $p$ had been less than 0.05, such a sample would have been even rarer.

Kiddiecorp has two choices. They can believe the supplier, assuming they have obtained a very unusual sample, or they can assume the claim is false (that more than 5 percent of this supplier's bolts are oversized). If they decide to reject his claim, then 0.0159 is the probability they have made an incorrect decision (incorrect because $p$ is really 0.05).

Of course if Kiddiecorp has a lot of money riding on the decision to purchase or not purchase bolts from that supplier (requiring 5 percent or fewer oversized), they would probably base the decision on a larger sample than the 20 used here. The sample size used in this example was merely convenient, permitting the use of the limited binomial tables available in this text. However, for a sample of size 20 our probability calculation was correct. The probability of 0.0159, a measure of the rarity of the observed event or one even more contrary to the claim, would at least cause Kiddiecorp to request more information; that is, to ask for a larger sample before making the purchasing decision.

## 8.6   THE NORMAL DISTRIBUTION

Historically the normal distribution arose from attempts to describe mathematically the behavior of errors of measurement. Give a ruler to 50 different people and ask them to tell you the length of a short piece of wooden dowel. You will probably hear 50 different lengths, some too short, some too long, but with the over- or undermeasurement (the error) tending to average out to zero. Most of the measurements will be very close to the true length of the dowel, or most of the errors will cluster closely around zero, with the number of large errors (positive or negative) tailing off rapidly as the magnitude of the error increases. That is, the probability of observing an error near zero is high, but the probabilities associated with larger errors get lower and lower as the magnitude of the errors becomes higher. A curve which suggests that situation appears as Figure 8.8

Suppose that Figure 8.8 represents the *population* (conceptually, the result of all possible measurements) of errors in the measurement of a dowel known to be exactly 6 inches long. The $x$ axis in the figure represents the magnitude of the error, with the scale in tenths of an inch. However, since error is a *continuous* random variable, it is impossible to associate a nonzero probability with every potential value of error because the error in any measurement could be any number in an interval about zero and there are an infinity of numbers in an interval. Thus while the curve in Figure 8.8 resembles a smoothed-out version of a histogram, in

*FIGURE 8.8*   Distribution of measurement error for a 6-inch dowel

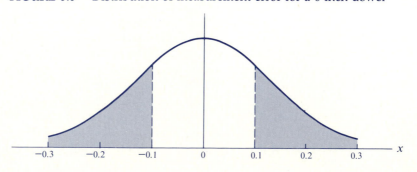

this case, the height to the curve cannot be made proportional to the probability for a particular error. Rather, the curve is intended to suggest a *probability density function*, with the *area* under the curve above a particular interval of interest being the probability that a random measurement error would fall in that interval.

To appreciate the concept, imagine the vertical scale in Figure 8.8 being adjusted so the entire area under the curve is unity. That area is then interpreted as the probability that the error will be any value on the real number scale: a certainty, with probability 1. Then the shaded area in the figure could represent the fraction of that unit area associated with the error exceeding the number 0.1 in magnitude, or the probability that the error will exceed a tenth of an inch.

The *normal distribution* is a generalization of this idea, where although the center of this symmetric distribution does not have to occur at zero, the "bell-shaped" curve of Figure 8.8 is preserved. The functional form of a general normal distribution is

$$f(x; \mu, \sigma) = \frac{1}{\sigma\sqrt{2\pi}} \exp\left[\frac{-1}{2\sigma^2}(x - \mu)^2\right]$$

with $-\infty < x < \infty$. The notation on the left means that this is a function of a variable $x$ with parameters (constants unique to a particular case of interest) $\mu$ and $\sigma$. That is, if the numbers $\mu$ and $\sigma$ are specified, the function may then be evaluated at any number $x$. The parameters $\mu$ and $\sigma$ are, as you might suspect, the mean and standard deviation of the normal distribution.

The graph of $f(x; \mu, \sigma)$, the general normal distribution, is suggested by Figure 8.9. It is symmetric about the mean $\mu$, and the distance from $\mu$ to the inflection points of the curve (where the curve stops "opening downward" and begins to "open upward," or where its concavity changes) is $\sigma$. The height of the curve at $x = \mu$ is $1/\sigma\sqrt{2\pi}$, establishing a vertical scale that makes the total area under the graph unity (even though $x$ ranges over the whole real number line, from $-\infty$ to $+\infty$).

**FIGURE 8.9**   The normal distribution

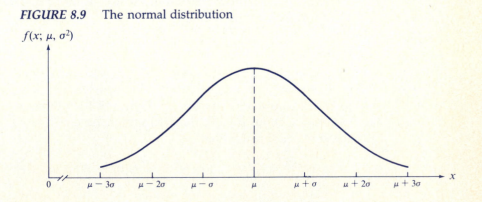

Now by the definition of probability for any continuous random variable, the probablity that the normal variable $X$ will assume a value in the interval from the number $a$ to the number $b$ is the area under the curve and above the interval from $a$ to $b$. Likewise, the probability that $X$ takes on a value less than $b$ is just the area under the curve and above the infinite interval from $-\infty$ to $b$. The determination of such areas is a difficult task mathematically. However, it is easy in practice because of the existence of a table of normal probabilities. To find a probability about any normal random variable, we first discover the relationship between the desired area and the corresponding area under a *standard normal curve*, and then use Table A.2.

> *Theorem 8.1.* If the random variable $X$ has the normal distribution with mean $\mu$ and variance $\sigma^2$, then the random variable $Z$, where
>
> $$Z = \frac{X - \mu}{\sigma}$$
>
> has the normal distribution with mean 0 and variance 1. That distribution of $Z$ is called the *standard normal distribution*.

### Example 8.23

Table A.2 in the Appendix gives areas (probabilities) under the standard normal curve to the left of a number of interest on the $z$ scale. The area to the left of a number $r$ will be denoted by $N(r)$. That is,

$$P(Z \le r) = N(r)$$

Figure 8.10 shows the appearance of the graph of the standard normal distribution as well as indicating, by shading, the area under the curve to the left of $z = 1.5$. That area, from Table A.2, is

$$N(1.5) = 0.93319$$

so a little more than 93 percent of the area under a standard normal curve lies to the left of the number 1.5.

### Example 8.24

We can utilize the symmetry of the normal curve and the fact that the total area under the curve is unity to obtain three more probabilities using just the information given on Figure 8.10. First, since the curve is symmetric about $\mu = 0$, the area under the curve to the left (and also to the right) of 0 is 0.5; that is,

$$P(Z \le 0) = N(0) = 0.50000$$

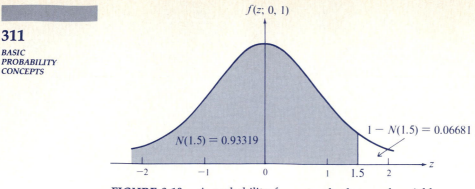

**FIGURE 8.10**    A probability for a standard normal variable

Second, since $N(1.5) = 0.93319$ and $N(0) = 0.50000$, then

$$P(0 \leq Z \leq 1.5) = N(1.5) - N(0)$$
$$= 0.93319 - 0.50000$$
$$= 0.43319$$

This is the probability that the standard normal variable $Z$ will assume a value in the interval from 0 to 1.5.   Finally, the area to the right of 1.5 may be obtained by subtracting $N(1.5)$ from unity, the total area under the curve, or

$$P(Z \geq 1.5) = 1 - N(1.5)$$
$$= 1 - 0.93319$$
$$= 0.06681$$

**Example 8.25**

The point of Theorem 8.1 was that *any* normal probability could be obtained by first *standardizing* the normal variable (turning it into $Z$) and then referring to a table of standard normal probabilities.   The following problem demonstrates how easy that is to do.

Scores on a certain IQ test are approximately normally distributed with mean $\mu = 100$ and standard deviation $\sigma = 10$ (variance 100).   Now the way tests are graded precludes the score $X$ being strictly a continuous variable, but experience with giving the test to thousands of people has suggested that areas under that smooth normal curve give close approximations to probabilities about $X$.

Presuming the normality assumption to be nearly correct, what is the probability that a randomly selected person would score 120 or more on the test?  By Theorem 8.1, $Z = (X - \mu)/\sigma = (X - 100)/10$, so

$$P(X \geq 120) = P\left(\frac{X - 100}{10} \geq \frac{120 - 100}{10}\right)$$

$$= P(Z \geq 2)$$

$$= 1 - N(2)$$

From Table A.2, $N(2) = 0.97725$, so

$$P(X \geq 120) = 1 - 0.97725$$

$$= 0.02275$$

Thus only a little over 2 percent of the people who take that test score 120 or more on it. Such a score would be regarded as exceptional. Figure 8.11 illustrates graphically the algebraic process suggested by Theorem 8.1.

Here the key idea was the standardization of $X$, subtracting its mean and dividing by its standard deviation so that

$$Z = \frac{X - 100}{10}$$

was a standard normal variable and Table A.2 could be used. To keep the events the same, so that their probabilities would be equal, that is, so that

$$P(X \geq 120) = P(Z \geq 2)$$

we also subtracted 100 from 120 and then divided by 10, the standard deviation.

What fraction of the scores lie between 105 and 117? This is

$$P(105 < X < 117) = P\left(\frac{105 - 100}{10} < \frac{X - 100}{10} < \frac{117 - 100}{10}\right)$$

$$= P(0.50 < Z < 1.70)$$

$$= N(1.70) - N(0.50)$$

From Table A.2 we learn that $N(1.70) = 0.95543$ and $N(0.50) = 0.69150$, so

$$P(105 < X < 117) = 0.95543 - 0.69150$$

$$= 0.26393$$

around 26 percent. Figure 8.12 shows the appropriate areas used in this calculation.

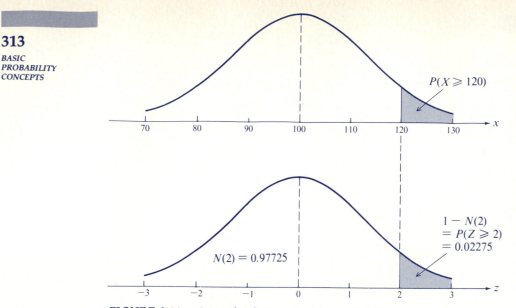

**FIGURE 8.11** Areas for first part of Example 8.25

Note that no difference between probabilities ensues if we ask for a probability that $X$ is less than some number or, equivalently, for the probability that $X$ is less than or equal to that number. The "equal" part of a probability statement for a continuous random variable does not add any additional probability. This is because of the area definition of probability for a continuous random variable. Since the area of a line segment is zero,

$$P(X = a) = 0$$

where $a$ is any number. This does not mean, of course, that it is impossible for $X$ to assume the value $a$. In practice this apparent paradox causes no difficulty, since it will be impossible to measure the value of a continuous random variable (like time, or length) accurately enough to know that $x$ is precisely the number $a$. Measurements themselves are always some small interval on the measurement scale, and anything in that interval is called the single measurement $a$. But the probability that $X$ will assume a value in some *interval*, however small, is *not* zero. This is how in practice $X$ can assume the value $a$ even though the probability for that event is zero.

The normal distribution plays an extremely important role in the theory of statistics. This importance stems primarily from various versions of an exciting mathematical result known as the *central limit theorem*, the most common version of which is stated here. Statisticians are often accused of assuming that every random variable in nature has the normal distribution just so they can fit all problems into their elegant normal-theoretic

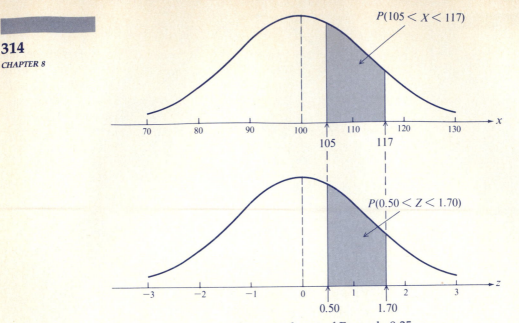

**FIGURE 8.12**   Areas for second part of Example 8.25

framework.  Those derisive detractors are usually simply dealing from a position of ignorance; they are not aware of the fact that even if *nothing* in nature has the normal distribution (and probably, nothing does), normal theory can still give excellent answers to many real probabilistic questions. The reason for that is the central limit theorem.

*Theorem 8.2: The central limit theorem.*   If $X$ is a random variable representing a quantity that may be observed in some population, and if the mean $\mu$ and variance $\sigma^2$ for $X$ exist, then if samples of size $n$ are taken from that population and for each sample the sample average $\overline{X}$ is computed, the distribution of

$$Z = \frac{\overline{X} - \mu}{\sigma/\sqrt{n}}$$

approaches the standard normal distribution as the sample size $n$ gets larger and larger.

This is a "large-sample" theorem; that is, to prove it mathematically it is necessary to let $n$ grow large without bound in a limit argument.  Since one never takes samples of size infinity in practice, why is the central limit theorem such a useful result?

The answer is easy to state.  Experience has shown that the standardized value of $\overline{X}$ (note the divisor $\sigma/\sqrt{n}$, not $\sigma$, in the theorem) has approximately the standard normal distribution for surprisingly small values of the sample size $n$.  As a rule of thumb, if $n \geq 20$, one usually obtains good approximate probabilities about $\overline{X}$ using the normality assumption, and very good approximations when $n$ is 30 or more.

It is extremely important to notice that the central limit theorem *does not* specify that the population from which we sample be *normal*. It only requires the existence of a mean and variance in the population (for only a few mathematically perverse distributions will either the mean or the variance not exist; rarely in the real world). Thus regardless of the type of real population from which we sample, the standardized sample average is still approximately standard normal for reasonable sample sizes.

### Example 8.26

Here we look at the use of the central limit theorem in a quality-control situation. Other examples will be seen in Chapter 10, where we take a closer look at useful statistical (pertaining to sampling) concepts.

In a cannery belonging to Yummy Food Company an automated process is used for filling cans with grape juice. The cans are advertised as containing 28 ounces of grape juice. The automated process is declared "in control" when the contents of the cans have an average of 28 ounces and a standard deviation of 0.1 ounces.

At regular intervals a random sample of 25 cans of grape juice is selected from the output of this process, and each can is weighed. Suppose that on one of those occasions the average weight of the contents of the 25 sampled cans is 27.95 ounces. Will the process be declared in control, or should the production line be shut down for possible adjustment of the equipment?

If the process is in control, then $\mu = 28$ and $\sigma = 0.1$. The sample size $n = 25$ is deemed large enough for the central limit theorem to apply approximately. Then the probability of observing a sample average at least as far below 28 as 27.95, if the process is in control, is

$$P(\overline{X} \le 27.95) = P\left(\frac{\overline{X} - 28}{\frac{0.1}{5}} \le \frac{27.95 - 28}{\frac{0.1}{5}}\right)$$

$$= P\left(Z \le \frac{-0.05}{0.02}\right)$$

$$= P(Z \le -2.50)$$

This is the area under a standard normal curve to the *left* of $-2.50$, which by the *symmetry* of the curve is the same as the area to the *right* of 2.50. Figure 8.13 shows the relationship. Thus

$$P(\overline{X} \le 27.95) = 1 - P(Z \le 2.50)$$

$$= 1 - N(2.50)$$

$$= 1 - 0.99379 \qquad \text{Table A.2}$$

$$= 0.00621$$

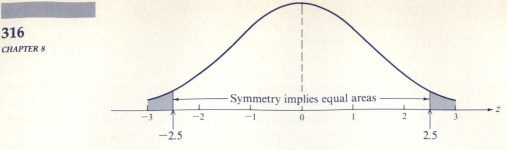

Symmetry implies equal areas

−2.5

2.5

**FIGURE 8.13**    Areas for Example 8.26

If the process had been in control, then in only about 6 of 1000 such samples would we have observed a sample average of 27.95 ounces or less.  The observed average is very rare, so Yummy would probably deem the process "out of control" and shut it down for adjustment.

A final reminder is in order about the standardization procedure for a random variable.  For standardization in a setting where Theorem 8.1 is to be used (the standardization of $X$, a general normal random variable), the divisor is the population standard deviation $\sigma$.  But if a *sample average* $\overline{X}$ is to be standardized for application of the central limit theorem, Theorem 8.2, the divisor must be $\sigma/\sqrt{n}$.  This is because the variance of a sample average is $\sigma^2/n$; that is, the variance of a sample average decreases as the sample size increases, and we know that the actual variance of $\overline{X}$ is the population variance divided by the sample size used to obtain $\overline{X}$.

## 8.7   SUMMARY AND CONCLUSIONS

Contained in this chapter are the elementary probability concepts most essential to understanding the business decision applications to appear throughout the remainder of this text.  The ideas and definitions found here are the same notions that one would encounter in the probability chapter of any good basic business statistics text.  However, although you will see some standard business statistics problems in Chapters 10 and 11, the purpose of introducing probability at this point is to enhance your appreciation of the decision criteria that will be exhibited immediately following, in Chapter 9.  Most of the applications in Chapter 9 require, along with some elementary economic concepts, only a direct appeal to probabilistic notions such as random variables, probability distributions, and expectation.

Probability interpretations and probability formulas such as the complementary event formula, the addition formula, and the multiplication formula, along with probability distributions and expectation, are necessary tools for many applied probabilistic business decision problems.  Further, the binomial and normal distributions and the central limit theorem that was introduced at the end of the chapter apply to a surprising variety of real problems in the areas of business, industry, and economics. In fact, every subsequent chapter of this text will contain some application of a probabilistic nature.

This chapter and the following two, Chapters 9 and 10, present most of the probabilistic and statistical concepts required for successful appreciation of applications to be presented in the remainder of this text. If you have already taken a substantial beginning business statistics course, you should find most of the material in these three chapters familiar. In that case, you should regard them as a fairly complete review of the most important portions of that course. If you have never studied any basic probability and statistics, then be advised that diligent study of this chapter and of Chapters 9 and 10 to follow will be extremely worthwhile during your study of the remainder of this text.

## KEY WORDS AND PHRASES

**Relative frequency**   The long-run proportion of outcomes representing the occurrence of an event of interest. The usual interpretation given to a probability.

**Subjective probability**   A probability representing an opinion about the occurrence of an event, usually based upon hypothetical betting odds. This probability may or may not permit a long-run relative-frequency interpretation.

**A priori probability**   A probability that may be obtained by pure reason, usually based upon known physical characteristics of the experiment that generates outcomes associated with the event of interest.

**Complementary event**   All of the outcomes that do not represent the occurrence of event $A$ are said to comprise the *complement* of $A$, and that set is called the event $A'$ ($A$ complement).

**Complementary event formula**   $P(A') = 1 - P(A)$.

**Addition formula**   $P(A \text{ or } B) = P(A) + P(B) - P(A \text{ and } B)$.

**Conditional probability**   The probability that an event will occur given that another event has occurred (or will occur), that given occurrence serving to reduce the total number of outcomes that must be considered. The usual notation is suggested by the symbols $P(A|B)$.

**Multiplication formula**   $P(A \text{ and } B) = P(A|B)P(B)$
$$= P(B|A)P(A).$$

**Independence**   Events $A$ and $B$ are independent if the occurrence or nonoccurrence of event $A$ in no way influences the probability that event $B$ will occur. If $A$ and $B$ are independent, $P(A|B) = P(A)$ and $P(B|A) = P(B)$.

**Random variable**   A function (variable) that takes on values according to the outcome of some random experiment. The actual value it assumes is not known until after the experiment has been performed.

**Probability distribution**   A list of values and associated probabilities for a discrete random variable.

**Cumulative distribution function**   A function whose value at the number $r$ gives the probability that the random variable will take on a value less than or equal to $r$.

**Mean (expectation, average)**   The weighted average of values of a random variable, with the weights being the associated probabilities.   A measure of central tendency of the random variable.

**Variance**   The average squared deviation of values of a random variable from its mean; a weighted average, with weights being associated probabilities.   It measures the spread, or dispersion, of values of the random variable about its mean.

**Standard deviation**   The square root of the variance.   A measure of dispersion expressed in the same units as the random variable.

**Binomial distribution**   The distribution of the number of successes in $n$ independent trials when the probability of success on any one trial remains the same from trial to trial.

**Normal distribution**   A bell-shaped distribution of a continuous random variable, symmetric about its mean $\mu$ and having inflection points at $\mu - \sigma$ and $\mu + \sigma$, where $\sigma$ is its standard deviation.

**Standard normal distribution**   A normal distribution with mean zero and variance unity.   If $X$ has a normal distribution with mean $\mu$ and variance $\sigma^2$, then $Z = (X - \mu)/\sigma$ has the standard normal distribution.   Tables of standard normal probabilities are used to evaluate a probability about any normal random variable.

**Central limit theorem**   The theorem which suggests that as the sample size gets larger and larger, the distribution of the sample average $\overline{X}$ approaches the normal distribution, regardless of the type of population from which the sample was taken.

## EXERCISES

♦ **8.1** Prestigious Press, subsidized by the Edsel Foundation, publishes books that sell very few copies upon initial release but that it anticipates will be studied as great literature in English classes 50 years from now.   So far this year they have released 10 such books, 5 of which sold 3,000 copies, 3 of which sold 2,000 copies, and 2 of which sold 1,000 copies.

Prestigious is about to release another such book, with reception by the public expected to be similar to that received by the other 10 books.

  **a** What is the probability that 2,000 copies of the book will be sold?

  **b** What is the probability that at least 2,000 copies of the book will be sold?

♦ **8.2** A new editor, recently hired by Prestigious Press (Exercise 8.1), believes strongly in the sales potential of the book due for release.   She remarks, "I'll bet $10 against $1 that this book will sell 3,000 copies or more."   What is her assessment of the probability that sales of the book will equal or exceed 3,000 copies?

**8.3** With reference to Figure 8.1, determine the probability that, if two fair dice are tossed, the following will occur:

a The total showing will be 6.
b The total showing will be 5 or less.
c The total showing will be 10 or more.

✦ **8.4** Management of a large fast-food chain is considering opening a new outlet in Laramie, Wyoming. Their subjective assessments of probabilities are $\frac{2}{5}$ that the outlet will gross over \$1,500 per day; $\frac{7}{15}$ that daily gross will be between \$500 and \$1,500, inclusive; and $\frac{7}{20}$ that daily gross will be less than \$500. Given your understanding of the conditions that must be satisfied by probabilities, are these subjective estimates consistent with each other? Why or why not?

**8.5** A national newsmagazine states: The probability that Senator Edward Kennedy will be the Democratic nominee for president in 1988 is $\frac{1}{5}$. How will you interpret that statement?

**8.6** Marketing analysts in the firm of which you are the chief executive officer report: The probability that public acceptance of our proposed new product will make its manufacture profitable is 0.55. Give two different interpretations of that report.

✦ **8.7** If $P(A) = 0.4$, $P(B) = 0.3$, and $P(A \text{ and } B) = 0.1$, find:
  a $P(A')$        d $P[(A \text{ and } B)']$
  b $P(B')$        e $P[(A \text{ or } B)']$
  c $P(A \text{ or } B)$

✦ **8.8** If $P(A) = 0.40$, $P(B) = 0.20$, and $P(A \text{ or } B) = 0.52$, find $P(A \text{ and } B)$.

**8.9** If $P(A) = 0.3$, $P(B) = 0.2$, and $A$ and $B$ are independent, find:
  a $P(A \text{ and } B)$
  b $P(A \text{ or } B)$

**8.10** If $P(A) = 0.60$, $P(B) = 0.20$, and $P(A \text{ and } B) = 0.15$, find:
  a $P(A \text{ or } B)$
  b $P(A|B)$
  c $P(B|A)$

✦ **8.11** Are the events $A$ and $B$ in Exercise 8.10 independent? How do you know?

✦ **8.12** A hunter with a license for either deer or antelope knows from past experience his probability of killing a deer during the season is 0.10, of killing an antelope is 0.40, and that those two events are independent.
  a What is the probability he will kill both a deer and an antelope?
  b What is the probability he will kill neither a deer nor an antelope?
  c What is the probability he will kill either a deer or an antelope, but not both?

**8.13** The two major employers in Laramie, Wyoming, are the University of Wyoming and the Union Pacific Railroad. The local Chrysler-Plymouth dealer has kept records on her most recent 200 customers, cross-classifying them according to place of employment and sex of the person to whom she sold a car. The following table exhibits her data:

|          |      | Sex    |       |
| Employer | Male | Female | Total |
|----------|------|--------|-------|
| University | 50 | 30 | 80 |
| Railroad | 25 | 35 | 60 |
| Other | 40 | 20 | 60 |
| Total | 115 | 85 | 200 |

The car dealer regards that table as quite representative of the characteristics of her customers. Consider a particular customer who walks into the dealership.

a What is the probability the customer is male?

b What is the probability the customer is employed by neither the University nor the Railroad?

c If the customer is male, what is the probability he is employed by the University?

d If the customer is employed by the Railroad, what is the probability the customer is female?

e Are the events "female" and "employed by University" independent events? Why or why not?

◆ **8.14** Refer to the game of Chuck-a-Luck described in Example 8.15 in the body of this chapter. What is the probability that after the three dice are tossed, neither a 5 nor a 6 shows on any one of them?

◆ **8.15** A random variable $X$ has the following probability distribution:

| $x$ | 0 | 1 | 2 | 3 | 4 | 5 | 6 |
|-----|---|---|---|---|---|---|---|
| $p(x)$ | 0.10 | 0.15 | 0.25 | 0.30 | 0.10 | 0.07 | 0.03 |

a Find $P(1 \le X \le 5)$.

b Find $P(X < 4)$.

c Find $P(2 \le X)$.

d What is the cumulative distribution for $X$?

e Find $\mu$.

f Find $\sigma^2$.

**8.16** A random variable $X$ has the following probability distribution:

| $x$ | $-1$ | 0 | 2 | 5 | 7 |
|-----|------|---|---|---|---|
| $p(x)$ | 0.15 | 0.25 | 0.20 | 0.20 | 0.20 |

a What is the cumulative distribution for $X$?

b Using the cumulative distribution, find $P(-1 < X \le 5)$.

c Using the cumulative distribution, find $P(5 \le X)$.

**d** Find the mean of $X$.

**e** Find the variance and standard deviation of $X$.

◆ **8.17** The cumulative distribution for a random variable $Y$ is as follows:

| $r$ | 2 | 3 | 5 | 8 | 9 | 10 |
|-----|------|------|------|------|------|------|
| $F(r)$ | 0.05 | 0.30 | 0.45 | 0.65 | 0.90 | 1.00 |

**a** Find $P(Y \leq 8)$.

**b** Find $P(Y \leq 6)$.

**c** Find $P(2 < Y < 9)$.

**d** What is the probability distribution for $Y$?

**e** Find the mean of $Y$.

**f** Find the standard deviation of $Y$.

**8.18** During the past 15 years demand for Jester Romances in the month of December in a local book store has been as follows: 300 in 5 of those years, 250 in 4 years, 200 in 3 years, 100 in 2 years, and only 50 in 1 year. The store will take this information as being representative of December demand for Jester Romances. Let $X$ represent December demand.

**a** What is the probability distribution for $X$?

**b** What is the cumulative distribution for $X$?

**c** What is $P(X \leq 200)$?

**d** If the store will order Jester Romances for December in an amount equal to expected demand, what quantity will be ordered?

◆ **8.19** Macduff's Hamburgers operates franchises in 20 cities with a population between 30,000 and 40,000. Last year the distribution of $X$, the annual profit from such a franchise, was as follows:

| $x$ | \$10,000 | \$15,000 | \$20,000 | \$25,000 | \$30,000 |
|-----|----------|----------|----------|----------|----------|
| $p(x)$ | $\frac{3}{20}$ | $\frac{5}{20}$ | $\frac{7}{20}$ | $\frac{3}{20}$ | $\frac{2}{20}$ |

**a** If Macduff's is considering opening a new franchise in a city with a population of 35,000, what might they assume to be its expected profit?

**b** How should Macduff's interpret the expected profit figure in part $a$?

**8.20** The random variable $X$ has the binomial distribution with $n = 5$, $p = 0.40$. Find:

**a** $P(X = 2)$

**b** $b(3; 5, 0.4)$

**c** $B(2; 5, 0.4)$

**d** The expected value of $X$, using the definition of expectation

**e** The variance of $X$, using the definition of variance

◆ **8.21** The random variable $X$ has the binomial distribution with $n = 25$, $p = 0.30$. Find:

**a** $B(12; 25, 0.3)$     **d** $P(X \geq 10)$
    **b** $P(5 \leq X \leq 10)$    **e** $P(X > 10)$
    **c** $P(6 < X < 11)$

✦ **8.22** The random variable $X$ has the binomial distribution with $n = 50$, $p = 0.60$. Find:
    **a** $P(X \geq 33)$
    **b** $P(X < 26)$
    **c** $P(28 < X \leq 35)$
    *Hint:* If the probability of success on a single trial is $p$, the probability of failure is $1 - p$. To use Table A.1, you will want to phrase these probability statements in terms of $y$, the number of failures.

**8.23** It can be shown in general that the mean of a binomial random variable is $\mu = np$, while its variance is $\sigma^2 = np(1 - p)$.
    **a** Find the mean, variance, and standard deviation of the random variable in Exercise 8.21.
    **b** Find the mean, variance, and standard deviation of the random variable in Exercise 8.22.

✦ **8.24** On a 25-question, 4-answer multiple-choice examination taken by someone who knows absolutely nothing about the subject and must guess, independently, at each answer,
    **a** What is the expected number of correct answers? (See Exercise 8.23.)
    **b** What is the probability of answering 40 percent or more of the questions correctly?

**8.25** Semisolid, Inc., manufactures transistors for use in electronic equipment. Semisolid claims that no more than 10 percent of its Type S-7 transistors have defective leads.
    Blare, Inc., a producer of inexpensive portable radios, is considering the purchase of a large quantity of Type S-7 transistors from Semisolid. Blare has taken a sample of size $n = 100$ Type S-7 transistors from a large batch that Semisolid made available for sampling. Eighteen transistors with defective leads were observed in that sample.
    **a** Assuming that the conditions for the binomial distribution are essentially satisfied, approximate the probability of observing 18 or more transistors with defective leads in a sample of 100 if in fact 10 percent of the lot made available consisted of transistors with defective leads.
    **b** In view of your answer to part *a*, what action might Blare, Inc., take?

✦ **8.26** From a very large group of voters in Wyoming, 50 are randomly chosen and asked whether they favor a proposed constitutional amendment. If in fact 40 percent of the voters in the large group favor the amendment, what is the probability that a majority of the voters in the sample of 50 favor it?

**8.27** J. C. Montgomery, Inc., a large retailing firm with the majority of its business coming from catalog sales, has sent a questionnaire to a randomly selected 100 people who are catalog customers. On that questionnaire, five new products are described, and the recipients were asked to rank them in order of preference.
    J. C. Montgomery will include product $C$ in its catalog if it becomes convinced

that at least 30 percent of its catalog customers would prefer it over the other four products. In the sample of 100, 39 customers listed product C as their preferred product. Do you think product C will be included in the J. C. Montgomery catalog? (Use an argument based on binomial probabilities to support your conclusion.)

**8.28** Scores on a job-aptitude exam have approximately a normal distribution with mean 50 and variance 36. If X denotes the score made by a randomly selected job applicant, find:
  **a** $P(X < 50)$
  **b** $P(44 \leq X \leq 56)$
  **c** $P(X \geq 60)$

◆ **8.29** The time it takes a one-page letter to be typed in the company's typing pool has approximately a normal distribution with a mean of 10 minutes and a standard deviation of 4 minutes.
  **a** What is the probability that more than 15 minutes will be required to get a one-page letter typed in that pool?
  **b** What is the probability that for three one-page letters sent to the pool, two require more than 15 minutes and one requires less than 15 minutes for typing?

◆ **8.30** Specifications for a particular machined part require a diameter of 3 inches with a permissible tolerance of 0.03 inch (high or low). The machining process generates parts with diameters having the normal distribution with a mean of 3.0 inches and a standard deviation of 0.014 inch.
  **a** What percentage of the parts do not meet the permissible tolerance standard?
  **b** What is the probability that the average diameter for a random sample of nine such parts will be less than 2.99 inches?

**8.31** The standard deviation of lifetimes of cathode-ray tubes on the remote computer terminals manufactured by Buford Instruments is known to be 50 hours. If the average lifetime observed for a sample of 25 Buford tubes is 995 hours, is this sufficient evidence to warrant doubting Buford's claim that the average lifetime of their tubes is 1,000 hours? (Use the central limit theorem as a basis for your discussion.)

**8.32** The expected completion time for a frequently occurring task that is part of a large, multitask project is 50 days, and completion time for that task has a distribution with a standard deviation of 10 days. If 16 such tasks are involved in the project (among others), approximate the probability that the total time to complete all 16 tasks exceeds 832 hours.

## SELECTED REFERENCES

Drake, A. W.: *Fundamentals of Applied Probability Theory*, McGraw-Hill Book Company, New York, 1967.
Guenther, W. C.: *Concepts of Statistical Inference*, 2d ed., McGraw-Hill Book Company, New York, 1973.

Hamburg, M.: *Basic Statistics: A Modern Approach*, Harcourt Brace Jovanovich, New York, 1974.

Hogg, R. V., and A. T. Craig: *Introduction to Mathematical Statistics*, 2d ed., The Macmillan Company, New York, 1965.

Lapin, L. L.: *Statistics for Modern Business Decisions*, Harcourt Brace Jovanovich, New York, 1973.

Lindgren, B. W., and G. W. McElrath: *Introduction to Probability and Statistics*, 3d ed., Collier-Macmillan Limited, London, 1969.

Mosteller, R., R. E. Rourke, and G. B. Thomas: *Probability with Statistical Applications*, Addison-Wesley Publishing Company, Inc., Reading, Mass., 1961.

# DECISION CRITERIA

*D*ecision making in business, industry, and government is almost always accompanied by conditions of uncertainty. That uncertainty can assume many different forms. Demand for a product cannot be exactly predicted; current costs of materials may not be the costs of the same materials two months from now; a strike is threatened, making personnel planning difficult; the Federal Reserve Bank may drastically tighten up the money supply before negotiations for the plant-expansion loan are completed. The list could go on and on, ranging from big, important judgments, like assessing the potential for full-scale war in the Middle East and the influence of such a war on oil supplies, to little ones, like whether or not Smith will call in sick on Friday because the weather is gorgeous.

Obviously, the more information the decision maker has, the better will be the decision. The information need not be perfect; that is, the person charged with the responsibility for the decision does not have to be able to predict the future precisely. But usually that manager will have *some* information about conditions bearing on the decision. For example, an estimate of demand for a product next month can be made, utilizing input from sales staff, other executives, sample surveys, and so on. Even though that estimate may take the form of a probability distribution, based either on accumulated data or simply representing the experienced manager's best guess about the probabilities, such an estimate is *information*, and information can be used.

In this chapter we will consider some of the decision criteria available to the manager, criteria that will differ depending upon the type and the quality of information that can be obtained. Two basic types of decisions will be involved: decisions in the presence of little or *no information* about future conditions, and decisions for which *probabilistic information* is available. The emphasis of the chapter is on that second situation.

## 9.1 UNCERTAINTY: NO PROBABILISTIC INFORMATION AVAILABLE

In this section we will choose *strategies* in the presence of various *states of nature*, and we will know the *payoff* for each competing strategy in conjunction with every possible state. But no information will be available about which state is most likely to occur.

We will borrow some ideas from the theory of games and mathematical decision theory and will use them in very simple settings. Useful terms that come from those areas are *maximin*, *maximax*, and *minimax regret*. Each suggests a different *decision criterion*, the use of which will be dictated by the type of company or person responsible for the decision. These criteria are introduced in Example 9.1.

### Example 9.1
### Maximin, Maximax, and Minimax Regret Decision Criteria

Consider the problem of deciding upon the best of three possible advertising strategies for a new product. One strategy, $S_1$, involves a very extensive (and expensive) combination of television, magazine, and newspaper advertising; strategy $S_2$ is advertising limited to a single television "special" and a few high-quality magazines; $S_3$ involves only a minimal newspaper campaign and some local radio commercials.

Your company has decided that only one of three states of nature, $N_1$, $N_2$, and $N_3$, will occur at the time the product is introduced. State $N_1$ is an expanding economy, involving high inflation and easy availability of money. $N_2$ is a healthy growth economy with no drastic features, a noninflated growth. $N_3$ is a contracting economy, with tight money and mild recession relative to $N_2$.

The annual profit realizable under each strategy and each state of nature has been estimated. Those profits (payoffs) are shown in Table 9.1. Such a table is known as a *payoff table*.

## TABLE 9.1    THE PAYOFF TABLE

| Strategy | State of nature | | |
|---|---|---|---|
| | $N_1$ | $N_2$ | $N_3$ |
| $S_1$ | $500,000 | $200,000 | −$300,000 |
| $S_2$ | $300,000 | $100,000 | −$100,000 |
| $S_3$ | $100,000 | $ 50,000 | $ 25,000 |

From Table 9.1 we see, for example, that if the state of nature happens to be $N_1$ when the company is using strategy $S_2$, the profit would be $300,000.  Since a negative payoff should be interpreted as a loss, we also see that if the state of nature is $N_3$ while the company is using strategy $S_1$ (extensive advertising in a contracting economy), a loss of $300,000 occurs.

Under conditions of *certainty* about the state of nature the decision is very simple.  For instance, if it is known that $N_3$ will occur, then the company should choose $S_3$, making a sure profit of $25,000 and avoiding the losses associated with $S_1$ and $S_2$.  But suppose your company does not know what the state of nature will be, yet must decide upon a strategy.  Which strategy would you recommend?

First, suppose you are the kind of person (or company) that does not like risk.  You are a "sure thing" bettor only.  You would look with favor upon $S_3$, reasoning that regardless of the true state of nature you can do no worse than make a profit of $25,000.  By selecting $S_3$ you defend yourself against the worst eventuality, the occurrence of $N_3$.  You would be adopting a *pessimistic* strategy, called a *maximin* strategy.

### The Maximin Criterion

From Table 9.1, list the minimum payoff, across states, for each of the strategies.  After listing those minima, identify their maximum, as shown in Table 9.2.  Here that maximum of those minima occurs with strategy $S_3$.

By selecting $S_3$ you cannot incur a loss; if $N_3$ occurs, you will make $25,000, while if $N_1$ or $N_2$ occurs, you will do even better.  However, by selecting strategy $S_3$ you have also put an upper bound of $100,000 on

## TABLE 9.2    MINIMUM PAYOFFS

| Strategy | Payoff | |
|---|---|---|
| $S_1$ | −$300,000 | |
| $S_2$ | −$100,000 | |
| $S_3$ | $ 25,000 | ← max |

profit, ruling out, for example, the $500,000 profit that could be made by using $S_1$ when $N_1$ occurs.

This is the defensive, pessimistic approach. If your company cannot afford to take a loss—perhaps it is just starting out—then $S_3$ is a reasonable strategy to adopt. However, if your company can afford to risk loss in the hope of realizing substantial profit, or if you subscribe to the notion of a benevolent nature (your opponent in the "game" being played), you might prefer the *maximax* strategy.

### The Maximax Criterion

From Table 9.1 list the maximum payoff, across states, for each of the strategies. This list is given in Table 9.3.

Identify the maximum of the maxima. This occurs with strategy $S_1$. You are being as *optimistic* as possible by selecting $S_1$, assuming that nature will do you the favor of selecting state $N_1$.

This criterion might be used by a large, well-established firm to whom the possibility of a $300,000 loss is not too disturbing, given the opportunity to make a $500,000 profit. Remember, we are assuming no information about the likelihoods of the states $N_1$, $N_2$, and $N_3$. If, for instance, some of the company's executives feel that $N_1$ would be unlikely to occur, this is extra information. Then the pure maximax criterion might not be applicable.

Obviously the choice of either strategy $S_1$ (maximax) or strategy $S_3$ (maximin) could cause the decision maker (hence the company) to experience some *regret*. If you had chosen $S_1$ and state $N_3$ occurred, you would regret having chosen $S_3$ (see Table 9.1). You could have made a profit of $25,000 instead of losing $300,000. In fact, a *measure* of your regret is $325,000, the amount by which you would have been better off if you had chosen strategy $S_3$. If you had chosen $S_3$ and state $N_1$ had occurred, you would of course be happy with the $100,000 profit, but you would regret by $400,000 not having chosen $S_1$.

There is no way to assure that regret will be avoided in this situation. You can, however, avoid experiencing the *worst* regret by using the *minimax regret* criterion.

### The Minimax Regret Criterion

To help us find a strategy that will avoid high regret, we form the *regret table* shown as Table 9.4. The numbers in that table are obtained by

**TABLE 9.3**  *MAXIMUM PAYOFFS*

| Strategy | Payoff |
|----------|--------|
| $S_1$ | $500,000 ← max |
| $S_2$ | $300,000 |
| $S_3$ | $100,000 |

TABLE 9.4   THE REGRET TABLE

| Strategy | State of nature | | |
|---|---|---|---|
| | $N_1$ | $N_2$ | $N_3$ |
| $S_1$ | 0 | 0 | $325,000 |
| $S_2$ | $200,000 | $100,000 | $125,000 |
| $S_3$ | $400,000 | $150,000 | 0 |

subtracting every number in each column of Table 9.1 from the maximum number in that column.

From Table 9.1 we see that if $S_1$ is chosen given $N_1$, then there is no regret. But by choosing $S_2$ given $N_1$ you make $300,000 instead of the $500,000 you could have made by using $S_1$. This is a regret of $200,000. Similar reasoning applies to each of the nine regrets in Table 9.4.

In Table 9.5 we list the maximum regret for each strategy across all states. Reasoning that we would like to avoid high regret, we choose the strategy $S_2$. It is associated with the minimum of the maximum regrets. The worst regret that we could experience, regardless of the true state of nature that occurs, is $200,000. Thus $S_2$ is called the *minimax regret strategy*. Notice that if we use $S_2$, we would always experience *some* regret, but we will avoid the largest regrets. In this example $S_2$ appears to be a "happy medium" sort of strategy. It falls somewhere between abject pessimism and naive optimism.

"Regret" is more of a decision-theoretic term than a term commonly used in the business world. Perhaps more meaningful to the businessperson is the designation *opportunity loss*. An opportunity loss (synonymous with regret) is just the amount of payoff given up by not selecting the strategy that produces maximum payoff for the state of nature that actually occurred. In Section 9.2 and following, which deal with probabilistic information for the states, opportunity loss will be used when referring to the regret concept. For now, however, since we are in the realm of pure, nonprobabilistic decision theory, we will continue to use the term "regret."

The minimax regret strategy will not always differ from the strategies chosen by the other two criteria. Example 9.2 illustrates how the *same* strategy could be selected by *any* of the three criteria.

TABLE 9.5   MAXIMUM REGRETS

| Strategy | Maximum regret | |
|---|---|---|
| $S_1$ | $325,000 | |
| $S_2$ | $200,000 | ← min |
| $S_3$ | $400,000 | |

**TABLE 9.6** *PAYOFF AND REGRET TABLES*

| | PAYOFF TABLE State | | | | REGRET TABLE State | | |
|---|---|---|---|---|---|---|---|
| Strategy | $N_1$ | $N_2$ | $N_3$ | Strategy | $N_1$ | $N_2$ | $N_3$ |
| $S_1$ | $100 | $90 | $60 | $S_1$ | 0 | $5 | 0 |
| $S_2$ | $ 80 | $95 | $50 | $S_2$ | $20 | 0 | $10 |

**Example 9.2**

Table 9.6 contains a payoff table and the corresponding regret table for two competing strategies and three states of nature. Now consider the columns in Table 9.7. In this case the strategy $S_1$ is selected regardless of the decision criterion employed. Yet $S_1$ does not completely dominate $S_2$ (is not best under all states), since if $N_2$ occurs, we would want to have chosen $S_2$.

The decision criterion you decide to use depends upon the type of company requiring the decision or upon the basic philosophy of its management. Poor companies might like maximin; rich companies may prefer maximax; others, rich or poor or simply stable, may subscribe to minimax regret as a decision criterion. That is, decisions are not made in a total vacuum. Company executives must decide which criterion seems a favorable one for them before an attempt is made to reach a decision. Definitely do not strive for consensus among the three criteria. Each criterion is based upon a different philosophy; what is best under one viewpoint usually will not be best under another.

## 9.2 UNCERTAINTY WITH PROBABILISTIC INFORMATION: RISK

In this section we will look at some further examples, again under conditions of uncertainty, but this time there will be less uncertainty (more information). Specifically, we will know more about the states of nature.

The extra information will appear in the form of *probabilities* that the different states of nature will occur. Decision making in the presence of probabilistic information about uncertain events is sometimes called "decision making under conditions of *risk.*" A preferable designation is

**TABLE 9.7** *TABLES FOR MAXIMIN, MAXIMAX, AND MINIMAX REGRET*

| Strategy | Minimum payoff | Maximum payoff | Maximum regret |
|---|---|---|---|
| $S_1$ | $60 ← max | $100 ←max | $ 5 ← min |
| $S_2$ | $50 | $ 95 | $20 |

simply "uncertainty," since "risk" has a very specific, more precise definition in decision theory. Later on, when we consider Table 9.9, we will use the term "risk" in its more precise sense.

## Example 9.3
## The Principle of Equal Ignorance

For ease of reference the payoff table of Example 9.1 is repeated here as Table 9.8. Suppose that this time the company has no particular reason to assume that any one state is more or less likely to occur than any other. It may then wish to subscribe to the notion that each state is *equally likely* to occur. If so, then the decision makers are in fact specifying probabilities for each state. Because there are three states, this so-called principle of equal ignorance suggests that the probability associated with each state could be $\frac{1}{3}$, as indicated in the last row of Table 9.8.

### The Maximum-Expected-Payoff (Minimum-Risk) Criterion

We can regard state of nature as a random variable with three possible "values," $N_1$, $N_2$, and $N_3$, but better yet, think of the *payoffs* for a particular strategy as random variables, each with the same, known, probability distribution. Then with reference to Table 9.8 we can determine the expected payoff for each of the three strategies. Thus

$$E_1 = (\$500,000)(\tfrac{1}{3}) + (\$200,000)(\tfrac{1}{3}) + (-\$300,000)(\tfrac{1}{3})$$

$$= \frac{\$400,000}{3} \simeq \$133,333 \leftarrow max \qquad S_1 \text{ gives maximum expected payoff}$$

$$E_2 = (\$300,000)(\tfrac{1}{3}) + (\$100,000)(\tfrac{1}{3}) + (-\$100,000)(\tfrac{1}{3})$$

$$= \frac{\$300,000}{3} = \$100,000$$

$$E_3 = (\$100,000)(\tfrac{1}{3}) + (\$50,000)(\tfrac{1}{3}) + (\$25,000)(\tfrac{1}{3})$$

$$= \frac{\$175,000}{3} \simeq \$58,333$$

**TABLE 9.8**  *THE PAYOFF TABLE*

| Strategy | State of nature | | |
|---|---|---|---|
| | $N_1$ | $N_2$ | $N_3$ |
| $S_1$ | $500,000 | $200,000 | -$300,000 |
| $S_2$ | $300,000 | $100,000 | -$100,000 |
| $S_3$ | $100,000 | $ 50,000 | $ 25,000 |
| $P(N_i)$ | $\frac{1}{3}$ | $\frac{1}{3}$ | $\frac{1}{3}$ |

Our decision criterion is to choose that strategy associated with the *maximum expected payoff*. This would be the strategy with the best long-run average payoff, in this case, strategy $S_1$. That strategy is also called the *minimum-risk strategy*, as explained following.

In decision theory, if "loss" is a random variable, then *risk* is defined to be *expected loss*. In the problem above we dealt with payoffs, not losses, but a *payoff* can be regarded as a *negative loss*. Thus, if we had wanted to consider a loss table instead of a payoff table, we would have used Table 9.9.

The losses in the loss table are simply the negatives of the payoffs in the payoff table (Table 9.8). Thus the expected losses (risks) are just the negatives of the corresponding expected payoffs. So if $R_j$ denotes risk for strategy $S_j$, then

$$R_1 = \frac{-\$400,000}{3} \qquad S_1 \text{ gives minimum risk}$$

$$R_2 = \frac{-\$300,000}{3}$$

$$R_3 = \frac{-\$175,000}{3}$$

Since the minimum of a set of negative numbers is the most negative of the numbers, here $-\$400,000/3$ is the minimum of the three risks (occurring for the same strategy as the maximum expected payoff), and $S_1$ is the minimum-risk strategy.

Of course the phrase "minimum risk" has a very good sound to it, but do not conclude that it is the best decision criterion just because its name sounds good. It may not be the one you want to use. Using this approach, the selection of a strategy is highly dependent upon the set of probabilities used. To be confident that you have correctly assessed risk, you need to be confident that you have good estimates of the probabilities

**TABLE 9.9**    *THE LOSS TABLE*

| Strategy | State of nature | | |
|---|---|---|---|
| | $N_1$ | $N_2$ | $N_3$ |
| $S_1$ | $-\$500,000$ | $-\$200,000$ | $\$300,000$ |
| $S_2$ | $-\$300,000$ | $-\$100,000$ | $\$100,000$ |
| $S_3$ | $-\$100,000$ | $-\$\ 50,000$ | $-\$\ 25,000$ |
| $P(N_i)$ | $\frac{1}{3}$ | $\frac{1}{3}$ | $\frac{1}{3}$ |

involved. Further, remember that an expected value is a *long-run average* value. Using minimum risk as a decision criterion makes a lot of sense if it is to be used over a series of similar decisions, so that a "long run" will actually be involved. But even if it is only a one-time decision, a good case can be made for using minimum risk as a criterion, especially if you always use it, thus establishing a "long run" over all your decisions, even if they are dissimilar. However, if your company cannot afford a loss, you still might prefer to use strategy $S_3$, the maximin strategy discussed in Section 9.1. That is, a minimum-risk strategy would look good only to a company that could afford to stay in business over the long haul.

### Example 9.4
### Good Strategy; Bad Outcome

The following vignette is a true story. No names are used, to avoid embarrassing the author.

As an Army inductee in basic training player $A$ had the opportunity to make a very good bet during a hand of poker. The game was draw poker; table stakes; jacks or better to open. Player $A$ entered the hand with $30 before him, about three-eighths of the monthly salary of an E-2 Private in 1954.

Player $A$ was dealt four cards to a flush while sitting just on the dealer's right. The opportunity to open passed around to the dealer, player $D$, who was able to open the betting. Four other players, including $A$, stayed in for the draw. Player $A$ caught the fifth heart for his flush and also observed that the dealer drew three cards (which indicated that he had opened with only a pair).

The exact expected payoff for $A$ in this situation would be difficult to calculate, but if you have played a little poker, you can appreciate that if this same opportunity were to arise regularly, the long-run profit accruing to $A$ should be considerable. (This assumes, as was the case on this particular hand, that none of the other players was "sandbagging"; that is, none had openers but declined the opportunity to open.) Of course, there was a small probability that player $D$ would get lucky and improve a pair sufficiently to enable his hand to beat a flush.

After the draw the betting progressed through a series of raises and counterraises until all of $A$'s money was in the pot and everyone but $D$ had dropped. On showdown it transpired that $D$ had acquired a full house by drawing three cards to a pair. Player $A$ was short of funds for the remainder of the month.

The strategy (play to the bitter end), from a long-run viewpoint, was a good one. In this one-shot situation, however, the unlikely state of nature did occur. Now a good poker player might suggest that $A$ had misplayed the hand, being aware all along that $D$ was confident enough to raise twice in the face of a one-card draw. Nevertheless, a lesson on the interpretation of expected values is contained in the story.

### Example 9.5
### Changing Probabilities May Change the Decision

Assume the same payoffs as in Table 9.8, but now with different probabilities for the states. Specifically, assume that $N_1$ and $N_2$ are equally likely states but that $N_3$ is twice as likely to occur as either $N_1$ or $N_2$. Then $P(N_1) = \frac{1}{4}$, $P(N_2) = \frac{1}{4}$, and $P(N_3) = \frac{1}{2}$. Now the expected payoffs become

$$E_1 = (\$500{,}000)(\tfrac{1}{4}) + (\$200{,}000)(\tfrac{1}{4}) + (-\$300{,}000)(\tfrac{1}{2}) = \frac{\$100{,}000}{4}$$

$$E_2 = (\$300{,}000)(\tfrac{1}{4}) + (\$100{,}000)(\tfrac{1}{4}) + (-\$100{,}000)(\tfrac{1}{2}) = \frac{\$200{,}000}{4}$$

$$E_3 = (\$100{,}000)(\tfrac{1}{4}) + (\$50{,}000)(\tfrac{1}{4}) + (\$25{,}000)(\tfrac{1}{2}) = \frac{\$200{,}000}{4}$$

With the new set of probabilities the expected payoffs have changed so that now *either* $S_2$ or $S_3$ is the maximum-expected-payoff (minimum-risk) strategy.

Many of us would break the tie by reasoning that since the two strategies have the same expected payoff, we might as well choose strategy $S_3$. Using $S_3$ we cannot experience a loss. But of course by avoiding the potential $100,000 loss under $N_3$ we are also giving up the potential $300,000 profit under $N_1$. So once again the characteristics of the decision maker enter into the final decision. An optimist would reason that since the expected payoff is $50,000 for either strategy $S_2$ or strategy $S_3$ ($200,000/ 4 = $50,000), $S_2$ would be more attractive because of the possibility of a $300,000 payoff (being willing to risk the $100,000 loss). A pessimist would be more inclined to choose $S_3$ because of the guaranteed profit. The coolly analytic type of person, however, might be indifferent to the two choices; since the expected payoffs are the same, this person might just flip a coin to break the tie.

This type of problem will be reconsidered when the concept of *utility* is discussed in Section 9.6. There we will attempt to quantify the characteristics of the decision maker and to incorporate that approach into a more formal analysis.

### Example 9.6
### Expected Value in a Bidding Situation

Consider a contractor who makes many bids for contracts during a long time span. Maximum expected payoff is clearly a good decision criterion in this situation. The contractor will lose some bids and win some bids, but in the long run there exists the opportunity to realize predicted expected payoffs.

Suppose XL Construction wants to bid for the right to build a short portion of highway for the state. A certain fixed cost will be involved in

| | CONDITIONAL PROBABILITY OF |
|---|---|
| **TABLE 9.10** | **WINNING CONTRACT** |

| Bid | Probability (given bid) |
|---|---|
| $B_1$: $C + 0.1C = 1.1C$ | 0.60 |
| $B_2$: $C + 0.2C = 1.2C$ | 0.40 |
| $B_3$: $C + 0.4C = 1.4C$ | 0.15 |

making a study to estimate the cost of constructing the section of highway. In the past this fixed cost has been in the neighborhood of 1 percent of the estimated cost of the job, say $C$.

XL is considering three possible bids: cost plus 10 percent, cost plus 20 percent, and cost plus 40 percent. Knowing something about how their competitors assess costs and make bids, the executives of XL have decided that the probabilities in Table 9.10 apply. Notice that those probabilities do not have to sum to unity, since they are *conditional* probabilities. For example, 0.60 is interpreted as the proportion of time the bid is won when the bid has been cost plus 10 percent (the condition), while 0.15 is the proportion of the time the bid is won when the bid was cost plus 40 percent, a different condition.

Table 9.11 lists the profits associated with each of the three bids (including deduction of fixed cost, $0.01C$) and the loss of $0.01C$ (a negative profit) if the bid is lost. Probabilities for winning and losing the contract are also included.

Now we can calculate the expected profit for each bid.

$$E_1 = (0.09C)(0.60) - (0.01C)(0.40) = 0.05C$$

$$E_2 = (0.19C)(0.40) - (0.01C)(0.60) = 0.07C \leftarrow max$$

$$E_3 = (0.39C)(0.15) - (0.01C)(0.85) = 0.05C$$

Using the maximum-expected-profit criterion, we find that XL Construction's optimal bid is $B_2$: cost plus 20 percent. This yields an expected profit of 7 percent of cost. Over the long haul, if the probabilities and the formula for fixed cost remain the same, XL can plan to make an overall

| | |
|---|---|
| **TABLE 9.11** | **THE PAYOFF TABLE** |

| Bid | Profit if won | Profit if lost | $(P_{win}, P_{lose})$ |
|---|---|---|---|
| $B_1$ | $0.09C$ | $-0.01C$ | (0.60, 0.40) |
| $B_2$ | $0.19C$ | $-0.01C$ | (0.40, 0.60) |
| $B_3$ | $0.39C$ | $-0.01C$ | (0.15, 0.85) |

profit of 7 percent of the estimated costs on all contracts for which they bid, provided they bid cost plus 20 percent. Of course, if that strategy is used, the profit is 19 percent of cost on any *particular* contract won.

The interesting aspect of this example is that XL Construction can establish an overall bidding strategy prior to estimating the costs for the projects. If the contract itself is on a "cost-plus" basis, they may need to do no cost estimation whatsoever to make their bid. Still, costs would need to be estimated as they move into the planning stage for the project after the contract has been won.

## 9.3  EXPECTED VALUE OF PERFECT INFORMATION: OPPORTUNITY LOSS

If the decision maker can somehow come up with an infallible predictor of the future, then the *best* decision can always be made. With reference to Examples 9.1, 9.3, and 9.5 (payoff table again repeated as Table 9.12), for instance, if the "infallible predictor" were to predict the occurrence of state $N_1$, then strategy $S_1$ could be confidently chosen. Or, since the infallible predictor never makes a mistake, if it predicts $N_3$ we choose $S_3$.

What would the company that has this problem be willing to pay for such a predictor? That amount, whatever it is, will be called the *expected value of perfect information*, or EVPI for short.

### Example 9.7

Table 9.12 shows the payoff table and the probabilities used in Example 9.5. For a realistic frame of reference, remember that the states of nature $N_1$, $N_2$, $N_3$ represent future states of the economy, ranging from expanding ($N_1$) to contracting ($N_3$), while the strategies $S_1$, $S_2$, $S_3$ are advertising levels of diminishing intensity.

Now we want to know the expected value of perfect information, the price we would be willing to pay for that infallible predictor. To come up with the EVPI we must realize two things: we have to decide upon a

**TABLE 9.12    THE PAYOFF TABLE**

| Strategy | State of nature $N_1$ | $N_2$ | $N_3$ |
|---|---|---|---|
| $S_1$ | $500,000 | $200,000 | −$300,000 |
| $S_2$ | $300,000 | $100,000 | −$100,000 |
| $S_3$ | $100,000 | $50,000 | $25,000 |
| $P(N_i)$ | $\frac{1}{4}$ | $\frac{1}{4}$ | $\frac{1}{2}$ |

price *before* we receive the perfect information, and we must evaluate the infallible predictor *over the long run*, acting as if the opportunity to choose a strategy under these conditions will arise time after time.

Thus we would expect $N_3$ to be predicted half the time, and when it is predicted, we could choose strategy $S_3$ with supreme confidence that the payoff will be $25,000. Likewise, one-fourth of the time $N_1$ will be predicted, giving us the $500,000 payoff associated with $S_1$, and one-fourth of the time $N_2$ will be predicted, causing us to choose $S_1$ again, with its $200,000 payoff. (Note that with perfect information we would never select strategy $S_2$.) The results of this discussion are condensed in Table 9.13.

Then the expected *payoff* with perfect information, say EP (this is not yet EVPI), is

$$EP = (\$500,000)(\tfrac{1}{4}) + (\$200,000)(\tfrac{1}{4}) + (\$25,000)(\tfrac{1}{2})$$

$$= \$187,500$$

But in Example 9.5 we have already computed the maximum expected payoff *without* perfect information. In that example we learned that either strategy $S_2$ or strategy $S_3$ would yield an expected payoff of

$$\text{Maximum expected payoff} = E_2 = E_3 = \$50,000$$

So the *value* of perfect information, in the long run (on the average), is

$$EVPI = EP - (\text{maximum expected payoff})$$

$$= \$187,500 - \$50,000$$

$$= \$137,500$$

Therefore the company should be willing to pay any amount up to $137,500 for perfect information. Without extra information, the expected payoff would be $50,000. With *perfect* information, this expected payoff increases by $137,500, to $187,500.

Now of what practical use is this knowledge? Surely it is not possible to come up with an infallible predictor of the state of the economy in the future. But suppose the company is considering an intensive study to

**TABLE 9.13** PAYOFF TABLE WITH PERFECT INFORMATION

| State | Payoff | Probability |
|---|---|---|
| $N_1$ | $500,000 | $\tfrac{1}{4}$ |
| $N_2$ | $200,000 | $\tfrac{1}{4}$ |
| $N_3$ | $ 25,000 | $\tfrac{1}{2}$ |

gain extra information about that future state. The EVPI is the absolute upper limit they should put on the cost of that study; if the study is to be more expensive than the EVPI, the company should not undertake it. That is, the EVPI serves as a guideline, a bound above which the company should not go when considering paying for *any* extra information.

The same result may be achieved by considering *opportunity loss*, called *regret* back in Section 9.1. Table 9.14 repeats the information in Table 9.4, except now "regret" is replaced by "opportunity loss," and probabilities for the states are incorporated.

We will use the information in Table 9.14 to select a strategy based on *minimum expected opportunity loss* (not necessarily the same as the minimax regret strategy, where no expectation was involved). Using $EOL_j$ to denote the expected opportunity loss if strategy $S_j$ is used, we obtain

$$EOL_1 = \$162,500$$

$$EOL_2 = \$137,500$$

$$EOL_3 = \$137,500$$

Take particular note of two results of the above analysis. First, the minimum-expected-opportunity-loss strategy would be either $S_2$ or $S_3$, the same decision gained using maximum expected payoff or minimum risk as the decision criterion. The three approaches are equivalent; that is, each will choose the same optimal strategy. Second, the expected opportunity loss associated with an *optimal* strategy is the EVPI. Symbolically, we have

$$EVPI = EOL_k$$

where $S_k$ is the optimal (minimum-risk) strategy. This result can be formally proved in general, applying to *any* such decision problem.

**TABLE 9.14**  *THE OPPORTUNITY LOSS TABLE*

| Strategy | State of nature | | |
|---|---|---|---|
| | $N_1$ | $N_2$ | $N_3$ |
| $S_1$ | 0 | 0 | $325,000 |
| $S_2$ | $200,000 | $100,000 | $125,000 |
| $S_3$ | $400,000 | $150,000 | 0 |
| $P(N_t)$ | $\frac{1}{4}$ | $\frac{1}{4}$ | $\frac{1}{2}$ |

We have just been discussing the value of extra information. Here we consider the question of how, given information in a particular form, we might make good use of it.

So far we have assumed that the probabilities in a decision problem have been obtained either from past data or from expert opinion, and that these probabilities pertain to the states of nature. Now we consider extra information, also in the form of data-based or subjective probabilities, that pertain to the observation of events *related* to the states of nature. These additional observations may cause us to revise prior beliefs about the probabilities for the states.

### Example 9.8

Consider a general who is attempting to assess the chance that the enemy will attack at dawn tomorrow. Intelligence reports a 50/50 chance for a dawn attack, but after that report is received, scouts come in with the information that the enemy is moving a new division of troops toward the front under cover of darkness. Should the general still assume a 50/50 chance for the attack? Probably not. He would want to revise that probability, if not to some specific number, at least to the extent that the probability for attack now exceeds the probability there will be no attack.

In this case the probabilities received from the intelligence report, one-half for attack, one-half for no attack, would be called *prior* probabilities. After the extra information is received from the scouts, however, a new set of revised probabilities would be used, probabilities that reflect the condition that troops are being moved toward the front. These revised probabilities will be *conditional* probabilities, where the condition is the extra information that has been received. Such "after-extra-information" probabilities are often called *posterior* probabilities. These posterior (conditional) probabilities may be computed using a restatement of the multiplication formula that is called Bayes' theorem.

Recall the general multiplication formula (formula 3 of Chapter 8). It was

$$P(A \text{ and } B) = P(A|B)P(B) = P(B|A)P(A)$$

Suppose we divide the right-most two products by $P(B)$, obtaining

$$P(A|B) = \frac{P(B|A)P(A)}{P(B)}$$

Since the numerator of the fraction on the right-hand side is just $P(A$ and $B)$, you recognize this as the definition of conditional probability given in Chapter 8. In another format, it is also Bayes' theorem.

Suppose that event $B$ can occur in conjunction with any of $n$ mutually exclusive, exhaustive events $A_i$, $i = 1, 2, \ldots , n$, as suggested by Figure 9.1. Then

$$P(B \text{ and } A_i) = P(B|A_i)P(A_i)$$

and

$$P(B) = \sum_{i=1}^{n} P(B|A_i)P(A_i)$$

Of course, $P(B|A_i)$ could be zero for some of the $A_i$ (such as $A_1$ and $A_6$ in Figure 9.1), but still, the entire sum is $P(B)$ because we are determining the probability $P(B)$ by adding the probabilities for $n$ mutually exclusive events, $P(B \text{ and } A_i) = P(B|A_i)P(A_i)$, which comprise all of event $B$.

If we want a different conditional probability, say $P(A_j|B)$, where $A_j$ is one of the events $A_i$, $i = 1, 2, \ldots , n$, we need only use Bayes' theorem, which is just the general multiplication formula applied to this special situation.

*Bayes' theorem.* For $B$ and $A_i$, $i = 1, 2, \ldots , n$ satisfying the conditions given above,

$$P(A_j|B) = \frac{P(B|A_j)P(A_j)}{\sum_{i=1}^{n} P(B|A_i)P(A_i)}$$

In practice, the events represented by the $A_i$'s are usually quite obvious, so that the application of Bayes' theorem is fairly simple. Example 9.9 is a trivial problem designed to show you how easy this is to do.

### Example 9.9
### Revising Probabilities Using Bayes' Theorem

Reginald, the custodian for an old apartment building heated by a coal-fired furnace, is forgetful. Before he leaves work in the late evening, he is supposed to bank the coals in the furnace, but he often forgets to do it. The furnace is not in very good condition anyway; if Reginald remembers

*FIGURE 9.1*    The event $B$ (shaded) in Bayes' theorem

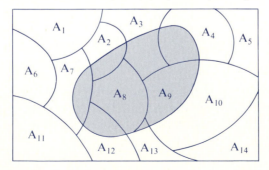

to bank the coals, the probability that the fire will go out in the furnace overnight is $\frac{1}{4}$. If Reginald forgets to bank the coals, the probability that the fire will go out is $\frac{3}{5}$. Past experience indicates probabilities of $\frac{3}{7}$ that he will remember to bank the coals and $\frac{4}{7}$ that he will forget.

Suppose that on a particular morning it is observed that the fire went out overnight. What is the probability that Reginald forgot to bank the coals?

Here we want to determine the *conditional* probability that Reginald forgot to bank the coals *given* that the fire went out overnight. This may be quite different from (and larger than) the *unconditional* probability ($\frac{4}{7}$) that he will forget to bank the coals. That is, the extra information would cause us to revise that probability upward.

To apply Bayes' theorem to this little problem,

Let $B$ = the event that the fire goes out overnight

$A_1$ = the event that Reginald remembers to bank the coals

$A_2$ = the event that Reginald forgets to bank the coals

Then we want to compute $P(A_2|B)$. We are given $P(B|A_1) = \frac{1}{4}$, $P(B|A_2) = \frac{3}{5}$, $P(A_1) = \frac{3}{7}$, and $P(A_2) = \frac{4}{7}$. Thus we have all the input required for the use of Bayes' theorem. In this instance the calculation is

$$P(A_2|B) = \frac{P(B|A_2)P(A_2)}{P(B|A_1)P(A_1) + P(B|A_2)P(A_2)}$$

$$= \frac{P(B|A_2)P(A_2)}{P(B)}$$

Here the event $B$, the fire going out overnight, can only occur in conjunction with two mutually exclusive events: Reginald remembering to bank the coals and Reginald forgetting to bank the coals.

Then the main computation is that for $P(B)$. We obtain

$$P(B) = P(B|A_1)P(A_1) + P(B|A_2)P(A_2)$$

$$= (\tfrac{1}{4})(\tfrac{3}{7}) + (\tfrac{3}{5})(\tfrac{4}{7})$$

$$= \tfrac{3}{28} + \tfrac{12}{35} = \tfrac{63}{140}$$

Then the desired conditional probability is

$$P(A_2|B) = \frac{P(B|A_2)P(A_2)}{P(B)}$$

$$= \frac{(\tfrac{3}{5})(\tfrac{4}{7})}{\tfrac{63}{140}}$$

$$= \tfrac{48}{63} \approx 0.76$$

Since $P(A_2) = \frac{4}{7} \approx 0.57$, we see that the given information (the fire went out) has indeed caused us to revise upward the probability that Reginald forgot to bank the coals.

Here we are reasoning from "observed effect" to "probable cause," one of the uses for Bayes' theorem. In this instance, the computation might indicate that Reginald's job could be in jeopardy if his supervisor notices that the fire went out. An extension of this idea to a more realistic business problem will be used in Example 9.10.

### Example 9.10
### A Business Application of Bayes' Theorem

ENC Corporation is considering three possible investment strategies for next year. Three states of nature can be anticipated: $E$, an expanding economy; $N$, basically no change from this year; and $C$, a contracting economy. Payoffs for each strategy and each state are given in Table 9.15.

In the absence of additional information ENC will assume that the three states are equally likely. Then $P(E) = P(N) = P(C) = \frac{1}{3}$. This gives

$$E(S_1 \text{ payoff}) = \frac{\$500,000}{3} \leftarrow$$
$$E(S_2 \text{ payoff}) = \frac{\$500,000}{3} \leftarrow \} \ max$$
$$E(S_3 \text{ payoff}) = \frac{\$450,000}{3}$$

If minimum risk is the decision criterion, then the corporation could choose either strategy $S_1$ or strategy $S_2$, which have equal, maximum expected payoffs.

However, ENC knows that the Council of Economic Advisers annually makes a prediction about the economy for the coming year. Historical records give the percentages shown in Table 9.16. These percentages are interpreted, for example, as: Whenever the economy has been in state $E$,

---

**TABLE 9.15** *THE PAYOFF TABLE: ENC, INC.*

| | State | | |
|---|---|---|---|
| Strategy | $E$ | $N$ | $C$ |
| $S_1$ | $400,000 | $200,000 | −$100,000 |
| $S_2$ | $350,000 | $150,000 | 0 |
| $S_3$ | $200,000 | $150,000 | $100,000 |

the Council has in the previous year predicted "E" 40 percent of the time, "N" 50 percent of the time, and "C" 10 percent of the time.

Suppose that this year the Council of Economic Advisers has said that next year will be a period of no change; that is, they have predicted "N." We want to incorporate this extra information into the problem by using it to revise the probabilities for the three states of nature. We need $P(E|"N")$, $P(N|"N")$, and $P(C|"N")$. Then we can calculate the *conditional expected payoffs*, where the condition is the prediction "N."

First, for the denominator in Bayes' theorem, we need $P("N")$. It is written symbolically as

$$P("N") = P("N"|E)P(E) + P("N"|N)P(N) + P("N"|C)P(C)$$

Converting the relevant percentages from Table 9.16 to probabilities yields $P("N"|E) = 0.50 = \frac{1}{2}$, $P("N"|N) = 0.40 = \frac{2}{5}$, and $P("N"|C) = 0.50 = \frac{1}{2}$. Then, since we already know the prior probabilities: $P(E) = P(N) = P(C) = \frac{1}{3}$, we obtain

$$P("N") = (\tfrac{1}{2})(\tfrac{1}{3}) + (\tfrac{2}{5})(\tfrac{1}{3}) + (\tfrac{1}{2})(\tfrac{1}{3})$$
$$= \tfrac{7}{15}$$

Now it is easy to calculate the three desired conditional (posterior) probabilities. For example,

$$P(E|"N") = \frac{P("N"|E)P(E)}{P("N")}$$

so that

$$P(E|"N") = \frac{(\tfrac{1}{2})(\tfrac{1}{3})}{\tfrac{7}{15}}$$
$$= \tfrac{5}{14}$$

**TABLE 9.16** *PREDICTION PERCENTAGES*

| Previous prediction | Actual state of economy | | |
|---|---|---|---|
| | E | N | C |
| "E" | 40 | 30 | 20 |
| "N" | 50 | 40 | 50 |
| "C" | 10 | 30 | 30 |

Similarly, the other two probabilities that we need are

$$P(N|''N'') = \frac{(\frac{2}{5})(\frac{1}{3})}{\frac{7}{15}} = \frac{4}{14}$$

$$P(C|''N'') = \frac{(\frac{1}{2})(\frac{1}{3})}{\frac{7}{15}} = \frac{5}{14}$$

Having revised the state probabilities using Bayes' theorem, we are ready to compute the conditional expected payoffs for the three strategies. They are

$$E(S_1 \text{ payoff}|''N'') = (\$400{,}000)(\tfrac{5}{14}) + (\$200{,}000)(\tfrac{4}{14}) + (-\$100{,}000)(\tfrac{5}{14})$$

$$= \frac{\$2{,}300{,}000}{14}$$

$$E(S_2 \text{ payoff}|''N'') = (\$350{,}000)(\tfrac{5}{14}) + (\$150{,}000)(\tfrac{4}{14}) + (0)(\tfrac{5}{14})$$

$$= \frac{\$2{,}350{,}000}{14} \leftarrow max$$

$$E(S_3 \text{ payoff}|''N'') = (\$200{,}000)(\tfrac{5}{14}) + (\$150{,}000)(\tfrac{4}{14}) + (\$100{,}000)(\tfrac{5}{14})$$

$$= \frac{\$2{,}100{,}000}{14}$$

The prediction "N" has changed the decision. Strategy $S_2$ is now the unique conditional minimum-risk strategy.

Be warned not to put too much faith in this approach unless you have quite a bit of confidence in the estimated probabilities. The assumption of equally likely states (prior probabilities of $\frac{1}{3}$ for each state) was a subjective assessment, being the opinion of the ENC executives. Historical data gave the other set of probabilities, but you would have to believe that the immediate future will not differ much from the recent past in order to trust their ability to produce accurate posterior probabilities.

Remember, calculations do not replace executives. The preceding example shows computations of a type that *assist* them in their decision-making deliberations. The output of the computations is no better than the data that are input, but even with good data the final decision may depend upon other considerations that have not been included in the conditional minimum-risk approach.

## 9.5 DECISION TREES

Often a company will find itself faced with a sequence of decisions to be made, with the final, overall strategy simply being the optimal decision *sequence*. In that sequential setting the concept of a *decision tree* can be very useful.

For a sequence of decisions that is short enough, it may be possible to lay out the whole set of potential decision sequences in a tree diagram. Then you can calculate the expected payoffs along each "branch" of the tree. The optimal sequence is determined by reasoning backward through the branches to find that sequence that yields the best expected payoff. This is the same kind of reasoning that will be used in the dynamic programming problems of Chapter 12; only the physical layout of the calculations differs; the concept is the same.

To introduce the notion of a tree, in Example 9.11 we consider only a single decision. Then in Example 9.12, to follow, a sequence of decisions will be involved.

**Example 9.11**
**A Tree with One Decision**

A specialty manufacturing firm is considering the production of a toy that might become a "fad," with high demand for a short period, then demand dropping off rapidly afterward. They plan to sell the toy to retailers for $3.00 per unit.

If the decision to manufacture the toy is made, special equipment will have to be purchased. The equipment will be scrapped at the end of the duration of the fad, with no salvage value. Units will be produced only as the demand develops, so no inventory will be on hand at the end of that time period.

If equipment costing $2,000 is purchased, the manufacturing cost per unit will be $2.50. If $6,000 equipment is purchased, the per-unit cost will only be $2.00.

Using past experience with similar items, the firm has estimated sales volumes (number of units that will be sold) and their associated probabilities. These are shown in Table 9.17. The firm wants to know if the toy should be produced and, if so, which type of equipment to purchase.

The firm decides the toy should be produced if a positive expected profit is associated with either type of equipment. If a positive expected profit is possible, the firm should purchase the equipment associated with the highest expected profit. The reasoning is assisted by the decision tree of Figure 9.2.

The tree for the toy problem exhibits two types of nodes and branches: a *decision node*, node 1, designated by a square, with *decision branches*

| | SALES VOLUMES | |
|---|---|---|
| *TABLE 9.17* | *AND PROBABILITIES* | |
| | **Volume** | **Probability** |
| | 2,000 | 0.30 |
| | 5,000 | 0.40 |
| | 10,000 | 0.20 |
| | 20,000 | 0.10 |

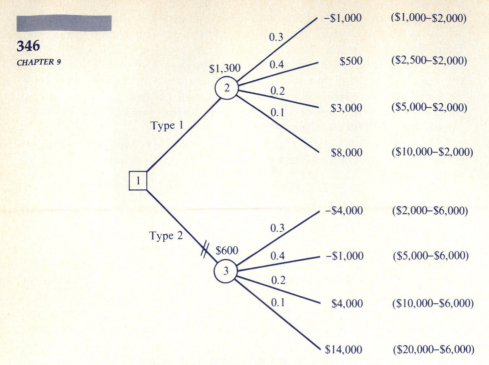

**FIGURE 9.2** Decision tree for the toy problem

leaving it, and *state nodes*, nodes 2 and 3, designated by circles, with *state branches* leaving them. On each state branch are the probabilities associated with each state, where sales volume represents state. Thus the four branches leaving node 2 correspond, from top branch to bottom branch, to sales volumes of 2,000, 5,000, 10,000, and 20,000 units. The branches leaving node 3 correspond to the same sequence of sales volumes.

At the tip of each state branch is the payoff associated with that branch. Now node 2 occurs on the "type 1" decision branch, which means that the units are to be produced with the $2,000 equipment. Since sales price is $3.00 per unit and each unit produced with the type 1 equipment costs $2.50, gross profit per unit is $0.50. Thus the payoff on the topmost branch emanating from node 2 is the $1,000 gross profit associated with producing 2,000 units at $0.50 per unit, *minus* the cost of the equipment, which is $2,000, or a payoff of −$1,000. Similarly, the $4,000 payoff at the tip of the third branch emanating from node 3 is obtained. Since type 2 ($6,000) equipment is to be used, the gross profit per unit is $3.00 − $2.00 = $1.00. On the third branch, 10,000 units will be produced, so the payoff is $10,000 minus the $6,000 cost of equipment, or $4,000. Payoffs at the tips of all other branches are determined in this manner, as indicated on Figure 9.2.

For each state node, the expected payoff is determined and written directly above the circled node. Thus

$$E(\text{node 2 payoff}) = (-\$1,000)(0.3) + (\$500)(0.4) + (\$3,000)(0.2)$$
$$+ (\$8,000)(0.1) = \$1,300$$

$$E(\text{node 3 payoff}) = (-\$4,000)(0.3) + (-\$1,000)(0.4) + (\$4,000)(0.2)$$
$$+ (\$14,000)(0.1) = \$600$$

Now the optimal decision can be made. First of all, since both expected payoffs are positive, *the toy should be produced.* Second, since the $2,000 type 1 equipment gives the largest expected payoff, *the $2,000 equipment should be used.* This decision is indicated by the double slashes on Figure 9.2, which "cut off" the type 2 branch of the tree.

This problem could have been solved using an ordinary payoff table, as shown in Table 9.18. It was worked using a decision tree only so you would have available a simple example in order to learn the decision-tree approach. Example 9.12, however, shows a decision tree that would not fit into this payoff-table format.

Before leaving this example, note that if demand (sales volume) turned out to be 20,000 units, the type 2 decision ($6,000 equipment) would produce the largest payoff. Further, if demand happened to be 2,000 units, the company would lose money under the type 1 decision. That is, actual payoff depends upon which state of nature does occur. The decision to use type 1 ($2,000) equipment was made using the criterion of maximum *expected* payoff.

**Example 9.12**
**A Tree with Four Decisions**

A representative of Sweepum Vacuum Cleaners has advertised he will be in town for one day only, interviewing for an experienced salesperson to handle their product in this region. He will only have time to interview four people thoroughly. The interviews will occur on a first-come, first-served basis.

The representative's experience indicates that people answering his ads are either adequate, good, or super salespersons. A super salesperson is twice as valuable to Sweepum as an adequate salesperson, with a good

**TABLE 9.18** THE PAYOFF TABLE FOR THE TOY PROBLEM

| Strategy | State (sales volume) | | | |
|---|---|---|---|---|
| | 2,000 | 5,000 | 10,000 | 20,000 |
| Type 1 | -$1,000 | $ 500 | $3,000 | $ 8,000 |
| Type 2 | -$4,000 | -$1,000 | $4,000 | $14,000 |
| Probability | 0.3 | 0.4 | 0.2 | 0.1 |

salesperson being intermediately valuable. Accordingly, the representative has arbitrarily assigned "values" of 2, 3, and 4, respectively, to adequate, good, and super.

The canny representative can tell with certainty what type of salesperson an interviewed person will be. It is understood that if he does not hire a person during the interview, the person is rejected. Then the salesperson hired would have to be one of the people interviewed later.

Past experience suggests that the "first-come, first-served" characteristic of the ad leads to the probabilities of Table 9.19 being associated with the prospects. What the interviewer wants to know, of course, is the optimal interview strategy. In terms of highest expected value to the company, *when should he hire a salesperson?*

Maximum value is measured by the number 4. Thus if the first person interviewed is super (value 4), that person would be hired on the spot and the interviews would be discontinued. If the first person interviewed is adequate (value 2), however, he or she would not be hired since the representative can do no worse by continuing to interview. But if the first person interviewed is good (value 3), a dilemma results. By not interviewing further, a super salesperson could be missed, but the representative could wind up after the fourth interview with only an adequate salesperson.

The decision tree of Figure 9.3 is very helpful in this situation. A sequence of decisions is definitely involved. Every possible sequence is exhibited on the tree, except for those involving the strategy "stop with an adequate salesperson," which could never be optimal. As in Example 9.11, both decision nodes and state nodes are involved, as are decision branches and state branches. In Figure 9.3, $I$ and $D$ on decision branches mean, respectively, "interview" and "don't interview." On the state branches, a good salesperson is indicated by the letter $G$, $A$ means adequate, and $S$ means super. Probabilities for each of those states are also indicated on every state branch, and the values of each type of salesperson are on the tips of the final branches.

We start the solution by supposing that the interviewer conducts a *fourth* interview. These fourth interviews could occur following nodes 24, 25, 27, 28, 30, 31, 33, and 34 on Figure 9.3. Ignore the sequence that would have brought him to one of those nodes. Reference to just any one of

**TABLE 9.19**  *PROBABILITIES ASSOCIATED WITH PROSPECTS*

| Prospect | Adequate | Good | Super |
|----------|----------|------|-------|
| 1st in line | 0.2 | 0.3 | 0.5 |
| 2d in line | 0.3 | 0.3 | 0.4 |
| 3d in line | 0.4 | 0.3 | 0.3 |
| 4th in line | 0.5 | 0.3 | 0.2 |

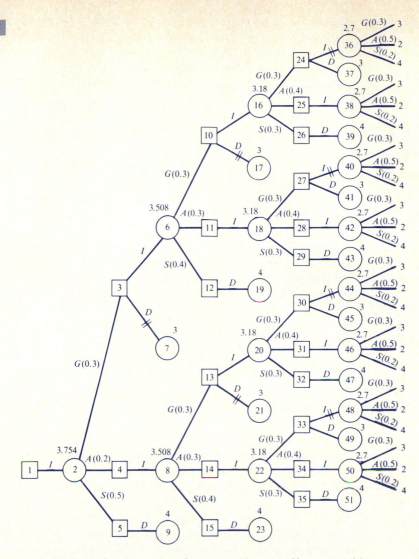

**FIGURE 9.3**   Decision tree: Sweepum Vacuum Cleaner problem

the sets of three branches from nodes 36, 38, 40, 42, 44, 46, 48, and 50 gives the expected value of a fourth interview.   It is

$$E_4 = (3)(0.3) + (2)(0.5) + (4)(0.2) = 2.7$$

We write 2.7 above each circled, even-numbered node in the last column of nodes on Figure 9.3.   This expected value is called the "value" of a fourth interview.

Now we can put double slashes through the branches to nodes 36, 40, 44, and 48, since the decision "don't interview" produces the value 3 we see above nodes 37, 41, 45, and 49, and the decision to *not* interview after a third interview gives a higher value, 3, than the decision *to* interview, *provided* that on the third interview we interviewed a good salesperson.

Now let's look at the expected value of a third interview. From the *I* branches leaving nodes 10, 11, 13, and 14, using the new set of state probabilities following nodes 16, 18, 20, and 22, we compute

$$E_3 = (3)(0.3) + (2.70)(0.4) + (4)(0.3) = 3.18$$

Thus 3.18 is the value of a third interview at nodes 16, 18, 20, and 22 and is written above those nodes. Since this exceeds the value 3 at nodes 17 and 21, double slashes are placed through the "don't interview" branches emanating from decision nodes 10 and 13. Here, if a good salesperson were interviewed on the second interview, the number 3.18 indicates a higher expected value for the decision to continue interviewing than the decision to stop with that good salesperson.

Continuing in this fashion, we see that the expected value of a second interview is

$$E_2 = (3.18)(0.3) + (3.18)(0.3) + (4)(0.4) = 3.508$$

This number is written above nodes 6 and 8 and indicates that a double slash should be put through the *D* branch emanating from decision node 3.

Although we now have enough information to determine the interviewer's optimal strategy just by following our reasoning through the tree in reverse, from node 1 to the end, let's go ahead and determine the expected value of that optimal decision sequence (strategy). It is

$$E_1 = (3.508)(0.3) + (3.508)(0.2) + (4)(0.5) = 3.754$$

This is a fairly high value relative to 4, the value of a super salesperson. The expected value of the optimal strategy is almost as good as the value we would achieve by just getting lucky and encountering a super salesperson. In fact, it indicates that the probability for finding a super salesperson is quite high if that optimal strategy is used.

The optimal strategy is now obvious from the tree in Figure 9.3. It is

*First interview:* If super, hire the prospect and stop. If adequate or good, conduct a second interview.

*Second interview:* If super, stop. If adequate or good, conduct a third interview.

*Third interview:* If super, stop. If good, stop. If adequate, conduct a fourth interview.

To conclude this section, let's calculate the probabilities of ending the day of interviewing with an adequate, good, or super salesperson. If the optimal policy is used, then

$$P(\text{adequate}) = (0.5)(0.6)(0.4)(0.5) = 0.06$$

$$P(\text{good}) = (0.5)(0.6)[0.3 + (0.4)(0.3)] = 0.126$$

$$P(\text{super}) = 0.5 + (0.5)\{0.4 + (0.6)[0.3 + (0.4)(0.2)]\} = 0.814$$

These probabilities, as they should, add to unity. It would be an excellent exercise for you to follow through the reasoning (look at the tree) used to obtain them. Just as we anticipated, there exists a high probability (0.814) that the strategy will produce a super salesperson. Further, an alternate calculation of the expected value of the optimal strategy is

$$E_1 = (2)(0.06) + (3)(0.126) + (4)(0.814) = 3.754$$

This simply verifies the validity of our treatment of expected values as "values" like 2 or 3 or 4 when we worked our way through the decision tree.

## 9.6   UTILITY

The concept of expected payoff and of selecting the maximum-expected-payoff (minimum-risk) strategy has seemed a reasonable approach to decision problems for which probabilistic information is available. But sometimes it *does not* direct us to the strategy *actually selected* by a decision maker. Often, especially in order to avoid the event of a large loss, albeit one with a small probability, a person may choose to adopt a strategy different from the one declared optimal by the minimum-risk criterion. Or it may be that a person will choose a riskier strategy in the hope of realizing a large payoff.

Such decision makers are not necessarily behaving irrationally; we have already seen situations in which a different decision criterion than minimum risk might be used because of the "philosophy" of the company or of the decision maker. When relatively small amounts of money are at stake, the rational person will ordinarily be quite satisfied with the maximum-expectation philosophy of the minimum-risk criterion. But as the stakes get higher, as potential losses or profits become very large, the *preference* of the decision maker begins to play a greater role in the decision-making process. These preferences may be incorporated into that process using the concept called *utility*.

Now there are various types of settings in which the idea of utility proves useful, not all of which specifically involve monetary payoffs. "Utility" as used here simply means one's perception of the real value of a promised payoff from that person's unique, individual point of view. For most people, for instance, "respect" has a fairly high utility in terms of satisfaction value, not necessarily a monetary concept. A simple ranking of opportunities would imply that a higher-ranked opportunity has a higher utility to a person, but another person might rank them differently, so the same opportunity would have different utilities to different people. However, since the types of decisions we have been considering have involved monetary payoffs, we will continue in that mode, discussing henceforth only the *utility for money*.

Central to incorporating the utility for money (utility) into a decision problem is the *utility curve*. This is just a smooth curve that exhibits one's utility as a function of monetary units, say dollars. In the mathematical theory of utility it is proved that a maximum-expected-utility strategy is always the same as the most preferred strategy of a rational decision maker. Theoretically, then, if we have a procedure for determining maximum expected utility, we have the *ideal decision rule*. But that theory assumes we are using the precise utility curve unique to that decision maker, in practice very nearly an impossibility. Still, the theory suggests it is worthwhile to try approximating that utility curve and to incorporate it into the decision-making process.

Although various mixes are sometimes encountered because of a person's changing perceptions of money over time, there are really only three basic shapes for utility curves, the shapes shown in Figure 9.4. All of these curves reflect the tendency for everyone (except antiestablishment types, perhaps) to have a "positive marginal utility for money," that is, for higher monetary amounts to have higher utilities. The concave downward curve in Figure 9.4 (I) is characteristic of a person averse to risk, with a decreasing (though still positive) marginal utility for money. To such a person, the $100 difference between having $500 and having $600 has more utility than the $100 difference between having $10,000 and having $10,100. Most of us who work for wages would be characterized as averse to risk in the sense that, to us, $10,000 is so much money to have on hand that we can't see much difference between that amount and $10,100, while $500 and $600 are more commonplace quantities, and the $100 difference seems more important. We would not accept the same risk at the $10,000 level to acquire an extra $100 as we would at the $500 level.

Figure 9.4 (II) characterizes a person whose marginal utility is linear, who perceives a $100 difference as simply that; $100 more than $10,000 is just as worthwhile seeking as $100 more than $500. For this person, maximum expected utility is equivalent to maximum expected payoff. The curve in Figure 9.4 (III) is the gambler's utility curve, or the curve associated with speculative management. It implies a willingness to take more risk for large payoffs, the utility for large amounts of money being quite high.

From curves such as those shown in Figure 9.4, payoffs in dollars can be converted to utilities. One simply reads up to the curve from the dollar amount, then across to the vertical axis for the corresponding utility. Once the utilities are known, the calculation of expected utility is done in the same way it was for expected payoffs, only now utilities are substituted for payoffs.

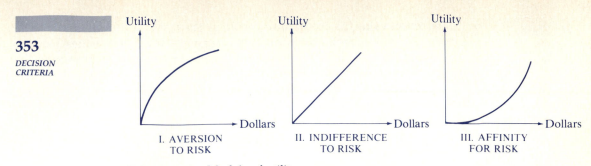

*FIGURE 9.4*    Models of utility curves

### Example 9.13
### Approximating a Utility Curve

To approximate the utility curve for a particular decision maker we use the idea of the *expected utility of a gamble*. This idea is fairly simple. The gamble is this: The decision maker is offered two theoretical choices, receive an amount of money $A$ with certainty, or participate in a lottery for which the probability of winning an amount $A_1$ is $p$ and of winning an amount $A_2$ is $(1 - p)$. The decision maker is asked to specify the probability $p$ for which she would be indifferent to the two choices. Then the utility of amount $A$ is the same as the expected utility of the lottery, or

$$u(A) = pu(A_1) + (1 - p)u(A_2)$$

where $u(A_i)$ means the utility of the amount $A_i$.

The way this is usually done in practice will be illustrated within the framework of Example 9.10 and the payoff table that was Table 9.15. We will not want to go on to the revision of probabilities using Bayes' theorem, however. It suffices for this utility example to assume equiprobable states and no extra information. Table 9.20 just repeats Table 9.15 for easy reference, and includes the probabilities.

Now in the lottery mentioned previously, we will want $A_1$ to be less than or equal to the minimum payoff in Table 9.20 and $A_2$ to be greater

*TABLE 9.20*   *THE PAYOFF TABLE*

| | | State | |
|---|---|---|---|
| **Strategy** | *E* | *N* | *C* |
| $S_1$ | $400,000 | $200,000 | -$100,000 |
| $S_2$ | $350,000 | $150,000 | 0 |
| $S_3$ | $200,000 | $150,000 | $100,000 |
| **Probability** | $\frac{1}{3}$ | $\frac{1}{3}$ | $\frac{1}{3}$ |

than or equal to the maximum payoff in that table. But we should not make the amounts too different from those low and high values because we want the decision maker's mind to be thinking about quantities in the neighborhood of the quantities in the problem to be solved. This also gives a dollar scale that includes all payoffs in the table.

A utility scale (not the money scale, but the vertical scale for the utility curve) can have any arbitrary range, since really it is only relative utilities that will interest us. For convenience, however, a commonly used scale is the interval from zero to one; that is, for any amount $A$ the utility of $A$ is a number between zero and one. Symbolically then, we have

$$0 \leq u(A) \leq 1$$

Suppose we choose $A_1 = -\$200,000$ and $A_2 = \$500,000$, assigning the following two utility values:

$$u(-\$200,000) = 0$$

$$u(\$500,000) = 1$$

Then any amount $A$ between $-\$200,000$ and $\$500,000$ (all payoffs in the table fall in that range) has a utility between 0 and 1.

Now we proceed to the lottery for determining the decision maker's utility curve. We already know two points on the curve: $(-\$200,000, 0)$ and $(\$500,000, 1)$. One more point, along with the knowledge that the decision maker tends to be conservative, optimistic, or neither, and in conjunction with the appropriate model curve from Figure 9.4, should suffice for a fair approximation to the curve.

We establish the hypothetical setting of a jar that contains 100 marbles, some white and some black. We tell the decision maker that if she draws a white marble, she loses $\$200,000$ (only theoretically, of course), while if she draws a black marble, she wins $\$500,000$. Or, as an alternative, she could receive, say, $\$100,000$ for certain and not play the marble game at all.

Once the decision maker has fully understood these two choices, we next ask her to tell us how many white marbles in that jar of 100 would cause her not to favor one option over the other. For example, if there were *no* white marbles, she would elect to draw from the jar, being assured of $\$500,000$. If there were *100* white marbles, she would want to take the $\$100,000$-certain option. Somewhere between those two extremes lies her indifference point.

Suppose she decides that 20 white marbles represents her indifference point. Then she is telling us that $p = 0.2$ in the equation

$$u(\$100,000) = pu(-\$200,000) + (1 - p)u(\$500,000)$$

Since we know that $u(-\$200,000) = 0$, $u(\$500,000) = 1$, and $p = 0.2$, then

$$u(\$100,000) = (0.2)(0) + (0.8)(1) = 0.8$$

That is, according to her individual preference, the utility of $100,000 is 0.8 if the utility of $-$200,000 is 0 and the utility of $500,000 is 1.

Is she a risk avoider, a risk seeker, or neither? Well, the expected *payoff* for her indifference gamble is

$$E(\text{payoff}) = (0.2)(-\$200,000) + (0.8)(\$500,000)$$

$$= \$360,000$$

Thus, by saying she would accept $100,000 or the opportunity to draw a marble, with indifference, she is really saying she would willingly give up the opportunity to gamble with an expected payoff of $360,000 for a sure-thing payment of $100,000. Thus she has the tendency to be averse to risk. This says that her utility curve would be best approximated by a shape like Figure 9.4 (I). Knowing that, we know that Figure 9.5 would be a fair representation of her personal utility curve.

### Example 9.14
### The Maximum-Expected-Utility Decision

Now we can work Example 9.10, just with equally likely states, using the criterion of maximum expected utility. All we have to do is replace Table 9.20, the payoff table, with Table 9.21, the utility table, converting payoffs to utilities using Figure 9.5. The entries in the table, of course, are only as accurate as they can be read from the curve.

Then, with $E(u_j)$ denoting the expected utility of strategy $S_j$, we obtain

$$E(u_1) = (0.99)(\tfrac{1}{3}) + (0.90)(\tfrac{1}{3}) + (0.40)(\tfrac{1}{3})$$

$$\approx 0.763$$

$$E(u_2) = (0.97)(\tfrac{1}{3}) + (0.84)(\tfrac{1}{3}) + (0.66)(\tfrac{1}{3})$$

$$\approx 0.823$$

$$E(u_3) = (0.90)(\tfrac{1}{3}) + (0.84)(\tfrac{1}{3}) + (0.80)(\tfrac{1}{3})$$

$$\approx 0.847 \leftarrow max$$

The strategy selected by the criterion of maximum expected utility, using the approximate utility curve for this particular individual, is strategy $S_3$. But back in Example 9.10 the maximum expected *payoff* occurred when either strategy $S_1$ or strategy $S_2$ was used (only assuming equiprobable states and no extra information). The concept of utility in this situation completely changed the decision.

Note that our decision maker has been identified as a conservative, risk-avoiding person. Reference to the payoff table, Table 9.20, reminds us that strategy $S_3$ would be a safe, conservative strategy (it is, in fact, the maximin strategy that was discussed in Section 9.1). Utility has success-fully incorporated into the problem the decision maker's preference, or

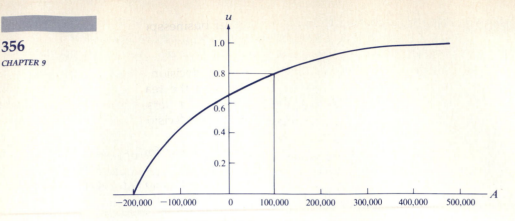

**FIGURE 9.5**    The decision maker's utility curve

philosophy, and in a fairly objective manner.  Essentially we have, for this individual, *quantified* the philosophy "conservatism."

Finally, you should realize that such utility analyses can be substituted anywhere for analyses involving monetary values.  You only need to convert monetary amounts to utilities using the appropriate utility curve.  That is, analyses such as the ones we have done with payoff tables and decision trees can be done in exactly the same fashion as we have done them, except with utilities being substituted for payoffs.

## 9.7   SUMMARY AND CONCLUSIONS

Decision theory may be studied as a mathematical theory of economic behavior which includes not only the basic ideas presented in this chapter but also the theory of games.  Here we have chosen to abstract from that mathematical theory the most elementary and useful notions as applied to real business decision problems.  Some ideas from game theory have been included, but only in the sense that we have regarded the decision problem as a "game" played against nature rather than a game played

**TABLE 9.21**    *THE UTILITY TABLE*

| Strategy | State | | |
|---|---|---|---|
| | E | N | C |
| $S_1$ | 0.99 | 0.90 | 0.40 |
| $S_2$ | 0.97 | 0.84 | 0.66 |
| $S_3$ | 0.90 | 0.84 | 0.80 |
| **Probability** | $\frac{1}{3}$ | $\frac{1}{3}$ | $\frac{1}{3}$ |

against a competitor such as another businessperson. Although mathematical game theory does consider such competitive situations, very little of a useful, practical nature has come from it.

The central, most applicable ideas in decision theory are the notions of expected payoff or expected utility and the realization that the type of decision made depends upon the type of person making the decision. Further, any information pertinent to the decision should be incorporated into the decision-making process.

The two basic types of decisions are those for which only the payoffs and the possible states of nature are known, and those for which extra information in the form of probabilities is also included. Only in the second of those two situations, the presence of probabilistic information, does analysis involving expectations apply. Otherwise, one is obliged to use a nonprobabilistic decision criterion such as maximin, maximax, or minimax regret.

Bayesian analysis can be used to modify prior probabilities by computing posterior (conditional) probabilities that reflect updating of the problem after extra information becomes available. Then the standard minimum-risk analysis used throughout most of this chapter becomes a modified, *conditional* minimum-risk approach. Problems in which the extra information for a Bayesian analysis comes from sampling, or is statistical in nature, will be considered in Chapter 10.

The concept of utility is a very interesting way of incorporating personal characteristics of a decision maker into an ordinary analysis involving expectations. It offers a formalized approach to merging the idea of a person's individual philosophy with the more mathematical notion of expected value. Since theoretically a theory of utility can produce an ideal decision rule, an appreciation of the basic notion of utility can be most helpful to the businessperson who wishes to be successful.

The fact that expected value is only a long-run average value cannot be overemphasized. Even the decision to use a strategy with a high expected payoff can produce an unsatisfactory outcome if an unfavorable state of nature occurs. The phrase "minimum risk" sounds very good, but the key word in that phrase is *risk*. You must understand that because of risk, even the best of decision criteria can produce, in a particular instance, a bad decision.

## KEY WORDS AND PHRASES

**Payoff table**  A table listing all possible payoffs associated with each strategy and for every potential state of nature.

**Maximin criterion**  The decision criterion that selects the strategy associated with the maximum of the minimum payoffs for each strategy. The pessimistic criterion.

**Maximax criterion**  The decision criterion that selects the strategy associated with the maximum of the maximum payoffs for each strategy. The optimistic criterion.

**Regret table**   A table showing, for each state and strategy, the monetary amount by which one would regret having chosen that strategy if the state actually did occur.

**Minimax-regret criterion**   The decision criterion that selects the strategy associated with the minimum of the maximum regrets for each strategy.

**Maximum-expected-payoff criterion**   The decision criterion used if probabilities for each state are known and the objective is to select the strategy with the highest expected payoff.

**Loss table**   A table listing all possible losses (negative payoffs) associated with each strategy and for every potential state of nature.

**Risk**   The expected loss for a given strategy.

**Minimum-risk criterion**   Another name for the maximum-expected-payoff criterion. It chooses the strategy associated with the smallest of the risks for all strategies.

**Expected value of perfect information (EVPI)**   The difference between the expected payoff given perfect information and the payoff associated with the minimum-risk strategy.

**Opportunity loss**   The amount of payoff given up by not selecting the strategy that produces maximum payoff for a given state of nature. The same thing as regret.

**Minimum-expected-opportunity loss**   Equal to the expected value of perfect information; it provides an alternative procedure for finding EVPI.

**Bayes' theorem**   A restatement of the multiplication theorem in such a way that the conditional probability for a state given extra information may be computed.

**Decision tree**   A diagram of a sequential decision problem, with individual branches associated with potential decisions and upon which sequential results of expected value calculations may be exhibited.

**Utility**   A person's perception of the real value of a promised payoff.

**Utility curve**   A curve that exhibits a person's utility as a function of monetary units.

**Expected utility of a gamble**   $pu(A_1) + (1 - p)u(A_2)$, where $A_1$ will be won with probability $p$ and $A_2$ will be won with probability $1 - p$. Used to approximate a person's utility curve.

**Utility table**   A table listing utilities for each strategy and each state of nature, those utilities being obtained from the approximate utility curve of the decision maker.

**Maximum-expected-utility criterion**   The decision criterion which selects the strategy that has the highest expected utility among all possible strategies. The strategy selected may differ from the one selected by the minimum-risk criterion.

## EXERCISES

**9.1** Consider the following payoff table for two strategies in the presence of two possible states of nature:

| | State | |
|---|---|---|
| **Strategy** | $N_1$ | $N_2$ |
| $S_1$ | $100 | $ 50 |
| $S_2$ | −$100 | $200 |

Select a strategy using each of the following decision criteria:
**a** Maximax     **c** Minimax regret
**b** Maximin     **d** Minimum risk, assuming equiprobable states

◆ **9.2** Following is a payoff table for three strategies and two states of nature:

| | State | |
|---|---|---|
| **Strategy** | $N_1$ | $N_2$ |
| $S_1$ | $40 | $60 |
| $S_2$ | $10 | −$20 |
| $S_3$ | −$40 | $150 |

Select a strategy using each of the following decision criteria:
**a** Maximax     **c** Minimax regret
**b** Maximin     **d** Minimum risk, assuming equiprobable states

**9.3** Consider the following payoff table (payoffs in thousands of dollars) for three strategies in the presence of four possible states of nature:

| | State | | | |
|---|---|---|---|---|
| **Strategy** | $N_1$ | $N_2$ | $N_3$ | $N_4$ |
| $S_1$ | 200 | 400 | −100 | 100 |
| $S_2$ | 300 | 200 | 100 | 0 |
| $S_3$ | 300 | 300 | 200 | −200 |

Select a strategy using each of the following decision criteria:
**a** Maximax     **c** Minimax regret
**b** Maximin     **d** Minimum risk, assuming equiprobable states
**e** For each of the above four criteria, hypothesize a type of company or decision situation where you think the choice of criterion is meaningful.

◆ **9.4** You are a general faced with the problem of deciding between two competing strategies for the battle to begin tomorrow. You will make many similar decisions throughout the war. The loss table for the battle appears below, where the entries are the anticipated numbers of casualties on your side.

| | State | |
|---|---|---|
| **Strategy** | **Win battle** | **Lose battle** |
| $S_1$ | 100,000 | 300,000 |
| $S_2$ | 50,000 | 350,000 |

Your current estimates of the strength of the enemy forces and the opinions of your senior officers have suggested that the following two probabilities hold, regardless of the strategy chosen:

$$P(\text{win battle}) = 0.6 \qquad P(\text{lose battle}) = 0.4$$

What is your minimum-risk strategy?

✦ **9.5** Your company has $50,000 available for investment. You are considering two competing investment strategies: (1) invest in municipal bonds with a guaranteed annual interest rate of 5 percent and (2) purchase new equipment costing $50,000 which, if a favorable state of the economy occurs, will yield an annual profit of $10,000. However, if an unfavorable state of the economy occurs, this approach will generate a $20,000 annual loss.

What probability must you ascribe to the favorable state of the economy in order to be indifferent between strategy 1 and strategy 2? How would that hypothetical probability help you make a decision between the two?

**9.6** You are in the habit of attending weekend races at a small quarterhorse track near your home. The starting gate at this track can only accommodate six horses, and there are enough breeders in the area to assure that each race will always have six horses in it.

You know nothing about quarterhorses, but you have a friend who does. You have kept records on your friend's selections and have learned that on the average he picks the winner in one of every three races. On the other hand, you have been picking horses at random and have been averaging one winner per seven races.

The bookies at this little track always assign odds of 1 to 1 (even money), 2 to 1, 3 to 1, 4 to 1, 6 to 1, and 10 to 1 to the six horses. Your friend's selections never get better than 4 to 1 odds.

You have two potential betting strategies in mind: (1) $S_1$: Wager on friend's selection if it has 4 to 1 odds. Otherwise, pass the race; that is, don't bet. (2) $S_2$: Wager on random selection if it has 10 to 1 odds. Otherwise, pass the race.

　**a** Which strategy will you choose?

　**b** Suppose that in a given race you make a random selection and find that it is assigned 10 to 1 odds, while your friend makes his educated selection and it is assigned 4 to 1 odds. Would you be willing to buy win tickets on *both* horses in the same race?

　**c** Do you think that your average of one winner per seven races using random selection is consistent with there being only six horses in any race? That is, does your experimental probability agree with the theoretical probability? If not, would you like to reconsider your answers in parts *a* and *b* above, using the theoretical probability? If so, do so.

　**d** What critical assumptions have you made about observed relative frequencies of winners and the assignment of odds in order to say that $S_1$ and $S_2$ are profitable?

✦ **9.7** You have just started a small company devoted to the manufacture of specialty items on a contract basis. The company has been invited to bid for the right to supply 50,000 whimmers to the Abecee Corporation.

Two different whimmer-making machines are available: type $X$ and type $Y$. A type $X$ machine costs $25,000 and type $Y$ costs $40,000. Using type $X$ the variable cost per whimmer manufactured is $1.75, while with type $Y$ the cost per whimmer is only $1.20.

Both suppliers, the X Company and the Y Company, will cancel your order for a machine if you don't get the contract since they have the machines already in stock. You should allocate the entire cost of a machine to your bid because there will be no salvage value and you probably will never again make any whimmers.

The bid is to be quoted on a "price per whimmer" basis. You are considering two bids, and have estimated probabilities, as shown below:

|  | Price per whimmer | Probability of winning bid |
|---|---|---|
| Bid 1 | $2.50 | $\frac{1}{3}$ |
| Bid 2 | $2.20 | $\frac{3}{4}$ |

a Is it possible to win the bid yet lose money in this situation?
b Using the minimum-risk criterion, what should you bid and what type of machine should be purchased if you win the bidding contest?

◆ **9.8** Consider Exercise 9.2. With equiprobable states, compute the expected value of perfect information using two different procedures.

**9.9** Consider Exercise 9.3. With equiprobable states, compute EVPI using two different procedures.

◆ **9.10** Consider the payoff table for Example 9.10, Table 9.15, and assume $P(E) = \frac{1}{4}$, $P(N) = \frac{1}{4}$, $P(C) = \frac{1}{2}$.
  a Construct the opportunity loss table.
  b What is the minimum-expected-opportunity-loss strategy?
  c What is the expected value of perfect information?

◆ **9.11** Suppose, in Exercise 9.4, that if you were to win the battle, it would be extremely unlikely that the enemy would have used their new "weapon $X$." In fact, you can say

$$P(\text{enemy used weapon } X|\text{we win}) = 0.1$$

$$P(\text{enemy used weapon } X|\text{we lose}) = 0.7$$

If G-2 reports that the enemy will use weapon $X$ tomorrow, what is your conditional minimum-risk strategy?

**9.12** Suppose that in the absence of additional information you would assume equiprobable states in Exercise 9.3. However, now you have received further information, $I$. You know that

$$P(I|N_1) = 0.3 \qquad P(I|N_2) = 0.5 \qquad P(I|N_3) = 0.4 \qquad P(I|N_4) = 0.3$$

Using the criterion of conditional minimum risk, which strategy will you select?

◆ **9.13** East Bygd, Greenland, is inhabited by two Eskimos, husband and wife. The man hunts daily, and if he makes a kill, it will be either a seal or a walrus. If he kills nothing by 4:00 P.M., he will fish for an hour or so. He can always catch fish.

He returns daily between 5:00 and 6:00 P.M. and, upon nearing the igloo, shouts either "Walrus!" or "Seal!" or "Fish!" The wife will reply in kind, shouting one of those three words. Depending upon her answer, she will gain or lose some leisure time—hours' relief from chores, such as skinning a walrus by herself—according to the following payoff table:

| Strategy (wife's reply) | State (what husband brings home) | | |
|---|---|---|---|
| | Walrus | Seal | Fish |
| Walrus | 5 | 2 | −1 |
| Seal | 2 | 3 | −$\frac{1}{2}$ |
| Fish | −4 | −1 | 1 |

Over a period of time, the wife has been keeping records of how often certain events occur. A portion of her record appears below:

$$P(\text{husband brings walrus}) = \tfrac{1}{20}$$

$$P(\text{husband brings seal}) = \tfrac{1}{10}$$

$$P(\text{husband brings fish}) = \tfrac{17}{20}$$

$$P(\text{husband shouts "Walrus!"}|\text{he brings walrus}) = \tfrac{3}{5}$$

$$P(\text{husband shouts "Walrus!"}|\text{he brings seal}) = \tfrac{1}{5}$$

$$P(\text{husband shouts "Walrus!"}|\text{he brings fish}) = \tfrac{1}{5}$$

What is the wife's conditional minimum-risk strategy whenever her husband shouts "Walrus!"?

**9.14** Using the probabilities $P(E) = \tfrac{1}{4}$, $P(N) = \tfrac{1}{4}$, $P(C) = \tfrac{1}{2}$, and the percentages in Table 9.16, find the conditional minimum-risk strategy for the ENC Corporation problem, Example 9.10.

◆ **9.15** Producto Corporation has experienced a substantial increase in sales during the past few years. In order to keep up with demand it appears necessary to expand production facilities. Of course, Producto could decide to do nothing to keep up with anticipated demand, simply keeping up existing facilities with minimal maintenance. They could also modernize the existing facilities, contract some of the work to a subcontractor, or build a new, additional plant.

The four potential strategies will produce different profits in conjunction with any of five perceived states of nature in the future: drastically declining demand ($D_1$), slightly declining demand ($D_2$), no change in demand ($D_3$), moderately increasing demand ($D_4$), and substantially increasing demand ($D_5$). Profits for each strategy under each state have been estimated, as well as probabilities for the occurrences of each state. These estimates are given in the following table (profits are in dollars):

| | Type of future demand | | | | |
|---|---|---|---|---|---|
| **Strategy** | $D_1$ | $D_2$ | $D_3$ | $D_4$ | $D_5$ |
| Maintenance | 300,000 | 200,000 | 25,000 | − 50,000 | − 100,000 |
| Modernization | 200,000 | 100,000 | 10,000 | − 25,000 | − 50,000 |
| Subcontracting | − 25,000 | − 10,000 | 0 | 25,000 | 100,000 |
| New plant | − 500,000 | − 400,000 | − 200,000 | 200,000 | 500,000 |
| $P(D_i)$ | 0.15 | 0.15 | 0.15 | 0.30 | 0.25 |

**a** What is Producto's minimum-risk strategy?

**b** Suppose now that Producto receives word $W$ that the price of a commodity whose demand is highly correlated with demand for their product is going up. Producto has established the following probabilities: $P(W|D_1) = 0.05$, $P(W|D_2) = 0.10$, $P(W|D_3) = 0.15$, $P(W|D_4) = 0.25$, $P(W|D_5) = 0.30$. Is Producto's conditional minimum-risk strategy different from the minimum-risk strategy found in part $a$?

**9.16** In Exercise 9.15, change the probabilities in the table to $P(D_1) = 0.05$, $P(D_2) = 0.10$, $P(D_3) = 0.15$, $P(D_4) = 0.40$, $P(D_5) = 0.30$. Now what are the answers to part $a$ and part $b$? (Keep the given conditional probabilities in part $b$ the same as before.)

◆ **9.17** In Exercise 9.15, find the optimal strategy using:
  **a** The maximin criterion
  **b** The maximax criterion
  **c** The minimax-regret criterion

◆ **9.18** In Exercise 9.15, find EVPI (ignoring the information $W$).

**9.19** In Exercise 9.16, find EVPI (ignoring the information $W$).

◆ **9.20** A produce buyer for a local grocery faces the same problem every morning. She competes with a buyer from another grocery for tomatoes. In the produce market there are two stalls displaying tomatoes coming from two farms in the area. Each morning the buyers pass along, one behind the other, inspecting tomatoes. Once the decision is made to purchase from a stall, the whole supply is purchased. This leaves the remaining stall for the other buyer.

The two buyers have agreed that each morning they will flip a coin to see who gets to proceed first. This morning our first buyer has won the toss. She has the following information available.

The probabilities that stall 1 will have good, fair, or bad tomatoes are 0.5, 0.3, and 0.2, respectively. The probabilities that stall 2 will have good, fair, or bad tomatoes are 0.4, 0.3, and 0.3. If the first buyer obtains good tomatoes, profit to her store is $100 for the day. If fair, the profit is $50, and if bad tomatoes are purchased, the store will lose $20.

If she passes by stall 1 she cannot return, for in that case the other buyer will purchase the stall 1 tomatoes. What is her optimal strategy for buying tomatoes today? Is minimum risk a good criterion in this situation? (She can, of course, know the quality of tomatoes she sees.)

✦ **9.21** If the first buyer in Exercise 9.20 uses her optimal strategy, what is her store's expected profit?

✦ **9.22** If the first buyer in Exercise 9.20 uses her optimal strategy, what are the respective probabilities she will wind up with good, fair, or bad tomatoes? Use those probabilities to verify your answer for Exercise 9.21.

**9.23** Consider the problem in Exercise 9.20. Suppose that the other buyer had won the coin toss. Assume both buyers act optimally. Now what is the expected profit to the first buyer's store (she now proceeds second in line)? *Before* the toss of the coin, what is a store's expected profit?

**9.24** Newmaker, Inc., has been doing quite well distributing and selling its whuzzers within Wyoming but is considering the possibility of western regional or even national distribution. The more widely whuzzers are distributed, the more advertising will be necessary.

A whuzzer costs $5 to produce and sells for $10. Cost per whuzzer for advertising and distribution is $0.50 if they are only distributed locally, while the corresponding costs for regional and national distribution are, respectively, $1.50 and $3.00.

Probability distributions of annual demand ($d$ = number of whuzzers) for local, regional, and national distribution are given below.

| Local | | Regional | | National | |
|---|---|---|---|---|---|
| $d$ | $p(d)$ | $d$ | $p(d)$ | $d$ | $p(d)$ |
| 8,000 | 0.2 | 14,000 | 0.1 | 22,000 | 0.2 |
| 6,000 | 0.3 | 8,000 | 0.4 | 14,000 | 0.2 |
| 4,000 | 0.3 | 5,000 | 0.3 | 8,000 | 0.3 |
| 2,000 | 0.2 | 3,000 | 0.2 | 4,000 | 0.3 |

Using a decision tree and the criterion of maximum expected profit, determine whether Newmaker should advertise and distribute whuzzers locally, regionally, or nationally.

✦ **9.25** Trustworthy Oil Company has $60,000 to invest. They are considering four alternatives: investing in a wildcat well, drilling deeper in a dry but once-producing well, refurbishing a producing well, or investing in municipal bonds at 5 percent annual interest. Investment in the wildcat will cost $60,000, drilling deeper costs $50,000, and refurbishing the producing well will cost $20,000. If an option costing less than $60,000 is elected, the remainder of the available money will be invested in municipal bonds at 5 percent.

The following table gives relevant probabilities and profits on an annual basis. Which alternative gives the maximum expected annual profit?

| Wildcat | | Drilling deeper | |
|---|---|---|---|
| **Probability** | **Profit** | **Probability** | **Profit** |
| $P(\text{oil}) = 0.10$ | \$385,000 | $P(\text{oil}) = 0.20$ | \$200,000 |
| $P(\text{gas}) = 0.20$ | \$ 50,000 | $P(\text{gas}) = 0.05$ | \$ 75,000 |
| $P(\text{dry}) = 0.70$ | $-\$ 60,000$ | $P(\text{dry}) = 0.75$ | $-\$ 50,000$ |

| Refurbishing | |
|---|---|
| **Probability** | **Profit** |
| $P(\text{improve}) = 0.60$ | \$20,000 |
| $P(\text{no change}) = 0.30$ | $-\$20,000$ |
| $P(\text{worse}) = 0.10$ | $-\$40,000$ |

**9.26** Refer to Exercise 9.25. Suppose that after six months' time there will arise the opportunity to earn 10 percent annually in the next six months on money that has been invested in municipal bonds. Considering only the annual profit for the first year, which alternative is best now? Which alternative is best if the six-months' earnings rate is 12 percent?

✦ **9.27** Refer back to Example 9.13. Suppose the decision maker states that 80 white marbles represents her indifference point between drawing a marble or accepting \$100,000 certain.
    **a** Is this decision maker a risk avoider or a risk seeker?
    **b** What is her approximate utility curve?

✦ **9.28** Using the utility curve established in Exercise 9.27, part *b*, find the maximum-expected-utility strategy for the problem worked earlier in Chapter 9 as Example 9.14.

**9.29** For the payoff table in Exercise 9.3 and with equiprobable states, use the utility curve developed in Example 9.13 to find the maximum-expected-utility strategy.

**9.30** For the payoff table in Exercise 9.3 and with equiprobable states, use the utility curve developed in Exercise 9.27, part *b*, to find the maximum-expected-utility strategy.

**9.31** Assume that the decision maker of Exercise 9.27 has the responsibility for the Trustworthy Oil Company decision in Exercise 9.25. If she uses a maximum-expected-utility criterion, which alternative will she choose?

## SELECTED REFERENCES

Ackoff, R. L., and M. W. Sasieni: *Fundamentals of Operations Research,* John Wiley
    & Sons, Inc., New York, 1968.

Anderson, D. R., D. J. Sweeney, and T. A. Williams: *An Introduction to Management Science*, 3d ed., West Publishing Company, St. Paul, Minn., 1982.

Cooke, W. P.: "Beginning Statistics at the Track," *Mathematics Magazine*, vol. 46, 1973, pp. 250–255.

Gaver, D. P., and G. L. Thompson: *Programming and Probability Models in Operations Research*, Brooks/Cole Publishing Company, Monterey, Calif., 1973.

Hamburg, M.: *Basic Statistics: A Modern Approach*, Harcourt Brace Jovanovich, New York, 1974.

Hoel, P. G., and R. J. Jessen: *Basic Statistics for Business and Economics*, John Wiley & Sons, Inc., New York, 1974.

Levin, R. I., C. A. Kirkpatrick, and D. S. Rubin: *Quantitative Approaches to Management*, 5th ed., McGraw-Hill Book Company, New York, 1982.

Thierauf, R. J., and R. C. Klekamp: *Decision Making Through Operations Research*, 2d ed., John Wiley & Sons, Inc., New York, 1975.

# STATISTICAL ESTIMATION AND FORECASTING

*I*n Chapter 8 you reviewed some basic probability notions, learned about random variables and probability distributions, and worked with the binomial and normal distributions. In Chapter 9 you considered decision making in the presence of probabilistic information. But most of that work involved just elementary probability theory, not statistics. Statistics implies the use of *sampling*.

This distinction is not always appreciated. If no sampling is done, no statistics are involved. The central interest of statisticians is in learning about populations using information contained in *samples* from those populations.

If you have taken a basic statistics course you will already be familiar with the two main types of statistical problems: estimation and hypothesis testing. In this chapter we consider only statistical *estimation* of population characteristics, including regression and forecasting techniques.

In Examples 8.22 and 8.26 of Chapter 8 you encountered problems involving sampling. Now we are ready to proceed further with the idea of using sampling information in managerial decision making. Since the notion of a statistic will be central to this discussion, first we must define a statistic.

A *statistic* is a random variable that takes on values according to the outcome of sampling.

The two most commonly used statistics are the sample mean, $\overline{X}$, and $S^2$, the sample variance. Another statistic is $\hat{P}$, the proportion of successes observed in a sample. Each of these statistics is used as an *estimator* for its population counterpart, here $\mu$, $\sigma^2$, and $p$, respectively.

Suppose that a random sample of size $n$ is taken from some population, and that numbers measuring the same characteristic for each unit in the sample are designated $x_1, x_2, \ldots, x_n$. Then the *values* of the statistics $\overline{X}$ and $S^2$ are calculated using the following formulas:

$$\overline{x} = \sum_{i=1}^{n} \frac{x_i}{n} \qquad s^2 = \sum_{i=1}^{n} \frac{(x_i - \overline{x})^2}{n - 1}$$

Suppose further that each unit in the sample is categorized as being either a success or a failure, and that $y$ is the number of successes observed in the sample. Then the value of $\hat{P}$ is

$$\hat{p} = \frac{y}{n}$$

Note the relationship of these three values to their counterparts in a population: $\mu$, $\sigma^2$, and $p$. The population mean $\mu$ is the weighted average for the population, with the weights being probabilities. The sample mean $\overline{x}$ is the average of the numbers in the sample. Because of the averaging procedure we might say that each number in the sample is given the weight $1/n$, which resembles a probability. Likewise, the population variance $\sigma^2$ is a weighted average squared deviation of population values from their mean $\mu$, while the sample variance $s^2$ is an "average" squared deviation of sample values from $\overline{x}$, the sample mean (the quotes on "average" remind us that the divisor is $n - 1$, not $n$). Finally, if $A$ is the number of successes in a population of size $N$, then $p = A/N$, while $\hat{p} = y/n$.

You should particularly notice the use of a lowercase letter to denote the value of a statistic, while a capital letter denotes the statistic itself. It is extremely important to distinguish between the *statistic*, which is a *random variable*, and *one of its values*, which is a *number*.

A statistic, remember, is a random variable, *not* a number. Although for a *particular* sample the *value* of $\overline{X}$ is a number, this value will be a different number for a different sample. That is, many different samples of the same size might be taken from the same population, with each sample having a different sample average $\bar{x}$. Thus $\overline{X}$ is a *variable* because its value may change from sample to sample, and it is a *random* variable because we cannot predict that value before sampling. The statistics $S^2$ and $\hat{P}$, of course, behave similarly.

A statistic that is used to estimate a population parameter is called an *estimator*, and its value for a particular sample is called the *estimate* of the parameter. The estimator is the *procedure* to be used (such as: Take a sample and calculate its average.), while the estimate is the *number* that the procedure yields for the particular sample that has been selected. Thus in an estimation problem the terms *estimator* and *statistic*, and *estimate* and *value*, respectively, may be used interchangeably, since they are synonymous.

## 10.2  SAMPLING DISTRIBUTIONS

The *sampling distribution* is the principal concept in the study of statistics. The sampling distribution ties together the important notions of probability, random variables and their distributions, and sampling. It is particularly important in the estimation problem, since it is the sampling distribution of an estimator that permits us to assess the *quality* of an estimator. For example, if we are planning to use $\hat{P}$ to estimate the true proportion $p$ of defective items in some large lot (population) of items, it would be a good idea to be able to say how well $\hat{P}$ performs as an estimator.

A *sampling distribution* is the probability distribution for a statistic (estimator).

The preceding definition reminds us that since an estimator is a random variable it could have an associated probability distribution (or density, if it is a continuous random variable). But the value of an estimator varies only from sample to sample, so one must, at least conceptually, consider many samples to appreciate the notion of a sampling distribution.

You have already studied, in Chapter 8, two very useful sampling distributions, although at that point we did not choose to emphasize that characteristic. Both the binomial and the standard normal distributions can be sampling distributions. The $n$ "trials" in the assumptions for the binomial distribution can represent a sample of size $n$, and $Y$, the number of successes observed in the sample of size $n$, is then a statistic whose sampling distribution is the binomial distribution. $Y$ of course varies from sample to sample, but given $p$ we can talk about the probabilities that $Y$ will take on various values or sets of values. From those probabilities we can also make probability statements about the estimator $\hat{P} = Y/n$. Likewise $\overline{X}$, the sample mean, when standardized, becomes a standard normal variable $Z$ (by the central limit theorem, Theorem 8.2 of Chapter

8). Since $\overline{X}$ is a statistic, so is $Z$, making the standard normal distribution a sampling distribution from which probabilities about $\overline{X}$ may be computed.

In a beginning statistics course you will have encountered other sampling distributions. The $t$ distribution of the statistic $(\overline{X} - \mu)/(S/\sqrt{n})$ is a sampling distribution since the statistics $\overline{X}$ and $S$ are involved in its definition. When $\sigma_1^2 = \sigma_2^2$, the ratio of two sample variances, $S_1^2/S_2^2$, has the $F$ distribution, a sampling distribution because $S_1^2$ and $S_2^2$ are statistics. Various forms of the chi-square distribution are sampling distributions whenever the value of the chi-square random variable is determined from sample data. In each case, whether binomial, normal, $t$, $F$, or chi-square statistics are involved, the sampling distribution permits us to discuss probabilistically how the values of the statistic vary from sample to sample.

## 10.3 ESTIMATING A MEAN: APPLYING THE CENTRAL LIMIT THEOREM

In Chapter 8 the central limit theorem was given as Theorem 8.2. It is stated again here for ease of reference:

*The central limit theorem.* If $X$ is a random variable representing a quantity that may be observed in some population, and if the mean $\mu$ and the variance $\sigma^2$ for $X$ exist, then if samples of size $n$ are taken from that population and for each sample the value of the sample average $\overline{X}$ is computed, the distribution of

$$Z = \frac{\overline{X} - \mu}{\sigma/\sqrt{n}}$$

approaches the standard normal distribution as $n$ gets larger and larger.

As was stated in Chapter 8, in practice the central limit theorem is interpreted as meaning that the random variable $\overline{X}$ has approximately a normal distribution with mean $\mu$ and variance $\sigma^2/n$ for sufficiently large $n$. In fact, if the sample size $n$ is 30 or more, the approximation is usually very good.

The basic result of the central limit theorem is the approximate normality of the estimator $\overline{X}$. But disregarding normality for the moment, let us look at two other interesting properties of $\overline{X}$.

Its average value, over all possible samples of the same size $n$, is $\mu$, the parameter it is trying to estimate. That is,

$$E(\overline{X}) = \mu$$

or the mean of the sampling distribution of the sample mean happens to be the population mean. This property of an estimator, its average value being the parameter it is estimating, is called *unbiasedness*. We say that $\overline{X}$ is an *unbiased* estimator for $\mu$. The statistics $S^2$ and $\hat{P}$ are also unbiased estimators for $\sigma^2$ and $p$, respectively. In fact, the divisor $n - 1$ in the definition formula for $s^2$ is used instead of the more logical $n$ since then $E(S^2) = \sigma^2$. Unbiasedness is generally a good property for an estimator to have.

But more than just unbiasedness is required of an estimator for it to be a "good" estimator. Unbiasedness means that the average value of the estimator, or the mean of its sampling distribution, is the parameter being estimated. However, if the variance of that sampling distribution is large, the estimator will vary considerably in value from sample to sample. On the other hand, if the estimator has small variance *and* is unbiased, then it is a *good* estimator since from sample to sample its values vary very little and tend to be near the parameter. The variance of $\overline{X}$, for instance, is $\sigma^2/n$, so we know that for larger and larger sample sizes, $\overline{X}$ becomes more dependable in the sense that its value, computed from *any* sample, will tend to be close to $\mu$. Figure 10.1 suggests the situation.

In Figure 10.1 the implications of the central limit theorem are made evident. The distribution of $\overline{X}$ for samples from almost any population, normal or not, is approximately normal. Further, $\overline{X}$ is an unbiased estimator for $\mu$, and its variance decreases with increasing sample size.

These observations have a definite bearing on assessments of the quality of $\overline{X}$ when used as an estimator for $\mu$. In Example 10.1 you will see how the central limit theorem permits us to discuss, in a probabilistic manner, the goodness of the estimator $\overline{X}$.

### Example 10.1

A government testing agency wants to estimate the average gasoline mileage for a new compact automobile. The agency has randomly selected $n = 49$ of the autos from the group of all such compacts manufactured

**FIGURE 10.1**    Implications of the central limit theorem

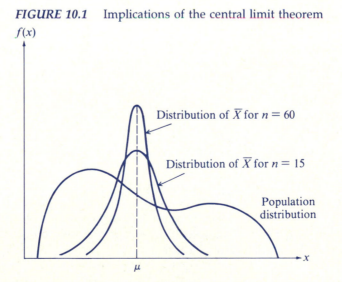

over a two-month period. Each of the 49 automobiles was driven for the same number of miles over the same range of varying driving conditions, and a gasoline mileage figure was obtained for each. The average miles per gallon was observed to be $\bar{x} = 38.4$, and the variance for that sample was $s^2 = 4.0$.

If $\mu$ is the average miles per gallon for the whole group of cars, then obviously the estimate of $\mu$ is $\bar{x} = 38.4$. But how close is 38.4 to the actual value of $\mu$; that is, how good is this estimate? Without knowing the true value of $\mu$, that question is impossible to answer.

Instead, we ask: How well does $\overline{X}$ perform as an *estimator* for $\mu$? To be more specific, we might ask: What is the probability (Pr) that $\overline{X}$ will assume a value within 0.5 miles per gallon of the true $\mu$? This is a question that can be answered using the central limit theorem, provided we assume that $n = 49$ is a large enough sample to cause us to believe that $s$ is approximately $\sigma$.

We write

$$\Pr(-0.5 \le \overline{X} - \mu \le 0.5) = \Pr\left(\frac{-0.5}{s/\sqrt{n}} \le \frac{\overline{X} - \mu}{s/\sqrt{n}} \le \frac{0.5}{s/\sqrt{n}}\right)$$

$$\approx \Pr\left(\frac{-0.5}{\frac{2}{7}} \le Z \le \frac{0.5}{\frac{2}{7}}\right)$$

$$= \Pr(-1.75 \le Z \le 1.75)$$

$$= 0.95994 - 0.04006 \qquad \text{From Table A.2}$$

$$= 0.91988$$

Thus if $\sigma$ is approximately 2 ($s = 2$), in about 92 percent of all such samples of size $n = 49$, the value of $\overline{X}$ will be within 0.5 miles per gallon of the true population mean, $\mu$.

This probability statement measures the quality of $\overline{X}$ as an estimator. What has it to say about the estimate from our *single* sample, the number $\bar{x} = 38.4$? Nothing. But we behave as if 38.4 is close to $\mu$, since before sampling there was a fairly high probability $\overline{X}$ would take on a value close to $\mu$.

### Example 10.2

Suppose the testing agency in Example 10.1 wants the probability to be 0.99 that $\overline{X}$ will assume a value within 0.5 miles per gallon from $\mu$. If again we assume $\sigma = 2$, how large a sample must be selected?

This is a *decision* problem, with the decision being the sample size $n$. How many cars should be selected from the group in order to be 99 percent sure that $\overline{X}$ will take on a value within 0.5 of $\mu$?

We begin as in Example 10.1, except this time the probability is known and we want to find $n$. Write

$$\Pr(-0.5 \le \overline{X} - \mu \le 0.5) = 0.99$$

$$\Pr\left(\frac{-0.5}{2/\sqrt{n}} \le Z \le \frac{0.5}{2/\sqrt{n}}\right) = 0.99$$

or

$$\Pr(-0.25\sqrt{n} \le Z \le 0.25\sqrt{n}) = 0.99$$

From Table A.2 we discover that

$$\Pr(-2.57 \le Z \le 2.57) \simeq 0.99$$

Then $0.25\sqrt{n}$ must equal 2.57. So we have

$$0.25\sqrt{n} = 2.57$$

$$\sqrt{n} = 10.28$$

$$n = 105.68$$

Thus to increase the probability from 0.92 to 0.99 we must increase the sample size from $n = 49$ to $n = 106$.

Examples 10.1 and 10.2 exhibit the role of a sampling distribution in an estimation problem. Knowledge of the sampling distribution allows us to make a probability statement about the quality of an estimator. Our faith in the *estimate* obtained from a *single sample* is strong if the probability is high that the estimator will take on a value close to the parameter it is trying to estimate.

Note that the variance was the key to probability in those examples. Since the variance of $\overline{X}$ is $\sigma^2/n$, for larger sample sizes $\overline{X}$ is less variable from sample to sample. Since $\overline{X}$ is also an unbiased estimator for $\mu$, small variance implies a high probability that $\overline{X}$ will be close to $\mu$.

Examples 10.1 and 10.2 were examples of what is commonly known as *point estimation*. We used $\bar{x}$, a single number, as our estimate of $\mu$. Another approach would be to obtain an *interval estimate* of $\mu$. In that approach we determine a random interval that has a high probability of capturing $\mu$. This probability is called the *confidence coefficient* for the interval, and the interval itself is called a *confidence interval*.

For the estimation of a mean the appropriate endpoints of the confidence interval with confidence coefficient $1 - \alpha$ are

Lower limit:
$$\overline{X} - z_{\alpha/2}\frac{\sigma}{\sqrt{n}}$$

Upper limit:
$$\overline{X} + z_{\alpha/2}\frac{\sigma}{\sqrt{n}}$$

where $z_{\alpha/2}$ is the value of a standard normal variable that cuts off an area to its right equal to $\alpha/2$. Figure 10.2 illustrates this definition of $z_{\alpha/2}$.

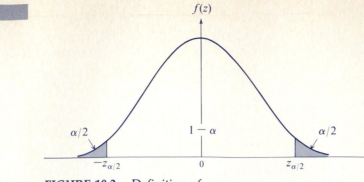

**FIGURE 10.2** Definition of $z_{\alpha/2}$

It is easy to verify that this random interval ($\overline{X}$ is a random variable *before* sampling) has a probability $1 - \alpha$ of capturing the true population mean $\mu$. Write

$$\Pr\left(\overline{X} - z_{\alpha/2}\frac{\sigma}{\sqrt{n}} < \mu < \overline{X} + z_{\alpha/2}\frac{\sigma}{\sqrt{n}}\right)$$

A bit of algebra will convert this to

$$\Pr\left(-z_{\alpha/2} < \frac{\overline{X} - \mu}{\sigma/\sqrt{n}} < z_{\alpha/2}\right) = \Pr(-z_{\alpha/2} < Z < z_{\alpha/2})$$

$$= 1 - \alpha \qquad \text{See Figure 10.2}$$

This probability statement can only be made *before sampling*, of course, since after the sample is obtained, $\bar{x}$ is a number, not a random variable. For a particular sample, we use the formulas for upper and lower limits to determine the endpoints of a specific interval. If we use $\alpha = 0.10$, for instance, we are 90 percent confident that our interval has captured $\mu$. That confidence comes from the observation that before sampling there was a probability of 0.90 that we would obtain a sample that would give an interval that catches $\mu$.

Before proceeding to an example of an interval estimate, we should notice that the formulas imply knowledge of $\sigma$, the population standard deviation. But just as we did in the point-estimation examples, for large samples we can replace $\sigma$ by $s$.

### Example 10.3

A retailer wishes to audit his inventory by randomly selecting $n = 200$ purchase invoices for unsold items in his stock. He desires a 99 percent confidence interval for the average purchase price per unsold item.

In this case $\alpha = 0.01$, so

$$z_{\alpha/2} = z_{0.005} = 2.58$$

The sample size $n = 200$ is large enough for him to safely presume that $s$ (the sample standard deviation) is approximately $\sigma$.

After sampling, the retailer determines that the average price per invoice in the sample is $\bar{x} = \$24.83$ and that the standard deviation of sampled invoice prices is $s = \$7.05$. Then

$$\text{Lower limit} = \bar{x} - 2.58\frac{s}{\sqrt{n}}$$

$$= 24.83 - 2.58\frac{7.05}{\sqrt{200}} = 23.54$$

$$\text{Upper limit} = \bar{x} + 2.58\frac{s}{\sqrt{n}}$$

$$= 24.83 + 2.58\frac{7.05}{\sqrt{200}} = 26.12$$

Thus the 99 percent confidence interval for $\mu$, the average purchase price for all unsold items, is the interval from \$23.54 to \$26.12.

Suppose further that the retailer has 2,500 unsold items in stock. Then multiplying the endpoints by 2,500 gives the interval

$$\$58{,}850 \text{ to } \$65{,}300$$

as a 99 percent confidence interval for the *total* purchase price of his entire remaining stock. (This result ignores the finite population correction factor we will be using in Section 10.5, but is still an adequate approximation.)

## 10.4 ESTIMATING PROPORTIONS IN LARGE POPULATIONS

A sample of size $n$ from a population in which $p$ is the proportion of elements in a certain class can be regarded as $n$ trials for which the probability of success (element is in the class) is $p$. If the sample is random, then successive trials are independent. If the population is very large relative to the sample size $n$, then $p$ does not vary appreciably from trial to trial. So we see that this experiment leads naturally to the binomial distribution of $Y$, the number of successes in the $n$ trials. Thus the binomial distribution becomes the basic sampling distribution in the following problem.

If $p$ is unknown, its natural estimator is

$$\hat{P} = \frac{Y}{n}$$

the proportion of successes in the sample. Now we know that the expected value of $Y$ in a binomial distribution is $np$ and that its variance (Var) is $npq$, where $q = 1 - p$. This means that

$$E(\hat{P}) = E\left(\frac{Y}{n}\right) = \left(\frac{1}{n}\right)E(Y) = \left(\frac{1}{n}\right)(np) = p$$

or $\hat{P}$ is an unbiased estimator for $p$. Further,

$$Var\,(\hat{P}) = Var\left(\frac{Y}{n}\right) = \left(\frac{1}{n^2}\right)Var(Y)$$

$$= \left(\frac{1}{n^2}\right)(npq) = \frac{pq}{n}$$

and its standard deviation is

$$\sqrt{Var(\hat{P})} = \sqrt{\frac{pq}{n}}$$

Now if the sample size $n$ is large, the central limit theorem also applies to the estimator $\hat{P}$ (it is an average number of successes per trial, or a random variable similar to $\overline{X}$). That is,

$$\frac{\hat{P} - p}{\sqrt{pq/n}} = Z$$

is approximately a standard normal variable. This result forms the basis for estimation procedures for $p$, the true population proportion of successes.

Recall that when we didn't know $\sigma$ but the sample was large, we could use $s$ instead. Here, since in the standard deviation of $\hat{P}$ occurs the product $pq$, and we don't know $p$, we are in a similar situation. The solution is to replace $pq$ by $\hat{p}\hat{q}$, where $\hat{q} = 1 - \hat{p}$.

**Example 10.4**

A political pollster randomly selects a sample of $n = 400$ people from a list of registered voters, asking each person whether or not she or he will vote for a particular candidate. Suppose that 180 of the people polled say that they will vote for the candidate. Then

$$\hat{p} = \frac{180}{400} = 0.45$$

is a point estimate of the true proportion $p$ of registered voters who will *say* they will vote for the candidate. (This might be different from the proportion who *will* vote for the candidate, but let's presume for the sake of the pollster that everyone responds honestly and that no one changes his or her mind.)

Nothing much to that problem, was there? But now let's investigate the *quality* of the estimation procedure. Specifically, let us approximate the probability that $\hat{P}$ from a sample like this will estimate $p$ to within 0.03. Write

$$\Pr(|\hat{P} - p| \le 0.03) = \Pr(-0.03 \le \hat{P} - p \le 0.03)$$

Standardizing by dividing by $\sqrt{pq/n}$ we see

$$\Pr\left(\frac{-0.03}{\sqrt{pq/400}} \le Z \le \frac{0.03}{\sqrt{pq/400}}\right)$$

$$\simeq \Pr\left(\frac{-0.03}{\sqrt{\hat{p}\hat{q}/400}} \le Z \le \frac{0.03}{\sqrt{\hat{p}\hat{q}/400}}\right)$$

$$= \Pr\left\{\frac{-0.03}{\sqrt{[(0.45)(0.55)]/400}} \le Z \le \frac{0.03}{\sqrt{[(0.45)(0.55)]/400}}\right\}$$

$$= \Pr(-1.21 \le Z \le 1.21) = 0.88686 - (1 - 0.88686) \qquad \text{Table A.2}$$

$$= 0.77372$$

Thus the pollster estimates about a 77 percent chance that his sample has estimated $p$ to within 0.03. If he wants a higher probability than that, he will have to sample some additional voters.

### Example 10.5

The assembler of inexpensive cassette tape recorders-players has received a large lot of cheap transistors from a new Hong Kong supplier. He knows that a fairly large proportion of these cheap transistors will have defective connectors (one of the wires sticking out of the transistor might be too short, or broken off, for instance). In order to plan for reordering if necessary, he wants to estimate the proportion of the lot with defective connectors.

He decides to estimate the proportion with a 90 percent confidence interval. Thus his lower and upper limits will be

$$\text{Lower limit} = \hat{p} - 1.645 \sqrt{\frac{\hat{p}\hat{q}}{n}}$$

$$\text{Upper limit} = \hat{p} + 1.645 \sqrt{\frac{\hat{p}\hat{q}}{n}}$$

Here $z_{\alpha/2} = z_{0.05} = 1.645$, and we are again appealing to the central limit theorem.

A sample of size $n = 100$ contains 24 transistors with defective connectors. Thus

$$\hat{p} = 0.24 \qquad \text{and} \qquad \sqrt{\frac{\hat{p}\hat{q}}{n}} = \sqrt{\frac{(0.24)(0.76)}{100}} = 0.043$$

Then the lower and upper limits of the 90 percent confidence interval are

$$\text{Lower limit} = 0.24 - (1.645)(0.043) = 0.17$$

$$\text{Upper limit} = 0.24 + (1.645)(0.043) = 0.31$$

The assembler has 90 percent confidence that the true proportion of transistors with defective connectors is between 0.17 and 0.31. If the lot is large enough so that 30 percent defectives will still leave enough good transistors for his assemblies, he will probably not reorder. If not, then he will probably base his reorder quantity on the assumption that 30 percent of the next lot will be similarly defective.

## 10.5   SURVEYS: SAMPLING FROM FINITE POPULATIONS

Often a company will use the results of a sample survey to help it make a rather major decision. For example, consider the decision of whether or not to introduce a product into a particular region. This decision may be based in part on the results of a sample survey designed to estimate the proportion of that region's population who would be interested in seeing a demonstration of the product. Or, for another example, the decision about where to locate a proposed new plant might involve consideration of survey results that estimate the number of workers in the work force, the proportion of potentially employable recent college graduates interested in the availability of certain cultural advantages like libraries or symphony orchestras, the average income of workers in the area, and so on.

When it is known that the population from which we are sampling is finite and when sampling is done without replacement (as it usually is), some of the results from "infinite population theory," which we used in Sections 10.3 and 10.4, do not apply directly. The basic difficulty in sample survey estimation problems is that not much is known, or assumed, about the populations from which we are sampling. Consequently, the sampling distributions for the statistics we use are not easy to determine. For that reason much of the estimation theory in sample survey problems is concerned with achieving high precision (low variance) of estimators, without being overly concerned about their sampling distributions. Whenever a probability must be approximated, however, a sampling distribution is required. Then one usually appeals to the central limit theorem, as is done in the second of the two examples to follow.

**Example 10.6**

Consider an auditor faced with the problem of determining the total dollar amount of accounts receivable for a large retail store. This store has 3,000 accounts. Now an auditor will usually be interested in other things besides just the amount of accounts; it would be very time consuming (thus expensive) for the auditor to look carefully at all 3,000 accounts.

Suppose it is decided to estimate the total dollar amount by taking a simple random sample, without replacement, from the population of size $N = 3000$. Obviously the auditor should take a sample of size $n$, then compute

$$\bar{y} = \frac{\sum_{i=1}^{n} y_i}{n}$$

This gives an estimate of the average account size $\bar{Y}$ for the population (traditionally, Greek letters are not used for population parameters in sample surveys of finite populations). The population total, denoted by $Y$, can then be estimated by

$$\hat{Y} = N\bar{y}$$

But what about the *quality* of the estimator $\hat{Y}$? How good is it? To an auditor this is a very important question; the accounting firm might be *sued* if the estimate is far from the true total.

Recall that one way to address the quality of an estimator is to speak in terms of two properties: unbiasedness and small variance. Even without knowing the sampling distribution for $\hat{Y}$ it is easy to prove that $\hat{Y}$ is indeed unbiased (see Cochran, 1963, p. 21), that is, that $E(\hat{Y})$ equals $Y$. Further, in the same reference it is proved that the variance of $\hat{Y}$, $V(\hat{Y})$, is

$$V(\hat{Y}) = \frac{N^2 S^2}{n}\left(1 - \frac{n}{N}\right)$$

where

$$S^2 = \sum_{i=1}^{N} \frac{(y_i - \bar{Y})^2}{N - 1} = \left(\frac{N}{N - 1}\right)\sigma^2$$

is referred to as the population variance (remember, here $\bar{Y}$ denotes the population mean). Thus the larger is $n$, the smaller is $V(\hat{Y})$.

In infinite population theory, where $\bar{X}$ estimates $\mu$, we know that

$$V(\bar{X}) = \frac{\sigma^2}{n}$$

Here we have

$$V(\hat{Y}) = V(N\bar{y}) = N^2 V(\bar{y})$$

so that $V(\bar{y})$ must be

$$V(\bar{y}) = \frac{S^2}{n}\left(1 - \frac{n}{N}\right)$$

Thus $V(\bar{y})$ looks a lot like $V(\bar{X})$, except $S^2/n$ is multiplied by $(1 - n/N)$. This multiplier is called the *finite population correction* factor (fpc).

Suppose the auditor has a good idea that $S^2 = 14{,}400$ (based on observations during previous audits), or that he may safely assume the standard deviation of the population of account balances is \$120. He desires an estimate of the population total $Y$ so that the standard deviation of the estimator $\hat{Y}$, sometimes called the *standard error of the estimate*, is no more than \$20,000. What size sample will be required?

Here the auditor has specified

$$\sqrt{V(\hat{Y})} = \frac{NS}{\sqrt{n}}\sqrt{1 - \frac{n}{N}} \leq 20{,}000$$

Now a sample size sufficient to make this an equation will be acceptable, since any larger sample will only reduce $\sqrt{V(\hat{Y})}$. Thus

$$\frac{N^2S^2}{n}\left(1 - \frac{n}{N}\right) = 4 \times 10^8$$

or

$$n = \frac{N^2S^2}{(4 \times 10^8 + NS^2)}$$

$$= \frac{1{,}296 \times 10^8}{4.432 \times 10^8}$$

$$\approx 293$$

So a sample size slightly less than 10 percent of the population size is required to achieve the auditor's desired precision for the estimator.

What *decisions* were involved here? First, the auditor had to make a decision about the precision of his estimator. It was probably assisted by past data or by the experience of the auditor. For instance, he might have guessed that the total should be roughly near \$600,000. The standard error of the estimate, \$20,000, is about 3 percent of that total. This decision would yield a high probability that his estimate would be within 5 percent of the true total, as could be verified using the central limit theorem.

The *statistical decision*, however, was the determination of the sample size. Thus we see how a statistical decision assists in the making of another decision of more primary interest, in this case determining the estimate of the total of accounts receivable.

**Example 10.7**

Here a probability, requiring the use of a sampling distribution, is involved. Consider a company wishing to introduce a product into a new territory. If they knew $P$, the proportion of households in this market that would allow a demonstration of the product, then they would have a good idea of $P_1$, the proportion who will actually buy the product (the objective here is only the estimation of $P$). Then they could decide if it is profitable to move into the new territory.

$P$ must be estimated rather accurately before the final decision can be made. The company requires the following of a survey designed to estimate $P$:

> There should be a probability of at least 0.95 that the sample estimate will fall within 0.02 of the true $P$.

There are 20,000 households in the territory. The statistical decision is again a decision about sample size. How large a sample is required to meet the stated objective of the survey?

Obviously, once the sample is taken, to estimate $P$ we should use:

$p$ = proportion of households in the sample who agree to a demonstration

Further, from Cochran (1963) we know

$$V(p) = \frac{P(1-P)}{n}\left(\frac{N-n}{N-1}\right)$$

where $N$ and $n$, respectively, are the population and sample sizes. It is also known that $p$ is an unbiased estimator for $P$.

Appealing to the central limit theorem we assume that

$$Z = \frac{p-P}{\sigma_p}$$

is approximately a standard normal variable. But to be able to use this to find the required sample size, we need to know $\sigma_p = \sqrt{V(p)}$. This in turn means we have to know the true value of $P$, which is unknown (we are trying to estimate $P$). Looks like a vicious circle, doesn't it?

But suppose the company's past experience with similar products indicates that $P$ cannot exceed 0.20. If $0 \le P \le 0.20$, the maximum possible value for $P(1-P)$ is $(0.20)(0.80) = 0.16$. Thus, to be on the safe side (high side) in the sample size determination, we decide to use 0.16 for $P(1-P)$.

Mathematically, the objective of the survey may be stated as

$$\Pr(|p - P| \le 0.02) \ge 0.95$$

Now we can rearrange that statement to read

$$\Pr(|p - P| \le 0.02) = \Pr(-0.02 \le p - P \le 0.02)$$

$$= \Pr\left(\frac{-0.02}{\sigma_p} \le Z \le \frac{0.02}{\sigma_p}\right) = 0.95$$

Here we set the probability *equal* to 0.95 to obtain the smallest sample size that will just meet the specifications if $P(1 - P) = 0.16$.

From the standard normal probability table, Table A.2, we learn that

$$\Pr(-1.96 \le Z \le 1.96) = 0.95$$

Therefore, we write

$$\frac{0.02}{\sigma_p} = 1.96$$

and solve that equation for $n$. Here

$$V(p) = \sigma_p^2 = \frac{0.16}{n}\left(\frac{20,000 - n}{19,999}\right)$$

so that

$$\frac{(0.02)^2 n(19,999)}{(0.16)(20,000 - n)} = (1.96)^2$$

Solving that equation for $n$ gives the sample size

$$n = 1,427$$

The required sample size looks large, but it is only about 7 percent of the population. The expense of the survey, of course, depends upon how the survey is to be conducted: mail, telephone, personal interview, and so on. Whether the company will actually conduct the survey depends upon how important it is to estimate $P$ with the specified precision and probability, and upon the cost of obtaining that estimate. To reduce the sample size, thus reducing cost, the company may decide to estimate $P$ to within 0.04, or to reduce the specified probability to 0.90.

The example discussed in this section is very similar to those shown in Section 9.4 of Chapter 9. The basic difference is that some of the extra information originates from sampling. Secondarily, the states are values of a parameter from some hypothesized population. The selection of strategy, however, involves a standard conditional minimum-risk calculation.

### Example 10.8

A supplier distributes a certain part that we need. Some fraction $p$ of the parts will be defective. We know that $p$ will be either 0.10, 0.20, or 0.30. These different values of $p$ could arise, for instance, because the parts are manufactured at different plants.

We require 2,000 such parts during the next two months. We are considering the following two strategies:

$S_1$: Order 2,000 now at a price of $20 per part.

$S_2$: Order 1,000 now at a price of $20 per part, and 1,000 a month from now at a price of $19.80 per part.

Defective parts will result in production slowdowns for the device in which we use the parts. Associated costs of delay per defective part for different $p$'s are given in Table 10.1.

Our executives agree upon the following probabilities: a 0.6 probability that $p$ will be 0.10, a 0.3 probability that $p$ will be 0.20, and a 0.1 probability that $p$ will be 0.30. Note that these are subjective probabilities, being based on opinions of experts instead of on experimental data. They will be used, however, just the same way any other probabilities would be used.

The supplier has agreed to our inspecting a randomly selected lot of 100 parts, to be chosen from those made at the plant that will handle our order. We have inspected such a sample and have discovered that the number of defective parts in that sample of size 100 is $y = 18$. This gives

---

**TABLE 10.1**   *COST TABLE*

|  | Cost per defective part | | |
|---|---|---|---|
|  | $p = 0.10$ | $p = 0.20$ | $p = 0.30$ |
| Part ordered now | $1.00 | $2.00 | $3.00 |
| Part ordered later | $1.60 | $3.00 | $4.00 |

**TABLE 10.2**   TOTAL COST

|       | $p = 0.10$ | $p = 0.20$ | $p = 0.30$ |
|-------|-----------|-----------|-----------|
| $S_1$ | $200 | $800 | $1,800 |
| $S_2$ | $ 60 | $800 | $1,900 |
| **Probability** | 0.6 | 0.3 | 0.1 |

more information, objective in nature, about $p$. Now we are ready to select a strategy.

Incorporating information about the purchase price of the 2,000 parts as well as the costs per defective part, we arrive at the total cost table shown as Table 10.2. Here the entries have been coded by subtracting $40,000 to keep the numbers small.

Now we ask: What would be the probability of observing 18 defective parts in a random sample of size 100 for each of the three possible values of $p$? The binomial probability table, Table A.1, gives the following conditional probabilities:

$$\Pr(Y = 18 | p = 0.10) = 0.00543$$

$$\Pr(Y = 18 | p = 0.20) = 0.09090$$

$$\Pr(Y = 18 | p = 0.30) = 0.02538$$

Given these probabilities, the determination of the conditional minimum-risk strategy proceeds as in Section 9.4. We emphasize that the use of a sampling distribution to obtain the conditional probabilities makes this problem different from those in Chapter 9. Now this is a *statistical* problem.

We need $\Pr(p = 0.10 | y = 18)$, $\Pr(p = 0.20 | y = 18)$, and $\Pr(p = 0.30 | y = 18)$. To obtain these conditional probabilities using Bayes' theorem we first compute $\Pr(Y = 18)$. Thus

$$\Pr(Y = 18) = (0.00543)(0.6) + (0.09090)(0.3) + (0.02538)(0.1)$$

$$= 0.003258 + 0.027270 + 0.002538$$

$$= 0.033066$$

Then 
$$\Pr(p = 0.10 | y = 18) = \frac{0.003258}{0.033066} = 0.09853$$

$$\Pr(p = 0.20 | y = 18) = \frac{0.027270}{0.033066} = 0.82471$$

$$\Pr(p = 0.30 | y = 18) = \frac{0.002538}{0.033066} = 0.07676$$

The required expected values are now as follows, where we have added back in the $40,000 subtracted in the coding of Table 10.2.

$$E(S_1 \text{ cost}|y = 18) = \$40,000 + \$817.64 = \$40,817.64$$

$$E(S_2 \text{ cost}|y = 18) = \$40,000 + \$811.52 = \$40,811.52 \leftarrow min$$

Strategy $S_2$ is selected as that with the lowest expected cost under the condition that 18 defective parts in a sample of size 100 were observed. Note that the difference in the two expected costs is very small, as it would have been even if we had not elected to obtain some sample information. The cost of the sampling would probably exceed the gain in expected cost achievable by finding the "optimal" strategy in this situation.

Note further that the sampling information would not have changed the decision anyway; $S_2$ would have been selected without it. But if we had obtained a different outcome from sampling, say $y = 34$, we might have swung to strategy $S_1$.

## 10.7   ESTIMATION AND PREDICTION USING REGRESSION MODELS

So far we have considered only a single measurement on each element in a sample: to estimate an average income we would simply measure the income of each person in the sample; to estimate the proportion of undersized ball bearings we would measure the diameter of each bearing in a sample, noting for each whether it is undersized, and so on. Now we look at an estimation problem in which each sampled element has associated with it more than one measurement. Our objective is still basically the estimation of means, but to take advantage of extra information the sample can provide we also look at other variables that are *related* to the mean of interest.

Let $Y$ be called the dependent variable, and other variables, say $x_1$, $x_2$, $x_3$, be called independent variables. If the value of $Y$ is uniquely determined by some functional relationship, say $y = 2x_1 + x_2/x_3$, then it is possible to predict $y$ exactly if we know the corresponding values of $x_1$, $x_2$, $x_3$. Generally, this functional relationship is denoted in mathematics by $y = f(x_1, x_2, x_3)$.

Suppose, however, that $Y$ is a random variable; that is, its value is not precisely predictable even if the values of the $x$'s are known, but that the *mean of* $Y$ is functionally related to the $x$'s. The idea is this: average $Y$ depends on the $x$'s, but $Y$ varies about that mean according to some probability law. Then we could say

$$E(Y|x_1, x_2, x_3) = f(x_1, x_2, x_3)$$

where $E(Y|x_1, x_2, x_3)$ denotes the mean of $Y$ for particular given values of the $x$'s. $Y$ itself, however, is represented by the model

$$Y = E(Y|x_1, x_2, x_3) + \varepsilon$$
$$= f(x_1, x_2, x_3) + \varepsilon$$

where $\varepsilon$ is a random variable, usually called an *error* term. If the random variable $Y$ is modeled in this fashion, we call the model a *regression model*.

### Example 10.9

Suppose $Y$ is the yield in pounds of some product that occurs as the result of a chemical process, and let $x_1$ = temperature, $x_2$ = pressure, and $x_3$ = concentration of catalyst used to precipitate the reaction. Theoretically, if these three variables are the only ones upon which the yield $Y$ depends, it should be possible to predict the precise values of $Y$ if we know the levels of temperature, pressure, and concentration.

Practically, however, this is not what actually happens. In repeated runs of the process, with temperature, pressure, and concentration fixed at the same levels, the yield will vary from run to run. This kind of situation is usually modeled by the relationship

$$Y = E(Y|x_1, x_2, x_3) + \varepsilon$$

That is, yield is presumed to vary at random about some average value that depends upon the levels of the $x$'s, with the randomness being accounted for by an error term $\varepsilon$.

Note particularly the dependence of average $Y$ upon the $x$ levels. This suggests different average yields for different settings of the independent variables, a basic assumption in all regression models. Another common assumption in such models is that $\varepsilon$, the error term, *does not* depend upon the independent variables.

### The Simple Linear Regression Model

Suppose the mean of $Y$ is thought to be *linearly* related to a *single* independent variable $x$. Then we may write

$$E(Y|x) = \beta_0 + \beta_1 x$$

where $\beta_0$ is the $y$ intercept and $\beta_1$ is the slope of a straight line. Then the regression model becomes

$$Y = E(Y|x) + \varepsilon$$
$$= \beta_0 + \beta_1 x + \varepsilon$$

If we may assume that average $Y$ is linearly related to $x$, but we do not know the exact nature of the linear relationship ($\beta_0$ and $\beta_1$ are unknown), then we may wish to estimate the model parameters. To do that we will need a sample, and the sample will consist of $n$ elements, upon each of which are made two measurements, $x$ and $y$. This results in a sample of $n$ pairs:

$$(x_1, y_1), (x_2, y_2), \ldots, (x_n, y_n)$$

where $(x_i, y_i)$ denotes the respective $x$ and $y$ values for the $i$th element in the sample.

Although initially we set out to estimate $\beta_0$ and $\beta_1$, our real objective is to estimate the mean of $Y$ at any particular $x$ value. If in turn we want to be able to assess the *quality* of the estimation procedure, we will need to appeal to a *sampling distribution*.

A standard assumption in regression analysis is the *normality* and *independence* of error terms. This assumption permits us to appeal to a well-known sampling distribution, the *t distribution*, in order to make probability statements about estimators in a regression problem.

If $Y$ is related to $x$ according to the model above, then so is $y_i$ related to $x_i$ for the $i$th sample pair. Thus the usual *simple linear regression model* is stated as

$$y_i = \beta_0 + \beta_1 x_i + \varepsilon_i$$

where $\beta_0$ and $\beta_1$ are constants and the errors $\varepsilon_i$, $i = 1, 2, \ldots, n$ are independent of each other and are each distributed normally with mean 0 and variance $\sigma^2$. (This variance $\sigma^2$, which does not depend on $x$, measures the variability of the $y_i$'s about their mean $\beta_0 + \beta_1 x_i$.)

## Example 10.10
### Scatter Diagram

A life insurance company believes that the amount of whole-life insurance coverage acquired by a man in a middle-management position of his company is approximately linearly related to his annual income. An actuarial trainee employed by the insurance company is given the task of investigating this claim.

The first thing the trainee does is program the company computer to identify male policyholders who have middle-management jobs. She establishes criteria based on information from insurance applications that will allow the computer to print out a list of men in such positions. Then she writes a program so the computer will randomly sample $n = 16$ names from the list. She pulls the complete files on each of these men and records from insurance applications the annual income $x$ and the amount of whole-life insurance coverage $y$ for each man in the sample. Data from the sample are shown in Table 10.3, where both $x$ and $y$ are in thousands of dollars, rounded to the nearest thousand.

TABLE 10.3 ANNUAL INCOME (x) AND WHOLE-LIFE COVERAGE (y)

| Man (i) | $x_i$ | $y_i$ | Man (i) | $x_i$ | $y_i$ |
|---------|-------|-------|---------|-------|-------|
| 1 | 27 | 5 | 9 | 50 | 38 |
| 2 | 35 | 32 | 10 | 55 | 72 |
| 3 | 64 | 60 | 11 | 62 | 100 |
| 4 | 58 | 36 | 12 | 65 | 76 |
| 5 | 53 | 58 | 13 | 60 | 90 |
| 6 | 68 | 85 | 14 | 32 | 20 |
| 7 | 25 | 10 | 15 | 41 | 43 |
| 8 | 30 | 8 | 16 | 54 | 70 |

To obtain a first impression about the validity of the linearity presumption, the actuarial trainee makes a simple *scatter diagram* of the data. A scatter diagram is nothing more than a plot of the (x, y) pairs. The scatter diagram for the data in Table 10.3 is shown as Figure 10.3.

The scatter diagram of Figure 10.3 suggests an upward trend to insurance coverage as income increases. If the trend of average coverage given income is linear, then the "eyeballed line" shown on the figure could serve as an estimator for average Y given x. For instance, the line would estimate the mean whole-life coverage for male middle managers whose income is $50,000 per year as about $52,000. Since the one man in the sample whose income was $50,000 had whole-life coverage of only $38,000, we see that the line did not do a very good job of predicting his coverage. On the other hand, this should not surprise us; the line is supposed to be used to estimate an *average y* for a particular x, not an individual y.

**FIGURE 10.3**   Scatter diagram: Income versus whole-life coverage

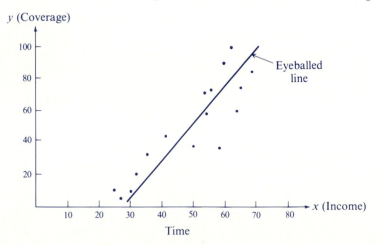

The actuarial trainee might be convinced by the scatter diagram that a linear model could be used to estimate average coverage for a particular income. But she would also wonder just *how good* that estimation procedure would be. Certainly, no matter what line is drawn through the points on the scatter diagram, the individual points will exhibit some definite variability relative to the line.

Now we will consider formulas that estimate the model parameters $\beta_0$ and $\beta_1$ in a "best-fit" sense. Various criteria for "bestness" could be proposed, but we will only use the one commonly employed in regression analyses, the criterion of *least squares*. That criterion, which mathematically is based on an important theorem called the Gauss-Markov theorem, is in its simplest terms merely a process that finds the line which, when drawn on the scatter diagram, minimizes the sum of squares of the vertical ($y$ direction) deviations of the points from the line.

At this point we elect not to follow the mathematics of proving that the subsequent formulas do indeed produce the best least-squares fitted line. That justification may be found in almost any elementary statistics text (see Hines and Montgomery, 1980, pp. 360–361, for instance). We will simply report the formulas and give examples of how to use them.

If $\hat{\beta}_0$, $\hat{\beta}_1$, and $\hat{\sigma}^2$, respectively, denote the estimators for $\beta_0$, $\beta_1$, and $\sigma^2$ in the regression model, then formulas for their values (the estimates) for a given set of $(x, y)$ pairs are

$$\hat{\beta}_1 = \frac{\Sigma x_i y_i - \dfrac{(\Sigma x_i)(\Sigma y_i)}{n}}{\Sigma x_i^2 - \dfrac{(\Sigma x_i)^2}{n}}$$

$$= \frac{S_{xy}}{S_{xx}}$$

$$\hat{\beta}_0 = \bar{y} - \hat{\beta}_1 \bar{x}$$

and
$$\hat{\sigma}^2 = \frac{S_{yy} - \hat{\beta}_1 S_{xy}}{n - 2}$$

where $S_{xy}$ and $S_{xx}$ are defined by the numerator and denominator of the first formula for $\hat{\beta}_1$, $\bar{y}$ and $\bar{x}$ are just the average $y$ and average $x$ for the sample, and

$$S_{yy} = \Sigma y_i^2 - \frac{(\Sigma y_i)^2}{n}$$

For later reference we also note that the numerator of $\hat{\sigma}^2$ is called the *error sum of squares*, often denoted by $SS_E$. That is,

$$SS_E = S_{yy} - \hat{\beta}_1 S_{xy}$$

so that

$$\hat{\sigma}^2 = \frac{SS_E}{n-2}$$

**Example 10.11**

Let us find the estimated regression line (the least-squares fit) for the insurance data of Example 10.10. A few minutes' work on a calculator with an accumulating memory gives the following basic input to the formulas:

$$n = 16 \qquad \bar{y} = 50.1875 \qquad \bar{x} = 48.6875 \qquad \Sigma y_i = 803$$

$$\Sigma y_i^2 = 54{,}351 \qquad \Sigma x_i y_i = 45{,}110 \qquad \Sigma x_i = 779 \qquad \Sigma x_i^2 = 41{,}187$$

We begin by determining $S_{xx}$, $S_{xy}$, and $S_{yy}$:

$$S_{xx} = \Sigma x_i^2 - \frac{(\Sigma x_i)^2}{n} = 41{,}187 - \frac{(779)^2}{16} = 3{,}259.44$$

$$S_{xy} = \Sigma x_i y_i - \frac{(\Sigma x_i)(\Sigma y_i)}{n} = 45{,}110 - \frac{(779)(803)}{16} = 6{,}013.94$$

$$S_{yy} = \Sigma y_i^2 - \frac{(\Sigma y_i)^2}{n} = 54{,}351 - \frac{(803)^2}{16} = 14{,}050.44$$

Then in sequence we obtain $\hat{\beta}_1$ and $\hat{\beta}_0$:

$$\hat{\beta}_1 = \frac{S_{xy}}{S_{xx}} = \frac{6{,}013.94}{3{,}259.44} = 1.845$$

$$\hat{\beta}_0 = \bar{y} - \hat{\beta}_1 \bar{x} = 50.1875 - (1.845)(48.6875) = -39.641$$

Thus we obtain the *estimated regression equation:*

$$\hat{y} = -39.641 + 1.845x$$

The graph of this equation is the *estimated regression line,* which will be exhibited in Figure 10.4.

To complete our point estimation task we must determine $\hat{\sigma}^2$. First, calculate $SS_E$:

$$SS_E = S_{yy} - \hat{\beta}_1 S_{xy}$$

$$= 14{,}050.44 - (1.845)(6{,}013.94) = 2{,}954.72$$

Then
$$\hat{\sigma}^2 = \frac{SS_E}{n - 2}$$

$$= \frac{2,954.72}{14} = 211.05$$

and $\hat{\sigma}$, the estimated standard deviation for error in the model, is

$$\hat{\sigma} = \sqrt{\hat{\sigma}^2} = 14.53$$

The results of the preceding calculations are shown in Figure 10.4.

In Figure 10.4 we see the plot of the estimated regression line as well as lines for $\hat{y} \pm 2\hat{\sigma}$. These $2\hat{\sigma}$ lines give a rough check on the correctness of our calculations, since we know that approximately 95 percent of the observations should fall between a mean plus and minus two standard deviations. The figure suggests that we have made no gross errors in our calculations.

### Example 10.12
### Point and Interval Estimates

Suppose we want to estimate the *average* whole-life coverage for male middle managers who earn $50,000 annually. We have already mentioned the point estimate, using the eyeballed line in Figure 10.3, but here we consider that problem a bit more formally. Symbolically, the problem is to estimate $E(Y|x_0)$, where $x_0 = 50$. That is, $x_0$ denotes the particular $x$ value at which we wish to estimate the mean of $Y$.

Since the estimated regression line is our best data-based guess about the location of the true regression line, we know that it is trying to pass

**FIGURE 10.4**   Estimated regression line and $2\hat{\sigma}$ lines

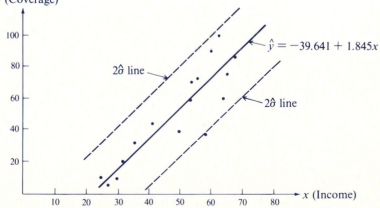

through mean $Y$ for every $x$. Thus the *point estimate* for $E(Y|x_0)$ is just $\hat{y}_0$, where

$$\hat{y}_0 = -39.641 + 1.845x_0$$

When $x_0 = 50$ (representing an income of $50,000), this yields

$$\hat{y}_0 = -39.641 + (1.845)(50)$$

$$= 52.609 \leftarrow point\ estimate$$

Thus, to the nearest thousand, we estimate that male middle managers who earn $50,000 per year carry an average of $53,000 whole-life coverage.

But point estimation is not the whole story in statistics. Suppose we want an *interval estimate* of the same mean. This is where we must appeal to a sampling distribution, in this case the $t$ distribution that was mentioned earlier.

Statistical theory tells us that a $(1 - \alpha)\ 100$ percent confidence interval for $E(Y|x_0)$ is given by the formula

$$\hat{y}_0 \pm t_{\alpha/2, n-2} \sqrt{\hat{\sigma}^2 \left[ \frac{1}{n} + \frac{(x_0 - \bar{x})^2}{S_{xx}} \right]}$$

Here $t_{\alpha/2, n-2}$ is the point in the tail of a $t$ distribution with $n - 2$ degrees of freedom that cuts off an area of $\alpha/2$ to its right.

If we want a 95 percent confidence interval for $E(Y|x_0)$ when $x_0 = 50$, then $\alpha = 0.05$. Since the sample size is $n = 16$, we use a 14-degree-of-freedom $t$ distribution. Table A.6 gives

$$t_{\alpha/2, n-2} = t_{0.025, 14} = 2.145$$

We already know that

$$x_0 = 50 \qquad \hat{y}_0 = 52.609 \qquad \bar{x} = 48.6875$$

$$\hat{\sigma}^2 = 211.05 \qquad \text{and} \qquad S_{xx} = 3{,}259.44$$

Then we have

$$52.609 \pm 2.145 \sqrt{211.05 \left[ \frac{1}{16} + \frac{(50 - 48.6875)^2}{3{,}259.44} \right]}$$

which becomes

$$52.609 \pm 7.823 \leftarrow interval\ estimate$$

So the 95 percent confidence interval for $E(Y|x_0 = 50)$ is the interval from 44.786 to 60.432. We would have 95 percent confidence that the *average* whole-life coverage for male middle managers who earn $50,000 annually is between $45,000 and $60,000.

### Example 10.13
### Prediction Interval

Earlier we commented that the eyeballed line did a poor job estimating the *actual* coverage for the one man in the sample whose annual income was $50,000. The reason was that his coverage is not an *average*, but merely a *single* observation from the population of coverages for middle managers making $50,000.

If we want to estimate a *single* value of $Y$ at a given $x_0$, we use what is called a *prediction interval*. A prediction interval is interpreted as an interval estimate for a single observation at a given $x_0$. That is, if we were to sample *one* person from the list of managers earning $50,000, the prediction interval is an interval estimate of *his* whole-life coverage.

The implication to managerial decisions is obvious. For instance, if you have done a similar regression analysis relating sales ($Y$) to advertising expenditures ($x$), a prediction interval will give you an estimate of *actual* sales whenever advertising expenditure is $x_0$, rather than the *average* sales for *all* those times your expenditure is $x_0$. If you are trying to decide on the level of advertising expenditure to produce sales of so much (a single expenditure; a single sales figure), then the notion of a prediction interval might be attractive to you.

The formula for a prediction interval for $y$ given $x_0$ appears to differ only slightly from the formula given for a confidence interval for average $Y$. Actually the resulting interval will be *much wider* than the confidence interval. This situation is reasonable when you recall that we are trying to capture, with high probability, a single observation in an entire population (which may have a large variance) rather than the *average* value for that same population (known to be centrally located).

Here is the formula for a $(1 - \alpha)$ 100 percent prediction interval:

$$\hat{y} \pm t_{\alpha/2, n-2} \sqrt{\hat{\sigma}^2 \left[ 1 + \frac{1}{n} + \frac{(x_0 - \bar{x})^2}{S_{xx}} \right]}$$

It looks just like the confidence interval for a mean except for the extra 1 underneath the square-root symbol (radical). The effect of including the 1, however, is to add $\hat{\sigma}^2$ to the entire number under the radical. This is because a single observation varies about the population mean with variance $\sigma^2$, and an estimate of $\sigma^2$ must be added into the original variance associated only with a sample mean.

For our insurance coverage problem, that of estimating the whole-life coverage for a single individual earning $50,000, the 95 percent prediction interval is

$$52.609 \pm 2.145 \sqrt{211.05\left[1 + \frac{1}{16} + \frac{(50 - 48.6875)^2}{3{,}259.44}\right]}$$

or $\qquad 52.609 \pm 32.129 \leftarrow prediction\ interval$

This is an interval ranging from 20.480 to 84.738, a much wider interval than the one we obtained for the mean of $Y$. We would be 95 percent confident that the coverage of a single middle-management male earning $50,000 is between $20,000 and $85,000. Another way of interpreting this is to say that we estimate that 95 percent of all managers earning $50,000 have whole-life coverage somewhere between $20,000 and $85,000. Not a very accurate prediction, but the best we can do given this limited data (small sample) that has lots of variability (in dollars, $\hat{\sigma} = \$14{,}530$). Finally, note that the one man in the sample who did earn $50,000 had whole-life coverage of $38,000, well within the prediction interval.

Before leaving this discussion of simple linear regression, it is worthwhile for the preceding series of examples to point out the *danger* inherent in *extrapolating beyond the range of the data*. Our assumption of linear relationship might be valid, but our fitted regression line was obtained using only *this* set of data. Had we acquired more data, including incomes less than $20,000 and/or over $70,000, we might have observed a very different estimated line. Furthermore, our assumption of linearity may have been a bad one, but our fitted linear function might still do a reasonably good job of estimating average $Y$ as long as we remain in the range of the data.

But suppose we have a middle manager who earns only $15,000 annually. Then a point estimate of his coverage (we would use the estimate of average $Y$ even though this is for a single coverage) is $\hat{y}_0$ at $x_0 = 15$. Here

$$\hat{y}_0 = -39.641 + (1.845)(15)$$
$$= -11.966$$

Try convincing your boss that statistical analysis is worthwhile when you report that the estimated whole-life coverage is *minus* $12,000. Moral: *Stay within the range of the data* and at least you will be able to report *reasonable* estimates and predictions.

### The Multiple Regression Model

No philosophical differences exist between simple linear regression models (one independent variable: $x$) and multiple linear regression models (more than one independent variable: say $x_1$, $x_2$, $x_3$). In multiple regression problems the objectives are still point and interval estimates of average $Y$ and prediction intervals for individual $Y$ values. Practically, however, the computations are more tedious since the mathematical basis for the estimates is matrix theory. Consequently we will depend upon a canned computer program for most of our arithmetic work.

In a multiple regression problem where $Y$ is the dependent variable and $x_1$, $x_2$, $x_3$ are the independent variables, the basic model is

$$Y = E(Y|x_1, x_2, x_3) + \varepsilon$$

That is, average $Y$ is a function of the independent variables only, but $Y$ itself is represented as average $Y$ plus a random error $\varepsilon$. If, further, the multiple regression model is assumed to be *linear* in the $x$'s, then

$$Y = \beta_0 + \beta_1 x_1 + \beta_2 x_2 + \beta_3 x_3 + \varepsilon$$

Our first task is the estimation of $\beta_0$, $\beta_1$, $\beta_2$, $\beta_3$, the coefficients in the linear function, and of $\sigma^2$, the variance of the random error.

The estimation is done statistically, meaning that a sample is involved. Here each sampled unit will supply four measurements, or a single data point will be an ordered quadruple, $(y, x_1, x_2, x_3)$. For instance, if $Y$ is the yield for the chemical process of Example 10.9, to get a data point we would measure yield, temperature, pressure, and concentration, respectively, for *one* run of the process, thus obtaining the four measurements required for *that* sample observation.

Then a sample that involves $n$ data points would yield $n$ ordered quadruples as follows:

| Observation ($i$) | $(y_i, x_{1i}, x_{2i}, x_{3i})$ |
|:---:|:---:|
| 1 | $(y_1, x_{11}, x_{21}, x_{31})$ |
| 2 | $(y_2, x_{12}, x_{22}, x_{32})$ |
| . | . |
| . | . |
| . | . |
| $n$ | $(y_n, x_{1n}, x_{2n}, x_{3n})$ |

Since the model for the $i$th observation would be written as

$$y_i = \beta_0 + \beta_1 x_{1i} + \beta_2 x_{2i} + \beta_3 x_{3i} + \varepsilon_i$$

the sample of $n$ data points would suggest the following system of $n$ equations:

$$y_1 = \beta_0 + \beta_1 x_{11} + \beta_2 x_{21} + \beta_3 x_{31} + \varepsilon_1$$
$$y_2 = \beta_0 + \beta_1 x_{12} + \beta_2 x_{22} + \beta_3 x_{32} + \varepsilon_2$$
$$.$$
$$.$$
$$.$$
$$y_n = \beta_0 + \beta_1 x_{1n} + \beta_2 x_{2n} + \beta_3 x_{3n} + \varepsilon_n$$

Another way to write that system involves matrix notation. The entire system is represented by the single equation

$$Y = X\beta + \varepsilon$$

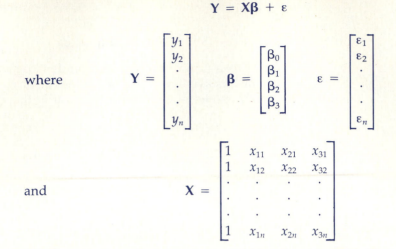

where
$$Y = \begin{bmatrix} y_1 \\ y_2 \\ \cdot \\ \cdot \\ \cdot \\ y_n \end{bmatrix} \quad \beta = \begin{bmatrix} \beta_0 \\ \beta_1 \\ \beta_2 \\ \beta_3 \end{bmatrix} \quad \varepsilon = \begin{bmatrix} \varepsilon_1 \\ \varepsilon_2 \\ \cdot \\ \cdot \\ \cdot \\ \varepsilon_n \end{bmatrix}$$

and
$$X = \begin{bmatrix} 1 & x_{11} & x_{21} & x_{31} \\ 1 & x_{12} & x_{22} & x_{32} \\ \cdot & \cdot & \cdot & \cdot \\ \cdot & \cdot & \cdot & \cdot \\ 1 & x_{1n} & x_{2n} & x_{3n} \end{bmatrix}$$

The reader familiar with matrix multiplication and matrix addition may easily verify that this is indeed our system of $n$ equations. The reader unfamiliar with matrix manipulations is referred to Appendix C.

The Gauss-Markov theorem (see Rao, 1965, pp. 179–182) of mathematical statistics tells us that the best linear unbiased estimator for the vector $\beta$ is given by

$$\hat{\beta} = \begin{bmatrix} \hat{\beta}_0 \\ \hat{\beta}_1 \\ \hat{\beta}_2 \\ \hat{\beta}_3 \end{bmatrix} = (X'X)^{-1}X'Y$$

where $X'$ is the transpose of the $X$ matrix and $(X'X)^{-1}$ is the inverse of the matrix $X'X$. Note that $X'X$ is only a $4 \times 4$ matrix when there are three $x$ variables, regardless of the sample size $n$. In general, the order of the square, symmetric matrix $X'X$ is always equal to the number of $\beta$ coefficients that are in the model and is not influenced by the sample size. In the simple linear regression model it is a $2 \times 2$ matrix; in fact, simple linear regression problems are nowadays usually phrased in this matrix notation, and the calculations are also usually done by computer.

Thus the estimation of the regression coefficients $\beta_0$, $\beta_1$, $\beta_2$, $\beta_3$ involves only matrix inversion and matrix multiplication. The *estimated regression equation* is then

$$\hat{y} = \hat{\beta}_0 + \hat{\beta}_1 x_1 + \hat{\beta}_2 x_2 + \hat{\beta}_3 x_3$$

Point estimates of average $Y$ and the center point of interval estimates for given $x_1$, $x_2$, $x_3$ are obtained from that equation.

TABLE 10.4

**TABLE 10.4** 1983 SALES (Y), POPULATION ($x_1$), INCOME ($x_2$), AND HOUSING STARTS ($x_3$) FOR EIGHT CITIES

| Y, hundreds | $x_1$, millions | $x_2$, \$1,000 | $x_3$, hundreds |
|---|---|---|---|
| 123 | 1.13 | 4.5 | 105 |
| 70 | 0.54 | 6.0 | 43 |
| 84 | 0.92 | 5.4 | 40 |
| 72 | 0.43 | 7.2 | 22 |
| 53 | 0.24 | 4.9 | 18 |
| 59 | 0.87 | 6.7 | 32 |
| 152 | 2.37 | 4.0 | 128 |
| 114 | 1.64 | 5.2 | 69 |

**Example 10.14**
**Point Estimates**

A television manufacturer operates "factory outlet" stores in eight large cities. The manufacturer is considering opening another store in a ninth city, yet to be determined, but wants to be able to predict annual sales in such a city before the final decision is made. Management feels that sales are most directly related to three characteristics of a city: population, per-capita income, and number of housing starts. It is decided that a multiple linear regression equation that includes those variables might be useful.

Let $Y$ = sales, in hundreds of units

$x_1$ = population, in millions

$x_2$ = per-capita income, in thousands of dollars

$x_3$ = number of housing units started, in hundreds

Values for each of these variables in each of the eight cities where stores already exist are determined for the year 1983 and are presented in Table 10.4.

The matrix **X** and the vector **Y** can be written out from the information in Table 10.4, and the parameter estimates $\hat{\beta}_0$, $\hat{\beta}_1$, $\hat{\beta}_2$, $\hat{\beta}_3$ could be determined by calculator-assisted pencil-and-paper computations. But almost every computer installation should have built into the system a general linear regression routine.

One such regression program is contained in the MINITAB* statistical package that is available at many colleges and universities. We will work the estimation problem of Example 10.14 using MINITAB. Figure 10.5 shows the input and a portion of the output supplied by the MINITAB routine.

* MINITAB is a proprietary computer software product of Minitab, Inc., and is currently available for use by license only on a variety of computers.

```
--  READ C1 C2 C3 C4
--  123 1.13 4.5 105
--  70 0.54 6.0 43
--  84 0.92 5.4 40
--- 72 0.43 7.2 22
--  53 0.24 4.9 18
--  59 0.87 6.7 32
--  152 2.37 4.0 128
--  114 1.64 5.2 69
--  NOBRIEF
--  REGRESS C1 3 C2 C3 C4

THE REGRESSION EQUATION IS
Y =     39.0 +   15.0 X1 +  .267 X2
   +   .615 X3

                                        ST. DEV.    T-RATIO =
          COLUMN      COEFFICIENT       OF COEF.    COEF/S.D.
            --           38.96           37.25        1.05
X1        C2             15.04           11.57        1.30
X2        C3             0.267           5.540        0.05
X3        C4             0.6152          0.2402       2.56

THE ST. DEV. OF Y ABOUT REGRESSION LINE IS
S = 10.50
WITH (    8- 4) =    4 DEGREES OF FREEDOM

R-SQUARED = 94.9 PERCENT
R-SQUARED = 91.0 PERCENT, ADJUSTED FOR D.F.

DURBIN-WATSON STATISTIC = 1.67

(X-PRIME X)INVERSE

                 0            1            2            3
  0      12.57779
  1       .27753      1.21311
  2     -1.83763      -.06960      .27822
  3      -.04641      -.01978      .00668       .00052
```

**FIGURE 10.5**   MINITAB output: Sales prediction problem

Inspection of the eight lines following READ C1 C2 C3 C4 will demonstrate the method of data entry. The NOBRIEF command asks the program for an extended output; here NOBRIEF was used because we want to be able to see the matrix $(\mathbf{X'X})^{-1}$. The command REGRESS C1 C2 C3 C4 tells MINITAB that the numbers in column C1 are $y$ values and that we have three independent $x$ variables, in columns C2, C3, and C4. The rest of the output in Figure 10.5 is generated automatically by the MINITAB routine (actually, more output than is shown would be seen, but this is all we need to analyze our problem from purely an estimation viewpoint).

The estimated regression equation is

$$\hat{y} = 39.0 + 15.0x_1 + 0.267x_2 + 0.615x_3$$

meaning that $\hat{\beta}_0 = 39.0$, $\hat{\beta}_1 = 15.0$, $\hat{\beta}_2 = 0.267$, and $\hat{\beta}_3 = 0.615$. Thus the first line of the MINITAB output estimates all the β's and even writes out the equation we will use to obtain point estimates of average $Y$. Suppose, for instance, that one of the cities under consideration for a new factory outlet had, in 1983, a population of 840,000, per-capita income of $5,400, and 3,600 housing units started. Then $x_1 = 0.84$, $x_2 = 5.4$, $x_3 = 36$, and the point estimate of sales is

$$\hat{y}_0 = 39.0 + (15.0)(0.84) + (0.267)(5.4) + (0.615)(36)$$

$$= 75.2 \quad (7,520 \text{ units})$$

Actually, the equation estimates *average* sales for all cities with $x_1 = 0.84$, $x_2 = 5.4$, $x_3 = 36$, but this number would also be our best *point estimate* of actual sales for that one city. In Example 10.15 we will consider interval estimates.

Continuing our interpretation of the numbers in Figure 10.5, the little table with X1, X2, X3 on the left and T-RATIO on the right comes next. The COEFFICIENT column just reports estimates of $\beta$ coefficients ($\hat{\beta}$'s) with another decimal place of accuracy. ST. DEV. OF COEF. gives the estimated standard deviations, $S(\hat{\beta})$, for the four regression coefficients, and T-RATIO is $\hat{\beta}/S(\hat{\beta})$, a quantity used for testing the hypothesis that the associated $x$ variable, given the other two $x$ variables, makes no significant extra contribution to the regression equation. Since hypothesis testing is not our objective here, we choose to ignore those $t$ ratios (values of $t$ statistics).

Next we see $S = 10.50$. This is a useful number for an interval estimation problem, since it is the estimate of $\sigma$, the standard deviation of the errors. That is, $S = \hat{\sigma} = 10.50$, or $S^2 = \hat{\sigma}^2 = (10.50)^2 = 110.25$, and we have also estimated $\sigma^2$, the variance of the errors.

An extremely informative number on the output in Figure 10.5 is R-SQUARED. This stands for $R^2$, the value of a statistic called the *coefficient of determination*. $R^2$ is a measure of the proportion of total variation in $Y$ that might be attributed to the linear relationship of its mean to the set of all $x$ variables. Here we see that 94.9 percent of the $Y$ variation is attributed to this presumed linear relationship or that a definite linear relationship seems to exist. $R^2$ values are thus a measure of the *strength* of the presumed linear relationship of average $Y$ to the $x$'s, with high $R^2$'s indicating strong relationships and low $R^2$'s indicating weak relationships. Here the 94.9 percent figure gives us quite a bit of faith in our assumption that $E(Y|x_1, x_2, x_3)$ might be well-approximated by a linear function.

We choose to ignore R-SQUARED, ADJUSTED FOR D.F. This is just an "adjusted" value of $R^2$ that reflects the degrees of freedom in the estimate of $\sigma^2$, often a more accurate measure of the strength of the linear relationship when the number of sample points is small relative to the number of $\beta$ coefficients. Even though this is precisely the situation in Example 10.14, the nuance is not sufficiently important for us to spend time with it here.

The DURBIN-WATSON STATISTIC is often a valuable piece of information to have. The Durbin-Watson statistic is used to judge whether any *autocorrelation* is present in the data, where autocorrelation implies more relationship among adjacent $y$ values than among those separated by greater distances or times. Particularly if the data points are collected over some period of time rather than all at once, the data should be tested for the presence of autocorrelation. *Low* values of the Durbin-Watson statistic (generally, values less than 1.0) suggest autocorrelated $y$ values. In the presence of autocorrelation a time-series analysis is usually more appropriate than a regression analysis. Since from Figure 10.5 we see a value of 1.64 for the Durbin-Watson statistic, we do not worry about autocorrelation in Example 10.14.

The final bit of information obtained from the MINITAB output in Figure 10.5 is the matrix $(\mathbf{X'X})^{-1}$. Since that matrix will always be a *symmetric* matrix (the elements in row $i$ are the same as the elements in column $i$), only enough numbers are printed to enable us to complete the matrix if we so desire. Here the entire matrix is

$$(\mathbf{X'X})^{-1} = \begin{bmatrix} 12.57779 & 0.27753 & -1.83763 & -0.04641 \\ 0.27753 & 1.21311 & -0.06960 & -0.01978 \\ -1.83763 & -0.06960 & 0.27822 & 0.00668 \\ -0.04641 & -0.01978 & 0.00668 & 0.00052 \end{bmatrix}$$

We will need this matrix to determine a confidence interval for average $Y$ or a prediction interval for a single $Y$ at given $x$ values.

**Example 10.15**
**Interval Estimates**

The following formulas are used to determine $(1 - \alpha) \, 100$ percent confidence intervals for average $Y$ or prediction intervals for a single $Y$, respectively. Here $\mathbf{x}_0$ is a vector with unity (one) as its first element and the $x$ values of interest as its remaining elements.

*Confidence interval* (for average $Y$ at $\mathbf{x}_0$).
$$\hat{y}_0 \pm t_{\alpha/2, n-p} \sqrt{S^2 \mathbf{x}_0'(\mathbf{X'X})^{-1}\mathbf{x}_0}$$

*Prediction interval* (for $Y$ at $\mathbf{x}_0$).
$$\hat{y}_0 \pm t_{\alpha/2, n-p} \sqrt{S^2[1 + \mathbf{x}_0'(\mathbf{X'X})^{-1}\mathbf{x}_0]}$$

The degrees of freedom for the $t$ statistic are $n - p$, where $n$ is the number of data points and $p$ is the number of $\beta$ coefficients in the regression model. $S^2$ is just the estimate of $\sigma^2$ (the square of $S$ on the MINITAB output). The number $\hat{y}_0$ is the point estimate of $y$ (or of average $y$) at $\mathbf{x}_0$.

Thus for the ninth city of Example 10.14, where $x_1 = 0.84$, $x_2 = 5.4$, and $x_3 = 36$, we have

$$\mathbf{x}_0 = \begin{bmatrix} 1 \\ 0.84 \\ 5.4 \\ 36 \end{bmatrix}$$

and from Example 10.14 we already know that $\hat{y}_0 = 75.2$. The degrees of freedom for $t$ are $n - p = 8 - 4 = 4$, and suppose we decide upon $\alpha = 0.05$ (95 percent intervals). From Table A.6 we find

$$t_{0.025,4} = 2.776$$

$S^2$ is known to be 110.25, so now all we need is $\mathbf{x}_0'(\mathbf{X}'\mathbf{X})^{-1}\mathbf{x}_0$. It is

$$\mathbf{x}_0'(\mathbf{X}'\mathbf{X})^{-1}\mathbf{x}_0$$

$$= (1, 0.84, 5.4, 36) \begin{bmatrix} 12.57779 & 0.27753 & -1.83763 & -0.04641 \\ 0.27753 & 1.21311 & -0.06960 & -0.01978 \\ -1.83763 & -0.06960 & 0.27822 & 0.00668 \\ -0.04641 & -0.01978 & 0.00668 & 0.00052 \end{bmatrix} \begin{bmatrix} 1 \\ 0.84 \\ 5.4 \\ 36 \end{bmatrix}$$

$$= (1, 0.84, 5.4, 36) \begin{bmatrix} 1.2115532 \\ 0.2086224 \\ -0.1532260 \\ -0.0082332 \end{bmatrix} = 0.2629804$$

So a 95 percent confidence interval for average $Y$ at $x_1 = 0.84$, $x_2 = 5.4$, $x_3 = 36$ is

$$75.2 \pm 2.776\sqrt{(110.25)(0.2629804)}$$

or $\qquad\qquad 75.2 \pm 14.95$

or the interval from 60.25 to 90.15. This means that our 95 percent interval estimate of *average* sales for cities of population 840,000, per-capita income of \$5,400, and 3,600 housing starts is between 6,025 and 9,015 units.

An interval estimate of sales for a *single* such city is

$$75.2 \pm 2.776\sqrt{(110.25)(1 + 0.2629804)}$$

or $\qquad\qquad 75.2 \pm 32.76$

or the interval from 42.44 to 107.96 (4,244 to 10,796 units). If sales of 4,500 units is an acceptable figure, then the city might be chosen as a location for a factory outlet; 4,500 is near the low end of the prediction interval, or is a conservative estimate.

## 10.8 TIME SERIES

The prediction of the value of a variable at some time in the future is called a *forecast*. Weather forecasting provides an obvious example of this type of endeavor: What will be tomorrow's temperature at 12:00 noon? A similar business question is: What will be the closing price tomorrow of a Hughes Tool share? Most of us would probably wager that the weatherperson could do a better job forecasting temperature than could the businessperson or economist at forecasting a stock price, yet occasionally weather forecasts, even those done by acknowledged weather experts, can be woefully inaccurate. Unanticipated changes in atmospheric conditions cause weather forecasts to be bad, just as unexpected variations in economic conditions adversely affect business forecasts.

Still, forecasting is central to business and economic activity. The money supply two months from now, the price in October of wheat harvested in July, the demand for electric toasters during the Christmas season, total employment in Chicago a year from now; all of these are numbers that someone needs to know, or at least needs to be able to predict with some accuracy. Forecasting methods include the intuitive judgment of a single individual, the experience-based consensus of a panel of experts, and the output of a mathematical model that uses historical data as input. Ideally, one might presume that a panel of experts possessing good historical data, extensive training in economics, and astute business sense would be able to make very accurate forecasts. Yet we all know that such expert panels are not infallible. Nevertheless, forecasting must be done, and it seems only reasonable that it is best done by experts.

To forecast the money supply in the future you should be a trained economist; to forecast demand for a new product you should have extensive market research experience; to forecast trends in the stock market you should have studied the market thoroughly. While nothing surpasses intimate understanding of the problem area for generating good forecasts, there are a few principles common to all forecasting endeavors that can be learned by nonexperts in the field to which the forecast will apply. Minimal background for forecasting is some appreciation of *time series* and the features that are common to all such series.

A *time series* is a sequence of observations of values of a variable obtained at regular time intervals.

A time series, by its definition, is necessarily a set of historical data. The values of the variable must be observed in order to be recorded, and we cannot observe a future value. But sometimes the past may be a reasonable guide to at least the immediate future, so time series are regarded as valuable information by forecasters.

A study of time series begins with the recognition of four *components*, some or all of which may be present in a sequence of data collected over time. These are (1) trend component, (2) seasonal component, (3) cyclic component, and (4) random component.

A *trend* component indicates a long-term tendency of the series and may be the result of population changes, inflation, governmental regulatory policies, or other factors that produce gradual changes over time. The general trend of a time series is often the principal basis of a forecast, but that basic number will usually be adjusted for one or more of the other components.

A *cyclic* component is associated with what is commonly called the business cycle, although that so-called cycle is by no means regular. Sales of a luxury item like a video tape recorder, for instance, might increase during a period of economic expansion and decrease in times of recession. When interest rates are high, sales might decline, and so on. This cyclic effect is as difficult to predict, of course, as the next recession or the next point drop in the prime rate, but such an economic cycle does exist. The cyclic component in a time series attempts to account for the effect of the business cycle.

A much more predictable component is the *seasonal* component. While the business cycle of expansion-contraction-expansion might occur over a period of, say, five years, the seasonal component is an annual phenomenon (and as such will not be present in a time series where the interval between observations is a year or more). Sales of many types of consumer goods tend to be highest in November and December and lowest in January and February. Special items like tennis rackets or fishing rods might enjoy peak sales in the summer and low sales in the winter. The available work force is greatest in the summertime when students become seekers of temporary jobs. A seasonal component in a time series is most easily predictable among all the components. In fact, its predictability is what distinguishes it from the cyclic component.

Least predictable is the *random* component. This component of a time series is analogous to "error" in a regression model. It is the source of variation that is left over after the contributions of all the other components have been considered. This random component is the result of irregular, short-term forces whose causes are simply too complex and too little understood to be modeled mathematically. If the random component is large relative to the other time-series components, it may so overwhelm them that forecasting using the time-series data becomes virtually impossible. But if the random component is relatively insignificant, then one might hope to achieve a fairly dependable forecast by projecting the observed series into the future.

The trend, seasonal, and cyclic components are often called the *systematic* components of the time series, what the electrical engineer would call the *signal*, while the random component is analogous to *noise* in engineering parlance. The objective of forecasting with time-series data is to filter out the noise and project the signal into the future.

### Example 10.16

Contemporary Electronics markets a popular brand of personal computer. Monthly sales, in hundreds of units, are shown for a four-year period in Table 10.5. This 48-month time series is graphed in Figure 10.6.

Close inspection of the time series plotted in Figure 10.6 suggests that at least three of the four components are present. Sales tend to be high near the end of the year and then drop off precipitously at the beginning of the next year, implying the presence of a seasonal component. Since

### TABLE 10.5    MONTHLY SALES: CONTEMPORARY PERSONAL COMPUTERS

| 1980 | Sales, hundreds | 1981 | Sales, hundreds | 1982 | Sales, hundreds | 1983 | Sales, hundreds |
|------|-----------------|------|-----------------|------|-----------------|------|-----------------|
| J | 5.6 | J | 5.6 | J | 2.8 | J | 4.0 |
| F | 5.3 | F | 7.3 | F | 2.8 | F | 4.6 |
| M | 7.6 | M | 7.9 | M | 5.6 | M | 6.4 |
| A | 7.1 | A | 7.7 | A | 3.5 | A | 5.6 |
| M | 7.9 | M | 7.8 | M | 5.4 | M | 6.7 |
| J | 8.0 | J | 7.4 | J | 4.0 | J | 8.0 |
| J | 7.5 | J | 5.1 | J | 4.4 | J | 9.5 |
| A | 6.9 | A | 5.9 | A | 4.9 | A | 10.4 |
| S | 6.7 | S | 6.3 | S | 3.1 | S | 9.7 |
| O | 7.0 | O | 5.0 | O | 4.7 | O | 8.4 |
| N | 9.2 | N | 6.8 | N | 3.3 | N | 10.4 |
| D | 8.9 | D | 4.4 | D | 5.8 | D | 12.3 |

### FIGURE 10.6    Monthly sales: Contemporary Personal Computers

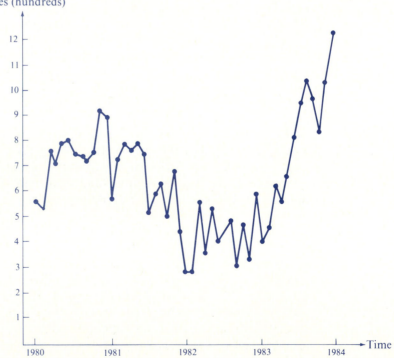

the pattern of variation changes from year to year, however, a random component also seems to be involved. Recalling that the economy was depressed in the years 1981 and 1982 but was recovering in 1983, we would conclude that a definite cyclic component is present, reflecting general business conditions. In fact, the cyclic component seems to have the most important effect on sales.

By simply observing the series as plotted in Figure 10.6 it is difficult to detect any regular trend (apart from the tendency of the data to follow the business cycle). We might guess that if we used simple linear regression, the trend would be represented by a gradually rising straight line. Note, however, that if the series had stopped at the end of the year 1982, our trend estimate would have been a steeply falling line.

The series depicted in Table 10.5 and Figure 10.6 was contrived in the following manner. A "trend," or "level of desire," line was drawn, a seasonal pattern was imposed, a curve representing the effect of the business cycle was drawn, and random variation was included. Then sales contributions associated with each component were added together to produce the final time series. Component curves used for this purpose are shown in Figure 10.7.

The four components illustrated in Figure 10.7 would not actually be seen for a set of real data; all we would see would be the series as depicted in Figure 10.6. For purposes of forecasting, however, we might want to identify trend, cyclic, and seasonal components. For instance, if we could establish a general trend, we might determine a way to adjust the trend for the seasonal component (establishing a seasonal index is one approach). Further, if the cyclic component could be detected, we could compare it to an actual graph of the business cycle to see if the cyclic component follows that graph or whether it tends to anticipate it or lag behind it. Such information would obviously be quite useful for making forecasts.

### Moving Averages

One way to assess general trend would be the application of regression analysis to the time-series data. To do this, however, we would have to assume some linear or quadratic (or cubic or exponential, and so on) model that might reflect trend. That is, we would have to impose upon the data an assumption that might not be true. One way to avoid such presumption is the use of *moving averages.*

Moving averages attempt to *smooth* the series so that its general trend might be easily observed. Such averages are computed using some fixed number of time units, and successively averaging values over that fixed interval, for each average in succession just shifting the interval over by one time unit. This process, which may sound vague when stated in words, is actually very simple. Example 10.17 illustrates the process of determining moving averages.

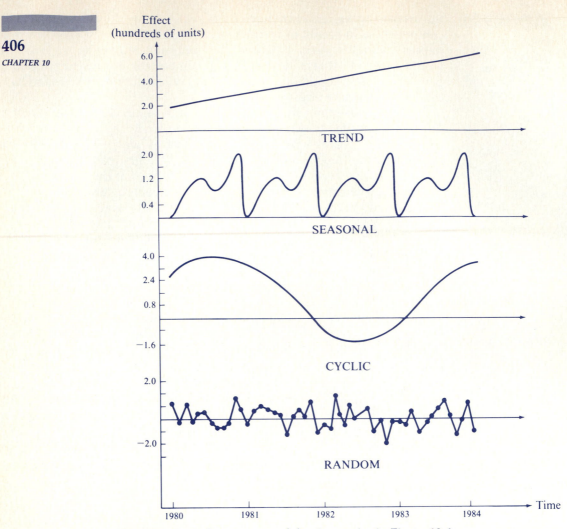

*FIGURE 10.7*    Components of the time series in Figure 10.6

### Example 10.17

Consider the first seven months of data that appear in Table 10.5.  We will obtain a succession of three five-month moving averages as follows:

$$\text{Average for first five months} \atop (J, F, M, A, M) = \frac{5.6 + 5.3 + 7.6 + 7.1 + 7.9}{5}$$

$$= 6.70$$

$$\text{Average for next five months} \atop (F, M, A, M, J) = \frac{5.3 + 7.6 + 7.1 + 7.9 + 8.0}{5}$$

$$= 7.18$$

$$\frac{\text{Average for next five months}}{\text{(M, A, M, J, J)}} = \frac{7.6 + 7.1 + 7.9 + 8.0 + 7.5}{5}$$

$$= 7.62$$

These averages, located at the middle of the interval used to construct them (the middle month of the five-month interval), are shown in Table 10.6.

Since each of the averages in Table 10.6 is over a five-month interval, the averages tend to vary less than individual monthly values or to be *smoother* than the original data. Note that the next average in succession drops out the first month in the previous average and adds in the next month that was not used in the previous average. Thus three numbers (out of five) that were used before are used again in the computation of the next average in succession.

Suppose we want to use the notion of a moving average to determine trend for a time series with a definite seasonal component. It would seem reasonable to use *12-month* moving averages, so that each average contains exactly one year's worth of monthly data. The only problem is that there is no middle month to associate with the average (it would fall between two months since 12 is an even number). To adjust for this we continue the process and average two adjacent averages, making a *centered moving average* that naturally falls on a month in the original series. This process facilitates plotting of the averages to make a judgment about trend.

### Example 10.18

We will compute all possible 12-month moving averages for the sales data of Table 10.5 and present them in Table 10.7. The first average is from January, 1980, to December, 1980:

$$\text{First average} = \frac{5.6 + 5.3 + \cdots + 9.2 + 8.9}{12} = 7.31$$

**TABLE 10.6** *FIVE-MONTH MOVING AVERAGES*

| Year | Month | Sales | 5-month average |
|------|-------|-------|-----------------|
| 1980 | J | 5.6 | |
| | F | 5.3 | |
| | M | 7.6 | 6.70 |
| | A | 7.1 | 7.18 |
| | M | 7.9 | 7.62 |
| | J | 8.0 | |
| | J | 7.5 | |

Likewise,

$$\text{Second average} = \frac{5.3 + 7.6 + \cdots + 8.9 + 5.6}{12} = 7.31$$

$$\text{Third average} = \frac{7.6 + 7.1 + \cdots + 5.6 + 7.3}{12} = 7.47$$

and so on.

Were we to plot the first average, it would naturally fall between June and July, 1980, while the second average would fall between July and August. But the *average* of the first two 12-month averages, the centered moving average, would be associated with July, while the average of the second and third averages would be associated with August. Thus

$$\text{First centered average} = \frac{7.31 + 7.31}{2} = 7.31 \qquad \text{July}$$

$$\text{Second centered average} = \frac{7.31 + 7.47}{2} = 7.39 \qquad \text{August}$$

Continuing in this fashion, we determine all the entries in Table 10.7.

To visualize the smoothing characteristic of moving averages the best way is to graph them. The original time-series data for the Contemporary Personal Computers sales records, along with the 12-month centered moving averages, are exhibited in Figure 10.8.

The 12-month centered moving averages are associated with a combination of the trend, if any, and the business cycle, as may be obvious (at least the cyclic portion) from inspection of Figure 10.8. The use of the moving averages to establish seasonal indices helpful in forecasting will be illustrated in Section 10.9. For the moment, simply observe the definite *smoothed* characteristic of the 12-month centered moving averages.

### Exponential Smoothing

One disadvantage of moving averages is the lack of an average associated with every point in the original time series. Table 10.7, for instance, has no centered moving average for the first six months and the last six months of the series. If the trend indicated by the smoothing technique is to be used for forecasting, then moving averages are not very suitable, since the trend near the end of the series is not available. Further, the averages do not contain all the information available in the series prior to the location of the average (remote observations in the series are not reflected in recent averages). A procedure that has neither of these shortcomings is the method of *exponential smoothing.*

Both the method and the reasoning behind the exponential smoothing process are very easy to understand. Basically, the concept is to "weight" all the previous observations as well as the most recent observation, but to assign weights in such a manner that as an observation becomes more

**TABLE 10.7** TWELVE-MONTH AVERAGES AND CENTERED MOVING AVERAGES

| Year | Month | Sales | 12-month average | Centered average |
|------|-------|-------|------------------|------------------|
| 1980 | J | 5.6 | | |
| | F | 5.3 | | |
| | M | 7.6 | | |
| | A | 7.1 | | |
| | M | 7.9 | | |
| | J | 8.0 | 7.31 | |
| | J | 7.5 | 7.31 | 7.31 |
| | A | 6.9 | 7.47 | 7.39 |
| | S | 6.7 | 7.50 | 7.48 |
| | O | 7.0 | 7.55 | 7.52 |
| | N | 9.2 | 7.54 | 7.54 |
| | D | 8.9 | 7.49 | 7.52 |
| 1981 | J | 5.6 | 7.29 | 7.39 |
| | F | 7.3 | 7.21 | 7.25 |
| | M | 7.9 | 7.17 | 7.19 |
| | A | 7.7 | 7.01 | 7.09 |
| | M | 7.8 | 6.81 | 6.91 |
| | J | 7.4 | 6.43 | 6.62 |
| | J | 5.1 | 6.20 | 6.32 |
| | A | 5.9 | 5.82 | 6.01 |
| | S | 6.3 | 5.63 | 5.72 |
| | O | 5.0 | 5.28 | 5.46 |
| | N | 6.8 | 5.08 | 5.18 |
| | D | 4.4 | 4.80 | 4.94 |
| 1982 | J | 2.8 | 4.74 | 4.77 |
| | F | 2.8 | 4.67 | 4.70 |
| | M | 5.6 | 4.39 | 4.53 |
| | A | 3.5 | 4.37 | 4.38 |
| | M | 5.4 | 4.08 | 4.22 |
| | J | 4.0 | 4.19 | 4.14 |
| | J | 4.4 | 4.29 | 4.24 |
| | A | 4.9 | 4.44 | 4.36 |
| | S | 3.1 | 4.51 | 4.48 |
| | O | 4.7 | 4.68 | 4.60 |
| | N | 3.3 | 4.79 | 4.74 |
| | D | 5.8 | 5.12 | 4.96 |
| 1983 | J | 4.0 | 5.55 | 5.34 |
| | F | 4.6 | 6.01 | 5.78 |
| | M | 6.4 | 6.56 | 6.28 |
| | A | 5.6 | 6.87 | 6.72 |
| | M | 6.7 | 7.46 | 7.16 |
| | J | 8.0 | 8.00 | 7.73 |
| | J | 9.5 | | |
| | A | 10.4 | | |
| | S | 9.7 | | |
| | O | 8.4 | | |
| | N | 10.4 | | |
| | D | 12.3 | | |

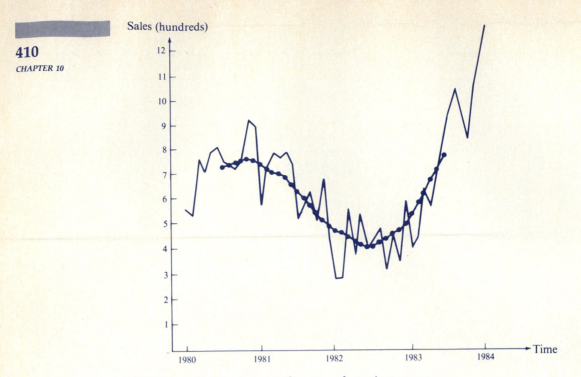

**FIGURE 10.8**   Twelve-month centered moving averages

and more remote (farther back in time from the current smoothed value), it receives less and less weight. This process becomes simpler in execution than in concept, for as we will see, a simple recursive equation does the weighting job for us once we have made an initial choice of a single weight $w$.

Let $y_1$ be the first observation in the series, $y_2$ be the second, and so on, so that $y_t$ is the $t$th observation. Let $S_t$ denote the smoothed value at time $t$. Choose a weight $w$, $0 \le w \le 1$, and let

$$S_1 = y_1 \quad \text{and} \quad S_t = wy_t + (1 - w)S_{t-1}$$

where $S_{t-1}$ is just the smoothed value at time $t - 1$. Thus

$$S_1 = y_1$$
$$S_2 = wy_2 + (1 - w)S_1 = wy_2 + (1 - w)y_1$$
$$S_3 = wy_3 + (1 - w)S_2$$
$$= wy_3 + (1 - w)[wy_2 + (1 - w)y_1]$$
$$= wy_3 + w(1 - w)y_2 + (1 - w)^2 y_1$$

$$S_4 = wy_4 + (1 - w)S_3$$

$$= wy_4 + (1 - w)[wy_3 + w(1 - w)y_2 + (1 - w)^2 y_1]$$

$$= wy_4 + w(1 - w)y_3 + w(1 - w)^2 y_2 + (1 - w)^3 y_1$$

and so on. Since $0 \leq w \leq 1$, $y_1$ receives less and less weight in each successive $S_t$ value, as does $y_2$, and all of the other $y$ values in successive smoothed values. The initial choice of $w$ automatically dictates the weights each $y$ term will receive in each $S$ term, and these weights, for a given $y$ term, get smaller and smaller as the $y$ term becomes more and more remote from the $S$ term.

The calculations, however, are done with the basic equation

$$S_t = wy_t + (1 - w)S_{t-1}$$

*not* with the individual $y$ terms. Example 10.19 illustrates that process.

**Example 10.19**

Consider the short time series $y_1 = 5$, $y_2 = 8$, $y_3 = 10$, $y_4 = 9$, $y_5 = 7$. Corresponding smoothed values, with $w = 0.4$, are

$S_1 = y_1 = 5$

$S_2 = 0.4y_2 + (1 - 0.4)S_1$

$\quad = (0.4)(8) + (0.6)(5) = 6.2$

$S_3 = 0.4y_3 + (1 - 0.4)S_2$

$\quad = (0.4)(10) + (0.6)(6.2) = 7.72$

$S_4 = 0.4y_4 + (1 - 0.4)S_3$

$\quad = (0.4)(9) + (0.6)(7.72) = 8.232$

$S_5 = 0.4y_5 + (1 - 0.4)S_4$

$\quad = (0.4)(7) + (0.6)(8.232) = 7.7392$

All that is required for any current exponentially smoothed value is the weight $w$, the current $y$ term, and the previous $S$ term.

The "art" of exponential smoothing lies in the choice of the weight $w$. If $w = 0.1$, for instance, then $1 - w = 1 - 0.1 = 0.9$, and the previous smoothed value is weighted much higher than the current value, implying that we want to give lots of weight to past data. If $w = 0.9$, then $1 - w = 1 - 0.9 = 0.1$, and now we want heavy weight on the most recent observation with previous data "dying out" rapidly in the computations. A basic rule of thumb suggested by those remarks is: If the series is fairly regular, with little random variation, then a small $w$ will permit the (fairly dependable) past data to remain prominent in the current $S$ value, while if the series is quite volatile, exhibiting substantial irregular variation, a large $w$ will put more weight on the terms in the series immediately preceding the current $S$ value.

## Example 10.20

To illustrate the method of exponential smoothing and to see what the resulting smoothed series looks like on a graph, we will consider an eight-year series of quarterly sales data, representing liquor sales in Wyoming. The data, along with associated exponentially smoothed values, is given in Table 10.8, and the original series and smoothed series are drawn in Figure 10.9.   A smoothing constant of $w = 0.3$ was used.

**TABLE 10.8**   *QUARTERLY LIQUOR SALES IN WYOMING FOR 1975–1982*

| Year | Quarter | $t$ | Sales, $ millions $y_t$ | $S_t$ |
|------|---------|-----|-------------------------|-------|
| 1975 | 1 | 1 | 3.5 | 3.5 |
|      | 2 | 2 | 4.5 | 3.8 |
|      | 3 | 3 | 5.0 | 4.2 |
|      | 4 | 4 | 6.2 | 4.8 |
| 1976 | 1 | 5 | 3.8 | 4.5 |
|      | 2 | 6 | 4.7 | 4.6 |
|      | 3 | 7 | 5.2 | 4.8 |
|      | 4 | 8 | 6.7 | 5.4 |
| 1977 | 1 | 9 | 4.0 | 5.0 |
|      | 2 | 10 | 5.1 | 5.0 |
|      | 3 | 11 | 6.0 | 5.3 |
|      | 4 | 12 | 7.8 | 6.1 |
| 1978 | 1 | 13 | 4.7 | 5.7 |
|      | 2 | 14 | 6.0 | 5.8 |
|      | 3 | 15 | 6.7 | 6.1 |
|      | 4 | 16 | 8.9 | 6.9 |
| 1979 | 1 | 17 | 5.5 | 6.5 |
|      | 2 | 18 | 7.2 | 6.7 |
|      | 3 | 19 | 7.0 | 6.8 |
|      | 4 | 20 | 9.6 | 7.6 |
| 1980 | 1 | 21 | 6.4 | 7.2 |
|      | 2 | 22 | 7.7 | 7.4 |
|      | 3 | 23 | 8.9 | 7.8 |
|      | 4 | 24 | 11.3 | 8.9 |
| 1981 | 1 | 25 | 6.8 | 8.3 |
|      | 2 | 26 | 9.4 | 8.6 |
|      | 3 | 27 | 9.4 | 8.8 |
|      | 4 | 28 | 11.4 | 9.6 |
| 1982 | 1 | 29 | 7.8 | 9.1 |
|      | 2 | 30 | 9.1 | 9.1 |
|      | 3 | 31 | 8.9 | 9.0 |
|      | 4 | 32 | 10.5 | 9.4 |

*Source:* Wyoming State Liquor Commission and the Data Retrieval System of the Institute for Policy Research, University of Wyoming.

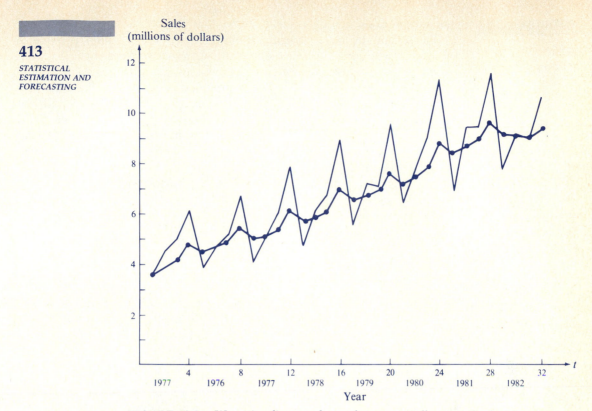

**FIGURE 10.9** Wyoming liquor sales and exponentially smoothed series

   The time series for quarterly liquor sales, depicted in Figure 10.9, appears to be surprisingly predictable. In every year the last quarter has the highest sales, which drop off drastically in the first quarter of a subsequent year. The trend up through 1981, as conveniently observable from the exponentially smoothed values, is regularly upward, with the annual pattern of quarterly sales being very similar from year to year. Yet the sales in 1982 are seen to be lower than an ordinary linear trend projection, perhaps obtained by linear regression methods, would have anticipated. The exponentially smoothed values, however, reflect this apparent change in trend and thus might serve as a good basis for forecasting.

## The Multiplicative Time Series Model

The analysis of time-series data often presumes that each component is a *factor* (a multiplier) in the actual observed value. Letting $Y_i$ be the $i$th observation, and $T_i$, $S_i$, $C_i$, and $R_i$ be the corresponding trend, seasonal, cyclic, and random factors, the multiplicative model of an observation is simply

$$Y_i = T_i \times S_i \times C_i \times R_i$$

This model does not necessarily mean that the terms in the series are caused strictly by such specific multiplication, but it does provide a convenient way for us to think about the structure of the series.

Time-series analysts are often interested in *decomposition* of a series. This decomposition is sometimes accomplished using *ratios*. For example, suppose we have estimated a combined series reflecting trend and the cyclic component, as was done with moving averages in Example 10.18 (also see Figure 10.8). Then we could use the estimates, say $\hat{Y}_i$'s (the moving averages), as divisors, forming the ratios $Y_i/\hat{Y}_i$. Since in the multiplicative model $\hat{Y}_i$ is supposed to reflect $T_i \times C_i$, we could identify the resulting ratio with $S_i \times R_i$, or with a combined seasonal and random effect. That is,

$$\frac{Y_i}{\hat{Y}_i} = \frac{T_i \times S_i \times C_i \times R_i}{T_i \times C_i}$$

$$= S_i \times R_i$$

Obviously the key to this type of analysis, which will be the basis for the seasonal indices of Section 10.9, is the assumption of a multiplicative model.

## 10.9   FORECASTING

The objective of the time-series discussions in Section 10.8 was to give you a feeling for time series and their components, as well as to illustrate certain smoothing methods useful for identifying trends and cycles. Now we are ready to extend some of those notions to the problem of forecasting future values.

A wide variety of forecasting techniques based on time-series data exists. Here we will illustrate the use of three methods: *seasonal indices*, forecasting using *exponential smoothing*, and *autoregressive models*.

### Seasonal Indices

A seasonal index for monthly (or quarterly) data attempts to account for month-to-month (or quarter-to-quarter) systematic fluctuations in a time series. These indices are essentially "average" values of $Y_i/\hat{Y}_i$, ratios that were described at the end of Section 10.8. When the $\hat{Y}_i$'s are moving averages, the ratios are called *ratios to moving averages*. The "averaging" of those ratios is in the sense of weighted medians. The "weighted median" characteristic of seasonal indices is best appreciated by example.

### Example 10.21

Refer to the monthly sales data for Contemporary Personal Computers, Example 10.16, and to Table 10.7, which gives the original data $(Y_i)$ and the centered moving averages $(\hat{Y}_i)$. We will compute 12 seasonal indices,

**TABLE 10.9**   *COMPUTING SEASONAL INDICES*

| Month | \multicolumn{4}{c}{Yearly ratios} | | | | Median ratio | Seasonal index |
|---|---|---|---|---|---|---|
| | 1980 | 1981 | 1982 | 1983 | | |
| January | — | 0.758 | 0.587 | (0.749) | 0.749 | 0.758 |
| February | — | 1.007 | 0.596 | (0.796) | 0.796 | 0.805 |
| March | — | (1.099) | 1.236 | 1.019 | 1.099 | 1.112 |
| April | — | 1.086 | 0.799 | (0.833) | 0.833 | 0.842 |
| May | — | (1.129) | 1.280 | 0.936 | 1.129 | 1.142 |
| June | — | 1.118 | 0.966 | (1.035) | 1.035 | 1.047 |
| July | (1.026) | 0.807 | 1.038 | — | 1.026 | 1.038 |
| August | 0.934 | (0.982) | 1.124 | — | 0.982 | 0.993 |
| September | (0.896) | 1.101 | 0.692 | — | 0.896 | 0.906 |
| October | (0.931) | 0.916 | 1.022 | — | 0.931 | 0.942 |
| November | (1.220) | 1.313 | 0.696 | — | 1.220 | 1.234 |
| December | 1.184 | 0.891 | (1.169) | — | 1.169 | 1.182 |
| | | | | | 11.865 | 12.001 |

one for each month of the year, in Table 10.9. The first four columns in Table 10.9, called "Yearly ratios," just report the ratios to moving averages available from Table 10.7. Then the median ratio, the middle ratio in magnitude among the three ratios available for each month, is reported. That median ratio is presumed to reflect a sort of "average" seasonal effect, leaving out high and low ratios from possibly unusual years. The median ratio would make a fairly good seasonal index, but one more step is usually taken. Notice that the sum of the median ratios in Table 10.9 is 11.865. To compute a set of seasonal indices, 12 of them, so that they sum to the number 12, we compute

$$\text{Seasonal index} = \frac{12 \times \text{median ratio}}{11.865}$$

Note that the indices in the last column of Table 10.9 actually sum to 12.001, but that is only due to rounding.

### Example 10.22

Now that we have established seasonal (monthly) indices, let us attempt to forecast the next six months of sales for Contemporary Personal Computers. To do that, we will have to extend the curve suggested by the centered moving averages in Figure 10.8 to establish a "trend" for the future. Our forecasts, even adjusted by the seasonal indices, will only be as good as our ability to guess that trend.

If we assume the business cycle might begin to level off again by the end of 1984, but continue to increase slightly, we might guess that the trend could rise from 9.0 to 10.0 (hundreds of units) through the first six months of 1984. Then we would apply the seasonal index as a multiplier to obtain our monthly forecasts. These forecasts, along with "actual" sales for the first six months of 1984 (obtained by extending the curves shown in Figure 10.7), are given in Table 10.10.

In this case little is achieved by discussing how good the forecasts are, since both actual sales and trend have been very arbitrarily determined. The example is included only to illustrate the method of seasonal indices.

### Forecasting Using Exponential Smoothing

A discussion of the rationale and the method of exponential smoothing has already been presented in Section 10.8. So we may go directly to the simple recursive equation that does forecasting by exponential smoothing. Let

$$F_t = WA_{t-1} + (1 - W)F_{t-1}$$

where $F_t$ is the forecast at time $t$ (what we want to determine), $A_{t-1}$ is the *actual* value observed at time $t - 1$, $F_{t-1}$ is the *forecasted* value at time $t - 1$, and $W$ of course is a weight chosen by the forecaster. When exponential smoothing is used in forecasting, experience has indicated that $W$ should usually not exceed 0.3.

This type of forecasting will give us a single number, the forecast for the very next time period, based on the most recent forecast and the most recent observation. For instance, we weight a forecast for April with what was actually observed in April to come up with a forecast for May. After observing the *actual* value for May, we may obtain a forecast for June, and so on.

### Example 10.23

We will use the quarterly liquor sales data, Table 10.8, as a basis for forecasting in this example. It is real data, not contrived, so we might also want to see how good a job our forecasting procedure does. To do

**TABLE 10.10**  *SIX-MONTH FORECAST USING SEASONAL INDICES*

| Month (1984) | Trend | Index | Forecast | Actual sales |
|---|---|---|---|---|
| January | 9.6 | 0.758 | 6.8 | 7.8 |
| February | 9.2 | 0.805 | 7.4 | 11.0 |
| March | 9.4 | 1.112 | 10.5 | 9.9 |
| April | 9.6 | 0.842 | 8.1 | 11.7 |
| May | 9.8 | 1.144 | 11.2 | 10.6 |
| June | 10.0 | 1.047 | 10.5 | 11.2 |

that, we must know actual values for liquor sales to have something to compare with the forecast. Consequently, we shall use the data up through the last quarter of 1980 as a basis for forecasting quarterly sales, quarter by quarter as the data become available, through 1981 and 1982.

From Figure 10.9 we observe the trend and seasonal effects up to the end of 1980. We might take the actual last-quarter sales for 1980, 11.3 (in millions), and use as the forecasted value the number 8.9, the exponentially smoothed value from Example 10.20. Then, using $W = 0.2$, our forecast for the first quarter of 1981 would be

$$F_1 = (0.2)(11.3) + (0.8)(8.9) = 9.38$$

Then, after observing actual sales in the first quarter of 1981 of only 6.8 million, we forecast second-quarter sales using

$$F_2 = (0.2)(6.8) + (0.8)(9.38) = 8.86$$

Similar calculations give the column headed "Smoothed forecast" in Table 10.11.

The numbers in that "Smoothed forecast" column are not entirely satisfactory (no forecast can be perfect, of course). They seem to do a pretty good job of forecasting the general trend of sales but do not reflect the definite seasonal effects that we know exist in this time series. However, they might be very good indicators of trend, and it would appear that for data *without* a seasonal component the method of exponential smoothing could supply adequate forecasts that smooth over effects of random variation.

However, since we are aware of the seasonal pattern in Wyoming liquor sales, it would seem reasonable to adjust the trend using seasonal indices. We can use the years 1976 through 1980 to establish seasonal indices for the data in Table 10.8 (1975 is a base year for getting the smoothed curve

**TABLE 10.11** SEASONALLY ADJUSTED EXPONENTIAL SMOOTHING FORECASTS: LIQUOR SALES

| Year | Quarter | Smoothed forecast | Seasonal index | Seasonally adjusted forecast | Actual sales |
|------|---------|-------------------|----------------|------------------------------|--------------|
| 1981 | 1 | 9.38 | 0.795 | 7.46 | 6.8 |
|      | 2 | 8.86 | 0.974 | 8.63 | 9.4 |
|      | 3 | 8.97 | 1.034 | 9.27 | 9.4 |
|      | 4 | 9.06 | 1.196 | 10.84 | 11.4 |
| 1982 | 1 | 9.53 | 0.795 | 7.58 | 7.8 |
|      | 2 | 9.18 | 0.974 | 8.94 | 9.1 |
|      | 3 | 9.16 | 1.034 | 9.47 | 8.9 |
|      | 4 | 9.11 | 1.196 | 10.90 | 10.5 |

started and would not give representative ratios). These indices (which you will be asked to verify in an end-of-chapter exercise), smoothed forecasts, seasonally adjusted forecasts for 1981 and 1982 (obtained quarter by quarter as data become available), and actual sales are shown in Table 10.11. The graph in Figure 10.10 provides a convenient means for us to observe the quality of our forecasts.

The seasonally adjusted, exponentialy smoothed forecasts do come very close to actual sales in all eight quarters during which forecasts were made. We should not be too surprised by that, since when we first saw this data, back in Example 10.20, we noticed that Wyoming liquor sales seemed easily predictable. Note also that the smoothed forecasts indicate the general trend of sales is no longer upward, as a superficial examination of Figure 10.9 might have suggested, but rather they show that sales are leveling off or even beginning to drop off by the end of 1982. So we seem to have pretty good quarter-by-quarter forecasts as well as a fair indication of a change in trend. Both types of forecasts could be useful to the state of Wyoming in planning budgets based on anticipated revenue from liquor sales, as well as to liquor wholesalers and retailers in Wyoming, who need to plan their inventories.

## Autoregressive Models

Economists use *autoregressive models* for forecasting when correlations exist between $y$ values separated by fixed time periods. For example, if we believe that a current observation is related to the observation two time periods ago, we might express that belief by the model

$$y_t = \beta_0 + \beta_1 y_{t-2} + \varepsilon$$

**FIGURE 10.10**   Forecasts of quarterly liquor sales

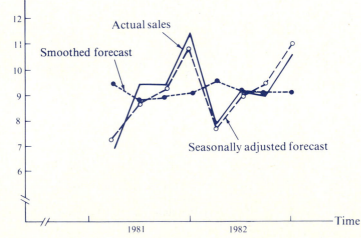

That is, we specify an ordinary regression model, but the $x$ variable is just one of the preceding $y$ variables. For another example, if we think that $y_t$ is related to the immediately preceding $y$ value as well as to the one 12 months ago, we would write

$$y_t = \beta_0 + \beta_1 y_{t-1} + \beta_2 y_{t-12} + \varepsilon$$

Such autoregressive models attempt to take advantage of autocorrelations in the data yet still use the convenience of a regression analysis for predictions.

### Example 10.24

The data in Table 10.12 are quarterly for the years 1978 through 1982, being revenues from the Wyoming sales and use tax, in millions of dollars. We will use the data from the years 1978 through 1980 and an autoregressive model to forecast quarterly revenue from the sales and use tax for 1981 and 1982. That is, we will use three years of data to forecast the known values for the next two, thereby being able to see how good the forecasts are.

**TABLE 10.12**
*QUARTERLY REVENUES:
WYOMING SALES AND USE TAX*

| Year | Quarter | Revenues, $ millions |
|------|---------|---------------------|
| 1978 | 1 | 34.28 |
|      | 2 | 38.97 |
|      | 3 | 40.90 |
|      | 4 | 42.02 |
| 1979 | 1 | 39.41 |
|      | 2 | 42.79 |
|      | 3 | 47.81 |
|      | 4 | 41.63 |
| 1980 | 1 | 48.51 |
|      | 2 | 58.93 |
|      | 3 | 59.63 |
|      | 4 | 57.55 |
| 1981 | 1 | 58.60 |
|      | 2 | 64.14 |
|      | 3 | 66.01 |
|      | 4 | 68.77 |
| 1982 | 1 | 73.83 |
|      | 2 | 66.76 |
|      | 3 | 65.90 |
|      | 4 | 61.21 |

*Source:* Wyoming Department of Revenue and the Data Retrieval System of the Institute for Policy Research, University of Wyoming.

Casual inspection of the data in Table 10.12 indicates no strong seasonal component, but it does suggest that adjacent values are similar. We might also suppose that values for the same quarters in different years might be correlated. These reflections suggest the following autoregressive model:

$$y_t = \beta_0 + \beta_1 y_{t-1} + \beta_2 y_{t-4} + \varepsilon$$

In Table 10.13 we set up the data for an ordinary multiple regression run using MINITAB, with $y_t$ playing the role of $Y$, $y_{t-1}$ acting like $x_1$, and $y_{t-4}$ acting like $x_2$. The horizontal lines setting off the data from $t = 5$ through $t = 12$ indicate the eight data points that are available from the first three years to establish the estimating (and forecasting) equation. The "Estimate" column in Table 10.13 shows the estimated values corresponding to data points used in estimating coefficients, $\beta$'s, in the equation, and the "Forecast" column shows forecasts for the eight quarters in 1981 and 1982. These forecasts are assumed to be made quarter by quarter, as the new data become available in the years 1981 and 1982.

The estimating equation, obtained from an ordinary MINITAB run, is

$$y_t = -10.7 + 0.478 y_{t-1} + 0.915 y_{t-4}$$

**TABLE 10.13**    TAX REVENUES: ESTIMATES AND FORECASTS

| Year | $t$ | $y_t$ | $y_{t-1}$ | $y_{t-4}$ | Estimate | Forecast | Actual, $y_t$ |
|------|-----|-------|-----------|-----------|----------|----------|---------------|
| 1978 | 1 | 34.28 | | | | | 34.28 |
|      | 2 | 38.97 | | | | | 38.97 |
|      | 3 | 40.90 | | | | | 40.90 |
|      | 4 | 42.02 | | | | | 42.02 |
| 1979 | 5 | 39.41 | 42.02 | 34.28 | 40.75 | | 39.41 |
|      | 6 | 42.79 | 39.41 | 38.97 | 43.80 | | 42.79 |
|      | 7 | 47.81 | 42.79 | 40.90 | 47.18 | | 47.81 |
|      | 8 | 41.63 | 47.81 | 42.02 | 50.60 | | 41.63 |
| 1980 | 9 | 48.51 | 41.63 | 39.41 | 45.26 | | 48.51 |
|      | 10 | 58.93 | 48.51 | 42.79 | 51.64 | | 58.93 |
|      | 11 | 59.63 | 58.93 | 47.81 | 61.21 | | 59.63 |
|      | 12 | 57.55 | 59.63 | 41.63 | 55.89 | | 57.55 |
| 1981 | 13 | | 57.55 | 48.51 | | 61.20 | 58.60 |
|      | 14 | | 58.60 | 58.93 | | 71.23 | 64.14 |
|      | 15 | | 64.14 | 59.63 | | 74.52 | 66.01 |
|      | 16 | | 66.01 | 57.55 | | 73.51 | 68.77 |
| 1982 | 17 | | 68.77 | 58.60 | | 75.79 | 73.83 |
|      | 18 | | 73.83 | 64.14 | | 83.28 | 66.76 |
|      | 19 | | 66.76 | 66.01 | | 81.61 | 65.90 |
|      | 20 | | 65.90 | 68.77 | | 83.72 | 61.21 |

Numbers in the "Estimate" and "Forecast" columns of Table 10.13 are obtained from that equation. The original time series, the estimates (for 1979 and 1980), and the forecasts (for 1981 and 1982) are plotted in Figure 10.11.

From Figure 10.11 we see that the autoregressive equation does a fairly good job of reproducing the pattern of the data used to obtain it, the pre-1981 data. Then its forecasts for 1981, while all on the high side, are not too far away from the actual revenues. But the year 1982 experienced a drastic drop in revenues that represented a distinct change from the previous pattern, and sure enough, the forecasts (based on 1978 to 1980 data) are much too high. This illustrates two points: the danger of extrapolating too far beyond the range of the data, and the ability of the autoregressive model we chose to only reproduce a previous pattern, not to anticipate a change.

In this instance of sales and use tax revenues, a bright economist working

**FIGURE 10.11**   Forecasting revenue from Wyoming sales and use tax

for the state of Wyoming would be expected to notice a downturn in the business cycle and to avoid projecting an upward trend with the autoregressive model. If only past data, and nothing else, are to be your forecasting base, you will be in trouble when current patterns differ from the patterns of the past. Again, the best forecaster will be the person with more knowledge about the problem than merely historical data.

One further point is in order here. The failure of the autoregressive model to do a good forecasting job two years ahead might be due to the particular form of the model that was chosen, and not to the notion of autoregression. For example, what is called the "naive" autoregressive model simply bases next quarter's forecast on the revenue from the immediately preceding quarter. For the data of Example 10.24, the model

$$y_t = \beta_0 + \beta_1 y_{t-1} + \varepsilon$$

might be better than the one we used. In an end-of-chapter exercise, you will be asked to try it out.

### Other Popular Forecasting Methods

Sometimes a worthwhile data base is not available, as would be the case, for example, with sales forecasting for a new product that has just been developed. Then forecasting methods that are not based on historical data must be used. Forecasts are often attempted by *consensus of an expert panel*, or by use of the *Delphi method*, which involves the use of a panel of experts but systematically attempts to avoid any "bandwagon" effect of majority opinion. *Market research* methods, which involve statistical sampling, are also worthwhile, especially in a new-product setting. The article by Geurts and Reinmuth (1980) discusses some of these *qualitative* forecasting methods.

Other data-based forecasting methods include *exponentially weighted moving averages, second-order exponential smoothing*, and what is called *Box-Jenkins forecasting*. The Mendenhall and Reinmuth text (1982) has good examples of the first two procedures, and Box-Jenkins forecasting, which is designed for time series with complex patterns, is presented by its originators in Box and Jenkins (1969). Another very good elementary treatment of time-series forecasting is found in the text by Mansfield (1983).

### 10.10  SUMMARY AND CONCLUSIONS

Estimation, prediction, and forecasting play important roles in business and economic activity. An appreciation of the basic principles of statistical estimation, regression, and time series enables the modern manager or executive to understand the value and the limitations of statistical techniques in helping him or her make decisions. This chapter strives to provide a working basis for that appreciation, mostly by example but with some elementary statistical theory included.

Central to measuring the quality of an estimator or a prediction technique is the notion of the sampling distribution of a statistic. That notion is in turn related to the probabilistic properties of a "good" estimator: unbiasedness and small variance. These properties assure "repeatability" of estimates: most samples would yield estimates close to the parameter being estimated if the estimation procedure is a good one. This repeatability property gives us faith that the estimate obtained from a *single* sample is good.

Both point and interval estimation of means and proportions are included, with some emphasis being placed upon the problem of determining an adequate sample size. Here "adequacy" is determined by the person who has the estimation problem to solve: a statement of one's expectations of the sample information is necessary. This statement usually involves a specification of closeness of the estimate to the target parameter as well as a declaration of an acceptable probability for being that close.

The important distinction between a confidence interval for a mean and a prediction interval for a single observation is emphasized. The second of those intervals is always much wider than the first, even though it is based on the same sample data. A prediction interval attempts to capture a single observation in a population rather than the population mean, which is the average of all observations in the population. Care must be exercised here. Do you want to estimate a mean, or do you want to predict a single future value?

The use of simple and multiple regression techniques is discussed. These methods take advantage of sample information from many variables that may be related to the variable of primary interest. Computations in regression problems are nowadays usually done by computers, so the emphasis is on interpretation of numbers on the computer output and upon use of the predicting equation to make both point and interval estimates. Again the distinction is made between a confidence interval and a prediction interval. Since regression analysis is often used for predictive purposes, this distinction is of primary importance.

The final unit of study in the chapter is time series and forecasting. Standard smoothing techniques useful in identifying trends and business cycles are included. The four basic components of a time series—trend, seasonal, cyclic, and random—are discussed. After demonstrating these components and smoothing methods so the reader has gained some appreciation of the features that distinguish time-series data from the "simultaneous" type of data contained in most statistical samples, the important topic of forecasting is taken up.

Forecasting based on historical (time-series) data is emphasized. Trend projections using smoothing techniques are considered, sometimes in conjunction with seasonal indices for "fine-tuning" the forecasts. Auto-regressive models, which basically convert the forecasting computations to familiar regression calculations, are introduced. The examples serve not only to demonstrate the mechanics of the methods, but also to illustrate the inability of historical data to forecast well when the current time-series pattern differs substantially from that observed in the past. Repeatedly the point is made that historical data are not the whole story in forecasting; expert knowledge about the subject to which the forecast applies is also very necessary to good forecasting practice.


## KEY WORDS AND PHRASES

**Statistic**   A function of observations obtained by sampling. A statistic is a random variable whose value changes from sample to sample.

**Sample mean**   The average of the numbers in a sample. Usually denoted by $\overline{X}$, the sample mean is a statistic that estimates the population mean $\mu$.

**Sample variance**   A statistic that measures the spread of numbers in a sample about the sample mean. It is denoted by $S^2$ and estimates $\sigma^2$, the population variance.

**Sample proportion** (of successes)   A statistic that estimates the proportion of successes in a population. Denoted by $\hat{P}$, its value is obtained by dividing the number of successes in the sample, $y$, by the sample size, $n$.

**Sampling distribution**   The probability distribution of a statistic.

**Estimator**   A statistic whose value, obtained from a particular sample, is a numerical estimate of a population parameter.

**Unbiased estimator**   An estimator whose average over all possible samples of the same size is the parameter it is estimating.

**Sample survey**   An experiment involving sampling from a finite population, with the objective the estimation of selected population parameters.

**Central limit theorem**   A theorem which implies, for large samples, the approximate normality of the sample mean, the statistic $\overline{X}$. It is the basis for most of the probability statements one can make about the estimators $\overline{X}$ and $\hat{P}$, and about $\hat{Y}$ in regression problems.

**Confidence interval**   An interval obtained from a sample to estimate a parameter of a population. Its endpoints are the values of the endpoints of a random interval which, before sampling, has a high, specified probability $(1 - \alpha)$ of capturing the parameter.

**Prediction interval**   Similar to a confidence interval in interpretation, except that it does not try to capture a fixed population parameter, but rather a single, particular observation in the population from which the sample was taken.

**Bayesian statistical decision**   A decision resulting from revision of prior probabilities according to the outcome of a sampling experiment.

**Regression model**   A mathematical model of an observation whose mean is presumed to be functionally related to some set of independent variables. The model is that mean plus a random error term which is usually assumed to be normally distributed.

**Simple linear regression**   Regression analysis in which the mean of the dependent variable $Y$ is assumed to be linearly related to the independent variable $X$.

**Multiple linear regression**   Regression analysis in which the mean of the dependent variable is assumed to be linearly related to more than one independent variable.

**Scatter diagram**   A graph of the sample points in a simple linear regression problem.

**Estimated regression equation**   The equation resulting from a least-squares fit of the sample data to the regression model.   It is the basis for point and interval estimates in a regression analysis.

**MINITAB**   A statistical computer package developed at Pennsylvania State University (Minitab, Inc.) for use by license on many types of computers.   The MINITAB regression routine was used here for multiple regression computations.

**Coefficient of determination**   Denoted by $R^2$, it measures the strength of the linear relationship of average $Y$ to the $X$ variables.   (In simple linear regression, the square root of $R^2$, $R$, is called the *correlation coefficient*.)

**Time series**   A sequence of observations of values of a variable, obtained at regular time intervals.

**Components** (of a time series)   Trend, seasonal, cyclic, and random components.

**Moving average**   A smoothing technique in time-series analysis that averages the observed values over successive, equal-length time intervals.

**Exponential smoothing**   A smoothing technique in time-series analysis that weights *all* observations prior to the point in time at which a smoothed value is desired.

**Multiplicative time-series model**   A conceptual model of an observation in a time series as the product of factors representing the four basic time-series components: trend, seasonal, cyclic, and random.

**Seasonal index**   A modified "ratio to trend" factor that attempts to account for systematic seasonal fluctuations in a time series.   It is used in forecasting as a multiplier of trend.

**Autoregressive model**   A forecasting model that takes advantage of intercorrelated values in a time series and that uses regression analysis to estimate coefficients in a forecasting equation.

**Qualitative forecasting**   Forecasting using expert judgment, market research methods, or some approach other than a purely historical data-based forecasting method.


## EXERCISES

For Exercises 10.1 through 10.5 you will find no worked-out examples in the body of the chapter.   To determine the required sampling distributions, simply list *all possible samples* that could be obtained and all associated values of the statistic, thus constructing the complete probability distribution for the statistic.   Other questions about the statistic are answered using the sampling distribution you have constructed.

✦ **10.1** Consider the population consisting of the five numbers 2, 4, 6, 8, 10. Let $\overline{X}$ be the average of a sample of size $n = 2$ selected *without replacement* from that population.
   **a** Develop the sampling distribution for $\overline{X}$.
   **b** Show that $\overline{X}$ is an unbiased estimator for the population mean $\mu$.
   **c** Show that $\overline{X}$ has a smaller variance than the variance of the original population.
   **d** What is the probability that $\overline{X}$ will assume a value within two units of the population mean?
   **e** What is the probability that $\overline{X}$ will exceed 7.50?

**10.2** From the population consisting of the five numbers 2, 4, 6, 8, 10, let $\overline{X}$ be the average of a sample of size $n = 2$ selected *with* replacement. Rework parts *a* through *e* of Exercise 10.1 for this different type of sampling. For which type of sampling is $\overline{X}$ less variable?

**10.3** Consider the population consisting of the five numbers 2, 4, 6, 8, 10. Let $S^2$ be the sample variance for a sample of size $n = 2$ selected *without* replacement from that population.
   **a** Develop the sampling distribution of $S^2$.
   **b** Show that $E(S^2) = [N/(N - 1)]\sigma^2$, where $\sigma^2$ is the population variance.

✦ **10.4** Repeat Exercise 10.3 using *with*-replacement sampling. In part *b*, however, show that $E(S^2) = \sigma^2$.

**10.5** Consider the population consisting of the six numbers 3, 6, 9, 15, 18, and 27. Let $\overline{X}$ be the sample average for a sample of size $n = 3$ selected *without* replacement from that population. Let $S^2$ be the sample variance.
   **a** Develop the sampling distribution of $\overline{X}$.
   **b** Show that $E(\overline{X}) = \mu$, that is, that $\overline{X}$ is an unbiased estimator for $\mu$.
   **c** Develop the sampling distribution for $S^2$.
   **d** Show that $E(S^2) = [N/(N - 1)]\sigma^2$.

✦ **10.6** The random variable $Z$ has a standard normal distribution. Use Table A.2 to find
   **a** $P(Z \le 1.00)$  **d** $P(1.65 \le Z)$
   **b** $P(Z \le -1.50)$  **e** $P(Z \le -2.50 \text{ or } 2.50 \le Z)$
   **c** $P(-2.00 \le Z \le 1.00)$

✦ **10.7** The random variable $Z$ has a standard normal distribution. Use Table A.2 to find
   **a** The number $z$ such that $P(Z \le z) = 0.8413$
   **b** The number $z$ such that $P(Z \le z) = 0.1587$
   **c** The number $z$ such that $P(z < Z) = 0.0099$
   **d** The number $z$ such that $P(-z < Z < z) = 0.9500$

✦ **10.8** The statistic $\overline{X}$ is the average of a sample of size $n = 25$ taken from a population with mean $\mu = 50$ and variance $\sigma^2 = 100$. Use the central limit theorem to find approximate answers for the following questions:

    **a** What is $P(\overline{X} \le 50)$?
    **b** What is $P(48 \le \overline{X} \le 52)$?
    **c** What is $P(55 \le \overline{X})$?
    **d** What is the number $k$ such that $P(\overline{X} \le k) = 0.0250$?

**10.9** The statistic $\overline{X}$ is the average of a sample of size $n$ taken from a population with mean $\mu = 10$ and variance $\sigma^2 = 25$. Approximately what size sample will assure that $P(\overline{X} \le 7) = 0.0228$?

✦ **10.10** An economist working for a federal commission wants to estimate the average value of assets for a large group of companies engaged in trade. A random sample of 50 of those companies had an average value of assets equal to $34.3 million with a standard deviation of asset values equal to $8.4 million. Estimate the probability that the point estimate of the true average assets for the large group of companies would have been within $2 million of that true average.

**10.11** The local telephone company wants to estimate the average duration in minutes of long-distance calls made by its customers in the month of December. Records from previous Decembers indicate that the standard deviation of those durations is 1.8 minutes. If the records of 100 long-distance calls in December will be randomly selected and their average duration determined, what is the probability that the sample average will be within 0.25 minute of the true average duration of all calls placed in December?

**10.12** An ingenious employee of Gougem Beauty Products has designed a new bottle for their main product: Helen of Troy's Favorite Shampoo. The new bottle looks just like the old bottle but has two ounces less capacity than before.

    Gougem has reset the bottle-filling machine to correspond to the new capacity. However, the amount of shampoo dispensed from the machine at each filling is a random variable. Because of long experience with the machine Gougem can assume that the standard deviation ($\sigma$) of the amount of shampoo dispensed is 0.2 ounce. But they are not sure about the average amount in ounces ($\mu$) dispensed using the new setting.

    An experiment is planned to estimate $\mu$. A random sample of filled shampoo bottles will be selected and weighed. The sample average $\overline{X}$ will be used as an estimator for $\mu$. How large a sample must be taken so that the probability is at least 0.99 that $\overline{X}$ will assume a value within 0.05 ounce of the true $\mu$?

✦ **10.13** Violent Reaction Chemicals (VRC) wants to investigate the mean yield of a new process for making chemical $Q$. A small pilot plant that used the process during experimentation has supplied data suggesting that the standard deviation of the hourly yields is 1 ton.

    The process is now in operation, running at full scale. VRC wants to take a random sample of hourly yields of chemical $Q$ in order to estimate $\mu$, the mean hourly yield in tons. How large should the sample be so that the probability that $\overline{X}$ will be within 0.2 ton of $\mu$ is at least 0.95?

**10.14** The U.S. Congress has directed the Department of Defense to estimate the average amount per meal spent by a certain defense contractor who entertains military officers and government officials. The standard deviation of those amounts is known to be $10. If the Department of Defense will be allowed to sample the meal receipts of that contractor, how large a sample must be selected so that there is a probability of 0.98 that the sample average will be within $1 of the true average amount?

✦ **10.15** State sales tax receipts in Cheyenne, Wyoming, are collected monthly. A sample of 40 Cheyenne retail stores' sales tax receipts had an average for the month of $15,000 with a standard deviation of $2,000. Determine a 95 percent interval estimate of average monthly sales tax receipts for all retail stores in Cheyenne.

**10.16** A new line of convenience frozen foods intended for preparation in microwave ovens was test-marketed for a month in 50 stores belonging to a large supermarket chain. The average dollar amount of sales during that test, in those 50 stores, was $2,540 with the standard deviation being $340. Establish a 90 percent interval estimate of average monthly sales of the product in all the stores of that chain.

✦ **10.17** David Harleyson Motorcycles, Inc., has the flywheels for its observed trials bikes made by Hong Kong Foundry. The flywheels are supposed to weigh exactly 4 pounds. Previous shipments from HKF have shown that the weight of flywheels is a random variable with a standard deviation of 0.08 pound.

David Harleyson has just received a large shipment of flywheels from HKF. They will accept the shipment if the average weight of flywheels in a random sample of size $n = 25$ is between 3.98 and 4.02 pounds. Otherwise the shipment will be returned to Hong Kong.

   **a** If the true mean weight of flywheels in the shipment is 3.96 pounds, what is the probability that the shipment will be accepted?

   **b** If the true mean weight of flywheels in the shipment is 4.01 pounds, what is the probability that the shipment will be returned to Hong Kong?

✦ **10.18** The random variable $X$ denotes the number of successes in 20 trials of an experiment with only two possible outcomes: success or failure. Successive trials are independent, and the probability of observing a success on any one trial is $p = 0.25$.

   **a** What is $P(X \le 4)$?    **d** What is $P(X \le 7 \text{ or } 9 < X)$?

   **b** What is $P(4 < X)$?    **e** What is $P(X = 6)$?

   **c** What is $P(4 < X \le 10)$?

✦ **10.19** The auditor for a wholesale auto parts distributor wants to estimate the error rate in billings to the distributor's customers. A random sample of 200 billings showed 15 which involved errors.

   **a** What is the point estimate of the true proportion of all billings that involve errors?

   **b** Determine a 95 percent confidence interval for the true error rate.

**10.20** The University Bookstore receives large shipments of ribbon cartridges for electric typewriters. For a certain large shipment, the bookstore manager wants to estimate the proportion of cartridges that are defective. A random sample of 100 cartridges from the shipment turned up 9 that were defective.

   **a** What is the point estimate of the proportion of defective cartridges in the shipment?

**b** Determine a 90 percent interval estimate for the proportion of defective cartridges in the shipment.

**c** Ignoring the finite population correction (fpc), if 2,000 cartridges were shipped, what is a 90 percent interval estimate of the number of defective cartridges in the shipment?

✦ **10.21** The manager of a bank in a small college town wants to estimate the proportion of her depositors who work for the college. How large a sample of depositors must she select in order to be 96 percent confident that the sample proportion falls within 0.06 of the true proportion?

✦ **10.22** Dominique Clouseau is an inspector in the quality control section of the Normandy Aircraft Factory. Her job is to inspect the strength of a particular welded connection on the Puce Panther, a new fighter-bomber.

The connection is supposed to be able to withstand 2,000 foot-pounds of torque. Randomly selected connections can be torque-tested by Inspector Clouseau on a testing machine.

Every morning Inspector Clouseau randomly selects 25 (French) connections for testing. If two or more connections fail to withstand the test, that is, break at torques under 2,000 foot-pounds, she orders the production line shut down for maintenance. On a given morning during which the true proportion of defective connections being produced is 0.10, what is the probability that Inspector Clouseau will shut down the production line?

**10.23** Herculite Luggage Company produces a line of vinyl-covered aluminum briefcases. The process for making the clasps for the briefcases is "in control" if the proportion of defective clasps being made is 0.10 or less.

Herculite regularly selects a random sample of 50 clasps and checks them to see if they operate satisfactorily. If eight or more of the clasps in the sample are found to be defective, then the process is declared "out of control" and is stopped for inspection.

**a** If the proportion of defective clasps being made is 0.10, what is the probability of selecting a sample that will cause the process to be needlessly stopped for inspection?

**b** If the proportion of defective clasps being made is 0.25, what is the probability of selecting a sample that will result in the process not being stopped when it should have been?

**10.24** Avant-Garde Cereals is interested in the public acceptance of a new product: orange-flavored oatmeal. A small pilot study is planned, a survey of the customers of a supermarket in a neighborhood in Chicago where the population is very representative of the population of the whole midwest. The supermarket manager estimates that his store has about 4,000 regular customers.

A representative of Avant-Garde will select a sample from those customers and obtain their opinions about the taste of the oatmeal. The objective is to estimate $P$, the proportion of the population who like the taste.

Avant-Garde's market analysts believe that the true $P$ will be somewhere between 0.10 and 0.40. How large a sample is required so there is a probability of at least 0.90 that the sample proportion will fall within 0.05 of the true population proportion?

✦ **10.25** At the 1996 National Convention of the Right-to-Loaf Party there are 500 delegates from the state of Euphoria. The chairperson of the Euphoria delegation knows that between 30 and 60 percent of the state's delegates plan to vote for Vera Cool as the party's nominee for president.

The chairperson of the convention has asked the chairperson of the Euphoria delegation for a quick estimate of the true proportion of Euphoria's delegates who plan to vote for Ms. Cool. What size sample can the delegation chairperson use to estimate that proportion and be at least 95 percent confident that the sample proportion $p$ will be within 0.04 of the true proportion $P$?

**10.26** Checkem and Adam, an accounting firm, is preparing to conduct its annual audit of the Albany County Bank. One of the figures required is the total amount of money deposited in savings accounts.

Checkem and Adam has just hired a bright young accounting graduate who has suggested that substantial efficiencies are possible by using statistical sampling in an audit. The firm has decided to let the new employee estimate total savings using sampling.

Previous audits indicate that the standard deviation of the distribution of savings deposits is $100, and Albany County Bank knows there are 1,000 savings accounts. What size sample is required if the standard deviation of the estimator of total savings cannot exceed $1,000?

✦ **10.27** In Example 10.8, suppose the company executives select a different set of subjective probabilities for the three values of $p$: a 0.3 probability that $p$ will be 0.10, a 0.3 probability that $p$ will be 0.20, and a 0.4 probability that $p$ will be 0.30. If the number of defectives observed in the sample of 100 is $x = 18$, what is the conditional minimum-risk strategy?

**10.28** In Example 10.8, suppose that the number of defectives observed in the sample of 100 is $x = 34$. What is the conditional minimum-risk strategy?

✦ **10.29** Average monthly demand for low-income housing in Rock Springs is thought to be linearly related to the employment rate in that small city. Over a 10-month period the number of low-income housing units sold in Rock Springs ($Y$) and the employment rate as a proportion of the work force ($X$) have been measured. The data are shown below:

| Y, sales | X, rate | Y, sales | X, rate |
|----------|---------|----------|---------|
| 4 | 0.84 | 6 | 0.86 |
| 10 | 0.87 | 7 | 0.88 |
| 9 | 0.92 | 7 | 0.93 |
| 5 | 0.92 | 0 | 0.80 |
| 11 | 0.90 | 2 | 0.82 |

a Determine the regression line that estimates average demand as a function of employment rate.

b Estimate the error variance $\sigma^2$.

c Plot the scatter diagram of the data and plot the estimated regression line on the same graph.

d Determine a 90 percent confidence interval for average demand for low-income housing in months for which the employment rate is 0.89.

e Determine a 90 percent prediction interval for demand for low-income housing in a particular month when the employment rate is 0.85.

f Do you think any of the assumptions underlying the simple linear regression model might be violated by this data? If so, which ones?

✦ 10.30 A small company that manufactures a particular spare part for automatic washing machines wants to estimate the number of person-hours required for production runs of different sizes (number of parts per run). Runs are made at irregular intervals and in different sizes as demand for the part develops.

A random sample of eight production runs yielded the following data. Suppose the production manager assumes number of person-hours is linearly related to run size.

| Y, person-hours | X, run size |
|---|---|
| 80 | 25 |
| 42 | 12 |
| 64 | 18 |
| 48 | 12 |
| 85 | 24 |
| 105 | 32 |
| 58 | 18 |
| 59 | 16 |

a Plot the scatter diagram for this data. Do the assumptions for a simple linear regression model seem to be satisfied?

b Determine the regression line for estimating average person-hours from run size.

c Estimate $\sigma^2$.

d What is your point estimate of the number of person-hours required for a production run size of 20 parts?

e Determine a 95 percent prediction interval for the number of person-hours required for a run size of 20 parts.

10.31 The personnel manager of a large photographic equipment manufacturer located in Golden, Colorado, believes that employee tardiness (being late for work) is linearly related to temperature. That is, during periods of low temperatures more employees seem to arrive late—because their cars won't start, or they want to transport children to school, and so on—while if temperatures are high, it seems that fewer people are tardy.

A random sample of 20 working days from the past year yielded the following information. Here Y is the number of tardy workers and X is the temperature in degrees Fahrenheit at 8:00 A.M.

| Y | X | Y | X |
|---|---|---|---|
| 26 | 65 | 33 | 80 |
| 56 | 40 | 94 | -20 |
| 39 | 45 | 70 | 10 |
| 78 | 0 | 33 | 60 |
| 70 | -10 | 39 | 50 |
| 51 | 25 | 73 | -12 |
| 25 | 65 | 51 | 54 |
| 37 | 70 | 51 | 20 |
| 12 | 90 | 62 | 48 |
| 62 | 30 | 61 | 36 |

a Plot the scatter diagram of the data. Does the personnel manager's assumption about the relationship of tardiness to temperature seem reasonable?

b Determine the regression line that would estimate the average number of tardy workers given temperature at 8:00 A.M., and estimate $\sigma^2$.

c Give a 90 percent interval estimate of the average number of tardy workers on days when the 8:00 A.M. temperature is 10°F.

d Give point and 90 percent interval estimates of the number of tardy workers on a particular day when the temperature at 8:00 A.M. is 50°F.

**10.32** A scientist working for the Environmental Protection Agency believes that gasoline mileage for automobiles is related to driving speed and weight of the automobile. She decides to use a multiple linear regression model to try to predict miles per gallon given speed and weight.

Four automobiles, weighing 2,000, 3,000, 4,000, and 5,000 pounds, respectively, are selected, and each is driven under controlled conditions at speeds of 30, 50, and 70 miles per hour. Mileage figures ($Y$) for all combinations of speed ($X_1$) in miles per hour and weight ($X_2$) in pounds appear below.

| Y, mi/gal | X₁, speed | X₂, weight |
|-----------|-----------|------------|
| 48.2 | 30 | 2,000 |
| 40.6 | 50 | 2,000 |
| 32.3 | 70 | 2,000 |
| 38.0 | 30 | 3,000 |
| 28.7 | 50 | 3,000 |
| 22.3 | 70 | 3,000 |
| 30.2 | 30 | 4,000 |
| 22.5 | 50 | 4,000 |
| 18.6 | 70 | 4,000 |
| 24.2 | 30 | 5,000 |
| 18.9 | 50 | 5,000 |
| 13.6 | 70 | 5,000 |

Partial output from a MINITAB computer run of this data appears at the top of page 433. Use that output to do the following exercises.

a What is the estimated regression equation for predicting gasoline mileage from speed and weight?

b What is the point estimate for gasoline mileage of a 3,500-pound automobile being driven at 60 miles per hour?

*EXERCISE 10.32*

```
-- READ C1 C2 C3
-- 48.2 30 2000
-- 40.6 50 2000
-- 32.3 70 2000
-- 38.0 30 3000
-- 28.7 50 3000
-- 22.3 70 3000
-- 30.2 30 4000
-- 22.5 50 4000
-- 18.6 70 4000
-- 24.2 30 5000
-- 18.9 50 5000
-- 13.6 70 5000
-- NOBRIEF
-- REGR C1 2 C2 C3
```

```
THE REGRESSION EQUATION IS
Y =    69.6 -  .336 X1 - .0070 X2
```

| | COLUMN | COEFFICIENT | ST. DEV.<br>OF COEF. | T-RATIO =<br>COEF/S.D. |
|---|---|---|---|---|
| | -- | 69.592 | 2.829 | 24.60 |
| X1 | C2 | -0.33625 | 0.03857 | -8.72 |
| X2 | C3 | -0.0070300 | 0.0005633 | -12.48 |

```
THE ST. DEV. OF Y ABOUT REGRESSION LINE IS
S = 2.182
WITH ( 12- 3) =   9 DEGREES OF FREEDOM
```

```
R-SQUARED = 96.3 PERCENT
R-SQUARED = 95.4 PERCENT, ADJUSTED FOR D.F.
```

```
(X-PRIME X)INVERSE
```

| | 0 | 1 | 2 |
|---|---|---|---|
| 0 | 1.681250 | | |
| 1 | -.015625 | .000313 | |
| 2 | -.000233 | -.000000 | .000000 |

c Interpret the number R-SQUARED on the MINITAB output. Do you think the equation should give reasonable estimates of average gasoline mileages?

d Establish a 95 percent confidence inteval for the average gasoline mileage of 4,500-pound automobiles being driven 55 miles per hour.

◆ **10.33** Consider the data for Exercise 10.32, but only look at gasoline mileage versus weight of the automobile.

a Plot the scatter diagram for mileage versus weight. Do the assumptions for simple linear regression seem to be satisfied?

b Determine the estimated regression line for mileage as a function of weight, and estimate $\sigma^2$.

c Establish a 95 percent confidence interval for the average gasoline mileage of 4,500-pound automobiles. Compare that interval to the one obtained in part *d* of Exercise 10.32.

d The value of R-SQUARED in this simple linear regression setting is 64.7 percent. What does that number tell you about the value of incorporating speed as well as weight into the estimating equation?

**10.34** An accountant working for Albany County wants to establish a multiple-regression predicting equation for property taxes on homes ($Y$, in dollars). Variables that affect assessments for tax purposes are

$X_1$ = original purchase price, in thousands of dollars

$X_2$ = number of rooms in home

$X_3$ = age of home in years

A random sample of 15 county tax records gives the following data:

| Y | $X_1$ | $X_2$ | $X_3$ |
|-----|-----|-----|-----|
| 338 | 26 | 8 | 14 |
| 486 | 54 | 10 | 10 |
| 710 | 75 | 10 | 5 |
| 425 | 32 | 6 | 8 |
| 623 | 64 | 5 | 3 |
| 837 | 105 | 11 | 6 |
| 894 | 140 | 10 | 3 |
| 113 | 15 | 4 | 20 |
| 96 | 15 | 6 | 32 |
| 516 | 84 | 7 | 10 |
| 84 | 13 | 6 | 38 |
| 503 | 110 | 9 | 16 |
| 52 | 6 | 5 | 42 |
| 372 | 43 | 6 | 12 |
| 284 | 40 | 8 | 28 |

Partial output from MINITAB is given at the top of page 435. Use that output to do the following exercises.

a What is the estimated regression equation for predicting property tax given original price, number of rooms, and age?

b Estimate the average tax on all homes in Albany County that originally cost $50,000, have 8 rooms, and are 15 years old. Give both a point estimate and a 90 percent interval estimate for that average.

c Determine the estimated regression equation for tax versus only the original purchase price, and estimate $\sigma^2$. Now determine a 90 percent interval estimate of the average tax on homes originally costing $50,000, and compare with the interval obtained in part b.

d Determine a 90 percent prediction interval for the tax on a single home originally costing $50,000, with 8 rooms, that is 15 years old. Compare with the interval obtained in part b.

◆ 10.35 The sales manager of a company that markets in supermarkets a popular frozen food item believes that sales per month in thousands of dollars (Y) is related to the following variables:

$X_1$ = regional advertising expenditures by the company in thousands of dollars

$X_2$ = local advertising expenditures by the supermarket in hundreds of dollars

$X_3$ = retail price in dollars of one unit of the item

$X_4$ = per-capita income in thousands of dollars of people in the region served by the supermarket

*EXERCISE 10.34*

```
-- READ C1 C2 C3 C4
-- 338 26 8 14
-- 486 54 10 10
-- 710 75 10 5
-- 425 32 6 8
-- 623 64 5 3
-- 837 105 11 6
-- 894 140 10 3
-- 113 15 4 20
-- 96 15 6 32
-- 516 84 7 10
-- 84 13 6 38
-- 503 110 9 16
-- 52 6 5 42
-- 372 43 6 12
-- 284 40 8 28
-- REGR C1 3 C2 C3 C4

THE REGRESSION EQUATION IS
Y =     257. +  2.91 X1 +  23.1 X2
      - 10.0 X3
```

|  | COLUMN | COEFFICIENT | ST. DEV.<br>OF COEF. | T-RATIO =<br>COEF/S.D. |
|---|---|---|---|---|
|  | -- | 257.10 | 92.61 | 2.78 |
| X1 | C2 | 2.9066 | 0.8194 | 3.55 |
| X2 | C3 | 23.15 | 12.54 | 1.85 |
| X3 | C4 | -10.049 | 2.069 | -4.86 |

```
THE ST. DEV. OF Y ABOUT REGRESSION LINE IS
S = 71.95
WITH ( 15- 4) =  11 DEGREES OF FREEDOM

R-SQUARED = 94.4 PERCENT
R-SQUARED = 92.9 PERCENT, ADJUSTED FOR D.F.

(X-PRIME X) INVERSE
```

|  | 0 | 1 | 2 | 3 |
|---|---|---|---|---|
| 0 | 1.656958 |  |  |  |
| 1 | -.001194 | .000130 |  |  |
| 2 | -.155909 | -.001210 | .030385 |  |
| 3 | -.022537 | .000185 | -.000161 | .000827 |

A sample of eight supermarkets in different regions gave the following data:

| $Y$ | $X_1$ | $X_2$ | $X_3$ | $X_4$ |
|---|---|---|---|---|
| 23 | 10 | 4 | 2.13 | 5.4 |
| 17 | 8 | 6 | 1.98 | 5.2 |
| 11 | 2 | 3 | 2.15 | 6.3 |
| 34 | 23 | 10 | 2.04 | 5.8 |
| 16 | 13 | 8 | 1.97 | 5.4 |
| 12 | 5 | 6 | 1.93 | 5.0 |
| 21 | 9 | 1 | 2.09 | 6.0 |
| 31 | 18 | 7 | 1.98 | 6.1 |

Partial MINITAB output follows. Use that output to do the following exercises.

*EXERCISE 10.35*

```
-- READ C1 C2 C3 C4 C5
-- 23 10 4 2.13 5.4
-- 17 8 6 1.98 5.2
-- 11 2 3 2.15 6.3
-- 34 23 10 2.04 5.8
-- 16 13 8 1.97 5.4
-- 12 5 6 1.93 5.0
-- 21 9 1 2.09 6.0
-- 31 18 7 1.98 6.1
-- REGR C1 4 C2 C3 C4 C5

THE REGRESSION EQUATION IS
Y = - 6.73 + 1.46 X1 - 1.00 X2


     + 9.76 X3 - .515 X4

                                    ST. DEV.    T-RATIO =
          COLUMN     COEFFICIENT    OF COEF.    COEF/S.D.
          --            -6.73        44.48       -0.15
X1        C2            1.4594        0.3152       4.63
X2        C3           -1.0014        0.8516      -1.18
X3        C4            9.76         23.43         0.42
X4        C5           -0.515         3.786       -0.14

THE ST. DEV. OF Y ABOUT REGRESSION LINE IS
S = 3.405
WITH (  8- 5) =   3 DEGREES OF FREEDOM

R-SQUARED = 93.0 PERCENT
R-SQUARED = 83.6 PERCENT, ADJUSTED FOR D.F.

    (X-PRIME X)INVERSE

             0         1         2         3         4
    0    170.634
    1      .362      .009
    2    -2.064     -.017      .063
    3    -80.350    -.054      .734     47.336
    4      .095     -.044      .073     -3.444     1.236
```

a What is the regression equation for estimating monthly sales in a region given regional advertising expenditure, local advertising expenditure, price per unit and per-capita income?

b Give a point estimate of average monthly sales for supermarkets in a region where $14,000 of regional and $600 of local advertising expenditure occurred, when the price per unit of the item is $2.02 and per-capita income of people in the region is $5,500.

c Determine a 95 percent prediction interval for monthly sales for a particular supermarket in a region with the same characteristics as the one in part *b*.

◆ 10.36 Using the canned multiple regression program that is available to you on your own computer, determine an estimating regression equation for monthly sales given only regional and local advertising expenditures (see Exercise 10.35). Use the results of that computer run to determine a 95 percent prediction interval for sales when regional and local advertising expenditures are $14,000 and $600, respectively. Compare this interval to the interval obtained in part *c* of Exercise 10.35.

**10.37** Consider the Contemporary Electronics sales data given in Table 10.5 of Example 10.16. Determine all 9-month moving averages, and plot the original time series and the moving averages on the same graph. Compare this graph to the graph of the 12-month centered moving averages shown in Figure 10.8. Do you get about the same kind of picture with 9-month moving averages?

✦ **10.38** Determine all 4-quarter centered moving averages for the Wyoming sales and use tax time series given in Table 10.12. Plot the time series and the centered moving averages on the same graph, and observe the smoothing that occurs.

**10.39** For the Wyoming sales and use tax time series given in Table 10.12, obtain smoothed values using exponential smoothing with $w = 0.4$. Plot the original series and the series of smoothed values on the same graph. Now do the same exercise again, but using $w = 0.1$. Compare the two pictures and say which choice of smoothing constant you prefer.

**10.40** Verify the seasonal indices used in Table 10.11 for forecasting Wyoming liquor sales.

**10.41** Using the years 1978 through 1980 as base years for the forecast, and a smoothing constant $W = 0.2$, make seasonally adjusted exponential smoothing forecasts of quarterly revenues from the Wyoming sales and use tax (data in Table 10.12) for the years 1981 and 1982. Plot the series, the smoothed values, and the adjusted forecasted values (like we did in Figure 10.10), and compare with the results obtained from autoregressive forecasting (Figure 10.11).

✦ **10.42** For the data of Example 10.24 (Table 10.12), use the following first-order autoregressive model:

$$y_t = \beta_0 + \beta_1 y_{t-1} + \varepsilon$$

to forecast 1981 and 1982 revenues from the Wyoming sales and use tax based on data from the years 1978 through 1980. Plot and compare with Figure 10.11.

**10.43** Using the multiple regression program available to you on your own computer, the second-order autoregressive model

$$y_t = \beta_0 + \beta_1 y_{t-6} + \beta_2 y_{t-12} + \varepsilon$$

and data from the years 1980 through 1982, forecast monthly sales in 1983 for the Contemporary Personal Computer problem, the data for which are given in Table 10.5. Plot the original series, the estimated values, and the forecasted values on the same graph (see Figure 10.11). In this instance, do you think the forecasting procedure is a good one?

## SELECTED REFERENCES

Berenson, M. L., and D. M. Levine: *Basic Business Statistics*, 2d ed., Prentice-Hall, Inc., Englewood Cliffs, N.J., 1983.

Box, G. E. P., and G. M. Jenkins: *Time Series Analysis, Forecasting and Control*, Holden-Day, Inc., San Francisco, 1969.

Cochran, W. G.: *Sampling Techniques*, 2d ed., John Wiley & Sons, Inc., New York, 1963.

Geurts, M. D., and J. E. Reinmuth: "New Product Sales Forecasting Without Past Sales Data," *European Journal of Operational Research*, vol. 4, 1980, pp. 84–94.

Guenther, W. C.: *Concepts of Statistical Inference*, 2d ed., McGraw-Hill Book Company, New York, 1973.

Hamburg, M.: *Basic Statistics: A Modern Approach*, Harcourt Brace Jovanovich, New York, 1974.

Hines, W. W., and D. C. Montgomery: *Probability and Statistics in Engineering and Management Science*, 2d ed., John Wiley & Sons, Inc., New York, 1980.

Hogg, R. V., and A. T. Craig: *Introduction to Mathematical Statistics*, 2d ed., The Macmillan Company, New York, 1965.

Mansfield, E.: *Statistics for Business and Economics*, 2d ed., W. W. Norton & Company, New York, 1983.

Mendenhall, W., and J. E. Reinmuth: *Statistics for Management and Economics*, 4th ed., Duxbury Press, Boston, 1982.

Rao, C. R.: *Linear Statistical Inference and Its Applications*, John Wiley & Sons, Inc., New York, 1965.

Tummala, V. M. R.: *Decision Analysis with Business Applications*, Intext, New York, 1973.

# INVENTORY MODELS

*T*he problem of *when* to order, produce, or otherwise acquire a quantity of items, and of *how many* items to acquire per order is called an *inventory* problem. The purpose of maintaining an inventory, or stockpile, of the items is to provide for future demand. If extremely large inventories are maintained, then lots of capital is tied up in inventory, storage and insurance costs are high, and periodic maintenance of the items may become expensive; that is, large inventories are costly. On the other hand, if very few items are held in inventory, then "production on demand" may be required, with its attendant large start-up costs and the inefficiencies of small production runs, or the cost of lost sales and possible customer ill will that shortages could cause might also become very expensive. Basically, then, an inventory problem involves consideration of the tradeoffs between building up inventory and operating with minimal or no inventory.

A large business handling thousands of different items is continually faced with many small inventory problems, as well as with one large, overall problem that considers all the items together. Small businesses, government agencies, educational institutions, and the military services also have inventory decisions to make. Even a homemaker shopping at the grocery store is, consciously or not, "solving" an inventory problem as he or she decides whether or not to purchase an item and, if so, how many units to buy.

This persistence of inventory problems continues to inspire research. Various mathematical models have been proposed to help solve a wide variety of such problems, these days much more complex problems than those that were earlier "solved," sometimes surprisingly well, by just the good guesses of experienced, successful businesspeople. Our purpose here is to consider a few of the most basic types of inventory models. They will introduce the terminology associated with inventory problems and some of the standard ways of thinking about them. Before launching a more formal introduction, let us look at a simple but representative example.

### Example 11.1
### A Very Common Type of Inventory Problem

The Campus Bookstore at State University stocks replacement film-ribbon cartridges for a popular brand of typewriter. Almost all of the departmental and administrative offices at State U. use that brand of machine, and many students and faculty members also own that brand. Consequently the demand for cartridges is very regular and fairly high. Although the bookstore manager is aware that minor, random fluctuations in demand do occur, she has determined through experience that demand for the cartridges occurs at a nearly constant rate of 100 cartridges per day.

The cartridges are ordered from a regional supplier at a cost of $2.00 each. For every order a fixed cost of placing the order is also involved. This fixed cost consists of salaries of personnel engaged in keeping records and making out the order, costs of paper, envelopes, postage, phone calls to the supplier, and so on. This fixed cost is independent of the number of cartridges ordered. The manager pegs that fixed cost, generally called *setup cost* in inventory terminology, at about $100 per order.

A large inventory of the cartridges keeps customers happy, since then any time a cartridge is needed, one is available. However, items in inventory are subject to *holding costs* that can be quite substantial. Holding costs consist of cost of storage space, insurance, maintenance, and the cost of capital that is tied up in inventory and cannot otherwise be used. In the case of the film-ribbon cartridges, the bookstore manager has assessed daily holding cost per cartridge at about 2 percent of acquisition cost, or $0.04 per cartridge per day.

For a large initial inventory of, say, 1,000 such cartridges (a 10-day supply), this holding cost is not insignificant. Since this inventory will be depleted after 10 days (at which time another order is placed), we observe that average inventory per day is 1,000/2 = 500 (this approach will be made to appear plausible in Section 11.2). Then total inventory holding cost for the 10 days will be (500)($0.04)(10) = $200. That is a significant amount of money just for the inventory of typewriter cartridges. If you consider how many different items like that would be stocked in a university bookstore, and that such holding costs are involved for *every* different item maintained in inventory, you should begin to gain an appreciation of the importance of inventory problems in the business world. It is very worthwhile to consider ways of reducing overall inventory costs.

The fairly large holding cost might suggest frequent ordering (maintenance of a small inventory). But since the setup cost per order is $100, perhaps that is not such a good idea. For instance, if 100 cartridges were ordered in each order, meaning the placement of one order per day, the combined daily setup cost plus holding cost would be $100 + $2 = $102 (here the holding cost of $2 is for an average inventory of 100/2 = 50 cartridges at $0.04 per day). If, however, 1000 cartridges (a 10-day supply) were to be ordered each time an order is placed, the overall 10-day cost (one setup cost per order) is $100 + $200 = $300, on the average only $30 per day.

So you see that the problem of determining an overall *inventory policy* (how many to order, and when to order) for typewriter cartridges is a very important one for the bookstore manager. If she can determine an *optimal* (minimum-cost) such policy, she could probably save the bookstore quite a lot of money, or at least the bookstore's customers, since the price they pay for cartridges would include a markup to cover inventory costs.

One other cost would ordinarily have to be considered in a situation like this: the *shortage cost* of not having a cartridge in stock when a customer comes in to buy one. Since demand is not truly constant at 100 cartridges per day—some fluctuations in demand rate can occur in practice—it would not be possible to guarantee that a shortage would never occur. Here, however, we will assume a constant demand rate and will take up the question of shortages in a later section. Further, the time between placement of an order and receipt of the order, called *lead time,* would also have to be considered. Here we assume the supplier is very dependable, so that lead time is constant (not random) and orders can be placed to allow for that constant lead time.

Then suppose demand occurs at a constant rate of 100 cartridges per day, setup cost per order is $100, and holding cost per cartridge per day is $0.04. If all demand is to be met on time (no shortage permitted), just what *is* the optimal inventory policy? That is, how frequently should the bookstore place an order, and how many cartridges should be ordered each time, so that average daily cost is a minimum?

In Section 11.2 we will develop a mathematical model called the EOQ (economic order quantity) model which can be solved in general for $S_0 =$ order quantity and $t_0 =$ time between orders. Formulas for $S_0$ and $t_0$ will be given in Section 11.2 in terms of the symbols used to derive them. For the moment, we simply state those formulas in words. Note that the $2.00 purchase price of the cartridges does not become part of the formulas for the optimal inventory policy, since if all demand is to be met, then the total purchase price of the cartridges is the same regardless of the inventory policy adopted.

The formulas for $S_0$ and $t_0$ are

$$S_0 = \text{Optimal order quantity}$$

$$= \sqrt{\frac{2(\text{demand rate})(\text{setup cost})}{(\text{holding cost per item per unit time})}}$$

$$t_0 = \text{Optimal time between orders}$$

$$= \sqrt{\frac{2(\text{setup cost})}{(\text{demand rate})(\text{holding cost per item per unit time})}}$$

Thus for the solution to the bookstore problem we have

$$S_0 = \sqrt{\frac{2(100)(100)}{0.04}} = 707.106 \text{ cartridges}$$

$$t_0 = \sqrt{\frac{(2)(100)}{(100)(0.04)}} = 7.071 \text{ days}$$

This fractional solution is a bit awkward to implement in a practical way, so the bookstore manager would probably adopt the following (nonoptimal, but more convenient) policy:

Place an order every 7 days for 700 cartridges.

The average daily cost of this policy can be shown to be \$28.2857. Since the average daily cost of the *optimal* (nonrounded) policy is \$28.2843, we see that the manager would be using a very practical, nearly optimal policy.

Notice that a superficial first impression that might lead you to place an order for 100 cartridges every day would have been much more expensive (about \$74 per day more costly). Also notice that while a trial-and-error approach might have given you a near-optimal policy (say 1,000 cartridges every 10 days, at an average daily cost of \$30), without the formal mathematical analysis to be presented in Section 11.2 you would be unable to *guarantee* the optimality (or even near-optimality) of your solution.

## 11.1  SOME TERMINOLOGY FOR INVENTORY PROBLEMS

Like linear programming problems, inventory problems are approached as *optimization* problems. If demand is fixed over the time span of interest, the *planning horizon*, the objective is to *minimize* the *cost* of meeting that

442

CHAPTER 11

future demand. If, however, an inventory policy itself might influence demand, the objective may be to maximize profit among various competing policies.

In either case the objective is to establish an inventory *policy* (strategy) that is in some sense *optimal*. All inventory policies eventually become simply stated by specifying *how many* items are to be acquired and *when* such acquisition is to occur.

Thus the *decision variables* in an inventory problem, that is, those variables over which the manager has some control, are the *quantity* to order and the *time* at which the order is to be placed. Of course, if the item is to be manufactured by the company facing the inventory problem, we would seek the quantity to produce per production run and the time between runs. The values of those decision variables that optimize the objective function (cost or profit) yield the solution for the problem.

Some variables in an inventory problem cannot be totally controlled by the executive responsible for the inventory decision, although occasionally his or her decision may influence some of them. Such variables are demand, production rate, production cost per unit, storage cost per unit, shortage costs, depreciation, cost of capital, lead time, and setup costs. These and other variables may enter into any inventory problem. Following is a discussion of some of the values that must be known (or estimated) to permit a solution.

Any time an inventory in excess of immediate demand is on hand, a *holding cost* is incurred. Holding cost is ordinarily a function of the number of units in inventory and the time for which the units are held. Involved in holding cost are costs attributable to things like storage, handling, maintenance, insurance, depreciation, and the cost of capital.

*Setup costs* are those costs associated with placing an order or with tooling up and getting ready to make a production run. A setup cost will ordinarily be independent of the number of units to be ordered or produced. Thus the setup cost *per unit* decreases as the number of units acquired increases. (This suggests certain efficiencies associated with large production runs, but those gains may be offset by increased holding costs; in fact, this is the essence of the inventory *problem*.) Setup cost is a fixed cost coming from such things as record keeping, administrative charges, putting the production line in shape, and hiring and training personnel.

When inventory is insufficient to meet immediate demand, a shortage (backlog of orders) occurs, and there is an attendant *shortage cost*. Contributors to shortage cost are the cost of idle equipment or penalties that may be a contractual consequence of a shortage. The more nebulous contributor, however, is the cost attributable to a loss of customers or a reduction in their good will toward the company. In a textbook, of course, we may simply specify a shortage cost, but in reality it is extremely difficult to assess.

*Demand* is another variable whose value is difficult to determine. Yet it is extremely important, since without demand for the product there is no reason to consider maintaining any inventory of the product. Some standard inventory models assume demand at a constant rate (as in Example 11.1), a fairly reasonable assumption for things like typewriter cartridges or staple grocery items, for instance. More frequently, however, demand is a random variable. In Sections 11.5 to 11.7 we will consider random demand by presuming that we know its probability distribution. But in the real business world we seldom have exact knowledge of even the probability distribution of demand. Instead, we must estimate it, either from past data or using the judgment of experienced people.

Thus the inventory models you will see in this chapter are necessarily designed for simplifications of real-world inventory problems. The assumptions underlying their solution never exactly prevail. Yet they have been used to great advantage by business and industry, since very often a near-optimal solution to the real problem may be achieved by using them. Further, the ideas you will encounter during your study of simple inventory models will suggest approaches you might be able to use in more complex situations.

## 11.2 EOQ: THE BASIC INVENTORY MODEL

The inventory model discussed here is called the *economic order quantity* (*EOQ*) model. This model has proved quite successful in practice even though its underlying assumptions are rarely exactly satisfied. Its solution yields a near-optimal policy for a surprising number of real inventory problems. The EOQ model as considered here is just the same type of problem we considered in Example 11.1, except now it is presented in general, symbolic terms.

Fundamental to this model is a periodic inventory over time. The demand rate is constant, and units are acquired into inventory instantaneously. Thus we expect to see an immediate buildup to maximum inventory, then demand at a constant rate depleting that initial inventory to zero. No shortage is allowed in this basic model. At the point where inventory becomes zero, another order is received. The inventory level as a function of time is depicted in Figure 11.1.

Here $S$ is the order quantity and $t$ is the time between receipt of orders. Assume that demand occurs at a constant rate of $r$ items per unit time and that the planning horizon is indefinite. The graph in Figure 11.1 indicates an initial inventory of $S$ units, and that after time $t$ the inventory has dropped to zero units, at which time another order of size $S$ is received, and the cycle repeats itself.

Since demand occurs at the rate of $r$ items per unit time, $rt$ is the demand during time $t$. But we already know that demand will have to be $S$, the order quantity, so we observe the relationship

$$S = rt$$

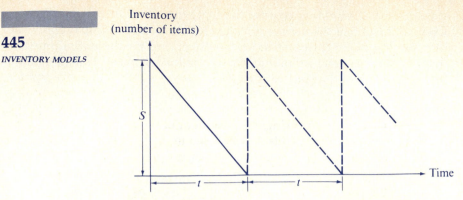

*FIGURE 11.1* The basic EOQ model

The equation for inventory level during the first cycle is

$$I = S - r(\text{time})$$

since when time $= 0$, the inventory level $I = S$, and when time $= t$, $I = 0$ because $S = rt$. Thus the slope of the line is $-r$, or the demand rate is the rate of decrease of inventory per unit time.

The objective is to discover $S$ and $t$ so that cost is minimized and all demand is met on time (no shortage allowed, a condition implied by Figure 11.1). Because of the indefinite planning horizon we will establish an inventory policy with the property that *average cost per unit time* is minimized. No other policy will give a lower overall cost over an arbitrary interval of time.

Let $c_1$ be the setup cost associated with placing an order, and let $c_2$ be the holding cost per item per unit time for items held in inventory. These are the only costs influencing the optimal policy. There is no shortage cost since the model permits no backlogging of orders, and the acquisition cost per item, exclusive of setup cost, is the same regardless of the inventory policy used to meet the demand.

Thus for one period, of length $t$, the cost of any inventory policy is

$$K = \text{setup cost} + \text{holding cost}$$

While setup cost for a single period is just $c_1$, it may not be clear just how the holding cost for a period should be computed.

Because we assume a constant demand rate $r$, during one period of length $t$ the level of inventory is changing continuously. If we knew that $n_1$ items were held for time $t_1$, $n_2$ for time $t_2$, and so on, we could calculate the sum of the $n_i t_i$'s, multiply by $c_2$, and have the holding cost. But Figure 11.1 implies that inventory is never the same during any two instants of time within the period.

In practice the holding cost for the EOQ model is taken to be $(S/2)(tc_2)$, where $S/2$ is called the *average inventory* for the period. This is equivalent to assuming that $S/2$ items are held in inventory for the entire time $t$, at the cost of $c_2$ per item per unit time. The following example demonstrates the plausibility of that line of reasoning.

**Example 11.2**
**Demonstration that Average Inventory is $S/2$**

Suppose that $S = 6$ and that items are demanded at the rate of one per two days (the demand rate $r$ is one-half an item per day). Then it will take 12 days to reduce the initial inventory to zero. Presuming that the one item demanded leaves inventory at the *end* of each two-day interval, daily inventory status is shown in Figure 11.2.

Let $c_2 = \$3$ per item per day. From Figure 11.2 it is clear that one of the original items is held for all 12 days, one for only 10 days, and so on. So the actual holding cost is

$$\text{Holding cost} = 1(12)(\$3) + 1(10)(\$3) + 1(8)(\$3) + 1(6)(\$3) \\ + 1(4)(\$3) + 1(2)(\$3)$$

$$= \$126$$

The dashed line in Figure 11.2 gives a fair approximation of inventory level as time progresses. If we were to call average inventory 6.5 items divided by 2, then $(S/2)(tc_2)$, with $S = 6.5$ and $t$ taken to be 13 (where the dashed line in Figure 11.2 intercepts the horizontal axis), becomes

$$\left(\frac{6.5}{2}\right)(13)(\$3) = \$126.75$$

*FIGURE 11.2*   Inventory level per day

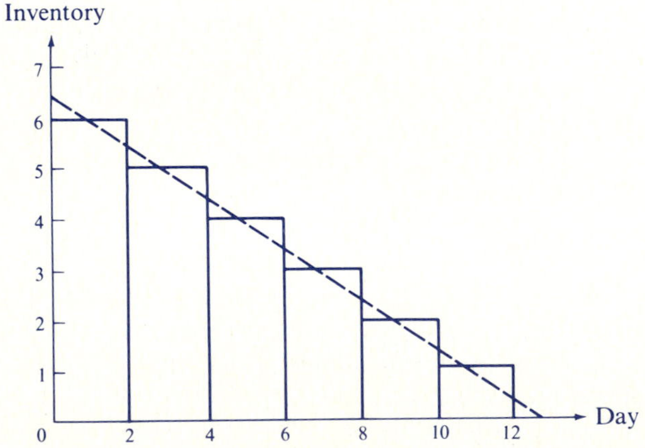

This gives a good approximation to the actual holding cost. Notice that the number \$126.75 is just the area of the triangle in Figure 11.2 (one-half the base $t$ times the altitude $S$) times the cost per item per unit time, $c_2$.

Now extend this line of reasoning and think about how Figure 11.2 would look if it consisted of many such rectangles, steadily diminishing in height as time increases. Picture each rectangle with much narrower width, and let the number of rectangles increase without bound (but still keep them all within a fixed time interval $t$). In the limit, as the widths of the rectangles approach zero while their number increases, the graph of inventory level will become the triangle depicted back in Figure 11.1. Finally, notice that the holding cost for the true situation shown in Figure 11.2 is just the *area* under the graph (sum of the areas of the rectangles) times \$3. Then it seems reasonable that the holding cost for the situation depicted in Figure 11.1 should also be area times $c_2$. But that results in the formula $(S/2)(tc_2)$, since $S$ is the altitude and $t$ is the base of the triangle in Figure 11.1.

Now we can write a mathematical expression for the cost of an inventory policy for the EOQ model, for one period of length $t$. We have already observed that the cost $K$ is setup cost plus holding cost for the period. Now we know that

$$K = c_1 + \frac{S}{2} tc_2$$

However, the original objective in the EOQ model was not to minimize the total cost $K$, but rather the *average cost per unit time*. Then divide $K$ by $t$ to obtain the objective function

$$C(S, t) = \frac{c_1}{t} + \frac{S}{2} c_2$$

This average cost function $C(S, t)$ involves as unknowns only the *decision variables* $S$ and $t$ (the order quantity and the time between orders), since the costs $c_1$ and $c_2$ are assumed to be known.

The fact that $S = rt$ allows $C$ to be written as a function of only *one* unknown quantity. By substituting $S = rt$ into $C(S, t)$ we obtain the simpler objective function

$$C(t) = \frac{c_1}{t} + \frac{rc_2}{2} t$$

Now our objective is to minimize $C(t)$, a function of the single variable $t$, since of course we also assume the demand rate $r$ is known.

Discovering the value of $t$ which minimizes $C(t)$ for given $r$, $c_1$, $c_2$ is a very easy calculus problem. However, a good plausibility argument for the solution can be made using only a simple graph and a little algebra.

The function $C(t)$ is the sum of two positive quantities, one of which is

$c_1/t$, the other being $(rc_2/2)t$. The function $c_1/t$ graphs as a branch of a hyperbola, while the graph of the function $(rc_2/2)t$ is just a straight line. Figure 11.3 suggests, as dashed lines, the general shape of graphs of these two constituent parts of $C(t)$ and shows the graph of their sum, the solid curve, which is the graph of $C(t)$ itself.

Figure 11.3 attempts to demonstrate that the value of $t$ which minimizes $C(t)$, the time $t_0$, occurs precisely at the point of intersection of the two dashed lines representing, respectively, average setup cost per unit time (the curved line) and average holding cost per unit time (the straight line). A point on the solid-line graph of $C(t)$ itself is just the sum of the vertical distances to each of the dashed lines at any time $t$. Careful inspection of Figure 11.3 might convince you that the sum of distances is least at the point $t = t_0$, where the dashed lines intersect.

Thus to find $t_0$ we merely set $c_1/t$ equal to $(rc_2/2)t$, realizing that when we do, the value of $t$ becomes $t_0$. Therefore,

$$\frac{c_1}{t_0} = \frac{rc_2}{2} t_0 \qquad \text{or} \qquad t_0^2 = \frac{2c_1}{rc_2}$$

This gives the solution

$$t_0 = \sqrt{\frac{2c_1}{rc_2}}$$

Here we use the positive square root because time cannot be negative.

Now we know $t_0$, the optimal time between orders. What about the optimal (economic) order quantity? That is easy to find, since $S = rt$ for any $t$. Thus

$$S_0 = rt_0 = \sqrt{\frac{2r^2c_1}{rc_2}} \qquad \text{or} \qquad S_0 = \sqrt{\frac{2rc_1}{c_2}}$$

**FIGURE 11.3**    Locating the minimum of $C(t)$

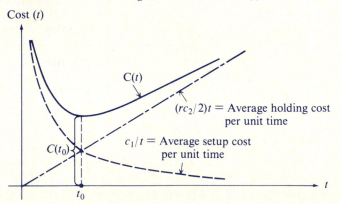

Now we have formulas for the optimal values of the decision variables, expressed in terms of the known quantities $r$, $c_1$, and $c_2$, which are, respectively, the demand rate, the setup cost, and the holding cost per item per unit time. It is also fairly easy to determine the optimal average cost per unit time, $C(t_0)$, which we denote for consistency by $C_0$, in terms of those same known quantities. Substitution of $t_0 = \sqrt{2c_1/rc_2}$ into our expression for $C(t)$ yields, after some fairly interesting algebra, the expression

$$C_0 = \sqrt{2rc_1c_2}$$

### Example 11.3
### Solving an EOQ Model Using the Formulas

High Plains Tire Sales supplies a particular brand of large truck tire for very big trucks that haul ore at nearby uranium mines. These tires are demanded at an average rate of two per day, setup cost is $400 per order, and holding cost is $4 per tire per day. Here, because High Plains Tire Sales uses its own truck to transport the tires ordered, and the truck can carry a small order at about the same cost as it can carry a large order, transportation cost is deemed part of the setup cost. These enormous tires are very expensive, so cost of capital represents a substantial portion of the holding cost. Thus, while both setup cost and holding cost might seem high to you, in the scenario just described these costs might be fairly realistic.

For substitution into the EOQ formulas, we have $r = 2$, $c_1 = 400$, and $c_2 = 4$. Therefore,

$$t_0 = \sqrt{\frac{2(400)}{2(4)}} = 10$$

$$S_0 = \sqrt{\frac{2(2)(400)}{4}} = 20$$

$$C_0 = \sqrt{2(2)(400)(4)} = 80$$

Thus the optimal policy for High Plains Tire Sales is to order 20 tires every 10 days, for an average inventory cost per day of $80.

To demonstrate the meaning of optimality here, suppose we had tried 11 days or 9 days between orders. If $t = 11$, then $S = rt = 2(11) = 22$, and $C$ becomes

$$C(11) = \tfrac{400}{11} + (\tfrac{22}{2})(4) \simeq 36.36 + 44 = 80.36 > 80$$

If $t = 9$, then $S = rt = 2(9) = 18$, and $C$ is

$$C(9) = \tfrac{400}{9} + (\tfrac{18}{2})(4) \simeq 44.44 + 36 = 80.44 > 80$$

This shows that at $t_0 = 10$ we have a relative minimum for $C(t)$, relative to integer $t$ in the neighborhood of 10. Of course, our derivation of the EOQ formulas has already told us that this relative minimum must be the absolute minimum value of $C(t)$.

Since in this example the constants $r$, $c_1$, and $c_2$ are known, the function $C(t)$ as well as each of its two constituent functions may be graphed. Here

$$C(t) = \frac{400}{t} + 4t$$

The graph in Figure 11.4 shows the location of the minimum of $C(t)$ at the intersection of the curves associated with setup cost and holding cost.

While the graph does show a minimum for $C(t)$ at $t = t_0 = 10$, it also shows that small deviations from the optimal policy will not drastically increase cost. If a weekly or biweekly order date is more convenient, cost will not appreciably exceed the optimal cost. But High Plains Tire Sales must remember that $C(t)$ represents *average* cost per unit time, not total cost. Over a long time span the savings in *total* cost could be substantial if the precise optimal policy, order 20 tires every 10 days, is used.

The more critical insight to be gained from the graph in Figure 11.4 has to do with the relationship between setup cost and holding cost. Increasing the time between orders from, say, 1 day to 4 days allows the contribution per tire due to setup cost to fall rapidly. Beyond 10 days, however, this per-item efficiency is offset by increasing holding cost as inventory grows. Ten days is the optimal tradeoff point between pressures to order in large quantities and efforts to hold down cost of inventory.

**FIGURE 11.4**    Graph of $C(t)$ for High Plains Tire Sales problem

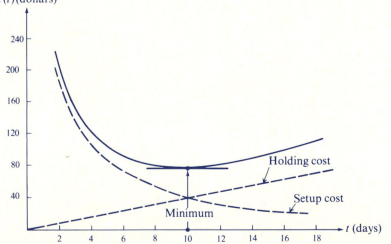

Here we consider the basic EOQ model from the previous section, but with the additional condition that "price breaks," in this case *quantity discounts*, are made available. That is, the purchase price per item is smaller if the quantity purchased in one order exceeds some fixed number of items, say $B$ ($B$ for "break point").

In this case the per-item acquisition cost, above setup cost, can no longer be ignored. In Section 11.2 that per-item cost was assumed to be constant regardless of the number of items purchased, so the total price of items necessary to meet demand was not affected by the choice of inventory policy. For instance, in the High Plains Tire Sales problem (Example 11.3), we did not even have to know the cost per tire to be able to determine the optimal policy. But in the case of quantity discounts, since the optimal inventory policy must specify the number of items to order, but the purchase price per item *depends* on the quantity ordered, then the cost of an inventory policy is *not* independent of the per-item acquisition cost. That is, the approach to determining the optimal order quantity must allow for the quantity discount.

A term that reflects purchase price per item may easily be incorporated into the cost function. In the basic EOQ model we saw the following expression for total cost:

$$K(S, t) = c_1 + \frac{S}{2} tc_2$$

If the per-item price is $p$, then the purchase of $S$ items adds to this cost function the term $pS$. Thus when purchase price is considered, the function for total cost is

$$K(S, t) = c_1 + \frac{S}{2} tc_2 + pS$$

Since we want to minimize $C$, the average cost per unit time, and the constraint $S = rt$ still applies, dividing $K(S, t)$ by $t$ and substituting $t = S/r$ gives

$$C(S) = \frac{c_1 r}{S} + \frac{c_2 S}{2} + pr$$

Notice that this cost function is just the function for the basic EOQ model (expressed as a function of $S$ instead of $t$) plus a *constant* term equal to $pr$. Here we have the mathematical justification for our statement that the optimal inventory policy did not depend upon the (constant) purchase price $p$. The value of $S$ that minimizes $C(S)$ is still $S_0 = \sqrt{2c_1 r/c_2}$, since the addition to a function of a constant term does not change the *location* of its minimum (value of $S$); it only changes its minimum *value*.

That is, this new function is minimized by the same value of $S$ as before, $S_0$, but its minimum value is now $\sqrt{2rc_1c_2} + pr$.

Now that we appreciate the effect of including purchase price in the inventory cost function, let's consider the EOQ model with a *quantity discount*. Suppose that whenever the quantity ordered $S$ is less than $B$ items, the price per item is $p_1$, but whenever $B$ or more items are ordered, the per-item price is reduced to $p_2$ ($p_2 < p_1$). Then the cost $C(S)$ must be described using *two* functions, depending on the level of $S$. That new expression for cost is

$$C(S) = \begin{cases} C_1(S) = \dfrac{c_1r}{S} + \dfrac{c_2S}{2} + p_1r & S < B \\[2mm] C_2(S) = \dfrac{c_1r}{S} + \dfrac{c_2S}{2} + p_2r & B \le S \end{cases}$$

Notice that $C_1(S)$ and $C_2(S)$ differ only in their third terms, which are constants in both expressions since $p_1$, $p_2$, and $r$ are all known constants. Thus the graphs of $C_1(S)$ and $C_2(S)$, shown in Figure 11.5, are identical in shape, both of course resembling the graph of $C(t)$ that was depicted in Figure 11.3. The graph of $C_2(S)$ looks the same as that of $C_1(S)$ but is shifted downward by the amount $p_1r - p_2r$, the difference in purchase price if the quantity discount is applied.

Clearly both $C_1(S)$ and $C_2(S)$ achieve their minimum at the same value of $S$, the point $S^*$ shown on Figure 11.5. However, $S^*$, which we know from Section 11.2 and our preceding discussion has the value

$$S^* = \sqrt{\frac{2c_1r}{c_2}}$$

**FIGURE 11.5**  The relationship between $C_1(S)$ and $C_2(S)$

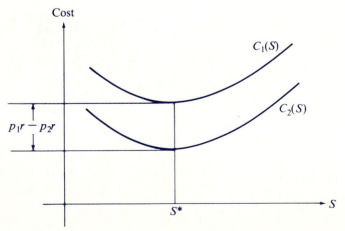

is not necessarily the solution (optimal order quantity) for our quantity-discount inventory problem. As you will see, that solution depends on the relative locations of $S^*$ and $B$, where $B$ is the point at which the quantity discount applies.

The reasoning that gives the optimal order quantity $S_0$ for this quantity-discount problem is best appreciated with reference to the two curves in Figure 11.5. Suppose first of all that $B$ is a number on the $S$ axis to the left of $S^*$. Then the lowest possible value of $C(S)$ would occur at $S^*$, and would in fact be $C_2(S^*)$, since if we order more than $B$ items, the cost is given by the lower of the two curves. Thus if $B < S^*$, $S_0 = S^*$. If $S^* = B$, of course, the solution is still $S_0 = S^* = B$.

Now suppose $S^* < B$; that is, the break point for the quantity discount occurs to the right of $S^*$ on Figure 11.5. Now for an order in the amount $B$ the cost would be $C_2(B)$, while an order of size $S^*$ would give a cost $C_1(S^*)$. Which of these two costs, $C_2(B)$ or $C_1(S^*)$, is smaller depends upon how far to the right of $S^*$ the break point $B$ is located. A simple solution procedure, which also incorporates the results of the discussion in the previous paragraph, is given by the following three steps, where $S_0$ is the optimal order quantity:

1 Find $S^*$.

2 If $B < S^*$, then $S_0 = S^*$.

3 If $S^* \le B$, find $C_1(S^*)$ and $C_2(B)$.
   If $C_2(B) \le C_1(S^*)$, then $S_0 = B$.
   If $C_1(S^*) < C_2(B)$, then $S_0 = S^*$.

### Example 11.4
### High Plains Tire Sales Problem with a Quantity Discount

In the High Plains Tire Sales problem of Example 11.3 the setup cost was $c_1 = \$400$ per order and the holding cost was $c_2 = \$4$ per tire per day. The large truck tires involved were demanded at an assumed constant rate of 2 tires per day. Suppose further that if fewer than 40 tires are ordered in any one order, the cost per tire is $560, while if 40 or more tires are ordered, a quantity discount is applied and the cost per tire is only $525. This is the quantity-discount problem described above, with $B = 40$, $p_1 = \$560$, and $p_2 = \$525$.

The two functions we need are determined by substituting the following quantities into the general formulas for $C_1(S)$ and $C_2(S)$: $c_1 = \$400$, $c_2 = \$4$, $r = 2$, $p_1 = \$560$, and $p_2 = \$525$. Thus

$$C_1(S) = \frac{(400)(2)}{S} + \frac{4S}{2} + (560)(2) = \frac{800}{S} + 2S + 1{,}120$$

and
$$C_2(S) = \frac{(400)(2)}{S} + \frac{4S}{2} + (525)(2) = \frac{800}{S} + 2S + 1{,}050$$

Step 1 of the solution procedure tells us to find $S^*$. This is just the optimal order quantity that we found for the constant-price problem in Example 11.3, but in this problem it is not necessarily the best solution. Thus

$$S^* = \sqrt{\frac{2c_1 r}{c_2}} = \sqrt{\frac{2(400)(2)}{4}} = 20$$

We check step 2 and find that it does not apply, since $B = 40$ while $S^* = 20$. Thus we must go to step 3. This tells us we must find $C_1(S^*)$ and $C_2(B)$.

$$C_1(S^*) = C_1(20) = \tfrac{800}{20} + 2(20) + 1{,}120 = 1{,}200$$
$$C_2(B) = C_2(40) = \tfrac{800}{40} + 2(40) + 1{,}050 = 1{,}150$$

Since $C_2(B) < C_1(S^*)$ because $1{,}150 < 1{,}200$, the optimal order quantity is

$$S_0 = 40 \qquad (= B)$$

Of course, since always in the EOQ model $S = rt$, we have

$$t_0 = \frac{S_0}{r} = \tfrac{40}{2} = 20$$

Thus High Plains Tire Sales' optimal inventory policy for this quantity-discount situation is:

Order 40 tires every 20 days.


## Example 11.5
### Tire Problem with Different Break Point

Suppose that in Example 11.4 the quantity discount did not apply unless 75 or more tires were purchased in one order. Here we would have $B = 75$ instead of 40.

Still, $S^* = 20 < B = 75$, so we have to reconsider step 3 of the solution procedure. We already know that $C_1(S^*) = C_1(20) = 1{,}200$. But now

$$C_2(B) = C_2(75) = \tfrac{800}{75} + 2(75) + 1{,}050 = 1{,}210.67$$

In this case $1{,}200 < 1{,}210.67$, or $C_1(S^*) < C_2(B)$, so the solution is:

Order 20 tires every 10 days.

Here the break point is so high (we must order 75 or more tires to gain the advantage of the price discount) that the holding cost prohibits ordering that many tires. That is, very large orders imply high holding costs as more tires are maintained in inventory, so in the long run the quantity discount does not change the old, undiscounted policy.

## 11.4   A GENERALIZED EOQ MODEL

We now consider a more general *production-inventory* situation. Here items are *produced* at a rate of $k$ per unit time, while items are demanded at a rate of $r$ per unit time. Production and demand may occur simultaneously and, in order to satisfy overall demand, necessarily $r < k$. Shortages are allowed, and production is halted after inventory reaches a prescribed level. This situation is suggested by Figure 11.6.

Here one complete period in the inventory cycle is of length $T = t_1 + t_2 + t_3 + t_4$, with production being initiated periodically when maximum shortage $s$ is attained. In formulating the model mathematically we shall use the following notation:

$S$ = maximum inventory during a period (where production is stopped)

$s$ = maximum shortage during a period (where production is begun)

$k$ = production rate (number of items per unit time)

$r$ = demand rate (number of items per unit time)

$t_1$ = time required to bring the level of inventory from $-s$ to zero items

$t_2$ = time required for inventory to build from zero to $S$

$t_3$ = time required for demand to exhaust maximum inventory (while no production occurs)

$t_4$ = time required for demand alone to produce a shortage of $s$ items

$c_1$ = setup cost per production run

*FIGURE 11.6*   The generalized EOQ model

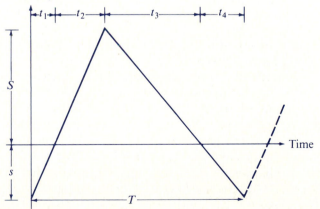

$c_2$ = holding cost per item per unit time

$c_3$ = shortage cost per item per unit time

In this model production occurs only during the time interval of length $t_1 + t_2$ (see Figure 11.6). At the end of that time the maximum inventory $S$ is achieved. Then production is stopped for a time of duration $t_3 + t_4$. During that time the demand depletes the inventory through the zero level until the maximum shortage $s$ is reached. At that point production is resumed and the cycle repeats.

The objective, of course, is an optimal production-inventory policy. We want to minimize $C$, the average cost per unit time for an indefinite planning horizon. Setup cost, holding cost, and shortage cost are all involved in that average cost, as are the production rate and the demand rate.

Here the per-item production cost, above setup cost, is assumed fixed over the planning horizon and consequently will not be included in the average cost function. Demand, which must be met eventually, is there regardless of the policy adopted. That is, the amount $r(t_1 + t_2 + t_3 + t_4)$ = $rT$ is the total demand for one period and *must* be produced. *When* to begin production of those $rT$ items, and *how many* to produce each production run, is the production-inventory policy, but every possible policy involves exactly the same production cost, the cost of producing $rT$ items.

The average cost per unit time for one period is

$$C = \frac{\text{setup cost} + \text{holding cost} + \text{shortage cost}}{\text{duration of one period}}$$

Using the "area times cost" analogy of Section 11.2, we reason that holding cost is $(S/2)(t_2 + t_3)c_2$, and that shortage cost is $(s/2)(t_1 + t_4)c_3$ (see Figure 11.6). Then $C$, as a function of six decision variables, is

$$C(S, s, t_1, t_2, t_3, t_4) = \frac{c_1 + (S/2)(t_2 + t_3)c_2 + (s/2)(t_1 + t_4)c_3}{t_1 + t_2 + t_3 + t_4}$$

Needless to say, it would be much nicer to have an expression for $C$ that involves fewer variables.

Fortunately there are constraints in this problem that permit $C$ to be expressed as a function of only *two* decision variables. Consider the implications of Figure 11.6. First of all, during time $t_1$ both production and demand occur. At the rate $k$, the number of items produced in time $t_1$ is $kt_1$. During that same time, however, $rt_1$ items are demanded. The net gain of production over demand in time $t_1$ is $kt_1 - rt_1 = t_1(k - r)$. This also happens to be $s$, since during time $t_1$ the inventory moves from the level $-s$ to the level zero. Thus

$$s = t_1(k - r)$$

During time $t_4$, where the inventory begins at zero level but no production occurs, the demand produces the shortage $s$. Then we also have the equation

$$s = rt_4$$

Similar reasoning yields two other equations:

$$S = t_2(k - r) \qquad S = rt_3$$

Now we have a system of four equations in the six unknowns $S$, $s$, $t_1$, $t_2$, $t_3$, and $t_4$. You are encouraged to satisfy yourself that these equations are valid (see Figure 11.6). That consideration will enhance your understanding of the model.

We can solve that system of four equations for any two variables, expressed in terms of the other four. Suppose that we arbitrarily decide to solve the system for $t_3$ and $t_4$. Then $C$ can be written as a function of just those two variables. Substitution and some algebraic simplification yields the objective function

$$C(t_3, t_4) = \frac{2(1 - r/k)c_1 + r(t_3^2 c_2 + t_4^2 c_3)}{2(t_3 + t_4)}$$

The point $(t_3, t_4)$ at which $C$ is minimum will allow an optimal production-inventory policy to be stated. $S$, $s$, $t_1$, and $t_2$ can be determined from the four constraining equations once $t_3$ and $t_4$ are known. The methods of multivariable calculus may be used to determine the optimal values of $t_3$ and $t_4$.

The optimal solution is

$$t_3^* = \sqrt{\frac{2(1 - r/k)c_1 c_3}{rc_2(c_2 + c_3)}} \qquad t_4^* = \sqrt{\frac{2(1 - r/k)c_1 c_2}{rc_3(c_2 + c_3)}}$$

Then $S^*$ and $s^*$, the optimal maximum inventory and maximum shortage, respectively, are

$$S^* = rt_3^* \qquad s^* = rt_4^*$$

The optimal policy may be stated in many ways. One such statement is:

Start production when a shortage of $s^*$ is reached, and stop production when inventory level reaches $S^*$.

Or, since

$$t_1^* = \frac{s^*}{k - r} \qquad t_2^* = \frac{S^*}{k - r}$$

then $T^* = t_1^* + t_2^* + t_3^* + t_4^*$ can be determined. Then the same optimal policy could be stated as:

Start a production run every $T^*$ time units and produce for the duration $t_1^* + t_2^*$.

In the usual "how many" and "when" format, the policy could be stated as:

Start a production run every $T^*$ time units and produce $k(t_1^* + t_2^*)$ items in each run.

### Example 11.6
### Production-Inventory Policy for Stagheart Trumpets

Stagheart Musical Instruments can produce student-line trumpets at the rate of 24 trumpets per day. These reasonably inexpensive ($300 retail) trumpets are ordered by music stores at the rate of 6 trumpets per day. Setup cost per production run is $1,600, holding cost per trumpet per day is $2, and shortage cost per trumpet per day has been assessed at $9. What production policy will minimize Stagheart's average inventory-related cost per day?

Here $k = 24$, $r = 6$, $c_1 = \$1,600$, $c_2 = \$2$, and $c_3 = \$9$. Thus

$$t_3^* = \sqrt{\frac{2(1 - \frac{6}{24})(1,600)(9)}{6(2)(2 + 9)}} = 12.79 \text{ days}$$

$$t_4^* = \sqrt{\frac{2(1 - \frac{6}{24})(1,600)(2)}{6(9)(2 + 9)}} = 2.84 \text{ days}$$

$$S^* = 6(12.79) = 76.74 \text{ trumpets}$$

$$s^* = 6(2.84) = 17.04 \text{ trumpets}$$

$$t_1^* = \frac{17.04}{24 - 6} = 0.947 \text{ days}$$

$$t_2^* = \frac{76.74}{24 - 6} = 4.263 \text{ days}$$

$$T^* = 0.947 + 4.263 + 12.79 + 2.84 = 20.84 \text{ days}$$

Since $k(t_1^* + t_2^*) = 24(0.947 + 4.263) = 24(5.21) = 125.04$, an almost-optimal production-inventory policy is:

Start a production run every 21 days, and produce 125 trumpets per run.

This means that production would start at the point when approximately 17 of the student-line trumpets are on back-order by music stores.

Production would occur for a little over 5 days per cycle, with maximum inventory during one cycle being about 77 trumpets. During the last nearly 15 days of the cycle no production occurs, and demand at the rate of 6 trumpets per day reduces this maximum inventory through the zero level down to a shortage of about 17 trumpets, at which point another run begins. Note that it takes almost 3 days for the maximum shortage to develop, but a little less than 1 day to make up the shortage.

These numbers are only approximate, of course, since the precise optimal policy has been modified slightly for administrative convenience. Here production occurs at three-week intervals, with the run occupying a little more than five working days of the first week. The average cost per day of this policy, obtained by substituting $t_3^*$ and $t_4^*$ into $C(t_3, t_4)$, is about $153.50. Since the total cost for 20.84 days would then be $3,198.94, during which time 125.04 trumpets are produced, the portion of the wholesale price of such a trumpet attributable to inventory cost is about $25.58.

## 11.5 AN EOQ PROBLEM WITH SAFETY STOCK

In the basic EOQ model that was introduced in Section 11.2 we assumed a constant demand rate $r$. Now suppose that demand is *random*, with $r$ being the *average* number of items demanded per unit time. We also assume that a *constant lead time* $t_1$ occurs between placement of an order and its receipt. Otherwise, conditions for the basic EOQ model remain the same; $S$ is the order quantity, $t$ is the time between orders, $c_1$ is setup cost per order, and $c_2$ is holding cost per item per unit time.

If demand is deterministic, occurring at a constant rate $r$, then all we have to do is place the order at time $t_1$ prior to the date on which we must receive the order. This is the situation shown in Figure 11.7. The

*FIGURE 11.7*    EOQ with constant lead time and constant demand rate

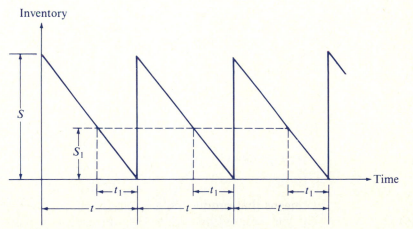

inventory level at which the order is placed, $S_1$, is called the *reorder point*.

With random demand, we can still place the order when the level of inventory reaches the reorder point $S_1$. However, although $r$ is the average demand rate, the variability in demand means that on occasion we could reach zero inventory before the next order is received. In this case a shortage will occur. Other times we may still have some items in inventory upon receipt of the next order. Figure 11.8 suggests that situation.

From Figure 11.8 we see that a backlog of orders is assumed. That is, whenever a shortage occurs, that shortage is made up from the next order of size $S$. Note also that the time between receipt of orders is no longer constant (although lead time $t_1$ *is* constant). Orders are placed at the reorder point $S_1$, but that reorder point occurs at different times during each period because of the random demand.

However, the basic EOQ model does not provide for a shortage. If the order quantity $S$ is to be near optimal for this situation, then we really should not permit a shortage to develop. One way to do this is to always carry some *safety stock* in inventory, sufficient to overcome any potential shortage. On the other hand, because demand is random, the amount of safety (buffer) stock required to guarantee *no* shortage could be substantial. The cost of carrying the safety stock in inventory might be very large.

Instead of carrying extremely high levels of safety stock, inventory managers often determine a safety stock so that the *probability* of a shortage developing is small. This will not guarantee no shortage, but it will guarantee that a shortage will occur only rarely.

Now while the situation depicted in Figure 11.8 is the true state of nature, we will act as if the average demand rate $r$ is really a constant demand rate, putting us in the position illustrated by Figure 11.7. From

**FIGURE 11.8**    EOQ with constant lead time and random demand

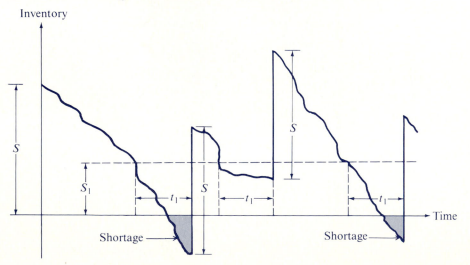

that figure we see that $S_1 = rt_1$. Let $B$ (for buffer) equal the amount of safety stock to keep on hand. Then the new reorder point, including provision for the buffer, is $B + rt_1$. We want the probability that all of this inventory is exhausted during the lead time to be small. Suppose we fix that probability at the level $\alpha$. Then if $D_1$ denotes the random demand during the lead time, $t_1$, we need to determine $B$ so that

$$P(D_1 \geq B + rt_1) \leq \alpha$$

To determine $B$, the distribution of demand during time $t_1$ is required. Obviously the average (mean) demand during time $t_1$ is just

$$\mu_1 = rt_1$$

since $r$ is the mean demand per unit time. Also, the variance of the demand during lead time is

$$\sigma_1^2 = t_1^2 \sigma^2$$

where $\sigma^2$ is the variance of the distribution of demand per unit time.

### Example 11.7
### A Safety Stock Problem with a Normal Demand Distribution

Suppose that the distribution of daily demand for an item is normal with mean $\mu = r = 20$ items per day and variance $\sigma^2 = 25$. Daily inventory cost is $c_2 = \$10$ per item, and setup cost per order is $c_1 = \$1,600$. Known lead time is $t_1 = 3$ days. We want the probability of a shortage developing during the lead time to be less than or equal to $\alpha = 0.05$.

Now demand during lead time will also have a normal distribution; its mean is $\mu_1 = rt_1 = (20)(3) = 60$ items, and its standard deviation is $\sigma_1 = t_1\sigma = (3)(5) = 15$. We need to find $B$ so that

$$P(D_1 \geq B + 60) \leq 0.05$$

We can standardize $D_1$ and work with the standard normal random variable $Z$ (see Section 8.6 of Chapter 8). Thus

$$P\left(\frac{D_1 - 60}{15} \geq \frac{B + 60 - 60}{15}\right) \leq 0.05$$

or

$$P\left(Z \geq \frac{B}{15}\right) \leq 0.05$$

From Table A.2 we find

$$P(Z \geq 1.64) = 0.05$$

Therefore, set $B/15$ equal to 1.64 and solve for $B$. This gives, to the nearest item,

$$B = 25$$

Then we should maintain a safety stock of 25 items. The reorder point is $25 + S_1 = 25 + rt_1 = 25 + 60 = 85$ items. All that remains is to determine $S_0$, the number of items to order.

$$S_0 = \sqrt{\frac{2rc_1}{c_2}} = \sqrt{\frac{2(20)(1,600)}{10}} = 80 \text{ items}$$

Thus our strategy is:

Order 80 items whenever inventory level reaches 85 items.

Since $t_0 = 4$ days, we would expect to place an order on the average every 4 days, although the random demand means that orders are not made quite so regularly. The situation is depicted in Figure 11.9.

The solution of Example 11.7 is not necessarily an optimal one. It is simply the result of one easy way to use the EOQ model and still incorporate lead time and random demand. Note that the buffer stock of 25 items adds approximately $25(\$10)(4) = \$1,000$ to the inventory cost per period, or $250 per day to the average inventory cost per unit time. Without the safety stock we would have had

$$C_0 = \sqrt{2rc_1c_2} = \sqrt{2(20)(1,600)(10)} = \$800$$

**FIGURE 11.9**   Symbolic result of the solution of Example 11.7

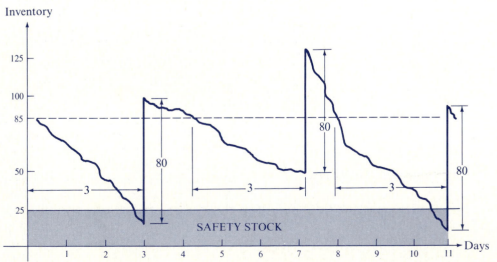

This is the average daily cost without any buffer. With the safety stock, the average daily cost is about $1,050.

Since the objective of the safety stock is to give a small probability for a shortage, we assume that this method presumes a substantial shortage cost per unit. Otherwise this "quick and dirty" method of handling lead time and random demand may yield a solution that is far from optimal. There does exist a standard inventory model that makes provision for *random* lead time and random demand, and which includes provision for cost of shortage, but the study of that model is beyond the scope of this text. It could be used, however, with fixed lead time incorporated as a special case.

## 11.6  A SINGLE-PERIOD, RANDOM-DEMAND INVENTORY PROBLEM

Some inventory problems are characterized by a single order for the entire demand period. Demand is random but occurs only once. No opportunity is available to replenish depleted stock.

A problem of this type is called a *newsboy problem*. The newsboy on the streetcorner faces an inventory problem daily. He must purchase enough newspapers to supply his customers, but he does not know precisely how many papers he will need. His experience only allows him to say that demand will fall within a certain range.

If he purchases too few newspapers from the circulation department, he will lose sales. If he purchases too many, he will be stuck with unsold papers; a newspaper has a very short useful life. Now these unsold papers may have some salvage value, say he can sell them to a pet shop for use as cage liners, but the salvage value will be less than he paid for the papers. The newsboy's problem is buying enough papers to realize as much profit as possible, yet not so many that unsold papers begin to eat away his profits.

You can easily think of other newsboy-type inventory problems. How much firewood must a local supplier cut in the summer for sale in the winter? How many chocolate-chip cookies should a bakery prepare in order to meet today's demand? How many pairs of currently fashionable shoes should a department store order for the spring sale? Note that time is not a decision variable in a newsboy problem; only the *order quantity* is important.

Vendors of food and drink at sporting events have newsboy-type problems, most especially since they deal with perishable food items. In Example 11.8 we look at the problem of a concessionaire at a football game.

**Example 11.8**
**A Concessionaire's Problem**

Playing conditions for a University of Wyoming football game in October can range from a frozen, snow-covered field to the mildness of Indian

Summer. Wyoming fans habitually eat more during football games as temperatures get colder. Some know this helps them stay warmer; others just use a trip to the concession stand as a reason for moving about.

The concessionaire who has purchased the privilege of purveying food and drink to the fans must order a supply of hot dogs for this Saturday's game. She purchases packaged hot dogs from a caterer for $0.30 each and sells them for $0.50 each. Unsold hot dogs at the end of the afternoon can be sold for $0.05 apiece to a local service organization that provides inexpensive meals for senior citizens.

The concessionaire knows that the eating habits of the fans depend upon temperature. She also has a pretty good idea of how the demand for hot dogs is related to temperature at game time. She is able to obtain a probabilistic prediction of temperature from the weather bureau. Table 11.1 shows the demand she anticipates for various possible game-time temperatures, and the associated probabilities. She must make her order on Thursday; these are Thursday predictions of Saturday's temperature. Demand units are numbers of hot dogs. How many hot dogs should the concessionaire order to maximize expected gross profit from the sale of hot dogs?

First we will calculate profit for every combination of demand and inventory. For instance, what is the profit if the concessionaire orders 2,100 hot dogs but the demand is only 1,800 (game-time temperature is between 51 and 60°F)? She will sell 1,800 hot dogs with a profit of $0.50 − $0.30 = $0.20 each, a profit of 1,800($0.20) = $360. However, she will have 300 hot dogs left over. These can be sold for $0.05 apiece but cost her $0.30 apiece, so she loses 300($0.25) = $75 on the unsold hot dogs. Total gross profit is $360 − $75 = $285. What if she orders 1,800 but the demand is 2,400? Then she can sell all 1,800 for a gross profit of $360, since there is no penalty for a shortage.

A formula for computing all possible gross profits follows. Suppose that $D$ is demand and $X$ is the order quantity. Then

**1** If $D < X$, gross profit = $0.20D − $0.25(X − D).

**2** If $X \leq D$, gross profit = $0.20X$.

**TABLE 11.1**  *THE PROBABILITY DISTRIBUTION OF DEMAND*

| Temperature, °F | Demand | Probability |
|---|---|---|
| 61–70 | 1,500 | 0.05 |
| 51–60 | 1,800 | 0.10 |
| 41–50 | 2,100 | 0.25 |
| 31–40 | 2,400 | 0.25 |
| 21–30 | 2,700 | 0.20 |
| 11–20 | 3,000 | 0.15 |

The gross profits in dollars for every combination of order quantity (inventory) and demand are shown in Table 11.2. That payoff table, where demand is the state of nature and order quantity is the strategy, also shows the probability for each demand level and, in the right margin of the table, the expected gross profit for each of the possible strategies.

Expected gross profits for Table 11.2 were calculated in the same fashion as we computed expected payoffs in the tables of Chapter 9. For example, expected gross profit when inventory is 2,100 hot dogs is

$$E_{2,100} = \$150(0.05) + \$285(0.10) + \$420(0.25)$$
$$+ \$420(0.25) + \$420(0.20) + \$420(0.15)$$
$$= \$393.00$$

We do a similar calculation for all rows in the table, then choose as the concessionaire's optimal strategy the inventory level associated with the maximum expected gross profit.

Thus the concessionaire should order 2,400 hot dogs from the caterer, a strategy with a $399.00 expected gross profit. This presumes, of course, that maximum expectation is the criterion the concessionaire wants to use. Since expectation is a long-run average value, but only two or three football games will be played at home in October, the concessionaire might choose a different decision criterion, which could of course change her decision.

For instance, she might choose to be pessimistic about game-time temperature, or her capitalization might be such that she prefers to choose the strategy with the best guaranteed payoff. Then, of course, she would only order 1,500 hot dogs from the caterer, knowing that regardless of temperature she could sell all of her hot dogs at a guaranteed gross profit of $300.00.

On the other hand, she might like the "happy medium" feature that often characterizes the minimax regret criterion. Then she may choose to ignore the probabilities and order 2,100 hot dogs from the caterer (you

**TABLE 11.2**    PAYOFF TABLE: GROSS PROFITS IN DOLLARS

| Inventory, $X$ (order quantity) | Demand, $D$ | | | | | | Expected profit |
|---|---|---|---|---|---|---|---|
| | 1,500 | 1,800 | 2,100 | 2,400 | 2,700 | 3,000 | |
| 1,500 | 300 | 300 | 300 | 300 | 300 | 300 | $300.00 |
| 1,800 | 225 | 360 | 360 | 360 | 360 | 360 | $353.25 |
| 2,100 | 150 | 285 | 420 | 420 | 420 | 420 | $393.00 |
| 2,400 | 75 | 210 | 345 | 480 | 480 | 480 | $399.00 ← max |
| 2,700 | 0 | 135 | 270 | 405 | 540 | 540 | $371.25 |
| 3,000 | −75 | 60 | 195 | 330 | 465 | 600 | $316.50 |
| Probability | 0.05 | 0.10 | 0.25 | 0.25 | 0.20 | 0.15 | |

should set up a regret table to verify that this is indeed her minimax regret strategy). The decision to order 2,100 hot dogs has almost as high an expected gross profit as the decision to order 2,400, and only if game-time temperature exceeds 50°F will she make less profit than that generated by a totally pessimistic viewpoint.

Expectation, however, is the most frequently used concept in these newsboy problems. In Section 11.7 you will see an approach to solution of a generalization of the newsboy problem, one that uses *minimum expected cost* as the decision criterion.

## 11.7 ANOTHER SINGLE-PERIOD, INSTANTANEOUS-DEMAND MODEL

The model presented here is a generalization of the newsboy problem, except that once again we are interested in minimizing cost of an inventory policy instead of maximizing profit as we did in Example 11.8. While the derivation of its solution is omitted because of the complexities involved, it is included here as an example of a *critical-ratio policy*, a type of solution that occurs frequently in this and even more intricate inventory problems.

Demand is a discrete random variable, but occurs instantaneously (one value of demand for the entire period) according to some probability distribution. Only one time period is involved, and we assume no setup cost. Other similar models exist, with continuous demand distributions and provisions for setup cost, but the determination of their optimal solutions, even if the critical ratios are known, is beyond the scope of this elementary text.

This general model is very similar to the newsboy problem, except that a penalty for a shortage is included. To discuss it, we require some new notation.

Let $p$ = price per item

$c_2$ = holding cost per item during the single time period

$c_3$ = shortage cost per item during the single time period

$D$ = demand during the period

$P(d)$ = probability that demand $D$ takes on the value $d$

$I$ = inventory on hand when an order is placed

$x$ = amount on hand after an order is received

Note particularly that $x - I$ will be the order quantity, provided that $I$ is not so large that nothing should be ordered.

The problem is to find the optimal value of $x$, say $x^*$, which in turn will specify the optimal order quantity (either zero or $x^* - I$). The optimal policy is the one that *minimizes the expected cost* for the single period.

The situation is indicated graphically in Figure 11.10. Two cases arise: demand less than $x$ or demand greater than $x$. The first case results in inventory being on hand; the second results in a shortage. Since demand is random, even if we do discover the optimal inventory level $x^*$ that minimizes expected cost, only after demand occurs do we know whether we have ordered too much (case 1) or too little (case 2). Thus the analysis of this model must include an expected holding cost and an expected shortage cost. Further, the price paid for the items ordered is included as part of the overall expected cost for the period.

This total expected cost may be expressed as a function of $x$, the inventory level after the order is received. In words, that function is

Expected cost
    = purchase price + expected holding cost + expected shortage cost

Some rather intricate algebraic manipulations, basically involving $x$ and $P(d)$, the demand distribution, are required to derive the optimal solution. Here we leave out the analysis and just report the solution.

This model has a solution that is specified by what is generally called a *critical ratio* (CR) in inventory analyses. That critical ratio is

$$CR = \frac{c_3 - p}{c_2 + c_3}$$

The solution of the model is that value of $x$, $x^*$, such that

$$P(D \le x^* - 1) \le CR \le P(D \le x^*)$$

That is, the critical ratio must be in between the values of the cumulative demand distribution at $x^* - 1$ and $x^*$. Example 11.9 illustrates the simplicity of the resulting solution process.

**FIGURE 11.10**    Two cases for a single-period model

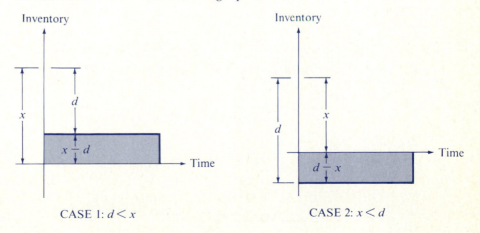

CASE 1: $d < x$          CASE 2: $x < d$

**Example 11.9**
**Winter Inventory of Engine Heaters**

The Big J Auto Parts outlet in Laramie has been offered a special price for the August purchase of Warmit block-plug engine heaters. These are little electrical devices that are inserted in place of the drain plug in an automobile engine and that heat the antifreeze mixture in the engine's cooling system to make cold-weather starts easier. Suppose that the following costs apply, where the period is winter in Laramie, the months from September through June.

$$p = \$10 \text{ per heater}$$

$$c_2 = \$5 \text{ per heater in inventory}$$

$$c_3 = \$20 \text{ per heater in shortage}$$

Because most of the long-time residents of Laramie already have some type of winter heating device installed in their cars, demand for the heaters is assumed to be small: anything from zero to six heaters during the whole winter season. But whenever someone requires such a heater, that person really needs one badly; this is why Big J assesses such a large shortage cost. The anticipated probability distribution of demand is shown in Table 11.3.

First we calculate the critical ratio. It is

$$CR = \frac{c_3 - p}{c_2 + c_3} = \frac{20 - 10}{5 + 20} = 0.40$$

Next we need the cumulative distribution of demand. It is shown in Table 11.4.

The critical ratio $CR = 0.40$ falls between the cumulative probability 0.30 at $k = 2$ and the cumulative probability 0.50 at $k = 3$. Then the solution must be $x^* = 3$.

Now $x^* = 3$ is the optimal number of Warmit heaters to have *on hand*

| TABLE 11.3 | DEMAND DISTRIBUTION | |
|---|---|---|
| | *d* | *P(d)* |
| | 0 | 0.05 |
| | 1 | 0.10 |
| | 2 | 0.15 |
| | 3 | 0.20 |
| | 4 | 0.30 |
| | 5 | 0.10 |
| | 6 | 0.10 |

| TABLE 11.4 | CUMULATIVE DISTRIBUTION | |
|---|---|---|
| | *k* | *P(D < k)* |
| | 0 | 0.05 |
| | 1 | 0.15 |
| | 2 | 0.30 ← CR = 0.40 |
| | 3 | 0.50 |
| | 4 | 0.80 |
| | 5 | 0.90 |
| | 6 | 1.00 |

after the order is received. Thus if $I = 0$ (Big J Auto Parts has no such heaters in stock when the order is placed), the optimal order quantity is *three*. If the auto parts outlet happens to have two Warmit heaters already in stock, left over from last year's purchase, then it should only order *one* heater this year. If Big J has three or more Warmit heaters already in stock, it should order *nothing* this year.

## 11.8 SUMMARY AND CONCLUSIONS

Inventory problems are probably the most persistent types of problems encountered by businesses and industrial organizations. All managers of organizations engaged in the sale of commodities face critically important cost and profit questions that are related to inventories. The manufacturer who produces the commodity, the wholesaler who distributes the commodity, the retailer who sells the commodity to consumers—all of those businesspeople remain engaged in profitable business partly because of their ability to make good inventory decisions.

As considered in this chapter an inventory problem is an optimization problem, the search for the quantity to order or produce and the time at which acquisition must occur so that inventory cost is minimized (or profit due to the inventory policy is maximized). Three basic costs exist in most inventory problems: setup cost, holding cost, and shortage cost. Each of the various models considered here endeavors to establish policies that represent optimal tradeoffs among these basic costs.

The most elementary and most-used models in practice are the so-called EOQ models. These basic models assume essentially constant demand rates and production rates, and include provision for shortages and for quantity discounts. Even in the more realistic cases, where demand rate is not really constant but where the average rate may be considered reasonably constant, these EOQ models work quite well. Incorporation of safety stock is one way that variations from theoretical assumptions may be handled.

The case of random demand is much more difficult to handle theoretically and in practice can be particularly bothersome since the exact distribution of demand is usually unknown. In this chapter only single-period models with random demand have been considered. The ideas that were used to solve them may be extended to multiple-period situations, and to one other type of inventory model that was not discussed here: the multiple-item model. When many different kinds of items are to be considered simultaneously in one large, overall inventory model, constraints on space and capital become involved, and usually the solutions are "satisficing" rather than theoretically optimal solutions.

Many inventory models beyond those considered here have been developed for application to problems that recur again and again in practice. One such model, which handles a multiple-period situation where setup costs, production costs, holding costs, and demand may differ from period to period, will be taken up in the next chapter, where it will be solved using the methods of dynamic programming. Simulation methods are also used quite frequently to handle some types of theoretically intractable inventory problems. You will see a simple example of solution by simulation in Chapter 16.

## KEY WORDS AND PHRASES

**Inventory problem**  A problem requiring the determination of an order quantity and a time at which to place the order so that overall policy cost is minimized or else profit coming from that ordering decision is maximized.

**Inventory policy**  The strategy decided upon as a result of analysis of an inventory problem.

**Planning horizon**  The length of time for which an inventory policy is desired. In this chapter the planning horizons were either indefinite or were one period in length, but in Chapter 12 you will see planning horizons of fixed length and involving more than one period.

**Setup cost**  The cost associated with placing an order or with getting ready to begin a production run.

**Holding cost**  The cost of keeping items in inventory, a function of the number of items in stock and the time for which they are held as inventory.

**Shortage cost**  A cost that develops when the number of items on hand is insufficient to meet immediate demand.

**Economic order quantity (EOQ) model**  An inventory model for the case of periodic orders over time, with instantaneous acquisition and no shortage allowed. The solution states how many items should be ordered and the time interval between orders. Modifications of the EOQ model include provision for production, quantity discounts, and shortages.

**Quantity discount**  The situation in which the per-item price is reduced if the quantity ordered exceeds a specified number of items.

**Lead time**  The time between the placing of an order and its receipt.

**Production rate**  The number of items produced per unit time.

**Demand rate**  The number of items per unit time required by customers.

**Reorder point**  The level of inventory that triggers placing of an order. That is, when inventory level drops to the reorder point, place an order.

**Safety stock**  Extra items carried in inventory to reduce the probability that a shortage will develop.

**Single-period, random-demand problem**  An inventory problem in which demand for an item is a random variable with known probability distribution, and in which only one opportunity to order is provided.

**Instantaneous demand**  The situation in which demand may be random, but assumes only one value during the period of interest.

**Initial inventory**  The number of items on hand when an order is placed.

**Critical ratio** A ratio involving known costs in an inventory problem, this ratio being the key to determining an optimal policy for many inventory problems.

## EXERCISES

✦ **11.1** Assume that in the basic EOQ model demand occurs at the rate of 20 items per day, setup cost is $250 per order, and holding cost per item per day is $1. Find the optimal inventory policy.

**11.2** A particular liquid chemical is required in the manufacture of an item in your company's product line. The chemical is used at the rate of 8 tons per week. Each time an order for the chemical is placed a setup cost of $2,400 is incurred (this includes cost of transportation and containers). It costs $24 to hold 1 ton of chemical for one week, and in the interest of regular production of the items no shortage is permitted. What is the company's optimal inventory policy for this chemical?

✦ **11.3** Seers and Warlock, a mail-order house specializing in occult paraphernalia, regularly sells 40 crystal balls per month. Making contact with their suppliers, the Dwarves of Mystic Mountain, is difficult; a setup cost of $2,000 is incurred each time an order is placed. Once placed, however, orders are received promptly; in fact, the industrious dwarves guarantee same-day service.

The cost of keeping one crystal ball in inventory for a week is $2. A fraction of a ball may be ordered, although this often results in an unhappy medium.

Assume four-week months and that no shortage is permitted. What is Seers and Warlock's optimal inventory policy for crystal balls? What is the average cost per week of that optimal policy?

**11.4** In the problem described as Exercise 11.3, suppose that communication difficulties have raised the setup cost to $4,000, while inflation has increased the holding cost of a crystal ball to $3 per week. Now what is the optimal inventory policy and its average weekly cost? Could you have anticipated the type of change you observed in the policy? How?

✦ **11.5** A furniture store sells 600 Languid Man recliners per year. These recliners cost the store $200 each and sell for $360. The annual holding cost per recliner is $20 and it costs $375 to place an order (including transportation cost).
   **a** What is the optimal inventory policy for Languid Man recliners in that store?
   **b** How many orders per year will be placed?
   **c** What is the total holding cost per year for Languid Man recliners?
   **d** What is the store's annual gross profit on these recliners?

**11.6** Suppose that the cost of placing an order in the problem described as Exercise 11.5 is $1,500 instead of $375. What is the change in the inventory policy, and what is the new annual gross profit if that policy is used?

✦ **11.7** Suppose that in Exercise 11.5 the cost per recliner is $200 if fewer than 200 recliners are purchased in an order, but if 200 or more recliners are ordered, the per-recliner cost becomes $160. What then is the optimal inventory policy for Languid Man recliners?

✦ **11.8** Consider the following quantity-discount inventory problem. The demand rate for an item is 10 per day, with a setup cost of $500 and a holding cost of $5 per item per day. The purchase price is $21 per item for orders of fewer than 50 items. For orders of 50 or more, the per-item price is only $19. What is the optimal order quantity? The optimal time between orders?

**11.9** Refer to the problem described as Exercise 11.8.
   a What is the optimal policy if the price break occurs at an order of 40 items?
   b What is the optimal policy if the price break occurs at an order of 70 items?

**11.10** Charlie's Cab Company regularly needs 10 new taxicabs per (30-day) month. Surplus taxicabs, those on hand but not yet needed, are kept in storage. Storage cost is $5 per day per cab. Charlie must always have a new cab available whenever one is needed.

When an order for cabs is placed, a setup cost of $400 is involved. The cabs are received almost as soon as an order is placed. The cab manufacturer will sell cabs to Charlie for $5,500 per cab if the order involves fewer than 8 cabs, but on orders of 8 or more the price per cab drops to $5,100.
   a What is Charlie's optimal policy for ordering cabs? (If the solution involves a fraction of a taxicab, round to the nearest integer.)
   b If the price break occurs at $B = 6$ cabs, what is his optimal policy?

✦ **11.11** Icon Novelty Company, Inc., produces replicas of 1972 Nixon-for-President buttons at the rate of 2,000 per day. Buttons are demanded at the rate of 300 per day. Backlogs of orders are allowed, with shortage cost deemed to be $0.10 per button per day.

Each time a production run is begun, a setup cost of $400 is incurred. Holding cost is $0.01 per button per day. What is Icon, Inc.'s optimum production-inventory policy for Nixon buttons?

✦ **11.12** Seers and Warlock, the occult paraphernalia mail-order house of Exercise 11.3, has become dissatisfied with the service received from the Dwarves of Mystic Mountain. Shipments of crystal balls have arrived late, some of the balls have had opaque centers (generating strident complaints from unhappy mediums), and now Seers has learned that its competitor, Montgomery Weird, has been purchasing crystal balls from the dwarves at a lower price. Consequently, they have just purchased Mystic Mountain and have begun producing their own crystal balls.

Demand for crystal balls is still 10 balls per week, and the cost of keeping one crystal ball in inventory for a week remains $2. Setup cost, however, has now changed to $1,500 per production run, and the production rate is 12.5 balls per week.

Seers and Warlock will now permit a shortage, with shortage cost being $8 per crystal ball per week. What is their optimal production-inventory policy for crystal balls?

**11.13** In Exercise 11.12 the setup cost was only reduced by a fourth of what it was in Exercise 11.3, and there is now a substantial shortage cost. Explain how such a dramatic decrease in average cost of the inventory policy (compared to the solution of Exercise 11.3) is possible.

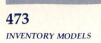
◆ **11.14** Refer to Exercises 11.3 and 11.12. Suppose that the purchase price for Mystic Mountain was $30,000. How long will it take Seers and Warlock to recover the purchase price through inventory savings alone? (Ignore the time value of money.)

**11.15** Refer to Exercise 11.12. Assume that the cost of producing a crystal ball is $10 (excluding setup cost; this is the per-item cost). Considering only per-item cost and inventory cost (ignoring marketing costs), for what price should a ball be sold in order for Seers and Warlock to just break even in the crystal ball business?

**11.16** Verify the formula for the objective function $C(t_3, t_4)$ in Section 11.4 of this chapter. This verification simply involves utilization of the four constraint equations that precede the formula.

**11.17** (Calculus required)  The figure below suggests a special case of the general EOQ model. Here production occurs only during time $t_2$, and no shortage is allowed.

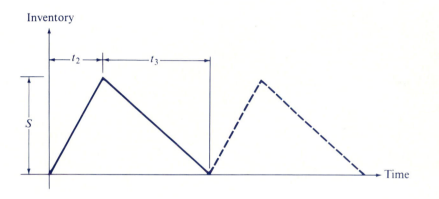

Show that the optimal $t_3$ is given by

$$t_3^* = \sqrt{\frac{2(1 - r/k)c_1}{rc_2}}$$

Start by establishing an objective function expressed as a function of $t_3$ only. Then differentiate and set the derivative equal to zero. Further, establish other formulas necessary to specify the optimal production-inventory policy.

**11.18** The problem described in Exercise 11.17 can also be solved starting from the formulas given in Section 11.4 for the optimal solution of the general EOQ model. Consider what happens to those formulas as $c_3$ gets large without bound. This is equivalent to making the cost of a shortage so prohibitive that the optimal solution must include $s^* = 0$. Use this line of reasoning to verify the formula for $t_3^*$ given in Exercise 11.17.

◆ **11.19** In Exercise 11.2 a liquid chemical was used at the rate of 8 tons per week during the manufacture of one of your company's products. It still costs $24 to store 1 ton of the chemical for one week.
　Suppose that for a capital outlay of $100,000 you can acquire equipment to

produce the chemical at the rate of 20 tons per week, with setup cost per production run being $800. To maintain production of items at the desired level, no shortage of the chemical is allowed.

   **a** Using the results from Exercise 11.17 (or Exercise 11.18), determine the optimal production-inventory policy.

   **b** Suppose that the purchase price per ton of the chemical in Exercise 11.2 had been $1,000, while if the chemical is produced by the new equipment, the production cost per ton is only $500. Assuming that the return on investment of capital in other areas is ignored, is it possible to recover the capital outlay of $100,000 from savings due to producing the chemical yourself? If so, approximately what length of time is required to regain the $100,000?

**11.20** The distribution of daily demand for an item is normal with a mean of 100 items and a standard deviation of 60 items. Setup cost per order is $200 and holding cost per item per day is $1. Time between placement and receipt of an order is one day. The probability of a shortage developing during that day must be 0.10 or less.

   **a** Find $S_0$, the ordinary optimal order quantity if no shortage had been permitted.

   **b** Find $B$, the safety stock required.

   **c** What is the reorder point?

   **d** What is the average time between receipt of orders?

**11.21** The J. Sears Montgomery store in Ptarmigan, Alaska, markets Mucklucks, a very popular brand of durable denim jeans. The 5-day demand for Mucklucks in Ptarmigan is normally distributed with a mean of 20 pairs and a variance of 100. Lead time for orders is 10 days. Setup cost per order is $400, and holding cost per pair of Mucklucks per day is $0.50.

The manager of the store does not want a shortage to develop during lead time but realizes that an extremely large safety stock could be very expensive; a probability of 0.05 or less is deemed acceptable for shortage. Determine the necessary safety stock $B$, the order quantity $S_0$, and the reorder point.

**11.22** Refer to the concessionaire's problem described as Example 11.8 in this chapter. Suppose that prior to a home game on another Saturday in October the weather bureau supplies the following prediction of temperatures:

| Temperature, °F | 61–70 | 51–60 | 41–50 | 31–40 | 21–30 | 11–20 |
|---|---|---|---|---|---|---|
| Probability | 0.20 | 0.30 | 0.25 | 0.10 | 0.10 | 0.05 |

Now what is the ordering strategy that will maximize expected gross profit, and what is that expected profit?

**11.23** Refer to the concessionaire's problem described in Example 11.8. Suppose that the service organization will no longer buy left-over hot dogs. Unsold hot dogs are now a total loss. Assume that the original probabilities of Example 11.8 still apply. Does this change the concessionaire's strategy? If so, what is the new ordering strategy and the associated expected gross profit?

**11.24** Work Exercise 11.23 using the following additional assumption: there is a penalty for shortage; the concessionaire believes that the cost per hot dog demanded but not available is $0.10. This cost is figured on the basis of lost customers in the future (some fans will start bringing their own food to the games).

**11.25** Work Exercise 11.24 using the probabilities in Exercise 11.22.

✦ **11.26** Woody Burns sells firewood in Chillsville, Wyoming. Although most Chillsvillites cut their own pine logs for firewood, some of Woody's customers like to add piñon. Piñon does not grow locally; Woody has the opportunity, once a year in September, to order piñon from a supplier in New Mexico. It costs him $40 per cord, delivered in Chillsville.

Woody can sell piñon as firewood for $60 per cord. Any left-over piñon at the end of the winter (the first of July) is delivered for $25 per cord to Reconstituted Cabins, Inc., in nearby Shiversville. If piñon is not available when a customer calls for it, a shortage cost is involved. Past experience tells Woody to measure shortage cost at $10 per cord.

Piñon consumption in Chillsville depends upon the severity of the winter. Woody has obtained a probabilistic prediction about the severity of the coming winter from an itinerant astrologer. Anticipated demand for piñon in cords and the associated probabilities are given in the following table. What is the order quantity that will maximize Woody's expected gross profits from the sale of piñon this winter?

| Winter | Demand | Probability |
|---|---|---|
| Marvelous | 100 | 0.10 |
| Copacetic | 200 | 0.20 |
| Discommoding | 400 | 0.30 |
| Ghastly | 700 | 0.25 |
| Terrifying | 900 | 0.15 |

✦ **11.27** Consider a single-period, instantaneous-demand problem where demand is random and there is no setup cost. The price per item ordered is $20, the holding cost per item in inventory is $2 per period, and the shortage cost per period per item is $30. Demand occurs according to the following probability distribution.

| d | P(d) | d | P(d) |
|---|---|---|---|
| 0 | 0.05 | 3 | 0.10 |
| 1 | 0.05 | 4 | 0.40 |
| 2 | 0.10 | 5 | 0.30 |

**a** Find the optimal number of items to be kept on hand after an order is received.

**b** If two items are on hand before the order is placed, how many items should be ordered? If four items are initially on hand?

**11.28** Alexander's Super Service is a small service station operating on limited capital. In one day, Alexander never needs more than four air-filter elements (assume a standard size for all automobiles he services). Daily demand for air-filter elements follows the probability distribution given below:

| $d$ | $P(d)$ |
| --- | --- |
| 0 | 0.30 |
| 1 | 0.30 |
| 2 | 0.20 |
| 3 | 0.15 |
| 4 | 0.05 |

The station is a one-person operation. Alexander always makes an early-morning trip to the local auto parts store to obtain supplies for the day. Otherwise he must remain on the job at his station.

Cost of an air-filter element to Alexander is $2. Setup cost of an order is negligible since the auto parts store is on his way to work. Alexander has determined that daily holding cost of one element is $0.10, and he believes that shortage cost per element per day is $6. On a day when he starts with one element in stock, how many should he buy from the auto parts store?

## SELECTED REFERENCES

Ackoff, R. L., and M. W. Sasieni: *Fundamentals of Operations Research*, John Wiley & Sons, Inc., New York, 1968.

Buchon, J., and E. Koenigsberg: *Scientific Inventory Management*, Prentice-Hall, Inc., Englewood Cliffs, N.J., 1963.

Hadley, G., and T. Whitin: *Analysis of Inventory Systems*, Prentice-Hall, Inc., Englewood Cliffs, N.J., 1963.

Hillier, F. S., and G. J. Lieberman: *Introduction to Operations Research*, 3d ed., Holden-Day, Inc., San Francisco, 1980.

Love, S.: *Inventory Control*, McGraw-Hill Book Company, New York, 1979.

Phillips, D. T., A. Ravindran, and J. J. Solberg: *Operations Research: Principles and Practice*, John Wiley & Sons, Inc., New York, 1976.

Stockton, R.: *Basic Inventory Systems: Concepts and Analysis*, Allyn and Bacon, Inc., Boston, 1965.

Taha, H. A.: *Operations Research*, 3d ed., Macmillan Publishing Company, Inc., New York, 1982.

# DYNAMIC PROGRAMMING

*D*ynamic programming is a computational technique used for optimization in problems that may be modeled with a very special kind of structure. The technique depends upon a very basic optimization principle that applies in a wide variety of settings, depending for its utility in a large part upon the ingenuity of the problem solver. For instance, example problems that will be solved here using dynamic programming include an inventory problem, a capital budgeting problem, and a reliability problem. Decision trees and certain nonlinear programming problems also may be solved using that procedure. Thus the unifying concepts in dynamic programming are the *optimization principle* that is used and the type of *structure* imposed upon the model, not any particular physical category of problems.

Some people regard dynamic programming as a difficult topic to understand. This need not be true of you; to understand dynamic programming you need only understand its basic principle of optimality, which is an extremely simple concept. The *concept* underlying dynamic programming should not be confused with the practical *applications* of the concept. Admittedly, some of these applications, even a couple that have been chosen as representative examples for this chapter, *are* difficult to follow. They require notation that is a bit more complex than what you have seen up until now, quite a bit of ingenuity is required to recognize that the problems fit the desired structure, and there is a lot of tedium involved in the computations for dynamic programming tables.

Still, the topic is an extremely important one for the tool kit of the practicing management scientist. It is included in this position of the text, between a chapter on inventory models and a chapter on network models, for two reasons. First, one of the most important types of problems solvable by dynamic programming is a production-inventory problem, so the study of the first parts of this chapter is really a continuation of your study of inventory models. Second, many features of problems solvable by dynamic programming are shared by network problems, and network models are to be considered in Chapter 13.

In general, a dynamic programming solution is used for a problem that can be broken down into *stages,* with each stage in turn associated with a number of *states.* A *decision* is required for *each* stage. The *optimal policy* (strategy) that solves the problem is just the optimal sequence of decisions. If every possible policy involves the *same number of stages,* then dynamic programming can be used.

Characteristic of the technique itself is the notion of *recursive relationships.* These involve the successive application of the same concept, or the same type of function, to obtain each decision in the optimal sequence. The specific relationships used in the recursive argument, however, change from problem to problem.

## 12.1   A CLASSIC EXAMPLE: THE STAGECOACH PROBLEM

Professor Harvey M. Wagner (1969), formerly of Yale University, has created a beautiful introductory example of the application of dynamic programming. It is known as *the stagecoach problem.* He conceived the problem in such a way that the key words *stage, state,* and *policy* arise quite naturally within the physical setting for the problem. More importantly, they occupy the same positions in the stagecoach problem that they would in *any* problem to which dynamic programming applies. Example 12.1 uses a new scenario, but credit for the original idea must go to Wagner.

**Example 12.1**
**The Stagecoach Problem**
Look at a late-nineteenth-century miner in Colorado who was fortunate to strike a rich vein of gold. He had left his home and lady love in New Jersey to go west to seek his fortune; now he is anxious to return home with bulging pockets and a proposal of marriage.

The trip must be made by stagecoach, and our moonstruck miner is a cautious man. Some danger exists that during the trip the stage may be held up by bandits. Upon checking with the stagecoach company, however, he learns that they will sell him an insurance policy covering loss of property during a stage holdup.

He further learns that the stage line can offer him a variety of routes through different states for his journey from Colorado to New Jersey. Interestingly, no matter which overall route he selects, exactly five different stages will be boarded. Because of the varying likelihood of robbery of the different coaches, the cost of his insurance policy will depend upon the route chosen.

Our prudent miner reasons that the route associated with the cheapest policy will also be the safest. Not only can he save a little money by choosing it, but there will be less hazard to his person.

The stage line has provided him with the schematic diagram shown in Figure 12.1. It shows the states in which the line operates. Numbers above the arrows are the cost in dollars of an insurance policy for travel on that particular stage. The sum of those numbers over the route chosen will be the cost of his insurance policy for the whole trip.

The miner begins by reading from left to right, constructing the various five-stage routes that he might choose. After only a little of this, he realizes how time-consuming that process is becoming, and he begins to worry that he might leave out some options. There must be a better way.

Staring out the window of the station, he finds himself daydreaming. What if he had not come to Colorado when he had? Was it not a curious set of circumstances that led him to this particularly fortunate state? If in the past he had made only one different decision, he might not be here now.

Eureka! The answer to his problem is obvious. Forget the past—let

**FIGURE 12.1** Schematic diagram: Stage routes

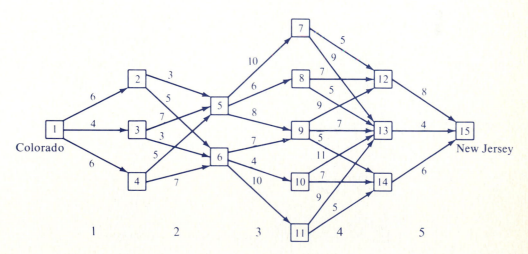

bygones be bygones. He should have been attacking the problem from *right to left*. Although he might not have stated it in just this fashion, our miner has discovered the following principle:

> *Optimality principle.* An optimal policy must have the characteristic that regardless of the route taken to a particular state, the decision for leaving that state must result in an optimal policy thereafter.

The miner begins to sketch the schematic on a separate piece of paper. Above each state he circles the cost of the *optimal* policy for leaving that state. His picture evolves in the following manner.

He starts with the last stage, the one to New Jersey. It is numbered stage 5. The first step in the analysis is shown in Figure 12.2.

Then he considers the next-to-last (fourth) stage, Figure 12.3, ignoring travel to state 15 since he has already allowed for that in stage 5. The (circled) optimal policy costs above state 7 through state 11, respectively, come from the following analysis. They are the costs of traveling from the indicated state *all the way* to state 15.

$$\text{⑬} = \text{minimum of } (5 + 8, 9 + 4) = \min (13, 13)$$

$$\text{⑨} = \text{minimum of } (7 + 8, 5 + 4) = \min (15, 9)$$

$$\text{⑪} = \text{minimum of } (9 + 8, 7 + 4, 5 + 6) = \min (17, 11, 11)$$

$$\text{⑬} = \text{minimum of } (11 + 4, 7 + 6) = \min (15, 13)$$

$$\text{⑪} = \text{minimum of } (9 + 4, 5 + 6) = \min (13, 11)$$

Now our miner moves to stage 3, shown in Figure 12.4. Here again, the costs for traveling from states 5 and 6 all the way to state 15 (New Jersey) by the cheapest route are, respectively,

$$\text{⑮} = \text{minimum of } (10 + 13, 6 + 9, 8 + 11) = \min (23, 15, 19)$$

$$\text{⑰} = \text{minimum of } (7 + 11, 4 + 13, 10 + 11) = \min (18, 17, 21)$$

Proceeding in this fashion, he sees the way to the answer for his problem.

**FIGURE 12.2**   Stage 5

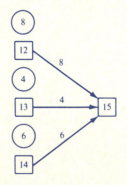

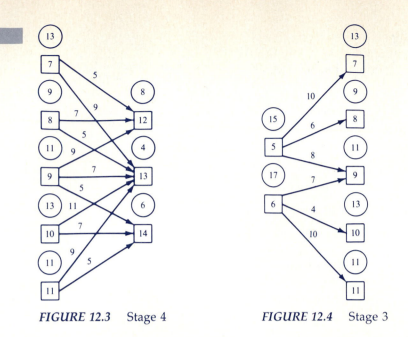

**FIGURE 12.3**   Stage 4          **FIGURE 12.4**   Stage 3

The final figure for stage 1, Figure 12.6, shows the optimal policy cost: $24.   It also shows that there are two alternative choices for the first stage. The miner can start his journey by first going to either state 2 or state 3.

Suppose he travels first to state 2.   What is the optimal policy thereafter? Figure 12.5 yields the decision "go to 5."   After that, Figure 12.4 says, "go to 8," Figure 12.3 says, "go to 13," and Figure 12.2 says, "go to 15." Then one optimal route is

$$1 \rightarrow 2 \rightarrow 5 \rightarrow 8 \rightarrow 13 \rightarrow 15$$

Similar reasoning gives the alternative optimal route

$$1 \rightarrow 3 \rightarrow 6 \rightarrow 10 \rightarrow 14 \rightarrow 15$$

**FIGURE 12.5**   Stage 2          **FIGURE 12.6**   Stage 1

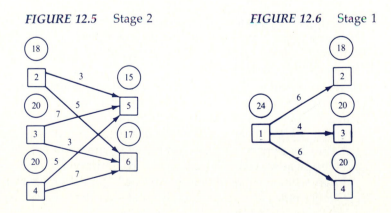

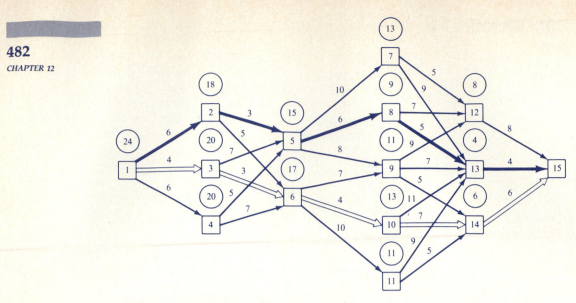

**FIGURE 12.7**  The two alternate optimal routes

Both routes give the minimal policy cost, and no other alternative is as inexpensive. Finally, note that to save lots of time, the miner could have just used the original schematic (Figure 12.1) as a worksheet. Its appearance after solution of the problem, along with the two alternate optimal routes, is shown in Figure 12.7.

Our delighted miner chooses to start by going to state 3 and enjoying the warmth of the southern route. We last see him dozing through Missouri, blissfully ignorant of the fact he has predated Richard Bellman's (1957) elegant formulation of the dynamic programming process by about three-quarters of a century.

## 12.2   THE RECURSIVE ARGUMENT: USE OF DP TABLES

The repeated (recursive) application of the optimality principle to the stagecoach problem made it unnecessary for us to enumerate all possible routes. In fact, no route was considered in its entirety until after all of the calculations were completed.

The problem was contrived in such a way that the sequence of decisions to be made was obvious. A decision was made about *each stage*, each stage was associated with a number of *states*, and the objective was an optimal *policy*. That is, all of the characteristics of a problem permitting solution by dynamic programming were there. As a matter of fact, the problem was solved *using* dynamic programming.

Then what is dynamic programming? Just *the repeated application of the optimality principle*. Conceptually, that's all there is to it.

But imagine a much larger problem, with more stages and more states associated with each stage. At this point you may want a computer to do the computational busywork for you. But you would have to teach that computer the optimality principle; that is, you would have to program it to carry out the recursive argument.

Thus it is very convenient to have a more general, mathematical way to describe the recursion. This not only facilitates computer programming, but helps in the hand computations as well. The following three symbols are used to construct mathematical expressions of the recursive argument:

$f_n(s)$ = the optimal policy cost from state $s$ to the end of the sequence of decisions, when there are $n$ stages remaining

$x_n(s)$ = the decision made in state $s$ when there are $n$ stages remaining [so that $f_n(s)$ is optimal]

$c_n(s, q)$ = the cost of moving from state $s$ in one stage to state $q$ in the next stage, when there are $n$ stages remaining

The utility of these symbols will be demonstrated by a reworking of the stagecoach problem. We will use *dynamic programming (DP) tables*, tables commonly associated with a dynamic programming solution.

In stage 5 of that problem, one stage remains. Thus $n = 1$. The only cost involved in the stage is $c_1(s, 15)$. Consider the DP table labeled Table 12.1.

Here state $s$ indicates the current status of the problem. This is where we find ourselves with $n = 1$ stage to go. Up to the heavy vertical rule in Table 12.1 is a "scratch pad" for entering cost computations for various values of $q$, a state we might enter from state $s$. Here there is no choice; $q$ must be state 15.

Note the designation $q = x$ at the left of the top row of Table 12.1. In other DP problems we will find it convenient to express $q$ in terms of the *decision* $(x)$ that leads us to that state $q$. In other words, $q$ will be a function of $x$. In this simple network problem the decision is just the specification of the state to which we move.

Finally, for complete understanding of the entries in Table 12.1, we

**TABLE 12.1**   STAGE 5: $n = 1$, $f_1(s) = c_1(s, 15)$

| $s$ \ $q = x$ | 15 | $x_1(s)$ | $f_1(s)$ |
|---|---|---|---|
| 12 | 8 | 15 | 8 |
| 13 | 4 | 15 | 4 |
| 14 | 6 | 15 | 6 |

**TABLE 12.2**   *STAGE 4:* $n = 2$, $f_2(s) = \min_x[c_2(s, x) + f_1(x)]$

| s \ x | 12 | 13 | 14 | $x_2(s)$ | $f_2(s)$ |
|---|---|---|---|---|---|
| 7 | 5 + 8 | 9 + 4 | | 12 or 13 | 13 |
| 8 | 7 + 8 | 5 + 4 | | 13 | 9 |
| 9 | 9 + 8 | 7 + 4 | 5 + 6 | 13 or 14 | 11 |
| 10 | | 11 + 4 | 7 + 6 | 14 | 13 |
| 11 | | 9 + 4 | 5 + 6 | 14 | 11 |

observe that 15 means the decision "go to state 15." Now $f_1(s)$ obviously gives the same information as the circled numbers above states 12, 13, and 14 in Figure 12.7, the optimal policy cost from state $s$ to the end of the sequence when there is only one stage to go.

Now consider stage 4. The number of stages remaining is $n = 2$, and $f_2(s)$ is given by

$$f_2(s) = \min_x[c_2(s, x) + f_1(x)]$$

In this stage, $s$ may assume the values 7, 8, 9, 10, or 11. To find $f_2(s)$, we find the minimum of the expression in brackets over all possible values of $x$. Here $x$ can take on the values 12, 13, or 14, the terminal states for stage 4.

The number $f_2(s)$ is the optimal policy cost for leaving state $s$ and traveling *all the way* to state 15. The subscript 2 reminds us that there are 2 stages involved. Then $c_2(s, x) + f_1(x)$ is the sum of the cost of moving from state $s$ to state $x$ when there are 2 stages to go and the *optimal* cost of leaving state $x$ given that we have arrived there [$f_1(x)$]. The DP table shown as Table 12.2 gives the cost computations and the optimal decisions.

A clarification of the method used to compute $f_2(s)$ is also provided by

**TABLE 12.3**   *STAGE 3:* $n = 3$, $f_3(s) = \min_x[c_3(s, x) + f_2(x)]$

| s \ x | 7 | 8 | 9 | 10 | 11 | $x_3(s)$ | $f_3(s)$ |
|---|---|---|---|---|---|---|---|
| 5 | 10 + 13 | 6 + 9 | 8 + 11 | | | 8 | 15 |
| 6 | | | 7 + 11 | 4 + 13 | 10 + 11 | 10 | 17 |

**TABLE 12.4**   STAGE 2: $n = 4$, $f_4(s) = \min\limits_x [c_4(s, x) + f_3(x)]$

| s \ x | 5 | 6 | $x_4(s)$ | $f_4(s)$ |
|---|---|---|---|---|
| 2 | 3 + 15 | 5 + 17 | 5 | 18 |
| 3 | 7 + 15 | 3 + 17 | 6 | 20 |
| 4 | 5 + 15 | 7 + 17 | 5 | 20 |

Table 12.2. Consider $f_2(9)$, for instance. It is just the minimum of the three costs in the row corresponding to $s = 9$. That minimum occurs when we go from state 9 to either state 13 or state 14. Thus the decision $x_2(9)$ is "go to state 13 *or* state 14." Finally, note that the only information required from Table 12.1 is found in its right-most column. This is where we get the costs 8, 4, and 6.

Now the pattern of the recursive argument has been established. In Tables 12.3, 12.4, and 12.5 we complete the computations for the stagecoach problem.

Clearly the optimal policy cost, $24, is indicated by $f_5(1)$ in Table 12.5. This is the cost of the optimal policy starting from state 1 when there are five stages to go; that is, the original policy that was the objective of the exercise. The optimal route (or routes) that produces that cost, however, is not indicated. It is discovered in much the same fashion as it was when we used the schematic diagrams of the preceding section. Here the key column of the tables is the one under $x_n(s)$.

The optimal decision when in state 1 and there are five stages to go is given by $x_5(1)$ in Table 12.5. It is, "go either to state 2 or state 3." Assume that we decide to go to state 3. Then $x_4(3)$, from Table 12.4, tells us to go to state 6. Now we are in state 6, and $x_3(6)$ (Table 12.3) says for us to go to state 10. From state 10, $x_2(10)$ (Table 12.2) says, "go to state 14." Finally, in Table 12.1 the decision $x_1(14)$ is to go to state 15, the end of the journey. This sequence of decisions, each optimal for its particular stage, produces one of the alternate optimal routes: $1 \rightarrow 3 \rightarrow 6 \rightarrow 10 \rightarrow 14 \rightarrow 15$. The other optimal route can be similarly constructed using the DP tables.

Then the right-most column in each table is used as a basis for cost

**TABLE 12.5**   STAGE 1: $n = 5$, $f_5(s) = \min\limits_x [c_5(s, x) + f_4(x)]$

| s \ x | 2 | 3 | 4 | $x_5(s)$ | $f_5(s)$ |
|---|---|---|---|---|---|
| 1 | 6 + 18 | 4 + 20 | 6 + 20 | 2 or 3 | 24 |

computations for the next table. The $x_n(s)$ column, or decision column, is used for determining the optimal policy once all the tables have been completed. This is characteristic of the use of all DP tables in this chapter.

## 12.3   DP SOLUTION OF A SMALL INVENTORY PROBLEM

A common type of production-inventory problem is nicely amenable to solution by DP techniques. This is the situation where a sequence of production decisions is required, one decision for each period in a planning horizon, when costs and demand may be different in each period. Here *periods* are *stages*, and *inventory* on hand at the beginning of a period will characterize the current *state* of the system. Since every possible decision sequence involves the same number of stages (periods), the conditions required for DP solution are satisfied.

### Example 12.2
### A Three-Period Production-Inventory Problem

Consider the following very simple production-inventory problem. Suppose that over a three-month planning horizon there is a known demand of *one* unit per month. No shortage is allowed, so we must then produce or have in inventory at least one unit every month. Further, suppose that we enter the first month with no inventory, and that we require zero inventory at the end of the planning horizon.

Obviously we must produce at least one unit in the first month to meet demand in that month. We could choose to produce all three units (exactly three units are demanded during the entire planning horizon) in the first month and then nothing in each of the other two months. This would mean that some units must be held in inventory, resulting in some holding cost. We could decide to produce exactly one unit per month, but this would mean incurring a setup cost for each production run, not necessarily a good idea.

Because of the season, changes in costs of raw materials, worker vacation schedules, and so on, the setup, production, and holding costs may differ in different months. Table 12.6 gives relevant cost figures.

**TABLE 12.6**   *COSTS FOR EACH MONTH*

| Cost | Month 1 | Month 2 | Month 3 |
|------|------|------|------|
| Setup cost | $14 | $8 | $12 |
| Production cost per unit | $10 | $8 | $10 |
| Holding cost per unit ending inventory | $ 4 | $2 | $ 6 |

The meaning of the costs in the first two rows of Table 12.6 should be clear. But the definition of holding costs in the third row may need clarification. These are costs per unit in inventory at the *end* of the month. For example, if three units are produced in the first month, there will be two units in inventory at the end of the first month (since one unit was used to meet demand for that month). Then the holding cost for the first month is 2($4) = $8.

At first glance one might try to produce everything in month 2, since all costs are smaller there. But necessarily there must be one unit available in month 1 to meet its demand. Since we have to produce something in month 1 anyway, why not produce all three units there and avoid further setup costs? But then we will be faced with larger production and holding costs. In sum, an optimal policy, even for this small problem, may not be obvious.

Here the stages are the months themselves, and a production decision is required for each month. To determine the minimum-cost production-inventory schedule (policy) using DP, we start with stage 3 (third month). The state of the system from which we enter stage 3 is given by the amount of ending inventory from the previous month (stage). Since there must be zero inventory at the end of the third month, and because demand is only one unit in that month, it is not feasible to leave month 2 with more than one unit in inventory. This gives us the values 0 and 1 for the state variable $s$ in stage 3 (Table 12.7).

State $s$ in Table 12.7 means the ending inventory from stage 2, or the entering inventory in stage 3. The decision variable $x$ is the number of units to produce in this stage; it can only take on the value 1 if $s = 0$ or the value 0 if $s = 1$, since demand is 1 and ending inventory must be 0. Thus, for example, $x_1(0) = 1$ is the production decision when there is one stage to go and entering inventory to that stage is zero. The cost of the optimal policy when entering inventory is zero and there is one stage to go is $f_1(0) = 22$. That cost is the sum of the $12 setup cost and the $10 production cost for the single unit produced. If $s = 1$, however, no production occurs and ending inventory is zero, so no cost accrues.

A comment is in order on the meaning of the notation $c_1(s, s + x - 1)$. Entering inventory is $s$ and $x$ is the amount produced, while the demand

**TABLE 12.7**    STAGE 3: $n = 1$, $f_1(s) = \min\limits_{x}[c_1(s, s + x - 1)]$

| $s$ \ $x$ | 0 | 1 | $x_1(s)$ | $f_1(s)$ |
|---|---|---|---|---|
| 0 | | 22 | 1 | 22 |
| 1 | 0 | | 0 | 0 |

**TABLE 12.8**   STAGE 2: $n = 2$, $f_2(s) = \min_x[c_2(s, s + x - 1) + f_1(s + x - 1)]$

| $s$ \ $x$ | 0 | 1 | 2 | $x_2(s)$ | $f_2(s)$ |
|---|---|---|---|---|---|
| 0 |  | 16 + 22 | 26 + 0 | 2 | 26 |
| 1 | 0 + 22 | 18 + 0 |  | 1 | 18 |
| 2 | 0 + 0 |  |  | 0 | 0 |

in that month is 1. The subscript 1 means one stage to go, and $q = s + x - 1$ is the next state achieved, that is, ending inventory.

In stage 2 the state variable $s$ can be no more than 2 since total demand for the next two periods is two units. Here $f_2(s)$ is the minimum of production and inventory cost in stage 2 plus the previously computed cost of the optimal policy in stage 3. A similar analysis applies to stage 1, the first month of the planning period. Computations are shown in Tables 12.8 and 12.9.

Table 12.9 has $s = 0$ as the only possibility since we know that the planning horizon is entered with nothing in inventory. The computations in the scratch pad to the left of the heavy vertical rule in Table 12.9 can be illustrated by showing how the numbers under $x = 2$ are obtained. Here we produce two units, setup cost is \$14, and production cost per unit is \$10. This leaves an ending inventory of one unit (since demand is 1), costing \$4. Thus $c_3(0, 0 + 2 - 1) = c_3(0, 1) = 14 + 20 + 4 = 38$. Further, $f_2(0 + 2 - 1) = f_2(1) = 18$. This last number is obtained from the last column of Table 12.8.

Table 12.9 says that the cost of the optimal production-inventory policy is \$50. The policy itself is established by working back through the tables in the $x_n(s)$ columns. If we enter stage 1 with 0 inventory, the optimal decision, $x_3(0)$, is to produce one unit. Demand of one unit in the first month means that we enter the second month with zero inventory. From Table 12.8 we find $x_2(0) = 2$, so two units are produced in the second month. Then we enter stage 3 with one unit in inventory, and $x_1(1) = 0$ (Table 12.7) says to produce nothing in the third month. This overall

**TABLE 12.9**   STAGE 1: $n = 3$, $f_3(s) = \min_x[c_3(s, s + x - 1) + f_2(s + x - 1)]$

| $s$ \ $x$ | 1 | 2 | 3 | $x_3(s)$ | $f_3(s)$ |
|---|---|---|---|---|---|
| 0 | 24 + 26 | 38 + 18 | 52 + 0 | 1 | 50 |

sequence of decisions is, by the optimality principle, the minimum-cost solution. That is, the optimal strategy is:

> Produce one unit in the first month, two units in the second, and nothing in the third month, for an overall minimum production-inventory cost of $50.

## 12.4   A MORE GENERAL DYNAMIC INVENTORY PROBLEM

Now let's move to a larger, more general version of the type of problem we just solved in Section 12.3. That problem could have been solved by just writing down all the possibilities and then choosing the policy with the minimum cost. As these kinds of problems get larger, however, dynamic programming procedures begin to look better and better.

### Example 12.3
### A Production-Inventory Problem with
### an Unspecified Planning Horizon

Assume basically the same type of problem as in Example 12.2, except that the length of the planning horizon is unspecified. There is no restriction on initial inventory. We *do* require knowledge of inventory at the *end* of the horizon; a reasonable specification is that it be zero. Given that specification, and costs and demand, a minimum-cost production-inventory policy can be determined for *any* horizon of reasonable length.

Suppose there is a constant demand of two units per period (stage) in all periods constituting the planning horizon. Suppose further that setup cost is the same for all periods, $10, and that production cost per unit in any period is $4. Holding cost per unit of ending inventory in any period is $2. However, restrictions are placed on the number of units that may be produced and held in inventory in any one period. Specifically, no more than *four* units may be produced in any one period, and no more than *three* units of ending inventory are allowed per period.

Regardless of the length of the planning horizon, the first DP table is the one for the last period. We know there will be zero units of ending inventory there, so we may construct the stage $L$ ($L$ for last) table, Table 12.10. Demand is 2 units, so $s + x - 2$ is the ending inventory if $s$ is entering inventory and $x$ is the number of units produced.

The portion of Table 12.10 to the left of the heavy rule, the "scratch pad," could have been made much smaller, but we want to emphasize that entering inventory cannot exceed two units and that production plus previous inventory cannot exceed two units, the demand for this last period. This is the end of the planning horizon, and ending inventory must be zero. Now we move on to Table 12.11, the table for the next-to-last stage.

The calculations in Table 12.11 are easy to follow. For example, if

**TABLE 12.10**    STAGE L: $n = 1$, $f_1(s) = c_1(s, s + x - 2)$

| $s$ \ $x$ | 0 | 1 | 2 | 3 | 4 | $x_1(s)$ | $f_1(s)$ |
|---|---|---|---|---|---|---|---|
| 0 |  |  | 18 |  |  | 2 | 18 |
| 1 |  | 14 |  |  |  | 1 | 14 |
| 2 | 0 |  |  |  |  | 0 | 0 |
| 3 |  |  |  |  |  |  |  |

entering inventory is $s = 1$, then we must produce at least one unit in order to meet demand. We cannot produce more than three units because total demand in the last two periods is only four units. If $x = 1$, then setup cost is \$10, production cost is \$4, and inventory cost is zero because the two-unit demand exhausts the units on hand after production. The number $f_1(1 + 1 - 2) = f_1(0) = 18$ is obtained from the table for the last stage, Table 12.10. Thus the cost of producing one unit in this period when entering inventory is one unit is \$14, and the optimal cost for the next period is \$18. The sum of these two costs, \$32, is thus a two-period cost.

Tables 12.10 and 12.11 allow the determination of an optimal two-period policy for *any* feasible initial inventory. For instance, if initial inventory is three units, the policy is: Produce nothing in the first period and one unit in the second, for a total minimum cost of \$16. If a policy is desired for three periods, we simply go on to the next DP table, Table 12.12.

From Table 12.12 we see that two alternate optimal three-period policies exist if $s = 0$ or $s = 1$. For example, suppose entering inventory is 1. In Figure 12.8 are two optimal production-inventory policies.

**TABLE 12.11**    STAGE L − 1: $n = 2$, $f_2(s) = \min\limits_{x}[c_2(s, s + x - 2) + f_1(s + x - 2)]$

| $s$ \ $x$ | 0 | 1 | 2 | 3 | 4 | $x_2(s)$ | $f_2(s)$ |
|---|---|---|---|---|---|---|---|
| 0 |  |  | 18 + 18 | 24 + 14 | 30 + 0 | 4 | 30 |
| 1 |  | 14 + 18 | 20 + 14 | 26 + 0 |  | 3 | 26 |
| 2 | 0 + 18 | 16 + 14 | 22 + 0 |  |  | 0 | 18 |
| 3 | 2 + 14 | 18 + 0 |  |  |  | 0 | 16 |

**TABLE 12.12** STAGE $L - 2$: $n = 3$, $f_3(s) = \min_x[c_3(s, s + x - 2) + f_2(s + x - 2)]$

| $s$ \ $x$ | 0 | 1 | 2 | 3 | 4 | $x_3(s)$ | $f_3(s)$ |
|---|---|---|---|---|---|---|---|
| 0 | | | 18 + 30 | 24 + 26 | 30 + 18 | 2 or 4 | 48 |
| 1 | | 14 + 30 | 20 + 26 | 26 + 18 | 32 + 16 | 1 or 3 | 44 |
| 2 | 0 + 30 | 16 + 26 | 22 + 18 | 28 + 16 | | 0 | 30 |
| 3 | 2 + 26 | 18 + 18 | 24 + 16 | | | 0 | 28 |

With the completion of Table 12.13 we elect to stop work on this example. Enough information is now at hand for constructing optimal policies for any number of periods up to four, given initial inventory. For instance, if initial inventory is two units in a four-period planning horizon, we know that the cost of an optimal production-inventory policy is $48, achieved by producing nothing in the first period, four units in the second, nothing in the third, and nothing in the fourth period, or else, alternatively, nothing in the first period, two units in the second, four units in the third, and nothing in the fourth period.

Some opportunity for sensitivity analysis exists here. The pattern "4, 3, 0, 0" under the $x_n(s)$ columns in each DP table suggests that an optimal policy (or at least the production decision in the first period) is not at all sensitive to the length of the planning horizon. On the other hand, the policies are extremely sensitive to initial inventory. For example, in Table 12.13 we see that a change from an initial inventory of one unit to an initial inventory of two units alters the production decision in the first period from three units to zero units.

This problem could be modified so that demand, setup cost, holding

**FIGURE 12.8** $s = 1$: Two alternate optimal three-period policies

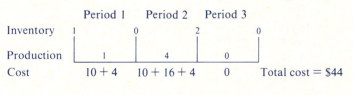

**TABLE 12.13**   STAGE $L - 3$: $n = 4$, $f_4(s) = \min_x [c_4(s, s + x - 2) + f_3(s + x - 2)]$

| $s$ \ $x$ | 0 | 1 | 2 | 3 | 4 | $x_4(s)$ | $f_4(s)$ |
|---|---|---|---|---|---|---|---|
| 0 |  |  | 18 + 48 | 24 + 44 | 30 + 30 | 4 | 60 |
| 1 |  | 14 + 48 | 20 + 44 | 26 + 30 | 32 + 28 | 3 | 56 |
| 2 | 0 + 48 | 16 + 44 | 22 + 30 | 28 + 28 |  | 0 | 48 |
| 3 | 2 + 44 | 18 + 30 | 24 + 28 |  |  | 0 | 46 |

cost, and production cost per unit all vary from period to period (a common situation when the demands, and even some of the costs, change with the season of the year). This makes the problem no more difficult conceptually, but you have to be a bit more careful with the recursion relationships. For instance, if $d_n$ is the demand in that period with $n$ periods to go, and $d_n$ changes from period to period, you would have to change notation from $s + x - 2$ to the sum $s + x - d_n$, reflecting the ending inventory as a function of initial inventory, the production decision, and the demand $d_n$. Examples of this and other modifications appear in the exercises at the end of this chapter.

## 12.5   DP SOLUTION OF A CAPITAL BUDGETING PROBLEM

So far we have applied dynamic programming to only two types of problems, a very special network problem and an inventory problem. In both types the objective was the minimum policy cost. But DP is not uniquely associated with any one physical setting, or even exclusively with cost minimization. The *structure* of a problem will suggest whether dynamic programming might be applicable.

Sometimes a bit of ingenuity is required merely to *recognize* that structure. The following *capital budgeting* problem has as its objective the *maximization of revenue*. It requires a different type of characterization of its states and stages.

### Example 12.4

Expando Corporation owns four factories. They are interested in the potential increase in revenue coming from expansion of those factories by allocating limited amounts of capital. The total amount of capital to be made available for expansion will not exceed $10 million.

For factory $A$ there are two alternative plans. One is simply the plan of "no expansion." The other requires some capital outlay to generate additional revenue. Similarly, for factories B, C, and D there are, respectively, three, four, and four plans (including for each the plan of no expansion). The capital outlays required and the ancipated increases in revenue are given in Table 12.14.

Expando's objective is to discover the particular set of four expansion plans, one for each factory, that will maximize total anticipated increased revenue obtainable from the allocation of a given amount of capital. They are not certain of the exact amount of capital that will be made available for expansion, except they know it will not exceed $10 million. Then our DP tables will allow for any number of millions of dollars, restricted to integer values, up to and including 10.

Here we may regard a *factory* as a *stage* in the problem. While no particular sequence is necessary for expansion decisions, at least every possible combination involves exactly four decisions. We can artificially create a sequence by calling factory A stage 1, and so on to stage 4 (factory D). As we have done in the previous DP examples, we will start our analysis with the last stage (stage 4).

Now we have to decide what variable to use to define the *state* of the system. In this case, *capital* allocated to the stages is a way of indicating state. Accordingly, let's define $s$ as the capital allocated to the project when there are $n$ stages to go. This includes the capital for the current stage as well as for all subsequent stages. Thus at any stage we require $0 \leq s \leq 10$, and that $s$ be an integer.

The specification of a plan for a factory is equivalent to specifying the amount of capital allocated to its expansion. For example, plan 2 for factory A means a $2 million capital outlay, while plan 3 for factory C requires an outlay of $3 million. We shall find it convenient to use capital as the decision variable $x$ in each stage. We know that $x$ will automatically imply the corresponding plan.

Let $r_n(s, x)$ denote the increased revenue when total capital allocation is $s$, $x$ is the capital allocation decision, and there are $n$ stages to go. Then our first DP table can be constructed, Table 12.15.

**TABLE 12.14**  *CAPITAL AND REVENUE IN MILLIONS OF DOLLARS*

| | Factory | | | | | | | |
|---|---|---|---|---|---|---|---|---|
| | A | | B | | C | | D | |
| Plan | Capital | Revenue | Capital | Revenue | Capital | Revenue | Capital | Revenue |
| 1 | 0 | 0 | 0 | 0 | 0 | 0 | 0 | 0 |
| 2 | 2 | 3 | 2 | 3 | 1 | 3 | 1 | 2 |
| 3 | — | — | 3 | 5 | 3 | 5 | 2 | 4 |
| 4 | — | — | — | — | 4 | 7 | 3 | 6 |

**TABLE 12.15**  STAGE 4: FACTORY D, $n = 1$, $f_1(s) = \max_x[r_1(s, x)]$

| s \ x | 0 | 1 | 2 | 3 | $x_1(s)$ | $f_1(s)$ |
|---|---|---|---|---|---|---|
| 0 | 0 | — | — | — | 0 | 0 |
| 1 | 0 | 2 | — | — | 1 | 2 |
| 2 | 0 | 2 | 4 | — | 2 | 4 |
| 3 | 0 | 2 | 4 | 6 | 3 | 6 |
| 4 | 0 | 2 | 4 | 6 | 3 | 6 |
| 5 | 0 | 2 | 4 | 6 | 3 | 6 |
| 6 | 0 | 2 | 4 | 6 | 3 | 6 |
| 7 | 0 | 2 | 4 | 6 | 3 | 6 |
| 8 | 0 | 2 | 4 | 6 | 3 | 6 |
| 9 | 0 | 2 | 4 | 6 | 3 | 6 |
| 10 | 0 | 2 | 4 | 6 | 3 | 6 |

Entries in Table 12.15 are quite easily understood. We assume we could arrive at the last stage with any amount of capital up to 10 units (for example, we could have elected plan 1 for each of factories $A$, $B$, and $C$, using no capital at all up to this point). If capital has been exhausted ($s = 0$) by the time we reach stage 4, then we could only implement plan 1 for factory $D$ ($x = 0$), gaining no extra revenue. If one unit of capital is available ($s = 1$) when $n = 1$, then we could let $x = 0$ or $x = 1$ (plan 1

**TABLE 12.16**  STAGE 3: FACTORY C, $n = 2$, $f_2(s) = \max_x[r_2(s, x) + f_1(s - x)]$

| s \ x | 0 | 1 | 3 | 4 | $x_2(s)$ | $f_2(s)$ |
|---|---|---|---|---|---|---|
| 0 | 0 + 0 | — | — | — | 0 | 0 |
| 1 | 0 + 2 | 3 + 0 | — | — | 1 | 3 |
| 2 | 0 + 4 | 3 + 2 | — | — | 1 | 5 |
| 3 | 0 + 6 | 3 + 4 | 5 + 0 | — | 1 | 7 |
| 4 | 0 + 6 | 3 + 6 | 5 + 2 | 7 + 0 | 1 | 9 |
| 5 | 0 + 6 | 3 + 6 | 5 + 4 | 7 + 2 | 1, 3, 4 | 9 |
| 6 | 0 + 6 | 3 + 6 | 5 + 6 | 7 + 4 | 3, 4 | 11 |
| 7 | 0 + 6 | 3 + 6 | 5 + 6 | 7 + 6 | 4 | 13 |
| 8 | 0 + 6 | 3 + 6 | 5 + 6 | 7 + 6 | 4 | 13 |
| 9 | 0 + 6 | 3 + 6 | 5 + 6 | 7 + 6 | 4 | 13 |
| 10 | 0 + 6 | 3 + 6 | 5 + 6 | 7 + 6 | 4 | 13 |

**TABLE 12.17** **STAGE 2: FACTORY B, $n = 3$, $f_3(s) = \max_x[r_3(s, x) + f_2(s - x)]$**

| $s$ \ $x$ | 0 | 2 | 3 | $x_3(s)$ | $f_3(s)$ |
|---|---|---|---|---|---|
| 0 | 0 + 0 | — | — | 0 | 0 |
| 1 | 0 + 3 | — | — | 0 | 3 |
| 2 | 0 + 5 | 3 + 0 | — | 0 | 5 |
| 3 | 0 + 7 | 3 + 3 | 5 + 0 | 0 | 7 |
| 4 | 0 + 9 | 3 + 5 | 5 + 3 | 0 | 9 |
| 5 | 0 + 9 | 3 + 7 | 5 + 5 | 2, 3 | 10 |
| 6 | 0 + 11 | 3 + 9 | 5 + 7 | 2, 3 | 12 |
| 7 | 0 + 13 | 3 + 9 | 5 + 9 | 3 | 14 |
| 8 | 0 + 13 | 3 + 11 | 5 + 9 | 2, 3 | 14 |
| 9 | 0 + 13 | 3 + 13 | 5 + 11 | 2, 3 | 16 |
| 10 | 0 + 13 | 3 + 13 | 5 + 13 | 3 | 18 |

or plan 2). The maximum increase in revenue occurs when $x = 1$, yielding $f_1(1) = 2$. If, however, we enter the last stage with three or more units of capital, only three units can be used. This means that the maximum increased revenue possible in stage 4 is 6.

To be able to follow the calculations in Table 12.16 it is only necessary to recall that $s$ is defined as the capital allocated when there are two stages to go. Thus $s - x$ is the amount of capital remaining to be used in stage

**TABLE 12.18** **STAGE 1: FACTORY A, $n = 4$, $f_4(s) = \max_x[r_4(s, x) + f_3(s - x)]$**

| $s$ \ $x$ | 0 | 2 | $x_4(s)$ | $f_4(s)$ |
|---|---|---|---|---|
| 0 | 0 + 0 | — | 0 | 0 |
| 1 | 0 + 3 | — | 0 | 3 |
| 2 | 0 + 5 | 3 + 0 | 0 | 5 |
| 3 | 0 + 7 | 3 + 3 | 0 | 7 |
| 4 | 0 + 9 | 3 + 5 | 0 | 9 |
| 5 | 0 + 10 | 3 + 7 | 0, 2 | 10 |
| 6 | 0 + 12 | 3 + 9 | 0, 2 | 12 |
| 7 | 0 + 14 | 3 + 10 | 0 | 14 |
| 8 | 0 + 14 | 3 + 12 | 2 | 15 |
| 9 | 0 + 16 | 3 + 14 | 2 | 17 |
| 10 | 0 + 18 | 3 + 14 | 0 | 18 |

TABLE 12.19    THE OPTIMAL POLICY: $10 MILLION CAPITAL

| Factory | A | B | C | D |
|---|---|---|---|---|
| Plan | 1 | 3 | 4 | 4 |
| Capital | 0 | 3 | 4 | 3 |
| Total: $10 million | | | | |
| Revenue | 0 | 5 | 7 | 6 |
| Total: $18 million | | | | |

4 (factory $D$ expansion).  Otherwise the entries are obtained from the capital and revenue figures for plans for factory $C$ (Table 12.14) and the previously computed $f_1(s)$ column in Table 12.15 (replacing $s$ by $s - x$).

Clearly, the type of reasoning used in constructing the DP tables for this capital budgeting problem is identical to that used in the inventory problem of Section 12.4.  Accordingly, we exhibit the remaining two tables required for solution of the budgeting problem as Tables 12.17 and 12.18.

Information is now at hand for making optimal allocations of any feasible amount of capital that might be made available for factory expansion.  For example, if the full $10 million were to become available, then from Table 12.18 the decision $x_4(10) = 0$ says to use plan 1 for factory $A$.  This leaves $10 million available at stage 2, where $x_3(10) = 3$ (Table 12.17).  We would use plan 3 for factory $B$.  Then $s = 7$ in Table 12.16, where $x_2(7) = 4$.  Thus plan 4 would be used for factory $C$.  Finally, three units of capital remain, and $x_1(3) = 3$ (from Table 12.15) says to use plan 4 for factory $D$.  The overall policy and attendant increased revenue are indicated in Table 12.19.

Suppose, however, that only $9 million in capital is made available.  Then Table 12.20 gives the optimal policy.  The overall policy seems to be fairly sensitive to the amount of capital made available for expansion.

Finally, suppose that for reasons unrelated to optimality, it is not possible to expand factory $A$ (we can only use plan 1).  Further suppose that only $8 million in capital is made available for factory expansion.  From Table 12.17 we see that only $7 million in capital is actually necessary to produce

TABLE 12.20    THE OPTIMAL POLICY: $9 MILLION CAPITAL

| Factory | A | B | C | D |
|---|---|---|---|---|
| Plan | 2 | 3 | 2 | 4 |
| Capital | 2 | 3 | 1 | 3 |
| Total: $ 9 million | | | | |
| Revenue | 3 | 5 | 3 | 6 |
| Total: $17 million | | | | |

a $14 million increase in revenue. The extra million, $8 - 7$, might just as well be used for some other purpose. The policy for $s = 7$ in stage 2 should be adopted on the grounds that the extra million in capital in this case produces no extra revenue.

## 12.6   DP DESIGN OF A SYSTEM FOR MAXIMUM RELIABILITY

Reliability of a component or of a system of components is simply its probability of survival. Systems are classified as either series or parallel. A series system is one that survives only if *all* its components survive; a parallel system survives if any *one* of its components survives. If components survive or fail independently of one another, computation of system reliability given component reliabilities is just a straightforward application of probability formulas from Chapter 8.

In the absence of constraints, such as restrictions on weight, volume, or cost, one could design a system with as high a reliability as desired. For example, consider system $S$, with reliability $R_S = 0.9$. To increase its reliability, simply put another complete system $S$ in parallel with it. The reliability of that new parallel system, which does the same job as the original system $S$, is $R_{SS} = 1 - (0.1)(0.1) = 0.99$. Still another system $S$ added in parallel would give the reliability $R_{SSS} = 0.999$, and so on. Such an approach to increasing reliability has been used effectively by public utilities; power-generating stations have been connected in parallel so that if one of the stations fails all the consumer experiences is a momentary flickering of lights during the time it takes to switch over to the other station.

With constraints, say on cost or configuration, there is a limit to the number of systems that could be included in parallel. Thus in practice the attainable reliability has an upper bound. Example 12.5 shows how to use dynamic programming to design a constrained system for maximum reliability.

### Example 12.5

We are to design a device consisting of three main components arranged in series. Reliability may be improved by installing parallel units on each component. Each component may include no more than three units in parallel. The total capital available for the device is $11,000. Data for the reliability $R_i$ and cost $C_i$ for a unit on the $i$th component are given in Table 12.21. Costs are in thousands of dollars, and time is not a factor; that is, over the time span for which the device is to be used, reliabilities of units remain essentially constant.

Let $m_i$ denote the number of units $i$, $i = 1, 2, 3$, to put in parallel on the $i$th component. We need to determine $m_1$, $m_2$, and $m_3$ so that total reliability of the system is maximized without exceeding the total capital available.

TABLE 12.21   RELIABILITY AND COST PER UNIT

| | Unit 1 | | Unit 2 | | Unit 3 | |
|---|---|---|---|---|---|---|
| | $R_1$ | $C_1$ | $R_2$ | $C_2$ | $R_3$ | $C_3$ |
| | 0.5 | 2 | 0.7 | 3 | 0.6 | 1 |

A representative system of this type is shown in Figure 12.9. Here $m_1 = 2$, $m_2 = 2$, and $m_3 = 1$; that is, two units are in component 1, two units are in component 2, and one unit is in component 3.
The reliability of that system is

$$R_S = [1 - (0.5)(0.5)][1 - (0.3)(0.3)](0.6)$$

$$= (0.75)(0.91)(0.6) = 0.4095$$

The cost of the system is $11,000, and no more than three units are included in any component, so the constraints on the system are satisfied. However, we can beat that reliability with a system described by $m_1 = 2$, $m_2 = 1$, and $m_3 = 2$, which will give a reliability of 0.441 but will only cost $9,000. We seek, of course, the optimal such system subject to the constraints.

We are assuming that costs are additive. Then Table 12.22 becomes convenient for reference. It shows the reliabilities and costs of components consisting of $m_i$ units. Here $R_{im_i}$ is the reliability of the $i$th component consisting of $m_i$ units, and $C_{im_i}$ is the corresponding cost of the component. The results in Table 12.22 come from preliminary calculations of reliability and cost of all possible parallel systems that could be the components in the final system.

Let $R_{im_i}(C_{im_i})$ denote the reliability of the $i$th component as a function of the cost $C_{im_i}$ that is allocated to it. Let $x_i$ be the capital allocated to all $i$ components and let $f_i(x_i)$ be the reliability of the system of $i$ components. Then the *states* used in dynamic programming are represented by $x_i$ while the components are the *stages* in the problem. Thus

$$f_1(x_1) = \max_{\substack{m_1 \\ 0 \le C_{1m_1} \le x_1}} [R_{1m_1}(C_{1m_1})]$$

FIGURE 12.9   A nonoptimal, $11,000 system

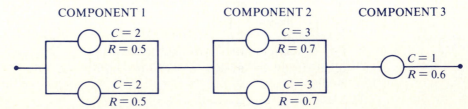

| COMPONENT 1 | COMPONENT 2 | COMPONENT 3 |
|---|---|---|
| $C = 2$  $R = 0.5$ | $C = 3$  $R = 0.7$ | $C = 1$  $R = 0.6$ |
| $C = 2$  $R = 0.5$ | $C = 3$  $R = 0.7$ | |

## TABLE 12.22 RELIABILITY AND COST OF PARALLEL COMPONENTS

| | $i = 1$ | | $i = 2$ | | $i = 3$ | |
|---|---|---|---|---|---|---|
| $m_i$ | $R_{1m_1}$ | $C_{1m_1}$ | $R_{2m_2}$ | $C_{2m_2}$ | $R_{3m_3}$ | $C_{3m_3}$ |
| 1 | 0.5 | 2 | 0.7 | 3 | 0.6 | 1 |
| 2 | 0.75 | 4 | 0.91 | 6 | 0.84 | 2 |
| 3 | 0.875 | 6 | 0.973 | 9 | 0.936 | 3 |

and
$$f_i(x_i) = \max_{\substack{m_i \\ 0 \le C_{im_i} \le x_i}} [R_{im_i}(C_{im_i}) \times f_{i-1}(x_i - C_{im_i})] \qquad i = 2, 3$$

For example, if a capital of 4 is allocated to component 1, then we maximize the reliability attainable for that allocation to get $f_1(4)$. Next, if 6 is allocated to *two* components, 1 and 2, then $C_{2m_2}$ is the cost for component 2, and only $6 - C_{2m_2}$ is available for component 1. Thus $f_2(6)$ is the maximum two-component system reliability. These calculations appear in Tables 12.23, 12.24, and 12.25.

From Table 12.25 we see that the optimal reliability is 0.5145, occurring with $m_3 = 2$ (two units in parallel in component 3). This leaves $11 - 2 = 9$ units of capital for the other two components. Table 12.24 shows that the optimal $m_2$ is 1 (only one unit in component 2). Since the cost of that one unit is 3, this leaves 6 units of capital, and from Table 12.23 we learn that the optimal $m_1$ is 3 (three units in parallel in component 1). The resulting optimal system is shown in Figure 12.10.

## TABLE 12.23 ONE-COMPONENT SYSTEM

| $x_1$ | $m_1 = 1$ | | $m_1 = 2$ | | $m_1 = 3$ | | $m_1^*$ | $f_1^*(x_1)$ |
|---|---|---|---|---|---|---|---|---|
| | $R_{1m_1} = 0.5$ | $C_{1m_1} = 2$ | $R_{1m_1} = 0.75$ | $C_{1m_1} = 4$ | $R_{1m_1} = 0.875$ | $C_{1m_1} = 6$ | | |
| 0 | — | | — | | — | | — | — |
| 1 | — | | — | | — | | — | — |
| 2 | 0.5 | | — | | — | | 1 | 0.5 |
| 3 | 0.5 | | — | | — | | 1 | 0.5 |
| 4 | 0.5 | | 0.75 | | — | | 2 | 0.75 |
| 5 | 0.5 | | 0.75 | | — | | 2 | 0.75 |
| 6 | 0.5 | | 0.75 | | 0.875 | | 3 | 0.875 |
| 7 | 0.5 | | 0.75 | | 0.875 | | 3 | 0.875 |
| 8 | 0.5 | | 0.75 | | 0.875 | | 3 | 0.875 |
| 9 | 0.5 | | 0.75 | | 0.875 | | 3 | 0.875 |
| 10 | 0.5 | | 0.75 | | 0.875 | | 3 | 0.875 |
| 11 | 0.5 | | 0.75 | | 0.875 | | 3 | 0.875 |

## TABLE 12.24 TWO-COMPONENT SYSTEM

| $x_2$ | $m_2 = 1$ $R_{2m_2} = 0.7$ | $C_{2m_2} = 3$ | $m_2 = 2$ $R_{2m_2} = 0.91$ | $C_{2m_2} = 6$ | $m_2 = 3$ $R_{2m_2} = 0.973$ | $C_{2m_2} = 9$ | $m_2^*$ | $f_2^*(x_2)$ |
|---|---|---|---|---|---|---|---|---|
| 0 | — | | — | | — | | — | — |
| 1 | — | | — | | — | | — | — |
| 2 | — | | — | | — | | — | — |
| 3 | — | | — | | — | | — | — |
| 4 | — | | — | | — | | — | — |
| 5 | (0.7)(0.5) = 0.35 | | — | | — | | 1 | 0.35 |
| 6 | (0.7)(0.5) = 0.35 | | — | | — | | 1 | 0.35 |
| 7 | (0.7)(0.75) = 0.525 | | — | | — | | 1 | 0.525 |
| 8 | (0.7)(0.75) = 0.525 | | (0.91)(0.5) = 0.455 | | — | | 1 | 0.525 |
| 9 | (0.7)(0.875) = 0.6125 | | (0.91)(0.5) = 0.455 | | — | | 1 | 0.6125 |
| 10 | (0.7)(0.875) = 0.6125 | | (0.91)(0.75) = 0.6825 | | — | | 2 | 0.6825 |
| 11 | (0.7)(0.875) = 0.6125 | | (0.91)(0.75) = 0.6825 | | (0.973)(0.5) = 0.4865 | | 2 | 0.6825 |

The solution suggested by Figure 12.10 is the optimal system attainable for $11,000, with maximum reliability of 0.5145. If you want to know the effect of another $1,000 of capital, you only need to add to each table a line corresponding to $x_i = 12$. If you do that, you will discover two alternate optimal systems, each costing $12,000, with reliabilities of 0.5733. Also, you can immediately see (from the preceding tables) the effect of having less capital. For example, if $10,000 is available, the maximum

## TABLE 12.25 THREE-COMPONENT SYSTEM

| $x_3$ | $m_3 = 1$ $R_{3m_3} = 0.6$ | $C_{3m_3} = 1$ | $m_3 = 2$ $R_{3m_3} = 0.84$ | $C_{3m_3} = 2$ | $m_3 = 3$ $R_{3m_3} = 0.936$ | $C_{3m_3} = 3$ | $m_3^*$ | $f_3^*(x_3)$ |
|---|---|---|---|---|---|---|---|---|
| 0 | — | | — | | — | | — | — |
| 1 | — | | — | | — | | — | — |
| 2 | — | | — | | — | | — | — |
| 3 | — | | — | | — | | — | — |
| 4 | — | | — | | — | | — | — |
| 5 | — | | — | | — | | — | — |
| 6 | (0.6)(0.35) = 0.21 | | — | | — | | 1 | 0.21 |
| 7 | (0.6)(0.35) = 0.21 | | (0.84)(0.35) = 0.294 | | — | | 2 | 0.294 |
| 8 | (0.6)(0.525) = 0.315 | | (0.84)(0.35) = 0.294 | | (0.936)(0.35) = 0.3276 | | 3 | 0.3276 |
| 9 | (0.6)(0.525) = 0.315 | | (0.84)(0.525) = 0.441 | | (0.936)(0.35) = 0.3276 | | 2 | 0.441 |
| 10 | (0.6)(0.6125) = 0.3675 | | (0.84)(0.525) = 0.441 | | (0.936)(0.525) = 0.4914 | | 3 | 0.4914 |
| 11 | (0.6)(0.6825) = 0.4095 | | (0.84)(0.6125) = 0.5145 | | (0.936)(0.525) = 0.4914 | | 2 | 0.5145 |

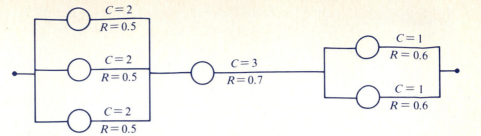

**FIGURE 12.10**  The optimal solution for Example 12.5

reliability is 0.4914; if $9,000, 0.441, and so on.  Thus a sensitivity analysis based on available capital is fairly easy to perform.

## 12.7  OTHER ASPECTS OF DYNAMIC PROGRAMMING

Many other applications of dynamic programming exist.  Sometimes a nonlinear programming problem whose solution would be difficult to obtain by any other method is solvable by DP.  Most decision-tree problems like those in Chapter 9 can be solved efficiently using DP.  Even some *linear* programming problems are nicely suited to these DP techniques. The optimality principle that is the basis of dynamic programming is very simple and very obvious, but as you can see from Examples 12.4 and 12.5, the capital budgeting and reliability problems, successful use of DP procedures depends quite heavily upon the ingenuity of the user.

To conclude our basic discussion of dynamic programming we point out a difficulty unique to that method.  It is called the *curse of dimensionality*. So far it has been possible to characterize the state of the system by the use of a single variable.  When more than one variable is required to describe a state (for instance, capital *and* person-hours), the DP problem is said to have a *multidimensional state vector*.  This multidimensionality means that more calculations are required for the comparisons of alternatives in any one stage.

Suppose, for example, a four-variable state vector $(x_1, x_2, x_3, x_4)$.  What if each $x_i$ can assume any of 10 values in any one stage?  Then there will be $10^4 = 10,000$ distinct states to consider, and in any one table a number of computations may be required for just one of those state vectors. Compound this by the fact that $f_n(x_1, x_2, x_3, x_4)$ must be recorded for every state vector in every stage, as well as the decisions $x_n(x_1, x_2, x_3, x_4)$.  It is no surprise that the memory capacity of even a large computer could be taxed by a DP problem of only modest dimensionality.

Of course, the advantage of DP over complete enumeration of all possible decision sequences resides in the fact that only one decision at a time is considered.  However, this advantage diminishes if an inordinate amount of computation and memory is required to make that single decision. Sometimes the curse of dimensionality can be lifted by the incantation called ingenuity; it remains, however, a very real difficulty in the application of dynamic programming.

## 12.8 SUMMARY AND CONCLUSIONS

Dynamic programming is a computational technique useful when a problem can be broken down into stages, with a decision required at each stage, where each stage is associated with a number of states and every possible decision sequence (policy) involves the same number of stages. It discovers the optimal policy without having to consider all possible decision sequences. The procedure is not unique to any particular problem setting, such as inventory, network, capital budgeting, and so on, but rather it may be used for any problem that has the special structure just described.

Probably the most important application of dynamic programming is to production-inventory problems of the type considered in Sections 12.3 and 12.4. These combined production and inventory problems are regularly encountered by manufacturing concerns. Often the planning horizons in those real problems will be longer than the three- or four-month horizons we have considered here, but as long as inventory at the end of the horizon may be specified, then, conceptually at least, the real problem will be no more difficult to solve; it will only take longer to solve it. However, in our textbook examples we have used only a few states within each stage, while in a real problem of this type there could be hundreds or even thousands of states in each stage (demand may be 900 units in one month, 1,200 in another, and so on). Again, the many-states-per-stage problem may be solved quite readily given the power of the modern computer. But if a state must be described by a multidimensional vector, application of dynamic programming procedures might not be feasible.

Other applications of dynamic programming exist, even beyond the inventory, capital budgeting, reliability, and decision-tree problems that have been mentioned here. A good reference for more examples is Bellman and Dreyfus (1962). Wagner (1969) could be chosen for a much more complete discussion of the application of dynamic programming to inventory problems.

## KEY WORDS AND PHRASES

**Stage**   A point in a DP problem at which a decision is required.

**State**   A characterization of the status of a DP problem in any stage, often the position achieved as a result of a decision in a previous stage.

**Policy**   An entire sequence of decisions that must be made in the problem.

**Optimality principle**   Regardless of the sequence of decisions that led to a particular state, the decision for leaving that state must result in an optimal policy thereafter.

$f_n(s)$   The optimal policy cost from state $s$ to the end of the sequence of decisions, when $n$ stages remain.

$x_n(s)$   The decision made if the problem is in state $s$ when $n$ stages remain.

$c_n(s, q)$   The cost of moving from state $s$ in one stage to state $q$ in the next stage when $n$ stages remain.

**DP table**   A table that organizes the calculations and exhibits the decisions and policy costs for one stage of a DP problem.

## EXERCISES

◆ **12.1** Unbeknown to our complacent gold miner of Section 12.1, now bouncing along through Tennessee, his inamorata has grown tired of waiting in New Jersey and has decided to travel to Colorado. She will make the journey by way of a different stage line and is concerned about surviving the trip to the Wild West. Her stagecoach company has given her the following schematic diagram outlining alternative routes. The numbers above the arrows indicate the corresponding costs of life insurance policies.

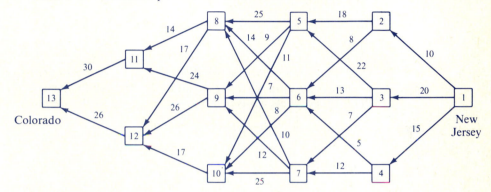

Her objective is to discover the route that will result in the minimum-cost life insurance policy for the complete trip to Colorado. Use the optimality principle for dynamic programming to determine the route (or routes) she should select.

**12.2** A convicted embezzler of government funds is to be transported from jail in state 1 to federal prison in state 13. The following diagram indicates the different routes by which travel between states may be accomplished. Numbers above the arrows are the number of hours travel time required for each stage of the journey.

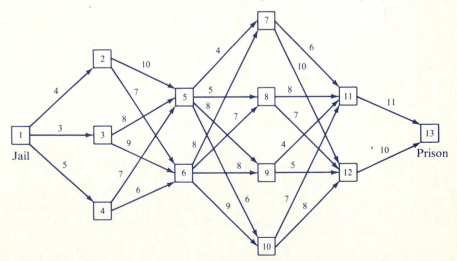

The U.S. marshal in charge of the transfer has decided to let his prisoner choose the route to be taken (the embezzler majored in accounting in college and took a beginning operations research course). If he wants to *maximize* total travel time using the methods of dynamic programming, what route will he choose? What will be the total (maximum) travel time?

◆ **12.3** The attorney general, a classmate of the embezzler in Exercise 12.2, has learned of a plot hatched during a drunken reunion of some of the prisoner's fraternity brothers. They plan to stop the marshal's automobile by creating a magnetic field that will incapacitate the ignition system, distract the marshal by regaling him with stories based on the humorous pronouncements of Ralph Nader, and remove the prisoner's handcuffs by laser beam.

Accordingly, the attorney general has telegraphed an order for his marshal to travel by the *fastest* route to state 13. If the marshal also knows the procedures of dynamic programming, what route will he elect?

**12.4** A man living in Chicago has allowed himself five days for a trip to Los Angeles by automobile. With gasoline prices the way they are, he wishes to travel by the shortest route. However, he also does not wish to incur motel expenses during the trip. Consequently he has sketched the following diagram. The cities represent places of residence of relatives with whom he can spend the night during his journey, while numbers above the arrows are distances in miles between cities.

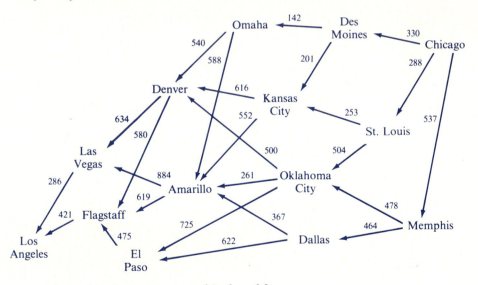

  **a** What is his shortest route and its length?
  **b** Suppose that he must visit his son in Dallas during the trip. What is his shortest route to Los Angeles and its length?
  **c** Suppose that he takes his wife along, who will not allow him to drive more than 620 miles in one day. She also must stay one night with her mother in Kansas City. What is their shortest route to Los Angeles and its length?

◆ **12.5** Following is a PERT network (see Chapter 14) that might be encountered during the planning of some project. Nodes in the network represent the start or finish of some task. Arrows indicate the task, and show which tasks must be

completed before the start of other tasks. In this case the numbers on the arrows
are the times in weeks required for the completion of the tasks.

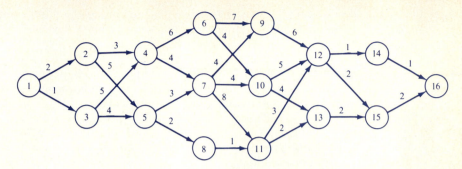

In such a project, *all* tasks must be completed. Consequently the *longest* path
through the network is called the *critical path*. Only if the completion time for a
task along the critical path can be shortened will it be possible to shorten the
completion time for the entire project.

   **a** Find the critical path and the corresponding project duration.

   **b** Suppose that the task $6 \to 9$, now requiring 7 weeks, is shortened to a duration
      of 2 weeks (perhaps by the allocation of additional labor power). Now what
      is the critical path and the project duration?

◆ **12.6** The following PERT networks do not have all of the characteristics usually
associated with problems solvable by dynamic programming (different numbers
of stages on the various paths). Nevertheless, use the optimality principle upon
which dynamic programming procedures are based to find the critical path in each
network (see Exercise 12.5 for the definition of a critical path).

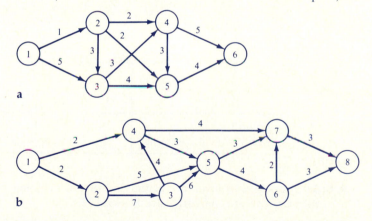

◆ **12.7** Consider a dynamic production-inventory problem with a planning horizon
of three periods. Inventory at the end of the horizon is to be zero, and there are
restrictions on ending inventory and production in each period. Specifically, no
more than four units may be produced in any period, and ending inventory in
any period cannot exceed four units.

    Assume a constant demand of three units per period. Setup cost per production
run is $14 in each period. Production cost per unit is $3, and holding cost per
unit of ending inventory is $2 (the same in each period). Determine optimal

production-inventory policies for initial inventories of zero, one, two, and three units, respectively.

♦ **12.8** Solve Exercise 12.7 using a planning horizon of four periods instead of three. Comment on similarities and differences among the policies for three and four periods.

♦ **12.9** In Exercise 12.7, change the setup cost to $40 per period and the production cost per unit to $8 (otherwise leave the problem unchanged). Are the three-period policies changed? Explain why or why not.

♦ **12.10** In Exercise 12.7, change the setup cost to $5 per period and the production cost to $10 per unit (otherwise leave the problem unchanged). Are the three-period policies changed? Explain why or why not.

**12.11** Suppose everything else remains the same, except that ending inventory may be no more than six units in any period.
  **a** Solve Exercise 12.7.
  **b** Solve Exercise 12.10.

♦ **12.12** Using a five-period planning horizon, solve **(a)** Exercise 12.7, **(b)** Exercise 12.10 (for a five-period policy), and **(c)** Exercise 12.11*b*.

**12.13** Assume a four-period planning horizon for a dynamic production-inventory problem. Production in any given period cannot exceed five units. Ending inventory in any period cannot exceed three units. Setup cost in any period is $10, and inventory at the end of the horizon must be zero. Holding cost per unit of ending inventory in all periods is $1.
  The following table gives, per period, the demand and the production cost per unit. Determine the optimal production-inventory policies for any level of initial inventory up to and including three units.

|  | **Period** | | | |
|---|---|---|---|---|
|  | **1** | **2** | **3** | **4** |
| Demand | 2 | 1 | 3 | 5 |
| Production cost per unit | $2 | $2 | $8 | $6 |

♦ **12.14** Suppose that inventory at the end of the planning horizon must be two units. Under this condition, solve Exercise 12.13.

**12.15** Assume a five-period planning horizon for a dynamic production-inventory problem. Production is limited to four units per period. Ending inventory is limited to five units per period. Inventory at the end of the horizon must be zero. Holding cost per unit of ending inventory is $2 for all periods.
  The following table gives, per period, the demand, setup cost, and production cost per unit. Determine the optimal production-inventory policies for any level of initial inventory up to and including five units.

| | Period | | | | |
|---|---|---|---|---|---|
| | 1 | 2 | 3 | 4 | 5 |
| Demand | 2 | 5 | 3 | 1 | 4 |
| Setup cost | $2 | $10 | $2 | $1 | $5 |
| Production cost per unit | $4 | $ 1 | $4 | $3 | $1 |

✦ **12.16** Refer to the capital budgeting problem of Section 12.5. Suppose that there are three factories and that no more than $8 million in capital will be made available for factory expansion. The plans, capital requirements, and additional revenues are shown in the following table. Determine the company's optimal expansion policies for capital outlays of $6, $7, and $8 million.

*CAPITAL AND REVENUE IN MILLIONS OF DOLLARS*

| | Factory | | | | | |
|---|---|---|---|---|---|---|
| | A | | B | | C | |
| Plan | Capital | Revenue | Capital | Revenue | Capital | Revenue |
| 1 | 0 | 0 | 0 | 0 | 0 | 0 |
| 2 | 2 | 3 | 1 | 3 | 2 | 4 |
| 3 | 5 | 7 | 3 | 5 | 4 | 7 |
| 4 | — | — | 5 | 8 | 6 | 10 |

**12.17** Refer to the capital budgeting problem of Section 12.5. Suppose that there are four factories and that no more than $13 million in capital will be made available for factory expansion. The following table gives plans, capital requirements, and additional revenues.

*CAPITAL AND REVENUE IN MILLIONS OF DOLLARS*

| | Factory | | | | | | | |
|---|---|---|---|---|---|---|---|---|
| | A | | B | | C | | D | |
| Plan | Capital | Revenue | Capital | Revenue | Capital | Revenue | Capital | Revenue |
| 1 | 0 | 0 | 0 | 0 | 0 | 0 | 0 | 0 |
| 2 | 2 | 4 | 1 | 3 | 2 | 5 | 3 | 5 |
| 3 | 5 | 7 | 5 | 8 | 4 | 7 | — | — |
| 4 | — | — | 6 | 9 | 6 | 9 | — | — |
| 5 | — | — | — | — | 7 | 11 | — | — |

**a** Determine the company's optimal expansion policies for capital outlays of $9, $11, and $13 million.

**b** Suppose that plan 2 *must* be used for factory A. Now what are the company's optimal expansion policies for $9, $11, and $13 million?

**12.18** We are asked to design a device consisting of three main components arranged in series. Reliability may be improved by installing parallel units on each component. We are limited to the case where no more than three units in parallel may be included on components 1 and 2, and no more than four units in parallel may be included in component 3.

Costs in thousands of dollars and reliabilities of the units are given below:

| $i = 1$ | | $i = 2$ | | $i = 3$ | |
|---------|---------|---------|---------|---------|---------|
| $R_1$ | $C_1$ | $R_2$ | $C_2$ | $R_3$ | $C_3$ |
| 0.8 | 2 | 0.7 | 2 | 0.6 | 1 |

Let $m_i$ denote the number of units to put in parallel in the $i$th component. Assume that costs are additive. Determine each $m_i$ so that total system reliability is maximized given that total available capital is \$14,000.

## SELECTED REFERENCES

Anderson, D. R., D. J. Sweeney, and T. A. Williams: *An Introduction to Management Science*, 3d ed., West Publishing Company, New York, 1982.

Bellman, R.: *Dynamic Programming*, Princeton University Press, Princeton, N.J., 1957.

Bellman, R., and S. Dreyfus: *Applied Dynamic Programming*, Princeton University Press, Princeton, N.J., 1962.

Cooper, L, U. N. Bhat, and L. J. LeBlanc: *Introduction to Operations Research Models*, W. B. Saunders, Philadelphia, 1977.

Hadley, G.: *Nonlinear and Dynamic Programming*, Addison-Wesley Publishing Company, Inc., Reading, Mass., 1964.

Hillier, F. S., and G. J. Lieberman: *Introduction to Operations Research*, 3d ed., Holden-Day, Inc., San Francisco, 1980.

Taha, H. A.: *Operations Research*, 3d ed., Macmillan Publishing Company, Inc., New York, 1982.

Wagner, H. M.: *Principles of Operations Research*, Prentice-Hall, Inc., Englewood Cliffs, N.J., 1969.

Wagner, H. M., and T. M. Whitin: "Dynamic Version of the Economic Lot Size Model," *Management Science*, vol. 5, 1958, pp. 89–96.

# NETWORK MODELS

*T*he networks you will see in this chapter have a general structure that differs from the network you saw in the stagecoach problem described as Example 12.1 of Chapter 12. That structure is simpler in one way: states are simply nodes in the network, while stages are only individual branches between nodes. But in another way the solution of a network problem is conceptually more complicated than the solution of a problem permitting a DP approach; the possible routes to a particular destination (node) may not all involve the same number of stages.

Yet there exist a few special types of network problems (besides those solvable by DP) whose solutions are fairly easy to obtain. They are usually identified by terms that indicate the type of real problem that they solve. Here we will consider the *minimal spanning tree* for a network, the *shortest route* between nodes in a network (probably the most frequently applied network procedure), and what is called the *maximal flow* problem for a network. Then in Chapter 14 we consider a network approach that is very useful in planning and scheduling problems: *PERT* networks.

The *minimal spanning tree* is that set of branches in a network that connects all nodes in such a way as to give a minimum total length for the set. Such a problem occurs in transportation or distribution networks and in situations involving the establishment of efficient communications networks.

The logic for solution of a minimal spanning tree problem is completely straightforward. In fact, such a problem offers one of the few opportunities in an operations research setting to make a decision that is immediately optimal without having to worry about its subsequent effect on other decisions. The approach will be illustrated by an example involving a communications network.

**Example 13.1**
**Minimal Spanning Tree for a Network of Computer Terminals**

The University of Wyoming has recently acquired a new computer that is to be installed in a location different from the one occupied by its older, smaller computer. As part of the new computer system, remote terminal facilities will also be installed in various buildings around campus. Lines linking up the system will be installed by the telephone company.

The telephone company must connect all terminal rooms to the central computer, but terminal rooms can share lines in the sense that, instead of connecting every room directly to the computer, the rooms themselves may be linked by telephone lines. That is, a terminal room is connected to the computer if it is connected to any other room that is connected to the computer.

Figure 13.1 depicts a schematic network showing distances (as fractions of miles) along routes between terminal rooms and the computer center, in locations where the telephone company will be permitted to install lines. The company's objective is to link up the system in such a way that the number of miles of line used is minimized. The resulting set of lines (the set that minimizes total distance) is the minimal spanning tree for the network.

Steps in an algorithm for determining the minimal spanning tree are listed following:

1 Arbitrarily choose any node.

2 Find the node nearest that node and connect the two.

3 Find the unconnected node nearest any connected node and connect those two.

4 Repeat step 3 until all nodes are connected.

Let's arbitrarily choose node 2 in the network of Figure 13.1. The nearest node to node 2 is node 4. Thus the results of steps 1 and 2 in the algorithm are shown as Figure 13.2.

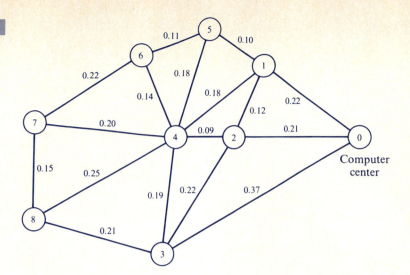

**FIGURE 13.1** Allowable connections for computer network

Now node 2 and node 4 are the connected nodes. From Figure 13.2 we see that node 1 is the nearest unconnected node to a connected node (0.12 miles from node 2). The result of step 3 in the algorithm is to connect node 1 to node 2, producing Figure 13.3.

At this stage nodes 1, 2, and 4 are connected nodes. Obviously (from Figure 13.3), node 5 is now nearest a connected node, node 1, and after that node 6 will be the nearest unconnected node to a connected node (node 5). So after those connections have been made, the partial spanning tree looks like Figure 13.4.

**FIGURE 13.2** First connection

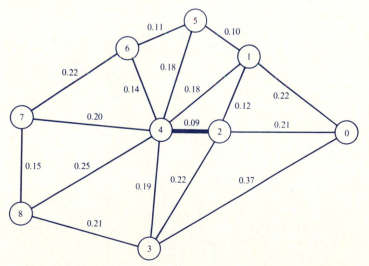

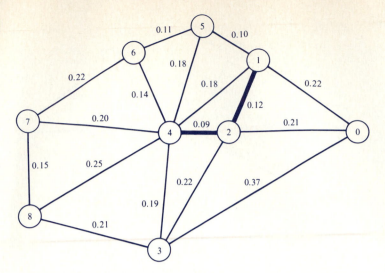

***FIGURE 13.3*** Second connection

Now the connected nodes are nodes 1, 2, 4, 5, and 6. Although the next-smallest branch length in the network is 0.14 miles in length, the associated branch is between nodes that have already been connected. And the branch 0.15 miles in length is between two as yet unconnected nodes, while the two branches 0.18 miles in length are again between nodes that are already connected. Thus the nearest *unconnected* node to a *connected* node is node 3, 0.19 miles from node 4. The partial tree at this stage is shown in Figure 13.5.

By now the pattern of the procedure should be crystal clear. The next

***FIGURE 13.4*** Third and fourth connections

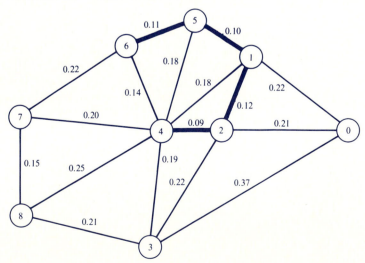

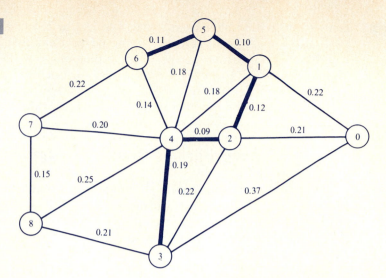

**FIGURE 13.5**  Fifth connection

connection is node 7 to node 4, then node 8 is connected to node 7, and, finally, node 0 (the computer center) is connected to node 2. This completes the minimal spanning tree, which is shown in Figure 13.6.

The (minimum) length of line required for linking up the network is the sum of the lengths of branches on the minimal spanning tree, 1.17 miles. We should observe that the same minimal spanning tree would have resulted from the choice of *any* original node. For instance, if node 0 had been the original choice in step 1 of the algorithm, then the sequence of

**FIGURE 13.6**  The minimal spanning tree

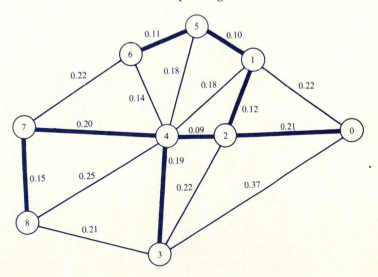

connections would have been 2 to 0, 4 to 2, 1 to 2, 5 to 1, 6 to 5, 3 to 4, 7 to 4, and 8 to 7. And certainly it should be clear that all of this work could have been carried out on a single diagram, say the original Figure 13.1. Figures 13.2 through 13.6 were only included to illustrate the steps in the algorithm. So once the original network has been drawn, the determination of the minimal spanning tree is an extremely simple task.

## 13.2 THE SHORTEST ROUTE THROUGH A NETWORK

Particularly in a transportation or distribution problem, sometimes the shortest distance from a point of origin to a destination is desired. But *shortest-route* problems are not confined to considerations of merely distance. Minimum time and minimum cost can often be determined by finding the "shortest route" through a network. For instance, the stagecoach problem, a related network for which is shown in Figure 12.1 of Chapter 12, can be regarded as a shortest-route problem if distances are replaced by policy costs. If the numbers in the network of Figure 12.1 happen to be travel times instead of policy costs, then the "shortest route" would become the minimum travel time. So we see that a procedure for finding the shortest route through a network can be applied to problems involving distance, time, or cost. Because of this versatility, a shortest-route algorithm is one of the most important procedures for a management scientist to know.

The algorithm to be illustrated by Example 13.2 successively finds the shortest route to each node in the network, arranged in order of their shortest distances from the point of origin. Since the ultimate destination is always one of the nodes in the network, the shortest route to the destination is also determined in the process. A nice feature of this shortest-route algorithm is that it gives the shortest route from the origin to *every* node in the network, not just to the destination.

As was the case when we applied DP to the network of Figure 12.1, either tables or graphs (of networks) may be used during the solution process. Here we elect to look at the algorithm graphically, since then the characteristics of the network being considered are always right there for us to see. As you will notice, the procedure implied by our solution of Example 13.2 has a lot of similarities to a dynamic programming analysis.

### Example 13.2
### Shortest Route from Timbering Site to Railhead

Clearcut Corporation has timbering operations going on at six different sites in Medicine Bow National Forest west of Laramie. Clearcut has built roads through that mountainous terrain, connecting sites and the railhead at the little tourist and ranching town of Centennial. On the network in Figure 13.7 the nodes are sites (except for the railhead node, node Y) and the associated road distances in miles are indicated. Many of these roads

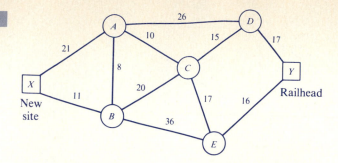

**FIGURE 13.7** Clearcut Corporation's timbering roads

are very winding, with switchbacks and wide, sweeping curves to avoid steep grades or obstacles like cliffs and ravines, so the straight-line paths on the figure do not reflect the actual appearance of the network on a map. Thus in some of the triangles, for example, the sum of two legs does not exceed the third, or the network is not drawn to scale.

Node $X$ in the network is Clearcut Corporation's newest timbering site, while node $Y$ represents the railhead at Centennial. Clearcut wants to determine the shortest route from its new site to the railhead. In the process of that determination, the corporation also wants to find the shortest routes from site $X$ to all of its other sites.

The shortest-route algorithm may be described concisely in words. First we find the nearest node to the origin, node $X$. Then we find the next-nearest node to node $X$, then the next-nearest node to node $X$ after that, and so on. During that process, we cross off any branch of the network that is not on the shortest path from a previously considered node to the next-nearest node we have just determined.

This process is much easier to understand by following through a sequence of pictures. For our first step, we see that only nodes $A$ and $B$ are contenders for the nearest node to node $X$. Clearly, node $B$ is that nearest node, being only 11 miles from node $X$. On our network we write that distance in a little box at node $B$. The result of this first step, with the shortest route from node $X$ to node $B$ indicated by a bold line, is shown in Figure 13.8.

The next-nearest node would have to be chosen from among those nearest $X$ and those nearest $B$. Node $A$ is the nearest node to node $B$, 8 miles from $B$, and the $8 + 11 = 19$ miles $A$ is from $X$ by way of $B$ is shorter than the 21-mile direct distance from $A$ to $X$. Thus node $A$ is the next-nearest node to node $X$. Further, since any shortest route from another node that passes through node $A$ would involve going through $B$ to get to $X$, we may cross off the 21-mile direct route from $A$ to $X$. This branch is not on the shortest route from a previously considered node to node $A$. The current status of the process is indicated by Figure 13.9.

The next-nearest node to node $X$ would be chosen from among those nodes nearest to nodes $A$ and $B$. The nearest node to $A$ is node $C$, a

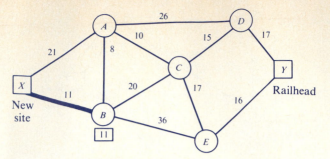

**FIGURE 13.8**   The nearest node to node $X$ is node $B$

distance of 10 miles from node $A$.   Node $C$ also happens to be the nearest node (not previously considered) to node $B$ since, by way of $A$, node $C$ is 18 miles from $B$.   Thus node $C$ is the next-nearest node to node $X$, and the shortest route from $C$ to $X$ has length $10 + 19 = 29$ miles.   At this stage we may also cross off the 20-mile branch from $B$ to $C$.   The current status is shown in Figure 13.10.

The next-nearest node to node $X$ will now be chosen from among those nodes nearest to $A$, $B$, and $C$, in this case, nodes $D$ and $E$.   The shortest distance from node $D$ to node $X$ is the minimum of $26 + 19$ and $15 + 29$, or $15 + 29 = 44$ miles.   The shortest distance from node $E$ to node $X$ is the minimum of $17 + 29$ and $36 + 11$, or $17 + 29 = 46$ miles.   Thus node $D$ is the next-nearest node to $X$, and we may cross off the 26-mile branch from $A$ to $D$, as indicated in Figure 13.11.

The next-nearest node to node $X$ is node $E$.   Here we see that the shortest distance from $E$ to $X$ is the minimum of $36 + 11$ and $17 + 29$, which is $17 + 29 = 46$ miles, while node $Y$ would have to be farther away from $X$ since by way of $D$ the distance to $X$ is $17 + 44 = 61$ miles, while the distance from $E$ to $Y$ is 16 miles ($E$ is closer to $X$ than $Y$).   We can also cross off the 36-mile branch from $B$ to $E$, as shown in Figure 13.12.

Last, the shortest distance from node $Y$, the railhead, to node $X$, the

**FIGURE 13.9**   The next-nearest node is node $A$

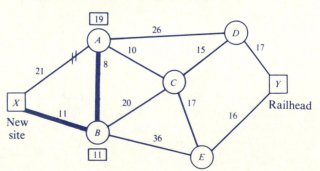

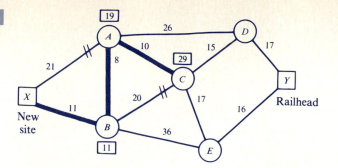

**FIGURE 13.10**  The next-nearest node is node C

new timbering site, is the minimum of 17 + 44 and 16 + 46, or 17 + 44 = 61 miles.  Figure 13.13 shows the final, completely solved network.

Reference to Figure 13.13 will immediately give us the shortest route from the new timbering site, node *X*, to any other site or to the railhead itself, node *Y*.  Thus from the new site to the railhead the shortest route is

$$X \to B \to A \to C \to D \to Y$$

a distance of 61 miles.  From node *X* to node *E* the shortest route, 46 miles in length, is

$$X \to B \to A \to C \to E$$

All of the pictures that have been drawn to illustrate the algorithm are not actually needed once the procedure is completely understood.  In fact, only one picture of the entire network is required; your worksheet for solving a shortest-route problem should just look like Figure 13.13.

**FIGURE 13.11**  The next-nearest node is node *D*

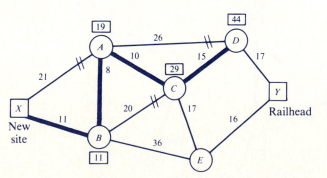

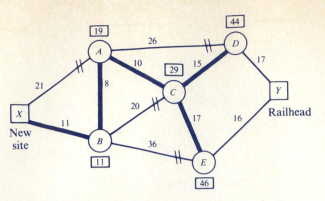

**FIGURE 13.12** The next-nearest node is node *E*

## 13.3 MAXIMAL FLOW IN A NETWORK

A *maximal flow* problem involves a network with one input node (the *source*) and one output node (the *sink*). It seeks the maximum amount of flow (number of vehicles, barrels of oil, and so on) that can enter the network at the source and leave by way of the sink during a specified period of time. The total amount of flow is restricted by flow capacities on the branches in the network. Pipe sizes or pump capacities can restrict flow in a pipeline system for distributing oil; the number of lanes, speed limits, and the condition of the roadway limit traffic flow on highways and streets.

In a network for a maximal flow problem, each branch will have an upper limit on the flow permitted in a given direction during the time interval of interest. These limits are the *flow capacities*. Nodes in the network are not considered to have capacities, but we must assume that flow into a node has to equal the flow out of the node.

The algorithm used to solve a maximal flow problem is a very simple one. We just follow a recursive cycle of easy steps that increase or

**FIGURE 13.13** Shortest routes from all nodes to node *X*

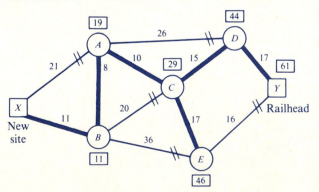

decrease flows along branches until no greater total flow from source to sink may be achieved. During our work on Example 13.3 we will state the algorithm and exhibit, step by step, its execution. You should see some analogies between the steps in the maximal flow algorithm and the steps we followed using the assignment method back in Chapter 7. This should be no big surprise, since to work the maximal flow problem we *assign* flow amounts to branches in the network.

### Example 13.3
### Maximal Flow in a Pipeline Network

The coal-slurry pipeline that will be used to send a mixture of coal and water from Gillette, Wyoming, to Minneapolis, Minnesota, was built piece by piece across Minnesota, North Dakota, and South Dakota before reaching Montana and Wyoming. Since coal-slurry pipelines are a recently conceived, innovative method for transporting coal, the network that developed during the construction phase of the project was largely experimental. Coal from North Dakota and South Dakota was transported through the earliest-constructed portions of the network using a variety of types of pumps and sections of pipeline of varying sizes. The terrain through which the branches pass also exhibits considerable variation from Minnesota to Wyoming. Thus different branches in the completed network have different flow capacities.

Suppose we measure flow of coal slurry in tons of coal transported per hour. Figure 13.14 exhibits the manner in which flow capacities, in either direction, will be indicated on our network.

The number 8 to the *right* of node 1 on the branch between nodes 1 and 2 indicates a flow capacity of 8 tons per hour directed *from* node 1 *toward* node 2. The number 0 to the *left* of node 2 implies that *no* flow is permitted *from* node 2 *toward* node 1. Likewise, the number 6 to the right of node 2 tells us that flow capacity from node 2 toward node 5 is 6 tons per hour, while the number 8 to the left of node 5 implies that 8 tons per hour may flow from node 5 toward node 2. With this notation understood, we exhibit the complete coal-slurry pipeline network in Figure 13.15.

Node 1, the rectangle to the left in Figure 13.15, represents Gillette, the *source* in this network. As we can see from the numbers on the three branches leaving node 1, a total of $8 + 5 + 4 = 17$ tons of coal per hour

*FIGURE 13.14*    Example branches and flow-capacity designations

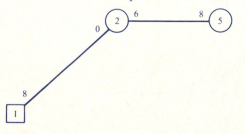

may be input at the source, provided that the network has the capacity to handle the flow. The rectangle on the right, node 8, represents Minneapolis, the *sink* in the network. We can see that nodes 5 and 7 are final supply points for node 8, and since the combined total flow capacity from node 5 to node 8 and node 7 to node 8 is only $7 + 8 = 15$ tons per hour, this is the maximum possible flow that could be received by the sink. But other branches in the network have restrictions on their flow capacities, so the *maximal* flow may *not* be 15 tons per hour; it might be something *less* than that. Here is our problem. Just what *is* the maximal flow permitted, in tons per hour, from Gillette to Minneapolis, and what flows should be assigned to what branches in order to achieve that maximal flow?

Before we state the maximal flow algorithm and then apply it to this pipeline network, let's look at the rationale of part of the procedure. Consider once more the little three-node network indicated in Figure 13.14. Remember, the numbers on the branches indicate the flow capacities *permitted* along the branches, not flow that has been assigned to the branches; we have yet to *assign* any flow. Now suppose we want *maximal* flow from node 1 to node 5. The number 6 to the right of node 2, the *smallest flow capacity on the path, in the direction of flow,* is the *maximal* flow allowed in that direction. So we could assign a flow, say $F$, of 6 tons per hour along that path.

Now we revise the numbers on the little network to indicate *remaining* flow capacities. In the direction of flow, change the first 8 to $8 - 6 = 2$, and change the 6 to $6 - 6 = 0$. These are remaining flow capacities, not yet assigned, in the direction of flow, for branches 1-2 and 2-5, respectively. But later on we might change our minds (because other portions of the large network in Figure 13.15 suggest better flow assignments), so we want the freedom to be able to "send" at least 6 tons per hour *back* to

**FIGURE 13.15**   Pipeline network with flow capacities

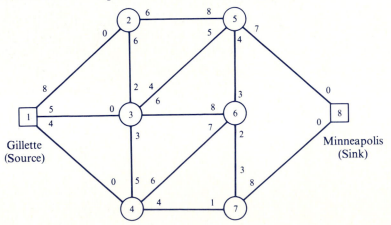

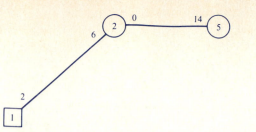

**FIGURE 13.16**    Remaining flow capacities after $F = 6$ is assigned to path 1-2-5

node 1 (we don't actually do that; we just assign less flow toward node 5). We make provision for this by simply *increasing* the permitted flows in the *other* direction by 6. Thus the 0 in Figure 13.14 becomes $0 + 6 = 6$, while the second 8 becomes $8 + 6 = 14$. This critical *accounting* procedure (accounting for flow that has been assigned and for remaining flow permitted) is used as we execute the steps in the maximal flow algorithm. The new look of the little network in Figure 13.14 is shown in Figure 13.16. Later on, in Figure 13.18, you will see this repeated as part of the look of the larger network.

Now we are ready to state the maximal flow algorithm. It is just a mechanical procedure for implementing the rationale we have most recently been discussing, along with steps that show how to determine the maximal flow and the assignments that yield it.

**THE MAXIMAL FLOW ALGORITHM**

1  Assume initially that no flow has been assigned to any branch of the network.

2  Find *any* path from source to sink that has flow capacities *in the direction of flow* that *exceed zero* for all branches on the path. If you cannot find such a path, go to step 5.

3  Find the smallest flow capacity on the path (in the direction of flow), say *F*, assign flow *F* to all branches on the path, and then
   a  Reduce all flow capacities on the path in the direction of flow by *F*.
   b  Increase all flow capacities on the path in the opposite direction by *F*.

4  Go back to step 2.

5  The *maximal flow* is the sum of all the flows *F* assigned during executions of step 3.

6  The flow assignments that yield maximal flow are the sums of the flows assigned to each branch during executions of step 3.

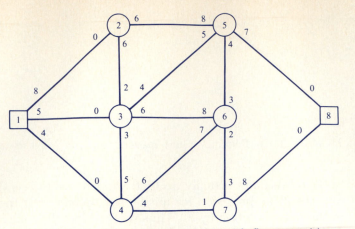

**FIGURE 13.17** The original network with flow capacities

Now let's apply the algorithm to the coal-slurry pipeline network of Example 13.3. To get started, we repeat Figure 13.15 as Figure 13.17 for ready reference, and we suppose that no flow has as yet been assigned to any branch (step 1).

The topmost path in the network, path 1-2-5-8, goes from source (node 1) to sink (node 8) and has positive flow capacities in the direction of flow. Here we have executed step 2 of the algorithm. Be reminded that we could have begun differently, since *any* such path, such as path 1-4-7-8, could have been chosen.

On path 1-2-5-8 the smallest flow capacity in the direction of flow is 6. Thus assign the flow $F = 6$ to all branches on the path. Further, reduce capacities in the direction of flow by 6, and increase capacities in the opposite direction by 6. Now we have completed a first execution of step 3. The result of this analysis, with the path 1-2-5-8 indicated by bold line segments, is shown in Figure 13.18.

**FIGURE 13.18** Remaining capacities after assigning $F = 6$ to path 1-2-5-8

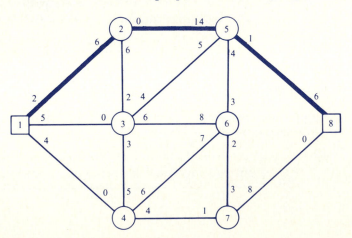

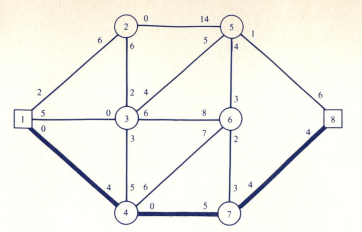

**FIGURE 13.19**   Remaining capacities after assigning $F = 4$ to path 1-4-7-8

Step 4 tells us to go back to step 2, which in turn instructs us to again find a path from source to sink with positive flow capacity. One such path is path 1-4-7-8. The smallest capacity on the path is 4 tons per hour, so assign flow $F = 4$ to all branches on the path, and complete parts *a* and *b* of step 3. Remaining capacities are shown in Figure 13.19.

Continuing the process, another path from source to sink with positive flow capacity is path 1-3-4-6-7-8. The smallest capacity on the path is 2, so assign flow $F = 2$ to all branches on that path. The current status of the network is given in Figure 13.20.

A path with positive flow capacity still exists. It is path 1-3-6-5-8. Assign flow $F = 1$ to all branches on this path, since that is the smallest capacity on the path. Revision of the network yields Figure 13.21.

At this stage, Figure 13.21, we see that it is no longer possible to find a path from node 1 to node 8 that does not have a 0 flow capacity somewhere

**FIGURE 13.20**   Remaining capacities after assigning $F = 2$ to path 1-3-4-6-7-8

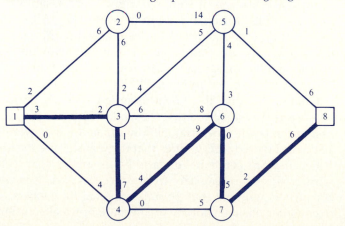

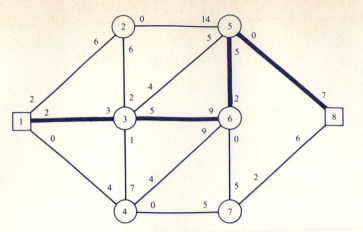

**FIGURE 13.21**  Remaining capacities after assigning $F = 1$ to path 1-3-6-5-8

on the path.  No path with positive remaining flow capacity leads into either node 5 or node 7, the final supply nodes for node 8.  Thus we are ready to determine maximal flow by executing step 5 in the algorithm.

Since every flow assignment has been made to a path that is directed all the way from the source to the sink, the total flow—in this case, the *maximal flow*—is just the sum of all the flow assignments that have been made.  Reference to the captions of Figures 13.18, 13.19, 13.20, and 13.21 reminds us what those assignments were.  Thus

$$\text{Maximal flow} = 6 + 4 + 2 + 1$$

$$= 13 \text{ tons per hour}$$

The facility at Gillette may be able to mix 17 tons of coal in slurry per hour, but the pipeline network (the distribution system) can handle only 13 tons per hour.  Likewise, while the processing facility on the other end, at Minneapolis, might be capable of processing 15 tons of coal per hour, it may expect to receive only 13 tons per hour at maximum flow capacity.

Finally, execution of step 6 will give flow assignments for each branch that permit the maximal flow to be achieved.  All you have to do is trace back through the history of the flow assignments, noting for each branch the amount of flow assigned to it.  A convenient way to record that information is simply to indicate the assigned flows on the network itself. This record is shown in Figure 13.22.

Finally, we sum the flows assigned to each branch.  This gives the combined flow assignments, shown in Figure 13.23.  Comparison of these assignments with the original flow capacities that were indicated in Figure 13.15 (or Figure 13.17) verifies that these assignments are indeed permitted.

Because we could have started this analysis by considering *any* path with positive flow capacity from source to sink, it is very possible that an *alternate* assignment that permits maximal flow exists.  You will be asked to consider this question of an alternate optimal solution in Exercise 13.10.

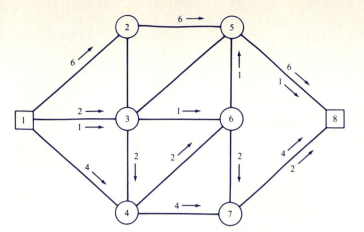

**FIGURE 13.22**   Record of assigned flows

## 13.4   SUMMARY AND CONCLUSIONS

Five basic types of network problems are considered in this book.   In this chapter were introduced three of them: the *minimal spanning tree* problem, the *shortest-route* problem, and the *maximal flow* problem.   In Chapter 12 you saw *dynamic programming* solutions for network-type problems when the networks had a very specialized structure.   In Chapter 14 you will see *PERT* and *critical path* analyses of networks related to project planning.

Those five types of analyses are the network procedures most used by management scientists.   But network problems solvable by dynamic programming or PERT–critical path procedures require that special structures be featured in the networks.   Conversely, the networks considered in this chapter were not required to have any particular features.   Their

**FIGURE 13.23**   Combined flow assignments yielding maximal flow

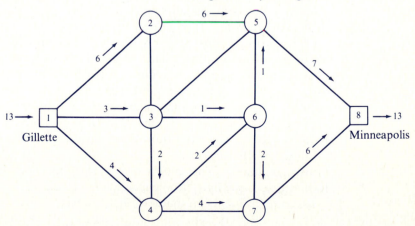
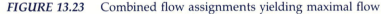

nodes and branches could be connected up in any pattern, so the networks themselves were completely *general*. The three *problems* addressed here, of course, required three very *particular* types of solutions.

The algorithms for the minimal spanning tree and for maximal flow are completely mechanical procedures that simply formalize the underlying logic behind solution of such problems; if you carefully follow the steps in those algorithms, it is unlikely that you will make an error. The shortest-route algorithm, however, was stated in such a way that a bit of *reasoning* on your part is required as you seek the next-nearest node to the initial node of interest. Thus you have to be much more careful when you work on a shortest-route problem. For small networks such as those that can be presented conveniently on one page of a textbook, only a little patience is required to discover all shortest routes. For very large, complex networks, however, you would probably want to make the steps more mechanical and let your computer do the busywork. A more formalized statement of the shortest-route algorithm may be found in Hillier and Lieberman (1980, p. 235).

Shortest-route problems are the types of network problems most frequently encountered in practice. Remember, there is no reason why a "route" has to be measured only in terms of *distance*. *Time* and *cost* are measures that often need to be minimized, and the shortest-route algorithm may just as easily be applied to those measures.

## KEY WORDS AND PHRASES

**Minimal spanning tree**  The set of branches in a network that connects all nodes in a way which minimizes the total length for the set.

**Connected node**  A node in a network that is connected to another node by a branch on the minimal spanning tree.

**Unconnected node**  A node that has not yet been connected to another node by a branch on the minimal spanning tree.

**Shortest-route problem**  The problem of determining the shortest distances from a specified node to other nodes in a network. The measure used need not be distance; it could be time or cost.

**Next-nearest node**  The node in a network that is nearest the origin after other, nearer nodes have already been determined.

**Maximal flow problem**  The problem of determining the maximum amount of flow that can enter a network at the source and leave at the sink, and the flow assignments that yield that maximal flow.

**Source**  The input node in a maximal flow problem.

**Sink**  The output node in a maximal flow problem.

**Flow capacity**  The maximum flow permitted in a given direction on a branch in the network.

**Flow assignment**  The amount of flow assigned to a branch in the network.

**Remaining capacity**  Flow capacity remaining on a branch after a flow assignment has been made to that branch.

## EXERCISES

**13.1** Reconsider Example 13.1 (Figure 13.1), which involved a network for a computer system. Find the minimal spanning tree using (**a**) node 1 and (**b**) node 2 as the arbitrary initial node. (Indicate the sequence of connections made in both cases.)

◆ **13.2** Find the minimal spanning tree for the following network:

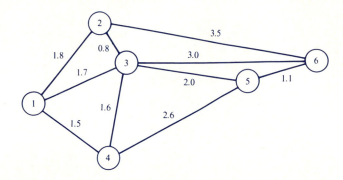

◆ **13.3** The University of Alaska at Point Barrow (UAPB) is faced with an austerity budget. Successful lobbying by energy companies for reduced mineral severance taxes has resulted in declining state revenues. The governor of Alaska has ordered all state institutions to cut expenditures by 10 percent.

  The president of UAPB has observed that snow removal from walks on campus is very expensive. In order to achieve substantial savings without hurting the instructional budget, she has directed the university maintenance supervisor to have snow-removal crews only clear enough walks to constitute a minimal spanning tree that connects all campus buildings.

  The following network indicates the layout of buildings and walks on the UAPB campus. Lengths of the walks in miles are also indicated. Find the minimal spanning tree and its total length.

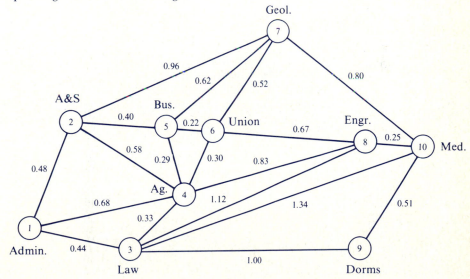

◆ **13.4** Clearcut Corporation (Example 13.2, Figure 13.7) has been informed by the U.S. Forest Service that the area in which the corporation is timbering is under consideration for wilderness designation. Clearcut will only be allowed to use those roads that constitute a minimal spanning tree for its network of timbering sites; the others will be closed to vehicular traffic.

    **a** Find the two alternative minimal spanning trees for Clearcut Corporation's timbering sites, including the railhead.

    **b** Which of the two alternative minimal spanning trees would enable Clearcut's trucks to travel from site X to the railhead at Y by the shortest route, given that the route must follow roads on the tree?

    **c** Suppose the Forest Service stipulates that the road from site A to site C must be closed. Now what is the minimal spanning tree that will produce the shortest route between site X and the railhead Y? What is that new shortest route and its length?

**13.5** Find the shortest routes, and their lengths, from node 1 to all of the other nodes in the network of Exercise 13.2.

◆ **13.6** A sales representative based at node 1 in the following network must on occasion drive from his office directly to each of the other nodes to respond to requests from his customers. Numbers on the branches are distances in miles, and the routes indicated on the network are the only roads in the region. Find the shortest routes he can use to drive from his office to the location of each of his customers. (The network is not drawn to scale.)

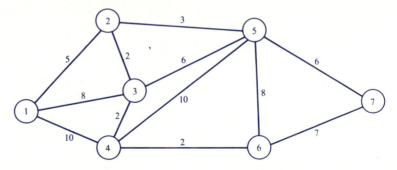

**13.7** The shortest routes for the sales representative of Exercise 13.6 will not necessarily be the minimum-time routes. Traffic along the routes, the features of the roadways, whether the road is a city or a country road, and so on, may result in longer routes taking him less travel time. Travel times in minutes are indicated on the following network. Find the minimum-travel-time routes (and the associated minimum times) from node 1 to each of the other nodes.

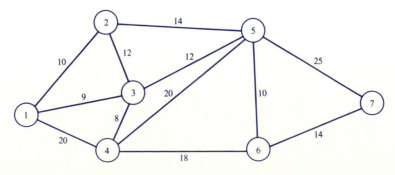

**13.8** Untied Parcel Service of Denver offers delivery of packages to eight locations east of Denver. The network following shows possible routings available for package deliveries and the costs in dollars associated with deliveries between nodes. Node $D$ represents the Denver point of origin. Find the minimum-cost routings, and the associated costs, from Denver to all other nodes in the network.

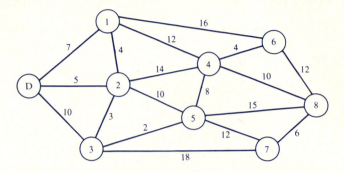

◆ **13.9** One of the CIA's contingency plans for dealing with a shutoff of oil from the Middle East has resulted in the following secretly negotiated deal. In return for the right of the United States to purchase camels from Saudi Arabia (the right to purchase sand to build roads for the camels is still under negotiation), the Saudi Arabian Oil Company has been given an extensive oil lease in Wyoming. Any oil found there will of course be exported to Japan.

The oil company is planning to drill seven test holes on the lease. The proposed sites for test holes are nodes in the following network, which also shows distances in miles along potential roads that could be built between the holes.

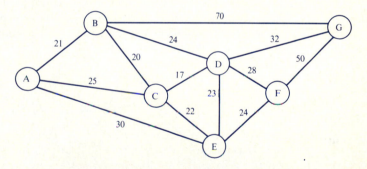

**a** Initially the oil company will only build roads along the minimal spanning tree. Find that minimal spanning tree and its length.

**b** Find the shortest route from node $A$ to node $G$ and its length. What additional roads (if any) will have to be built to supplement the minimal spanning tree roads so that the shortest route from $A$ to $G$ can be taken?

**13.10** Reconsider Example 13.3 (Figure 13.15), the maximal flow problem for the coal-slurry pipeline. Make initial flow assignments to path 1-3-5-8, and then finish solving the maximal flow problem from that point on using any positive-flow paths you wish. Do you get the same maximal flow (you should), but by way of an alternate flow assignment? If so, indicate the alternate assignment that will yield maximal flow.

**13.11** Reconsider the coal-slurry pipeline network of Example 13.3 (Figure 13.15). Suppose that an earthquake has caused a break in the line between node 2 and node 5, so that during repair that branch is no longer in the network. Now what is the maximal flow and the flow assignments that yield it?

◆ **13.12** The following network represents a highway system. Flow capacities indicated are in thousands of vehicles per hour. If node 1 is the source and node 7 is the sink, what maximal flow can the system handle and how should the traffic be routed in order to achieve it?

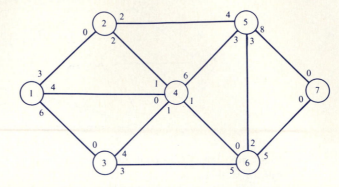

◆ **13.13** In the highway system of Exercise 13.12, would it increase maximal flow if highway engineers were able to increase flow capacity on only one branch in the network? If so, which branch (if you have a choice, just arbitrarily select one branch), and how much extra flow capacity on that branch would be worthwhile?

**13.14** Zorba Miraculous, the famous shipping magnate, has recently purchased a pipeline system that extends across Turkey. He will use it to transport Soviet oil from Leninakan, U.S.S.R., to Istanbul, where the oil will then be loaded into his tankers. Engineers in Zorba's organization have supplied him with the following schematic of the pipeline network and have determined for him the flow capacities indicated, in thousands of barrels of oil per hour.

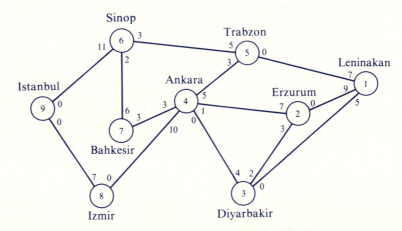

You are sharing a table and a bottle of ouzo with Zorba in a Paris bistro. He shows you the schematic and admits that he can't figure out how many barrels of oil per hour his new pipeline system can deliver to Istanbul. You rashly remark that in 15 minutes' time you not only can tell him the maximal flow from Leninakan to Istanbul, but you can also give him the routings (flow assignments) through the network which produce the maximal flow.

Mr. Miraculous is a high roller. He will bet you $100,000, against your agreeing to work for him for a year for no salary beyond subsistence, that you cannot do what you say you can in 15 minutes.

You have accepted the terms of the wager. See if you can win it.

**13.15** You had one too many shots of ouzo in that Paris bistro of Exercise 13.14; it took you 17 minutes to solve Zorba's problem. However, you did casually mention that if Mr. Miraculous were to build one more link (branch) into his pipeline network, connecting two unconnected nodes that already exist, he could increase the maximal flow by 20 percent.

Zorba declares that if you will tell him how to do that, he not only will forgive your debt to him, but he will also pay you $100,000. With reference to distances on a map of Turkey, where would you tell him to build the link, and what should be its flow capacity, to increase maximal flow by as much as possible?

## SELECTED REFERENCES

Anderson, D. R., D. J. Sweeney, and T. A. Williams: *An Introduction to Management Science*, 3d ed., West Publishing Company, St. Paul, Minn., 1982.

Bradley, S. P., A. C. Hax, and T. L. Magnanti: *Applied Mathematical Programming*, Addison-Wesley Publishing Company, Reading, Mass., 1977.

Hillier, F. S., and G. J. Lieberman: *Introduction to Operations Research*, 3d ed., Holden-Day, Inc., San Francisco, 1980.

Levin, R. I., C. A. Kirkpatrick, and D. S. Rubin: *Quantitative Approaches to Management*, 5th ed., McGraw-Hill Book Company, New York, 1982.

# PLANNING AND SCHEDULING: PERT-CPM

*P*lanning, scheduling, and controlling the work during any worthwhile project is a task calling for talented management.  The project may be extremely complex, involving hundreds or even thousands of separate, interrelated activities.  It could be practically impossible for one responsible person to keep any but a small portion of the project in manageable perspective; impossible, that is, without some assistance.  Here a convenient analytical and visual aid for scheduling and control, the PERT network of a project, is discussed.

The initials P E R T stand for Project Evaluation and Review Technique.  The original PERT approach was developed about 1958 by the Navy Special Projects Office with the assistance of the consulting firm of Booz, Allen, and Hamilton.  The particular application at that time was to the research and development effort involved in the Navy's Polaris missile program.

A bit earlier in time, but essentially simultaneously and independently, the I. E. du Pont de Nemours Company and Remington Rand initiated a similar technique called the Critical Path Method (CPM).  Their first application of CPM was to construction projects in the chemical industry.

First reports on these two very similar techniques, PERT and CPM, appear in Malcom et al. (1959) and Kelley and Walker (1959), respectively. Both reports are dated in the same year, 1959, and the techniques are related because of the type of network used in the analyses; the critical path is the heart of the PERT analysis of a project network. At their inception certain basic differences existed between PERT and CPM. Now, however, they have become commonplace in the realm of enlightened management, and in fact are regarded as one overall project-scheduling technique. PERT-CPM, or more simply, PERT, commonly denotes network analyses involving the combination and subsequent modification of the basic ideas of those first two innovative research groups.

In the years between World War I and the development of PERT-CPM, project coordination and control was almost universally assisted by a very simple visual aid called a *Gantt chart*. This chart, developed by the scientific management pioneer Henry L. Gantt, is basically a set of horizontal bar graphs. A bar represents a *task,* and within the bar may be a number of *milestones* representing the completion of *activities* that must take place during the task. The horizontal axis is a time scale, and the desired (or required) start and finish times for each task may be conveniently displayed on the chart. If someone takes the time to update the chart at regular intervals, indicating (perhaps by shading the bars) the stage of completion of all tasks at a particular point in time, the Gantt chart affords the manager an excellent visual aid for assessing project progress. Its disadvantage for planning purposes is its lack of adequate depiction of the *interrelationships* between the separate activities.

Gantt charts are still quite commonly used, especially for small projects or day-to-day operations like production scheduling. But their utility for large, one-shot projects like research and development for a new product is diminishing relative to that of PERT networks. A PERT network will convey all of the information available from a Gantt chart, as well as additional information about how all activities are related to each other. Further, while completion times for activities are also part of a PERT network, in PERT provision is made for those times to be random variables.

The original planning effort results in the first schematic PERT network for the project. In the planning phase PERT forces the planner to think through all activities and their interrelationships carefully. Particularly, the planner must determine which activities must precede which other activities and what resources (time, personnel, space, and so on) must be allocated to the completion of an activity. Two other managerial responsibilities, scheduling and control of activities, are also assisted by the network analysis. These functions of PERT will be considered later on, after we look at the development of the network in the planning phase of a project.

## 14.1 PERT NETWORK FOR A SMALL-BUSINESS PROJECT

In Example 14.1 we consider the steps involved in the construction of a PERT network for the project of starting up a small business. Before proceeding, we define the terms *activity* and *event* as they are used in PERT-CPM.

An *activity* is a clearly definable portion of a project that requires for its completion the consumption of resources (for example, time, money, or energy).

An *event* is a point in time during a project, consuming no resources. An event will always occur at the initiation and at the completion of an activity.

### Example 14.1
### Establishing a Small Bookstore

Colonel Read has retired from the Army to a small city in southern California. After a year of tending his garden and sunning himself, he begins to look for a more interesting way to spend his time. He has saved a little money, not enough to finance a small business but enough to merit a good credit rating, and is considering establishing a bookstore. The store would offer quality hardcover books to a reasonably affluent clientele and would not be in direct competition with other stores specializing in magazines and paperbacks. Being a discriminating and avid reader of both fiction and nonfiction, Colonel Read believes himself capable of choosing an attractive selection of books for his customers. Besides, all his adult life he has envisioned himself the respected proprietor of a small shop simply identified by the sign: READ BOOKS.

During his Army career Colonel Read participated in PERT analyses of weapons systems projects. He decides to apply that procedure to his project of establishing the bookstore.

The first task to be carried out, the initial project-planning phase, is the identification of activities, events, and precedence relationships. This can be managed conveniently by a listing of events and activities according to the following notation.

A number, such as 3, will denote an *event*. A pair of numbers, like 3-4, will denote an *activity* that is to take place between the events numbered three and four. The *ordered* pair 3-4 also indicates that event 3 must *precede* event 4. Table 14.1 gives the list of events and activities Colonel Read has determined apply to his project. The list is brief enough to avoid excessive complexity in an introductory example, yet has sufficient detail to be nontrivial.

The activities listed in Table 14.1 were not initially just written down in the form you see there. Quite likely Colonel Read attempted to sketch the PERT network at the same time he was anticipating the required activities, thereby keeping the precedence relationships straight. He probably started over a few times and made many erasures and modifications before being satisfied that the network and the listed activities and events did in fact adequately describe his project. In Figure 14.1 is the schematic of the PERT network he finally drew.

**TABLE 14.1**

## BOOKSTORE PROJECT: ACTIVITIES AND EVENTS

| Activity | Event |
|---|---|
| **1-2** Assess need for new bookstore | 1 Project begins |
| **1-3** Discuss loan feasibility with banker | 2 Need assessed |
| **2-3** (Need must be demonstrated before continuing project) | 3 Loan discussed and need assessed |
| **2-8** Plan advertising campaign | 4 Inventory and space require- |
| **3-4** Approximate inventory and space required | ments approximated |
| **3-5** Obtain verbal agreements from wholesale distributors | 5 Agreements secured and option to lease building acquired |
| **4-5** Locate suitable building and acquire option to lease it | 6 Loan approved |
| **5-6** Submit proposal to bank and await loan approval | 7 Contracts with distributors signed |
| **6-7** Sign contracts with distributors | 8 Orders placed, building leased, advertising planned |
| **6-8** Exercise option and lease building | 9 Building remodeled |
| **7-8** Refine inventory requirements and place orders | 10 Assistant hired, inventory on hand |
| **8-9** Remodel building | 11 Grand opening |
| **8-10** Store inventory as it arrives | |
| **8-11** Advertise grand opening | |
| **9-10** Conduct interviews and hire assistant | |
| **10-11** Stock shelves | |

The network shown in Figure 14.1 merely displays the activities and events involved and their correct precedence relationships. For instance, node 8 represents the event that the orders are placed, the building has been leased, and the advertising has been planned (event 8 in Table 14.1). Certainly activities 8-9 and 8-10, remodeling the building and storing the inventory, cannot begin until after the building has been leased, and advertising cannot begin (activity 8-11) until after it has been planned.

**FIGURE 14.1**    Network representation of the bookstore project

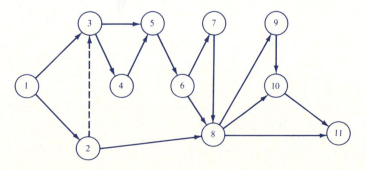

For keeping the precedence relationships straight the network of Figure 14.1 is very helpful, but if it is to be used further for *scheduling* the activities of the project, then *activity times* (as well as other resources that will be consumed besides time) must be estimated. That is, Colonel Read must also estimate the time required to complete each activity in order to be able to gain full benefit from his PERT network. This is the reason for the use of a *dashed line* to make the arrow representing "activity" 2-3 in the network of Figure 14.1. The arrows in the network depict activities and indicate which activities must precede other activities, and activities have been defined as portions of a project that consume resources, particularly, time. Yet activity 2-3 requires no time; it is included only to indicate that activity 1-2 must be completed before the activities that follow event 3 may be undertaken. Thus it is called a *dummy activity*. Dummy activities are used only to indicate precedence relationships when no other scheme for doing that seems feasible and always have *zero* activity times. In Table 14.1 the "dummy" characteristic of activity 2-3 was implied by putting the description of the activity in parentheses.

## 14.2 ACTIVITY TIMES AND THE CRITICAL PATH

*Time* is the basic resource of interest in PERT-CPM analyses. Other resources, such as personnel and money, may also be analyzed with PERT procedures and in fact will be considered in Sections 14.5 and 14.7. For the moment, however, we concentrate on one extremely important piece of information for any project: its overall *completion time*. Since to complete a project *all* of its activities must be completed, it is necessary to know (or to have estimates of) completion times for each activity (in PERT terminology, the *activity times*). But because some activities can be going on simultaneously during the project (activities 3-4 and 3-5 on Figure 14.1, for instance), the overall completion time is *not* just the sum of all activity times.

**Example 14.2**
**Activity Times and the Critical Path**

Colonel Read (Example 14.1) has made what he considers to be reasonable estimates of the times in weeks required for the completion of all activities in his project of establishing a bookstore. He realizes that the actual times may differ from his estimates, that in fact those times are random variables, but for his planning and control purposes he believes his estimates will suffice. Estimated activity times for the 16 activities in the project are given in Table 14.2.

A true PERT network for a project indicates activity times as well as precedence relationships. The PERT network for Colonel Read's bookstore project is shown in Figure 14.2, with activity times in weeks indicated on the appropriate arrows.

**TABLE 14.2**    *ESTIMATED ACTIVITY TIMES FOR THE BOOKSTORE PROJECT*

| Activity | Time, weeks | Activity | Time, weeks |
|----------|-------------|----------|-------------|
| 1-2 | 1.0 | 6-7 | 1.5 |
| 1-3 | 0.2 | 6-8 | 0.6 |
| 2-3* | 0* | 7-8 | 0.8 |
| 2-8 | 2.5 | 8-9 | 4.5 |
| 3-4 | 1.0 | 8-10 | 6.0 |
| 3-5 | 0.8 | 8-11 | 3.0 |
| 4-5 | 3.0 | 9-10 | 1.0 |
| 5-6 | 2.0 | 10-11 | 1.0 |

* Activity 2-3 is a dummy activity.

Now, with Figure 14.2 available, Colonel Read can begin to make some *scheduling* decisions for the activities. For instance, at the beginning of the project activities 1-3 and 1-2, discussing loan feasibility and assessing need for the store, respectively, must be completed before the approximation of inventory and space requirements can begin. Thus Colonel Read knows that in order to keep project completion time as short as possible, he should complete activity 1-3 (talk to the banker) sometime during the two weeks he is also assessing need (activity 1-2). The two-tenths of a week (part of a day) he has estimated for discussion of loan feasibility could be scheduled at any convenient time during the first two weeks of the project. Likewise, the 2.5 weeks allocated to planning for advertising (activity 2-8) could be scheduled during the time all activities between event 3 and event 8 are being completed, or he has a lot of flexibility available for scheduling activity 2-8.

Just how much flexibility *does* he have for scheduling activity 2-8, still with the objective of completing the project in minimum time? The answer to that question may be determined by discovering the time it takes to

**FIGURE 14.2**    PERT network for the bookstore project

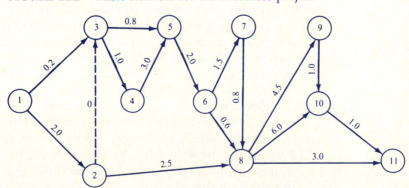

complete all activities on the *longest path* (measured in weeks) between nodes 3 and 8 in the network. Remember, *all* activities prior to event 8 must be completed before any of the remaining activities can begin, *including* those activities on the longest path between nodes (events) 3 and 8. Thus the *shortest* completion time for those activities will be the sum of the activity times on the *longest* path. Such activities (those on the longest path) are called *critical activities* because they fall along the *critical path* through the network, as defined following.

The *critical path* for any PERT network is defined to be the *longest path* through the entire network (in Figure 14.2, from event 1 to event 11). Since *all* activities must be completed in order to complete the entire project, the length of the critical path is also the *shortest time allowable* for completion of the project. Thus if the project is to be completed in that shortest time, all activities on the critical path must be started *as soon as possible*. Those activities are called *critical activities*. If the project is to be completed *ahead* of the schedule dictated by the critical path, then the time required for at least one of the *critical* activities must be *reduced*.

On the other hand, activities *not* on the critical path may have some *slack*. In this context, slack is the amount of time by which the start of an activity may be delayed without affecting the overall completion time for the project. This has implications for project control and scheduling; a delay in starting a noncritical activity may permit a temporary reallocation of resources to critical activities. Also, an unavoidable delay of a noncritical activity may not have drastic consequences.

A critical activity, however, has no slack. To reduce overall project completion time, *more resources* (less time implies more effort; probably, more cost) would need to be assigned to a *critical* activity.

The preceding discussion anticipates the critical path method (CPM), and the notions involved in that discussion are basic to a PERT analysis of a project. However, we will defer a formal procedure for *finding* the critical path until after the idea of expected activity times has been introduced. Meanwhile, we simply *indicate* the critical path for the bookstore project by the bolder arrows in Figure 14.3. You could verify that it is the longest path from event 1 to event 11 by determining the lengths of *all* paths in the network.

The length of the critical path in Figure 14.3 is 17.3 weeks (about four months), representing the shortest possible completion time for the project. The sum of critical activity times on that portion of the critical path between events 3 and 8 is 8.3 weeks. So the latest possible time that Colonel Read could start activity 2-8 and still not affect overall minimum completion time would be $8.3 - 2.5 = 5.8$ weeks after the occurrence of event 3 (or 7.8 weeks after the project begins, looking at the $2.0 + 0 = 2.0$ weeks prior to event 3 that are associated with the critical path). This presumes, of course, that his estimated activity times are the true activity times. That 5.8 weeks, by the way, is the *slack* for activity 2-8.

An assumption implied by the previous discussion is that sufficient resources exist for some activities to be conducted simultaneously. In the

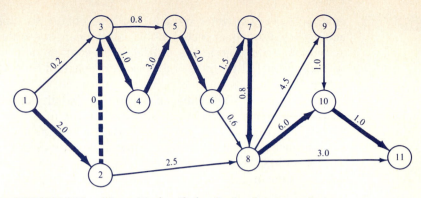

*FIGURE 14.3*   The critical path for the bookstore project

bookstore project of Example 14.1, until he hires an assistant near the end of the project, Colonel Read would have to carry out all of the activities himself. Thus it might not be possible for him to spend 2.5 weeks planning for advertising and *also* complete all activities between event 3 and event 8 in 8.3 weeks. This apparent oversight is not the fault of our analysis; it is the fault of Colonel Read. He should have drawn his PERT network in a way that would preclude impossible simultaneous activity. Here we are behaving as if Colonel Read has available to him the resources of some organization. In an ordinary PERT network for an industrial or governmental project the planner might rightly assume that adequate resources, particularly personnel, will be made available for work on the project.

## 14.3   EXPECTED ACTIVITY TIMES

The creators of PERT had intended to incorporate the random nature of activity times by allowing for the input of the probability density functions of time for each activity. Quite early in the history of PERT applications, however, it was discovered that managers had difficulty quoting opinions about activity times in the form of density functions. Moreover, many activities, such as those in a one-time research and development (R&D) project, are such that little or no past data or experience exists for the estimation of a density function for activity time.

On the other hand, the experienced manager seemed to have little difficulty expressing an opinion in the form of a "three-time estimate." Nowadays the manager is ordinarily asked for a best estimate of three times for each activity in the project: the earliest completion time, the anticipated completion time, and the latest completion time. These times are also called the *most optimistic, most likely,* and *most pessimistic* estimates. The letters *a, m,* and *b,* respectively, have been traditionally used to denote those time estimates.

The original CPM approach simply used the most likely time *m* as the best realistic estimate of activity time. In PERT, however, all three time estimates are combined by a formula to obtain an *expected time* for an activity. After all expected times have been computed, one for each activity in the project, the critical path is then determined by simply treating expected times as if they were the actual times required by each activity.

Practitioners of PERT have chosen the probability density called the *beta distribution* as a density of activity time that is most compatible with the philosophy of using three time estimates. The beta distribution is a continuous density with a finite range; it is quite flexible for practical use. For the right choice of parameters it can approximate the true distribution of a random time for a wide variety of situations. If the true density of activity time is known, then of course you should use it. If not, practice has indicated that the assumption of a beta distribution will provide estimates for expected times (and also standard deviations, useful when we want to discuss completion times probabilistically) that are very near the actual expected times.

To make the basic philosophy behind the use of the beta distribution more evident, we exhibit Figure 14.4. It shows the general shape of a beta density function and the relative locations assumed for the time estimates $a$, $m$, and $b$. It also shows the relative location of expected time $t_e$ to be calculated following.

Experience indicates that a good approximation to the expected time for a beta distribution like the one in Figure 14.4 is

$$t_e = \frac{a + 4m + b}{6}$$

Obviously this is just a weighted average of the three time estimates, where the most likely estimate $m$ receives four times the weight of the optimistic and pessimistic estimates. In Figure 14.4 $t_e$ is to the right of $m$, but if the distance from $a$ to $m$ had exceeded the distance from $m$ to $b$, $t_e$ would have been to the left of $m$.

## Example 14.3
## Expected Activity Times

Consider a project consisting of seven activities with three time estimates for each activity, shown in Table 14.3. The column headed $t_e$ is obtained using the formula for expected time. For instance, the expected time for activity 3-4 is

$$t_e = \frac{3 + 4(4) + 9}{6} = \frac{28}{6} = 4.67 \text{ weeks}$$

while the expected time for activity 3-5 is

$$t_e = \frac{5 + 4(8) + 10}{6} = \frac{47}{6} = 7.83 \text{ weeks}$$

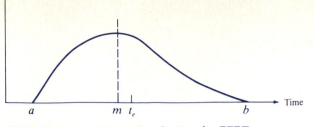

**FIGURE 14.4**   A beta distribution for PERT

Note the effect of the pessimistic time estimate on expected time for activity 3-4 and the effect of the optimistic time estimate on expected time for activity 3-5.  One expected time is above $m$ and the other is below $m$. In statistical terminology, in the first case the mean is greater than the mode ($m$), while in the second the mean is less than the mode, where the mode is the most likely time, or the time associated with the highest point on the graph of the beta distribution.  This result points out the ability of the beta distribution to allow for skewness; that feature is not offered by a symmetric distribution.

The PERT network for this project is shown in Figure 14.5.  The expected times are indicated along the activity arrows.

## 14.4  PERT-CPM: DETERMINING SLACK AND THE CRITICAL PATH

In Example 14.2 were introduced the notions of *slack* for an activity and the *critical path* for a project.  Now that we can determine expected activity times, we are ready to formally consider slack and its use in determining the critical path, and to see how these ideas are useful in project scheduling and control.  For its illustrations our discussion will employ the project of Example 14.3.

Associated with each activity of a project are four times of particular

**TABLE 14.3**   *TIME ESTIMATES IN WEEKS*

| Activity | $a$ | $m$ | $b$ | $t_e$ |
|----------|-----|-----|-----|-------|
| 1-2 | 1 | 2 | 4 | 2.17 |
| 1-3 | 5 | 8 | 11 | 8.00 |
| 2-3 | 3 | 5 | 8 | 5.17 |
| 2-4 | 4 | 6 | 8 | 6.00 |
| 3-4 | 3 | 4 | 9 | 4.67 |
| 3-5 | 5 | 8 | 10 | 7.83 |
| 4-5 | 1 | 2 | 3 | 2.00 |

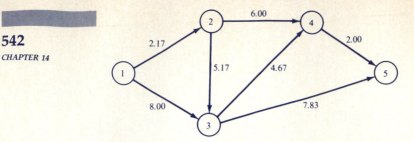

**FIGURE 14.5**    PERT network with expected activity times

interest in scheduling: the *earliest starting* time, the *earliest finishing* time, the *latest starting* time, and the *latest finishing* time.  Here "earliest time" means "earliest possible time permitted" and "latest time" means "latest possible time without increasing overall project duration."  These times, denoted by ES, EF, LS, and LF, respectively, will be computed assuming that the *expected* activity time is the *actual* time required to complete the activity.  The four basic times will all be measured from the *beginning* of the project, where we assume a *zero* value of time.

### Example 14.4
### Determining ES, EF, LS, and LF

To begin, we will determine ES and EF for all activities in the project of Example 14.3 (Figure 14.5).  Remember, for a given activity,

$$ES = \text{earliest starting time}$$

$$EF = \text{earliest finishing time}$$

Since $t_e$, the expected activity time, will be regarded as the true activity time, then clearly

$$EF = ES + t_e$$

that is, the earliest finishing time possible for an activity is its earliest starting time plus its expected completion time.  To determine earliest starting time (ES) for any activity, we refer to the project network and use the following rule:

The *earliest starting time* for an activity leaving a node equals the *maximum* of the earliest finishing times for all activities entering the node.

For any project, the values of ES and EF for every activity are determined by making a *forward pass* through the network, that is, by working through the network from the starting node to the ending node.  For ease of reference, we repeat the network of Figure 14.5 as Figure 14.6.

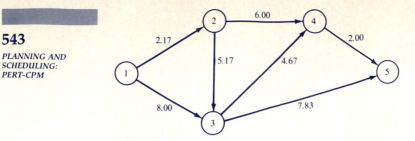

**FIGURE 14.6** Network for Example 14.3

Now we start our forward pass through the network, beginning at node 1. Consider activity 1-2. Its earliest starting time is ES $= 0$, the time at which the project begins. Its expected completion time is $t_e = 2.17$ weeks, so its earliest finishing time is

$$EF = ES + t_e = 0 + 2.17 = 2.17 \quad \text{activity 1-2}$$

Similarly, for activity 1-3, ES $= 0$ and

$$EF = ES + t_e = 0 + 8.00 = 8.00 \quad \text{activity 1-3}$$

For activity 2-3, we notice that only one activity enters node 2: activity 1-2. Thus the earliest starting time for activity 2-3 is the earliest *finishing* time for activity 1-2, or

$$ES = 2.17 \quad \text{activity 2-3}$$

Then $$EF = 2.17 + 5.17 = 7.34 \quad \text{activity 2-3}$$

Now consider activity 3-4. Its earliest starting time is the *maximum* of the *two* earliest finishing times for activities entering node 3, activity 1-3 and activity 2-3. Thus

$$ES = \max(8.00, 7.34) = 8.00 \quad \text{activity 3-4}$$

Its earliest finishing time is just

$$EF = 8.00 + 4.67 = 12.67 \quad \text{activity 3-4}$$

Continuing in this systematic fashion on a forward pass through all activities in the network yields ES and EF for every activity. Those "earliest times" are shown in Figure 14.7, where for each activity ES is at the tail of the arrow and EF is at the head of the arrow. The expected activity times are shown in parentheses.

Already we have much useful information. For instance, since the

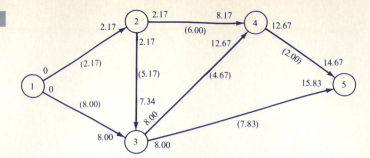

**FIGURE 14.7** Earliest starting and earliest finishing times

maximum earliest finishing time, EF for activity 3-5, is 15.83, we know that the shortest possible time in which the entire project may be finished is 15.83 weeks (this will be the length of the critical path, of course). Also, the project manager would know, for example, that at least 12.67 weeks are available for acquiring the resources necessary to carry out activity 4-5, since it cannot possibly be started any earlier.

Of as much interest, of course, are latest starting times (LS) and latest finishing times (LF) for the activities. These are determined by making a *backward pass* (from end to beginning) through the network. Here we make the latest finishing times for activities entering the last node equal to the *maximum* of the *earliest finishing times* for those same activities in order to get started. Then latest starting times are computed using the formula

$$LS = LF - t_e$$

and all the other latest finishing times are determined by the following rule:

> The *latest finishing time* for an activity entering a node equals the *minimum* of the latest starting times for all activities leaving the node.

Thus for the project of Figure 14.6 we can refer to Figure 14.7 and see that the maximum earliest finishing time for activities 4-5 and 3-5 is max(14.67, 15.83) = 15.83. Then 15.83 is the latest finishing time for *both* activity 4-5 and activity 3-5. Thus for activity 4-5 we have

$$LS = LF - t_e = 15.83 - 2.00 = 13.83 \qquad \text{activity 4-5}$$

and for activity 3-5 the latest starting time is

$$LS = LF - t_e = 15.83 - 7.83 = 8.00 \qquad \text{activity 3-5}$$

Now consider activity 3-4. The only activity leaving node 4 is activity 4-5, so

$$LF = 13.83 \qquad \text{activity 3-4}$$

and
$$LS = 13.83 - 4.67 = 9.16 \qquad \text{activity 3-4}$$

Now look at activity 2-3. Two activities, 3-4 and 3-5, leave node 3. Thus

$$LF = \min(9.16, 8.00) = 8.00 \qquad \text{activity 2-3}$$

Then
$$LS = 8.00 - 5.17 = 2.83 \qquad \text{activity 2-3}$$

Completing the backward pass all the way through the network (to node 1) gives LS and LF for every activity. These "latest times," and the expected times (in parentheses), are shown on Figure 14.8.

Again, this most recent analysis gives some worthwhile information. In order to be able to complete the project in its minimum possible completion time, the *latest* possible time we could initiate activity 4-5, for instance, would be 13.83 weeks into the project. Then adding on its expected activity time of 2.00 weeks, we get the 15.83 weeks representing the earliest finishing time for the project.

### Example 14.5
### Slack and the Critical Path

The *most useful* information about the project of Example 14.3 derives from *combining* all the ES, EF, LS, and LF times we have available from Figures 14.7 and 14.8. Particularly, we are now able to compute *slack* for each activity and thereby to determine the *critical path* for the project.

Slack is just the amount of time the start of an activity may be delayed without changing the minimum completion time for the project. Thus for any activity we can compute slack by *either* of the following two formulas:

$$\text{Slack} = LS - ES$$

$$= LF - EF$$

**FIGURE 14.8**   Latest starting and latest finishing times

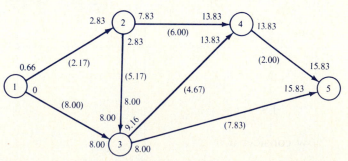

For example, look at activity 2-4. From Figure 14.7 we get ES = 2.17 and EF = 8.17. From Figure 14.8 we get LS = 7.83 and LF = 13.83. Then

$$\left.\begin{array}{l} \text{Slack} = 7.83 - 2.17 = 5.66 \\ \phantom{\text{Slack}} = 13.83 - 8.17 = 5.66 \end{array}\right\} \text{activity 2-4}$$

This means that once activity 1-2 has been completed (so we are *permitted* to start activity 2-4), we may delay the start of activity 2-4 by any duration up to 5.66 weeks without lengthening the overall completion time of the project.

But consider activity 3-5. From Figure 14.7 we get ES = 8.00 and EF = 15.83, and from Figure 14.8 we get LS = 8.00 and LF = 15.83. Thus

$$\left.\begin{array}{l} \text{Slack} = 8.00 - 8.00 = 0 \\ \phantom{\text{Slack}} = 15.83 - 15.83 = 0 \end{array}\right\} \text{activity 3-5}$$

Then we *may not delay* the start of activity 3-5 without lengthening the duration of the project, since that activity has *zero slack*. It is thus a *critical activity*, falling on the critical path. And thereby we see a way to *determine* the critical path in the project network. We simply find all critical (zero-slack) activities and connect them up. The easiest way to do that, and to also have a nice, concise record of all of our previous analysis, is to form a table like Table 14.4.

Thus Table 14.4 gives the amount of time each activity may be delayed after it *may* be begun (the slacks) without increasing overall project duration. It also reports earliest and latest starting times and earliest and latest finishing times for each activity, information that is obviously useful for activity-scheduling decisions. Finally, it indicates the *critical* activities about which those scheduling decisions must revolve, those activities with no slack. Here only activity 1-3 and activity 3-5 are critical. Thus a path

**TABLE 14.4**   *STARTING TIMES, FINISHING TIMES, AND SLACK FOR EXAMPLE 14.3*

| Activity | ES | LS | EF | LF | Slack | Critical? |
|----------|-------|-------|-------|-------|-------|-----------|
| 1-2 | 0 | 0.66 | 2.17 | 2.83 | 0.66 | No |
| 1-3 | 0 | 0 | 8.00 | 8.00 | 0 | Yes |
| 2-3 | 2.17 | 2.83 | 7.34 | 8.00 | 0.66 | No |
| 2-4 | 2.17 | 7.83 | 8.17 | 13.83 | 5.66 | No |
| 3-4 | 8.00 | 9.16 | 12.67 | 13.83 | 1.16 | No |
| 3-5 | 8.00 | 8.00 | 15.83 | 15.83 | 0 | Yes |
| 4-5 | 12.67 | 13.83 | 14.67 | 15.83 | 1.16 | No |

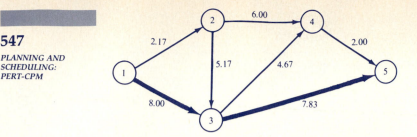

**FIGURE 14.9**    The critical path for the project of Example 14.3

through the network that includes only those critical activities is a *critical path*. The critical path for the project is shown in Figure 14.9, along with the original expected activity times.

## 14.5   PROJECT SCHEDULING AND RESOURCE LEVELING

For the project originally described as Example 14.3, we now know the earliest and latest possible starting times for each activity and all of the slacks.   The starting times for activities with slack may be adjusted to achieve objectives other than just finishing the project early.

One such objective is the leveling of resources allocated to the overall project.   The time for each activity would most certainly have been estimated by someone who also has estimated the amount of resources needed for the activities.   That is, those resources should be known in the project-scheduling phase of the problem.   Often one wants to keep the total amount of resources in use during the project as nearly constant as possible through time.   Perhaps certain constraints will be imposed as well.   An easy version of that process of resource leveling is discussed in Example 14.6.

### Example 14.6

To make the problem simple, suppose that personnel is the only resource to be considered.   Assume that at no time during the course of the project will more than 10 people be assigned to it.   Our objective is to keep the number of people working as nearly constant as possible throughout the entire project duration.   Personnel required for each activity are shown in Table 14.5.

It is helpful to exhibit activities on a time scale that shows ranges of time allowable for each activity.   These are the dashed lines in Figure 14.10.   On the same time chart we show each activity at its earliest and latest possible starting time.   These are represented by the solid lines. The times are obtained from Table 14.4.

Next we may construct two pictures, one giving personnel requirements over time if each activity is scheduled at its earliest starting time, the other

TABLE 14.5    PERSONNEL PER ACTIVITY

| Activity | Personnel | Activity | Personnel |
|----------|-----------|----------|-----------|
| 1-2 | 1 | 3-4 | 2 |
| 1-3 | 4 | 3-5 | 5 |
| 2-3 | 3 | 4-5 | 3 |
| 2-4 | 2 | | |

giving the same information for latest starting times. It might be that for one or both of the schedules the constraint that no more than 10 people be working at once is satisfied. If so, then the only problem is that of shifting starting times for those activities with slack to keep the number working as nearly constant as possible. If not, then the resource leveling must be attempted with the constraint in mind.

Figures 14.11 and 14.12 show the number of people working at any one time under both schedules. We first note that the constraint is satisfied by both of the potential work schedules. The only problem is that of resource leveling.

In this instance there is not much leveling that can be done. We would probably just try to get rid of the "chimneys," where extra people would be working for a short duration. Figure 14.13 shows the result if we take advantage of the slack in activity 2-4 to achieve a slightly more level schedule.

FIGURE 14.10    Activities at earliest and latest starting times

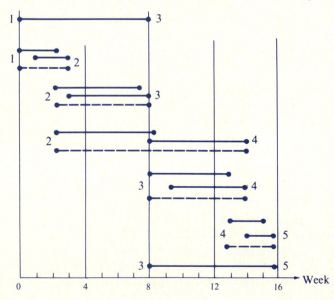

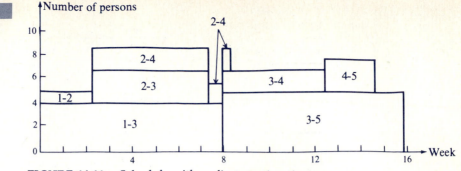

**FIGURE 14.11**   Schedule with earliest starting times

To date no technique has been created to assure an optimal leveled schedule.   The one shown in Figure 14.13 may or may not be the best that can be done, provided that expected times for the activities remain as originally computed.

If we are given the freedom to adjust those expected times, by adding or deleting resources to or from activities, there is another, simpler way to overcome the chimney problem.   The chimney arises because in the schedules of Figures 14.11 and 14.12 activity 2-4 must overlap both activities 3-4 and 2-3.   It might be possible to take advantage of the slack of 1.16 weeks in activity 3-4 and assign, for a while, one of the people on 3-4 to activity 2-4.   This could have the effect of shortening the expected time for 2-4 just enough so it may be scheduled to overlap only one of those activities in one or the other of the two basic schedules.   Probably this would not increase the expected time of activity 3-4 by more than 1.16 weeks, and both of the original schedules could be made smoother.

As managers you might be free to reassign resources to any activities you wish.   You should be aware, however, that the reassignment may affect the critical path.   It will certainly change the slacks for some of the activities.   Consequently, the whole PERT analysis should be redone to reflect the changes in expected times.

**FIGURE 14.12**   Schedule with latest starting times

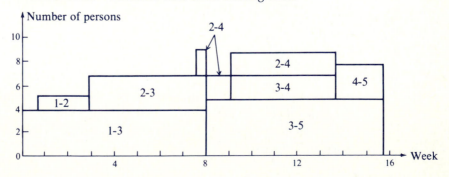

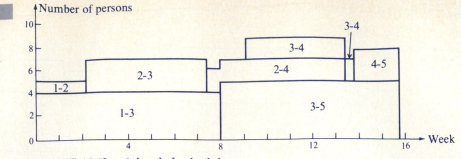

**FIGURE 14.13**    A leveled schedule

## CHAPTER 14

## 14.6   PROBABILITY IN PERT

Throughout the previous three sections we have been essentially ignoring the fact that activity times are random variables.  In Section 14.3 the beta distribution was assumed for the random activity times, but up to this point we have behaved as if the expected activity time $t_e$ is the actual time required for completing each activity.  Scheduling was carried out under that assumption, and of course if some activity in reality uses more or less time than $t_e$, the schedule may be disrupted.  This might not cause any problem if the activity is one having some slack.  But an activity on the critical path taking more time than $t_e$ could be troublesome.

Then it is important to investigate the network from a *probabilistic* point of view.  You may want to know, for instance, the probability of completing the project of Example 14.3 ahead of schedule, say in 14.50 weeks instead of 15.83.  Or, because of its implications for the critical path, the probability that some other path through the network will have duration more than 15.83 weeks may be of interest.  How to answer those and other probabilistic questions is the subject of this section.

A knowledge of the variance of each activity time is important.  In PERT the true variance of the assumed beta distribution is not used; rather, one appeals to the fact that for most random variables almost all of their values will fall within three standard deviations of the mean, or will *range* through an interval approximately six standard deviations in length.  If we assume a symmetric distribution with finite range $b - a$, and if $\sigma$ denotes the standard deviation, then

$$6\sigma \simeq b - a \qquad \text{or} \qquad \sigma \simeq \frac{b - a}{6}$$

Although the beta distribution is not in general symmetric, PERT analysts have found that the formula above gives a fair approximation in practice for the standard deviation of an activity time.  Thus we have two approximation formulas available for our probabilistic investigations.  For a particular activity,

$$\text{Expected activity time} = t_e = \frac{a + 4m + b}{6}$$

$$\text{Variance of activity time} = \sigma^2 = \frac{(b - a)^2}{36}$$

The second formula just uses the fact that the variance is the square of the standard deviation.

If our project happened to involve only a series of activities, one right after the other, so there is only one path through the network, and if the duration of each activity is a random variable independent of other activity durations, then project duration is a random variable with known mean and variance. Let $T$ denote project duration. Then under the conditions stated above,

$$\text{Expected project duration} = E(T) = \sum_{\substack{\text{all} \\ \text{activities}}} t_e$$

$$\text{Variance of project duration} = V(T) = \sum_{\substack{\text{all} \\ \text{activities}}} \sigma^2$$

That is, the mean of a sum of random variables is the sum of their means, and the variance of a sum of *independent* random variables is the sum of their variances.

Unfortunately, for a fairly complex set of *interrelated* activities such as most PERT networks are, project duration is a random variable that is difficult to handle. Because of the random character of the activity times, the true project duration could be dictated by some path other than the critical path. Nevertheless, just as the assumption of a beta distribution simplifies the practical task of determining expected times and variances, so another assumption simplifies probabilistic analyses of project durations.

The specific assumption is that *project duration will be measured along the critical path.* Assuming independence of critical activities, then for a PERT project we have

$$E(T) = \sum_{\substack{\text{all activities} \\ \text{on critical path}}} t_e \qquad\qquad V(T) = \sum_{\substack{\text{all activities} \\ \text{on critical path}}} \sigma^2$$

## Example 14.7
### Probabilities in a PERT Analysis

Now let's take a look at some probabilistic implications of the previous discussion. To make things more interesting, we will consider a slightly more complicated project than the one used in the illustrations based on Example 14.3. Table 14.6 lists 10 project activities, along with the most optimistic ($a$), most likely ($m$), and most pessimistic ($b$) time estimates for

TABLE 14.6    EXPECTED TIMES AND VARIANCES

| Activity | a | m | b | $t_e$ | $\sigma^2$ |
|----------|---|---|---|-------|-----------|
| 1-2 | 3 | 5 | 7 | 5 | 0.4444 |
| 1-3 | 1 | 2 | 9 | 3 | 1.7778 |
| 1-4 | 5 | 7 | 15 | 8 | 2.7778 |
| 2-4 | 1 | 2 | 3 | 2 | 0.1111 |
| 3-4 | 5 | 6 | 7 | 6 | 0.1111 |
| 3-5 | 5 | 6 | 13 | 7 | 1.7778 |
| 4-6 | 2 | 4 | 6 | 4 | 0.4444 |
| 4-7 | 3 | 10 | 11 | 9 | 1.7778 |
| 5-7 | 1 | 3 | 5 | 3 | 0.4444 |
| 6-7 | 1 | 8 | 9 | 7 | 1.7778 |

each activity.   The table also shows expected activity time ($t_e$) and the variance of activity time ($\sigma^2$).   Those quantities, in the last two columns of Table 14.6, were computed using the formulas

$$t_e = \frac{a + 4m + b}{6} \quad \text{and} \quad \sigma^2 = \frac{(b - a)^2}{36}$$

The times in Table 14.6 are given in weeks, that usually being the smallest manageable time unit for most projects with some substance to them.   The PERT network for this project is shown in Figure 14.14, with expected activity times shown for each activity (the $t_e$'s from Table 14.6) and with the critical path depicted by the bolder arrows.

The length of the critical path is 20, so we can say that the expected project duration is 20 weeks.   The variance of that duration, measured along the critical path, is 4.1111 square weeks, or the standard deviation of duration is $\sqrt{4.1111} = 2.03$ weeks.   Computations of the mean and variance are indicated in Table 14.7.

**FIGURE 14.14**    Project network and critical path

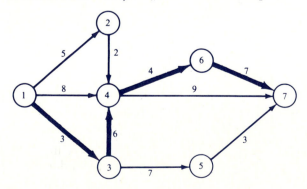

**TABLE 14.7** *MEAN AND VARIANCE ALONG CRITICAL PATH*

| Critical activity | $t_e$ | $\sigma^2$ |
|---|---|---|
| 1-3 | 3 | 1.7778 |
| 3-4 | 6 | 0.1111 |
| 4-6 | 4 | 0.4444 |
| 6-7 | 7 | 1.7778 |
| | 20 | 4.1111 |

A high percentage (about 99 percent) of the values of almost any random variable should lie within three standard deviations of its mean. Since the standard deviation of duration along the critical path is $\sqrt{4.1111} \simeq 2.03$ and the mean duration is 20 weeks, then

$$20 - 3(2.03) = 13.91$$

$$20 + 3(2.03) = 26.09$$

Thus we can say it is almost certain that the project will be completed in a time somewhere between 13.9 weeks and 26.1 weeks.

That is a very wide range. If better probabilistic statements are to be made, then more needs to be known about the distribution of the random variable $T$, the project duration in weeks.

Here we may appeal to a different *central limit theorem*. Back in Chapter 8 we observed that a sample average $\overline{X}$ is approximately normally distributed for reasonably large sample sizes. The central limit theorem which gave that result was only a special case of a much more general theorem. Generally, the *sum* of *independent* random variables may be treated as if its distribution is approximately normal, and that approximation becomes better as the number of random variables that comprise the sum gets larger.

In a PERT analysis, the project duration $T$ is considered to be the sum of activity times along the critical path, and those activity times are assumed to be independent. Thus project duration is approximately normal when many activities fall on the critical path. In practice we simply assume normality of $T$ anyway, even if the critical path involves only a few activities. This assumption has proved its worth after years of application in PERT analyses.

**Example 14.8**
**A Probability for Project Duration**

Suppose that completion of the project of Example 14.7 (Figure 14.14) within 22 weeks is extremely important. We may compute an associated probability using the usual operation of standardizing a normal variable. Here $\mu = E(T) = 20$ and $\sigma = \sqrt{V(T)} = \sqrt{4.1111} \simeq 2.03$. Thus

$$P(T \leq 22) = P\left(\frac{T - 20}{2.03} \leq \frac{22 - 20}{2.03}\right)$$

$$= P(Z \leq 0.98) = 0.83646 \qquad \text{Table A.2}$$

Then we can say there is about an 84 percent chance of completing the project within 22 weeks. Of course, the actual meaning of that probability statement is that if many, many identical projects were to be undertaken, about 84 percent of them would be completed within 22 weeks.

Suppose that management is not satisfied with an 84 percent chance. It wants a higher probability of completing the project within 22 weeks. If that probability is to be increased, then *additional resources* will have to be allocated to *critical* activities. This is called "crashing" the project.

### Example 14.9
### Expected Duration Required for a Probability of 0.95

Suppose management wants a 95 percent chance of completing the project within 22 weeks. Then we require $P(T \leq 22) = 0.95$. The standardized value of 22 would then have to become 1.64, since, from Table A.2, $P(Z \leq 1.64) = 0.95$. This just suggests the equation

$$\frac{22 - E(T)}{2.03} = 1.64 \qquad \text{or} \qquad E(T) = 18.67$$

Thus *expected* project duration would have to be reduced from 20 weeks to 18.67 weeks in order to have a probability of 0.95 for project completion within 22 weeks. This assumes, however, that (1) the new critical path will be the same as before [before "crashing" to reduce $E(T)$ to 18.67] and (2) the variances of activity times along the critical path, or at least their sum, will remain the same. Unfortunately, the crashing effort will change $a$, $m$, and $b$ for some of the activities; it is doubtful that the variances would remain the same as they were before. Nevertheless, 18.67 weeks could be taken as an approximate target for the crashing operation. Adjustments due to changes in the PERT network could be made later on in the analysis.

### Example 14.10
### Probability of Positive Slack

Another important probabilistic consideration is that of approximating the probability of positive slack for an activity. Remember, an activity with positive (not zero) slack is not a critical activity. So the probability of positive slack is equivalent to the probability that the activity will *not* become a *critical* activity during the project.

Consider activity 2-4 in the network of Figure 14.14. It is not on the critical path. What is the probability that it will not *become* critical?

Here we must consider *slack* for activity 2-4, say *S*, as the random variable of interest. We want $P(S > 0)$. To obtain it, we need $E(S)$ and $V(S)$, and will again assume normality.

Since slack (in this case, *expected* slack) may be computed by subtracting earliest starting time from latest starting time, we have

$$E(S) = LS - ES$$

To compute LS we have to make a backward pass through the network to node 2. Involved in that calculation are activities 6-7, 4-6, 4-7, and 2-4, yielding LS = 7. To compute ES a forward pass, involving only activity 1-2, gives ES = 5. Thus

$$E(S) = 7 - 5 = 2$$

To obtain $V(S)$, we remember that *five* activities—1-2, 2-4, 4-6, 4-7, and 6-7—had to be considered. However, it is unlikely that activity 4-7 would contribute to variability of slack, since the path from node 4 to node 7 by way of activities 4-6 and 6-7 is part of the critical path. Thus we would obtain $V(S)$ by summing the variances of activities 1-2, 2-4, 4-6, and 4-7. We obtain those variances from Table 14.6, which yields

$$V(S) = 0.4444 + 0.1111 + 0.4444 + 1.7778$$

$$= 2.7777$$

Finally, the appropriate standard deviation is $\sqrt{V(S)} = \sqrt{2.7777} = 1.67$. Therefore,

$$P(S > 0) = P\left(\frac{S - 2}{1.67} > \frac{0 - 2}{1.67}\right)$$

$$= P(Z > -1.20)$$

$$= P(Z < 1.20) \qquad \text{symmetry}$$

$$= 0.88493 \qquad \text{Table A.2}$$

This fairly high probability means that it is unlikely that activity 2-4 will become a critical activity during the course of the project. The manager would know that the progress of activity 2-4 would not need to be monitored with quite the same care as that which would apply to some other activity with a lower probability of positive slack, that is, with a greater chance of becoming critical.

As you finish your consideration of this probabilistic material, remember that a number of *assumptions* have been made in obtaining our probabilities. For that reason they should only be regarded as *approximations* of the true probabilities of interest.

## 14.7  COST IN PERT

In this section we consider the cost of crashing activities so a project might be completed at its earliest possible date. By "crashing" we mean the allocation of more resources to an activity. These additional resources involve some additional cost, so it is no longer possible just to deal with the time variable; time-cost tradeoffs are now involved.

Direct costs are the only type of costs to be considered here. These are costs attributable to the actual conducting of the activities and not those indirect costs coming from supervision or coordination within the project. Indirect costs are not unimportant, and in fact most real PERT analyses make provision for indirect costs. Often such indirect costs are functions of time, so as project time is reduced, so are indirect costs. However, to keep the analyses simple we choose here to consider only direct costs.

Two kinds of times will be involved, along with their associated costs. One is the *normal* time for completing an activity and its associated normal cost. The other is the *crash* time and the attendant crash cost. For instance, suppose that the normal time for activity 1-3 is eight weeks, and the cost of completing that activity in eight weeks is $20,000. Management judges that the infusion of another $10,000 in resources will permit activity 1-3 to be completed in only six weeks. Further, the activity is such that regardless of the additional resources channeled to it, the completion time cannot be reduced to less than six weeks. This is the meaning of "crash time" for an activity. Crash time for activity 1-3 is six weeks and its crash cost is $30,000, the $20,000 normal cost plus $10,000 for crashing the activity by two weeks.

The concept of *incremental cost* is fundamental to the PERT cost analysis. Incremental cost is simply the increase in cost *per unit* of time saved by crashing. Another term for this is *marginal cost*. It may be possible for those responsible for the project to determine actual cost curves for each activity, from which incremental cost at any point in time may be determined. However, it has been discovered in practice that the effort required to determine those cost curves is rarely worthwhile. The simple assumption that the curve is *linear* for each activity has usually worked quite well.

With a linear cost assumption, incremental cost is the same regardless of the point in time from which the activity is viewed. Figure 14.15 suggests the situation. Here NT is normal time, NC is normal cost, CT is crash time, and CC is crash cost.

The incremental cost of a saving of one time unit is just the negative of the slope of the line segment connecting crash cost with normal cost. More simply,

$$\text{Incremental cost} = \frac{\text{CC} - \text{NC}}{\text{NT} - \text{CT}}$$

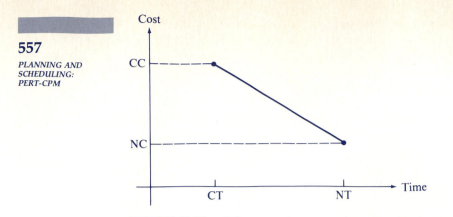

**FIGURE 14.15** A linear cost curve

For example,

$$\text{Incremental cost for activity 1-3} = \frac{30,000 - 20,000}{8 - 6}$$

$$= \frac{10,000}{2} = \$5,000 \text{ per week}$$

Thus to shorten activity 1-3 by one week we must pay an additional cost of \$5,000. This is the incremental cost for the activity.

Table 14.8 gives normal and crash times (weeks) and the associated costs (thousands of dollars) for a project. Although the network for this project looks like the network we used in Example 14.3, this is actually a different project. Incremental costs are also included in Table 14.8, but no probabilistic considerations will be involved in this problem.

**TABLE 14.8** *TIMES, COSTS, AND INCREMENTAL COSTS*

| Activity | Normal | | Crash | | Incremental cost |
|:---:|:---:|:---:|:---:|:---:|:---:|
| | Time | Cost | Time | Cost | |
| 1-2 | 2 | 2 | 1 | 5 | 3 |
| 1-3 | 8 | 20 | 6 | 30 | 5 |
| 2-3 | 5 | 10 | 4 | 12 | 2 |
| 2-4 | 6 | 8 | 4 | 12 | 2 |
| 3-4 | 4 | 6 | 3 | 10 | 4 |
| 3-5 | 8 | 12 | 5 | 21 | 3 |
| 4-5 | 2 | 5 | 1 | 10 | 5 |

Now consider the PERT networks of Figures 14.16 and 14.17. Figure 14.16 is simply the network wherein each activity takes its normal time. The network in Figure 14.17 reflects *every* activity having been crashed. Indicated costs are just the sums of costs in the corresponding columns of Table 14.8.

The 16-week network (duration along critical path) of Figure 14.16 shows the project as it would look if all activities were to be completed in their normal times, with an associated cost of $63,000. The 11-week network of Figure 14.17 is the one that would result if all activities were to be crashed. Notice that it has the same critical path as the normal network, but that its associated cost would be $100,000. Obviously the minimum possible time for completing the project is 11 weeks. Every activity in Figure 14.17 was quoted at its crash time; no further time improvement would be possible.

The cost of the totally crashed project is $100,000. No shorter time may be achieved, but could we design the project network so the overall duration is 11 weeks while the total cost is less than $100,000? We can.

Consider activity 2-4. Suppose it had not been crashed. Then its duration would have been six weeks instead of four (Figure 14.16), but the critical path in Figure 14.17 would not have been affected. The incremental cost for activity 2-4 is $2,000, so $4,000 has been needlessly expended by crashing that activity. Clearly we can achieve an 11-week (minimum-time) network at a cost of only $96,000.

Since we have found a minimum-time network at lower cost, can we find a minimum-time network with the *minimum* cost? Again the answer is yes. The analysis in Example 14.11 shows how this is usually done in PERT. Here the concept of incremental cost plays an important role, that of assuring optimality.

### Example 14.11
### Finding the Minimum-Cost, Minimum-Time Network

We begin by looking at the original 16-week network, Figure 14.16. If its duration is to be shortened, then certainly one of the *critical* activities must be completed in less time than normal. In this case either activity 1-3 or

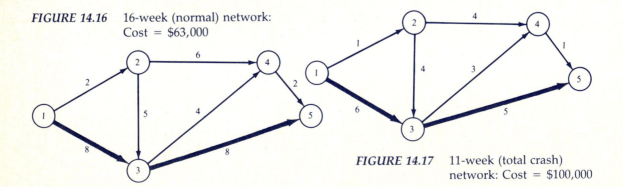

FIGURE 14.16    16-week (normal) network:
Cost = $63,000

FIGURE 14.17    11-week (total crash)
network: Cost = $100,000

activity 3-5 could be shortened by one week to begin the analysis. But if a week is to be saved, it might as well be saved as cheaply as possible. Consider the incremental costs in Table 14.9.

The decision is clear; shortening activity 3-5 is $2,000 per week less costly than shortening activity 1-3. This approach to decreasing project duration is obviously the best (optimal) approach to use at this stage of the analysis. To save a week by a more expensive method would be ridiculous.

Close observation of the part of the network involving events 3, 4, and 5 reveals that activity 3-5 can be shortened by *two* weeks without overrunning the slack in the other activities of that subnetwork. Also note that the crash time for activity 3-5 is five weeks, so what is proposed is feasible. Finally, observe that at this stage we should not try to achieve that crash time, since then activity 3-5 would no longer be critical.

This line of reasoning leads to the 14-week network of Figure 14.18, involving an additional cost of $6,000: 2 weeks times the incremental cost of $3,000 per week. Since the critical activity with the lowest incremental cost was used to achieve it, this is a *minimum-cost* 14-week network.

Because of using up the slack in activities 3-4 and 4-5, the 14-week network has *two* critical paths. We would like to decrease the duration further, again using critical activities with minimum incremental cost. But more care needs to be taken here because of the two critical paths. Activity 3-5 cannot be shortened further, for example, without also shortening either 3-4 or 4-5. That is, some critical activities can only be shortened in combination with others. When that happens their incremental costs should be *added* to reflect that combination. Table 14.10 shows all feasible

**FIGURE 14.18**    14-week network: Cost = $63,000 + $6,000 = $69,000

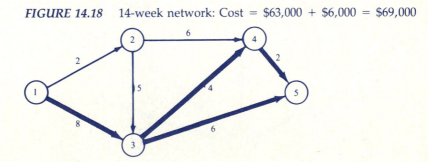

| TABLE 14.10 | INCREMENTAL COSTS FOR CRITICAL ACTIVITIES | |
| --- | --- | --- |
| | **Combination of critical activities** | **Combined incremental cost** |
| | 1-3 | $5,000 ← min |
| | 3-4, 3-5 | $7,000 |
| | 3-5, 4-5 | $8,000 |

sets of critical activities that can be considered for shortening at this stage, as well as combined incremental costs.

Here the decision is to shorten activity 1-3 rather than one of the combined sets. It can be shortened by only one week without losing its status as a critical activity. The result is the minimum-cost 13-week network of Figure 14.19.

Next, to gain another week, the combinations and associated incremental costs shown in Table 14.11 are involved. The decision here is to use *two* combinations. Shorten activities 1-3 and 2-3 by one week each *and* activities 3-4 and 3-5 by one week each. (This achieves the limiting crash time for all four activities.) The increase in cost for the overall two-week saving is $14,000, but the optimal network, minimum cost for minimum time, has now been reached. It is shown in Figure 14.20.

The final cost figure, $88,000, can be verified by consideration of Table 14.12. It lists all of the activities that have been crashed, the time in weeks by which each normal activity time has been reduced, the incremental costs, total cost per crashed activity, and overall crash cost. Since the cost of the project if all activities are completed in normal time is $63,000, and the overall crash cost is $25,000, the cost of the crashed project network of Figure 14.20 is $63,000 + $25,000 = $88,000. This is $12,000 under the cost of the project if *every* activity is crashed (Figure 14.17).

Certainly the saving of $12,000 justifies the effort that went into this analysis. But clearly the PERT cost analysis has other advantages. For instance, if you want the project to be completed in 14 weeks (minimum time is not the objective), you would know that it could be done at a cost

*FIGURE 14.19*    13-week network: Cost = $69,000 + $5,000 = $74,000

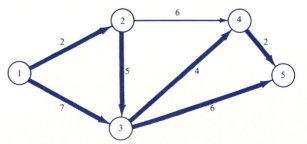

560

| TABLE 14.11 | INCREMENTAL COSTS FOR CRITICAL ACTIVITIES | |

| Combination of critical activities | Combined incremental cost |
|---|---|
| 1-2, 1-3 | $8,000 |
| 1-3, 2-3 | $7,000 ← min |
| 3-4, 3-5 | $7,000 ← min |
| 3-5, 4-5 | $8,000 |

of $69,000. Or, if no more than $75,000 is allocated to the project, you would know that the fastest it could be completed would be 13 weeks (costing only $74,000). Further, the manager who has worked through the analysis of Example 14.11 would certainly be more aware of potential time-cost tradeoffs that may be possible during the course of the project.

## 14.8 SUMMARY AND CONCLUSIONS

PERT-CPM is a network technique that is very useful to a project manager throughout all phases of a project. An understanding of events and activities and an appreciation of the interrelationships between them are necessary before a network for the project can be constructed, so even in the project's planning stage the PERT concept is particularly helpful. Scheduling and controlling activities that take place during the project are also made easier by analyses based on the PERT network.

The basis for all of the PERT analyses you saw in this chapter is the critical path through the project network. The length of the critical path, the longest path through the network, is the shortest time allowable for project completion. Activities along the critical path are termed critical activities and must be begun and completed on schedule if the project is to be finished in that shortest allowable time. A critical path may be determined simply on the basis of estimated activity times, or the normal times you saw in the PERT cost analysis, or it may come from expected

**FIGURE 14.20**   Optimal 11-week network: Cost = $74,000 + $14,000 = $88,000

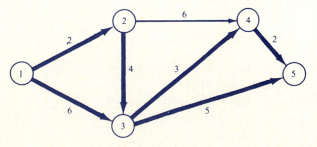

TABLE 14.12   SUMMARY OF CRASHED ACTIVITIES

| Activity | Time reduction | Incremental cost | Total cost |
|----------|----------------|------------------|------------|
| 1-3 | 2 | $5,000 | $10,000 |
| 2-3 | 1 | $2,000 | $ 2,000 |
| 3-4 | 1 | $4,000 | $ 4,000 |
| 3-5 | 3 | $3,000 | $ 9,000 |
|     |   |     Crash cost: | $25,000 |

times that have been computed from three time estimates: the most optimistic time, the most likely time, and the most pessimistic time. The random characteristic of activity times is handled in PERT using the beta distribution, with variances of sums of independent activity times being a central computation for probabilistic considerations.

The use of probability in PERT analyses enables the manager to obtain approximate probabilities to assist decisions about project scheduling and control. Two specific probabilities of particular interest are the probability that project duration will not exceed a specified time and the probability that a particular noncritical activity will not become critical during the course of the project.

Normal times and crash times for completing activities, and their associated normal and crash costs, can be used to solve the optimization problem of completing a project in minimum time at minimum cost. Central to that optimization problem is the notion of incremental cost, the per-unit-time cost of completing an activity in less than normal time.

It should be noted that an important managerial task, project control during the time the activities are being executed, has not been addressed during our discussions of ordinary PERT analyses. Some unforeseen circumstance may cause an activity to be delayed to the point that a new network, and a new PERT analysis, might be required. When that happens, one merely assigns zero time to those activities that have been completed, allocates a proportionate amount of time to those activities that are already under way, and redesigns the PERT network and the corresponding project schedule. Usually these revisions occur early in the execution phase of the project, when new experience with unfamiliar activities is being acquired.

## KEY WORDS AND PHRASES

**PERT**   Project evaluation and review technique.
**CPM**   Critical path method.
**Activity**   A clearly definable portion of a project that requires for its completion the consumption of resources, time in particular.

**Event**   A point in time during a project, occurring at the initiation or completion of an activity.   An event consumes no resources.

**Critical path**   The longest path through the network, consisting of activities with zero slack.   The length of the critical path is the shortest time allowable for project completion.

**Critical activity**   An activity with zero slack; one of the activities along the critical path.

**Slack**   The amount of time by which the start of an activity may be delayed without affecting the overall duration of the project.   It may be computed either by subtracting earliest starting time from latest starting time, or subtracting earliest finishing time from latest finishing time.

**Earliest starting time**   The earliest time at which work on an activity may begin.   Denoted by ES.

**Earliest finishing time**   The earliest possible time for completion of an activity.   Denoted by EF.

**Latest starting time**   The latest time at which an activity may begin without affecting overall project duration.   Denoted by LS.

**Latest finishing time**   The latest time at which an activity may be completed without affecting overall project duration.   Denoted by LF.

**Three-time estimate**   Three estimates of completion time for an activity: most optimistic, most likely, and most pessimistic.

**Expected activity time**   An estimate of the average completion time for an activity, based on the formula $t_e = (a + 4m + b)/6$.

**Beta distribution**   A probability density for a continuous random variable with a finite range.   Its ability to allow for skewness makes the beta distribution particularly useful as an approximate distribution for activity times.

**Resource leveling**   Keeping the amount of resources in use during the project as nearly constant as possible throughout the duration of the project.   An important example is personnel.

**Expected project duration**   The sum of the expected activity times for all activities on the critical path.

**Crashing**   The allocation of extra resources to an activity or to the project in order to reduce overall completion time.

**Crash time**   The minimum completion time that may be achieved for an activity (or the project) by the allocation of additional resources.

**Crash cost**   The total cost of completing an activity in its crash time.

**Incremental cost**   The increase in cost per unit of time saved by crashing an activity.


## EXERCISES

◆ **14.1** Assuming that the numbers on the arrows are expected times for activities, find the critical path in the following network.

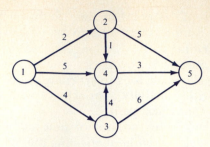

**14.2** Assuming that the numbers on the arrows are expected times for activities, find the critical paths in the network.

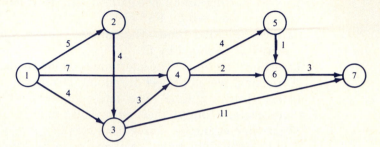

◆ **14.3** Following is a list of project activities and their expected times in weeks:

| Activity | $t_e$ | Activity | $t_e$ |
|----------|-------|----------|-------|
| 1-2 | 4 | 3-6 | 7 |
| 1-3 | 6 | 4-6 | 4 |
| 2-3 | 3 | 5-6 | 6 |
| 2-4 | 6 | 5-7 | 6 |
| 2-5 | 5 | 6-7 | 1 |
| 3-5 | 2 | | |

**a** Draw a PERT network for this project.
**b** Find the slack for each activity in the project.
**c** Find the critical path(s).

**14.4** Following is a list of project activities and their expected times in weeks:

| Activity | $t_e$ | Activity | $t_e$ |
|----------|-------|----------|-------|
| 1-2 | 2 | 4-7 | 4 |
| 1-4 | 2 | 5-6 | 4 |
| 2-3 | 7 | 5-7 | 3 |
| 2-5 | 5 | 6-7 | 2 |
| 3-4 | 4 | 6-8 | 3 |
| 3-5 | 6 | 7-8 | 3 |
| 4-5 | 3 | | |

**a** Draw a PERT network for the project.
**b** Find the slack for each activity in the project.
**c** If every event in a PERT network is on the critical path, does that mean that every activity is a critical activity?  Support your answer by citing an example from this project.

◆ **14.5** Assuming that the numbers on the arrows are expected times for activities, find the slack for each activity in the network and find the critical path(s).

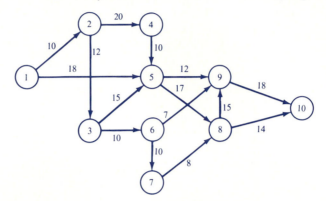

◆ **14.6** Refer to Chapter 12, Exercise 12.6a.  For that PERT network, find the slack for each activity and find the critical path(s).  (Treat the numbers on the arrows as expected activity times.)

**14.7** Natasha Samovara is a student at Moscow University, working toward the diploma in International Terrorism with a minor in Burglary.  Her senior term project is to blow up the United Nations Building in order to demonstrate the earnest desire of all peoples of the world for peace.

Natasha has decided that a PERT analysis of the project will be useful. Accordingly, she has prepared the following list of activities:

| Activity | Description of activity |
| --- | --- |
| 1-2 | Burgle Romanov crown jewels from Workers' Museum (includes planning). |
| 1-3 | Locate a fence for the jewels. |
| 1-5 | Hang around East European pipeline project until storage location for dynamite is discovered. |
| 2-3 | (Jewels must be available before they can be fenced.)  (Dummy activity) |
| 3-4 | Fence jewels. |
| 4-5 | Rent a U-Haul truck. |
| 4-6 | Locate suitable freighter in Murmansk and bribe captain. |
| 4-7 | Arrange forgery of Uruguayan passport. |
| 4-8 | Hire New York confederate. |
| 5-6 | Steal four tons of dynamite and drive to docks in Murmansk. |
| 6-7 | Load dynamite onto freighter. |
| 7-9 | Stow away on freighter. |

| Activity | Description of activity |
|---|---|
| 8-7 | (Confederate must be hired before stowing away.) (Dummy activity) |
| 8-11 | Confederate attempts to find five Communist stevedores to offload dynamite in New York. |
| 9-10 | Freighter travels to New York. |
| 10-11 | Steal a truck. |
| 10-12 | Rent a warehouse. |
| 10-13 | Marry a UN security guard; nag him into allowing you to park truck in basement of UN building. |
| 11-12 | Offload dynamite from freighter to truck. |
| 12-13 | Hide truck in warehouse and assemble bomb. |
| 13-14 | Drive truck to UN, park in basement, and light fuse. |
| 14-15 | Call a taxi and join a tour of UN building while awaiting taxi. |
| 14-16 | Fuse burns down. |
| 15-16 | Take taxi to airport; fly to Moscow. |

**a** Draw a PERT network for Ms. Samovara's term project.
**b** Identify verbally each event in the project.

**14.8** The administrative secretary in the statistics department has been given the project of getting out a brochure describing three short summer courses on applications of statistics in industry, to be taught by three different professors. A PERT network for the project as visualized by the secretary appears below. Dashed arrows indicate dummy activities (in this project dummy activities require either no time or else times that are insignificant relative to times required by the solid-line activities). Descriptions of the activities follow.

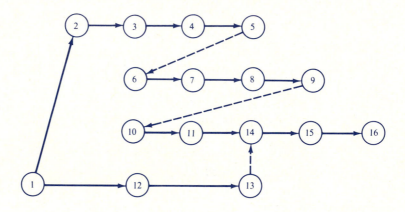

| Activity | Description |
|---|---|
| 1-2 | Decide upon the basic layout of the brochure. |
| 1-12 | Work up the mailing list. |
| 2-3 | Determine space restrictions for each section of brochure. |
| 3-4 | Discuss restrictions with each professor. |
| 4-5 | Professors write appropriate sections for brochure. |
| 5-6 | Professors return sections to secretary. |

| Activity | Description |
|----------|-------------|
| 6-7 | Rough out brochure in four copies. |
| 7-8 | Obtain final opinions from professors. |
| 8-9 | Incorporate final revisions and type brochure. |
| 9-10 | Deliver to printing and duplicating service. |
| 10-11 | Brochures are printed and duplicated. |
| 11-14 | Brochures delivered to secretary by printing and duplicating. |
| 12-13 | Address envelopes. |
| 14-15 | Stuff and seal envelopes. |
| 15-16 | Prepare bulk mailing and deliver to mail service. |

*Note:* Activity 13-14 in the figure is a true dummy activity requiring no time, but merely indicating logical precedence of events.

The following table gives three time estimates for each activity (in days). These are, from the secretary's viewpoint, activity times including the time she thinks will be wasted before the professors or the duplicating service get around to the tasks assigned to them. Dummy activities are not included since for them all time estimates are zero. It is assumed that the secretary will have available assistance from work-study students to conduct parallel activities.

| Activity | a | m | b |
|----------|-----|------|------|
| 1-2 | 0.2 | 0.5 | 1.0 |
| 1-12 | 5.0 | 10.0 | 15.0 |
| 2-3 | 0.1 | 0.2 | 0.5 |
| 3-4 | 0.3 | 0.5 | 1.0 |
| 4-5 | 2.0 | 3.0 | 5.0 |
| 6-7 | 0.4 | 0.5 | 1.0 |
| 7-8 | 0.2 | 0.3 | 0.5 |
| 8-9 | 0.5 | 0.7 | 1.0 |
| 10-11 | 4.0 | 8.0 | 14.0 |
| 12-13 | 2.0 | 4.0 | 7.0 |
| 14-15 | 0.8 | 1.5 | 2.0 |
| 15-16 | 0.1 | 0.2 | 0.4 |

**a** Find the critical path and the expected project duration. (Use two-decimal accuracy for all $t_e$'s.)

**b** Discuss which activities are "crucial" (not necessarily critical) in the sense that if project duration is to be decreased substantially, the time for conducting those activities would have to be shortened. (These are activities that should be watched in case they become critical; in fact, one might wish to see them shortened because it is easy for them to become critical.) How might the secretary be able to influence the duration of those crucial activities? When would a crucial activity become a critical activity?

♦ **14.9** Consider a project composed of the activities listed below. For each activity an optimistic, anticipated, and pessimistic time estimate is supplied. Perform the necessary PERT analysis to determine slack for all activities. All time estimates are in weeks.

| Activity | a | m | b | Activity | a | m | b |
|----------|---|---|---|----------|---|---|---|
| 1-2 | 1 | 2 | 5 | 4-6 | 4 | 6 | 10 |
| 1-3 | 1 | 3 | 4 | 5-6 | 3 | 4 | 9 |
| 2-3 | 1 | 2 | 3 | 5-7 | 1 | 3 | 4 |
| 2-5 | 2 | 4 | 8 | 6-7 | 2 | 3 | 5 |
| 3-4 | 2 | 3 | 5 | 6-8 | 4 | 8 | 10 |
| 4-5 | 2 | 4 | 5 | 7-8 | 1 | 4 | 6 |

**14.10** Consider the project suggested by Exercise 14.1. Assume that the times on the arrows are expected times in weeks for the activities. Suppose the following numbers of people must be assigned to the activities:

| Activity | Personnel | Activity | Personnel |
|----------|-----------|----------|-----------|
| 1-2 | 4 | 2-5 | 2 |
| 1-3 | 6 | 3-4 | 8 |
| 1-4 | 2 | 3-5 | 4 |
| 2-4 | 4 | 4-5 | 6 |

**a** Indicate graphically the number of people working on the project at any point in time if every activity is scheduled at its earliest starting time. Do the same thing if every activity is scheduled at its latest starting time.
**b** Design a leveled schedule for which the number of people working on the project at any time appears to be as constant as possible. Draw the appropriate graph.

**14.11** Answer questions *a* and *b* from Exercise 14.10 for the project described in Exercise 14.9, except use *m* in place of $t_e$ (this keeps the numbers simple). Personnel asignments follow:

| Activity | Personnel | Activity | Personnel |
|----------|-----------|----------|-----------|
| 1-2 | 2 | 4-6 | 3 |
| 1-3 | 5 | 5-6 | 5 |
| 2-3 | 1 | 5-7 | 4 |
| 2-5 | 3 | 6-7 | 2 |
| 3-4 | 6 | 6-8 | 6 |
| 4-5 | 5 | 7-8 | 1 |

✦ **14.12** Consider a project for which the following activities, time estimates, and personnel assignments apply (times are in weeks):

| Activity | a | m | b | Personnel |
|----------|---|---|---|-----------|
| 1-2 | 3 | 5 | 8 | 3 |
| 1-3 | 2 | 3 | 5 | 5 |
| 1-5 | 2 | 3 | 4 | 4 |
| 2-3 | 1 | 2 | 5 | 2 |
| 2-6 | 7 | 9 | 18 | 4 |
| 3-4 | 1 | 3 | 6 | 1 |

| Activity | $a$ | $m$ | $b$ | Personnel |
|----------|-----|-----|-----|-----------|
| 3-5 | 2 | 4 | 6 | 2 |
| 4-5 | 1 | 2 | 4 | 1 |
| 5-6 | 1 | 2 | 3 | 1 |

**a** Compute $t_e$ for each activity.

**b** Compute slack for each activity.

**c** Design as level a personnel schedule as you can, and indicate graphically the number of personnel assigned to the project at any point in time. (For realism, this time use $t_e$'s, not $m$'s.)

◆ **14.13** Each part of this exercise refers to the project in Exercise 14.12.

**a** Compute the variance of activity time for each activity.

**b** Approximate the probability that project duration will not exceed 18 weeks. Interpret that probability.

**c** Approximate the probability that activity 3-4 will have positive slack. What is the managerial implication of that probability?

**d** Approximate the probability that the sum of activity times along the path 1-2-3-4-5-6 will exceed the expected project duration.

**14.14** Refer to the secretary's problem in Exercise 14.8.

**a** Approximate the probability that the brochures will arrive at the mail service within 18 days.

**b** Approximate the probability that the brochures will arrive at the mail service within 15 days.

**c** What is the approximate probability that the combined times for activities 1-12 and 12-13 will exceed ES for activity 14-15? What is the implication of that probability?

◆ **14.15** Assume a project having two completely distinct critical paths (none of the activities on one path are on the other). What is the probability that the duration of the activities along at least one of those paths does not exceed the expected project duration? Is this the same thing as the probability that project duration will not exceed its expected value?

◆ **14.16** The following time-cost table (time in weeks, cost in thousands of dollars) applies to the project suggested by Exercise 14.1. Use it to arrive at the network associated with completing the project in minimum time at minimum cost.

| Activity | Normal | | Crash | |
|----------|--------|--------|--------|--------|
|  | Time | Cost | Time | Cost |
| 1-2 | 2 | 8 | 1 | 14 |
| 1-3 | 4 | 10 | 2 | 20 |
| 1-4 | 5 | 10 | 3 | 18 |
| 2-4 | 1 | 5 | 1 | 5 |
| 2-5 | 5 | 15 | 3 | 21 |
| 3-4 | 4 | 20 | 3 | 30 |
| 3-5 | 6 | 12 | 4 | 16 |
| 4-5 | 3 | 9 | 2 | 16 |

**14.17** The following time-cost table (time in weeks, cost in thousands of dollars) applies to the project suggested by Exercise 14.2:

| Activity | Normal | | Crash | |
|---|---|---|---|---|
| | Time | Cost | Time | Cost |
| 1-2 | 5 | 4 | 3 | 12 |
| 1-3 | 4 | 8 | 2 | 24 |
| 1-4 | 7 | 10 | 5 | 30 |
| 2-3 | 4 | 5 | 3 | 10 |
| 3-4 | 3 | 10 | 2 | 17 |
| 3-7 | 11 | 30 | 9 | 36 |
| 4-5 | 4 | 6 | 3 | 8 |
| 4-6 | 2 | 5 | 1 | 14 |
| 5-6 | 1 | 5 | 1 | 5 |
| 6-7 | 3 | 12 | 1 | 24 |

**a** What is the minimum time in which the project can be completed?
**b** What is the smallest cost for which the project can be completed in 16 weeks?
**c** What is the network associated with completing the project in minimum time at minimum cost?

## SELECTED REFERENCES

Giffin, W. C.: *Introduction to Operations Engineering*, Richard D. Irwin, Inc., Homewood, Ill., 1971.

Kelley, J. M., and M. R. Walker: "Critical Path Planning and Scheduling," Proceedings of the Eastern Joint Computer Conference, 1959.

Kerzner, H.: *Project Management*, Van Nostrand Reinhold Co., New York, 1979.

Levin, R. I., C. A. Kirkpatrick, and D. S. Rubin: *Quantitative Approaches to Management*, 5th ed., McGraw-Hill Book Company, New York, 1982.

Malcom, D. G., J. H. Roseboom, C. F. Clark, and W. Fazar: "Applications of a Technique for Research and Development Program Evaluations," *Operations Research*, 7, pp. 646–670, 1959.

Mood, A. M., and F. A. Graybill: *Introduction to the Theory of Statistics*, 2d ed., McGraw-Hill Book Company, New York, 1963.

Riggs, J. L., and M. S. Inoue: *Introduction to Operations Research and Management Science*, McGraw-Hill Book Company, New York, 1975.

Rosenau, M.: *Successful Project Management*, Lifetime Learning, Belmont, Calif., 1981.

Siemans, N., C. H. Marting, and F. Greenwood: *Operations Research*, The Free Press, New York, 1973.

Weist, J., and F. Levy: *A Management Guide to PERT/CPM*, Prentice-Hall, Inc., Englewood Cliffs, N.J., 1977.

# *QUEUEING PROBLEMS*

$W$henever customers arrive at a service facility and some of them must wait before they receive the desired service, a *queue*, or *waiting line*, is formed.  You have been part of a queue many times, and you have occasionally experienced either mental or physical discomfort because of the wait.  Examples are the long lines during university registration, queueing up to buy tickets to a popular movie, waiting for a haircut, and checking out at the supermarket.  Instances of queues occurring in business or industrial settings include letters waiting to be typed by a secretary, malfunctioning machinery awaiting repair, machinists queueing up to check out tools from a tool room in a factory, and manufactured products waiting for the next operation in an assembly line process.

The existence of a queue does not necessarily imply the existence of a problem.  If neither the queue nor the wait for service is inordinately long, then from the customers' viewpoint the service facility is functioning satisfactorily.  The person responsible for providing the service sees no problem if no appreciable costs are incurred because of the queue (for instance, costs due to customer dissatisfaction, production delays, or idle time of service workers). Only if unacceptable cost or unusual congestion arises within the system do we say that a queueing *problem* exists. In this chapter we will look at some examples of queueing problems as well as some of the simpler mathematics of queueing theory that help us to solve those problems.

## 15.1  DESCRIPTION FOR DECISION

Ordinarily the arrival times of customers are random; rarely will regular intervals be involved. The time required for the customer to receive service once the service facility is entered is also usually random. Thus the discipline known as *queueing theory* is a part of probability theory. Using queueing theory we study characteristics of situations in which queues may form. Random variables are involved, and the knowledge of their probability distributions is important if you want to understand the workings of a queueing system.

Queueing theory is description-oriented rather than decision-oriented. Mathematical results provided by the theory help you to describe critical facets of the queueing system. For example, the arrival pattern of customers or the service mechanism of the facility can often be completely described mathematically. But descriptions do not constitute decisions. They only assist you, the decision maker, by allowing you to understand the system better.

Cost, for instance, is often the criterion upon which the decision to modify a queueing system is based. If too many customers are in the queue for long periods of time, some costs due to bad feelings or lost productive time are incurred. You might want to shorten the expected waiting time by introducing more servers, people or machines, into the service facility. This will increase the rate at which customers receive service; it also costs something. If enough servers are supplied so that negligible waiting times are expected, then long periods of inactivity among the servers can ensue.

Queueing theory does not tell us what the best choice is for a number of servers to minimize total cost (cost of customer discontent plus cost of idle facilities). It is not a theory of optimization; it is a theory of description. On the other hand, better decisions can be made if better descriptions are available.

The point has been made that queueing theory does not solve queueing problems; it only helps us to solve them. Following the next section, which discusses characteristics common to all queueing systems, you will see two examples of problem solutions. Then we will look at basic queueing theory. The chapter closes with sections merging theory with observation. By then you should be able to distinguish between the descriptive and the decision-making aspects of a queueing problem.

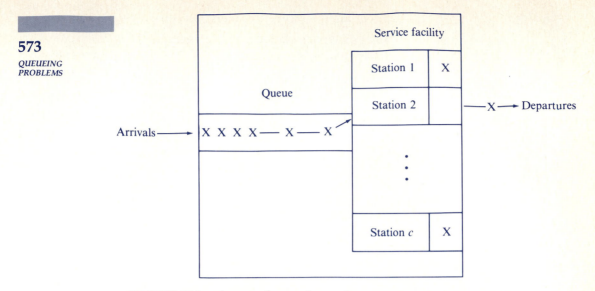

**FIGURE 15.1**   A general queueing system

## 15.2   CHARACTERISTICS OF QUEUEING SYSTEMS

A *queueing system* is comprised of two basic components: the *queue* and the *service facility*.   Within the queue are customers waiting to be served. Within the service facility are customers being served and the individual service stations, or *servers*.   The schematic diagram of Figure 15.1 suggests a general queueing system.

The cost of modifying the system in order to achieve some desirable objective has been mentioned, but other things besides cost can be important.   For example, in the case of aircraft maintenance the objective may be to determine the number of maintenance stations within the service facility to achieve a high probability of keeping enough aircraft operational to meet a published schedule.   The objective in a manufacturing process might be to keep the time between departures as regular as is feasible to avoid congestion or excess idle time in the next phase of the process.

To make good decisions about system modification, you must have good information.   In queueing theory the knowledge of six principal characteristics provides information sufficient to model the system mathematically.   These characteristics are listed below and discussed individually thereafter.

**1** The arrival pattern (arrival distribution)

**2** The service mechanism (departure distribution)

3 The queue discipline (how customers are chosen for service)

4 The number of service stations, or channels

5 The type of calling population (source of arrivals)

6 The number of customers allowed in the system

### The Arrival Pattern

Except in special situations such as articles moving along a conveyor belt in regular spacing, the precise instant that a customer may become a part of the queueing system is unpredictable. The arrival time for any customer and the number of customers arriving in any specified time interval are usually random variables. Often we can determine an average *arrival rate* for customers; usually this is done statistically. The arrival rate is quoted as a number of arrivals per unit time, as when we say: ten machine breakdowns per day, or forty machinists per hour calling at a tool crib.

Basic queueing theory assumes a knowledge of that arrival rate, which plays a paramount role in describing the arrival pattern. But the average arrival rate is only one parameter in the probability distribution of number of arrivals. Certainly the *variability* in that random variable is as important as its average. This variability is what renders it impossible to design a system in which no queue forms. Groups of arrivals, occurring at a rate much higher than the average, tend to cause the formation and building up of queues.

*Completely random* arrivals at a *constant rate* is a common assumption that seems to fit many real queueing systems. As we will demonstrate in Section 15.5, that assumption leads to a *Poisson distribution* of the number of arrivals. The Poisson distribution in turn implies an *exponential distribution* of the time between arrivals. Thus in the case of completely random arrivals the arrival rate specifies the distributions of two critical random variables in the queueing system. This is the reason for the emphasis in the theory on arrival rates.

Other types of arrival patterns are *regular* arrivals (assumed in Section 15.3) and *aggregated* (grouped) arrivals. Sometimes the rate of arrival is different for different times during the operation of the system. The rate can be influenced by such things as the number of customers already in the queue or the number of servers in the service facility. In the latter case we say that arrivals are *correlated* with other characteristics of the system. However, much of basic queueing theory only deals with completely random arrivals and with constant arrival rate.

### The Service Mechanism

The length of time required to serve a particular customer is called the *service time*. The service time is usually a random variable. We may not be able to say just how long it will take to complete the service for a given individual, but observation of the system may tell us an *average* service time. This is called the *service rate*. Each server may have a different service rate, and the whole service facility will have an overall service rate. These rates are stated in the form of a "number of customers served per unit time."

Just as with arrival times, the *distribution* of service times is important. Often we can assume that the time required to complete service for a customer is the same regardless of how long the customer has been in the facility. This unusual-sounding assumption fits quite well in many real queueing situations. It leads to an exponential distribution of service time. In the queueing theory sections to follow, that exponential distribution is assumed for all servers. It will also be assumed that after a server has completed service for one customer, the server will be available to give service to the next customer entering the facility.

### The Queue Discipline

In familiar situations like lining up to buy tickets or waiting for a haircut in a barber shop one assumes a "first-come, first-served" procedure for selecting the next customer to receive service. That assumption is made throughout this chapter.

Other queue disciplines besides first-come, first-served might be used; one such is a system of *priorities*. Here arriving customers are served according to their need for the service or for purposes of controlling the cost of customer waiting time. In extreme cases a server may even interrupt the service of a low-priority customer to attend to one with a higher priority. Other disciplines include "service in random order," where some random procedure is used to choose the next customer to receive service, and "last-come, first-served," such as when unserved products are placed in a container in such a way that the later arrivals are on top and become most readily available for service. General queueing theory incorporates these other types of queue disciplines, but we will not study them here.

### The Number of Service Stations

The greater the number of stations (channels) in the service facility, the greater the overall service rate of the facility. Since the combination of arrival rate and service rate is critical for the determination of operating parameters of the system, the number of parallel channels is very important. In fact, if we are to influence the system by modification, we often focus our attention here. It may be much easier or much less expensive to control waiting time by changing the number of servers than by trying to influence the arrival rate of customers. Mathematical results for both the single-server and multiple-server cases will be included in this chapter.

### The Type of Calling Population

Much of basic queueing theory assumes an infinite *source population*, the population from which arrivals originate. Although there are no truly infinite populations in real queueing situations, the assumption is quite adequate in the case of very large populations. Not only is it a fair approximation of the real situation, but the infinite population assumption serves to simplify the mathematical arguments.

An implication of that assumption is that if the service rate is smaller than the arrival rate, then the queue may be expected to grow (lengthen) indefinitely. In such a case, more than one server becomes an absolute necessity for a reasonably functioning queueing system. For a small, finite population of potential arrivals the situation is very different. If there are $N$ units in the population and one server in the system, then maximum queue length is only $N - 1$. Thus the type of calling population is a critical factor in mathematically determining the main parameters of the system.

### The Number of Customers Allowed in the System

Similar to the type of calling population, restrictions on the number of customers allowed in the system at any one time have a large effect on the description of the system. An internal effect could be to convert an infinite source population to only a finite one, as dictated by the restriction. Such a restriction can come from the size of the room in which the service facility is housed or from an appreciation of the fact that limited facilities imply that customers in the queue might have to be turned away at the close of business hours. These restrictions can be handled mathematically in the theory of queueing systems.

Now we are ready to consider some basic queueing theory. First, however, it is worthwhile to look at two simple queueing problems (Sections 15.3 and 15.4). After seeing those illustrations you can begin to appreciate the kind of information that will be desirable.

### 15.3 UNIFORM ARRIVALS AND SERVICE: AN ILLUSTRATION

Envision a large room in a factory, containing hundreds of identical machines—drill presses, for instance—that regularly require maintenance. Assigned to a group of these machines is an attendant who is responsible for their maintenance.

Assume that the maintenance operation is routine and that the time required for that service is constant for each machine. Specifically, it takes an attendant eight minutes to perform the required maintenance on one machine. This converts to a *uniform service rate* of 7.5 machines per hour. In an eight-hour working day an attendant can service 60 machines, the size of the group for which the attendant is responsible.

Maintenance has been scheduled so that every five minutes another machine is stopped to receive service. The regular five-minute intervals between demands for service by the machines imply a *uniform arrival rate* of 12 machines per hour. Note that since the arrival rate exceeds the service rate, a queue of machines will build up as they are stopped to await service by the attendant.

*Idle time* for a machine is defined as the time the machine spends waiting for maintenance after it has been stopped and before the attendant begins servicing it. Service time is not counted as machine idle time. The cost of machine idle time has been determined to be $10 per hour. Idle time of an attendant is defined as time during which he or she is not busy performing maintenance; it costs $4 per hour.

The supervisor in this section of the factory has observed that too many machines seem to be idle and awaiting service, especially through the middle of the working day. He wants to convince management that at least one more attendant, with the same service rate, should be assigned to those 60 machines. He decides to investigate the total cost of idle time for both machines and attendants, and to use this as a basis for recommending an optimal number of attendants.

In this case, where no randomness at all is involved, his problem is very simple to solve. For example, we know that exactly 480 minutes (8 hours) are required to perform the maintenance on the 60 machines. Thus if two attendants are assigned, total idle time for both together must be 8 hours: 16 hours minus 8 hours in actual maintenance work. An extra 8 hours of attendant idle time is then added with each extra attendant. On the other hand, the more expensive machine idle time is reduced by this assignment of extra attendants.

First we consider the case of only one attendant. In this situation there is no attendant idle time. Exactly 8 hours are required to perform maintenance on the 60 machines. However, there will be quite a lot of machine idle time. To determine it, the diagram of Figure 15.2 is useful.

The horizontal scale in Figure 15.2 is a contracted 480 minutes. The first 25 minutes are considered in detail. Machine 1 "arrives" at time zero, experiences no waiting, and "departs" after 8 minutes. In the meantime, machine 2 has arrived and has waited 3 minutes to receive

**FIGURE 15.2** Arrivals, waiting times, and departures: One attendant

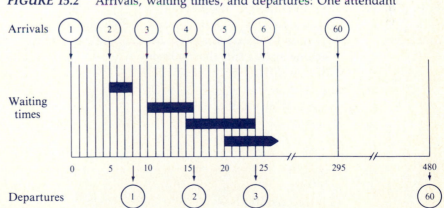

maintenance.  It departs at the sixteenth minute, while machine 3 has arrived at the tenth minute and has been required to wait 6 minutes for service.

At this point a pattern of machine waiting times is becoming evident. Each machine experiences a waiting (idle) time that is 3 minutes longer than that of the machine that arrived ahead of it.  (A first-come, first-served queue discipline is assumed.)  Table 15.1 records those idle times.

From Table 15.1 we see that the waiting time of machine 60 could be observed by continuing the arithmetic progression 0, 3, 6, 9, . . . , through 60 terms.  However, we know that machine 60 will complete service at precisely the 480th minute.  Thus it must enter service at the 472nd minute, and we know that its arrival time was the 295th minute.  Then $472 - 295 = 177$ minutes must be its waiting time.

Total waiting time is simple to compute, given a formula for the sum of the first $n$ positive integers.  That formula is

$$S_n = 1 + 2 + 3 + \cdots + n = \frac{n(n + 1)}{2}$$

Then total waiting time is

$$\text{Total} = 3 + 6 + 9 + 12 + \cdots + 177$$
$$= 3(1 + 2 + 3 + 4 + \cdots + 59)$$
$$= 3S_{59} = \frac{3(59)(60)}{2}$$
$$= 5{,}310 \text{ minutes} = 88.5 \text{ hours}$$

Finally, the cost of 88.5 hours of machine idle time at \$10 per hour is \$885.  There was no attendant idle time, so \$885 is the daily cost of idle time in the one-attendant (single-server) system.

**TABLE 15.1**  *MACHINE IDLE TIME: ONE ATTENDANT*

| Machine | Idle time, minutes |
|---|---|
| 1 | 0 |
| 2 | 3 |
| 3 | 6 |
| 4 | 9 |
| . | . |
| . | . |
| . | . |
| 60 | 177 |

Total: 5,310 minutes = 88.5 hours

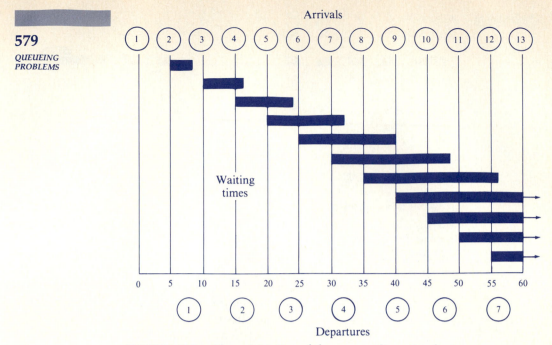

FIGURE 15.3    The origination of the queue: One-attendant case

Before proceeding to the cost of idle time with two attendants, it is of some interest to observe just how the *queue* of machines waiting for service starts to build up in the one-attendant case. Figure 15.3 shows the first 60 minutes of the day.

In Figure 15.3 the horizontal bars indicate the length of the waiting time for each machine, as well as the exact period during the hour when that waiting takes place. The vertical overlap of the bars then shows, at each minute, exactly how many machines are in the queue. The sequence of numbers representing the length of the queue (the number waiting) as the hour progresses is 0, 1, 0, 1, 2, 1, 2, 1, 2, 3, 2, 3, 4, 3, 4, 5, 4. The arrows at the ends of the bars for machines 9 through 12 show that they will wait beyond the sixtieth minute. But machine 13 arrives at that instant, so just beyond that instant five machines are again in queue. Thus, although queue length does not increase with each minute, the *trend* in queue length is an increasing one.

Maximum queue length occurs in the neighborhood of the arrival time of the sixtieth machine, since no more arrivals are allowed during the day. Beyond that point a departure occurs every eight minutes until the queue length becomes zero again at the end of eight hours.

Observe particularly that some kind of *description* of the state of the queueing system over time was required to work the *problem* involved here. That problem was to determine the total cost of idle time, in this case $885 for the day. In the presence of *random* arrivals and service rates,

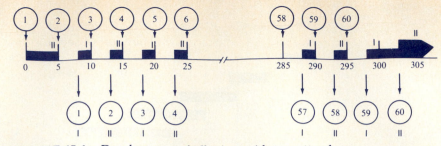

**FIGURE 15.4**    Development of idle time with two attendants

as we will consider in Section 15.4, such a nice, "clean" picture cannot be drawn. In that case the description of the system must be mathematical instead of pictorial.

Now consider the case of *two* attendants. It may be obvious to you that *no* machine idle time is experienced and that exactly 8 hours of attendant idle time are involved. The total cost of idle time here is only 8 hours at $4 per hour: $32. Again it is of value for us to see just how that idle time develops. Figure 15.4 shows the situation with two attendants.

Here the attendants are referred to as attendant I and attendant II. In this case the bars in Figure 15.4 indicate *idle times* for *attendants*. Assuming that attendant I performs the maintenance on machine 1, then attendant II is idle for the first five minutes—until machine 2 arrives. Meanwhile, attendant I completes service on the first machine and is idle for two minutes until machine 3 arrives, and so on.

First of all, observe that attendant I is idle for 2 minutes prior to the arrival of every odd-numbered machine, except machine 1. This accumulates to $(29)(2) = 58$ minutes. Further, attendant I is idle for the rest of the day after the 298th minute. Then $480 - 298 = 182$ minutes is the remaining idle time for attendant I. Therefore attendant I is idle for $58 + 182 = 240$ minutes, or exactly 4 hours. Similarly the idle time for attendant II is $5 + 58 + (480 - 303) = 240$ minutes, or 4 hours. We have thus verified what was obvious earlier: total idle time of attendants is 8 hours, and the cost is $32.

Clearly a dramatic reduction in cost of idle time occurs with the assignment of two attendants to the 60 machines; cost drops from $885 to only $32. Also it would be illogical to consider adding a third attendant, since with two attendants there is no machine idle time. Bringing in one more attendant must increase cost by one day's pay: $32. Thus the optimal modification of the system is to employ two attendants. The queueing problem has been solved.

## 15.4    RANDOM ARRIVALS AND SERVICE: AN ILLUSTRATION

Now consider the same machine-maintenance problem, except that here both arrival time and service time will be random variables. Specifically, assume completely random arrivals with constant arrival rate (Poisson arrivals) and an exponential distribution of service times (constant service rate). Be reminded that "constant" here is not the same as "uniform" in Section 15.3. The *rate* of arrival does not change, but the time intervals between arrivals vary randomly. The theoretical results needed here will not be developed until Section 15.8, but we will use them anyway, understanding that the purpose is to illustrate their application, not their derivation.

Assume Poisson arrivals at the average arrival rate of 12 machines per hour and exponential service at the average service rate of 7.5 machines per hour. Thus the *expected* time required to perform the maintenance on 60 machines is still eight hours. Because of the random nature of service time, however, on some days one attendant could complete all maintenance on 60 machines in less than eight hours, while on other days the maintenance would require more than eight hours. But the average, over many days, is assumed to be eight hours. Similarly, machines do not arrive in a regular pattern now. *On the average*, one machine arrives every five minutes.

These observations promote the minimization of *expected* total cost of idle time as the decision criterion. Now we cannot say what the exact cost of idle time will be for a given day. So when we compare with the answer obtained in Section 15.3, we have to remember that exact costs were involved there. In this section the expected costs are interpreted as averages over many eight-hour days.

The queueing formulas that we will use were developed for infinite calling populations with no limitation on the number of customers allowed in the queue. Then the average cost of idle time must be interpreted as the expected cost attributable only to the first 60 arrivals of the day. Since a first-come, first-served queue discipline is assumed, that interpretation is not unreasonable. We also assume that the system reaches a *steady state*, where system behavior is independent of the time of day, early in the eight-hour period. Such assumptions are the rule, not the exception, in practical applications of queueing theory. They often serve to simplify the requisite computations while still adequately approximating the true situation.

The first thing to notice as we begin work on the solution of this problem is that large expected costs of idle time should still result with only one attendant. So in this case we ignore the one-attendant queue.

Now concentrate on expected costs with two or more attendants. A relevant admonition is "Caveat lector!" Do not trust your intuition in this case. The fact that two attendants are assigned to the 60 machines *does not* imply no machine idle time. Because arrival times are random, it is perfectly feasible that on many occasions during the day both attendants are busy when yet another machine arrives for service. Thus we know in advance that providing two (or even three or more) attendants will not reduce expected machine idle time to zero.

Expected cost of attendant idle time is the same as it was in the uniform case of Section 15.3. The expected number of hours required to complete service on 60 machines is still eight. The expected cost of an extra attendant's idle time is $32.

To find the expected cost of machine idle time in the presence of more than one attendant we must first compute the expected idle time itself. The approach is to compute that expected idle time for one machine, multiply by 60 (number of machines), and multiply that figure by $10. This is where a *mathematical characterization* (queueing theory) comes in. Formulas may be developed that allow the computation of expected waiting time per customer. Specifically, the formulas required are those for $p_0$, $L_q$, and $W_q$ in Section 15.8. At the moment we only point out that $W_q$ denotes the expected waiting time per customer in the queue. $L_q$ (the expected length of the queue) and $p_0$ (the probability that the queue contains no customers) are required to obtain $W_q$. The value of $W_q$ with two, three, and four attendants is given in Table 15.2. The computations of these $W_q$'s are shown as examples in Section 15.8.

Clearly, from Table 15.2, the optimal number of attendants to recommend is *three*. Thus even though the average arrival rate and average service rate were identical to the uniform rates assumed in Section 15.3, the decision is different. Changes in the *distribution* of arrivals and service were the reasons.

This illustration anticipates the need for mathematical results that can only be supplied by theory—for example, the formula for $W_q$. The next four sections are a very basic introduction to queueing theory.

## 15.5   THE POISSON AND EXPONENTIAL DISTRIBUTIONS

Both the Poisson and the exponential distribution have been mentioned as occupying prominent positions in queueing theory. A general discussion of those probability distributions is included here so you can develop

**TABLE 15.2**   *EXPECTED COST OF IDLE TIME*

|  | Number of attendants | | |
|---|---|---|---|
|  | 2 | 3 | 4 |
| $W_q$ = expected waiting time per machine in hours | 0.237 | 0.026 | 0.005 |
| Total expected waiting time in hours for 60 machines | 14.22 | 1.56 | 0.30 |
| Expected cost of machine idle time | $142.20 | $15.60 | $ 3.00 |
| Expected cost of attendant idle time | $ 32.00 | $64.00 | $96.00 |
| Total expected cost of idle time | $174.20 | $79.60 min | $99.00 |

a better appreciation of the nomenclature *Poisson arrivals, exponential interarrival times,* and *exponential service.*

First we look at a formula that gives values of the Poisson probability function. Consider the problem of determining the probability of $n$ "successes" being observed during a time interval of length $t$, where the following assumptions hold:

1 The probability that a success is observed during a small time interval (say of length $v$) is proportional to the length of the interval. Let the proportionality constant be $\lambda$, so that the probability is $\lambda v$.

2 The probability that more than one success is observed during a very small time interval is negligible relative to the probability of one success. That is, the probability of two or more successes in such a small interval is assumed to be zero.

3 The number of successes in any time interval is independent of the number in any nonoverlapping time interval.

These assumptions have been found to hold fairly well for situations such as the number of particles per unit time recorded by a particle counter, the number of typing errors per page made by a typist, and the number of animals per unit area for certain wildlife populations. They also hold for completely random arrivals (successes) into a queueing system.

The three assumptions listed above, some ingenuity, and the definition of a derivative (a basic notion in the calculus) may be combined to yield what is called a system of difference-differential equations whose solution is the Poisson distribution. Suppose we define a function $p$ as follows:

$p(n, t) =$ the probability that $n$ successes will be observed in a time interval of length $t$

Then our previous assumptions give the formula

$$p(n, t) = \frac{(\lambda t)^n e^{-\lambda t}}{n!} \qquad n = 0, 1, 2, \ldots$$

This is the *Poisson probability distribution* for the discrete random variable $n$, the number of successes, where the length of the time interval of interest, $t$, is assumed to be given.

You may be used to a different expression for the Poisson distribution. Often it is written as follows:

$$P(X = n) = \frac{\alpha^n e^{-\alpha}}{n!} \qquad n = 0, 1, 2, \ldots$$

Here $\alpha$ is the mean of the random variable $X$. We only have to observe that our $p(n, t)$ has the same form, except that $\alpha$ has been replaced by $\lambda t$.

What has all of this to do with queueing problems? Let $\lambda$ be the average arrival rate of customers into a queueing system. This rate is an average number of arrivals per unit time; so if $\lambda$ is multiplied by $t$, the result must be the average number of arrivals in an interval of length $t$. That is, an interpretation of $\lambda t$ as the mean of a Poisson distribution seems reasonable. So if in the list of assumptions you replace the word "success" by the word "arrival," you will have described the situation of completely random arrivals with constant arrival rate. In queueing theory this situation is called the case of *Poisson arrivals*. Since only arrivals, not departures, are considered, it is also called a *pure birth process*.

For our descriptions of queueing systems we will also need to consider the time between successive arrivals. These are called *interarrival times*. In the case where the number of arrivals in a given time interval has the Poisson distribution, interarrival times can be shown to have the *exponential distribution*. If we let $f(t)$ denote the probability density of time between arrivals (we use a density function because time is a continuous random variable), then the value of that density function is

$$f(t) = \lambda e^{-\lambda t} \qquad t > 0$$

Because $\lambda$ is an arrival rate, necessarily $\lambda > 0$. Thus for Poisson arrivals at the constant rate $\lambda$ per unit time, the time between successive arrivals (interarrival time) has the exponential distribution. A graph of this exponential distribution is shown in Figure 15.5. The area to the left of time $t_0$ represents the probability that interarrival time will be less than $t_0$.

The probability that interarrival time is less than time $t_0$, the shaded area in Figure 15.5, is useful to know. Since the exponential distribution is a density function, the total area under its graph is the number one. So if we know $P(T \le t_0)$, where $T$ is the random interarrival time, we also know $P(T > t_0) = 1 - P(T \le t_0)$. A very simple calculus operation (integration) gives us that basic probability, also denoted by $F(t_0)$ since it is a cumulative probability. The formula is

$$F(t_0) = P(T \le t_0) = 1 - e^{-\lambda t_0}$$

**FIGURE 15.5**  The exponential distribution of interarrival time

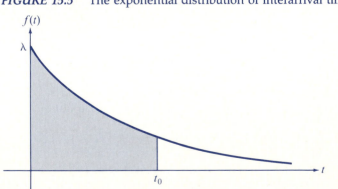

**Example 15.1**
**Probabilities for Number of Arrivals**

Suppose that machines in a factory break down and require service according to a Poisson distribution at the average rate of two per day. What is the probability that exactly three machines break down in two days?

Here one day is the time unit, so $\lambda = 2$, $n = 3$, and $t = 2$. We want $p(n, t) = p(3, 2)$ when $\lambda = 2$. This is

$$p(3, 2) = \frac{(2 \times 2)^3 e^{-2 \times 2}}{3!}$$

$$= \frac{4^3 e^{-4}}{6} = 0.1953668$$

We can also compute this quantity from Table A.3. That table gives cumulative Poisson probabilities for selected values of $\alpha$, where for our problem $\alpha = \lambda t$. Table entries are

$$P(r) = P(X \leq r) = \sum_{n=0}^{r} \frac{\alpha^n e^{-\alpha}}{n!} = \sum_{n=0}^{r} p(n, t)$$

with the understanding that $\alpha = \lambda t$.

We want $P(X = 3)$ when $\alpha = \lambda t = 4$. This is

$$p(3, 2) = P(3) - P(2) = 0.43347 - 0.23810$$

$$= 0.19537$$

This number agrees (to the five-decimal accuracy of Table A.3) with the more precise answer computed previously. Clearly Table A.3 provides a convenient way to compute such a Poisson probability, but on the other hand, given an "$e^x$" key on your pocket calculator, our first mode of computation was even more convenient. Table A.3 holds the edge, however, for computing a cumulative probability.

Suppose we want the probability of three or fewer machines breaking down in two days. This is just

$$P(X \leq 3) = \sum_{n=0}^{3} p(n, 2) \qquad \text{for } \lambda = 2$$

or, from Table A.3 with $r = 3$, $\alpha = 4$, we have

$$P(X \leq 3) = P(3) = 0.43347$$

Computing that cumulative probability with your pocket calculator would require the calculation of four distinct Poisson probabilities, then summing them.

Be reminded that our objective is always to find out useful information, not just to learn how to do computations. By determining probabilities like these, the managerial function of providing for maintenance of the machinery in the factory would be enhanced. That is, these *descriptive* probabilities have made no *decisions* for us, but they would be useful in *helping* us to arrive at good decisions.

**Example 15.2**
**Probability for Interarrival Time**

For the machine-breakdown situation described in Example 15.1, what is the probability that the time between two successive breakdowns exceeds $1\frac{1}{2}$ days?

Here we use the exponential density of interarrival times, and the associated formula for cumulative probability, $F(t_0)$. The time of interest is $t_0 = \frac{3}{2}$ days, and $\lambda = 2$. Thus

$$P(T > \tfrac{3}{2}) = 1 - P(T \le \tfrac{3}{2})$$
$$= 1 - F(\tfrac{3}{2}) = 1 - (1 - e^{-2(3/2)})$$
$$= e^{-3} = 0.04979$$

So we see that if machines break down at an average rate of two per day, it is fairly unlikely that the time between breakdowns would be as much as $1\frac{1}{2}$ days; it is much more likely to be less than that.

The discussions of the Poisson and exponential distributions and the two examples we have just looked at serve to justify the emphasis in queueing problems on the arrival rate. The formula for $p(n, t)$ gives the probability of $n$ arrivals in an interval of length $t$ if $\lambda$ is known. Likewise, the probability that the time between arrivals will be $t_0$ or more may be determined if we know $\lambda$. In Examples 15.1 and 15.2, all we had to know was $\lambda$ and the fact that the number of arrivals followed a Poisson distribution (which in turn is assured if we know that the arrival rate, $\lambda$ again, is constant).

The exponential density also occurs in another context in queueing problems. If customers leave the queueing system at random but at a *constant departure rate* $\mu$, then this situation is referred to as a *Poisson departure* case. Here

$$g(t) = \mu e^{-\mu t} \qquad t > 0$$

is the associated *exponential service time* distribution.

An exponential density has a unique property that is important for consideration of service times. Using conditional probability arguments it can be shown that the probability that service time will exceed time $t_1 + t_2$ *given* that the customer has been in service for time $t_2$ is just the probability that service time will exceed time $t_1$ for any customer. This is known as the "memoryless" property of the exponential density. It simply says that no matter how long a customer has been in service, the probability of completing service in a specified additional time $t_1$ is the same as it would have been if the customer had *just entered* the service facility. Then regardless of when we observe the system, the probability that a customer in service will complete service within a specified time can be obtained from the density $g(t)$.

Since no derivation of the service time distribution was presented, we should at least consider the plausibility of $g(t)$ in this context. The mean of that exponential density, in this case the mean service time, is $1/\mu$. If $\mu$ is a departure rate of the form "number of customers per unit time," then $1/\mu$ has the form "number of units of time per customer." This of course exactly agrees with the notion that $1/\mu$ is an average service time per customer.

## 15.6 BASIC SINGLE-SERVER QUEUEING FORMULAS

Most basic queueing models involve Poisson arrivals and exponential service times. Such models are called *Poisson queues* and are the only types of queues we will consider here. The most elementary Poisson queue assumes one server, a first-come, first-served queue discipline, and no restrictions on the number of customers in the calling source or in the system.

Two characteristics of the queue are of particular interest: the number of customers in the system at any given time, and the waiting time per customer. Recall that in Section 15.4 (Table 15.2) we investigated the cost of idle time using the expected (average) waiting time per machine (or customer, in general). Thus expected waiting time becomes an important consideration in queueing problems; essentially, knowledge of expected waiting time (a mathematical description of a system characteristic) is required if we must make a decision that will improve the operation of the system. Likewise, knowledge of the average number of customers in the system is also very helpful. To obtain such averages (expected values), we need the associated probability distributions.

First we will consider the number of customers in the system. Assume Poisson arrivals at arrival rate $\lambda$ and exponential service with service rate $\mu$. Define $p_n(t)$ as follows:

$p_n(t)$ = the probability that exactly $n$ customers are in the system at time $t$

Notice that $p_n(t)$ is different from $p(n, t)$ used in Section 15.5. There $p(n, t)$ was the probability of $n$ *arrivals* in time $t$. Now, because of the service facility, both arrivals *and* departures must be considered.

Using assumptions very like those underlying the Poisson distribution in Section 15.5, it is possible to develop a formula for $p_n(t)$. That formula is called the *transient* solution for the queueing model, where "transient" means that the system is time-dependent, as implied by the "*t*" in $p_n(t)$. More usually, however, people use what are called *steady-state* probability formulas, where the system has been in operation long enough, and where of course the right assumptions are satisfied, so that the probability of *n* customers in the system no longer depends upon the particular time at which we look at the system. Early in the life of a queueing system, its characteristics are strongly dependent upon the initial conditions, the state of the system near time zero. As time progresses, however, the dependence of $p_n(t)$ upon time diminishes as the effect of the initial conditions becomes less pronounced. Eventually, if it is possible for the system to achieve steady state, the probability of *n* customers in the system is approximately constant regardless of the point in time at which we view the system. Until the system reaches (or approaches) steady state, the time-dependent probabilities are *in transition* toward that constant value and are thus called transient probabilities.

The requirement for the single-server Poisson queue to be able to achieve steady state is that the ratio of arrival rate to service rate be less than unity, that is, $\lambda/\mu = \rho < 1$. Here the parameter $\rho$ is called the *traffic intensity*. If the arrival rate exceeds the service rate, then the length of the queue might be expected to grow indefinitely, since customers arrive at a rate faster than the rate at which they can be served. If the arrival rate is *less* than the service rate, however, then the service facility is able to handle the traffic and the queue might be expected to settle down to some finite length. Thus if the traffic intensity $\rho$ is a number less than unity, then it is possible for the system to reach the steady-state condition.

In steady state, the probability of *n* customers in the system no longer depends upon time. Thus the notation $p_n$ will suffice, where

$p_n =$ the probability that exactly *n* customers will be in the system at any point in time after the system has achieved its steady state

The solution for the steady-state system is

$$p_n = (1 - \rho)\rho^n \qquad n = 0, 1, 2, \ldots$$

where $\rho = \lambda/\mu$, and $\rho < 1$. This probability function is called the *geometric distribution* because its cumulative probabilities turn out to be sums of geometric progressions.

### Example 15.3
### Probabilities for the Number of Customers in the System

Customers of a retail mail-order store arrive at the order–pick-up station at the average rate of nine per hour. On the average, it takes five minutes to find the customer's order and fill out the necessary form, thus completing service. Therefore, the arrival rate is $\lambda = 9$ customers per hour, and the service rate is $\mu = 12$ customers per hour, so the traffic intensity for that queueing system is $\lambda/\mu = \frac{9}{12} = 0.75 = \rho$.

Suppose we want the probability that exactly four customers are in the system (three in line and one being served) at any time after the system is in steady state. This is just

$$p_4 = (1 - 0.75)(0.75)^4$$

$$= 0.0791$$

This probability may be interpreted to mean that approximately 8 percent of the time there will be exactly four customers in the system.

What is the probability that *no more than four* customers will be in the system at any time during steady state? This is a *cumulative* probability. If $X$ denotes the number of customers in the system, then

$$P(X \le 4) = \sum_{n=0}^{4} p_n = \sum_{n=0}^{4} (1 - 0.75)(0.75)^n$$

$$= (0.25)[1 + (0.75)^1 + (0.75)^2 + (0.75)^3 + (0.75)^4]$$

$$= (0.25)(3.0507813) = 0.7627$$

Thus about 76 percent of the time no more than four customers will be observed in the system.

Of course, an implication is that about 24 percent of the time there will be *more than four* customers in the system, or at least four in line waiting for service. Then we might also be interested in the distribution of waiting time for a customer.

Suppose we let $T$ denote the time elapsed from the arrival of a customer to the departure of that customer from the system. Then $T$ stands for the total time from entry to departure from the *system*, not just the queue or the service facility. Then the probability density function that is the *waiting time distribution* may be shown to be

$$g(t) = \mu(1 - \rho)e^{-\mu(1-\rho)t} \qquad t > 0$$

That expression describes an exponential density with parameter $\mu(1 - \rho)$. Thus waiting time in the *system* (the total time it takes an arriving customer to get through the queue and into and out of service) has an exponential distribution when arrivals are Poisson and service is exponential.

This density is like the exponential density of interarrival times you saw in Section 15.5, except now the parameter is $\mu(1 - \rho)$ instead of $\lambda$. Therefore, the probability that total time in the system is less than or equal to time $t_0$ would be

$$F(t_0) = P(T \le t_0) = 1 - e^{-\mu(1-\rho)t_0}$$

### Example 15.4
### Probabilities about Waiting Times

Suppose that for the queueing system described in Example 15.3 we want the probability that a particular arriving customer will spend no more than 25 minutes in the system. Here we would want to convert that waiting time to hours, since the arrival rate and service rate are quoted as "number of customers per hour." Thus $t_0 = \frac{25}{60} = 0.4167$ hours, $\mu = 12$ customers per hour, and $\rho = 0.75$. Then

$$P(T \leq 0.4167) = F(0.4167)$$
$$= 1 - e^{-12(1-0.75)(0.4167)}$$
$$= 1 - 0.2865 = 0.7135$$

Thus it is fairly likely that a customer would get through the system within 25 minutes, since about 71 percent of all customers do.

Of course, the probability that a given customer will spend *more* than 25 minutes in the system is just

$$P(T > 0.4167) = 1 - F(0.4167) = 1 - 0.7135$$
$$= 0.2865$$

So about 28 percent of the customers will spend more than 25 minutes in the system.

The probabilities observed in Examples 15.3 and 15.4 suggest that the queueing system for the order–pick-up station works pretty well with just the single service station. However, we have just seen that a fairly large fraction (28 percent) of the customers will experience waits (for completion of service) of more than 25 minutes. We might want to consider adding another service station to the service facility. Descriptive numbers that would be helpful in making that decision would be the *average* (expected) *number of customers* in the system and the *expected waiting time* for a customer.

Since we know the probability distribution for number of customers in the system and the probability density function for waiting time, those expected values may be computed. Before doing that (in the next section of the chapter), however, be reminded that the solutions of Examples 15.3 and 15.4, and in fact the general formulas used to obtain them, depended upon the assumption that the single-server queueing system was in steady state. In the case of the order–pick-up station, early in the morning when the facility has just opened and late in the afternoon when it is about to close, the system will be in a transient condition. We don't know for sure when it reaches approximately its steady-state condition, but a reasonable supposition might be that if the facility is open from 8:00 A.M. until 5:00 P.M., the probabilities we have computed might be good approximations during the hours from 9:00 A.M. until 4:00 P.M.

Here we concentrate on two kinds of expected values that are important for analyses of queueing problems. They are the expected number of customers and the expected waiting time. A system in steady state is assumed.

Expected values for both the whole system *and* only the queue (the waiting line, excluding the service facility) are of interest. To distinguish between the two cases:

Let $L_s = E(n)$ = expected number of customers in the system

$L_q$ = expected number of customers in the queue

$W_s = E(T)$ = expected waiting time of a customer in the system (including service time)

$W_q$ = expected waiting time of a customer in the queue (excluding service time)

Here we will develop formulas for these important expected values for the basic single-server Poisson queue. We will also note some general relationships between the $L$'s and the $W$'s that hold in even more complex queueing models.

First of all, consider $L_s$ for the simple Poisson queue of Section 15.6. The expected number of customers in the system is

$$L_s = E(n) = \sum_{n=0}^{\infty} np_n = \sum_{n=0}^{\infty} n(1-\rho)\rho^n$$

$$= (1-\rho)\sum_{n=0}^{\infty} n\rho^n$$

$$= (1-\rho)(0 + \rho + 2\rho^2 + 3\rho^3 + \cdots)$$

$$= \frac{(1-\rho)\rho}{(1-\rho)^2}$$

You can verify that the infinite sum following the factor $(1-\rho)$ is $\rho/(1-\rho)^2$ using algebraic long division. Therefore

$$L_s = \frac{\rho}{1-\rho} = \frac{\lambda}{\mu - \lambda}$$

is the expected number of customers in the system at any time after it has reached steady state.

The expected waiting time of a customer in the system $W_s$ is even easier to determine. From Section 15.6 we know that waiting time has the exponential density with parameter $\mu(1-\rho)$. But the expected value of an exponential random variable is just the reciprocal of its parameter. Then

$$W_s = \frac{1}{\mu(1 - \rho)} = \frac{1}{\mu - \lambda}$$

This is the expected waiting time per customer in the steady-state system, including service time.

### Example 15.5
### Expected Values for the Order–Pick-Up Problem

Now we are able to determine the average number of customers in the system and the average waiting time per customer for the problem discussed in Examples 15.3 and 15.4. There we had $\lambda = 9$ customers per hour (arrival rate), $\mu = 12$ customers per hour (service rate), and $\rho = 0.75$ (traffic intensity). Thus

$$L_s = \frac{\rho}{1 - \rho} = \frac{0.75}{0.25} = 3.0$$

and

$$W_s = \frac{1}{\mu(1 - \rho)} = \frac{1}{(12)(0.25)} = \frac{1}{3}$$

Then on the average there will be three customers in the system, and the average waiting time per customer (from arrival to completion of service) is 20 minutes (one-third of an hour).

If you were to consider using these averages to help you decide whether or not to change the system (improve the service rate or add another service station, for instance), you should remember that random variables do exhibit *variability* as well as central tendency (an average only measures central tendency). For example, although the *average* waiting time per customer is 20 minutes, we have already found out (Example 15.4) that about 28 percent of all customers spend more than 25 minutes within the system. Nevertheless, knowledge of average number of customers and average waiting times is obviously very useful in considerations of queueing problems.

A very natural relationship exists between the two expected values $L_s$ and $W_s$. If $W_s$ is the expected waiting time per customer and $\lambda$ is the arrival rate of customers, then $\lambda W_s$ should be, on the average, the number of customers in the system. That is, the equation $L_s = \lambda W_s$ is quite plausible. For the basic single-server Poisson queue that equation is immediately demonstrable.

$$L_s = \frac{\lambda}{\mu - \lambda} \qquad \text{and} \qquad W_s = \frac{1}{\mu - \lambda}$$

so

$$L_s = \lambda W_s$$

Under very general conditions on almost any queueing system, the expression

$$L = \lambda W$$

has been proved to hold (see Jewell, 1967, and Little, 1961). Note the absence of subscripts; the expected number of customers should equal the arrival rate times the expected waiting time per customer regardless of whether we are speaking about the queue or about the system. Again, for the basic single-server Poisson queue, it is quite easy to demonstrate that

$$L_q = \lambda W_q$$

The relationship $L = \lambda W$ is usually considered to be the most basic in queueing theory.

Two other relationships among the $L$'s and $W$'s may be easily established, but we will not derive them here. The following four formulas apply in general:

$$L_s = \lambda W_s \qquad W_s = W_q + \frac{1}{\mu}$$

$$L_q = \lambda W_q \qquad L_s = L_q + \rho$$

Since $\lambda$ and $\mu$ must be assumed known to make any progress at all, and then $\rho = \lambda/\mu$ would also be known, the discovery of *any one* of the four expected values $L_s$, $L_q$, $W_s$, and $W_q$ implies that the *other three* may be obtained from the four equations above. Those general relationships are common to many queueing models other than just the basic single-server Poisson queue.

### Example 15.6
### Using the Expected Value Formulas

Assume a single-server Poisson queue in steady state. Customers arrive at the average rate of 10 per hour and the average service rate is 16 customers per hour. Then $\lambda = 10$, $\mu = 16$, and $\rho = \frac{10}{16} = \frac{5}{8}$.

Suppose we start out by using the formula for $L_s$, the expected number of customers in the system at any time, the one that was derived from knowledge of the geometric distribution of number of customers in the system. Then

$$L_s = \frac{\rho}{1 - \rho} = \frac{\frac{5}{8}}{1 - \frac{5}{8}}$$

$$= \frac{5}{3} \qquad \text{average number of customers in the system}$$

Then if we were to look at the system many times while it is in steady state, the average of the number of customers observed in the system at those times should be near $1\frac{2}{3}$.

We can obtain the rest of the expected values by using the general formulas most recently observed. For instance, we can obtain $W_s$ from the equation $L_s = \lambda W_s$. Dividing by $\lambda$, we have

$$W_s = \frac{L_s}{\lambda} = (\tfrac{1}{10})(\tfrac{5}{3})$$

$$= \tfrac{1}{6} \qquad \text{average waiting time in the system, in hours}$$

Similarly, $\quad W_q = W_s - \dfrac{1}{\mu} = \tfrac{1}{6} - \tfrac{1}{16}$

$$= \tfrac{5}{48} \qquad \text{average waiting time in the queue, in hours}$$

and $\qquad L_q = L_s - \rho = \tfrac{5}{3} - \tfrac{5}{8}$

$$= \tfrac{25}{24} \qquad \text{average number of customers in the queue}$$

Thus the expected number of customers in the system is approximately 1.67, the expected number of customers in the queue, waiting for service, is approximately 1.04, the average waiting time per customer in the system is 10 minutes, and the average time a customer spends in the queue, awaiting service, is 6.25 minutes.

Obviously these general formulas will be extremely worthwhile in a queueing *problem*. Expected values of critical importance can be obtained quite easily given that any *one* of them can first be calculated using the theoretical description of the system. This indicates the position of queueing theory within the framework of a queueing problem.

## 15.8 FORMULAS FOR OTHER POISSON QUEUES

The preceding two sections exhibited formulas for the analysis of the basic single-server Poisson queue. No restrictions were placed on the calling source or on the number of customers allowed in the system, and only one server was made available to provide service. Now we will consider some other common Poisson queues, specifically those with more than one server and those with restrictions on the number of customers permitted in the system.

### Multiple Servers

Consider a queueing system in which arrivals are Poisson and service is exponential, but which has $c$ servers in its service facility. This system is identical to the one in Section 15.5 except for the number of servers.

A steady-state system is assumed. The relevant formulas follow:

$$p_0 = \left[ \sum_{n=0}^{c-1} \frac{\rho^n}{n!} + \frac{\rho^c}{c!(1 - \rho/c)} \right]^{-1}$$

$$p_n = \begin{cases} \dfrac{\rho^n}{n!} p_0 & \text{when } 0 \le n \le c \\[3mm] \dfrac{\rho^n}{c^{n-c}c!} p_0 & \text{when } n > c \end{cases}$$

$$L_q = \frac{\rho^{c+1}}{(c-1)!(c-\rho)^2} p_0$$

In order for a steady-state condition to be able to occur, the ratio $\rho/c$ must be less than unity. That is, the arrival rate $\lambda$ must be less than the maximum *facility* service rate $\mu c$.

With these three formulas we can calculate the probability that any number of customers will be in the system at any point in time after the system is in steady state, as well as $L_q$, the expected number of customers in the queue. The other expected values $W_q$, $L_s$, and $W_s$ can of course be computed using the general relationships at the end of Section 15.7.

You must be careful to note the exponent $-1$ in the expression for $p_0$. Correct computation of $p_0$ is essential for obtaining both $p_n$ and $L_q$. That calculation, as well as the computation of $W_q$, is demonstrated in Example 15.7.

### Example 15.7

Now we can do the calculations that were only reported in Table 15.2 of Section 15.4. This was the machine-maintenance problem with random arrivals and service. It contained the parameters $\lambda = 12$ machines per hour and $\mu = 7.5$ machines per hour. The ratio of those parameters, $\rho$, exceeds unity. That is why in Section 15.4 we did not consider expected waiting time with one server; the system would have been in a transient condition.

We want to find $W_q$ for $c = 2$, 3, and 4 in order to find the expected costs of idle time that were computed in Table 15.2. The multiple-server formulas will be used, along with the general relationship $L_q = \lambda W_q$.

First of all, note that $\rho = \lambda/\mu = 12/7.5 = 1.6$. That number will recur in all calculations following. We now consider the case where there are two servers, each with service rate $\mu = 7.5$.

For $c = 2$,

$$p_0 = \left[ \sum_{n=0}^{1} \frac{(1.6)^n}{n!} + \frac{(1.6)^2}{2!(1 - 0.8)} \right]^{-1}$$

$$= (1 + 1.6 + 6.4)^{-1} = \tfrac{1}{9}$$

Then $\qquad L_q = \dfrac{(1.6)^3}{1!(2 - 1.6)^2}\left(\dfrac{1}{9}\right)$ or $\qquad L_q = 2.8444$ machines

Using $\lambda W_q = L_q$ we find

$$W_q = \frac{L_q}{\lambda} = \frac{2.8444}{12}$$

$$= 0.237 \text{ hours}$$

For $c = 3$,

$$p_0 = \left[\sum_{n=0}^{2} \frac{(1.6)^n}{n!} + \frac{(1.6)^3}{3!(1 - 0.5333)}\right]^{-1} = \left[1 + 1.6 + \frac{(1.6)^2}{2} + \frac{(1.6)^3}{6(0.4667)}\right]^{-1}$$

$$= (1 + 1.6 + 1.28 + 1.463)^{-1} = \tfrac{1}{5.343} = 0.187$$

Then $\qquad L_q = \dfrac{(1.6)^4}{2!(1.4)^2}(0.187) = 0.3126$ machines

Therefore, $\qquad W_q = \dfrac{L_q}{\lambda} = \dfrac{0.3126}{12} = 0.026$ hours

Similarly, when $c = 4$ we can show that $p_0 = 0.1993$, $L_q = 0.060$ machines, and $W_q = 0.005$ hours. Thus all of the $W_q$'s used in Table 15.2 have now been verified. They are correct only to the extent that we can reasonably assume the system satisfies the assumptions of a Poisson queue.

## A Maximum of $N$ Customers Allowed in the System

Here two cases will be considered: the single-server case and the multiple-server case with $c < N$. We will give formulas for $p_n$ in both cases and will include a discussion of the modifications required in the general expected value formulas because of the restriction $N$.

**Case 1: $c = 1$** In this single-server case the formula for $p_n$ is fairly simple. It is

$$p_n = \frac{1 - \rho}{1 - \rho^{N+1}}\rho^n \qquad n = 0, 1, 2, \ldots, N$$

Since $n$ cannot exceed $N$ because of the restriction, the random variable $n$ can only range from 0 to $N$. For very large $N$ and $\rho < 1$, the formula for $p_n$ can be approximated by $p_n \simeq (1 - \rho)\rho^n$. This is the formula used with no restrictions on the number permitted in the system. The approximation stems from the fact that $\rho^{N+1}$ would approach zero for large $N$ and $\rho < 1$.

However, the assumption $\rho < 1$ is unnecessary for the system to achieve steady state. The queue cannot become indefinitely long since the maximum queue length is $N - 1$. Customers arriving when there are already $N$ customers in the system are simply turned away. If $\rho > 1$ of course, the exact formula for $p_n$ must be used.

Because of the restriction on the number allowed in the system the true arrival rate is not always $\lambda$. If $n = N$, then no one else is allowed in the system. Customers arrive *wanting* to enter the system at the rate $\lambda$. But when the system is saturated ($n = N$), the true arrival rate is zero. Only when $n < N$ is the arrival rate $\lambda$.

Thus the general relationships between the expected values, cited in Section 15.7, must be modified to reflect this double-valued arrival rate. The modification is simple; just replace $\lambda$ in $L = \lambda W$ by $\lambda_e$, where $\lambda_e$ is the *effective arrival rate* of customers into the system.

The rate $\lambda_e$ is the weighted average of the two arrival rates: $\lambda$ and 0. The weights are the probabilities associated with the two rates. Now the true arrival rate is zero only when $n = N$. Thus the associated probability is $p_N$. The probability that $n$ is less than $N$ is simply $1 - p_N$, so $1 - p_N$ is the probability associated with $\lambda$. Thus

$$\lambda_e = 0(p_N) + \lambda(1 - p_N)$$

$$= \lambda(1 - p_N)$$

where the probability $p_N$ is obtained by substituting $N$ for $n$ in the formula for $p_n$.

Now $\lambda_e$ must be substituted for $\lambda$ in the expected value relationships of Section 15.7. But to use those relationships we have to obtain at least one of the expected values by means other than the relationships themselves. The easiest one to get is $L_s$. It can be shown that

$$L_s = E(n) = \frac{\rho[1 - (N + 1)\rho^N + N\rho^{N+1}]}{(1 - \rho)(1 - \rho^{N+1})}$$

Then from $W_s = L_s/\lambda_e$ we find

$$W_s = \frac{L_s}{\lambda(1 - p_N)}$$

You also have to be careful with the relationship involving $\rho$. Instead of $L_s = L_q + \rho = L_q + \lambda/\mu$, now you should use $L_s = L_q + \lambda_e/\mu$. Therefore,

$$L_q = L_s - \frac{\lambda_e}{\mu} \quad \text{or} \quad L_q = L_s - \frac{\lambda(1 - p_N)}{\mu}$$

Finally,

$$W_q = \frac{L_q}{\lambda_e} = \frac{L_s - [\lambda(1 - p_N)]/\mu}{\lambda(1 - p_N)}$$

or

$$W_q = \frac{L_s}{\lambda(1 - p_N)} - \frac{1}{\mu}$$

Now we know all of the expected values needed to analyze a queueing problem of this type. For $\rho > 1$ and large $N$, you might consider the use of logarithms to compute $p_N$. Terms like $\rho^{N+1}$ and $\rho^N$ can become awkward otherwise.

**Case 2: $1 < c < N$**  This is the case of multiple servers with no more than $N$ customers allowed in the system and where the number of servers is less than that limit $N$. Here the formula for $p_n$ looks just like the one we used in the multiple-server case with no restrictions. However, the formula for $p_0$ is different, so the probabilities $p_n$ will have different values than in the no-restriction case.

$$p_0 = \left[ \sum_{n=0}^{c-1} \frac{\rho^n}{n!} + \rho^c \frac{1 - (\rho/c)^{N-c+1}}{c!(1 - \rho/c)} \right]^{-1}$$

$$p_n = \begin{cases} \dfrac{\rho^n}{n!} p_0 & \text{when } 0 \le n \le c \\[2ex] \dfrac{\rho^n}{c!c^{n-c}} p_0 & \text{when } c \le n \le N, \text{ but } c < N \end{cases}$$

For this queueing system the determination of expected values is best begun from $L_q$, the easiest of the four to find from basic theory. We find

$$L_q = \left[ \frac{\rho^{c+1}}{(c - 1)!(c - \rho)^2} \right] \left[ 1 - \left( \frac{\rho}{c} \right)^{N-c} - (N - c)\left( \frac{\rho}{c} \right)^{N-c}\left( 1 - \frac{\rho}{c} \right) \right] p_0$$

The other three expected values are found using the relationships from Section 15.7. Again $\lambda$ is replaced by $\lambda_e$ and $\rho$ is replaced by $\lambda_e/\mu$. Here $\lambda_e$ is still $\lambda(1 - p_N)$, but of course $p_N$ for this new system should be used. Because of the restriction on the number of customers allowed in the system it is not necessary that $\rho/c$ be less than unity.

## 15.9  APPLICATIONS: OBSERVATION PLUS THEORY

To apply the theoretical formulas developed so far, you must know the arrival rate $\lambda$ and the per-server service rate $\mu$, or else have good estimates of those rates. Also you must be convinced that the assumptions of Poisson arrivals and exponential service are at least approximately satisfied for your real queueing system.

Now we will do some sampling and use some statistics. Recall that a statistic is a random variable that takes on values according to the outcome of sampling.

### Statistical Estimation of $\lambda$ and $\mu$

Regardless of the arrival or service-time distributions, it is a simple matter to estimate $\lambda$ and $\mu$ for a queueing system. Both of these parameters are in the units "number of customers per unit time." Then if data are to be gathered from the system by just watching it operate for a while, the following estimators $\lambda^*$ and $\mu^*$ appear to be a logical approach:

$$\lambda^* = \frac{\text{number of arrivals observed}}{\text{time interval of observation}}$$

$$\mu^* = \frac{\text{number of departures observed}}{(\text{time interval of observation})(\text{number of servers})}$$

This last formula for $\mu^*$ assumes that $\mu$ is the same for each of the servers.

But we also know that $\lambda$ is the reciprocal of the average interarrival time and that $\mu$ is the reciprocal of the average service time. If you were to use $\lambda^*$ and $\mu^*$ as estimators for $\lambda$ and $\mu$, you would always be worried about possibly noticing another arrival or departure if you had only observed the system for an instant longer. On the other hand, if you use the following estimators $\hat{\lambda}$ and $\hat{\mu}$, you would not have that difficulty:

$$\hat{\lambda} = \frac{1}{\text{observed average time between arrivals}}$$

$$\hat{\mu} = \frac{1}{\text{observed average service time}}$$

### Example 15.8

Suppose that a queueing system is observed for one hour and that five arrivals and three departures are observed. Then

$$\lambda^* = \frac{5}{1} = 5 \text{ customers per hour}$$

If there is only one server in the system,

$$\mu^* = \frac{3}{(1)(1)} = 3 \text{ customers per hour}$$

However, the actual times between arrivals and service times were recorded. The information is shown in Table 15.3.

Notice that a whole hour is not accounted for by either of the sets of times in Table 15.3. We must assume that no arrival was observed in,

**TABLE 15.3**   *INTERARRIVAL AND SERVICE TIMES*

| Interarrival time, minutes | Service time, minutes |
|:---:|:---:|
| 15 | 20 |
| 10 | 10 |
| 5 | 15 |
| 10 | |
| 10 | |

say, the first five minutes and last five minutes of the hour. Likewise, the system may have come under observation just as a customer had departed, and perhaps a customer has been in service for 15 minutes but has not left the system at the end of the hour of observation.

The information in Table 15.3 gives the following estimates:

$$\text{Average time between arrivals} = \frac{15 + 10 + 5 + 10 + 10}{5}$$

$$= 10 \text{ minutes per arrival}$$

$$= \tfrac{1}{6} \text{ hour per arrival}$$

$$\text{Average service time} = \frac{20 + 10 + 15}{3}$$

$$= 15 \text{ minutes per service}$$

$$= \tfrac{1}{4} \text{ hour per service}$$

Therefore, the estimates of $\lambda$ and $\mu$ by our alternate method are

$$\hat{\lambda} = \frac{1}{\tfrac{1}{6}} = 6 \text{ customers per hour} \qquad \hat{\mu} = \frac{1}{\tfrac{1}{4}} = 4 \text{ customers per hour}$$

The values of $\hat{\lambda}$ and $\hat{\mu}$ are different from the values of $\lambda^*$ and $\mu^*$. Yet the same data were used for both pairs of estimates; only the estimation methods were different. Practically, it is more sensible to use $\hat{\lambda}$ and $\hat{\mu}$ because the actual observed interarrival and service times were used. That is, we had those times available, and if we do not use them, we are throwing away information. Also, the use of those reciprocal-type estimators removes most of the worry about the duration of observation of the system. Another argument in favor of that second type of estimator is that they will be maximum likelihood estimators if the queue is Poisson. Thus $\hat{\lambda}$ and $\hat{\mu}$ are recommended.

### Testing the Poisson Assumption

By "Poisson assumption" we mean of course the assumption of a Poisson queue. That is really *two* assumptions, as follows:

1 Number of arrivals per unit time has the Poisson distribution. Alternatively, interarrival times are exponential.

2 Service times have the exponential density.

Thus "testing the Poisson assumption" means testing *both* of those assumptions.

To test the hypothesis that a particular random variable has a certain probability distribution or density we could consider any of a number of statistical tests of *goodness of fit*. But there is a very good chance that you are already familiar with the *chi-square test,* so we will use it. The chi-square test can be used to test both assumption 1 and assumption 2 above: individually, of course.

In the case of the first assumption, we have a choice. We could either test whether the number of arrivals has a Poisson distribution or whether the interarrival times have an exponential density. For consistency, let's test both assumptions 1 and 2 by way of the exponential density.

The sampling experiment is just the observation of the queueing system for some time period. We will not list the times in detail; rather, we will condense them into frequency distributions. These are just tabular organizations of the data showing the frequencies with which sample observations fall within certain predetermined categories. The observed frequencies become the "observed" part in the evaluation of the well-known chi-square statistic:

$$\chi^2 = \sum_{\substack{\text{all} \\ \text{categories}}} \frac{(\text{observed} - \text{expected})^2}{\text{expected}}$$

### Example 15.9

Assume that the sampling of a continuously operating single-server queueing system is initiated by randomly selecting a time to begin observation. The system is observed for five days (120 hours). Arrival and departure times are recorded, and from that record every interarrival time and service time is computed. We arbitrarily decide to choose 20-minute intervals as the categories for both interarrival times and service times.

The sample frequency distributions are determined by counting and tabulating the number of times that fall in each of the categories. These appear in Table 15.4. The estimates $\hat{\lambda}$ and $\hat{\mu}$ may be computed from the tables. We use an approximating form of the mean when data appear in a frequency distribution; that approximation assumes that every observation occurs at a class midpoint.

Mean interarrival time

$$= \frac{110(10) + 70(30) + 24(50) + 21(70) + 6(90) + 5(110)}{236}$$

$$= 29.49 \text{ minutes} = 0.4914 \text{ hours}$$

$$\text{Mean service time} = \frac{160(10) + 52(30) + 22(50) + 6(70)}{240}$$

$$= 19.5 \text{ minutes} = 0.3250 \text{ hours}$$

$$\hat{\lambda} = \frac{1}{0.4915} = 2.0346 \text{ customers per hour}$$

$$\hat{\mu} = \frac{1}{0.3250} = 3.0769 \text{ services per hour}$$

The hypotheses to be tested statistically are (1) interarrival times have the exponential density and (2) service times have the exponential density. We must compute the *expected* frequencies in each category under the assumption that the hypotheses are true. To do that, we act as if $\lambda$ and $\mu$ are really $\hat{\lambda}$ and $\hat{\mu}$ as determined from the data, remembering when we perform the chi-square tests to *subtract a degree of freedom* because we were using an *estimated* parameter to determine expected values.

Then we estimate the probability that an interarrival time will have duration from 0 to 20 minutes ($\frac{1}{3}$ hour) as

$$P(0 < T \leq \tfrac{1}{3}) = F(\tfrac{1}{3})$$

$$= 1 - e^{-2.0346(1/3)} = 0.49338$$

**TABLE 15.4**  *OBSERVED FREQUENCY DISTRIBUTIONS*

| Interarrival times | | Service times | |
|---|---|---|---|
| **Duration, minutes** | **Number** | **Duration, minutes** | **Number** |
| $0^+$–20 | 110 | $0^+$–20 | 160 |
| $20^+$–40 | 70 | $20^+$–40 | 52 |
| $40^+$–60 | 24 | $40^+$–60 | 22 |
| $60^+$–80 | 21 | $60^+$–80 | 6 |
| $80^+$–100 | 6 | $80^+$– | 0 |
| $100^+$–120 | 5 | | 240 |
| $120^+$– | 0 | | |
| | 236 | | |

This probability is interpreted as the proportion of interarrival times that are 20 minutes or less in duration. We know that 236 interarrival times were observed. Thus the expected number of interarrival times in the first category (if our hypothesis is true) is 236(0.49338) = 116.

Similarly, for the expected number of service times that are between 40 and 60 minutes in duration, we compute

$$240[F(1) - F(\tfrac{2}{3})] = 240[(1 - e^{-3.0769(1)}) - (1 - e^{-3.0769(2/3)})]$$

$$= 240(e^{-2.05} - e^{-3.08}) = 20$$

Proceeding in this fashion for all categories and both hypothesized densities, we get the "observed versus expected" tables shown as Table 15.5.

Now we go to the chi-square goodness-of-fit test. Its philosophy is simple: if the numbers in the observed column differ substantially from those in the expected column, then the value of the chi-square test statistic will be large. Whether that value is large enough to be statistically significant depends upon the significance level we choose and the degrees of freedom of the statistic. Here the degrees of freedom are two less than the number of categories.

In the case of interarrival times there are 7 categories (5 degrees of freedom). Suppose we choose $\alpha = 0.05$ as the significance level. Then we would reject the hypothesis when it is true in only 5 of every 100 such experiments, on the average. We go to the table of chi-square values, Table A.4, to determine the critical region for the test. We find $\chi^2_{5;0.95} = 11.07$. Then we will reject the hypothesis of exponential interarrival times if our computed $\chi^2$ exceeds 11.07.

Use the observed and expected frequencies under interarrival times in Table 15.5. They give

**TABLE 15.5** *OBSERVED AND EXPECTED FREQUENCIES*

| Number of interarrival times | | | Number of service times | | |
|---|---|---|---|---|---|
| Category | Observed | Expected | Category | Observed | Expected |
| 0⁺–20 | 110 | 116 | 0⁺–20 | 160 | 154 |
| 20⁺–40 | 70 | 59 | 20⁺–40 | 52 | 55 |
| 40⁺–60 | 24 | 30 | 40⁺–60 | 22 | 20 |
| 60⁺–80 | 21 | 15 | 60⁺–80 | 6 | 7 |
| 80⁺–100 | 6 | 8 | 80⁺– | 0 | 4 |
| 100⁺–120 | 5 | 4 | | 240 | 240 |
| 120⁺– | 0 | 4 | | | |
| | 236 | 236 | | | |

$$\chi^2 = \frac{(110 - 116)^2}{116} + \frac{(70 - 59)^2}{59} + \frac{(24 - 30)^2}{30} + \frac{(21 - 15)^2}{15}$$

$$+ \frac{(6 - 8)^2}{8} + \frac{(5 - 4)^2}{4} + \frac{(0 - 4)^2}{4}$$

$$= 10.46$$

The calculated value, 10.46, is less than the critical value, 11.07. We *accept* the hypothesis that interarrival times have the exponential density. Perhaps the better way to say this is that we have insufficient evidence to warrant rejecting the hypothesis at the chosen level of significance.

What about the other hypothesis? Here, with $\alpha = 0.05$ and 3 degrees of freedom, we will reject it if the calculated chi-square value exceeds $\chi^2_{3;0.95} = 7.82$. That calculated value is

$$\chi^2 = \frac{(160 - 154)^2}{154} + \frac{(52 - 55)^2}{55} + \frac{(22 - 20)^2}{20} + \frac{(6 - 7)^2}{7} + \frac{(0 - 4)^2}{4}$$

$$= 4.74$$

The observed value of the statistic, 4.74, is less than the critical value, 7.82. We have failed to reject the hypothesis that service times have the exponential density.

The preceding results imply that we have no sample evidence to cause us to doubt that the assumption of a Poisson queue holds. If we wish to investigate the system further, we can now appeal to the theoretical formulas that were developed earlier. This is the relationship between observation and theory that leads to intelligent application of queueing formulas to queueing problems.

## 15.10   SUMMARY AND CONCLUSIONS

Queueing theory, or the theory of waiting lines, is a descriptive process. Unlike most of the other procedures presented in this text, it does not solve optimization problems. However, it does give good mathematical descriptions of queueing systems, descriptions that prove to be quite useful to a person responsible for making decisions about modifications of the systems.

Six characteristics of any queueing system must be specified if the system is to be modeled mathematically. These characteristics are the arrival distribution, the departure distribution, the queue discipline, the number of channels in the service facility, the type of source population, and the number of customers allowed in the system.

In the case of Poisson queues, the only types of queues discussed in this chapter, the most important parameters to know are the average arrival rate of customers into the system and the average service rate of a channel in the service facility. The Poisson arrival distribution results from the assumption of a constant rate of arrival and the independence of number of arrivals in nonoverlapping time intervals. The exponential densities of interarrival times and of service times follow from similar assumptions. In many real-world queueing situations those assumptions are at least approximately satisfied, justifying the emphasis here on Poisson queueing models.

In Section 15.9 of this chapter the statistical estimation of arrival and service rates is discussed, and a procedure for testing the hypotheses of Poisson arrivals and exponential service times is presented. If those hypotheses may be accepted, then one may use the formulas of this chapter with reasonable confidence that they give adequate descriptions of the queueing system. If those hypotheses were to be *rejected*, however, then nothing was said about how to proceed. One approach to the analysis of queues that may not be Poisson queues is to use *simulation* procedures such as those to be introduced in Chapter 16. Other more formally mathematical arguments for non-Poisson queues may be found in Saaty (1961) or Cooper (1972).

The more critical thing to watch out for when considering applying the queueing formulas of this chapter is the *steady-state* assumption. Unless you are reasonably sure that initial conditions of the system no longer influence its behavior, you would be better advised to use formulas that apply to systems in their *transient* state (again, see Saaty, 1961). But formulas for transient solutions can be extremely complex, involving functions of types not familiar to anyone but professional mathematicians, or, worse yet, for some systems precise transient solutions are not known. In such cases the common approach is to use simulation to obtain descriptions of system characteristics.

## KEY WORDS AND PHRASES

**Queueing theory**  That part of probability theory pertaining to the study of systems in which waiting lines (queues) may form.

**Queueing problem**  The case of high cost or unusual congestion in a queueing system, requiring a decision to modify the system.

**Queueing system**  The combination of the waiting line and the service facility.

**Queue**  A waiting line. That part of a queueing system where customers wait before their service begins.

**Service facility**  That part of a queueing system where customers receive service after leaving the queue.

**Arrival distribution**  The probability distribution that describes the random arrivals of customers into the queueing system.

**Service distribution**  The probability density for random service times associated with an individual server.

**Queue discipline**  The process by which customers in the queue are selected to receive service. In this chapter a first-come, first-served discipline is assumed for all queueing models considered.

**Channel**   A service station within a service facility. A channel can serve one customer at a time.

**Source population**   The type of population from which arrivals into the queueing system are generated.

**Idle time**   Time during which machines or people are doing no productive work.

**Poisson distribution**   The distribution of number of arrivals in a time interval when the arrival rate is constant and the number of arrivals in a time interval is independent of that number in any nonoverlapping interval.

**Interarrival time**   The time between successive arrivals into a queueing system. If the number of arrivals has a Poisson distribution, interarrival times are distributed exponentially.

**Exponential distribution**   The probability density for interarrival times if the arrival rate is constant, or for service times if the service rate is constant.

**Poisson queue**   A queueing system involving Poisson arrivals and exponential service times.

**Steady state**   The state of a queueing system characterized by a lack of dependence on time or initial condition of the system.

**Transient condition**   The condition that the state of the queueing system still depends on time and initial conditions, usually occurring early in the life of the system.

**Traffic intensity**   The ratio of arrival rate to service rate.

**Geometric distribution**   The distribution of number of customers in the system during steady state of a single-server Poisson queue.

$L = \lambda W$   The basic equation connecting expected number of customers ($L$) with expected waiting time ($W$), where $\lambda$ is the arrival rate.

**Multiple servers**   The case where more than one channel is available in the service facility.

**Effective arrival rate**   A modified arrival rate used when restrictions on the number of customers allowed in the queue can cause some arriving customers to be turned away.

**Goodness-of-fit test**   A test based on the chi-square distribution, designed to test whether observed sample data might differ significantly from what would be expected from a hypothesized form of a probability density or distribution.

## EXERCISES

◆ **15.1** Hi-Mileage Tire Store sells a very popular brand of automobile tire. The only way this particular brand is sold is in complete sets of four tires. Because of the popularity of the tire a customer must make an appointment to have a new set of tires installed.

Suppose that appointments are made so that a customer arrives every 10 minutes. Customers are never late for their appointments (uniform arrivals). One attendant can install a new set of tires in 15 minutes. This time is not variable (uniform service).

Over a period of time Hi-Mileage has been investigating the cost due to customer dissatisfaction when customers have had to wait for service to begin. That cost of customer waiting time is determined to be $20 per hour. Attendants, on the other hand, are paid $5 per hour. This is the cost of attendant idle time.

The first customer is scheduled to arrive at the instant the store opens. Consider only the first two hours of operation of the store, including the customer who arrives at the 120th minute. With only one attendant,

   a When is service for the sixth arrival completed? The thirteenth arrival?
   b What is the total cost of customer waiting time and attendant idle time attributable to arrivals during those first two hours?

◆ **15.2** Under the same conditions as in Exercise 15.1, but with two attendants,
   a When is service for the sixth arrival completed? The thirteenth arrival?
   b What is the total cost of customer waiting time and attendant idle time attributable to arrivals during those two hours? (Ignore idle time after completion of the thirteenth service.)

**15.3** For the Hi-Mileage Tire Store of Exercises 15.1 and 15.2,
   a What is the number of customer appointments that can be made so that all services can be completed if only one attendant is available and he or she only works an eight-hour day?
   b If the number of customer appointments is the same as that decided upon in part *a*, but if two attendants are available, what is the total cost of waiting and idle time for an eight-hour day?
   c Assuming that the number of appointments is fixed by that determined in part *a*, what is the optimum number of attendants that will minimize total cost of waiting and idle time?

◆ **15.4** The Off-Beat Engine Company manufactures three-cylinder engines for use on irrigation wells. Each day during production 16 engine blocks are sent along the assembly line toward the cylinder-boring station. One block is started down the line precisely every 15 minutes, and it takes a boring machine exactly 40 minutes to finish the cylinders on each block.

Therefore, exactly $10\frac{2}{3}$ hours are required each day for the boring operation. (When comparing waiting and idle times when different numbers of boring machines are involved, you should use a period of $10\frac{2}{3}$ hours even though only 16 blocks are started, regardless of the number of borers.)

Compute the total block waiting time and machine (borer) idle time when one, two, and three borers, respectively, are made available at the boring station.

◆ **15.5** For the uniform-arrival, uniform-service queueing situation described in Exercise 15.4, suppose that the cost of block waiting time is $100 per hour and the cost of borer idle time is $150 per hour. How many borers should Off-Beat make available at the boring station to minimize total cost of waiting and idle time?

**15.6** With reference to Exercises 15.4 and 15.5, suppose that the cost of block waiting time is $120 per hour and the cost of borer idle time is only $90 per hour.

Is Off-Beat's optimal decision changed from the one you determined in Exercise 15.5?

◆ **15.7** Letters to be typed arrive at a secretary's desk according to a Poisson distribution with average arrival rate $\lambda = 2$ per hour.

  **a** What is the expected number of letters arriving in a two-hour period? A four-hour period?

  **b** What is the probability that exactly one letter will arrive in a particular hour? That one or fewer will arrive in an hour? That more than one will arrive in an hour?

**15.8** Customers arrive at a barber shop according to a Poisson distribution and at the average rate of one every 15 minutes.

  **a** What is the probability that exactly two customers will arrive in the next 30 minutes?

  **b** What is the average number of arrivals per hour?

  **c** What is the probability that six or more customers will arrive during the next hour?

◆ **15.9** Airplanes arrive for maintenance at a central service facility at the rate of one every two days and according to a Poisson distribution. The facility is said to be "congested" if four or more airplanes arrive during a (seven-day) week. What is the probability that the facility will become congested during the next seven days?

◆ **15.10** Refer to the airplane arrivals in Exercise 15.9. What is the probability that the time between two successive arrivals will be three days or more?

**15.11** A physicist has designed a particle counter that emits a distinctive sound when struck by a particular rare particle, dubbed the alfalfa particle. Alfalfa particles strike the counter according to a Poisson distribution and at an average rate of one per 30 minutes. The physicist has been aurally monitoring the counter, but wishes to take a 15-minute coffee break. She decides to start her break at the time that she hears the next alfalfa particle strike.

  Use the fact that interarrival times have the exponential density to compute the probability that none of the rare particles strike the counter while she is on her coffee break. Also, what is the probability that she will have to wait at least 30 minutes from the time she makes her decision before she can begin her break? (Don't forget the memoryless property of the exponential density.)

◆ **15.12** Nippoff Electronics manufactures inexpensive electronic calculators. After assembly the calculators are placed on a conveyor belt leading to a test facility according to a Poisson distribution and at an average rate of two per minute. What is the probability that the time between the placing of two successive calculators on the belt will be less than 30 seconds? Will exceed one minute?

**15.13** Automobiles arrive at a toll gate according to a Poisson distribution and at the rate of two per minute. Time to complete service (paying fee) after the car reaches the gate has an exponential density with a mean of 20 seconds. Assume that the system is in steady state.

  **a** What percentage of the time is the attendant manning the toll gate idle? (This is the percentage of the time that there are no customers in the system.)

**b** What is the probability of two or more automobiles in the system at any time?

**c** What is the average number of automobiles in the system?

**d** What is the average waiting time of an automobile before it enters the toll gate for service?

✦ **15.14** Customers arrive at a drive-in banking window at the rate of one customer every two minutes and according to a Poisson distribution. On the average it takes one minute to transact business at the window; this transaction time has an exponential density. Assume that this single-server queueing system is in steady state.

    **a** What fraction of the working day is the teller at the drive-in window busy with a customer?

    **b** What is the probability of fewer than three customers in the system at any time?

    **c** What is the expected number of customers in the queue (excluding any at the window)?

    **d** What is the expected length of time that a customer will spend in the system (including transaction time)?

    **e** If the teller has to close the window for a five-minute period, how many customers may be expected to arrive during that time? Would this suggest to you that upon the teller's return the system will no longer be in steady state? Why or why not? If you thought that the closing of the window means that the system will go to a transient state, do you think that the system has a chance to settle down to steady state again? Why or why not?

✦ **15.15** During the height of the construction season in Laramie (when the ground is sufficiently thawed—local wags maintain this means the month of August) trucks arrive at a ready-mix concrete plant according to a Poisson distribution at the rate of 15 trucks per hour. The present capacity of the plant permits 20 trucks per hour to be loaded with concrete (on the average). This service time has the exponential density. Truck drivers earn $8 per hour and are considered idle during the time their trucks are waiting to be loaded but not during the loading operation itself. Assume that this queueing system is in steady state throughout the eight-hour working day.

    **a** What is the average length of time a truck will be in the system (including loading time)?

    **b** What is the expected waiting time in queue for a truck (excluding loading time)?

    **c** What is the expected total cost of driver idle time during a working day?

    **d** Suppose the capacity of the plant can be increased so that on the average 30 trucks per hour can be loaded. The exponential density still applies. What is the effect on your answers to parts *a*, *b*, and *c*?

**15.16** Suppose that in Exercise 15.15 the cost of facility (plant) idle time is $20 per hour. What is the expected cost of facility idle time during the eight-hour day for both a 20-truck and 30-truck per hour average service rate? What is the expected total cost of idle time (drivers and facility) for each service rate? If the increased service rate can be achieved at a cost of $60 per day, can that increase from 20 to 30 trucks per hour be justified?

**15.17** Consider the toll-gate queueing system described in Exercise 15.13. Suppose that another toll gate is made available with the same density of service time. If cars line up in single file and move for service in first-come, first-served order to whichever gate becomes free, what is the effect of the extra gate on your answers to parts a, b, c, and d in Exercise 15.13?

✦ **15.18** Suppose that another banking window is made available in the system described in Exercise 15.14, with the same density of transaction time as the original window. Customers wait in a single line and move in turn to the window that becomes free.

    **a** What is the effect of the extra window on the answers to the questions stated in parts b, c, and d of Exercise 15.14?

    **b** What fraction of the working day is neither window busy?

✦ **15.19** The chain of Croesus Muffler Shops has franchised a very large shop in Denver, employing many mechanics. These mechanics are inexperienced when hired, being put through Croesus' training program in removing and installing mufflers. Not being experienced mechanics who have their own sets of tools, they use those made available by Croesus.

The tools are available to be checked out and checked in at a centrally located tool room. The tool room is manned by clerks; it takes about the same time for a clerk to check out a tool to a mechanic as it does for a clerk to check in a tool.

Mechanics have been complaining that they have spent too much time in line waiting for service at the tool room; they contend that more clerks should be hired. On the other hand, the shop manager does not want to hire so many clerks that much of the time they have nothing to do. But because idle time of mechanics is more expensive than idle time of clerks, he decides to investigate the problem.

It is determined that time between arrivals of mechanics at the tool room appears exponentially distributed with a mean of one minute, and that service time of any clerk seems exponentially distributed with a mean of $1\frac{1}{2}$ minutes. Mechanics are paid $6 per hour while clerks receive $2 per hour. These wages are thus taken as the respective costs of idle time for mechanics and clerks. Finally, a mechanic being served by a clerk is regarded as working, not idle.

Croesus' manager decides to staff the tool room with clerks in such a way that the expected total cost of idle time for an eight-hour day is minimized. Assuming that he uses steady-state queueing formulas with no restrictions on the number allowed in the system, what is his solution for the optimal number of clerks?

**15.20** In Exercise 15.19, suppose that mechanics earn $8 per hour while clerks are paid only $1.50 per hour. Now what is the solution for the optimal number of clerks?

**15.21** In Exercise 15.19, suppose that mechanics arrive at the rate of one every 50 seconds and that the average service time per clerk is one minute. What is the optimal number of clerks if mechanics earn $6 per hour and clerks earn $2 per hour? What is that number if the respective wages are $8 and $1.50?

✦ **15.22** For the system described by Exercise 15.19, what is the probability

    **a** That there will be one mechanic in the system when there are two clerks?

    **b** That there will be three mechanics in the system when there are two clerks?

    **c** That there will be four mechanics in the system when there are three clerks?

**15.23** Using the arrival and service rates given in Exercise 15.21, answer parts *a*, *b*, and *c* as stated in Exercise 15.22.

◆ **15.24** Reconsider Exercise 15.5 under the assumption that arrivals of engine blocks are Poisson and boring time has the exponential density. In computing expected costs assume that only 16 blocks are involved per day, but use formulas having no restrictions on the number allowed in the system. Is Off-Beat's optimal decision changed?

**15.25** Reconsider Exercise 15.6 using the same assumptions used in Exercise 15.24. What is the optimal number of boring machines to make available?

◆ **15.26** Mini-Q Car Wash is situated on a very small lot. There is space available for washing only one car at a time, with parking available for only three other cars. If Mini-Q's space is all occupied (one car is being washed while three are waiting in line), other arriving customers will drive on to another location.

Suppose that potential customers arrive according to a Poisson distribution at the rate of 10 per hour. The time required to wash a car is exponentially distributed with a mean of 10 minutes. Assume that the system is in a steady-state condition.

**a** What is the probability that exactly two cars will be in the system?
**b** What is the probability that a potential customer will arrive to find the system at capacity and will have to drive to another location?
**c** What is the effective arrival rate of customers into the system?
**d** What is the expected number of customers in the system?
**e** What is the average time that a customer spends in the system? In the waiting line?

**15.27** Suppose that Mini-Q Car Wash of Exercise 15.26 acquires another space for washing cars at the expense of losing one space for parking while waiting. There are now two service stations but still only four customers permitted in the system. Answer parts *a*, *b*, *c*, *d*, and *e* as stated in Exercise 15.26. Note particularly the effect of the extra washing station on the probability that a potential customer will not be able to enter the system. (Assume that the service time for the new space has the same exponential density as the original space.)

**15.28** Suppose that Mini-Q of Exercise 15.26 acquires better equipment so that its mean service time is cut to four minutes. Now what is the probability of losing a potential customer? Contrast that probability with the approximate probability that would result from using $p_n \simeq (1 - \rho)\rho^n$.

**15.29** Rework Exercises 15.26 and 15.27 using a mean service time of four minutes. Comment on the effect on Mini-Q's business brought about by the acquisition of better equipment.

◆ **15.30** Outway Supermarket is curious about customer utilization of a particular checkout stand. The manager decides to observe the next 10 customers arriving at the stand, measuring the time of arrival and the time required for the clerk to serve the customer. The data appear below.

| Customer | Time of arrival | Service time, minutes | Customer | Time of arrival | Service time, minutes |
|----------|-----------------|-----------------------|----------|-----------------|-----------------------|
| 1 | 10:15 | 2 | 6 | 10:27 | 5 |
| 2 | 10:20 | 5 | 7 | 10:28 | 3 |
| 3 | 10:21 | 3 | 8 | 10:30 | 6 |
| 4 | 10:22 | 1 | 9 | 10:40 | 4 |
| 5 | 10:25 | 10 | 10 | 10:42 | 2 |

a Without doing any estimation, but looking at a time scale showing observed arrivals and departures, try to form an opinion as to whether this system appears to be capable of achieving a steady state.

b Estimate the arrival rate at this checkout stand.

c Estimate the service rate of the checkout stand.

d Estimate $\rho$, the traffic intensity, and comment on the relationship of this estimate to the conclusion you reached in part $a$.

**15.31** The warehouse supervisor for the local outlet of a nationwide retail chain is interested in the service given at the customer pick-up station of the warehouse. Over a period of two weeks the operation has been carefully observed and data have been recorded. A condensation of the data yields the following frequency tables for interarrival times and service times:

| Duration, minutes | Number of interarrival times | Duration, minutes | Number of service times |
|-------------------|------------------------------|-------------------|-------------------------|
| $0^+$–10 | 630 | $0^+$–5 | 524 |
| $10^+$–20 | 132 | $5^+$–10 | 170 |
| $20^+$–30 | 30 | $10^+$–15 | 70 |
| $30^+$–40 | 8 | $15^+$–20 | 21 |
| $40^+$– | 0 | $20^+$–25 | 10 |
| | 800 | $25^+$–30 | 3 |
| | | $30^+$–35 | 2 |
| | | $35^+$– | 0 |
| | | | 800 |

a Estimate the average arrival rate and service rate for the system.

b Estimate the traffic intensity for the system.

c Use a significance level of either 0.05 or 0.01 (as you prefer) to test the hypothesis that the number of arrivals per unit time has the Poisson distribution. Discuss why you chose the particular level of significance you used.

d Use a significance level of either 0.05 or 0.01 to test the hypothesis that service times have the exponential density.

e If the supervisor wishes to study the system in more depth, can she safely use Poisson queueing formulas?

**15.32** Regardless of whether you rejected one or the other of the hypotheses in parts $c$ and $d$ of Exercise 15.31, assume that the system is a Poisson queueing system.

**a** Estimate the average number of customers in the system.

**b** Estimate the proportion of the time that the pick-up station is idle.

**c** Estimate the average waiting time in the queue (excluding service) per customer.

**d** Investigate the effect of another identical pick-up station being made available at the warehouse. Particularly, estimate the change in the probability of idle stations and the change in expected waiting time per customer.

## SELECTED REFERENCES

Cooper, R. B.: *Introduction to Queueing Theory*, Macmillan Publishing Company, Inc., New York, 1972.

Cox, D. R., and W. L. Smith: *Queues*, John Wiley & Sons, Inc., New York, 1961.

Jewell, W. S.: "A Simple Proof of: $L = \lambda W$," *Operations Research*, vol. 15, 1967, pp. 1109–1116.

Kosten, L.: *Stochastic Theory of Service Systems*, Pergamon Press, New York, 1973.

Lee, A. M.: *Applied Queueing Theory*, St. Martin's Press, New York, 1966.

Little, J. D. C.: "A Proof for the Queueing Formula: $L = \lambda W$," *Operations Research*, vol. 9, 1961, pp. 383–387.

Morse, P. M.: *Queues, Inventories, and Maintenance*, John Wiley & Sons, Inc., New York, 1958.

Panico, J. A.: *Queueing Theory*, Prentice-Hall, Inc., Englewood Cliffs, N.J., 1969.

Prabhu, N. U.: *Queues and Inventories*, John Wiley & Sons, Inc., New York, 1965.

Saaty, T. L.: *Elements of Queueing Theory*, McGraw-Hill Book Company, New York, 1961.

Taha, H. A.: *Operations Research*, 3d ed., Macmillan Publishing Company, New York, 1982.

# SIMULATION

*T*hroughout this text you have studied mathematical models of real problems. Those models have had analytic solutions, solutions obtainable by straightforward mathematical techniques. Sometimes, however, we might not be able to model the whole problem completely, or else we could have a model so complex that an analytic solution is impossible. In such a situation a *simulation* of the problem can often offer a near-optimal solution.

There is no all-inclusive definition for "simulation" as it is used in management science and operations research. Often simulation involves numerical experimentation with a large computer model of a very complex system, but simulation could also be nothing more than an experimental verification of an analytic solution that has been proposed for a simple mathematical model. Regardless of the complexity of the problem, or whether or not a computer is required, *experimentation* is the essence of simulation.

A simulation model in operations research usually involves mathematical models. But often the simulation model will consist of *many* mathematical models, each describing some facet of the problem, and a way of connecting those models to reflect interactions between them. That is, a simulation model may not be one single mathematical model of the whole problem. For instance, suppose you want to simulate a simple single-server queue. You would need a model of the arrival distribution, a model of the departure distribution, and a description of the relationships between those two models.

Most simulation models involve random variables and statistical sampling. A simple example of simulation applied to a statistics problem is the experimental approximation of the distribution of an estimator. Suppose that $\overline{X}$ is the average of a sample of size $n = 3$ from some population. We are interested in the distribution of $\overline{X}$, but the sample size is too small to permit our citing the central limit theorem. Further, it may not be possible to derive its distribution mathematically. If we know the distribution for the population from which we will sample (a mathematical model), then we can simulate selecting many samples of size $n = 3$, compute the value of $\overline{X}$ for each simulated sample, and build up a picture of what the distribution of $\overline{X}$ might look like. In statistics, simulated sampling from a mathematical model is called *model sampling*. The combination of the population model and the simulated sampling is a simulation model.

In management decision problems model sampling is often a part of a simulation model. For the single-server queue simulation we would conduct model sampling on the arrival distribution to simulate the random arrivals, and model sampling on the service-time distribution to help simulate departures.

The best way to learn about simulation techniques is to study examples of simple simulation models. That approach is taken throughout the chapter. Our first illustration requires no mathematics beyond arithmetic; later examples will get a bit more complicated.

## 16.1 TESTING A STRATEGY FOR ROULETTE

Simulation does not always require a mathematical model. Sometimes we just experiment with a scale model of the actual system. In this illustration our scale model is a small roulette wheel purchased by the author in a toy store for $3.95. We do not expect its balance to be as true as that of a wheel in an honest casino, but we believe that it will suffice.

The following "system" has been proposed for playing roulette: Wagers are placed on any of the even-money chances: Red, Black, High, Low, Odd, or Even. The number of units, say dollars, wagered depends upon whether you won or lost on the previous wager. The wagering plan is based on the original sequence 1-2-3. Each number represents a quantity of units to bet. As betting progresses, the sequence changes according to the following plan:

1 Bet the sum of the outside two numbers.

2 If you win, cross off those numbers and again bet the sum of the outside two numbers *or* bet the single remaining number if only one remains.

3 If you lose, write the number of units lost as the next number in the sequence.

4 Start a new sequence (1-2-3) whenever all of the numbers in the old sequence are crossed off. At the end of any sequence, when all numbers are crossed off, you will have won six units.

This is an example of a *martingale,* any system of betting where bets are increased after a loss. (Doubling one's bet after a loss is the most common martingale.) Our objective is to test the strategy proposed above to see how profitable (or unprofitable) it is. We will use simulation; many sequences will be played vicariously using our small roulette wheel as a scale model. This type of simulation is actually done in industry; it allows us to test a proposed strategy without actually having to make the real investment called for by the proposal.

Before looking at the results of simulation let's be sure that you understand the wagering system. Example 16.1 describes a hypothetical sequence.

**Example 16.1**

Write down the sequence 1-2-3. You place a bet of $1 + 3 = 4$ units and lose. Write the loss at the end of the sequence, producing the new sequence 1-2-3-4. Bet the sum of the outside two numbers, $1 + 4 = 5$. You lose again, so now your sequence is 1-2-3-4-5 and you will bet $1 + 5 = 6$ units. Suppose you win. Now your sequence looks like this:

$$\cancel{1}\text{-}2\text{-}3\text{-}4\text{-}\cancel{5}$$

and you next bet the sum of the remaining outside two numbers, $2 + 4 = 6$. You lose, and your scratch pad now shows the sequence

$$\cancel{1}\text{-}2\text{-}3\text{-}4\text{-}\cancel{5}\text{-}6$$

The next bet is $2 + 6 = 8$ units. You lose again; your pad reads as follows:

$$\cancel{1}\text{-}2\text{-}3\text{-}4\text{-}\cancel{5}\text{-}6\text{-}8$$

So you wager $2 + 8 = 10$ units and win, yielding the sequence

$$\cancel{1}\text{-}\cancel{2}\text{-}3\text{-}4\text{-}\cancel{5}\text{-}6\text{-}\cancel{8}$$

Next you bet 9 units and lose, yielding

$$\cancel{1}\text{-}2\text{-}3\text{-}4\text{-}\cancel{5}\text{-}6\text{-}\cancel{8}\text{-}9$$

then 12 units.  You win, producing the sequence

$$\cancel{1}\text{-}2\text{-}\cancel{3}\text{-}4\text{-}\cancel{5}\text{-}6\text{-}\cancel{8}\text{-}\cancel{9}$$

Now you wager $4 + 6 = 10$ units, crossing your fingers in the process, and are fortunate enough to win.  This gives

$$\cancel{1}\text{-}2\text{-}\cancel{3}\text{-}\cancel{4}\text{-}\cancel{5}\text{-}\cancel{6}\text{-}\cancel{8}\text{-}\cancel{9}$$

and you have worked your way to the completion of the sequence.  You should now be 6 units ahead (or will have increased your capital by 6 units).  Let's see if this is so.  Table 16.1 shows losses and wins encountered during the sequence; sure enough, you have won exactly 6 units more than you have lost.

Table 16.1 also displays the attraction of this system to the undereducated gambler (one who does not appreciate the concept of expected value). We have been playing an unfair game (the percentages favor the house, not the bettor), have won fewer times than we have lost, and have made a profit!  The system has us writing down only one number when we lose but crossing off two when we win, so on an essentially even-money chance we should always be able to cross off all the numbers (eventually).

In theory, of course, that line of reasoning seems valid enough; it should be possible to complete any sequence eventually.  In practice, however, one encounters restrictions on the game, either in the form of limited capital or else a maximum wager, or limit, imposed by the casino.  For example, with the martingale system of doubling one's bet after a loss (which only requires *one* win in the sequence to recover all previous losses plus a profit equal to the initial unit wagered), one could anticipate a win *eventually*.  As this author remembers a bit of trivia he once read, the

**TABLE 16.1**   *LOSSES AND WINS*

| Loss | Win |
| --- | --- |
| 4 | 6 |
| 5 | 10 |
| 6 | 12 |
| 8 | 10 |
| 9 | |
| 32 | 38 |

maximum number of times in succession that "Red" has occurred in the casino at Monte Carlo is 55, so if one had initially wagered $1 on "Black" and had doubled the wager on each subsequent bet, always on "Black," the final winning wager in the sequence would have been $2^{55}$, at which point, of course, the bettor would have increased his initial capital by $1, the original wager. That final winning wager would have been in the approximate amount of $36 quadrillion, with $18 quadrillion, of course, having just been lost on the previous wager. Thus one would have required capital far in excess of the United States' national debt (at the date of this writing) to survive that long sequence of losses.

"Unfair!" you protest. "We have been discussing a much less drastic martingale, one that shouldn't require the same order of capital necessitated by the doubling system. That original martingale still looks good to me!"

Does it? Suppose you had been at Monte Carlo when that string of 55 Reds in a row occurred, betting on Black, of course. Then somewhere in one of your sequences you would have encountered 55 straight losses, requiring at least 29 subsequent wins to cross off all the numbers. You would probably have exhausted your capital or else run up against a limit on the wheel before completing your sequence.

Oh, all right, so you probably wouldn't be so unlucky as to be at Monte Carlo at just the wrong time. Let's simulate experience with the more modest martingale using our little roulette wheel.

## Example 16.2

Suppose we enter the casino with $25 available to play roulette. The casino will accept a minimum wager of $2, and, for the sake of realism, suppose the limit on the wheel is a $1,000 bet (this would allow a gambler to double an original $2 wager only eight times).

The following sequences were those actually encountered by the author on his little toy roulette wheel. Since seven sequences will be involved before catastrophe strikes, a concise notation for describing them is worthwhile. To explain the notation, consider a different description of the final sequence in Example 16.1, as follows:

```
Win    3 6 8 9 3 9 6 8      number of the spin
       1-2-3-4-5-6-7-8
Loss        1 2 4 5 7       number of the spin
```

The numbers opposite "Win" and "Loss" represent the particular spin of the wheel on which the win or loss occurred; we lost $4 on the first spin and lost $5 on the second spin, but won $6 (1 + 5) on the third spin, and so on. That notation will permit you to reconstruct the string of wins and losses encountered in each of the following sequences:

```
              Win   1 3 1 3
Sequence 1:         1-2-3-2        Capital = $25 + $6 = $31
              Loss      2
```

Sequence 2:

Win  1 3 1 3

1-2-3-2          Capital = $37

Loss     2

Sequence 3:

Win  1 2 1

1-2-3          Capital = $43

Loss

Sequence 4:

Win  1 3 1 3

1-2-3-2          Capital = $49

Loss     2

Sequence 5:

Win  1 5 1 6 6 5

1-2-3-2-4-6          Capital = $55

Loss     2 3 4

Sequence 6:

Win  3 5 6 6 3 5

1-2-3-4-5-6          Capital = $61

Loss     1 2 4

Sequence 7:

Win  2 4 7 2 4 11 7 15    11        15

1-2-3-4-5-  3-6-  3-6-  9-  9-12-15-18-?

Loss        1 3   5 6   8 9 10 12 13 14 16

We have been unable to complete sequence 7. Starting with a capital of $61, by the sixteenth spin of the wheel, on which we lost $18, our capital has been reduced to only $22. The next wager required by the system is the sum of the remaining outside two numbers, $6 + 18 = 24$, and our capital is insufficient to permit the wager. We could either risk the whole $22 on one spin of the wheel or quit and accept the $3 loss. Either way, we would no longer be pursuing the original strategy.

This brief simulation shows that we can learn a lot more from a simulation experiment than just an approximate answer to one question (Can we go broke?). The simulation has shown that we can easily lose our capital, even if no long runs of losses are encountered (the longest run of successive losses in sequence 7 was three). But now we can also see, from sequence to sequence, just what to expect from the strategy. We have learned not to get excited about early success; one bad sequence will demolish all early accumulations of capital. Further, if sequence 7 had been the *first* sequence at the roulette table, our $25 would have disappeared rapidly. Even the $61 available at the end of sequence 6 did not survive that sequence.

Of course, the physical construction of a roulette wheel should have told us that a loss was inevitable. A roulette wheel has 38 slots: the numbers 1 through 36, half colored red and half colored black, and the two "house" slots 0 and 00, which are colored green and which are not included in the Red-Black, Odd-Even, or High-Low fields. Thus on any even-money wager the probability of winning is $\frac{18}{38} \approx 0.47$. This is less than $\frac{1}{2}$, so the expected profit on even-money wagers is negative. Specifically, for a bet of $1 on Red,

$$\text{Expected profit} = \$1(\tfrac{18}{38}) - \$1(\tfrac{20}{38})$$

$$= -\$\tfrac{1}{19} \simeq -\$0.05263$$

No system of money management can overcome the implications of this expected profit. In the long run you should average losing about $0.05 for every $1 invested. The more you bet, the more you lose.

In this instance we have invested a total of $243 (the sum of all bets made during the seven sequences) and have lost exactly $3. This is an average loss of $3/243 ≃ $0.012, or a little over $0.01 per $1 wagered, very different from the predicted $0.0526. That result anticipates the major disadvantage of a simulation approach to solution; to obtain a good approximation of that theoretical expectation we would have needed to simulate the experience with *thousands* of such sequences. Our little group of seven may not be at all representative of long-run experience with the system. In the real world of business applications, where accurate simulation solutions are needed, those extremely large simulation runs chew up large chunks of computer time, a very expensive approach to solution. On the other hand, the cost of the computer time may in no way approach the loss that might be incurred by not doing the simulation at all and thereby using a very bad investment strategy. Nevertheless, when considering a simulation approach to the solution of some problem you must incorporate the anticipated cost of the simulation into your deliberations. One can anticipate that on occasion the cost of the simulation might exceed the savings that could result from using an optimal solution (obtained from the simulation) rather than a near-optimal one.

## 16.2 RANDOM NUMBERS

In the simulation of Example 16.2 we used an actual model of the real device to generate the random outcomes of simulated wagers. For simulations in business we want to avoid building a physical model if we can. Random samples from uniform, exponential, and normal densities will often be required. We would prefer not to have to sample from the actual populations; mathematical models are so much easier to use.

Sometimes we just want to simulate sampling from a population of fixed size, where the units in the population can be conveniently numbered. For this type of sampling, as well as for sampling from a theoretical population, *random digits* can be used.

Random digits are the result of sampling from the following *uniform distribution:*

$$f(x) = \tfrac{1}{10} \qquad x = 0, 1, 2, \ldots, 9$$

That is, $X$ is a random variable that may take on any integral value from 0 to 9 with probability $\tfrac{1}{10}$ for each value. Those values are just the 10 digits in the decimal system.

A *spinner* is a simple mechanical device for simulating a random sample from the uniform distribution. You could build a spinner resembling the one suggested by Figure 16.1 and use it to generate random digits. The accuracy of the $\frac{1}{10}$ probability for each digit depends upon the balance of the pointer and the precision of your division of the circle into sectors. You would also need a decision rule for cases when the pointer falls on a line, such as a coin flip to decide which digit to choose.

The use of the spinner of Figure 16.1 to generate random digits needs no explanation. But what if you want to use it to select a random sample of size $n = 8$ from a population consisting of 100 units?

You could number the population units consecutively from 00 to 99. Then each sequence of two spins could be used to select a population unit randomly. For instance, if you spin the spinner twice and observe 3 on the first spin and 7 on the second, you have randomly selected the population unit numbered 37. Continuing this process 8 times (16 spins) will give the sample of 8 units.

This process could take a long time if your hypothetical population contains 10,000 units and you want a sample of size $n = 500$ (units labeled 0000, 0001, and so on up to 9999, with four spins required to select one unit at random and 500 repetitions required). Worse yet, what if you propose to sample from the *uniform density* on the unit interval by selecting five-place decimals? That uniform density is

$$f(x) = 1 \qquad 0 \le x \le 1$$

with $X$ being a continuous random variable.

The spinner could still be used to create the digits in a decimal number; it would give you numbers such as 0.53002 or 0.03193, using one spin per digit to the right of the decimal point. We ignore the discrepancy between the continuity of $X$ and the discreteness of five-digit decimals; this is no practical drawback. But the spinner is obviously impractical for selecting large samples of random uniform *numbers* (not just digits).

If you do not have access to a computer, this is where a *table of random digits* comes in handy. Quite a few such tables have been generated, and

**FIGURE 16.1** A 10-digit random digit generator

some will be found in the reference section of any university library. One such table is *A Million Random Digits with 100,000 Normal Deviates*, generated at the RAND Corporation in 1947 and published by The Free Press, Glencoe, Illinois, in 1955. This tabulation is nearly equivalent to the result of 1 million spins of a perfectly balanced spinner like that shown in Figure 16.1. In reality, it was generated using an "electronic roulette wheel" with 32 "slots" representing binary digits. An electronic pulse was used to "stop" the wheel.

Random digits tables report groups of random digits that can be used to represent random numbers containing as many digits as you might want. Table 16.2 is a brief table of random digits generated using a TI-59 programmable calculator with its Statistics Module implanted. A larger table generated similarly appears as Table A.5 in the Appendix.

### Example 16.3

Suppose we want to use the digits in Table 16.2 to randomly select five numbers from the uniform density on the unit interval. Let three-decimal numbers suffice. Arbitrarily enter the table at the second line and the tenth digit. Then reading across we can group the digits into three-digit groups. Putting a decimal in front gives the following five random numbers:

$$0.278 \qquad 0.066 \qquad 0.091 \qquad 0.429 \qquad 0.530$$

Obviously a table of random digits beats a spinner for convenience in this situation.

Even better than a table of random digits is to let your *computer* generate random numbers for you. In effect the computer can simulate your selecting from such a table by generating digits or numbers as you need them. Any computer center will have a subroutine available for you to call up when you need random numbers (even fairly inexpensive pocket calculators now provide the capability of generating random uniform numbers). Some of these computer programs just use modular arithmetic, with a large modulus. Others may be tied in electronically to counters on the computer. At any rate, the generation of random numbers no longer requires spinners or tables, provided a computer is available to

---

**TABLE 16.2** *A SHORT TABLE OF RANDOM DIGITS*

| | | | | | | | | | |
|---|---|---|---|---|---|---|---|---|---|
| 03410 | 55858 | 06874 | 34736 | 76524 | 48504 | 44120 | 81127 | 73314 | 04046 |
| 66876 | 70172 | 78066 | 09142 | 95305 | 09809 | 54723 | 29840 | 33254 | 02907 |
| 44703 | 62845 | 28541 | 60941 | 32333 | 79604 | 75912 | 88507 | 02491 | 64107 |
| 62652 | 71132 | 27047 | 40532 | 07773 | 25550 | 76981 | 46829 | 02586 | 40776 |
| 49244 | 84963 | 96038 | 86717 | 14900 | 97634 | 76951 | 08750 | 71738 | 42336 |

you. But for ease of reference we will use the random digits tables (either Table 16.2 or Table A.5) in the examples and exercises of this chapter.

## 16.3 MODEL SAMPLING

Many simulation problems in operations research will require that we simulate random sampling from a known probability distribution or density. A convenient way to simulate sampling from such theoretical populations is based upon the uniform density and what is called the *probability transformation*. The key idea is that values of the *cumulative* distribution function must be numbers from zero to one, inclusive; this is so because those values are probabilities.

### Example 16.4

Consider the probability distribution function shown in Table 16.3. It is the distribution of a discrete random variable $X$ that can take on the values 1, 2, 3, 4, and 5.

We want to simulate taking a random sample of size $n = 20$ from a population wherein the values of $X$ occur in the proportions shown in Table 16.3. One easy way to do that is to collect 10 slips of paper, number one of them 1, three of them 2, two of them 3, one of them 4, and three of them 5, put them in a bowl and draw 20 times, with replacement, from the bowl. Another way is to use a table of random digits and the relationship of the uniform density to the cumulative distribution function of Table 16.4.

Now enter the short table of random digits, Table 16.2, at row 3, column 13. Select the next two digits moving across; they are 4 and 1. Call this the number 0.41. Note that 0.41 falls between the probability 0.40 and the probability 0.60 in the cumulative distribution in Table 16.4. Associate that number with the value 3 for the random variable $X$. We have randomly sampled and obtained $x = 3$ as the first number in our sample.

The reasoning behind this probability transformation is simple. Twenty percent of the population is associated with $x = 3$; 20 percent of all uniform

| TABLE 16.3 | PROBABILITY DISTRIBUTION | |
|---|---|---|
| | $x$ | $p(x)$ |
| | 1 | 0.10 |
| | 2 | 0.30 |
| | 3 | 0.20 |
| | 4 | 0.10 |
| | 5 | 0.30 |

| TABLE 16.4 | CUMULATIVE DISTRIBUTION | |
|---|---|---|
| | $r$ | $P(X \leq r)$ |
| | 1 | 0.10 |
| | 2 | 0.40 ← 0.41 |
| | 3 | 0.60 |
| | 4 | 0.70 |
| | 5 | 1.00 |

**TABLE 16.5** SELECTIONS FOR THE SAMPLE

| Random number | $x$ | Random number | $x$ |
|---|---|---|---|
| 0.41 | 3 | 0.12 | 2 |
| 0.60 | 3 | 0.88 | 5 |
| 0.94 | 5 | 0.50 | 3 |
| 0.13 | 2 | 0.70 | 4 |
| 0.23 | 2 | 0.24 | 2 |
| 0.33 | 2 | 0.91 | 5 |
| 0.79 | 5 | 0.64 | 4 |
| 0.60 | 3 | 0.10 | 1 |
| 0.47 | 3 | 0.76 | 5 |
| 0.59 | 3 | 0.26 | 2 |

numbers on the unit interval fall between 0.40 and 0.60. Thus the proportion of times $x = 3$ is selected by this process would be, in the long run, 0.20.

Now let's finish obtaining the other 19 numbers for our sample. First we need a "borderline" decision rule. If we get the random number 0.40, will we select $x = 2$ or $x = 3$? We decide upon $x = 2$; that is, for a borderline random number choose the lower value of $x$. For any random number falling between two probabilities in Table 16.4 choose the higher value of $x$. Table 16.5 shows the selections corresponding to just continuing horizontally in the short random digits table from our starting point at row 3, column 13.

A frequency distribution for the sample gives the proportions shown in Table 16.6. Comparing observed and expected numbers (obtained from the population distribution of Table 16.3) yields $\chi_4^2 = 1.67$. Since about 80 percent of 4-degree-of-freedom chi-square values lie to the right of that number, it is not statistically significant, implying that the sampling scheme was appropriate.

We already know how to use a table of random digits to sample from

**TABLE 16.6** SAMPLE PROPORTIONS

| $x$ | Proportion |
|---|---|
| 1 | $\frac{1}{20} = 0.05$ |
| 2 | $\frac{6}{20} = 0.30$ |
| 3 | $\frac{6}{20} = 0.30$ |
| 4 | $\frac{2}{20} = 0.10$ |
| 5 | $\frac{5}{20} = 0.25$ |

the uniform density on the unit interval. In fact, that was the source of the random numbers in Table 16.5. Now let's use those random numbers to simulate sampling from the *exponential density*. Again, the cumulative distribution is the key idea. Here we anticipate the model sampling to be needed in the queueing simulation of Section 16.5.

### Example 16.5

Consider the specific exponential density

$$f(t) = 2e^{-2t} \qquad t > 0$$

This could represent the interarrival times of customers arriving at the rate of two customers per unit time. We want to sample from this model or, equivalently, simulate random times between arrivals of customers.

The cumulative distribution is required. It is

$$C(t) = P(T \leq t)$$
$$= 1 - e^{-2t}$$

The graph of $C(t)$ is shown in Figure 16.2.

The vertical axis in Figure 16.2 reminds us that the values of $C(t)$ are probabilities; they only range from 0 to 1, just like the uniform numbers on the unit interval. To simulate sampling from the exponential density, first select a random uniform number. Then find the associated $t$ on the horizontal scale of the cumulative distribution in Figure 16.2. This is a *random exponential number*.

Suppose that we go to a table of random digits and select the number 0.85. Horizontal and vertical lines drawn on Figure 16.2 suggest that the associated $t$ is about 0.95. Thus we have randomly selected the number 0.95 from the *exponential* density using the random *uniform* number 0.85.

*FIGURE 16.2*    The cumulative distribution

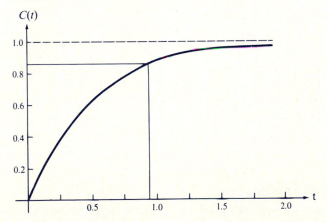

This process is called the *probability integral transformation*. It will work for any density of a continuous random variable, provided that a convenient expression for the cumulative distribution exists.

We cannot always depend upon the scale of the graph to yield an accurate value for $t$, especially if our random uniform number has many decimal places. Also, drawing the graph of $C(t)$ is inconvenient. Fortunately, we can find the exact $t$ algebraically.

Assume that the random uniform number 0.85 has been selected. Just set this equal to $C(t)$ and solve for $t$.

$$C(t) = 0.85 = 1 - e^{-2t}$$

Then
$$e^{-2t} = 1 - 0.85 = 0.15$$

Take the natural logarithm of both sides of the equation. This gives

$$-2t = \ln(0.15)$$

or
$$t = -\tfrac{1}{2}\ln(0.15)$$
$$= (-\tfrac{1}{2})(-1.897)$$
$$= 0.9485$$

Then the exact random exponential number is 0.9485 instead of the 0.95 we estimated from the graph in Figure 16.2.

The preceding algebra suggests a convenient formula for simulating sampling from *any* exponential density. Let $R$ be the random uniform number selected and let $\theta$ be the parameter of the exponential density. Then the randomly selected value of the exponential random variable is

$$t = -\frac{1}{\theta}\ln(1 - R)$$

In queueing simulations, let $\theta = \lambda$ for the interarrival times and let $\theta = \mu$ for the service times.

One more example of model sampling is in order. Earlier we noted that the method used in Example 16.5 works fine if the cumulative distribution may be expressed in a convenient form. The cumulative distribution for the *normal* probability density is not a nice closed algebraic expression, yet often we need to simulate sampling from a normal distribution. A convenient method is based on the central limit theorem. This method, illustrated in Example 16.6, works all right if you can do without values from the extreme "tails" of the normal density.

### Example 16.6

It is easy to show that the uniform random variable on the unit interval has a mean of $\tfrac{1}{2}$ and a variance of $\tfrac{1}{12}$. Random uniform numbers, because they are random, are independent. Then the central limit theorem says that the *sum* of N independent random uniform numbers has approximately the normal density with mean N/2 and variance N/12, or standard deviation $\sqrt{N/12}$. For convenience we usually take $N = 12$, a large enough N so that we can trust the approximation. Also, when $N = 12$, the mean is 6 and the standard deviation is 1.

This suggests a way to get *random standard normal* values. Randomly select 12 uniform numbers $R_1, R_2, \ldots, R_{12}$, denoting their sum by S. Then the number

$$Z = \frac{S - 6}{1} = S - 6$$

is a randomly selected *standard* normal value.

Usually our objective is to sample from a normal density with mean $\mu$ and variance $\sigma^2$. But we know that such a random variable X, when standardized as $(X - \mu)/\sigma$, has the standard normal density. Set this equal to Z (replacing the random variable X by its value x) and solve for x:

$$\frac{x - \mu}{\sigma} = S - 6$$

$$x = \mu + \sigma(S - 6)$$

Then to obtain a random value for X, where X is normal with mean $\mu$ = 5 and standard deviation $\sigma = 2$, first select 12 random uniform numbers and find their sum S. Then calculate x using the given formula. For instance, let's just use the first 12 random numbers in Table 16.5. Their sum is $S = 6.09$. Thus

$$x = 5 + 2(6.09 - 6) = 5.18$$

We have simulated the random selection of the number 5.18 from a normal density with mean 5 and standard deviation 2.

Doing this over and over with a table of random digits and an electronic calculator gets tedious; a computer offers a real advantage here. Call upon its random number generating routine for 12 numbers, then write your own short program to calculate S and x. A simple DO loop will rapidly produce a large random sample from a specified normal density.

Now we are ready to use these model-sampling concepts in other simulation studies. Section 16.4 presents an approximate solution for a simple inventory problem, while a queueing simulation is discussed in Section 16.5.

## 16.4 WOODY BURNS'S INVENTORY PROBLEM

Simulation is a handy tool for probabilistic inventory problems. Random demands and random lead times can be selected by model sampling.

**TABLE 16.7    PROBABILITY DISTRIBUTION OF DEMAND**

| Demand, number of cords | Probability |
|---|---|
| 100 | 0.10 |
| 200 | 0.20 |
| 400 | 0.30 |
| 700 | 0.25 |
| 900 | 0.15 |

Then competing strategies can be compared using many simulation runs for each strategy. Average profits or costs can be used as a basis for choosing a strategy.

A simple example, where only demand is random, is described as Exercise 11.26 at the end of Chapter 11. There Woody Burns, a firewood dealer, had to choose an optimal order quantity. The assumed probability distribution of demand is repeated in Table 16.7.

Suppose that this probability distribution will hold from year to year. We want to see how Woody can use simulation to determine his optimal order quantity.

Piñon is the type of firewood involved. A cord of piñon is delivered to Woody for $40. Each cord sold for use as firewood brings in $60, or $20 in profit. Unsold piñon at the end of the winter is sold elsewhere for $25 per cord, a loss of $15. If a cord of piñon is demanded after Woody runs out of stock, a shortage cost of $10 is incurred. The only possible order quantities that Woody will consider are the demands themselves. He wants to know which of those five possibilities is optimal in the sense of maximizing expected profit.

The critical-ratio method of Chapter 11 gives the solution as 700 cords. Theoretically, if Woody always orders 700 cords per winter, he should in the long run average $4,950 profit per year from piñon transactions. Let's see how close we come to those figures using a brief simulation to approximate the solution.

We will simulate 20 years' experience with each possible strategy. First we need the cumulative distribution shown in Table 16.8.

**TABLE 16.8    CUMULATIVE DISTRIBUTION OF DEMAND**

| $d$ | $P(D \leq d)$ |
|---|---|
| 100 | 0.10 |
| 200 | 0.30 |
| 400 | 0.60 |
| 700 | 0.85 |
| 900 | 1.00 |

Next, obtain 20 random numbers to simulate demand for each of the 20 years. Start from row 2, column 3 of Table 16.2 and read two-digit decimals horizontally. The resulting random numbers, random demands, and associated profits for each possible order quantity are given in Table 16.9.

Profit entries in Table 16.9 are obtained as follows. Suppose that the order quantity is 400 but the demand is 700. Then only 400 cords are sold at a profit of $20 per cord, giving $8,000. However, the shortage of 300 cords at a shortage cost of $10 per cord costs $3,000. The net profit is $8,000 − $3,000 = $5,000. On the other hand, if 700 cords are ordered but only 400 cords are demanded, then again 400 cords are sold at a profit of $8,000. But the 300 excess cords must be sold at a loss of $15 per cord, $4,500 total loss. Then $8,000 − $4,500 = $3,500 is the net profit here. The other entries are computed in the same way.

The average annual profit is highest if 700 cords are ordered each year. This is the same conclusion that would arise from the critical-ratio method.

**TABLE 16.9**   SIMULATED 20-YEAR PROFIT RECORD

| Year | Random number | Demand | Profit per order quantity, in dollars | | | | |
|------|------|------|------|------|------|------|------|
| | | | 100 | 200 | 400 | 700 | 900 |
| 1 | 0.87 | 900 | −6,000 | −3,000 | 3,000 | 12,000 | 18,000 |
| 2 | 0.67 | 700 | −4,000 | −1,000 | 5,000 | 14,000 | 11,000 |
| 3 | 0.01 | 100 | 2,000 | 500 | −2,500 | −7,000 | −10,000 |
| 4 | 0.72 | 700 | −4,000 | −1,000 | 5,000 | 14,000 | 11,000 |
| 5 | 0.78 | 700 | −4,000 | −1,000 | 5,000 | 14,000 | 11,000 |
| 6 | 0.06 | 100 | 2,000 | 500 | −2,500 | −7,000 | −10,000 |
| 7 | 0.60 | 400 | −1,000 | 2,000 | 8,000 | 3,500 | 500 |
| 8 | 0.91 | 900 | −6,000 | −3,000 | 3,000 | 12,000 | 18,000 |
| 9 | 0.42 | 400 | −1,000 | 2,000 | 8,000 | 3,500 | 500 |
| 10 | 0.95 | 900 | −6,000 | −3,000 | 3,000 | 12,000 | 18,000 |
| 11 | 0.30 | 200 | 1,000 | 4,000 | 1,000 | −3,500 | −5,500 |
| 12 | 0.50 | 400 | −1,000 | 2,000 | 8,000 | 3,500 | 500 |
| 13 | 0.98 | 900 | −6,000 | −3,000 | 3,000 | 12,000 | 18,000 |
| 14 | 0.09 | 100 | 2,000 | 500 | −2,500 | −7,000 | −10,000 |
| 15 | 0.54 | 400 | −1,000 | 2,000 | 8,000 | 3,500 | 500 |
| 16 | 0.72 | 700 | −4,000 | −1,000 | 5,000 | 14,000 | 11,000 |
| 17 | 0.32 | 400 | −1,000 | 2,000 | 8,000 | 3,500 | 500 |
| 18 | 0.98 | 900 | −6,000 | −3,000 | 3,000 | 12,000 | 18,000 |
| 19 | 0.40 | 400 | −1,000 | 2,000 | 8,000 | 3,500 | 500 |
| 20 | 0.33 | 400 | −1,000 | 2,000 | 8,000 | 3,500 | 500 |
| Average annual profit | | | −2,300 | 25 | 4,225 | 5,800 | 5,100 |

But the theoretical expected profit is only $4,950 while the average in the simulation run is $5,800. We conclude that more runs are needed before the results of simulation begin to approach those of theory. How many more runs (years)? That is the most difficult question to pose in a simulation experiment. Without bringing in some rather advanced statistical notions, about all you can do is just start simulating and hope that you can see when the process begins to settle down to some mode of regularity. Meanwhile, Woody Burns, unaware that we suspect we might have just been lucky, begins to behave optimally.

## 16.5  SIMULATING A POISSON QUEUE

A Poisson queue must have exponential interarrival times and exponential service times. Then the model-sampling part of the simulation only requires samples from two different exponential densities. But more than model sampling is necessary to simulate the behavior of a queueing system. We have to find some convenient way to keep track of the random arrivals and service completions. By hand, we can just use a time scale depicting real time. With a computer, that time scale itself would have to be simulated using counters.

A queueing system that is supposed to be operating in steady state is difficult to simulate. Important values such as the expected waiting time in the queue or the expected number of customers in the system might be the objective of the simulation. But if those numbers are unknown, then it is likely that you don't know other steady-state characteristics of the system. If you start the simulation at time zero and with no one in the system, then certainly the simulated system starts out in a *transient* state. Ideally, you want the initial conditions of the simulation to be as near those of steady state as possible. But if you don't know the steady-state characteristics, this becomes difficult to assure.

With a Poisson queue, we usually have adequate steady-state formulas. We really don't need to simulate the queue to learn its steady-state characteristics. Still, there are two obvious reasons for simulating a Poisson queue. First, we might not know how long it takes for the system to settle down to steady state; simulation can help us estimate that time. Second, the knowledge of transient characteristics of the system can be important. Example 16.7 involves simulating for that purpose.

### Example 16.7

Reconsider Exercise 15.19 at the end of Chapter 15. This is the Croesus Muffler Shop problem, where you are asked to determine the optimal number of clerks for staffing a tool room. Mechanics arrive at the tool room at the average rate of one per minute and the average service time is $1\frac{1}{2}$ minutes. A Poisson queue is assumed.

Using steady-state queueing formulas you will discover that three clerks should be used. However, Croesus' manager knows that some time must elapse before a steady state of the system is achieved. He is considering staggering the times at which clerks begin work. One of his alternatives is to have one clerk on duty at 8:00 A.M., with the other two clerks arriving at 8:15. He wants to simulate the effect of that policy on the system. He is particularly interested in the first 15 minutes of the day, when only one clerk is available to serve the mechanics. If too much mechanic idle time is involved, he will use a different policy.

Let's simulate those first 15 minutes. Interarrival times of mechanics have the exponential density with parameter $\lambda = 1$. Service times have the exponential density with parameter $\mu = \frac{2}{3}$ (the reciprocal of the mean). Time is measured in minutes.

First we randomly select the interarrival times using the random digits in Table 16.2 and the formula

$$t = -\frac{1}{\lambda} \ln (1 - R)$$

$$= -\ln (1 - R)$$

Arbitrarily start at row 1, column 6 of Table 16.2 and select two-digit numbers. For each such random number compute the associated inter-arrival time. When the sum of interarrival times exceeds 15 minutes, stop.

Now randomly select service times. Start at row 3, column 6 of Table 16.2, again selecting two-digit numbers. Use the formula

$$t = -\frac{1}{\mu} \ln (1 - R)$$

$$= -\tfrac{3}{2} \ln (1 - R)$$

to compute the associated service times. For convenience, again stop when the sum of service times exceeds 15 minutes, although we probably won't get to use every service time thus selected. Record all times to the nearest tenth of a minute. Results of this exercise are shown in Table 16.10.

We can look at the first 15 minutes of the simulated queueing system in the graph of Figure 16.3. Exactly 15 arrivals occurred during those 15 minutes—what we would expect on the average. The time of arrival of each mechanic is obtained by adding interarrival times. For example, the second arrival occurs at $0.8 + 1.9 = 2.7$ minutes into the time interval. Horizontal lines in Figure 16.3 are the actual service times. The thicker bars correspond to waiting times.

Croesus' manager can see from Figure 16.3 that things don't look too bad during the first 10 minutes. But the long service time of 4.5 minutes for the seventh arrival happened just as a series of short interarrival times

TABLE 16.10   INTERARRIVAL AND SERVICE TIMES IN MINUTES

| Interarrival times | | | Service times | | |
|---|---|---|---|---|---|
| Random number | Mechanic | Interarrival time | Random number | Mechanic | Service time |
| 0.55 | 1 | 0.8 | 0.62 | 1 | 1.4 |
| 0.85 | 2 | 1.9 | 0.84 | 2 | 2.7 |
| 0.80 | 3 | 1.6 | 0.52 | 3 | 1.1 |
| 0.68 | 4 | 1.1 | 0.85 | 4 | 2.8 |
| 0.74 | 5 | 1.3 | 0.41 | 5 | 0.8 |
| 0.34 | 6 | 0.4 | 0.60 | 6 | 1.4 |
| 0.73 | 7 | 1.3 | 0.94 | 7 | 4.5 |
| 0.67 | 8 | 1.1 | 0.13 | | 0.2 |
| 0.65 | 9 | 1.0 | 0.23 | | 0.4 |
| 0.24 | 10 | 0.3 | | | |
| 0.48 | 11 | 0.7 | | | |
| 0.50 | 12 | 0.7 | | | |
| 0.44 | 13 | 0.6 | | | |
| 0.41 | 14 | 0.5 | | | |
| 0.20 | 15 | 0.2 | | | |
| 0.81 | | 1.7 | | | |

developed.  This caused a lengthy queue to start building up.  At the end of 15 minutes the seventh mechanic is still in service and there are eight mechanics waiting in line.

More than 30 minutes of mechanic waiting time are involved.  At $6 per hour the cost is over $3.  On the other hand, clerk idle time only costs $2 per hour.  By not having three clerks on duty during the first 15 minutes of the day the manager would save $1, thirty minutes of clerk time for the two extra clerks.  Since the cost of mechanic idle time exceeds that saving by more than $2, he might like to consider a different policy for the first 15 minutes of the day.

Of course we could have obtained an unusual sample for this single simulation.  Better would be to repeat the simulation for *many* 15-minute intervals, each time starting with no one in the system to correspond to the opening of the shop.  Then look at *averages* over those simulations: average waiting time and average number in the queue at the end of 15 minutes.  This will give the manager a better experimental picture of the system.

You could also simulate early experience with the queueing system, during its transient state, by assuming two or three clerks on duty from the outset.  Here you would probably be interested in how long it takes for the system to settle down to steady state so that your formulas apply.  For the Croesus Muffler Shop problem, we might conjecture that steady

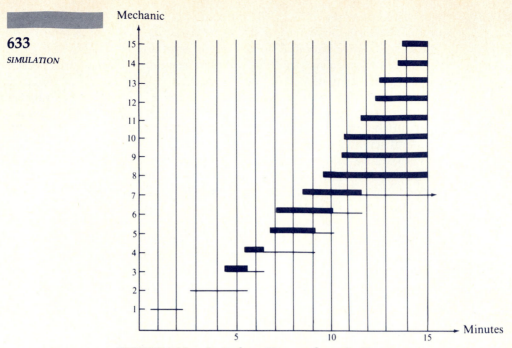

**FIGURE 16.3**    Arrival, waiting, and service times

state develops rather early in the day.  We could use simulation to verify that conjecture.

Finally, note that not all queues are Poisson queues.  For example, you could easily conceive of a system with Poisson arrivals but *normal* service times; that is, the service times have the normal probability density.  In such a situation simulation may be the *only* convenient way to obtain estimates of the important operating characteristics of the queueing system.

## 16.6   SUMMARY AND CONCLUSIONS

Simulation is an acceptable procedure for obtaining approximate solutions for management decision problems.  If it is possible to anticipate the long-run outcome associated with a particular strategy, without actually having to implement the strategy, substantial cost savings could result.  Simulation procedures offer an opportunity to compare competing strategies without incurring risk, although the cost of the simulation itself must sometimes be an important consideration.

The statistical concept of model sampling is the central idea in the simulation approach to many real problems.  If the random characteristics of the problem may be modeled using known probability distributions, then values of the associated random variables may be obtained conveniently using model sampling.  Further, random digits and cumulative distributions are the principal components of a model-sampling experiment. These notions have proved to be particularly useful in simulation approaches to inventory and queueing problems and could also be applied quite readily to analyses of PERT networks, where random observations from beta distributions would be required.

Most simulation studies would have to be done with the aid of a computer because of the large number of trials that are usually required before much faith can be placed in the solution indicated by the simulation. A general scientific programming language like FORTRAN could be used to write your own simulation program. However, because most simulation problems have many common features, such as model sampling, for instance, special simulation programming languages have been created to make the computer modeling of a problem simpler. Two examples of simulation languages that are readily available at many large computer installations are GPSS and SIMSCRIPT. Other such languages exist, geared specifically to the needs of people who must simulate, and surely more of these simulation languages will continue to be created as the problems addressed by simulation procedures become increasingly complex.

## KEY WORDS AND PHRASES

**Simulation**   The determination of long-run properties of a system using experimentation with scale models or mathematical models.

**Model sampling**   Simulated sampling from a mathematical (usually probabilistic) model.

**Random digits**   Integers selected at random from the uniform probability distribution of a random variable with values ranging through the integers 0 to 9.

**Random uniform numbers**   Numbers selected from the uniform probability density on the interval from 0 to 1.

**Probability transformation**   The process of transforming a random uniform number into a randomly selected value from a specified distribution.

## EXERCISES

**16.1** Refer to the roulette system and the simulated results in Example 16.2. If you have a model of a roulette wheel available, use it and bet on one of the even-money chances. Otherwise, a coin flip will suffice to simulate one spin of the wheel, even though with the coin your expected profit is zero, or at least the odds are not against you (nor are they with you). Bet on tails.

Give yourself $25 initial capital and use a betting unit of $1. See if you can complete 20 sequences of the martingale without going broke.

**16.2** Using an ordinary 52-card deck of playing cards, deal 100 five-card poker hands. Do this with 20 shufflings of the deck (to ensure randomness), dealing 5 hands after each shuffle.

    **a** Count the number of hands with a poker value equal to "a pair of Jacks or better." Divide by 100. This will approximate the probability of being dealt a pair of Jacks or better in a game of draw poker.

    **b** Count the number of deals (out of 20) on which at least one of the five hands contained a pair of Jacks or better. Divide by 20. This will approximate the probability that a hand will be "opened" in a poker game involving five people.

    **c** If your class is assigned this exercise, get together and pool your results. Use the pooled sample to approximate the probabilities in parts *a* and *b*. Now either compute those probabilities exactly or look them up in some reference on poker. How close are your class's simulated results to the actual probabilities? (The larger the class, the closer they should be.)

**16.3** In the game of craps as played in a casino, odds of 4 to 1 are given on the bet that you can toss a 7 with a pair of dice. The probability of tossing a 7 with a pair of fair dice is $\frac{1}{6}$, so that *fair* (break-even) odds should be 5 to 1.

    If you are not a gambler, locate the floating crap game in your dormitory and borrow a pair of dice from one of the participants (hope that they are fair). Simulate the results of 108 bets on the number 7 in a casino that offers 4 to 1 odds. Compare your profit or loss with that predicted by the $\frac{1}{6}$ probability.

◆ **16.4** Consider the probability distribution shown in the following table. Use random digits from Table A.5 to simulate taking a sample of size $n = 15$ from that distribution.

| $x$ | 1 | 2 | 3 | 4 | 5 | 6 |
|------|------|------|------|------|------|------|
| $p(x)$ | 0.10 | 0.05 | 0.25 | 0.20 | 0.25 | 0.15 |

**16.5** Consider the probability distribution shown in the following table. Use random digits from Table A.5 to simulate taking a sample of size $n = 40$ from that distribution. Conduct a chi-square test (use 4 degrees of freedom) at significance level $\alpha = 0.05$ to see if your sample differs significantly from the population. If it does, does that mean that you have incorrectly simulated the sampling?

| $x$ | 1 | 2 | 3 | 4 | 5 |
|------|------|------|------|------|------|
| $p(x)$ | 0.20 | 0.10 | 0.30 | 0.30 | 0.10 |

**16.6** Use random digits from Table A.5 to simulate taking a random sample of size $n = 10$ from a population where the random variable has the following exponential density:

$$f(t) = 3e^{-3t} \qquad t > 0$$

◆ **16.7** Simulate taking a random sample of size $n = 5$ from a population where the random variable has the probability density suggested by the following figure:

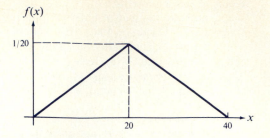

**16.8** Simulate selecting a random sample of size $n = 5$ from a normal distribution with mean 20 and standard deviation 7.

**16.9** Simulate selecting a random sample of size $n = 5$ from a normal distribution with mean $-10$ and variance 25.

**16.10** Refer to the concessionaire's problem stated as Example 11.8 of Chapter 11. Assume that the order quantity for hot dogs will be one of the six possible demands listed in Table 11.1. Simulate the profit experience with each order quantity over 10 home football games, assuming that the probabilities in Table 11.1 hold for each game. Recommend an order quantity based on this experiment. Does it agree with the strategy indicated in Table 11.2?

**16.11** Work Exercise 11.27 of Chapter 11 using simulation. Take average cost over 20 periods as the decision criterion.

**16.12** In Exercise 15.13 of Chapter 15 automobiles arrive at a toll gate according to a Poisson distribution and at the rate of two per minute. Time to complete service (paying fee) after the car reaches the gate has the exponential density with a mean of 20 seconds.

  Start simulating this queueing system assuming that one car is at the gate receiving service and one car is waiting in line. Simulate 20 minutes' experience with this queue. (*Hint:* The memoryless property of the exponential density applies.)

  **a** Estimate the percentage of the time that the attendant manning the toll gate is idle.

  **b** Estimate the average waiting time of an auto before it enters the toll gate for service.

  **c** Compare these estimates with your answers to parts *a* and *d* of Exercise 15.13. Do you think that they should be comparable?

**16.13** Consider the Croesus Muffler Shop problem discussed in Example 16.7. Assume that two clerks are made available at the tool room at 8:00. Simulate 40 minutes' experience with the system. Use the last 20 minutes of the simulation to estimate the average waiting time of mechanics in the queue. Does this estimate suggest that the system is in steady state after 20 minutes of operation? (*Hint:* Refer to Example 15.7 of Chapter 15.)

## SELECTED REFERENCES

Emshoff, J. R., and R. L. Sisson: *Design and Use of Computer Simulation Models*, Macmillan Publishing Company, New York, 1970.

Hammersley, J. M., and D. C. Handscomb: *Monte Carlo Methods*, John Wiley & Sons, Inc., New York, 1964.

Hillier, F. S., and G. J. Lieberman: *Introduction to Operations Research*, 3d ed., Holden-Day, Inc., San Francisco, 1980.

Meier, R. C., W. T. Newell, and H. L. Pazer: *Simulation in Business and Economics*, Prentice-Hall, Inc., Englewood Cliffs, N.J., 1969.

Mihram, G. A.: *Simulation: Statistical Foundations and Methodology*, Academic Press, New York, 1968.

Naylor, T. H., J. L. Balintfy, D. S. Burdick, and K. Chu: *Computer Simulation Techniques*, John Wiley & Sons, Inc., New York, 1966.

Phillips, D. T., A. Ravindran, and J. J. Solberg: *Operations Research: Principles and Practice*, John Wiley & Sons, Inc., New York, 1976.

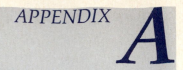

APPENDIX A

# TABLES

Tables A.1, A.2, and A.5 were generated using a TI-59 programmable calculator with its Statistics Module in place.  Tables A.3, A.4, and A.6 were generated on a CYBER 730/760 computer using programs written by Lee Plumb, programs which interact with programs in the International Mathematics and Statistics Library (IMSL).

**639**

CUMULATIVE BINOMIAL PROBABILITIES

Entries in the body of the table are

$$B(r;n,p) = P(X \le r) = \sum_{x=0}^{r} \binom{n}{x} p^x (1 - p)^{n-x}$$

where $r$ is given in the left-hand column and $p$ is given at the top of the table.

**n = 5**

| p \ r | .10 | .20 | .25 | .30 | .40 | .50 |
|---|---|---|---|---|---|---|
| 0 | .59049 | .32768 | .23730 | .16807 | .07776 | .03125 |
| 1 | .91854 | .73728 | .63281 | .52822 | .33696 | .18750 |
| 2 | .99144 | .94208 | .89648 | .83692 | .68256 | .50000 |
| 3 | .99954 | .99328 | .98438 | .96922 | .91296 | .81250 |
| 4 | .99999 | .99968 | .99902 | .99757 | .98976 | .96875 |
| 5 | 1.00000 | 1.00000 | 1.00000 | 1.00000 | 1.00000 | 1.00000 |

**n = 10**

| p \ r | .10 | .20 | .25 | .30 | .40 | .50 |
|---|---|---|---|---|---|---|
| 0 | .34868 | .10737 | .05631 | .02825 | .00605 | .00098 |
| 1 | .73610 | .37581 | .24403 | .14931 | .04636 | .01074 |
| 2 | .92981 | .67780 | .52559 | .38278 | .16729 | .05469 |
| 3 | .98720 | .87913 | .77588 | .64961 | .38228 | .17188 |
| 4 | .99837 | .96721 | .92187 | .84973 | .63310 | .37695 |
| 5 | .99985 | .99363 | .98027 | .95265 | .83376 | .62305 |
| 6 | .99999 | .99914 | .99649 | .98941 | .94524 | .82812 |
| 7 | 1.00000 | .99992 | .99958 | .99841 | .98771 | .94531 |
| 8 | | 1.00000 | .99997 | .99986 | .99832 | .98926 |
| 9 | | | 1.00000 | .99999 | .99990 | .99902 |
| 10 | | | | 1.00000 | 1.00000 | 1.00000 |

$$n = 15$$

| $r$ \ $p$ | .10 | .20 | .25 | .30 | .40 | .50 |
|---|---|---|---|---|---|---|
| 0 | .20589 | .03518 | .01336 | .00475 | .00047 | .00003 |
| 1 | .54904 | .16713 | .08018 | .03527 | .00517 | .00049 |
| 2 | .81594 | .39802 | .23609 | .12683 | .02711 | .00369 |
| 3 | .94444 | .64816 | .46129 | .29687 | .09050 | .01758 |
| 4 | .98728 | .83577 | .68649 | .51549 | .21728 | .05923 |
| 5 | .99775 | .93895 | .85163 | .72162 | .40322 | .15088 |
| 6 | .99969 | .98194 | .94338 | .86886 | .60981 | .30362 |
| 7 | .99997 | .99576 | .98270 | .94999 | .78690 | .50000 |
| 8 | 1.00000 | .99922 | .99581 | .98476 | .90495 | .69638 |
| 9 |  | .99989 | .99921 | .99635 | .96617 | .84912 |
| 10 |  | .99999 | .99988 | .99933 | .99065 | .94077 |
| 11 |  | 1.00000 | .99999 | .99991 | .99807 | .98242 |
| 12 |  |  | 1.00000 | .99999 | .99972 | .99631 |
| 13 |  |  |  | 1.00000 | .99997 | .99951 |
| 14 |  |  |  |  | 1.00000 | .99997 |
| 15 |  |  |  |  |  | 1.00000 |

$$n = 20$$

| $r$ \ $p$ | .10 | .20 | .25 | .30 | .40 | .50 |
|---|---|---|---|---|---|---|
| 0 | .12158 | .01153 | .00317 | .00080 | .00004 |  |
| 1 | .39175 | .06918 | .02431 | .00764 | .00052 | .00002 |
| 2 | .67693 | .20608 | .09126 | .03548 | .00361 | .00020 |
| 3 | .86705 | .41145 | .22516 | .10709 | .01596 | .00129 |
| 4 | .95683 | .62965 | .41484 | .23751 | .05095 | .00591 |
| 5 | .98875 | .80421 | .61717 | .41637 | .12560 | .02069 |
| 6 | .99761 | .91331 | .78578 | .60801 | .25001 | .05766 |
| 7 | .99958 | .96786 | .89819 | .77227 | .41589 | .13159 |
| 8 | .99994 | .99002 | .95907 | .88667 | .59560 | .25172 |
| 9 | .99999 | .99741 | .98614 | .95204 | .75534 | .41190 |
| 10 | 1.00000 | .99944 | .99606 | .98286 | .87248 | .58810 |
| 11 |  | .99990 | .99906 | .99486 | .94347 | .74828 |
| 12 |  | .99998 | .99982 | .99872 | .97897 | .86841 |
| 13 |  | 1.00000 | .99997 | .99974 | .99353 | .94234 |
| 14 |  |  | 1.00000 | .99996 | .99839 | .97931 |
| 15 |  |  |  | .99999 | .99968 | .99409 |
| 16 |  |  |  | 1.00000 | .99995 | .99871 |
| 17 |  |  |  |  | .99999 | .99980 |
| 18 |  |  |  |  | 1.00000 | .99998 |
| 19 |  |  |  |  |  | 1.00000 |
| 20 |  |  |  |  |  |  |

$n = 25$

| r \ p | .10 | .20 | .25 | .30 | .40 | .50 |
|---|---|---|---|---|---|---|
| 0 | .07179 | .00378 | .00075 | .00013 | | |
| 1 | .27121 | .02739 | .00702 | .00157 | .00005 | |
| 2 | .53709 | .09823 | .03211 | .00896 | .00043 | .00001 |
| 3 | .76359 | .23399 | .09621 | .03324 | .00237 | .00008 |
| 4 | .90201 | .42067 | .21374 | .09047 | .00947 | .00046 |
| 5 | .96660 | .61669 | .37828 | .19349 | .02936 | .00204 |
| 6 | .99052 | .78004 | .56110 | .34065 | .07357 | .00732 |
| 7 | .99774 | .89088 | .72651 | .51185 | .15355 | .02164 |
| 8 | .99954 | .95323 | .85056 | .67693 | .27353 | .05388 |
| 9 | .99992 | .98267 | .92867 | .81056 | .42462 | .11476 |
| 10 | .99999 | .99445 | .97033 | .90220 | .58577 | .21218 |
| 11 | 1.00000 | .99846 | .98927 | .95575 | .73228 | .34502 |
| 12 | | .99963 | .99663 | .98253 | .84623 | .50000 |
| 13 | | .99992 | .99908 | .99401 | .92220 | .65498 |
| 14 | | .99999 | .99979 | .99822 | .96561 | .78782 |
| 15 | | 1.00000 | .99996 | .99955 | .98683 | .88524 |
| 16 | | | .99999 | .99990 | .99567 | .94612 |
| 17 | | | 1.00000 | .99998 | .99879 | .97836 |
| 18 | | | | 1.00000 | .99972 | .99268 |
| 19 | | | | | .99995 | .99796 |
| 20 | | | | | .99999 | .99954 |
| 21 | | | | | 1.00000 | .99992 |
| 22 | | | | | | .99999 |
| 23 | | | | | | 1.00000 |
| 24 | | | | | | |
| 25 | | | | | | |

$n = 50$

| r \ p | .10 | .20 | .25 | .30 | .40 | .50 |
|---|---|---|---|---|---|---|
| 0 | .00515 | .00001 | | | | |
| 1 | .03378 | .00019 | .00001 | | | |
| 2 | .11172 | .00128 | .00009 | | | |
| 3 | .25029 | .00566 | .00050 | .00003 | | |
| 4 | .43120 | .01850 | .00211 | .00017 | | |
| 5 | .61612 | .04803 | .00705 | .00072 | | |
| 6 | .77022 | .10340 | .01939 | .00249 | .00001 | |
| 7 | .87785 | .19041 | .04526 | .00726 | .00006 | |
| 8 | .94213 | .30733 | .09160 | .01825 | .00023 | |
| 9 | .97546 | .44374 | .16368 | .04023 | .00076 | |
| 10 | .99064 | .58356 | .26220 | .07885 | .00220 | .00001 |
| 11 | .99678 | .71067 | .38162 | .13904 | .00569 | .00005 |
| 12 | .99899 | .81394 | .51099 | .22287 | .01325 | .00015 |
| 13 | .99971 | .88941 | .63704 | .32788 | .02799 | .00047 |
| 14 | .99993 | .93928 | .74808 | .44683 | .05396 | .00130 |
| 15 | .99998 | .96920 | .83692 | .56918 | .09550 | .00330 |
| 16 | 1.00000 | .98556 | .90169 | .68388 | .15609 | .00767 |
| 17 | | .99374 | .94488 | .78219 | .23688 | .01642 |
| 18 | | .99749 | .97127 | .85944 | .33561 | .03245 |
| 19 | | .99907 | .98608 | .91520 | .44648 | .05946 |
| 20 | | .99968 | .99374 | .95224 | .56103 | .10132 |
| 21 | | .99990 | .99738 | .97491 | .67014 | .16112 |
| 22 | | .99997 | .99898 | .98772 | .76602 | .23994 |
| 23 | | .99999 | .99963 | .99441 | .84383 | .33591 |
| 24 | | 1.00000 | .99988 | .99763 | .90219 | .44386 |
| 25 | | | .99996 | .99907 | .94266 | .55614 |
| 26 | | | .99999 | .99966 | .96859 | .66409 |
| 27 | | | 1.00000 | .99988 | .98397 | .76006 |
| 28 | | | | .99996 | .99238 | .83888 |
| 29 | | | | .99999 | .99664 | .89868 |
| 30 | | | | 1.00000 | .99863 | .94054 |
| 31 | | | | | .99948 | .96755 |
| 32 | | | | | .99982 | .98358 |
| 33 | | | | | .99994 | .99233 |
| 34 | | | | | .99998 | .99670 |
| 35 | | | | | 1.00000 | .99870 |
| 36 | | | | | | .99953 |
| 37 | | | | | | .99985 |
| 38 | | | | | | .99995 |
| 39 | | | | | | .99999 |
| 40 | | | | | | 1.00000 |
| 41 | | | | | | |
| . | | | | | | |
| . | | | | | | |
| . | | | | | | |
| 50 | | | | | | |

$n = 100$

| r \ p | .10 | .20 | .25 | .30 | .40 | .50 |
|---|---|---|---|---|---|---|
| 0 | .00003 | | | | | |
| 1 | .00032 | | | | | |
| 2 | .00194 | | | | | |
| 3 | .00784 | | | | | |
| 4 | .02371 | | | | | |
| 5 | .05758 | .00002 | | | | |
| 6 | .11716 | .00008 | | | | |
| 7 | .20605 | .00028 | | | | |
| 8 | .32087 | .00086 | .00001 | | | |
| 9 | .45129 | .00233 | .00004 | | | |
| 10 | .58316 | .00570 | .00014 | | | |
| 11 | .70303 | .01257 | .00039 | .00001 | | |
| 12 | .80182 | .02533 | .00103 | .00002 | | |
| 13 | .87612 | .04691 | .00246 | .00006 | | |
| 14 | .92743 | .08044 | .00542 | .00016 | | |
| 15 | .96011 | .12851 | .01108 | .00040 | | |
| 16 | .97940 | .19234 | .02111 | .00097 | | |
| 17 | .98999 | .27119 | .03763 | .00216 | | |
| 18 | .99542 | .36209 | .06301 | .00452 | | |
| 19 | .99802 | .46016 | .09953 | .00889 | .00001 | |
| 20 | .99919 | .55946 | .14883 | .01646 | .00002 | |
| 21 | .99969 | .65403 | .21144 | .02883 | .00004 | |
| 22 | .99989 | .73893 | .28637 | .04787 | .00011 | |
| 23 | .99996 | .81091 | .37108 | .07553 | .00025 | |
| 24 | .99999 | .86865 | .46167 | .11357 | .00056 | |
| 25 | 1.00000 | .91252 | .55347 | .16313 | .00119 | |
| 26 | | .94417 | .64174 | .22440 | .00240 | |
| 27 | | .96585 | .72238 | .29637 | .00460 | |
| 28 | | .97998 | .79246 | .37678 | .00843 | .00001 |
| 29 | | .98875 | .85046 | .46234 | .01478 | .00002 |
| 30 | | .99394 | .89621 | .54912 | .02478 | .00004 |
| 31 | | .99687 | .93065 | .63311 | .03985 | .00008 |
| 32 | | .99845 | .95540 | .71072 | .06150 | .00020 |
| 33 | | .99926 | .97241 | .77926 | .09125 | .00044 |
| 34 | | .99966 | .98357 | .83714 | .13034 | .00089 |
| 35 | | .99985 | .99059 | .88392 | .17947 | .00176 |
| 36 | | .99994 | .99482 | .92012 | .23861 | .00332 |
| 37 | | .99998 | .99725 | .94695 | .30681 | .00602 |
| 38 | | .99999 | .99860 | .96602 | .38219 | .01049 |
| 39 | | 1.00000 | .99931 | .97901 | .46208 | .01760 |
| 40 | | | .99968 | .98750 | .54329 | .02844 |

$n = 100$

| r \ p | .10 | .20 | .25 | .30 | .40 | .50 |
|---|---|---|---|---|---|---|
| 41 | | | .99985 | .99283 | .62253 | .04431 |
| 42 | | | .99994 | .99603 | .69674 | .06661 |
| 43 | | | .99997 | .99789 | .76347 | .09667 |
| 44 | | | .99999 | .99891 | .82110 | .13563 |
| 45 | | | 1.00000 | .99946 | .86891 | .18410 |
| 46 | | | | .99974 | .90702 | .24206 |
| 47 | | | | .99988 | .93621 | .30865 |
| 48 | | | | .99995 | .95770 | .38218 |
| 49 | | | | .99998 | .97290 | .46021 |
| 50 | | | | .99999 | .98324 | .53979 |
| 51 | | | | 1.00000 | .98999 | .61782 |
| 52 | | | | | .99424 | .69135 |
| 53 | | | | | .99680 | .75794 |
| 54 | | | | | .99829 | .81590 |
| 55 | | | | | .99912 | .86437 |
| 56 | | | | | .99956 | .90333 |
| 57 | | | | | .99979 | .93339 |
| 58 | | | | | .99990 | .95569 |
| 59 | | | | | .99996 | .97156 |
| 60 | | | | | .99998 | .98240 |
| 61 | | | | | .99999 | .98951 |
| 62 | | | | | 1.00000 | .99398 |
| 63 | | | | | | .99668 |
| 64 | | | | | | .99824 |
| 65 | | | | | | .99911 |
| 66 | | | | | | .99956 |
| 67 | | | | | | .99980 |
| 68 | | | | | | .99991 |
| 69 | | | | | | .99996 |
| 70 | | | | | | .99998 |
| 71 | | | | | | .99999 |
| 72 | | | | | | 1.00000 |
| . | | | | | | |
| . | | | | | | |
| . | | | | | | |
| 100 | | | | | | |

Entries in the body of the table are

$$N(z) = P(Z \le z) = \int_{-\infty}^{z} \frac{1}{\sqrt{2\pi}} e^{-x^2/2} dx$$

and the first decimal place in $z$ is in the left-hand column, the second at the top.

| z | .00 | .01 | .02 | .03 | .04 | .05 | .06 | .07 | .08 | .09 |
|---|-----|-----|-----|-----|-----|-----|-----|-----|-----|-----|
| 0.0 | .50000 | .50399 | .50798 | .51197 | .51595 | .51994 | .52392 | .52790 | .53188 | .53586 |
| 0.1 | .53983 | .54380 | .54776 | .55172 | .55567 | .55962 | .56356 | .56749 | .57142 | .57535 |
| 0.2 | .57926 | .58317 | .58706 | .59095 | .59483 | .59871 | .60257 | .60642 | .61026 | .61409 |
| 0.3 | .61791 | .62172 | .62552 | .62930 | .63307 | .63683 | .64058 | .64431 | .64803 | .65173 |
| 0.4 | .65542 | .65910 | .66276 | .66640 | .67003 | .67364 | .67724 | .68082 | .68439 | .68793 |
| 0.5 | .69146 | .69497 | .69847 | .70194 | .70540 | .70884 | .71226 | .71566 | .71904 | .72240 |
| 0.6 | .72575 | .72907 | .73237 | .73565 | .73891 | .74215 | .74537 | .74857 | .75175 | .75490 |
| 0.7 | .75804 | .76115 | .76424 | .76730 | .77035 | .77337 | .77637 | .77935 | .78230 | .78524 |
| 0.8 | .78814 | .79103 | .79389 | .79673 | .79955 | .80234 | .80511 | .80785 | .81057 | .81327 |
| 0.9 | .81594 | .81859 | .82121 | .82381 | .82639 | .82894 | .83147 | .83398 | .83646 | .83891 |
| 1.0 | .84134 | .84375 | .84614 | .84849 | .85083 | .85314 | .85543 | .85769 | .85993 | .86214 |
| 1.1 | .86433 | .86650 | .86864 | .87076 | .87286 | .87493 | .87698 | .87900 | .88100 | .88298 |
| 1.2 | .88493 | .88686 | .88877 | .89065 | .89251 | .89435 | .89617 | .89796 | .89973 | .90147 |
| 1.3 | .90320 | .90490 | .90658 | .90824 | .90988 | .91149 | .91308 | .91466 | .91621 | .91774 |
| 1.4 | .91924 | .92073 | .92220 | .92364 | .92507 | .92647 | .92785 | .92922 | .93056 | .93189 |
| 1.5 | .93319 | .93448 | .93574 | .93699 | .93822 | .93943 | .94062 | .94179 | .94295 | .94408 |
| 1.6 | .94520 | .94630 | .94738 | .94845 | .94950 | .95053 | .95154 | .95254 | .95352 | .95449 |
| 1.7 | .95543 | .95637 | .95728 | .95818 | .95907 | .95994 | .96080 | .96164 | .96246 | .96327 |
| 1.8 | .96407 | .96485 | .96562 | .96638 | .96712 | .96784 | .96856 | .96926 | .96995 | .97062 |
| 1.9 | .97128 | .97193 | .97257 | .97320 | .97381 | .97441 | .97500 | .97558 | .97615 | .97670 |
| 2.0 | .97725 | .97778 | .97831 | .97882 | .97932 | .97982 | .98030 | .98077 | .98124 | .98169 |
| 2.1 | .98214 | .98257 | .98300 | .98341 | .98382 | .98422 | .98461 | .98500 | .98537 | .98574 |
| 2.2 | .98610 | .98645 | .98679 | .98713 | .98745 | .98778 | .98809 | .98840 | .98870 | .98899 |
| 2.3 | .98928 | .98956 | .98983 | .99010 | .99036 | .99061 | .99086 | .99111 | .99134 | .99158 |
| 2.4 | .99180 | .99202 | .99224 | .99245 | .99266 | .99286 | .99305 | .99324 | .99343 | .99361 |
| 2.5 | .99379 | .99396 | .99413 | .99430 | .99446 | .99461 | .99477 | .99492 | .99506 | .99520 |
| 2.6 | .99534 | .99547 | .99560 | .99573 | .99585 | .99598 | .99609 | .99621 | .99632 | .99643 |
| 2.7 | .99653 | .99664 | .99674 | .99683 | .99693 | .99702 | .99711 | .99720 | .99728 | .99736 |
| 2.8 | .99744 | .99752 | .99760 | .99767 | .99774 | .99781 | .99788 | .99795 | .99801 | .99807 |
| 2.9 | .99813 | .99819 | .99825 | .99831 | .99836 | .99841 | .99846 | .99851 | .99856 | .99861 |
| 3.0 | .99865 | .99869 | .99874 | .99878 | .99882 | .99886 | .99889 | .99893 | .99896 | .99900 |

$N(1.28156) = .90000$    $N(1.6449) = .95000$    $N(2.3264) = .99000$

Entries in the body of the table are

$$P(X \le r) = \sum_{n=0}^{r} \frac{\alpha^n e^{-\alpha}}{n!}$$

where $r$ is given in the left-hand column and $\alpha$, the mean, across the top.

| $r$ \ $\alpha$ | 0.5 | 1.0 | 1.5 | 2.0 | 2.5 | 3.0 | 3.5 | 4.0 |
|---|---|---|---|---|---|---|---|---|
| 0 | .60653 | .36788 | .22313 | .13534 | .08208 | .04979 | .03020 | .01832 |
| 1 | .90980 | .73576 | .55782 | .40601 | .28730 | .19915 | .13589 | .09158 |
| 2 | .98561 | .91970 | .80885 | .67668 | .54381 | .42319 | .32085 | .23810 |
| 3 | .99825 | .98101 | .93436 | .85712 | .75758 | .64723 | .53663 | .43347 |
| 4 | .99983 | .99634 | .98142 | .94735 | .89118 | .81526 | .72544 | .62884 |
| 5 | .99999 | .99940 | .99554 | .98344 | .95798 | .91608 | .85761 | .78513 |
| 6 | 1.00000 | .99992 | .99907 | .99547 | .98581 | .96649 | .93471 | .88933 |
| 7 | | .99999 | .99983 | .99890 | .99575 | .98810 | .97326 | .94887 |
| 8 | | 1.00000 | .99997 | .99976 | .99886 | .99620 | .99012 | .97864 |
| 9 | | | 1.00000 | .99995 | .99972 | .99890 | .99668 | .99187 |
| 10 | | | | .99999 | .99994 | .99971 | .99898 | .99716 |
| 11 | | | | 1.00000 | .99999 | .99993 | .99971 | .99908 |
| 12 | | | | | 1.00000 | .99998 | .99992 | .99973 |
| 13 | | | | | | 1.00000 | .99998 | .99992 |
| 14 | | | | | | | .99999 | .99998 |
| 15 | | | | | | | 1.00000 | 1.00000 |
| 16 | | | | | | | | |
| 17 | | | | | | | | |
| 18 | | | | | | | | |
| 19 | | | | | | | | |
| 20 | | | | | | | | |
| 21 | | | | | | | | |
| 22 | | | | | | | | |
| 23 | | | | | | | | |

| 4.5 | 5.0 | 5.5 | 6.0 | 6.5 | 7.0 | 7.5 | 8.0 |
|---|---|---|---|---|---|---|---|
| .01111 | .00674 | .00409 | .00248 | .00151 | .00091 | .00055 | .00034 |
| .06110 | .04043 | .02656 | .01735 | .01128 | .00730 | .00470 | .00302 |
| .17358 | .12465 | .08838 | .06197 | .04304 | .02964 | .02026 | .01375 |
| .34230 | .26503 | .20170 | .15120 | .11185 | .08176 | .05914 | .04238 |
| .53210 | .44049 | .35752 | .28506 | .22367 | .17299 | .13206 | .09963 |
| .70293 | .61596 | .52892 | .44568 | .36904 | .30071 | .24144 | .19124 |
| .83105 | .76218 | .68604 | .60630 | .62652 | .44971 | .37815 | .31337 |
| .91341 | .86663 | .80948 | .74398 | .67276 | .59871 | .52464 | .45296 |
| .95974 | .93191 | .89436 | .84724 | .79157 | .72909 | .66197 | .59255 |
| .98291 | .96817 | .94622 | .91608 | .87738 | .83050 | .77641 | .71662 |
| .99333 | .98630 | .97475 | .95738 | .93316 | .90148 | .86224 | .81589 |
| .99760 | .99455 | .98901 | .97991 | .96612 | .94665 | .92076 | .88808 |
| .99920 | .99798 | .99555 | .99117 | .98397 | .97300 | .95733 | .93620 |
| .99975 | .99930 | .99831 | .99637 | .99290 | .98719 | .97843 | .96582 |
| .99993 | .99977 | .99940 | .99860 | .99704 | .99428 | .98974 | .98274 |
| .99998 | .99993 | .99980 | .99949 | .99884 | .99759 | .99539 | .99177 |
| 1.00000 | .99998 | .99994 | .99982 | .99957 | .99904 | .99804 | .99628 |
|  | .99999 | .99998 | .99994 | .99985 | .99964 | .99921 | .99841 |
|  | 1.00000 | .99999 | .99998 | .99995 | .99987 | .99970 | .99935 |
|  |  | 1.00000 | .99999 | .99998 | .99995 | .99989 | .99975 |
|  |  |  | 1.00000 | .99999 | .99998 | .99996 | .99991 |
|  |  |  |  | 1.00000 | .99999 | .99998 | .99997 |
|  |  |  |  |  | 1.00000 | .99999 | .99999 |
|  |  |  |  |  |  | 1.00000 | 1.00000 |

*CHI-SQUARE CRITICAL VALUES*

Entries in the body of the table are $\chi_p^2$, where

$$P(\chi^2 < \chi_p^2) = p = \int_0^{\chi_p^2} f(\chi^2)d\chi^2$$

Degrees of freedom, $v$, are in the left-hand column, and values of $p$ are given at the top of the table.

| $v$ \ $p$ | .90 | .95 | .975 | .99 | .995 | .999 |
|---|---|---|---|---|---|---|
| 1 | 2.706 | 3.841 | 5.024 | 6.635 | 7.879 | 10.828 |
| 2 | 4.605 | 5.991 | 7.378 | 9.210 | 10.597 | 13.816 |
| 3 | 6.251 | 7.815 | 9.348 | 11.345 | 12.838 | 16.266 |
| 4 | 7.779 | 9.488 | 11.143 | 13.277 | 14.860 | 18.467 |
| 5 | 9.236 | 11.070 | 12.832 | 15.086 | 16.750 | 20.515 |
| 6 | 10.645 | 12.592 | 14.449 | 16.812 | 18.548 | 22.458 |
| 7 | 12.017 | 14.067 | 16.013 | 18.475 | 20.278 | 24.322 |
| 8 | 13.362 | 15.507 | 17.534 | 20.090 | 21.955 | 26.125 |
| 9 | 14.684 | 16.919 | 19.023 | 21.666 | 23.589 | 27.877 |
| 10 | 15.987 | 18.307 | 20.483 | 23.209 | 25.188 | 29.588 |
| 11 | 17.275 | 19.675 | 21.920 | 24.725 | 26.757 | 31.264 |
| 12 | 18.549 | 21.026 | 23.337 | 26.217 | 28.300 | 32.909 |
| 13 | 19.812 | 22.362 | 24.736 | 27.688 | 29.820 | 34.528 |
| 14 | 21.064 | 23.685 | 26.119 | 29.141 | 31.319 | 36.123 |
| 15 | 22.307 | 24.996 | 27.488 | 30.578 | 32.801 | 37.697 |
| 16 | 23.542 | 26.296 | 28.845 | 32.000 | 34.267 | 39.252 |
| 17 | 24.767 | 27.587 | 30.191 | 33.409 | 35.718 | 40.790 |
| 18 | 25.989 | 28.869 | 31.526 | 34.805 | 37.156 | 42.312 |
| 19 | 27.204 | 30.144 | 32.852 | 36.191 | 38.582 | 43.820 |
| 20 | 28.412 | 31.410 | 34.170 | 37.566 | 39.997 | 45.315 |
| 25 | 34.382 | 37.652 | 40.646 | 44.314 | 46.928 | 52.618 |
| 30 | 40.256 | 43.773 | 46.979 | 50.892 | 53.672 | 59.703 |
| 40 | 51.805 | 55.758 | 59.342 | 63.691 | 66.766 | 73.402 |
| 60 | 74.397 | 79.082 | 83.298 | 88.379 | 91.952 | 99.607 |

| | | | | | | | | | |
|---|---|---|---|---|---|---|---|---|---|
| 21084 | 52384 | 90881 | 88346 | 88080 | 42040 | 44504 | 13731 | 95896 | 51478 |
| 75297 | 19178 | 43142 | 20844 | 25821 | 58060 | 11227 | 66971 | 24757 | 15436 |
| 36682 | 62562 | 03919 | 86715 | 53829 | 92581 | 93196 | 46671 | 86304 | 66195 |
| 59341 | 19901 | 16136 | 27705 | 35201 | 69267 | 07544 | 76757 | 96615 | 04938 |
| 44627 | 12821 | 84498 | 86313 | 83540 | 23070 | 06633 | 24105 | 62525 | 85875 |
| | | | | | | | | | |
| 55001 | 72583 | 73798 | 13047 | 77547 | 87513 | 47895 | 16996 | 35670 | 66523 |
| 41797 | 53138 | 03295 | 15724 | 18010 | 60607 | 82821 | 52565 | 76556 | 14588 |
| 11556 | 39614 | 98307 | 14384 | 64337 | 22367 | 45889 | 78328 | 77277 | 37358 |
| 76360 | 46081 | 33281 | 13729 | 59279 | 29520 | 38306 | 24640 | 76993 | 30114 |
| 74234 | 97353 | 44637 | 59847 | 12940 | 66751 | 71126 | 69911 | 70098 | 13120 |
| | | | | | | | | | |
| 41291 | 49821 | 16596 | 22909 | 99033 | 71430 | 58010 | 86990 | 38923 | 22362 |
| 21707 | 98793 | 26320 | 78389 | 49714 | 09980 | 54074 | 53303 | 20872 | 04343 |
| 77100 | 34267 | 77267 | 06318 | 67484 | 96811 | 84889 | 97889 | 57869 | 52929 |
| 33614 | 18692 | 34933 | 73136 | 15423 | 03812 | 76317 | 19871 | 94850 | 17306 |
| 62874 | 82101 | 46269 | 97976 | 77067 | 42164 | 67029 | 36192 | 47832 | 74149 |
| | | | | | | | | | |
| 26635 | 37507 | 07851 | 29155 | 69859 | 03429 | 82055 | 41865 | 10261 | 92527 |
| 94432 | 65660 | 66204 | 81473 | 91158 | 22196 | 88477 | 79185 | 09629 | 25403 |
| 07926 | 37101 | 45298 | 08083 | 54402 | 21183 | 77179 | 60356 | 50162 | 98108 |
| 92665 | 25894 | 37597 | 99419 | 44259 | 71266 | 89418 | 30337 | 83673 | 56937 |
| 06488 | 18871 | 78511 | 88493 | 54808 | 91986 | 36688 | 11376 | 64657 | 94301 |
| | | | | | | | | | |
| 18904 | 01930 | 52312 | 32834 | 72982 | 86620 | 56706 | 04828 | 61788 | 81760 |
| 67600 | 04275 | 40544 | 12543 | 22481 | 02840 | 66478 | 43749 | 77051 | 43240 |
| 97997 | 02171 | 21100 | 50278 | 09588 | 40362 | 83649 | 64517 | 03625 | 38972 |
| 02676 | 73204 | 66063 | 64469 | 41500 | 31869 | 23517 | 80141 | 23355 | 40942 |
| 64865 | 46934 | 75317 | 11650 | 24323 | 66163 | 98048 | 27860 | 95851 | 44315 |
| | | | | | | | | | |
| 80853 | 38207 | 14741 | 28294 | 56794 | 48643 | 77880 | 96414 | 26337 | 96922 |
| 65787 | 56618 | 61452 | 31761 | 98896 | 30226 | 97651 | 84414 | 41881 | 91983 |
| 63478 | 57930 | 44292 | 63065 | 19697 | 65200 | 80364 | 55124 | 71442 | 53571 |
| 25082 | 01960 | 81048 | 57654 | 42563 | 62028 | 26583 | 80596 | 78464 | 77091 |
| 22789 | 93376 | 20290 | 59408 | 48630 | 72260 | 35749 | 02503 | 74038 | 35911 |
| | | | | | | | | | |
| 72738 | 50534 | 28193 | 83975 | 77785 | 93085 | 40530 | 68374 | 03604 | 26527 |
| 18439 | 04033 | 52359 | 84525 | 53538 | 28909 | 01048 | 34018 | 40471 | 17834 |
| 93035 | 19806 | 10936 | 81587 | 57673 | 89015 | 39531 | 74480 | 76007 | 82372 |
| 41669 | 39762 | 02140 | 53337 | 36535 | 82945 | 50432 | 68555 | 01187 | 04166 |
| 76624 | 61319 | 89703 | 77451 | 61395 | 32804 | 33133 | 16136 | 33206 | 00136 |
| | | | | | | | | | |
| 89267 | 78056 | 60543 | 30762 | 21792 | 64033 | 30172 | 88961 | 27985 | 46951 |
| 68709 | 48279 | 40236 | 16136 | 29790 | 90908 | 48717 | 83951 | 93535 | 80243 |
| 10838 | 13980 | 46713 | 96614 | 98985 | 98585 | 69617 | 10207 | 65541 | 72232 |
| 50400 | 83073 | 73012 | 10494 | 43781 | 43189 | 59698 | 13701 | 71087 | 34135 |
| 67259 | 12976 | 60480 | 99230 | 54972 | 71294 | 56568 | 45362 | 62120 | 43120 |

Entries in the body of the table are $t_{p,v}$, where

$$P(t < t_{p,v}) = p$$

Degrees of freedom, $v$, are on the left, and values of $p$ are at the top.

| $v$ \\ $p$ | 0.90 | 0.95 | 0.975 | 0.99 | 0.995 |
|---|---|---|---|---|---|
| 1 | 3.078 | 6.314 | 12.706 | 31.821 | 63.657 |
| 2 | 1.886 | 2.920 | 4.303 | 6.965 | 9.925 |
| 3 | 1.638 | 2.353 | 3.182 | 4.541 | 5.841 |
| 4 | 1.522 | 2.132 | 2.776 | 3.747 | 4.604 |
| 5 | 1.476 | 2.015 | 2.571 | 3.365 | 4.032 |
| 6 | 1.440 | 1.943 | 2.447 | 3.143 | 3.707 |
| 7 | 1.415 | 1.895 | 2.365 | 2.998 | 3.499 |
| 8 | 1.397 | 1.860 | 2.306 | 2.896 | 3.355 |
| 9 | 1.383 | 1.833 | 2.262 | 2.821 | 3.250 |
| 10 | 1.372 | 1.812 | 2.228 | 2.764 | 3.169 |
| 11 | 1.363 | 1.796 | 2.201 | 2.718 | 3.106 |
| 12 | 1.356 | 1.782 | 2.179 | 2.681 | 3.055 |
| 13 | 1.350 | 1.771 | 2.160 | 2.650 | 3.012 |
| 14 | 1.345 | 1.761 | 2.145 | 2.624 | 2.977 |
| 15 | 1.341 | 1.753 | 2.131 | 2.602 | 2.947 |
| 16 | 1.337 | 1.746 | 2.120 | 2.583 | 2.921 |
| 17 | 1.333 | 1.740 | 2.110 | 2.567 | 2.898 |
| 18 | 1.330 | 1.734 | 2.101 | 2.552 | 2.878 |
| 19 | 1.328 | 1.729 | 2.093 | 2.539 | 2.861 |
| 20 | 1.325 | 1.725 | 2.086 | 2.528 | 2.845 |
| 21 | 1.323 | 1.721 | 2.080 | 2.518 | 2.831 |
| 22 | 1.321 | 1.717 | 2.074 | 2.508 | 2.819 |
| 23 | 1.319 | 1.714 | 2.069 | 2.500 | 2.807 |
| 24 | 1.318 | 1.711 | 2.064 | 2.492 | 2.797 |
| 25 | 1.316 | 1.708 | 2.060 | 2.485 | 2.787 |
| 30 | 1.310 | 1.697 | 2.042 | 2.457 | 2.750 |
| 40 | 1.303 | 1.684 | 2.021 | 2.423 | 2.704 |
| $\infty$ | 1.282 | 1.645 | 1.960 | 2.326 | 2.576 |

# MATRIX MANIPULATIONS

## B.1 DEFINITIONS OF MATRICES AND VECTORS

*Definition:* A *matrix* is a rectangular array of elements.

*Definition:* A *vector* is a matrix consisting of only one row or one column of elements.

**Examples**

The array

$$A = \begin{bmatrix} 2 & -3 \\ 4 & 6 \\ 5 & 7 \end{bmatrix}$$

is a *matrix* with three rows and two columns, a type referred to as a "3 × 2 matrix." The matrix

$$B = \begin{bmatrix} 4 & 2 \\ 7 & -3 \end{bmatrix}$$

is a 2 × 2 matrix, or a square matrix of order 2.

The matrix
$$C = \begin{bmatrix} 2 & -3 & 5 \\ 4 & 8 & 6 \end{bmatrix}$$

with two rows and three columns, is a $2 \times 3$ matrix, and matrices $D$ and $E$ are also *vectors*, since $D$ has only one row and $E$ has only one column.

$$D = (5, 3, -2) \qquad E = \begin{bmatrix} 6 \\ 3 \end{bmatrix}$$

## B.2 ADDING MATRICES

Matrices that are the *same size* may be *added* together to form another matrix of that size. To be the same size, the matrices being added must have the same number of rows and the same number of columns. The addition is done by simply adding corresponding elements of the two arrays.

**Examples**

Let

$$A = \begin{bmatrix} 2 & -3 \\ 4 & 6 \\ 5 & 7 \end{bmatrix} \quad \text{and} \quad B = \begin{bmatrix} -1 & 8 \\ -6 & -5 \\ 7 & 2 \end{bmatrix}$$

Then
$$A + B = \begin{bmatrix} 2 & -3 \\ 4 & 6 \\ 5 & 7 \end{bmatrix} + \begin{bmatrix} -1 & 8 \\ -6 & -5 \\ 7 & 2 \end{bmatrix}$$

$$= \begin{bmatrix} 2 + (-1) & -3 + 8 \\ 4 + (-6) & 6 + (-5) \\ 5 + 7 & 7 + 2 \end{bmatrix} = \begin{bmatrix} 1 & 5 \\ -2 & 1 \\ 12 & 9 \end{bmatrix}$$

Vectors may also be added using the same rule; this should be obvious, since a vector is also a matrix. Let

$$C = (8, 7, -2, 1) \quad \text{and} \quad D = (-3, 0, 4, -2)$$

two vectors of the same size. Then

$$C + D = (8, 7, -2, 1) + (-3, 0, 4, -2)$$
$$= (8 - 3, 7 + 0, -2 + 4, 1 - 2)$$
$$= (5, 7, 2, -1)$$

## B.3 MULTIPLYING MATRICES

Two matrices may be multiplied only if they are *conformable* for multiplication. Matrices are conformable for multiplication if the number of columns in the left-hand matrix equals the number of rows in the right-hand matrix.

Once we know that two matrices are conformable, we still need a rule for multiplying them. The easiest way to remember how to calculate the elements in a product matrix is to use the so-called two-finger rule. It is:

> To find the element in the *i*th row and *j*th column of a product of two matrices, move the index finger of your left hand *along* row *i* in the left-hand matrix and move the index finger of your right hand *down* column *j* in the right-hand matrix. Multiply corresponding left-hand and right-hand elements as they are encountered, adding up the products so produced.

**Example**

Let

$$A = \begin{bmatrix} 2 & 3 & 5 \\ 4 & 6 & 1 \end{bmatrix} \quad \text{and} \quad B = \begin{bmatrix} -2 & 5 \\ 3 & 1 \\ 4 & 2 \end{bmatrix}$$

Here the matrices $A$ and $B$ are conformable for multiplication in the order $AB$ since $A$ has three columns and $B$ has three rows. The product matrix $AB$ will have as many rows as the left matrix and as many columns as the right matrix, or in this case $AB$ will be a $2 \times 2$ square matrix. Applying the two-finger rule, we get

$$AB = \begin{bmatrix} 2 & 3 & 5 \\ 4 & 6 & 1 \end{bmatrix} \begin{bmatrix} -2 & 5 \\ 3 & 1 \\ 4 & 2 \end{bmatrix}$$

$$= \begin{bmatrix} (2)(-2) + (3)(3) + (5)(4) & (2)(5) + (3)(1) + (5)(2) \\ (4)(-2) + (6)(3) + (1)(4) & (4)(5) + (6)(1) + (1)(2) \end{bmatrix}$$

$$= \begin{bmatrix} 25 & 23 \\ 14 & 28 \end{bmatrix}$$

## B.4 IDENTITY AND INVERSE MATRICES

*Definition:* An *identity* matrix is a square matrix with ones on its main diagonal and zeros everywhere else.

**Examples**

$$I_2 = \begin{bmatrix} 1 & 0 \\ 0 & 1 \end{bmatrix}$$

is an identity matrix of order 2, and

$$I_3 = \begin{bmatrix} 1 & 0 & 0 \\ 0 & 1 & 0 \\ 0 & 0 & 1 \end{bmatrix}$$

is an identity matrix of order 3.

*Definition:* If $A$ is a square matrix of order $n$, then the *inverse* of $A$, denoted by $A^{-1}$, is a square matrix of order $n$ such that

$$AA^{-1} = A^{-1}A = I_n$$

**Example**

Let

$$A = \begin{bmatrix} -2 & 5 \\ 3 & 4 \end{bmatrix}$$

Then

$$A^{-1} = \begin{bmatrix} -\frac{4}{23} & \frac{5}{23} \\ \frac{3}{23} & \frac{2}{23} \end{bmatrix}$$

is the inverse of $A$, since

$$AA^{-1} = \begin{bmatrix} -2 & 5 \\ 3 & 4 \end{bmatrix} \begin{bmatrix} -\frac{4}{23} & \frac{5}{23} \\ \frac{3}{23} & \frac{2}{23} \end{bmatrix}$$

$$= \begin{bmatrix} (8 + 15)/23 & (-10 + 10)/23 \\ (-12 + 12)/23 & (15 + 8)/23 \end{bmatrix} = \begin{bmatrix} 1 & 0 \\ 0 & 1 \end{bmatrix}$$

There are many procedures for matrix inversion, but no information on how to obtain the inverse of a matrix is needed here. For the problems in this text you only need to know what an inverse matrix is, not how to obtain one.

# ANSWERS TO SELECTED EXERCISES

## Chapter 2

**2.2** Let $x_1$ = number of yellow squidgets to make

$x_2$ = number of thin squidgets to make

$x_3$ = number of smooth squidgets to make

Maximize $P$

where $\qquad P = 3x_1 + 6x_2 + 10x_3$

subject to $\qquad 8x_1 + 6x_2 + 4x_3 \leq 24{,}000$

$\qquad\qquad 10x_1 + 7x_2 + 3x_3 \leq 30{,}000$

$\qquad\qquad 4x_1 + 8x_2 + 12x_3 \leq 50{,}000$

$\qquad\qquad x_1, x_2, x_3 \geq 0$

**2.3 a** Let $x_1$ = number of Little Giant traps to produce

$x_2$ = number of Giant Little traps to produce

Maximize $P$

where
$$P = 2x_1 + 5x_2$$

subject to
$$0.2x_1 + 0.4x_2 \leq 400$$
$$1.0x_1 + 1.2x_2 \leq 1,200$$
$$0.1x_1 + 0.2x_2 \leq 150$$
$$x_2 \geq 300$$
$$x_1, x_2 \geq 0$$

**b** One redundant constraint is $x_2 \geq 0$, since we also require $x_2 \geq 300$. But one other constraint is redundant; see if you can find it.

**2.7** Let $x_1$ = number of type $A$ parts to produce per hour

$x_2$ = number of type $B$ parts to produce per hour

$x_3$ = number of type $C$ parts to produce per hour

Profit must allow not only for the cost of the casting, but for the cost of drilling, shaping, and polishing. Since 25 type $A$ parts per hour can be run on the drilling machine, at a cost of \$20, then \$20/25 = \$0.80 is the drilling cost per type $A$ part. Similar reasoning for shaping and polishing gives

Profit per type $A$ part = \$8 − \$5 − \$0.80 − \$1.20 − \$0.75 = \$0.25

On the drilling machine, one type $A$ part consumes one twenty-fifth of the available hour, a type $B$ part consumes one fortieth, and a type $C$ part consumes one twenty-fifth of an hour. Thus the drilling-machine constraint is

$$\frac{x_1}{25} + \frac{x_2}{40} + \frac{x_3}{25} \leq 1$$

The model is

Maximize $P$

where
$$P = 0.25x_1 + 1.00x_2 + 0.95x_3$$

subject to
$$\frac{x_1}{25} + \frac{x_2}{40} + \frac{x_3}{25} \leq 1$$

$$\frac{x_1}{25} + \frac{x_2}{20} + \frac{x_3}{20} \leq 1$$

$$\frac{x_1}{40} + \frac{x_2}{30} + \frac{x_3}{40} \leq 1$$

$$x_1, x_2, x_3 \geq 0$$

**2.8 a** Let $x_1, x_2, x_3, x_4, x_5$ be, respectively, the number of pounds of types $A$, $B$, $C$, $D$, and $E$ chocolates to buy.

Minimize $K$

where

$$K = 0.8x_1 + 1.0x_2 + 1.5x_3 + 1.2x_4 + 1.8x_5$$

subject to

$$0.6x_1 + 0.6x_2 - 0.4x_3 - 0.4x_4 - 0.4x_5 \geq 0$$

$$-0.3x_1 - 0.3x_2 - 0.3x_3 + 0.7x_4 + 0.7x_5 \leq 0$$

$$-x_1 - x_2 - x_3 - x_4 + 15x_5 \geq 0$$

$$x_1 + x_2 + x_3 + x_4 + x_5 \geq 600$$

$$x_1, x_2, x_3, x_4, x_5 \geq 0$$

**2.9 a** Let $x_1, x_2, x_3, x_4, x_5$ be the number of dollars to invest in areas 1, 2, 3, 4, 5, respectively.

Maximize $Y$

where

$$Y = 0.1x_1 + 0.2x_2 + 0.3x_3 + 0.4x_4 + 0.5x_5$$

subject to

$$x_1 + x_2 + x_3 + x_4 + x_5 \leq 1{,}000{,}000$$

$$x_1 + x_2 + x_3 \geq 250{,}000$$

$$x_1 - x_2 - x_3 \geq 0$$

$$-x_3 + x_4 \leq 0$$

$$-x_1 \qquad -x_4 + x_5 \leq 0$$

$$x_1 \geq 200{,}000$$

$$x_1, x_2, x_3, x_4, x_5 \geq 0$$

**2.10** Let $i = 1$ correspond to Goodstone and $i = 2$ correspond to Fireyear, and let $j = 1, 2, 3, 4$ correspond to Bosler, Federal, Woods Landing, and Buford, respectively. Let $x_{ij}$ = number of tires to order from company $i$ for shipment to terminal $j$.

Minimize $C$

where

$$C = 70x_{11} + 74x_{12} + 62x_{13} + 62x_{14} + 64x_{21} + 62x_{22} + 68x_{23} + 72x_{24}$$

subject to

$$x_{11} + x_{12} + x_{13} + x_{14} \leq 16{,}000$$

$$x_{21} + x_{22} + x_{23} + x_{24} \leq 8{,}000$$

$$x_{11} + x_{21} = 4{,}000$$

$$x_{12} + x_{22} = 8{,}000$$

$$x_{13} + x_{23} = 3{,}000$$

$$x_{14} + x_{24} = 5{,}000$$

$$x_{ij} \geq 0, \ i = 1, 2; \ j = 1, 2, 3, 4$$

**2.14** Let $x_1$, $x_2$, $x_3$, $x_4$, $x_5$, $x_6$ be the number of long tables, short tables, long benches, short benches, armchairs, and folding chairs to make during the month.

$$\text{Maximize } P$$

where

$$P = 50x_1 + 35x_2 + 25x_3 + 20x_4 + 45x_5 + 15x_6$$

subject to

$$10x_1 + 6x_2 + 6x_3 + 4x_4 + 7x_5 + 3x_6 \le 3{,}000$$
$$8x_1 + 5x_2 + 3x_3 + 2x_4 + 4x_5 + x_6 \le 2{,}000$$
$$6x_1 + 4x_2 + 2x_3 + 4x_4 + 4x_5 \le 1{,}800$$
$$4x_1 + 6x_2 + 6x_3 + 4x_6 \le 1{,}400$$
$$20x_1 + 14x_2 + 12x_3 + 10x_4 + 12x_5 + 8x_6 \le 4{,}000$$
$$8x_1 + 4x_2 + 5x_3 + 3x_4 + 8x_5 + 6x_6 \le 2{,}400$$
$$x_2 \ge 10$$
$$x_4 \ge 20$$
$$x_5 \le 50$$
$$x_1, x_2, x_3, x_4, x_5, x_6 \ge 0$$

**2.16** Let $x_1$, $x_2$, $x_3$, $x_4$, $x_5$, $x_6$ be the number of dollars allocated to home, industrial, commercial, auto, otherwise secured, and unsecured loans, respectively.

$$\text{Maximize } I$$

where

$$I = 0.14x_1 + 0.15x_2 + 0.17x_3 + 0.18x_4 + 0.20x_5 + 0.22x_6$$

subject to

$$x_1 + x_2 + x_3 + x_4 + x_5 + x_6 = 20{,}000{,}000$$
$$x_6 \le 3{,}000{,}000$$
$$x_1 + x_2 + x_3 \ge 10{,}000{,}000$$
$$x_3 + x_4 + x_5 \le 12{,}000{,}000$$
$$x_1, x_2, x_3, x_4, x_5, x_6 \ge 0$$

**2.18** Let $x_1$, $x_2$, $x_3$, $x_4$, $x_5$ be, respectively, the fraction of a pound of Phoenician, Greek, Etruscan, Assyrian, and Egyptian bronzes that should make up a pound of blend.

$$\text{Minimize } V$$

where

$$V = 20x_1 + 14x_2 + 10x_3 + 16x_4 + 18x_5$$

subject to

$$x_1 + x_2 + x_3 + x_4 + x_5 = 1$$
$$0.95x_1 + 0.60x_2 + 0.50x_3 + 0.70x_4 + 0.80x_5 = 0.70$$
$$0.04x_1 + 0.30x_2 + 0.30x_3 + 0.10x_4 + 0.05x_5 = 0.16$$
$$0.01x_1 + 0.05x_2 + 0.15x_3 + 0.15x_4 + 0.05x_5 = 0.10$$
$$0.05x_2 + 0.05x_3 + 0.05x_4 + 0.10x_5 = 0.04$$
$$x_1, x_2, x_3, x_4, x_5 \ge 0$$

(Note that the first constraint is redundant, since it is equivalent to the sum of the last four constraints.)

# Chapter 3

**3.1** Max $Z = 3$ at $(x_1, x_2) = (0, 3)$

**3.3** Max $P = 16$ at $(x, y) = (4, 4)$

**3.4** Min $C = \frac{310}{3}$ at $(A, B) = (5, \frac{8}{3})$

**3.7** Make 60 type $A$ belts and 100 type $B$ belts for maximum daily profit of $135.

**3.10** Make $166\frac{2}{3}$ Plain toasters and $66\frac{2}{3}$ Gaudy toasters for maximum daily profit of $1,366.67.

**3.12 a** No. The optimal $(x, y)$ is still $(4, 4)$, but of course now Max $P = 20$ instead of 16.
  **b** Max $P = 12$ at either $(x, y) = (4, 4)$ or $(x, y) = (\frac{80}{9}, \frac{14}{9})$.
  **c** Max $P = \frac{94}{9}$ at $(x, y) = (\frac{80}{9}, \frac{14}{9})$.
  **d** The coefficient of $y$ can range from 2 to *any* larger positive value without changing the fact that the optimal solution occurs at $(x, y) = (4, 4)$. The value of $P$ increases by 4 per unit increase in the coefficient of $y$.

**3.14** Make 2,250 square feet of laminate 1 and 1,500 square feet of laminate 2 for maximum profit of $12,750 for the production period.

**3.17** Alternate optimal solutions occur at $(x_1, x_2) = (\frac{500}{3}, \frac{200}{3})$ and at $(x_1, x_2) = (\frac{2000}{9}, \frac{200}{9})$, with Max $P = \$1,000$. An optimal integer solution occurs at $(x_1, x_2) = (200, 40)$.

**3.19** If $x_1$ = number of pounds of Family Mix and $x_2$ = number of pounds of Party Mix, her objective function should be $P = 0.75x_1 + 1.06x_2$. She should offer 3,000 pounds of Family Mix and 2,500 pounds of Party Mix per week, for maximum profit of $4,900.
  This solution would consume all the available pecans and cashews, but she would still have 500 pounds of peanuts available (that she cannot use). So more available pecans would be to her advantage, but not more peanuts.

**3.21** Max $Z = 15$ at $(x_1, x_2, x_3) = (0, 0, 5)$

**3.23** Universal Furniture Outlets should make no yellow squidgets, no thin squidgets, and $4,166\frac{2}{3}$ smooth squidgets, for maximum profit of $41,666.67.

**3.25** Max $P = \$570$ at $(X_A, X_B, X_C, X_D) = (0, 45, 0, 20)$

**Chapter 4**

| 4.1 Basic | Z | $x_1$ | $x_2$ | $x_3$ | $S_1$ | $S_2$ | Solution | Ratio |
|---|---|---|---|---|---|---|---|---|
| Z | 1 | $-1$ | $-2$ | $-3$ ↓ | 0 | 0 | 0 | |
| $S_1$ | 0 | 2 | 1 | 4 | 1 | 0 | 32 | 8 |
| ← $S_2$ | 0 | 3 | 2 | (5) | 0 | 1 | 30 | 6 ← |
| Z | 1 | $\frac{4}{5}$ | $-\frac{4}{5}$ ↓ | 0 | 0 | $\frac{3}{5}$ | 18 | |
| $S_1$ | 0 | $-\frac{2}{5}$ | $-\frac{3}{5}$ | 0 | 1 | $-\frac{4}{5}$ | 8 | 40 |
| ← $x_3$ | 0 | $\frac{3}{5}$ | $(\frac{2}{5})$ | 1 | 0 | $\frac{1}{5}$ | 6 | 15 ← |
| Z | 1 | 2 | 0 | 2 | 0 | 1 | 30 Optimal | |
| $S_1$ | 0 | $\frac{1}{2}$ | 0 | $\frac{3}{2}$ | 1 | $-\frac{1}{2}$ | 17 | |
| $x_2$ | 0 | $\frac{3}{2}$ | 1 | $\frac{5}{2}$ | 0 | $\frac{1}{2}$ | 15 | |

Max $Z = 30$ at $(x_1, x_2, x_3) = (0, 15, 0)$. There remain 17 units of slack in the first constraint, but since $S_2 = 0$ (nonbasic), there is no slack in the second constraint.

**4.3** Make no product A, 800 units of product B, and 440 units of product C for maximum profit of $7,520. No slack remains in either constraint at optimality. Three simplex tableaus, including the initial tableau, are required.

**4.4** Same answer as that given for Exercise 3.23.

**4.5** Make no product I, 120 units of product II, and 1,560 units of product III for maximum profit of $4,920. Solution obtained in three tableaus, including initial. (Don't forget to convert hours to minutes in right-hand sides of constraints—or minutes to hours on the left.)

**4.6** Same answer as that given for Exercise 3.14.

**4.8** Same answer as that given for Exercise 3.10.

**4.12** Justin should invest $200,000 in area 1, nothing in area 2, $200,000 in area 3, $200,000 in area 4, and $400,000 in area 5, for maximum yield of $360,000.

**4.13** Same answer as that given for Exercise 3.4

**4.14** Purchase 0.75 pound of $F_1$, 4.25 pounds of $F_2$, and no $F_3$, at minimum cost of $3.78 (strictly, $3.775).

**4.16** Max $Z = 24$ at $(x_1, x_2, x_3)$ of either $(12, 0, 0)$, $(0, 4, 0)$, or $(0, 0, 6)$. These are three alternate optimal basic feasible solutions. Note that slack in the second constraint is different for each solution.

**4.17** Problem has three alternate optimal basic feasible solutions: $(\frac{60}{7}, 0, \frac{36}{7})$, $(\frac{48}{5}, \frac{36}{5}, 0)$, and $(15, 0, 0)$. Max $Z = 120$.

**4.19** The problem has an unbounded solution. The variable $x_2$ can be increased indefinitely without violating the constraints.

**4.20** No feasible solution. "Optimal" tableau still has a nonzero artificial variable in the basis. ($c_j - z_j$ approach recommended.)

**4.23** Max $Z = 20$ at $(x_1, x_2) = (-10, 0)$

**4.25** Min $Z = -18$ at $(x_1, x_2) = (9, 0)$

**4.26** The feed company should prepare 300 tons of Standard feed, 500 tons of Special feed, and 200 tons of Super feed, thus filling the 1,000-ton order at a minimum cost of $164,000. (Four tableaus, using $c_j - z_j$ approach.)

**4.29** Dealer should order no S125 bikes, 50.851 S175 bikes, and 58.468 S250 bikes, for maximum gross profit of $55,421.28. (He would probably order 51 S175s and 58 S250s.)

**4.32** Produce 166.67 Plain toasters and 66.67 Gaudy toasters. Neither goal is achieved. Profit goal is underachieved by $33.33, and work-force goal is underachieved by 5.33 persons.

## Chapter 5

**5.1** Let $y_1 =$ implicit value in cents of one ounce of aluminum

$\qquad y_2 =$ implicit value in cents of one square inch of cardboard

$\qquad y_3 =$ implicit value in cents of one minute

Minimize Y

where $\qquad Y = 1,200y_1 + 32,000y_2 + 7,200y_3$

subject to
$$0.5y_1 + 10y_2 + 0.1y_3 \geq 0.5$$
$$0.8y_1 + 12y_2 + 0.2y_3 \geq 0.7$$
$$y_1 + 16y_2 + 0.2y_3 \geq 0.8$$
$$y_1, y_2, y_3 \geq 0$$

**5.2** Maximum profit is 1,200 cents ($12), achieved by making 2,400 type $A$ containers (no type $B$ and no type $C$). The implicit value of an ounce of aluminum is one cent, while a square inch of cardboard and a minute each have zero implicit value.

**5.5** The dual of the diet problem is a maximization problem with three "less-than-or-equal" constraints, so that only slack variables are involved (no artificial variables). Four tableaus are required. In the optimal $Z$ row, under $S_1$, $S_2$, $S_3$, we find $\frac{3}{4}$, $\frac{17}{4}$, and 0. Thus we should buy 0.75 pound of $F_1$ and 4.25 pounds of $F_2$ (no $F_3$) to achieve dietary requirements at a minimum cost of $3.775.

**5.7** Flour, sugar, and salt all have zero implicit values; so no ingredients should be purchased. An hour of mixing and baking time has implicit value of $0.50, and a minute of decorating time has implicit value \$0.15. Thus an hour of decorating time is worth \$9.00. So the bakery should hire more decorators at \$1.00 per hour.

**5.9**

$$\text{Minimize } Y$$

where

$$Y = 1{,}000y_1 + 50y_2$$

subject to

$$20y_1 + y_2 \geq 100$$
$$10y_1 + y_2 \geq 70$$
$$5y_1 + y_2 \geq 30$$
$$y_1, y_2 \geq 0$$

**5.11**

$$\text{Minimize } Z$$

where

$$Z = 400x_1 - 800x_2 + 200x_3$$

subject to

$$x_1 - 2x_2 + x_3 \geq 6$$
$$x_1 - 3x_2 - 10x_3 = 1$$
$$x_1 + 4x_2 + 20x_3 \geq 200$$

$$x_1, x_2 \geq 0 \qquad x_3 \text{ unrestricted in sign}$$

**5.13 a** The amount of change can be between $-3{,}900$ minutes and 600 minutes.
**b** Max $Z = \$5{,}160$ at $(x_1, x_2, x_3) = (0, 60, 1{,}680)$

**5.15 a** Let $\delta_1$ be the change in machine $A$ availability and $\delta_2$ be the change in machine $B$ availability. Then

$$-4\delta_1 + \delta_2 \leq 15{,}600$$
$$2\delta_1 - 3\delta_2 \leq 1{,}200$$

**b** $\delta_1 = (-5)(60) = -300$, and $\delta_2 = (20)(60) = 1{,}200$. Yes, the current basic solution is still feasible. The new optimal solution is

$$\text{Max } Z = \$5{,}040 \text{ at } (x_1, x_2, x_3) = (0, 540, 1{,}320)$$

**5.17** Let $\delta_1$ be the change in the $x_1$ coefficient and $\delta_2$ be the change in the $x_2$ coefficient. Then

$$-1 \leq \delta_2 \leq 4$$
$$5\delta_1 - 4\delta_2 \leq 9$$

**5.19** The number of parts $A$ can change by an amount between $-112.5$ and 450, inclusive.

**5.21 a** $\delta \leq \frac{4}{9}$   **b** Max $Z = \$4{,}387.50$ at $(x_1, x_2, x_3, x_4) = (0, 0, 56.25, 12.5)$

**5.22** Between $-\$0.50$ and \$94, inclusive.

## Chapter 6

**6.1 a** Produce 2,250 square feet of laminate 1 and 1,500 square feet of laminate 2 for maximum profit of $12,750.
   **b** Maple and process I time are the scarce resources. Implicit value of one board foot of maple is $1.25 and of one hour of process I time is $0.25.

**6.3 b** $7,100    **c** 200    **d** 300

**6.4 b** Maximum profit is $318,000, obtained by producing 4,000 type 3 transistors by method $P$ in plant $A$, 10,000 type 1 transistors by method $P$ in plant $B$, and 5,000 type 2 transistors by method $Q$ in plant $B$.
   **c** Plant $C$ is not involved in production, and method $R$ is not used.

**6.6 b** Minimum cost is $657, obtained by purchasing 225 pounds of type $A$ chocolates, 180 pounds of type $B$, 60 pounds of type $C$, 60 pounds of type $D$, and 75 pounds of type $E$.
   **c** $A$: 37.5%, $B$: 30%, $C$: 10%, $D$: 10%, $E$: 12.5%    **d** Yes

**6.8 b** 12,000 from Goodstone; 8,000 from Fireyear.    **c** No
   **d** If we bring in a unit of slack (effectively, decrease $x_{22}$ from 8,000 to 7,999), we would increase cost by $12. ($x_{21}$ would increase by 1, thereby removing a $62 cost but adding in $74.)

**6.11** Assign the Red crew to board 2, the White crew to board 4, the Blue crew to board 3, and the Mauve crew to board 1. The minimum total expected crew hours are 37.

**6.12** Assign Brown to client 1, Greene to client 4, White to client 2, Black to client 3. Minimum estimated cost is $835.

**6.14 c** 76.8 percent    **d** Mechanic time; $4.25
   **e** 105 cubic feet of storage and 214 hours of sales time could be diverted to other uses without affecting net profit on the three types of motorcycles.

**6.15 a** $200,000 in area 1, nothing in area 2, $200,000 in area 3, $200,000 in area 4, $400,000 in area 5. Rate of return is 36 percent.
   **b** It would be redundant; X1 .GE. 200000 is already included.
   **c** It is really the value of a surplus variable; $150,000 more than the required $250,000 was put into areas 1, 2, and 3.

**6.18 b** Produce 400 engines in July, 1,200 in August, 2,100 in September, and 200 in October.
   **c** 0 at end of July, 0 at end of August, 600 at end of September, 0 at end of October.
   **d** $290,100

## Chapter 7

**7.1** Max $Z = 15$ at $(x_1, x_2) = (0, 3)$

**7.2** Max $Z = 15$ at $(x_1, x_2) = (3, 0)$

**7.5** $x_{11} = 50$, $x_{12} = 150$, $x_{13} = 100$, $x_{21} = 200$, $x_{22} = 0$, $x_{23} = 0$.  Minimum cost = 4,200.

**7.7** VAM solution is optimal.  Minimum cost = 27,480.  $x_{11} = 250$, $x_{12} = 110$, $x_{13} = 140$, $x_{23} = 180$, $x_{32} = 250$, $x_{34} = 170$; all other $x_{ij}$'s are zero.

**7.9** Order 4,000 for Bosler from Goodstone, 8,000 for Federal from Fireyear, 3,000 for Woods Landing from Goodstone, 5,000 for Buford from Goodstone.

**7.10** Produce: 200 units at plant *A* for shipment to warehouse 2
100 units at plant *B* for shipment to warehouse 1
100 units at plant *B* for shipment to warehouse 2
300 units at plant *C* for shipment to warehouse 1
for maximum profit of $7,100.

**7.11** Allocate 8 high school dropouts to firm *A*, 7 high school graduates to firm *B*, 8 high school graduates to firm *C*, 3 college dropouts to firm *B*, and 12 college dropouts to firm *D*.  Minimum subsidy is $389,000.

**7.14** Two alternate optimal solutions exist, each giving minimum cost of $1,980:

*Solution 1:* 20 units of *C* and 80 units of *D* on line 1, 50 units of *A* and 100 units of *B* on line 2, and 50 units of *C* on line 3
*Solution 2:* 80 units of *D* on line 1, 50 units of *A* and 100 units of *B* on line 2, and 70 units of *C* on line 3

**7.18** Same answer as that given for Exercise 6.11.

**7.19** Refer to Figure 6.7.

**7.20** Assign Brown to client 1, Greene to client 3, White to client 4, Black to client 2.  Minimum time is 63 hours.

**7.21** Same answer as that given for Exercise 6.12.

## Chapter 8

**8.1 a** $\frac{3}{10}$    **b** $\frac{8}{10}$

**8.2** $\frac{10}{11}$

**8.4** No.  The sum of the probabilities for the three mutually exclusive events is $\frac{77}{60}$, more than unity.

**8.7 a** 0.6    **b** 0.7    **c** 0.6    **d** 0.9    **e** 0.4

**8.8** 0.08

**8.11** No.  $P(A|B) = 0.75 \neq 0.60 = P(A)$, or $P(B|A) = 0.25 \neq 0.20 = P(B)$.

**8.12 a** 0.04    **b** 0.54    **c** 0.42

**8.14** $\frac{8}{27}$

**8.15 a** 0.87    **b** 0.80    **c** 0.75

**d**

| $r$ | 0 | 1 | 2 | 3 | 4 | 5 | 6 |
|---|---|---|---|---|---|---|---|
| $F(r)$ | 0.10 | 0.25 | 0.50 | 0.80 | 0.90 | 0.97 | 1.00 |

**e** 2.48    **f** 2.1296

**8.17 a** 0.65    **b** 0.45    **c** 0.60

**d**

| $y$ | 2 | 3 | 5 | 8 | 9 | 10 |
|---|---|---|---|---|---|---|
| $p(y)$ | 0.05 | 0.25 | 0.15 | 0.20 | 0.25 | 0.10 |

**e** 6.45    **f** 2.7654

**8.19 a** $19,000

   **b** If many such franchises were to be opened, and if this year's experience is like last year's, the average annual profit per franchise will be near $19,000.

**8.21 a** 0.98253    **b** 0.81173    **c** 0.56155    **d** 0.18944    **e** 0.09780

**8.22 a** 0.23688    **b** 0.09781    **c** 0.61618

**8.24 a** 6.25    **b** 0.07133

**8.26** 0.05734

**8.29 a** 0.10565    **b** 0.2535

**8.30 a** 3.236 percent    **b** 0.01618

# Chapter 9

**9.2 a** $S_3$; maximax payoff = $150    **c** $S_3$; minimax regret = $80
   **b** $S_1$; maximin payoff = $40    **d** $S_3$; maximum expected payoff = $55

**9.4** $S_2$; expected casualties are 10,000 fewer using $S_2$.

**9.5** $P = 0.75$

**9.7 a** Yes.  Bid $2.20 per whimmer and use a type $X$ machine.  If you win the bid, you lose $2,500.
   **b** Bid $2.50 per whimmer.  Purchase type $Y$ machine.  Expected payoff = $8,333.

**9.8** EVPI = $40

**9.10 b** $S_3$    **c** \$62,500

**9.11** $P(W|X) = \frac{3}{17}$, $P(L|X) = \frac{14}{17}$.  Use strategy $S_1$.

**9.13** Wife replies "Seal," for maximum expected payoff of $\frac{7}{44}$ of an hour.

**9.15 a** Maintenance
   **b** Yes.  Subcontracting is new (conditional) minimum-risk strategy.

**9.17 a** Subcontracting    **b** New plant    **c** Subcontracting

**9.18** EVPI = \$236,500

**9.20** If stall 1 tomatoes are good or fair, buy them.  If stall 1 tomatoes are bad, buy stall 2 tomatoes.

**9.21** \$74.80

**9.22** $P(\text{good}) = 0.58$, $P(\text{fair}) = 0.36$, $P(\text{bad}) = 0.06$

**9.25** Drilling deeper.  Expected annual profit is \$6,750.

**9.27 a** A risk seeker.

**9.28** $S_1$; maximum expected utility is approximately 0.42.

# Chapter 10

**10.1 a** Sample: 2,4  2,6  2,8  2,10  4,6  4,8  4,10  6,8  6,10  8,10

$\bar{x}$: 3    4    5    6    5    6    7    7    8    9

| $\bar{x}$ | 3 | 4 | 5 | 6 | 7 | 8 | 9 |
|-----------|-----|-----|-----|-----|-----|-----|-----|
| $p(\bar{x})$ | 0.1 | 0.1 | 0.2 | 0.2 | 0.2 | 0.1 | 0.1 |

**b** $\mu = (2 + 4 + 6 + 8 + 10)/5 = 6$

$E(\bar{x}) = 3(0.1) + 4(0.1) + 5(0.2) + 6(0.2) + 7(0.2) + 8(0.1) + 9(0.1) = 6$

**c** $\sigma^2 = \frac{1}{5}\{(2 - 6)^2 + (4 - 6)^2 + (6 - 6)^2 + (8 - 6)^2 + (10 - 6)^2\} = 8$

$\sigma^2_{\bar{x}} = (3 - 6)^2(0.1) + (4 - 6)^2(0.1) + (5 - 6)^2(0.2) + (6 - 6)^2(0.2)$
$\quad + (7 - 6)^2(0.2) + (8 - 6)^2(0.1) + (9 - 6)^2(0.1)$

$\quad = 3 < 8$

**d** 0.8    **e** 0.2

**10.4 a**

| $s^2$ | 0 | 2 | 8 | 16 | 32 |
|-------|------|------|------|------|------|
| $p(s^2)$ | 0.20 | 0.32 | 0.24 | 0.16 | 0.08 |

**b** $E(s^2) = 0(0.2) + 2(0.32) + 8(0.24) + 18(0.16) + 32(0.08) = 8 = \sigma^2$

**10.6 a** 0.84134     **b** 0.06681     **c** 0.81859     **d** 0.04947     **e** 0.01242

**10.7 a** 1.00     **b** $-1.00$     **c** $-2.33$     **d** 1.96

**10.8 a** 0.5000     **b** 0.68268     **c** 0.00621     **d** 46.08

**10.10** 0.90704

**10.13** $n = 97$

**10.15** \$14,380 to \$15,620

**10.17 a** 0.09944     **b** 0.29638

**10.18 a** 0.41484     **b** 0.58516     **c** 0.37889     **d** 0.91205     **e** 0.16861

**10.19 a** 0.075     **b** 0.0385 to 0.1115

**10.21** $n = 292$

**10.22** 0.72879

**10.25** $n = 274$

**10.27** $Pr(p = 0.10|y = 18) = 0.0417$
$Pr(p = 0.20|y = 18) = 0.6983$
$Pr(p = 0.30|y = 18) = 0.2600$     Select strategy $S_1$.

**10.29 a** $\hat{y} = -42.7 + 55.8x$     **b** 6.662     **d** 5.4 to 8.5     **e** 0 to 9.8

**10.30 b** $\hat{y} = 9.03 + 2.99x$     **c** 13.24     **d** 68.8     **e** 59.3 to 78.3

**10.33 b** $\hat{y} = 52.8 - 0.007x_2$ and $\hat{\sigma}^2 = 40.46$
    **d** Since R-SQUARED for the full model (Exercise 10.32) is 96.3 percent, the proportion of explained $Y$ variation is increased by 31.6 percent when speed is included. We should have a much better predicting equation if both speed and weight are used.

**10.35 c** \$11,764 to \$37,422

**10.36** $\hat{y} = 11.0 + 1.48x_1 - 1.18x_2$. Prediction interval: \$17,118 to \$32,162

**10.38**

| Year | Quarter | Centered average | Year | Quarter | Centered average |
|------|---------|------------------|------|---------|------------------|
| 1978 | 1 | — | 1981 | 1 | 60.78 |
|      | 2 | — |      | 2 | 62.98 |
|      | 3 | 39.68 |      | 3 | 66.28 |
|      | 4 | 40.80 |      | 4 | 68.52 |
| 1979 | 1 | 42.14 | 1982 | 1 | 68.83 |
|      | 2 | 42.96 |      | 2 | 67.88 |
|      | 3 | 44.04 |      | 3 | — |
|      | 4 | 47.20 |      | 4 | — |
| 1980 | 1 | 50.70 |      |   |   |
|      | 2 | 54.17 |      |   |   |
|      | 3 | 57.42 |      |   |   |
|      | 4 | 59.33 |      |   |   |

**10.42** $\hat{y}_t = 9.91 + 0.827y_{t-1}$

| Year | Quarter | Forecast | Year | Quarter | Forecast |
|------|---------|----------|------|---------|----------|
| 1981 | 1 | 57.50 | 1982 | 1 | 66.78 |
|      | 2 | 58.37 |      | 2 | 70.97 |
|      | 3 | 62.95 |      | 3 | 65.12 |
|      | 4 | 64.50 |      | 4 | 64.41 |

## Chapter 11

**11.1** Order 100 items every 5 days.

**11.3** Order 141.42 crystal balls every 14.14 weeks, at an average cost per week of $282.84.

**11.5** **a** Order 150 recliners every three months.
**b** Four    **c** $1,500    **d** $93,000

**11.7** Order 200 recliners every four months.

**11.8** Optimal order quantity is 50 items.   Time between orders is 5 days.

**11.11** Start a production run every 18.6 days and produce 5,573 buttons per run.

**11.12** Start a production run when shortage is 15 balls, and stop production when inventory level reaches 240 balls.

**11.14** 90 years, 7 months, and 2 weeks.

**11.19** **a** Start a production run every 8.33 weeks and produce 66.67 tons per run.

**11.20** **a** 200 items    **b** $B = 77$ items

**c** Reorder 200 items when inventory level reaches the reorder point of 177 items.

**d** Two days

**11.22** Order 1,800 hot dogs, for maximum expected gross profit of $333.00.

**11.23** Order either 2,100 or 2,400 hot dogs, for maximum expected gross profit of $390.00 in either case.

**11.26** Order 700 cords, for maximum expected gross profit of $4,950.

**11.27 a** 4     **b** If $I = 2$, order 2.  If $I = 4$, order nothing.

## Chapter 12

**12.1** $1 \to 2 \to 6 \to 10 \to 12 \to 13$.  Cost of minimum-cost policy $= \$69$.

**12.3** $1 \to 3 \to 5 \to 7 \to 11 \to 13$.  Minimum travel time $= 32$ hours.

**12.5 a** Critical path: $1 \to 3 \to 4 \to 6 \to 9 \to 12 \to 15 \to 16$
Project duration: 29 weeks

    **b** There are three alternate critical paths:

        $1 \to 2 \to 5 \to 7 \to 11 \to 12 \to 15 \to 16$

        $1 \to 3 \to 4 \to 6 \to 10 \to 12 \to 15 \to 16$

        $1 \to 3 \to 4 \to 7 \to 11 \to 12 \to 15 \to 16$

    Project duration: 25 weeks

**12.6 a** Critical path: $1 \to 3 \to 4 \to 5 \to 6$
Length of critical path: 15

    **b** Critical path: $1 \to 2 \to 3 \to 4 \to 5 \to 6 \to 7 \to 8$
Length of critical path: 25

**12.7**

| Initial inventory | Number of units to produce | | | Minimum policy cost |
|---|---|---|---|---|
| | Period 1 | Period 2 | Period 3 | |
| 0 | 3 | 3 | 3 | $69 |
| 1 | 4 | 4 | 0 | $62 |
| 2 | 4 | 0 | 3 | $55 |
| 3 | 0 | 3 | 3 | $46 |

**12.8**

| Initial inventory | Number of units to produce | | | | Minimum policy cost |
|---|---|---|---|---|---|
| | Period 1 | Period 2 | Period 3 | Period 4 | |
| 0 | 4 | 4 | 4 | 0 | $92 |
| 1 | 4 | 4 | 0 | 3 | $85 |
| 2 | 4 | 0 | 3 | 3 | $78 |
| 3 | 0 | 3 | 3 | 3 | $69 |

**12.9** No. None of the three-period production policies change, although the associated minimum costs are higher, of course.

**12.10** Yes. Policies for initial inventories of one and two units change. Every optimal policy involves no ending inventory in any period. Here the ratio of setup cost to holding cost is low, resulting in a "production on demand" policy.

**12.12 a**

| | Initial inventory | Number of units to produce | | | | | Minimum policy cost |
|---|---|---|---|---|---|---|---|
| | | Period 1 | Period 2 | Period 3 | Period 4 | Period 5 | |
| Alternate optima { | 0 | 3 | 4 | 4 | 4 | 0 | $113 |
| | 0 | 4 | 4 | 4 | 0 | 3 | $113 |
| | 1 | 4 | 4 | 0 | 3 | 3 | $108 |
| | 2 | 4 | 0 | 3 | 3 | 3 | $101 |
| | 3 | 0 | 4 | 4 | 4 | 0 | $ 90 |

**12.14**

| Initial inventory | Number of units to produce | | | | Minimum policy cost |
|---|---|---|---|---|---|
| | Period 1 | Period 2 | Period 3 | Period 4 | |
| 0 | 5 | 0 | 3 | 5 | $103 |
| 1 | 4 | 0 | 3 | 5 | $101 |
| 2 | 0 | 4 | 2 | 5 | $ 91 |
| 3 | 0 | 3 | 2 | 5 | $ 90 |

**12.16** Outlay = 6 million: five alternate optimal policies.

| Factory A | Factory B | Factory C | Revenue (millions) |
|---|---|---|---|
| Plan 1 | Plan 1 | Plan 4 | 0 + 0 + 10 = 10 |
| Plan 1 | Plan 2 | Plan 3 | 0 + 3 + 7 = 10 |
| Plan 2 | Plan 1 | Plan 3 | 3 + 0 + 7 = 10 |
| Plan 2 | Plan 2 | Plan 2 | 3 + 3 + 4 = 10 |
| Plan 3 | Plan 2 | Plan 1 | 7 + 3 + 0 = 10 |

Outlay = 7 million: two alternate optimal policies.

| Factory A | Factory B | Factory C | Revenue (millions) |
|---|---|---|---|
| Plan 1 | Plan 2 | Plan 4 | 0 + 3 + 10 = 13 |
| Plan 2 | Plan 2 | Plan 3 | 3 + 3 + 7 = 13 |

Outlay = 8 million: only one optimal policy.

| Factory A | Factory B | Factory C | Revenue (millions) |
|---|---|---|---|
| Plan 3 | Plan 2 | Plan 2 | 7 + 3 + 4 = 14 |

## Chapter 13

**13.2** Connect 1-4, 2-3, 3-4, 3-5, 5-6.  Length of spanning tree = 7.0.

**13.3** Connect 1-3, 2-5, 3-4, 4-5, 5-6, 6-7, 6-8, 8-10, 9-10.  Length of spanning tree = 3.63 miles.

**13.4 b** Shortest route from $X$ to $Y$ along tree: $X \to B \to A \to C \to D \to Y$.  Length of shortest route = 61 miles.

**13.6** From node 1 to *Node 2:* $1 \to 2$.  Length = 5 miles.

*Node 3:* $1 \to 2 \to 3$.  Length = 7 miles.
*Node 4:* $1 \to 2 \to 3 \to 4$.  Length = 9 miles.
*Node 5:* $1 \to 2 \to 5$.  Length = 8 miles.
*Node 6:* $1 \to 2 \to 3 \to 4 \to 6$.  Length = 11 miles.
*Node 7:* $1 \to 2 \to 5 \to 7$.  Length = 14 miles.

**13.9 a** Connect $A$-$B$, $B$-$C$, $C$-$D$, $C$-$E$, $D$-$G$, $E$-$F$.  Length of spanning tree = 136 miles.
   **b** Shortest route from $A$ to $G$: $A \to C \to D \to G$.  Length = 74 miles.  Road $A$-$C$ would have to be built.

**13.12** Assign flows of 2 to 1-2, 6 to 1-3, 4 to 1-4, 2 to 2-5, 3 to 3-4, 3 to 3-6, 6 to 4-5, 1 to 4-6, 8 to 5-7, 4 to 6-7.  This gives maximal flow of 12,000 vehicles per hour from node 1 to node 7.

**13.13** Yes.  Extra flow capacity of 1,000 vehicles per hour on either branch 4-6 or branch 3-8 would increase maximal flow by 1,000 vehicles per hour.

## Chapter 14

**14.1** The critical path is path $1 \to 3 \to 4 \to 5$.  Length = 11.

**14.3 b**

| Activity | Slack | Activity | Slack |
|----------|-------|----------|-------|
| 1-2 | 0 | 3-6 | 1 |
| 1-3 | 1 | 4-6 | 1 |
| 2-3 | 0 | 5-6 | 0 |
| 2-4 | 1 | 5-7 | 1 |
| 2-5 | 0 | 6-7 | 0 |
| 3-5 | 0 | | |

   **c** The critical paths, each of length 16 weeks, are

$$1 \to 2 \to 5 \to 6 \to 7 \quad \text{and} \quad 1 \to 2 \to 3 \to 5 \to 6 \to 7$$

**14.5**

| Activity | Slack | Activity | Slack | Activity | Slack |
|----------|-------|----------|-------|----------|-------|
| 1-2 | 0 | 3-6 | 7 | 6-9 | 23 |
| 1-5 | 22 | 4-5 | 0 | 7-8 | 7 |
| 2-3 | 3 | 5-8 | 0 | 8-9 | 0 |
| 2-4 | 0 | 5-9 | 20 | 8-10 | 19 |
| 3-5 | 3 | 6-7 | 7 | 9-10 | 0 |

The critical path, of length 90, is $1 \rightarrow 2 \rightarrow 4 \rightarrow 5 \rightarrow 8 \rightarrow 9 \rightarrow 10$.

**14.6**

| Activity | Slack | Activity | Slack | Activity | Slack |
|---|---|---|---|---|---|
| 1-2 | 1 | 2-5 | 8 | 4-5 | 0 |
| 1-3 | 0 | 3-4 | 0 | 4-6 | 2 |
| 2-3 | 1 | 3-5 | 2 | 5-6 | 0 |
| 2-4 | 8 | | | | |

The critical path, of length 15, is $1 \rightarrow 3 \rightarrow 4 \rightarrow 5 \rightarrow 6$.

**14.9**

| Activity | Slack | Activity | Slack | Activity | Slack |
|---|---|---|---|---|---|
| 1-2 | 0 | 3-4 | 0 | 5-7 | 5.68 |
| 1-3 | 1.50 | 4-5 | 0 | 6-7 | 0.67 |
| 2-3 | 0 | 4-6 | 2.17 | 6-8 | 0 |
| 2-5 | 4.67 | 5-6 | 0 | 7-8 | 0.67 |

**14.12 a** and **b**

| Activity | $t_e$ | Slack |
|---|---|---|
| 1-2 | 5.17 | 0 |
| 1-3 | 3.17 | 4.83 |
| 1-5 | 3.00 | 10.34 |
| 2-3 | 2.33 | 0.50 |
| 2-6 | 10.17 | 0 |
| 3-4 | 3.17 | 0.50 |
| 3-5 | 4.00 | 1.84 |
| 4-5 | 2.17 | 0.50 |
| 5-6 | 2.00 | 0.50 |

**c** A pretty good leveled schedule would result from beginning activities 1-2 and 1-3 at time 0, 1-5 at 3.17 weeks, 2-6 at 5.17 weeks, 2-3 at 5.67 weeks, 3-4 at 8.00 weeks, 3-5 at 9.34 weeks, 4-5 at 11.17 weeks, and 5-6 at 13.34 weeks. At least 5 people would always be working on the project, with 10 people working for half of one week; otherwise, no more than 8 people working.

**14.3 a**

| Activity | Variance | Activity | Variance | Activity | Variance |
|---|---|---|---|---|---|
| 1-2 | 0.6944 | 2-3 | 0.4444 | 3-5 | 0.4444 |
| 1-3 | 0.2500 | 2-6 | 3.3611 | 4-5 | 0.2500 |
| 1-5 | 0.1111 | 3-4 | 0.6944 | 5-6 | 0.1111 |

**b** 0.90658    **c** 0.63307    **d** 0.36693

**14.15** 0.75. No. (Why not?)

**14.16** Crash activity 1-3 by 2 weeks, 4-5 by 2 weeks, and 3-5 by 1 week, giving an optimal 7-week duration project at a cost of $115,000.

## Chapter 15

**15.1 a** Service for sixth arrival completed 90 minutes after store opens; for thirteenth arrival, 195 minutes after store opens.
 **b** $130

**15.2 a** Service for sixth arrival completed 65 minutes after opening; for thirteenth arrival, 135 minutes after opening.
 **b** $5.83

**15.4** *One borer:* no borer idle time; 50 hours of block waiting time.
 *Two borers:* $10\frac{2}{3}$ hours of borer idle time; $9\frac{1}{3}$ hours of block waiting time.
 *Three borers:* $21\frac{1}{3}$ hours of borer idle time; no block waiting time.

**15.5** Make two borers available, for minimum total cost of $2,533.33.

**15.7 a** Expected number in 2-hour period = 4, expected number in 4-hour period = 8.
 **b** 0.27067, 0.40601, 0.59399

**15.9** 0.46337

**15.10** 0.22313

**15.12** 0.63212, 0.13534

**15.14 a** 0.50    **b** 0.875    **c** 0.50 customer    **d** 2 minutes    **e** 2.5 customers

**15.15 a** 12 minutes    **b** 9 minutes    **c** $144
 **d a** becomes 4 minutes; **b** becomes 2 minutes; **c** becomes $32

**15.18 a b** becomes 0.975; **c** becomes 0.03333 customer; **d** becomes 1.06667 minutes
 **b** 0.60

**15.19** Three clerks will minimize expected cost of idle time at $35.37.

**15.22 a** 0.21429    **b** 0.12054    **c** 0.05921

**15.24** Yes.  $\rho/c = \frac{4}{3}$ when $c = 2$, so system cannot even reach steady state unless at least three borers are used.

**15.26 a** 0.15614    **b** 0.43373    **c** 5.663 customers per hour
 **d** 2.92 customers    **e** $W_s$ = 0.5159 hour, $W_q$ = 0.34896 hour

**15.30 b** $\hat{\lambda}$ = 20 arrivals per hour    **c** $\hat{\mu}$ = 14.63 customers per hour
 **d** $\hat{\rho}$ = 1.367

## Chapter 16

**16.4** For example, if we read two-digit numbers from Table A.5, starting in row 6, column 12, we get the numbers: 0.37, 0.98, 0.13, 0.04, 0.77, 0.75, 0.47, 0.87, 0.51, 0.34, 0.78, 0.95, 0.16, 0.99, 0.63. This would yield one 1, one 2, three 3s, two 4s, four 5s, and four 6s.

**16.7** The cumulative density is given by the area under the curve to the left of $x$. That is, $Pr(X \leq x)$ = area to left of $x$.

For $0 \leq x \leq 20$, the area is $x^2/800$.

For $20 \leq x \leq 40$, the area is $1 - (40 - x)^2/800$. (Try to verify these areas.)

Of course, the area to the left of 20 is precisely 0.50. Then to do the simulation, first select a random number between 0 and 1. If that number is less than or equal to 0.50, set it equal to $x^2/800$ and solve for the $x$ between 0 and 20. If it exceeds 0.50, set it equal to $1 - (40 - x)^2/800$ and solve for the $x$ between 20 and 40.

# *INDEX*

# INDEX